ALASTAIR SAWDAY'S
SPECIAL PLACES TO STAY

FRENCH BED AND BREAKFAST

Nearly 800 remarkable and beautiful private houses, all of them visited – then chosen simply because we like them.

EDITED BY EMMA CAREY &
ANN COOKE-YARBOROUGH

Design: Caroline King

Maps & Mapping: Mapping ©Bartholomew Ltd 2002, part of Collins Information. Reproduced by permission of HarperCollins Publishers. www.bartholomewmaps.com

Printing: Canale, Italy

UK Distribution: Portfolio, Greenford, Middlesex

US Distribution: The Globe Pequot Press, Guilford, Connecticut

Published in October 2002

Alastair Sawday Publishing Co. Ltd
The Home Farm Stables, Barrow Gurney, Bristol BS48 3RW
Tel: +44 (0)1275 464891 Fax: +44 (0)1275 464887
E-mail: info@specialplacestostay.com Web: www.specialplacestostay.com

The Globe Pequot Press
P. O. Box 480, Guilford, Connecticut 06437, USA
Tel: +1 203 458 4500 Fax: +1 203 458 4601
E-mail: info@globe-pequot.com Web: www.globe-pequot.com

Eighth edition

A catalogue record for this book is available from the British Library.

ISBN 1-901970-40-X in the UK
ISBN 0-7627-2462-5 in the US

Printed in Italy

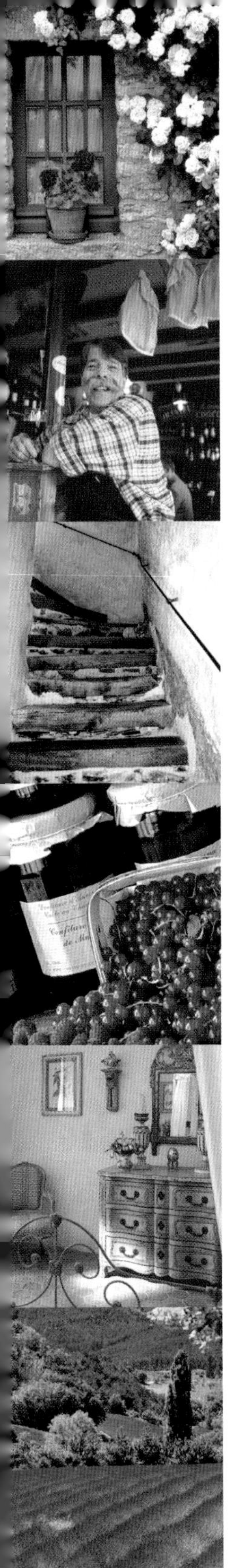

ALASTAIR SAWDAY'S
SPECIAL PLACES TO STAY

FRENCH BED AND BREAKFAST

Foreign travel, o reader, has very real advantages and all the pleasant scenes you have collected are so many medicine bottles stored on your shelves against the maladies of life.

Reginald Farrer (1917)

Guilford
Connecticut, USA

Alastair Sawday Publishing
Bristol, UK

EDITED BY EMMA CAREY &
ANN COOKE-YARBOROUGH

CONTENTS

CONTENTS

CONTENTS

CONTENTS

ACKNOWLEDGEMENTS

There are many perks and pleasures in putting this book together; the people who inhabit it are delightful and rewarding in their individual ways. If you are a Francophile, as we all are in this office, there is a gentle pleasure in writing to, and telephoning, France.

However, perks and pleasures apart, the creation and construction of 'French B&B' is a mammoth task. The book has more than doubled in size since the first edition in 1994. Every detail has to be gathered, checked, inspected and filed. The writing has to be done and checked, the placing on the map must be correct, every detail has to be pored over for possible error. And the whole process must be well-mannered and kindly, lest it become intolerable. So who does all this?

Ann Cooke-Yarborough, the presiding genius behind it all, has handed over the main baton to Emma Carey and focused on writing and inspecting from her bases in Paris and the south of France. Inspectors criss-cross France for months at her whim and she maintains the keenest of eyes for aesthetic detail and personal honesty and authenticity. It is greatly to her that we owe the continued very high quality of the houses and their owners, and the vividness and perception of the writing. The book 'sings', thanks to Ann.

Meanwhile, Emma has been indomitable and sweet-natured. She never flags, never complains, sees the humour in everything and has somehow emerged smiling from under mounting piles of paper. Backed up in the last months by Philippa Rogers' easy, efficient intelligence, she has done a terrific job and this book is proof of that.

Alastair Sawday

Series Editor: Alastair Sawday
Editors: Emma Carey, Ann Cooke-Yarborough
Editorial Director: Annie Shillito
Production Manager: Julia Richardson
Web Producer: Russell Wilkinson
Production Assistants: Rachel Coe, Tom Dalton, Paul Groom
Editorial Assistants: Jo Boissevain, Laura Kinch, Philippa Rogers
Additional Writing: Jo Boissevain, Lindsay Butler
Accounts: Jenny Purdy
Inspections: Richard & Linda Armspach, Helen Barr, Alyson & Colin Browne, Jill Coyle, Meredith Dickinson, Sue Edrich, John Edwards, Georgina Gabriel, Denise Goss, Diana Harris, Sarah Hidderley, Chantal Le Bot, Jo-Bell Moore, Joanna Morris, Caroline Portway, Catherine Wall, Elizabeth Yates. Special thanks to those people not mentioned here, who visited, – often at short notice – just one or two houses for us.

A WORD FROM ALASTAIR SAWDAY

We began with this book. It was easier then, for we knew little of the complexity that would come. Ignorance was bliss, and we got away with all sorts of strange things – like putting my family photographs in the place of those that never arrived from the owners. (Indeed, a photograph of my cousins in the bath would not do now – they are no longer so little.)

A word about our new cover design: we hope that it is fresher and more contemporary than those lovely watercolours – which we are sad to lose. They have always set us apart but we feel that our style is now well-entrenched and respected and we are free to branch out with a new design. This edition will last until Autumn 2004.

However, it is still fun to be able to include and write about so many remarkable places. This is a very personal selection and we are lucky to be able to make it without having to obey rules. Nobody can tell us whom to include, where to go, what criteria to use, whom to exclude. That means that we can be as intensely human as we have always been. The result is that the houses and their owners make up one of the most fascinating gatherings of their kind. You really can set off to France clutching this book in the full knowledge that you are being advised by 'friends'. It is an introduction to interesting people throughout France, and all of them will genuinely welcome you. You could spend your life painfully building up your own network of friends and contacts in France. We have done it for you. We cannot guarantee your travelling contentment, of course, but almost.

Having cast aside the usual rule books we are, nevertheless, tough on ourselves. We're good at spotting the owners who are pretending to be nicer than they really are: owners who get irritated, who charge you for tiny extras, who haul you out of bed for an early breakfast because it suits them, who are mean with the coffee or wine, who sneak stale bread onto your plates, who dislike each other, let alone guests – these we hope to have found and excluded. In their place are those who freely open another bottle of wine to enjoy with you, who make their own bread and jams, who can shed light on France as no tourist office can, who look for ways of making your stay special. Many of them are down-to-earth and have simple tastes; others are highly educated and sophisticated. Some live grandly; others live modestly. Some are eccentric: all are individuals doing things their own way. All are worth visiting; it is up to you to choose by reading the descriptions carefully. You will return from France richer in relationships – with the people and the country – no bad thing as Europe creaks under its own strain.

Alastair Sawday

INTRODUCTION

What to expect from a French B&B • Choosing the right place • How to use this book • Practical matters • Internet • Feedback

What's special about staying in French B&Bs (*chambresd'hôtes*)?

The conversations you can have, the unexpected encounters you can make. The people in this guide come from all walks of life – aristocrats and artisans, painters and *paysans*, teachers, writers, retired globetrotters: so many opportunities for enriching exchange. Some readers have formed enduring friendships with owners or other guests and we treasure the tale of a couple who sailed their yacht from Australia to visit Paris and stayed with a true Parisienne. And although most of our owners are simply down-to-earth, friendly individuals living in reliably French houses, they all have a touch of originality, are passionate about their area and want you to discover its hidden treasures.

How we choose our Special Places

We have visited every single house in this book. We search for the best of everything – atmosphere, welcome and value for money are the keys, each place is judged on its own merits, not by comparison – and write a book without fixed boundaries. If we discover a B&B where the art of hospitality is practised with flair, good humour and commitment, we want to include it. Good views and good walks count more than deluxe toiletries and jacuzzis and we like people who do their own thing, though eccentricity is no excuse for poor standards.

B&Bs are not hotels

Expect to feel a privileged guest in your chosen house and to gain a fascinating glimpse of a French way of life but, if you are new to B&B, remember they are not hotels – you are a paying guest in someone's home, so please don't expect hotel services. Don't expect your towels to be changed daily, your children's toys to be gathered or your late request for a vegetarian meal to produce anything more exciting than an omelette. Let your hosts know of any special needs well ahead and take your own tea bags if you are particular. Owners love guests to stay more than one night and it's really worth seizing the opportunity for genuine contact, but they often expect you to be out during the day - they have their own lives to lead so they can't be on hand all the time. If they are happy for you to be around, check which parts of the house or garden you may use during the day.

Breakfast is usually 'Continental': fruit juice, home-made jams and the freshest bread. Occasionally fruit, eggs, cheese or meats will be offered, or you can ask; there may be an extra charge.

Choosing the right place for you

Read carefully, sleep happily

Do remember to interpret what you see and read in this book. If you opt for a working farm, expect cockerels to crow or tractors to set off at dawn. If you choose a "rambling château with old-fashioned bathrooms", there could be some draughty corridors and idiosyncratic plumbing. If "antique beds" sounds seductively authentic, remember they are liable to be antique sizes, too (190 cm long, doubles 140 cm wide, singles 80 or 90 cm wide). Check on anything that is really important to you before confirming your booking, e.g. whether the swimming pool will be ready to use at Easter, whether the bicycles available have been booked by others.

A problem well defined is half-way solved

If you find anything we say misleading (things do change in the lifetime of a guide), or you think we miss the point – if, for example, you thought you'd chosen a child-friendly house and were surprised by elegant white carpets and delicate ornaments at toddler height – please let us know. And do discuss any problem with your hosts at the time – they are the only ones who can do something about it immediately. They would be mortified to discover, too late, that you were, for example, cold in bed when extra blankets could easily have been provided.

How to use this book

Non-French owners

Our aim is essentially to guide readers to meetings with French families in their homes, so non-French owners have a smaller chance of being chosen. But many of you have said how good it can be to relax in English from time to time, so we include a number of 'foreigners'. The choice is yours.

Bedrooms and how we describe them:

- 'double': one double bed
- 'twin': two single beds
- 'double/twin': two single beds that can become a large double
- 'triple' or 'family room': any mix of beds (sometimes sofabeds) for 3, 4 or more people
- 'suite': either one large room with a sitting area or two or more interconnecting rooms, plus one or more bathrooms

- 'apartment': similar to suite but with an independent entrance and possibly a small kitchen
- 'studio': bedroom, bathroom, sitting and cooking areas

Extra beds and cots for children, at an extra cost, can often be provided; ask when booking.

Bathrooms

There's a wonderful variety of washing arrangements in French homes – we've done our best to make the layouts clear: bathrooms directly off the bedroom = 'with'; not directly off the bedroom but not shared = 'private'; shared with others = 'sharing'. Most, but not all baths have shower attachments. A 'continental' bath is a half- or three-quarter-size tub with a shower attachment. Bathrooms are generally good but if you are wary of quirky arrangements go for the modernised places (which are probably more expensive).

Dinner – *Table d'Hôtes*: fixed-price menu to be booked ahead

A wonderful opportunity to eat honest, even gourmet, food in an authentic family atmosphere but don't expect a choice: *table d'hôtes* means the same food for all and absolutely must be booked ahead, so do specify any particular diet needs when you book. The number and type of courses you will be offered varies and we have not attempted to go into details, although price may be an indicator. It won't be available every day either but do please turn up if you have booked it – it's distressing to prepare a meal that no-one comes to enjoy. Very few places offer lunch but occasionally picnics can be provided.

Including wine?

When wine is included this can mean a range of things, from a standard quarter-litre carafe per person to a barrel of table wine; from a very decent bottle of local produce to, in some rare cases, an excellent estate wine. Whatever it is, it is usually good value but please do not abuse your hosts' *vin à volonté* (unlimited wine with meals).

If there is no *table d'hôtes*, we give an idea of other places to eat but beware, rural restaurants stop taking orders at 9pm and close at least a day a week.

Prices

The prices in this book are not guaranteed, but are presumed to be for 2003. Check our website for up-dates.

INTRODUCTION

Many places offer reductions for longer stays; attractive half-board terms, special prices for children: ask when you book.

There is a €/£/$ conversion table at the back of the book.

Gîte space

Gîte space for … people means there are that many self-catering spaces as well as the B&B rooms. You can then assess what the total number of people staying on the property might be. Some places are *Gîtes d'Étape* i.e. they welcome walkers, cyclists or riders, often on a half-board basis; others are *Gîtes de Séjour* or *Gîtes Ruraux* – self-contained holiday houses. We have not inspected these *gîtes* and are not necessarily recommending them. For those we do recommend see our French Holiday Homes guide.

Symbols

Symbols and their explanations are listed on the last page of the book. Use them as a guide rather than an unequivocal statement of fact and double-check anything that is important to you.

Our symbol shows where children are welcome with no age restrictions. Elsewhere, they may be welcome with restrictions as indicated in italics at the end of the description. e.g. Babies only, because of an unfenced pool.

Our symbol tells you which houses generally welcome pets but you must check whether this means the size and type of your pet. Your hosts will expect animals to be well behaved and you to be responsible for them at all times.

Practical Matters

Types of houses

For a definition of *château, bastide, mas*, see 'French words & expressions' at the back of the guide (where most French words used in the descriptions are explained).

Telephoning/Faxing

All phone numbers in France have ten digits, e.g. (0)5 05 25 35 45.

You should know that:

- the zero (bracketed above) is for use when telephoning from inside France only, e.g. dial 05 15 25 35 45 from any private or public telephone;
- when dialling from outside France use the international access code, then the country code for France (33) then the last 9 digits of the number you want, e.g. 00 33 5 15 25 35 45;

- numbers beginning (0)6 are mobile phone numbers;
- to telephone from France
  - to Great Britain: 00 44 then the number without the first 0.
  - to North America: 00 1 then the number without the first 0.

Télécartes phone cards are widely available in France and there are plenty of telephone boxes, even in the countryside (they often only take cards).

Travel to and from France

I hope it proves easy, and entertaining, to chose your Special Place to stay in France using this book. But getting there can be expensive and the poor person to whom the organisational task falls can have a horrible – and bewildering – time getting ferries and/or trains sorted out.

So, hoping to make things easier – and cheaper – for you, we have linked up with Bonnes Vacances. They are a small, family-run company in Surrey who have gradually built up a reputation for decent, personal service and good prices.

They are not the biggest fish in the pond but by all accounts they do a marvellous job and will treat you like human beings. Best of all, they will save you from those frustrating phone calls to ferry companies in your quest for the best route and best deal. They have a page at the back of this book with phone numbers etc. Note that in order to use them you have to have a booking at a Special Place. The ball is in your court.

Booking

There is a bilingual Booking Form at the back of this book. It is essential to book well ahead for July and August, and wise for other months. You may receive a *Contrat de Location* (Tenancy Contract) as confirmation. It must be filled in and returned, probably with a deposit, and commits both sides to the arrangement. Remember not to telephone any later than 9pm or 9.30pm at the latest and that Ireland and the UK are one hour behind the rest of Europe. Some country people have been quite upset by enquiries coming through when they were fast asleep. And please remember that owners count on you to stay as long as you have booked for. If you don't, they may feel justified in applying a cancellation charge.

Deposits

Some owners ask for a deposit. Many readers have found it virtually impossible or ridiculously expensive to do this by direct transfer but you can send an ordinary cheque which the owner will destroy when you arrive (so no-one pays the charges). When you leave, they will ask you for cash for your whole stay.

Paying

Most B&B owners do not take credit cards, but those who do have our credit card symbol. Virtually all ATMs in France take Visa and MasterCard. Euro travellers' cheques should be accepted; other currency cheques are unpopular because of commission charges.

Taxe de séjour

This is a small tax that local councils can levy on all visitors paying for accommodation. Some councils do; some don't – you may find your bill increased by a Euro or two per person per day.

Tipping

B&B owners would be taken aback by a tip, but if you encounter extraordinary kindness you may feel a thank-you letter, Christmas card or small gift would be appropriate.

Arriving

Most owners expect you to arrive between 5 and 7 pm. If you come earlier, rooms may not be ready or your hosts may still be at work. If you are going to be late (or early, unavoidably), please telephone and say so.

No-shows

Owners hope you will treat them as friends by being sensitive and punctual. It's obviously upsetting for them to prepare rooms – even meals – and to wait up late for 'guests' who give no further sign of life. So if you find you are not going to take up a booking, telephone right away.

By the way, there is a tacit agreement among some B&B owners that no-show + no-call by 8 pm (the deadline is 6 pm in some cases) can be taken as a refusal of the booking and they will re-let the room if another guest turns up.

Subscriptions

Owners pay to appear in this guide; their fee goes towards the huge costs of a sophisticated inspection system and the production of an all-colour book. We only include places and owners that we find positively special. There is a long waiting list of candidates and it is not possible for anyone to buy their way in.

Internet

www.specialplacestostay.com

Our web site has online entries for all the places featured here and in our other books, with up-to-date information and direct links to their own email addresses and web sites. You'll find more about the site at the back of this book.

Disclaimer

We make no claims to pure objectivity in choosing our Special Places to Stay. They are here because we like them. Our opinions and tastes are ours alone and this book is a statement of them; we hope that you will share them.

A huge Thank You to those of you who take the time and trouble to write to us about your *chambres d'hôtes* experiences – good and bad – or to recommend new places. This is what we do with them:

- Poor reports are followed up with the owners in question: we need to hear both sides of the story. Really bad reports lead to incognito visits, after which we may exclude a place.
- Owners are informed when we receive substantially positive reports about them.
- Recommendations are followed up with inspection visits where appropriate. If your recommendation leads us to include a place, you receive a free copy of the edition in which that house first appears.

We have done our utmost to get our facts right but apologise unreservedly for any mistakes that may have crept in. We would be grateful to hear of any errors that you find. Feedback from you is invaluable and we always act upon comments. With your help and our own inspections we can maintain our reputation for dependability.

And finally

We love your letters and value your comments which make a real contribution to this book, be they on our report form, by letter or by email to info@sawdays.co.uk. Or you can visit our website and write to us from there.

Bon Voyage – Happy Travelling!

Ann Cooke-Yarborough

HOW TO USE THIS BOOK

sample entry

AUVERGNE

The solid reality of this magical tower is deeply moving. Michel's skill in renovation (well, reconstruction from near-ruin), Anita's decorating talent, their passionate dedication, have summoned a rich and sober mood that makes the 15th-century *chastel* throb with authenticity: only 'medieval' materials; magnificent deep-tinted fabrics, many designed by Anita; antique tapestries, panelling and furniture – nothing flashy, all simply true to the density of the place. Spectacular bedrooms, amazing bathrooms of antique-faced modern perfection and a generous breakfast – this is a must. *Minimum 2 nights July-August.*

1 rooms — 3 doubles, all with bath/shower & wc.
2 price — €87-€122 for two.
3 dinner — Auberge & traditional restaurants 1-4km.
4 closed — January-February.
5 directions — From A75 exit 6 for St Nectaire; through Champeix to Montaigut le Blanc; follow signs up to château.

Anita & Michel Sauvadet
Le Chastel Montaigu,
63320 Montaigut le Blanc,
Puy-de-Dôme
tel (0)4 73 96 28 49
fax (0)4 73 96 21 60
web www.le-chastel-montaigu.com

6 

7 **map: 11 entry: 568**

explanations

❶ rooms

'with bath & wc' or 'with shower & wc' means en suite; 'with private bath & wc' means they are not en suite but you have them to yourself; 'sharing bath & wc' means sharing them with one or two other guests or family members.

❷ price

The prices given are for two people in one room and include breakfast. A price range incorporates differences between rooms or between seasons. They are presumed to be for 2003 but are not guaranteed, so please check.

❸ dinner

Prices are per person. Dinner must always be booked in advance. See Introduction for wine details.

❹ closed

When given in months, this means for the whole of the named months and the time in between.

❺ directions

See details above Maps 1 & 2.
Use them as a guide; owners can provide more details.

❻ symbols

See the last page of the book for details.

- working farm
- all children welcome
- pets can sleep in your bedroom
- vegetarians catered for with advance warning
- mostly home-grown/local/organic produce used
- step-free access to bathroom/bedroom
- wheelchair facilities for one bedroom/bathroom
- no smoking anywhere
- this house has pets
- credit cards accepted
- licensed premises
- Smoking restrictions exist.

❼ map & entry numbers

Map number – refers to detailed map on which the entry appears; entry number – links place on map to detailed entry in book (NB Paris flags are not positioned geographically).

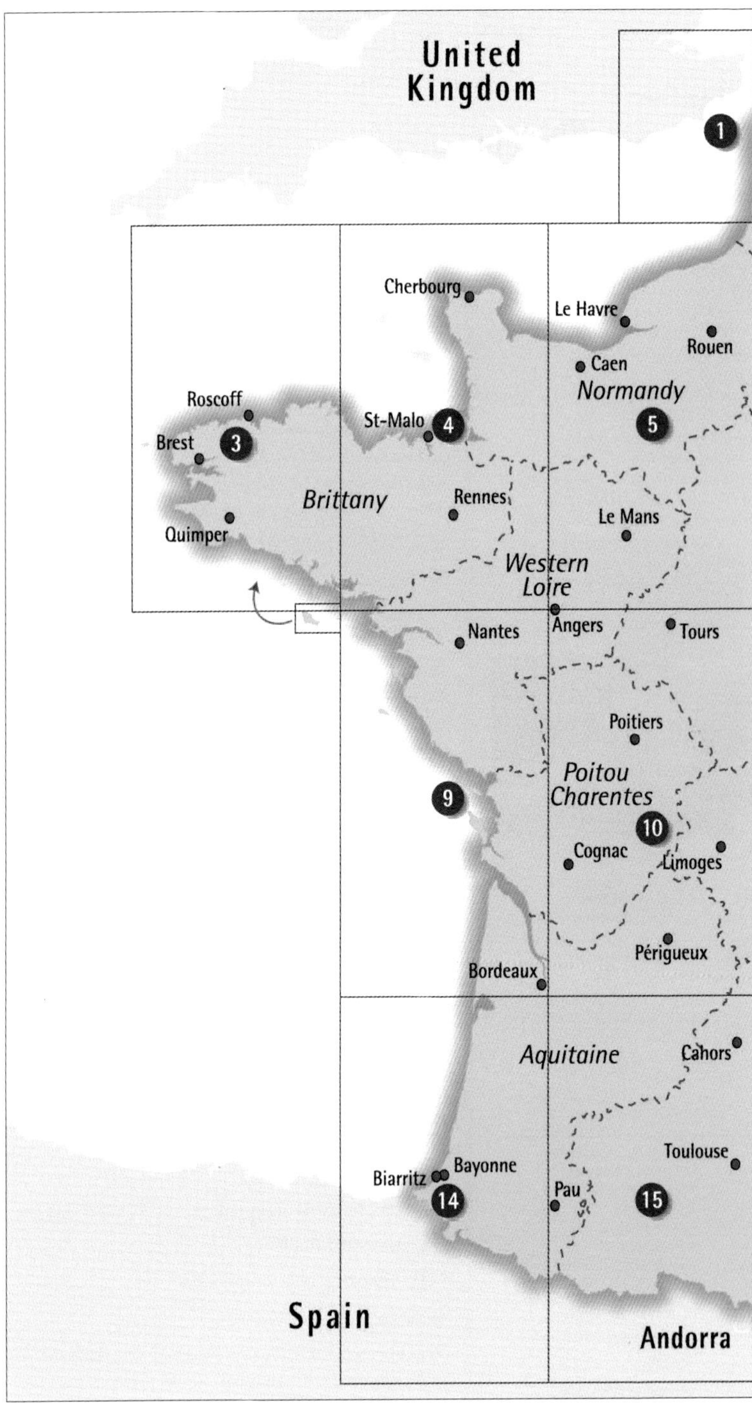

United Kingdom
1
Cherbourg
Le Havre
Rouen
Caen
Normandy
Roscoff
Brest
3
St-Malo
4
5
Brittany
Rennes
Le Mans
Quimper
Western Loire
Angers
Nantes
Tours
Poitiers
Poitou Charentes
9
10
Cognac
Limoges
Périgueux
Bordeaux
Aquitaine
Cahors
Toulouse
Biarritz
Bayonne
14
Pau
15
Spain
Andorra

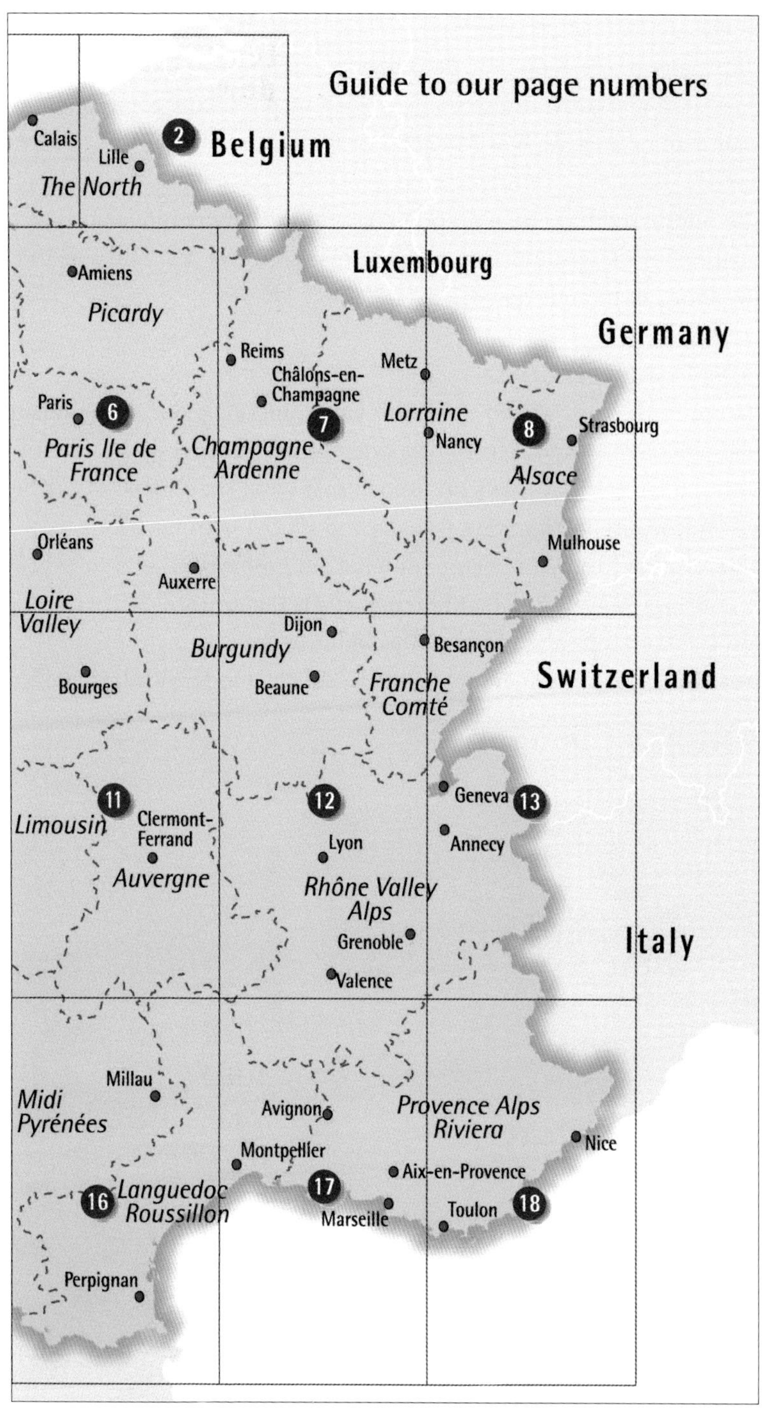

Guide to our page numbers
Calais
2
Belgium
Lille
The North
Luxembourg
Amiens
Picardy
Germany
Reims
Metz
Châlons-en-Champagne
Paris
6
7
Lorraine
8
Strasbourg
Paris Ile de France
Champagne Ardenne
Nancy
Alsace
Orléans
Mulhouse
Auxerre
Loire Valley
Dijon
Besançon
Burgundy
Switzerland
Bourges
Beaune
Franche Comté
11
12
Geneva
13
Limousin
Clermont-Ferrand
Annecy
Lyon
Auvergne
Rhône Valley Alps
Grenoble
Italy
Valence
Millau
Midi Pyrénées
Avignon
Provence Alps Riviera
Nice
Montpellier
Aix-en-Provence
16
Languedoc Roussillon
17
Marseille
Toulon
18
Perpignan

HOW TO USE OUR MAPS

Our maps are designed for B&B flagging only – you will be deeply frustrated if you try to use them as road maps! Take a good detailed road map or atlas such as Michelin or Collins.

The numbered flags have no pointers and are simply indications of position on the ground, not accurate markers. You will find specific directions in the relevant entry.

READING OUR DIRECTIONS

Except in the case of two-way motorway junctions, our directions take you to each house from one side only. French roads are identified with the letters they carry on French maps and road signs:
A = Autoroute. Motorways (mostly toll roads) with junctions that generally have the same name/number on both sides.
N = Route Nationale. The old trunk roads that are still fairly fast, don't charge tolls and often go through towns.
D = Route Départementale. Smaller country roads with less traffic.

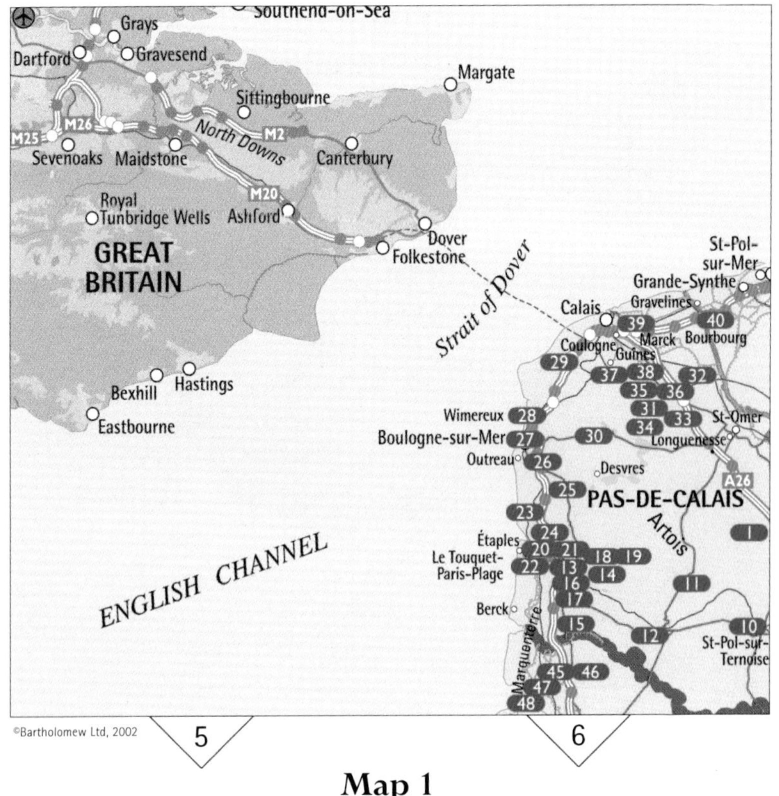

Map 1

Our directions are as succinct as possible.

For example: From A7 exit Valence Sud A49 for Grenoble; exit 33; right D538a for Beaumont 2.5km; right again at sign 800m; house on right.

Interpretation: Take A7 motorway going north or south; leave at junction named 'Valence Sud' and get onto motorway A49 going towards Grenoble; leave this road at junction 33 and turn right onto road D538a (the 'a' means there are probably roads numbered 538b, 538c... in the vicinity) towards Beaumont for 2.5km until you meet a meaningful sign (often 'Chambres d'Hôtes', the name of the house or a pictogram of a bed under a roof); turn right at this sign; the house is 800 metres down this road on the right.

Scale for maps 1:1 600 000

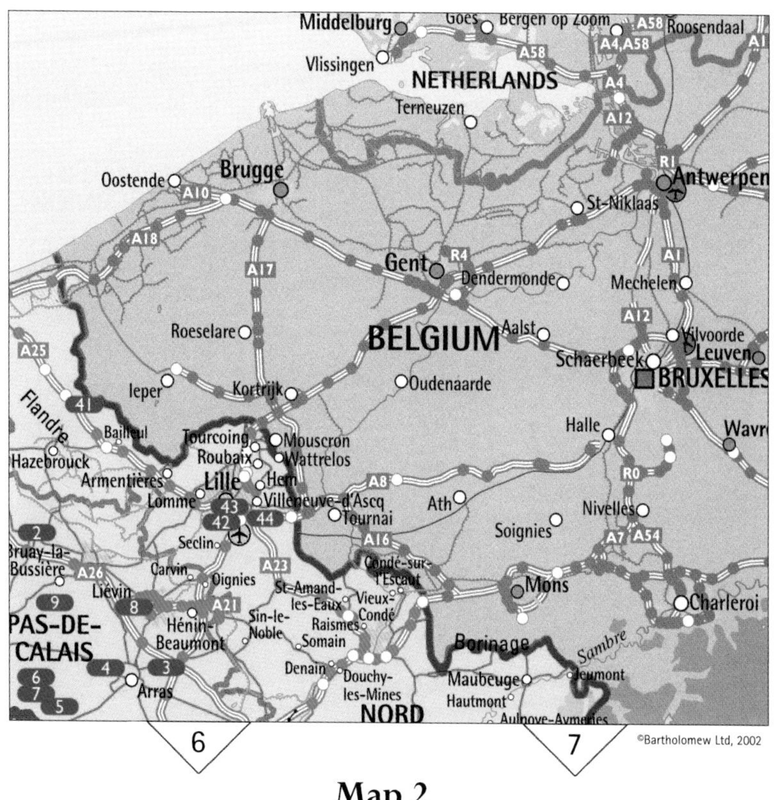

Map 2

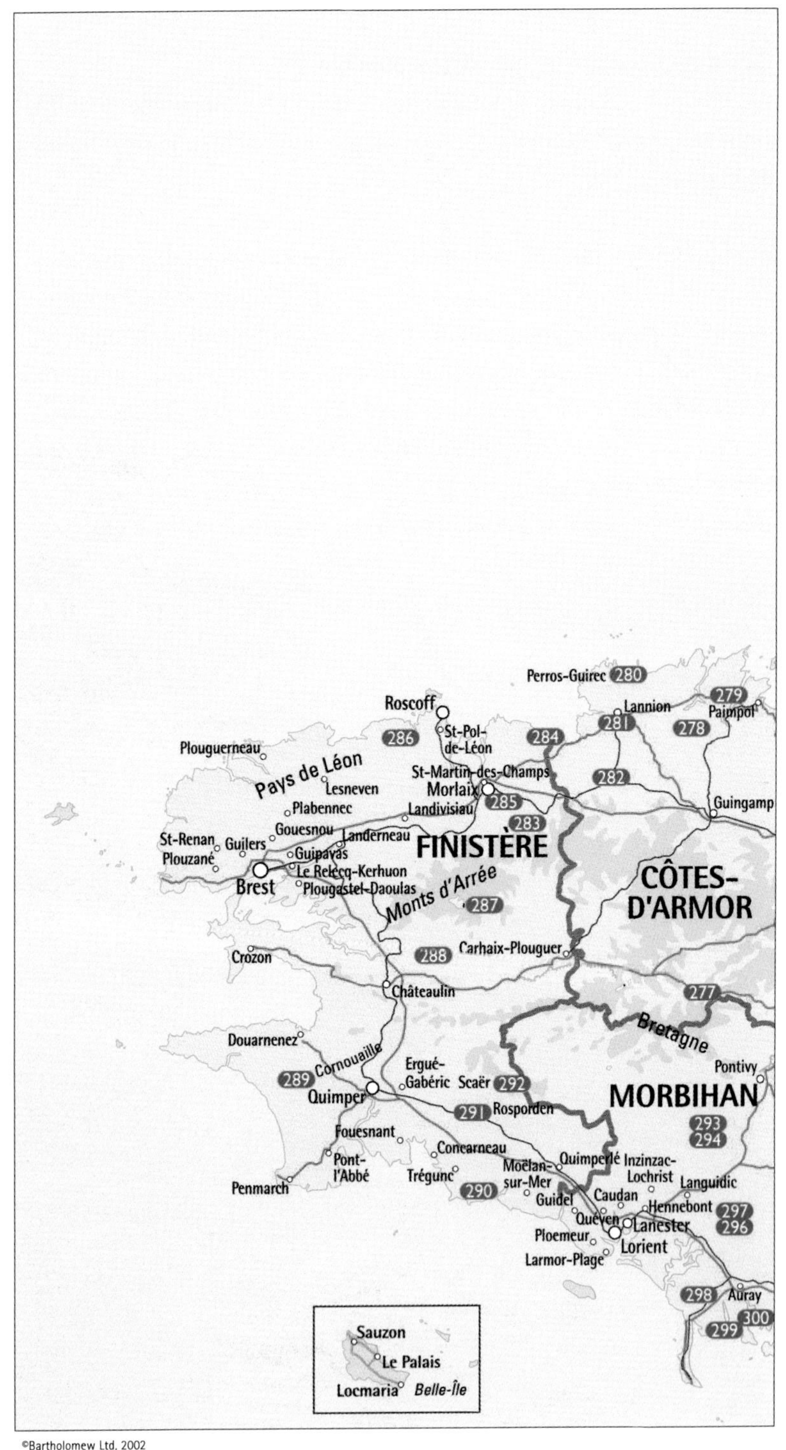

Perros-Guirec
280
279
Paimpol
Lannion
281
278
Roscoff
St-Pol-de-Léon
286
284
Plouguerneau
Pays de Léon
St-Martin-des-Champs
Morlaix
Lesneven
282
285
Guingamp
Plabennec
Landivisiau
283
Gouesnou
Landerneau
FINISTÈRE
St-Renan
Guilers
Guipavas
Plouzané
Le Relecq-Kerhuon
CÔTES-D'ARMOR
Brest
Plougastel-Daoulas
Monts d'Arrée
287
Crozon
288
Carhaix-Plouguer
Châteaulin
277
Bretagne
Douarnenez
Cornouaille
Pontivy
Ergué-Gabéric
289
Scaër
292
MORBIHAN
Quimper
291
Rosporden
293
294
Fouesnant
Concarneau
Pont-l'Abbé
Moëlan-sur-Mer
Quimperlé
Inzinzac-Lochrist
Trégunc
Languidic
Penmarch
290
Guidel
Caudan
Hennebont
297
Quéven
Lanester
296
Ploemeur
Lorient
Larmor-Plage
298
Auray
300
299
Sauzon
Le Palais
Locmaria
Belle-Île

Map 3

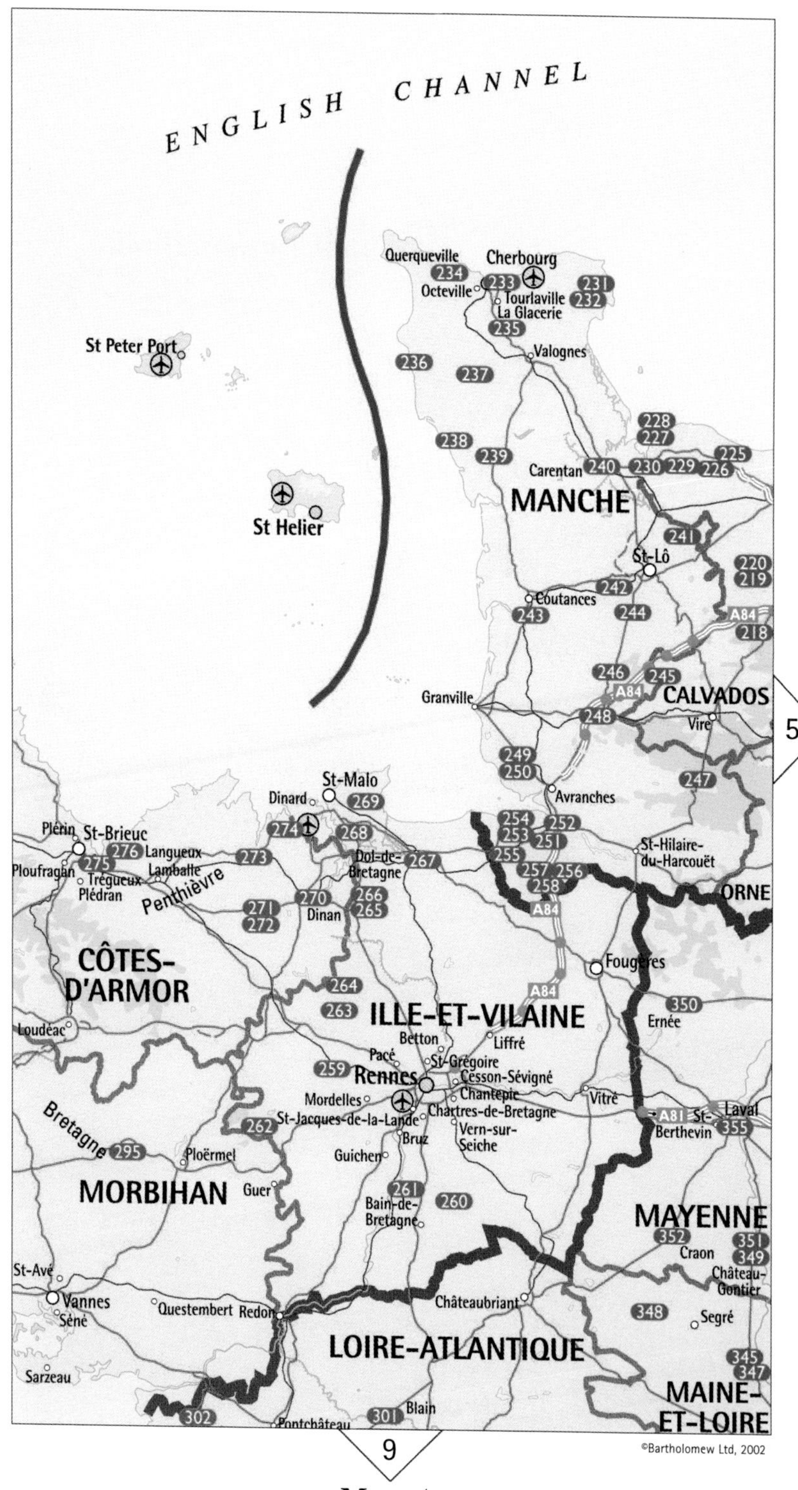
ENGLISH CHANNEL
Querqueville
Cherbourg
Octeville
Tourlaville
La Glacerie
Valognes
St Peter Port
St Helier
Carentan
MANCHE
St-Lô
Coutances
Granville
CALVADOS
Vire
5
Avranches
St-Malo
Dinard
Plérin
St-Brieuc
Langueux
Lamballe
Ploufragan
Trégueux
Plédran
Penthièvre
Dol-de-Bretagne
Dinan
St-Hilaire-du-Harcouët
ORNE
CÔTES-D'ARMOR
Fougères
ILLE-ET-VILAINE
Loudéac
Ernée
Betton
Liffré
Pacé
St-Grégoire
Rennes
Cesson-Sévigné
Chantepie
Mordelles
St-Jacques-de-la-Lande
Chartres-de-Bretagne
Vitré
Laval
St-Berthevin
Bretagne
Ploërmel
Bruz
Vern-sur-Seiche
Guichen
MORBIHAN
Guer
Bain-de-Bretagne
MAYENNE
Craon
Château-Gontier
St-Avé
Vannes
Séné
Questembert
Redon
Châteaubriant
Segré
LOIRE-ATLANTIQUE
Sarzeau
MAINE-ET-LOIRE
Blain
Pontchâteau
9

Map 4

1
4
10
ENGLISH CHANNEL
SOMME
Le Tréport
170
169
Eu
171
Dieppe
172
Neuville-lès-Dieppe
174
173
A28
Fécamp
175
SEINE-MARITIME
Neufchâtel-en-Bray
Pays de Bray
176
A29
Yvetot
Pavilly
A151
Montivilliers
Bolbec
Barentin
Notre-Dame-de-Bondeville
Ste-Adresse
Harfleur
Lillebonne
177
Mont-St-Aignan
Le Havre
Gonfreville-l'Orcher
Notre-Dame-de-Gravenchon
A150
178
Honfleur
Seine
Le Petit-Quevilly
180
179
Rouen
A131
Le Grand-Quevilly
Sotteville-lès-Rouen
181
Trouville-sur-Mer
194
Petit-Couronne
A29
192
Roumois
Grand-Couronne
St-Étienne-du-Rouvray
222
216
193
223
217
215
Cléon
224
Ouistreham
Dives-sur-Mer
213
Pont-Audemer
191
Elbeuf
Val-de-Reuil
A13
214
A13
Hérouville-St-Clair
195
189
Les Andelys
Colombelles
Pays d'Auge
Lieuvin
Louviers
221
Mondeville
Lisieux
190
188
Gaillon
Seine
Caen
Ifs
212
197
A84
Normandie
187
186
196
Bernay
Vernon
183
211
210
EURE
Évreux
185
184
CALVADOS
Condé-sur-Noireau
Falaise
204
209
208
198
Flers
206
205
203
L'Aigle
Dreux
166
Argentan
Verneuil-sur-Avre
Vernouillet
202
ORNE
Thymerais
368
207
La Ferté-Macé
201
167
199
Chartres
369
370
Alençon
200
Lucé
Luisant
357
358
359
EURE-ET-LOIR
Mamers
Maine
Mayenne
Nogent-le-Rotrou
A28
360
Loir
MAYENNE
La Ferté-Bernard
371
Évron
356
SARTHE
A11
Châteaudun
A81
361
Coulaines
Dunois
354
Le Mans
391
Allonnes
A11
Arnage
Mulsanne
353
A28
Sablé-sur-Sarthe
362
367
363
Loir
395
Vendôme
364
392
393
EURE-ET-CHER
Château-du-Loir
346
La Flèche
Loir
396
366
365
394
397
MAINE-ET-LOIRE
398
342
340
339
A10
343
344
405
407
399
338
341
Avrillé
Château-Renault
Blois
Vineuil
Gâtine
Angers
A85
337
406
INDRE-ET-COIRE

Map 5

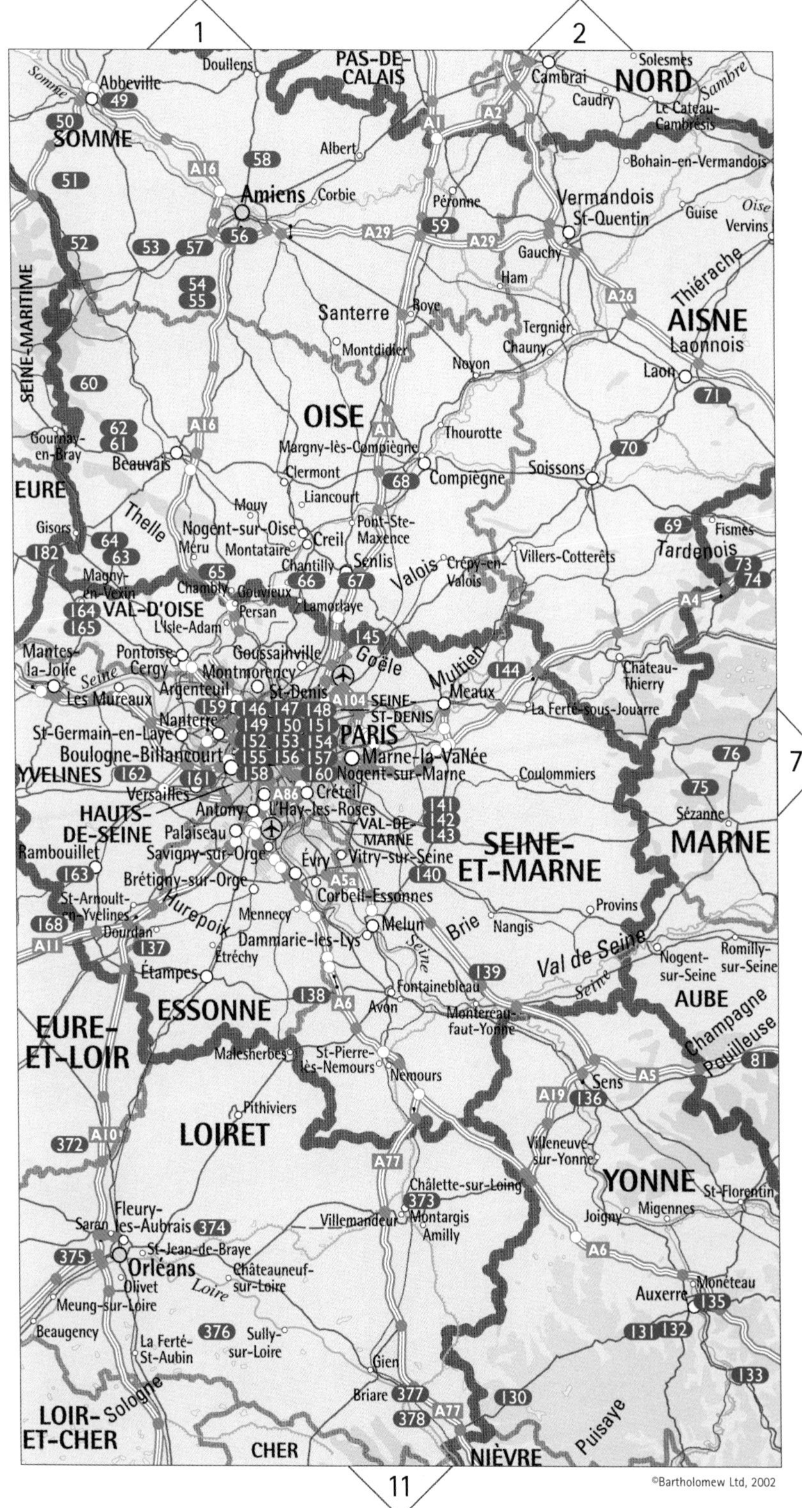
1
2
7
11
PAS-DE-CALAIS
NORD
Doullens
Abbeville
Cambrai
Solesmes
Caudry
Le Cateau-Cambrésis
Sambre
Somme
SOMME
Albert
Bohain-en-Vermandois
Amiens
Corbie
Péronne
Vermandois
St-Quentin
Guise
Oise
Vervins
Gauchy
Ham
Thiérache
AISNE
Laonnois
Santerre
Roye
Tergnier
Chauny
Montdidier
Noyon
Laon
SEINE-MARITIME
OISE
Thourotte
Margny-lès-Compiègne
Compiègne
Soissons
Gournay-en-Bray
Beauvais
Clermont
Liancourt
EURE
Mouy
Thelle
Gisors
Nogent-sur-Oise
Creil
Pont-Ste-Maxence
Fismes
Tardenois
Méru
Montataire
Chantilly
Senlis
Valois
Crépy-en-Valois
Villers-Cotterêts
Magny-en-Vexin
Chambly
Gouvieux
Lamorlaye
VAL-D'OISE
Persan
L'Isle-Adam
Mantes-la-Jolie
Pontoise
Cergy
Goussainville
Goële
Montmorency
Multien
Château-Thierry
Seine
Les Mureaux
Argenteuil
St-Denis
SEINE-ST-DENIS
Meaux
La Ferté-sous-Jouarre
Nanterre
St-Germain-en-Laye
PARIS
Boulogne-Billancourt
Marne-la-Vallée
YVELINES
Nogent-sur-Marne
Coulommiers
Versailles
Créteil
HAUTS-DE-SEINE
Antony
L'Haÿ-les-Roses
VAL-DE-MARNE
Sézanne
Palaiseau
SEINE-ET-MARNE
MARNE
Rambouillet
Savigny-sur-Orge
Évry
Vitry-sur-Seine
Brétigny-sur-Orge
Corbeil-Essonnes
St-Arnoult-en-Yvelines
Hurepoix
Provins
Mennecy
Melun
Brie
Nangis
Dourdan
Dammarie-les-Lys
Val de Seine
Nogent-sur-Seine
Romilly-sur-Seine
Étréchy
Étampes
Fontainebleau
AUBE
ESSONNE
Avon
Montereau-faut-Yonne
Champagne Pouilleuse
EURE-ET-LOIR
Malesherbes
St-Pierre-lès-Nemours
Nemours
Sens
Pithiviers
LOIRET
Villeneuve-sur-Yonne
Châlette-sur-Loing
YONNE
St-Florentin
Montargis
Amilly
Villemandeur
Joigny
Migennes
Fleury-les-Aubrais
Saran
St-Jean-de-Braye
Orléans
Châteauneuf-sur-Loire
Olivet
Loire
Meung-sur-Loire
Auxerre
Monéteau
Beaugency
La Ferté-St-Aubin
Sully-sur-Loire
Gien
Briare
Sologne
LOIR-ET-CHER
CHER
NIÈVRE
Puisaye
A1
A2
A16
A29
A26
A4
A104
A86
A5a
A11
A6
A5
A19
A10
A77
49
50
51
52
53
54
55
56
57
58
59
60
61
62
63
64
65
66
67
68
69
70
71
73
74
75
76
81
130
131
132
133
135
136
137
138
139
140
141
142
143
144
145
146
147
148
149
150
151
152
153
154
155
156
157
158
159
160
161
162
163
164
165
168
182
372
373
374
375
376
377
378

Map 6

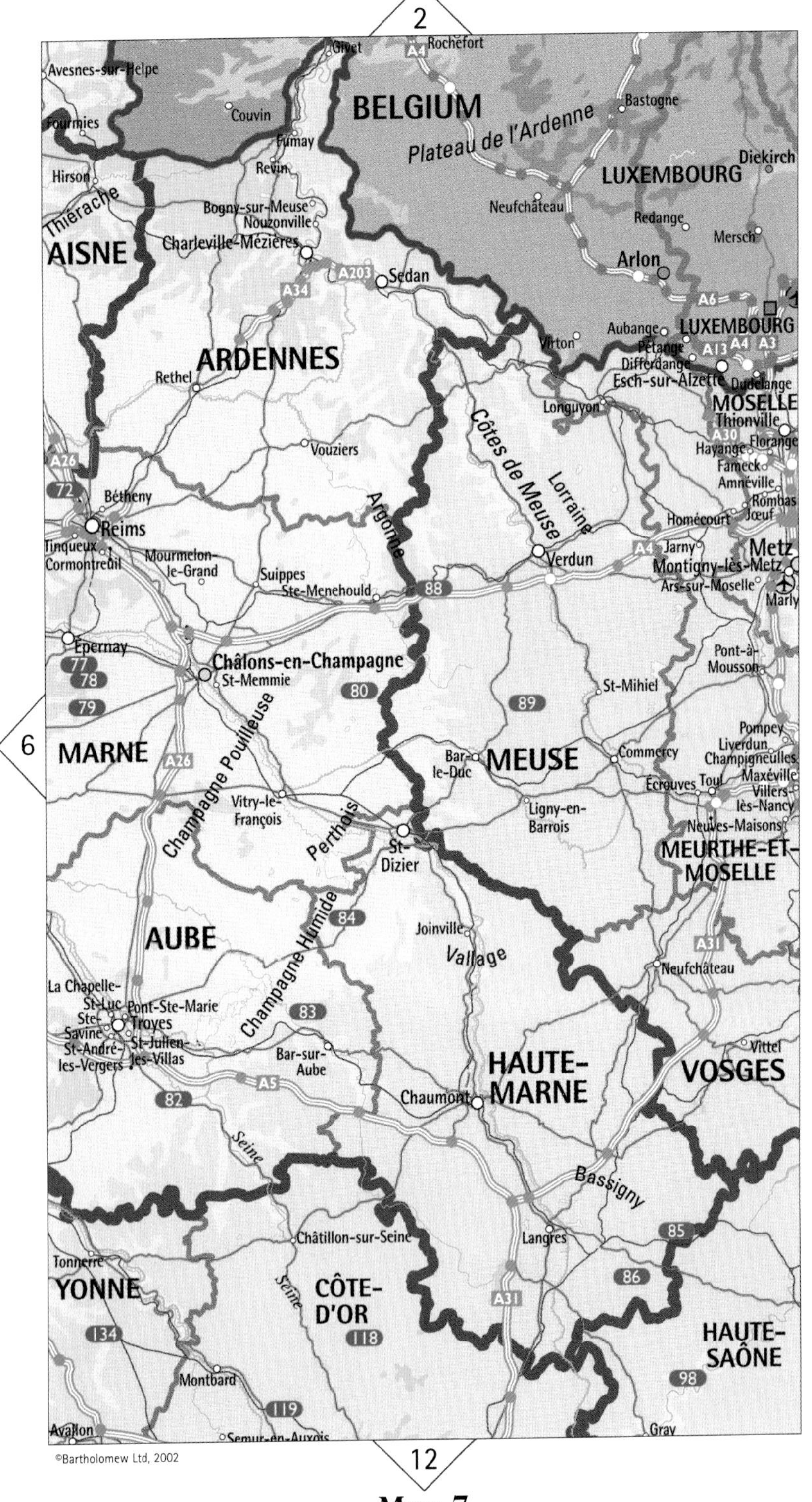
2
6
12
BELGIUM
Plateau de l'Ardenne
LUXEMBOURG
AISNE
ARDENNES
Thiérache
Argonne
Côtes de Meuse
Lorraine
MOSELLE
MARNE
MEUSE
MEURTHE-ET-MOSELLE
Champagne Pouilleuse
Perthois
Champagne Humide
Vallage
AUBE
HAUTE-MARNE
VOSGES
Bassigny
YONNE
CÔTE-D'OR
HAUTE-SAÔNE
Seine
Givet
Rochefort
Avesnes-sur-Helpe
Couvin
Bastogne
Fourmies
Fumay
Diekirch
Hirson
Revin
Neufchâteau
Redange
Mersch
Bogny-sur-Meuse
Nouzonville
Charleville-Mézières
Arlon
Sedan
Virton
Aubange
Pétange
Differdange
Esch-sur-Alzette
Dudelange
Rethel
Longuyon
Thionville
Vouziers
Hayange
Florange
Fameck
Amnéville
Rombas
Jœuf
Bétheny
Homécourt
Reims
Tinqueux
Cormontreuil
Mourmelon-le-Grand
Verdun
Jarny
Metz
Montigny-lès-Metz
Ars-sur-Moselle
Marly
Suippes
Ste-Menehould
Épernay
Châlons-en-Champagne
St-Memmie
Pont-à-Mousson
St-Mihiel
Pompey
Liverdun
Champigneulles
Bar-le-Duc
Commercy
Maxéville
Écrouves
Toul
Villers-lès-Nancy
Vitry-le-François
Ligny-en-Barrois
Neuves-Maisons
St-Dizier
Joinville
Neufchâteau
La Chapelle-St-Luc
Pont-Ste-Marie
Ste-Savine
Troyes
St-André-les-Vergers
St-Julien-les-Villas
Bar-sur-Aube
Vittel
Chaumont
Châtillon-sur-Seine
Langres
Tonnerre
Montbard
Gray
Avallon
Semur-en-Auxois
A4
A203
A34
A6
A13
A3
A30
A26
A31
A5
72
77
78
79
80
84
83
82
88
89
85
86
98
118
119
134

Map 7

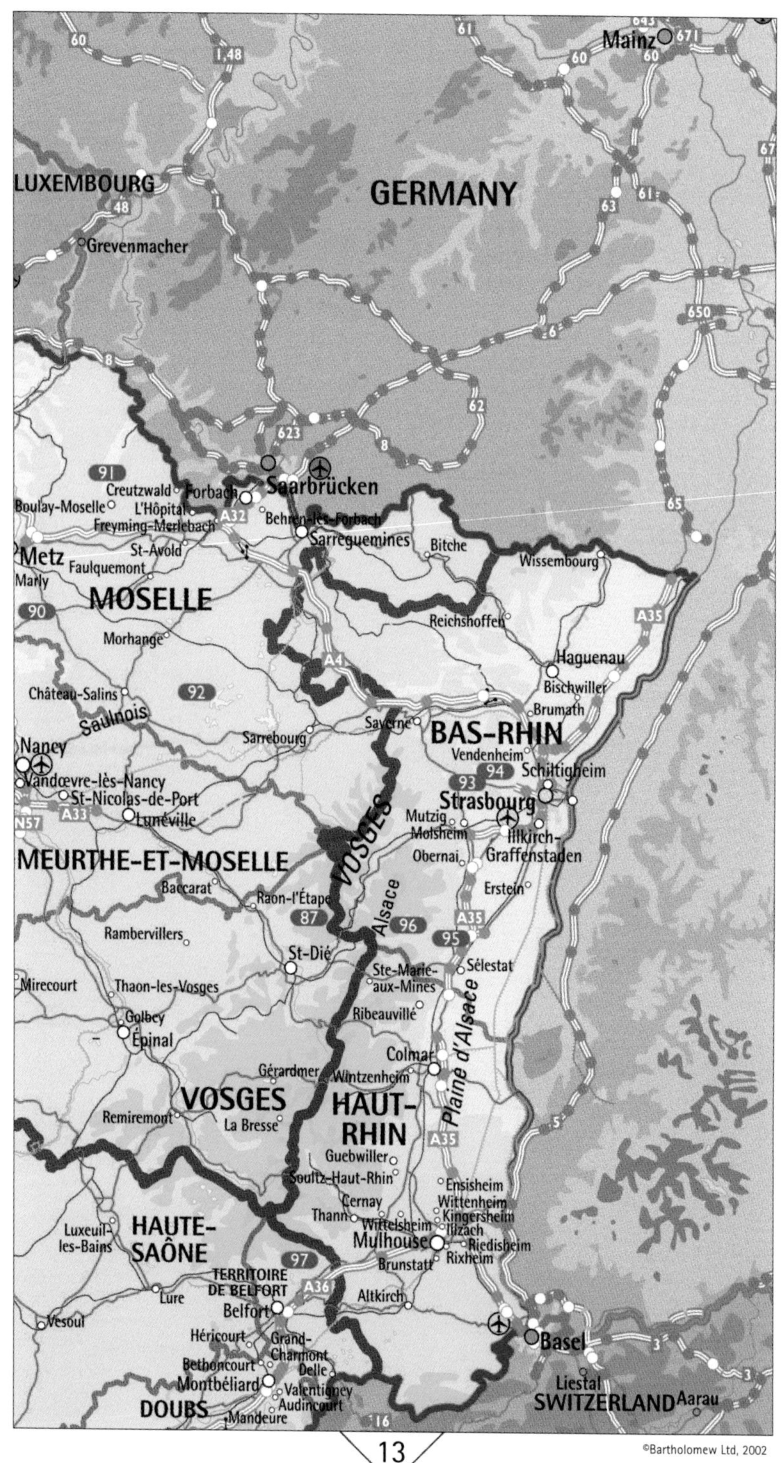
GERMANY
Mainz
LUXEMBOURG
Grevenmacher
Saarbrücken
Creutzwald
Forbach
Boulay-Moselle
L'Hôpital
Behren-lès-Forbach
Freyming-Merlebach
Sarreguemines
Bitche
Wissembourg
Metz
St-Avold
Faulquemont
Marly
MOSELLE
Reichshoffen
Morhange
Haguenau
Bischwiller
Château-Salins
Saulnois
Brumath
Saverne
Sarrebourg
BAS-RHIN
Vendenheim
Schiltigheim
Nancy
Vandœuvre-lès-Nancy
St-Nicolas-de-Port
Lunéville
Strasbourg
VOSGES
Mutzig
Molsheim
Illkirch-Graffenstaden
Obernai
MEURTHE-ET-MOSELLE
Baccarat
Raon-l'Étape
Alsace
Erstein
Rambervillers
St-Dié
Sélestat
Ste-Marie-aux-Mines
Mirecourt
Thaon-les-Vosges
Ribeauvillé
Golbey
Épinal
Colmar
Plaine d'Alsace
Gérardmer
Wintzenheim
VOSGES
Remiremont
La Bresse
HAUT-RHIN
Guebwiller
Soultz-Haut-Rhin
Ensisheim
Cernay
Wittenheim
Thann
Kingersheim
Wittelsheim
Illzach
Luxeuil-les-Bains
HAUTE-SAÔNE
Mulhouse
Riedisheim
Rixheim
Brunstatt
TERRITOIRE DE BELFORT
Lure
Altkirch
Belfort
Vesoul
Héricourt
Grand-Charmont
Basel
Bethoncourt
Delle
Montbéliard
Valentigney
Audincourt
Liestal
SWITZERLAND
Aarau
DOUBS
Mandeure
13

Map 8

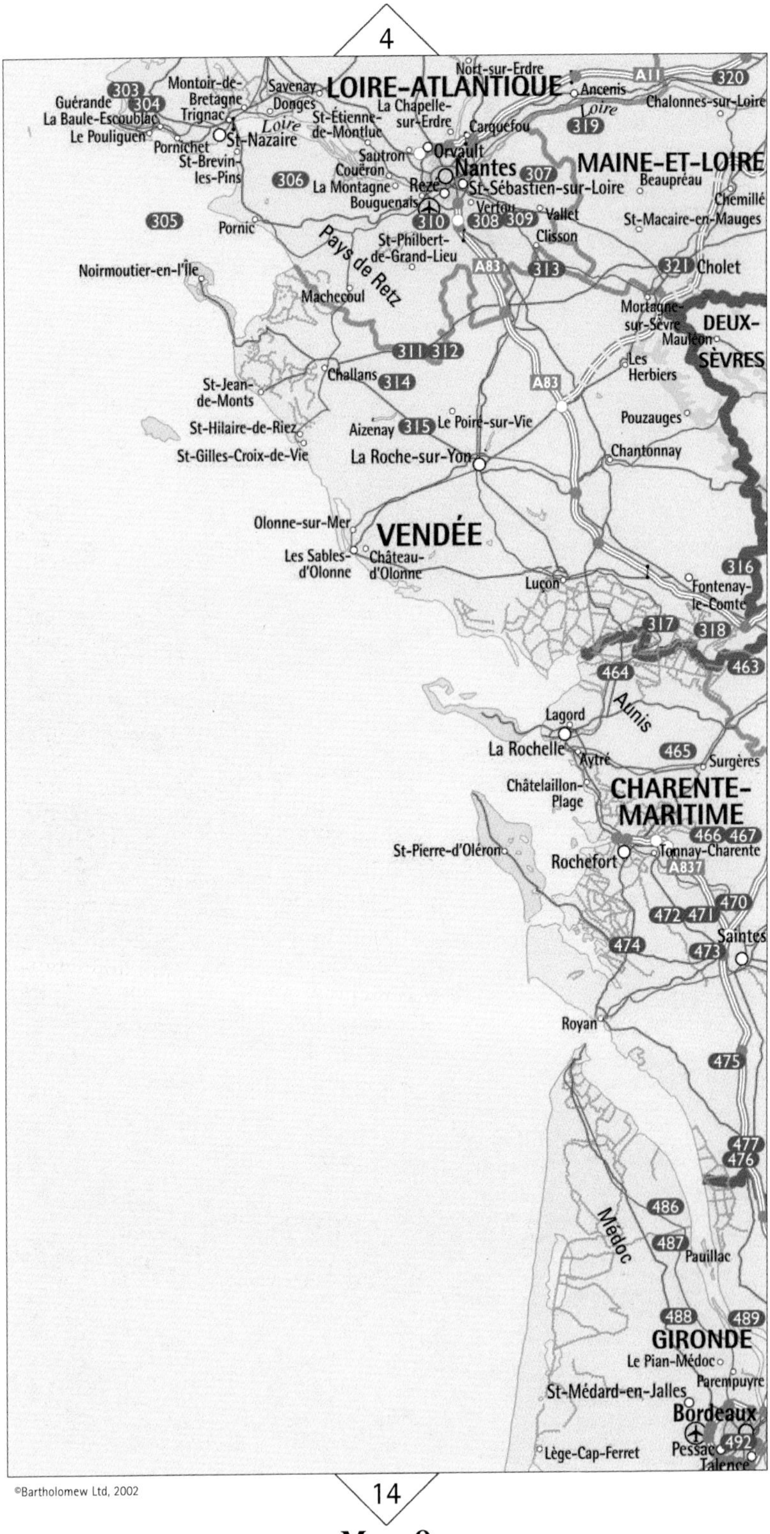

4

LOIRE-ATLANTIQUE
Nort-sur-Erdre
A11
320
Ancenis
Loire
Chalonnes-sur-Loire
319
303
304
Guérande
La Baule-Escoublac
Le Pouliguen
Montoir-de-Bretagne
Trignac
Pornichet
St-Nazaire
St-Brevin-les-Pins
Savenay
Donges
Loire
St-Étienne-de-Montluc
La Chapelle-sur-Erdre
Carquefou
Sautron
Orvault
Couëron
Nantes
307
MAINE-ET-LOIRE
306
La Montagne
Rezé
St-Sébastien-sur-Loire
Beaupréau
Bouguenais
Vertou
Vallet
Chemillé
305
Pornic
310
308
309
St-Macaire-en-Mauges
Pays de Retz
St-Philbert-de-Grand-Lieu
Clisson
Noirmoutier-en-l'Île
A83
313
321
Cholet
Machecoul
Mortagne-sur-Sèvre
Mauléon
DEUX-SÈVRES
311
312
Les Herbiers
St-Jean-de-Monts
Challans
314
A83
St-Hilaire-de-Riez
Aizenay
315
Le Poiré-sur-Vie
Pouzauges
St-Gilles-Croix-de-Vie
La Roche-sur-Yon
Chantonnay
Olonne-sur-Mer
VENDÉE
Les Sables-d'Olonne
Château-d'Olonne
316
Luçon
Fontenay-le-Comte
317
318
463
464
Aunis
Lagord
La Rochelle
Aytré
465
Surgères
Châtelaillon-Plage
CHARENTE-MARITIME
466
467
St-Pierre-d'Oléron
Rochefort
Tonnay-Charente
A837
470
472
471
Saintes
474
473
Royan
475
477
476
486
Médoc
487
Pauillac
488
489
GIRONDE
Le Pian-Médoc
Parempuyre
St-Médard-en-Jalles
Bordeaux
Pessac
492
Talence
Lège-Cap-Ferret

14

Map 9

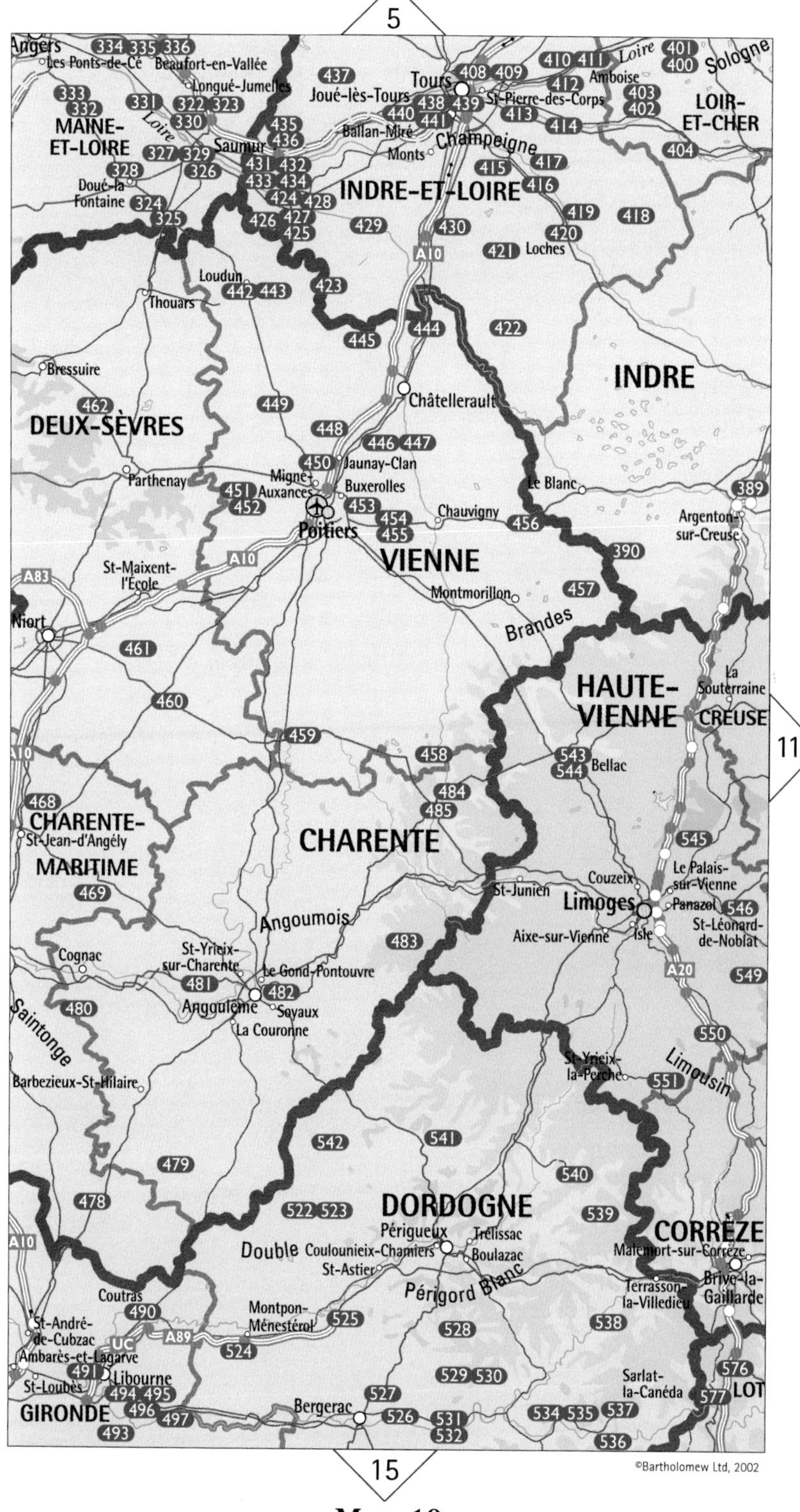
5
Angers
Les Ponts-de-Cé
Beaufort-en-Vallée
Longué-Jumelles
Loire
Saumur
MAINE-ET-LOIRE
Doué-la-Fontaine
Tours
Joué-lès-Tours
Ballan-Miré
Monts
Champeigne
St-Pierre-des-Corps
Amboise
Sologne
LOIR-ET-CHER
INDRE-ET-LOIRE
Loches
Loudun
Thouars
Bressuire
DEUX-SÈVRES
Parthenay
INDRE
Châtellerault
Jaunay-Clan
Migné-Auxances
Buxerolles
Poitiers
Chauvigny
Le Blanc
Argenton-sur-Creuse
VIENNE
St-Maixent-l'École
Niort
Montmorillon
Brandes
HAUTE-VIENNE
La Souterraine
CREUSE
11
Bellac
CHARENTE-MARITIME
St-Jean-d'Angély
CHARENTE
Couzeix
Le Palais-sur-Vienne
St-Junien
Limoges
Panazol
Aixe-sur-Vienne
Isle
St-Léonard-de-Noblat
Angoumois
Cognac
St-Yrieix-sur-Charente
Le Gond-Pontouvre
Angoulême
Soyaux
La Couronne
Saintonge
Barbezieux-St-Hilaire
St-Yrieix-la-Perche
Limousin
DORDOGNE
Périgueux
Trélissac
Double
Coulounieix-Chamiers
Boulazac
St-Astier
Périgord Blanc
CORRÈZE
Malemort-sur-Corrèze
Brive-la-Gaillarde
Terrasson-la-Villedieu
Coutras
St-André-de-Cubzac
Montpon-Ménestérol
Ambarès-et-Lagarve
Libourne
St-Loubès
GIRONDE
Bergerac
Sarlat-la-Canéda
LOT
A10
A83
A20
A89
15
©Bartholomew Ltd, 2002

Map 10

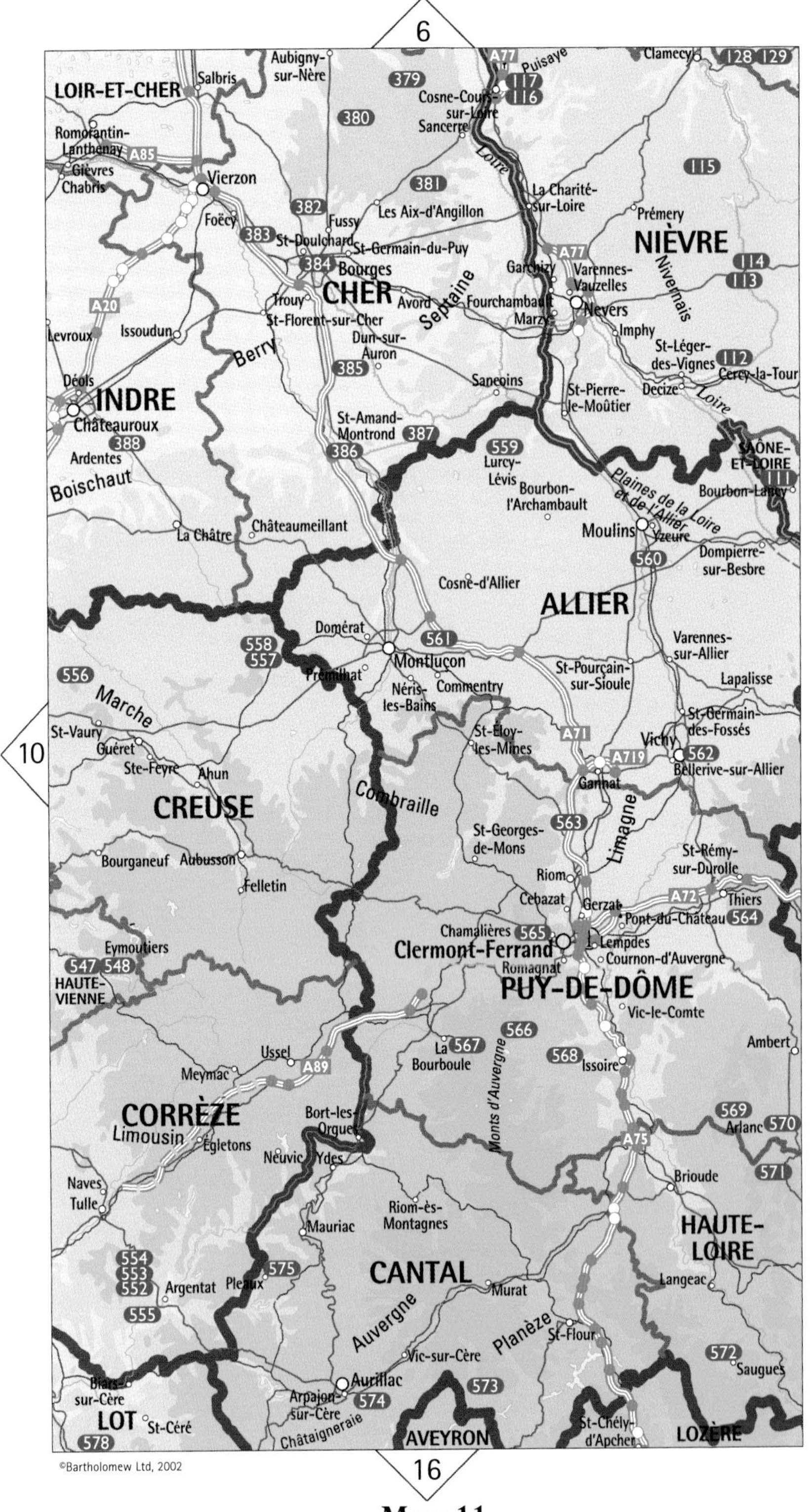

6
10
16
LOIR-ET-CHER
Salbris
Aubigny-sur-Nère
379
380
A77
Puisaye
117
116
Cosne-Cours-sur-Loire
Sancerre
Clamecy
128
129
Romorantin-Lanthenay
A85
Gièvres
Chabris
Vierzon
Loire
115
381
382
Fussy
Les Aix-d'Angillon
La Charité-sur-Loire
Prémery
Foëcy
383
St-Doulchard
St-Germain-du-Puy
NIÈVRE
384
Bourges
A77
Garchizy
Varennes-Vauzelles
Nivernais
114
113
CHER
Septaine
Trouy
Avord
Fourchambault
Nevers
A20
St-Florent-sur-Cher
Marzy
Imphy
Levroux
Issoudun
Berry
Dun-sur-Auron
St-Léger-des-Vignes
112
Cerey-la-Tour
385
Sancoins
Déols
INDRE
St-Pierre-le-Moûtier
Decize
Loire
Châteauroux
St-Amand-Montrond
387
388
386
559
SAÔNE-ET-LOIRE
Ardentes
Lurcy-Lévis
111
Boischaut
Bourbon-l'Archambault
Plaines de la Loire et de l'Allier
Bourbon-Lancy
Moulins
Yzeure
La Châtre
Châteaumeillant
560
Dompierre-sur-Besbre
Cosne-d'Allier
ALLIER
Domérat
558
557
561
Varennes-sur-Allier
556
Montluçon
Prémilhat
St-Pourçain-sur-Sioule
Lapalisse
Commentry
Néris-les-Bains
Marche
St-Germain-des-Fossés
St-Éloy-les-Mines
A71
St-Vaury
Guéret
Vichy
562
A719
Bellerive-sur-Allier
Ste-Feyre
Ahun
Gannat
Combraille
CREUSE
563
Limagne
St-Georges-de-Mons
St-Rémy-sur-Durolle
Bourganeuf
Aubusson
Riom
Felletin
Cebazat
Gerzat
A72
Thiers
Pont-du-Château
564
Chamalières
565
Lempdes
Clermont-Ferrand
Eymoutiers
Romagnat
Cournon-d'Auvergne
547
548
HAUTE-VIENNE
PUY-DE-DÔME
Vic-le-Comte
566
La Bourboule
567
568
Issoire
Ambert
Ussel
A89
Meymac
Monts d'Auvergne
CORRÈZE
Bort-les-Orgues
569
Arlanc
570
Limousin
Egletons
A75
Neuvic
Ydes
Brioude
571
Naves
Tulle
Riom-ès-Montagnes
Mauriac
HAUTE-LOIRE
554
553
552
575
CANTAL
Argentat
Pleaux
Murat
Langeac
555
Auvergne
Planèze
St-Flour
572
Saugues
Vic-sur-Cère
Biars-sur-Cère
Aurillac
573
Arpajon-sur-Cère
574
LOT
St-Céré
Châtaigneraie
AVEYRON
St-Chély-d'Apcher
LOZÈRE
578

Map 11

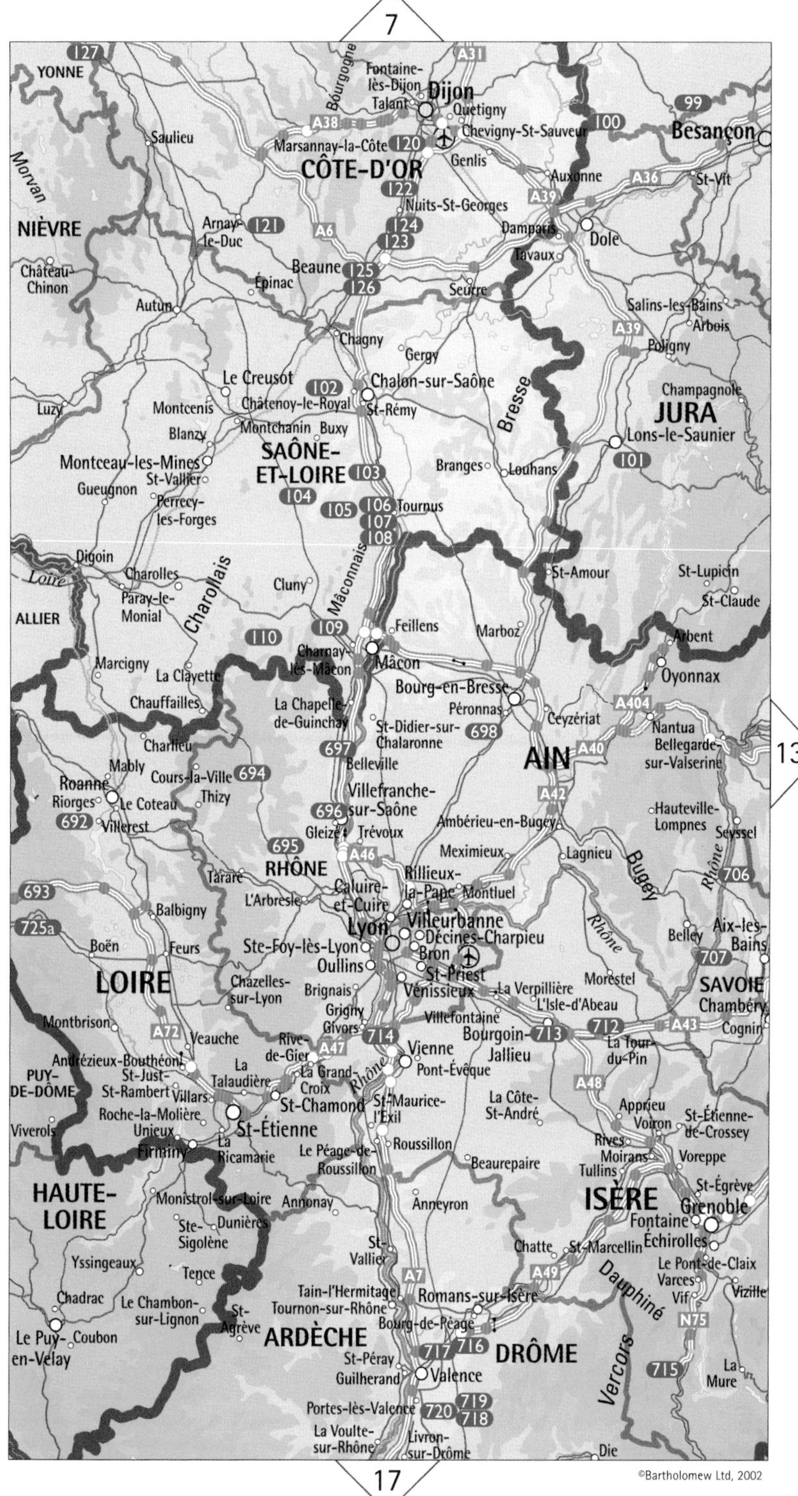
7
13
17
©Bartholomew Ltd, 2002

Map 12

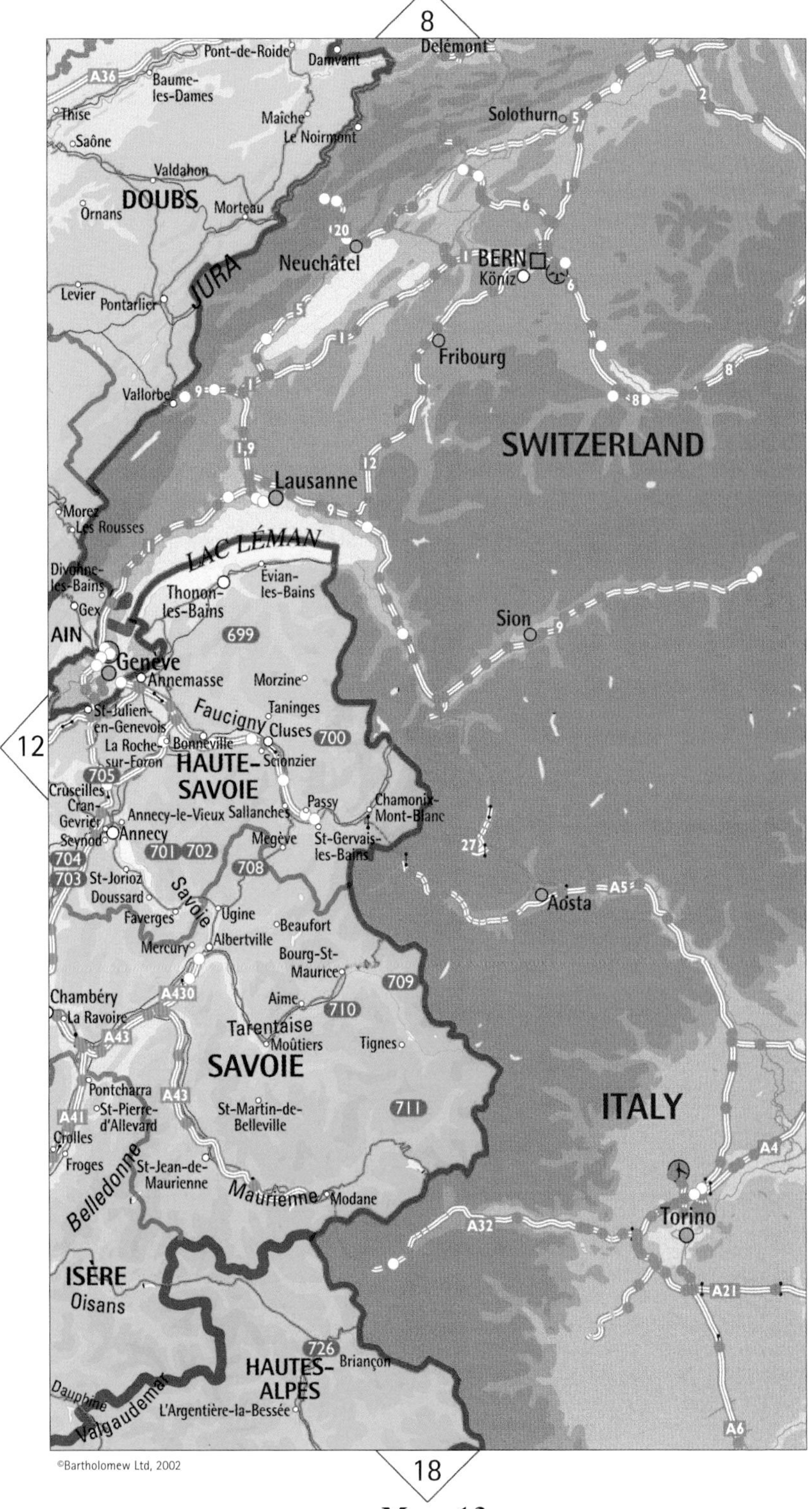
8
Pont-de-Roide
Damvant
Delémont
Baume-les-Dames
Thise
Maîche
Le Noirmont
Saône
Solothurn
Valdahon
DOUBS
Ornans
Morteau
Neuchâtel
JURA
BERN
Köniz
Levier
Pontarlier
Fribourg
Vallorbe
SWITZERLAND
Lausanne
Morez
Les Rousses
LAC LÉMAN
Divonne-les-Bains
Gex
Thonon-les-Bains
Évian-les-Bains
Sion
AIN
Genève
Annemasse
Morzine
Faucigny
Taninges
St-Julien-en-Genevois
Cluses
La Roche-sur-Foron
Bonneville
HAUTE-SAVOIE
Scionzier
Cruseilles
Cran-Gevrier
Annecy-le-Vieux
Sallanches
Passy
Chamonix-Mont-Blanc
Seynod
Annecy
Megève
St-Gervais-les-Bains
St-Jorioz
Doussard
Savoie
Aosta
Faverges
Ugine
Beaufort
Mercury
Albertville
Bourg-St-Maurice
Chambéry
Aime
La Ravoire
Tarentaise
Moûtiers
Tignes
SAVOIE
Pontcharra
St-Pierre-d'Allevard
St-Martin-de-Belleville
ITALY
Crolles
Froges
St-Jean-de-Maurienne
Belledonne
Maurienne
Modane
Torino
ISÈRE
Oisans
HAUTES-ALPES
Briançon
Dauphiné
Valgaudemar
L'Argentière-la-Bessée
12
18

Map 13

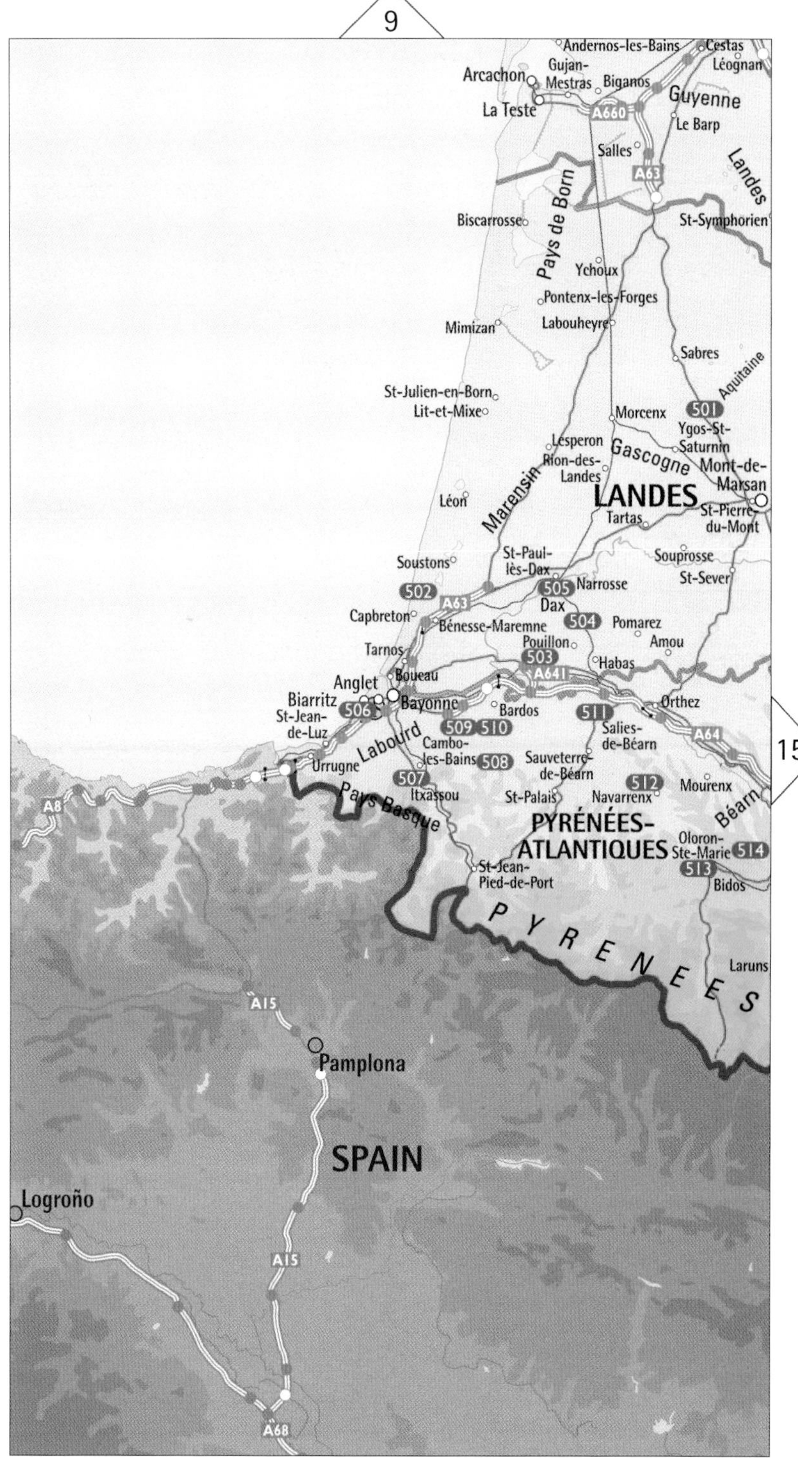
9
15
Andernos-les-Bains
Cestas
Léognan
Arcachon
Gujan-Mestras
Biganos
La Teste
A660
Guyenne
Le Barp
Salles
A63
Landes
Pays de Born
Biscarrosse
St-Symphorien
Ychoux
Pontenx-les-Forges
Mimizan
Labouheyre
Sabres
Aquitaine
St-Julien-en-Born
Lit-et-Mixe
Morcenx
501
Ygos-St-Saturnin
Lesperon
Gascogne
Rion-des-Landes
Mont-de-Marsan
Marensin
LANDES
Léon
Tartas
St-Pierre-du-Mont
St-Paul-lès-Dax
Souprosse
Soustons
St-Sever
502
505
Narrosse
A63
Dax
Capbreton
504
Pomarez
Bénesse-Maremne
Amou
Pouillon
Tarnos
503
Habas
Boueau
A641
Anglet
Biarritz
Bayonne
Orthez
506
Bardos
St-Jean-de-Luz
509
510
511
Salies-de-Béarn
A64
Labourd
Cambo-les-Bains
508
Sauveterre-de-Béarn
Urrugne
507
512
Mourenx
Itxassou
St-Palais
Navarrenx
A8
Pays Basque
PYRÉNÉES-ATLANTIQUES
Béarn
Oloron-Ste-Marie
514
513
St-Jean-Pied-de-Port
Bidos
PYRENEES
Laruns
A15
Pamplona
SPAIN
Logroño
A15
A68
©Bartholomew Ltd, 2002

Map 14

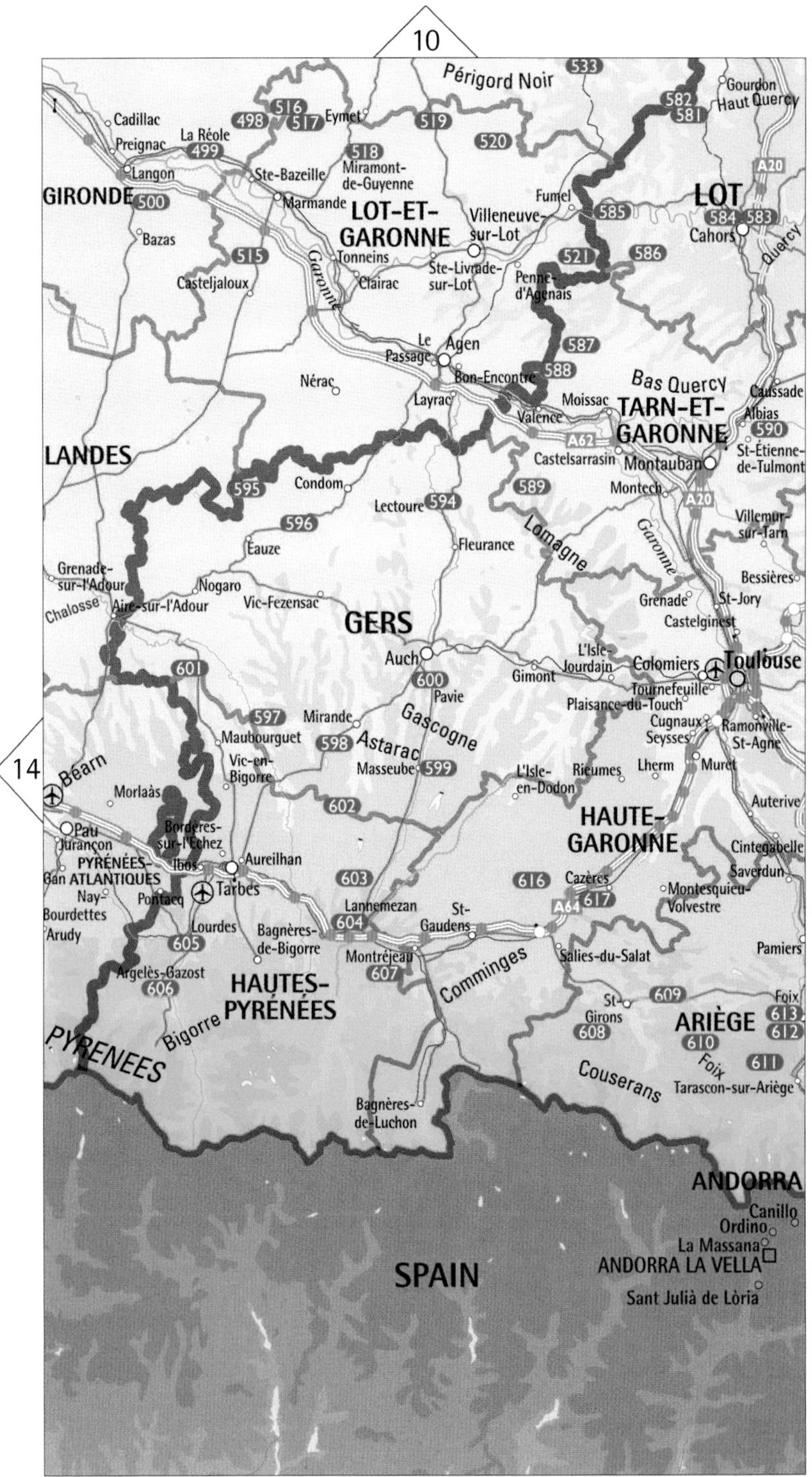

10
14
Périgord Noir
Gourdon
Haut Quercy
Cadillac
Preignac
La Réole
Eymet
Langon
Ste-Bazeille
Miramont-de-Guyenne
GIRONDE
Marmande
LOT-ET-GARONNE
Fumel
Villeneuve-sur-Lot
LOT
Cahors
Quercy
Bazas
Tonneins
Ste-Livrade-sur-Lot
Penne-d'Agenais
Casteljaloux
Clairac
Garonne
Le Passage
Agen
Bon-Encontre
Nérac
Layrac
Bas Quercy
Moissac
TARN-ET-GARONNE
Caussade
Albias
Valence
LANDES
Castelsarrasin
Montauban
St-Étienne-de-Tulmont
Condom
Lectoure
Montech
Fleurance
Lomagne
Villemur-sur-Tarn
Eauze
Grenade-sur-l'Adour
Nogaro
Bessières
Chalosse
Aire-sur-l'Adour
Vic-Fezensac
Grenade
St-Jory
GERS
Castelginest
Auch
L'Isle-Jourdain
Colomiers
Toulouse
Gimont
Pavie
Tournefeuille
Plaisance-du-Touch
Gascogne
Mirande
Cugnaux
Ramonville-St-Agne
Seysses
Maubourguet
Astarac
Béarn
Vic-en-Bigorre
Masseube
L'Isle-en-Dodon
Rieumes
Lherm
Muret
Morlaàs
Auterive
Pau
Bordères-sur-l'Echez
HAUTE-GARONNE
Jurançon
Cintegabelle
PYRÉNÉES-ATLANTIQUES
Ibos
Aureilhan
Saverdun
Gan
Tarbes
Cazères
Montesquieu-Volvestre
Nay-Bourdettes
Pontacq
Lannemezan
St-Gaudens
Arudy
Lourdes
Bagnères-de-Bigorre
Montréjeau
Salies-du-Salat
Pamiers
Comminges
Argelès-Gazost
HAUTES-PYRÉNÉES
St-Girons
Foix
ARIÈGE
Bigorre
PYRENEES
Couserans
Tarascon-sur-Ariège
Bagnères-de-Luchon
ANDORRA
Canillo
Ordino
La Massana
ANDORRA LA VELLA
Sant Julià de Lòria
SPAIN
A20
A62
A64
498
499
500
515
516
517
518
519
520
521
533
581
582
583
584
585
586
587
588
589
590
594
595
596
597
598
599
600
601
602
603
604
605
606
607
608
609
610
611
612
613
616
617

Map 15

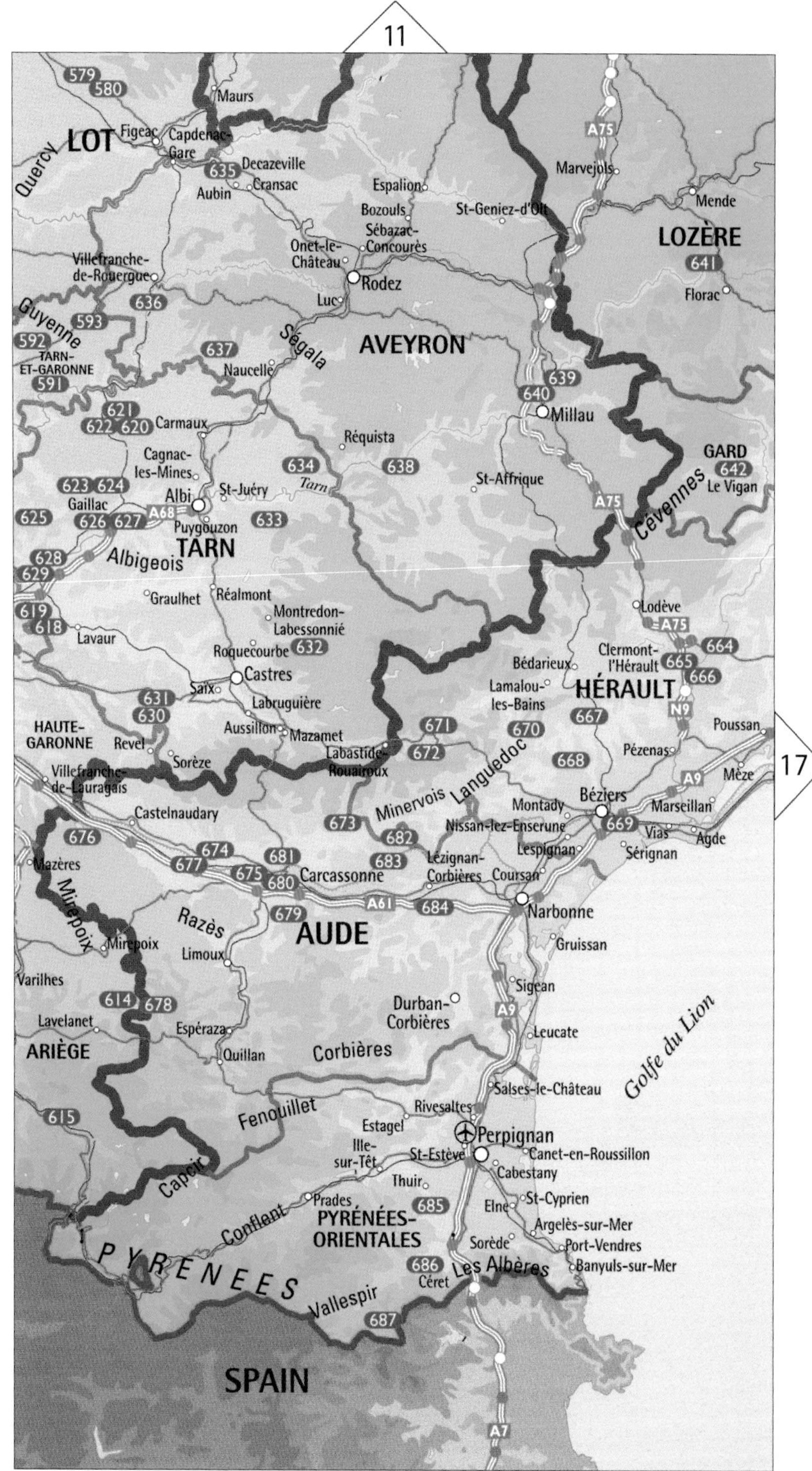

©Bartholomew Ltd, 2002

Map 16

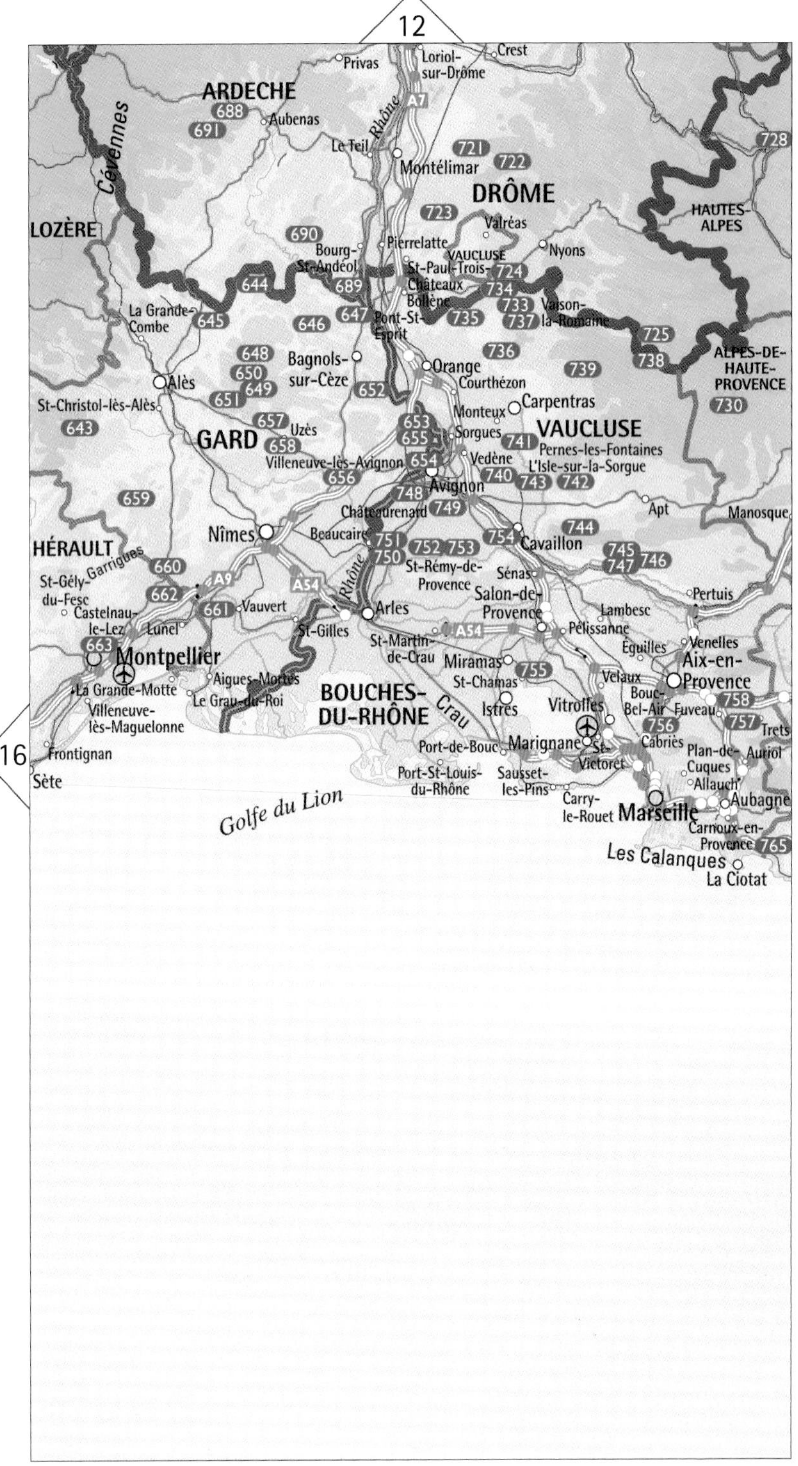
12
16
Privas
Loriol-sur-Drôme
Crest
ARDECHE
688
691
Aubenas
Cévennes
Rhône
A7
Le Teil
Montélimar
721
722
728
DRÔME
LOZÈRE
723
Valréas
HAUTES-ALPES
690
Bourg-St-Andéol
Pierrelatte
VAUCLUSE
Nyons
St-Paul-Trois-Châteaux
724
644
689
734
Bollène
733
Vaison-la-Romaine
La Grande-Combe
645
646
647
Pont-St-Esprit
735
737
725
738
ALPES-DE-HAUTE-PROVENCE
648
Bagnols-sur-Cèze
Orange
736
739
650
649
Alès
Courthézon
652
730
651
Carpentras
St-Christol-lès-Alès
Monteux
643
657
653
Uzès
GARD
655
Sorgues
741
VAUCLUSE
658
Pernes-les-Fontaines
Vedène
Villeneuve-lès-Avignon
654
740
L'Isle-sur-la-Sorgue
656
Avignon
743
742
748
659
Châteaurenard
749
Apt
Manosque
Nîmes
Beaucaire
744
HÉRAULT
751
752
753
754
Cavaillon
Garrigues
750
745
747
746
St-Rémy-de-Provence
660
Sénas
St-Gély-du-Fesc
A9
A54
Salon-de-Provence
Pertuis
662
Castelnau-le-Lez
661
Vauvert
Arles
Lambesc
Lunel
St-Gilles
A54
Pélissanne
663
Montpellier
St-Martin-de-Crau
Éguilles
Venelles
Miramas
755
Aix-en-Provence
La Grande-Motte
Aigues-Mortes
St-Chamas
Velaux
Villeneuve-lès-Maguelonne
Le Grau-du-Roi
BOUCHES-DU-RHÔNE
Crau
Istres
Vitrolles
Bouc-Bel-Air
Fuveau
758
756
757
Trets
Frontignan
Port-de-Bouc
Marignane
St-Victoret
Cabriès
Plan-de-Cuques
Auriol
Sète
Port-St-Louis-du-Rhône
Sausset-les-Pins
Allauch
Aubagne
Golfe du Lion
Carry-le-Rouet
Marseille
Carnoux-en-Provence
765
Les Calanques
La Ciotat

Map 17

13

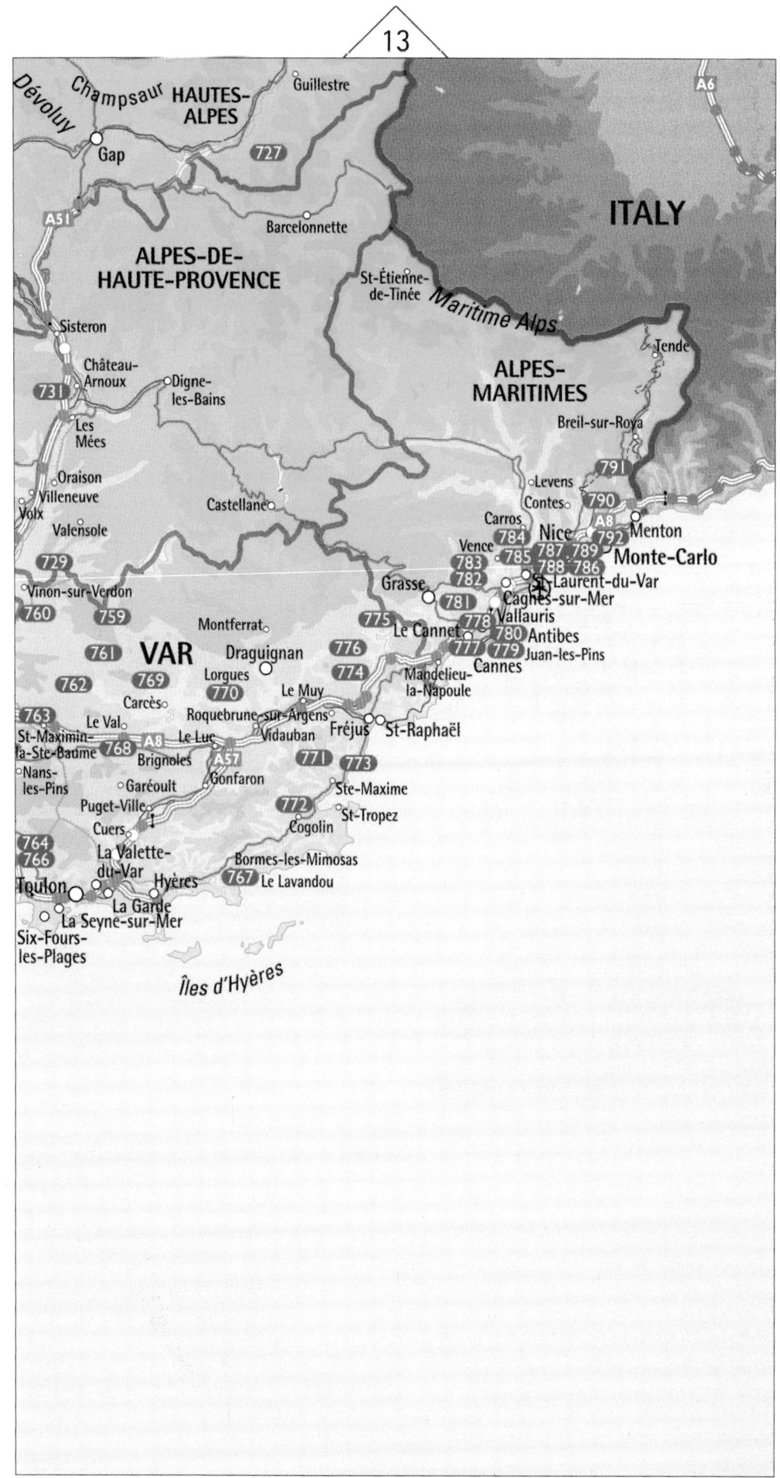

Dévoluy
Champsaur
HAUTES-ALPES
Guillestre
Gap
727
A51
Barcelonnette
ITALY
A6
ALPES-DE-HAUTE-PROVENCE
St-Étienne-de-Tinée
Maritime Alps
Sisteron
Tende
Château-Arnoux
Digne-les-Bains
ALPES-MARITIMES
731
Les Mées
Breil-sur-Roya
791
Oraison
Villeneuve
Volx
Levens
Castellane
Contes
790
Valensole
Carros
A8
Menton
784
Nice
792
Vence
787
789
Monte-Carlo
729
785
783
788
786
Grasse
782
St-Laurent-du-Var
Vinon-sur-Verdon
781
Cagnes-sur-Mer
760
759
775
778
Vallauris
Montferrat
Le Cannet
780
Antibes
761
VAR
Draguignan
776
777
779
Juan-les-Pins
Cannes
762
769
Lorgues
774
Mandelieu-la-Napoule
770
Le Muy
Carcès
763
Le Val
Roquebrune-sur-Argens
Fréjus
St-Raphaël
St-Maximin-la-Ste-Baume
768
A8
Le Luc
Vidauban
Brignoles
A57
771
773
Nans-les-Pins
Gonfaron
Garéoult
Ste-Maxime
Puget-Ville
772
St-Tropez
Cuers
Cogolin
764
766
La Valette-du-Var
Bormes-les-Mimosas
767
Le Lavandou
Toulon
Hyères
La Garde
La Seyne-sur-Mer
Six-Fours-les-Plages
Îles d'Hyères

Map 18

THE NORTH · PICARDY

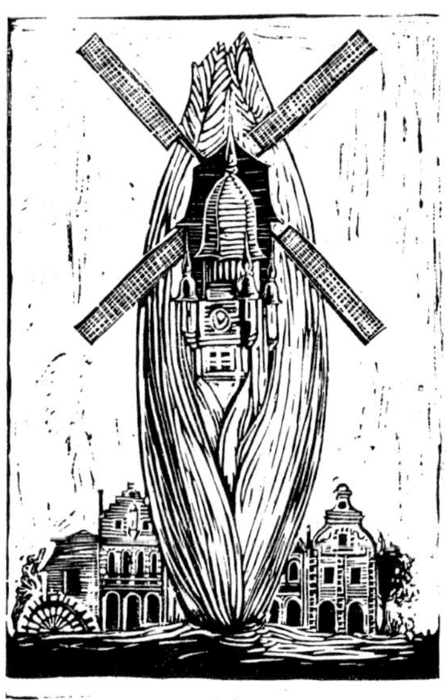

On the flat plains of Flanders, windmills, belfries and the arcades of lovely old Arras grow among the wheat and maize. In rolling, river-run Picardy, Gothic fervour spills from gargoyles' throats over the thirsty fields, twice quenched by Europe's young blood, and out to the misty bird sanctuary and the long low sea.

Calm countryside with neither cockerels nor dogs to alarm your early morning and a genuine, unpretentious hostess and house. It's fun too. There are garden games, *pétanque* tournaments in summer, informal wine-tastings, an outbuilding where you may use the cooking equipment. Bedrooms are colour coded; we preferred the fabrics and antiques of the three in the attic of this long low farmhouse (mind your head up there!). The new garden room is snug with its own little patio. Gina cares deeply that everyone should be happy, adores her guests and creates a really homely atmosphere. Ask about her themed weekends.

rooms	6: 4 doubles, 2 family rooms, all with bath or shower & wc.
price	€42-€46 for two.
dinner	€18.50 with wine, by arrangement.
closed	Rarely.
directions	From Calais A26, exit 4 to Thérouanne; D341 to Auchy au Bois, 12km. Right at Le Vert Dragon restaurant. 1st left; 2nd house on right after church.

	Gina Bulot
	Les Cohettes,
	28 rue de Pernes,
	62190 Auchy au Bois, Pas-de-Calais
tel	(0)3 21 02 09 47
fax	(0)3 21 02 81 68
e-mail	temps-libre-evasion@wanadoo.fr

This is a real farm, so don't expect pretty-pretty as you approach it, but Madame's welcome is top class. It was recommended by one of our readers who has been back many a time for the atmosphere... and the food. Furniture has been handed down or gleaned from careful perusal of local *brocantes* and is set off by impeccably French wallpaper. Good bedding, too. Small boys – and bigger ones – will love the Fifties table football. Or there's a billiard table and various other games to keep you occupied before supper, which will be delicious and probably all grown a stone's throw from the kitchen. A good, French place to stop.

rooms	3: 1 twin, 1 triple, 1 suite, all with shower & wc.
price	€39 for two.
dinner	€14 with wine, by arrangement.
closed	Rarely.
directions	Exit Thérouanne from A26; then D341 for Arras; after 'Vert Dragon' r'bout, 1st on right.

Brigitte de Saint Laurent
Ferme de la Vallée,
13 rue Neuve,
62190 Auchy au Bois, Pas-de-Calais
tel (0)3 21 25 80 09
fax (0)3 21 25 80 09

THE NORTH

A lovely surprise as you turn into the big farmyard: the old house is as splendid as the 19th-century brewery across the road with its curious double swastika emblem, and the people are simple, warm and gentle. Their children have grown and flown, they no longer farm and visibly enjoy good company. The homely décor is without pretension, the attic bedrooms are basic but perfectly adequate with their roof windows, screened-off showers (one outside the room), old timbers and floorboards; the welcome is family-friendly. A good-value stopover or an excellent base for battlefield visits or a day trip to fascinating old Arras.

rooms	5: 3 doubles, 1 twin, 1 quadruple, all with shower, sharing 2 wcs.
price	€33 for two.
dinner	Restaurants 5km.
closed	Christmas & New Year.
directions	From A26 exit 7 on N50 for Lille to Gavrelle then Fampoux; in village follow Chambres d'Hôtes signs; house on right.

Dominique & Marie-Thérèse Peugniez
17 rue Paul Verlaine,
62118 Fampoux, Pas-de-Calais
tel (0)3 21 55 00 90
fax (0)3 21 55 00 90

Madame is warmly relaxed and attentive, the pivot of her much-photographed family, and is passionate about interior design: beautifully made curtains, gently matched papers and fabrics, old-fashioned touches here (crochet, carving), modern details there in good comfortable bedrooms. Monsieur's domain, the sheltered garden going down to the little river, is splendid (swings for the children too) and the lime trees are a fitting backdrop to this imposing old manor built in soft grey stone. It originally belonged to the château next door and the drive is still flanked by a fine laurel hedge. A gentle, civilised place to stay.

rooms	2: 1 double, 1 family suite, both with bath or shower & wc.
price	€44 for two.
dinner	Choice of restaurants 4-7km.
closed	Rarely.
directions	From Arras, N39 for Le Touquet. After 6km under r'way bridge, 1st left along D56 to Duisans. House 1st on left.

Annie & Patrick Senlis
Le Clos Grincourt,
18 rue du Château,
62161 Duisans, Pas-de-Calais

tel (0)3 21 48 68 33
fax (0)3 21 48 68 33

THE NORTH

The re-lifted stately face looks finer than ever in its great park and orchards (producing delicious apples by 'Reasoned Agriculture'). Inside, it's a warm, embracing country house with a panelled breakfast room, a perfectly amazing, museum-worthy, multi-tiled gents cloakroom and, up the wide old stairs, delightful bedrooms, some very big, mostly done with fresh pine furniture and good strong colours on wooden floors with old fireplaces or mirrored *armoires*. Quiet and intelligent, Sylvie will make you feel deeply welcome in her redecorated rooms while serenely managing her young family.
Gîte space for 4.

rooms	5: 1 double, 2 triples, 2 suites for 4, all with bath or shower & wc.
price	€46 for two.
dinner	Choice of restaurants 5-9km.
closed	January.
directions	From Doullens N25 towards Arras 17km. In L'Arbret, 1st left to Saulty; follow signs.

Emmanuel & Sylvie Dalle
Château de Saulty,
82 rue de la Gare,
62158 Saulty, Pas-de-Calais

tel (0)3 21 48 24 76
fax (0)3 21 48 18 32
e-mail chateaudesaulty@nordnet.fr

An exceptional mix of place and people. After 12 years, this dynamic family, all eight of them, have almost finished rebuilding their château and brightening their escutcheon while being publishers in Paris and brilliant socialites – fascinating people, phenomenal energy, natural hospitality that makes up for any residual damp or slight winter chill. Built in 1745, the château has striking grandeur: come play lord and lady in vastly beautiful chandeliered, ancestored *salons*, enjoy an aristocratically graceful bedroom with big windows and a good bathroom and walk the rolling green parkland as if it were your own.

rooms	4 doubles/twins, all with bath or shower & wc.
price	€90 for two.
dinner	Two restaurants within 4km.
closed	Rarely.
directions	From Arras N39 for St Pol & Le Touquet 5km; left D339 to Avesnes le Comte; D75 for Doullens & Grand Rullecourt 4km. Château in village square; sign.

Patrice & Chantal de Saulieu
Château de Grand Rullecourt,
62810 Grand Rullecourt,
Pas-de-Calais
tel (0)3 21 58 06 37
fax (0)1 41 27 97 30
e-mail saulieu@routiers.com
web www.saulieu.com/chateau/

THE NORTH

You may just come for lovely old Arras or the military cemeteries of the Vimy Ridge but the rural simplicity of this low house, hugging its little garden behind the church, could entice you to stay longer. The very personal rooms with their air of family history are a delightful mix of modern and old: spriggy wallpaper among the timbers, an unusual old desk in the ground-floor room, a super multi-purpose piece on the red-carpeted landing (an armchair/desk/bookcase said to have belonged to Jules Verne), plus well-fitted bathrooms. Madame is shyly proud of her house and serves a generous, imaginative breakfast.

rooms	3: 2 doubles, 1 twin, all with bath or shower & wc.
price	€30 for two.
dinner	Basic bar/restaurant 5km.
closed	Rarely.
directions	From Arras N25 towards Doullens. At Bac du Sud right on D66 to Gouy en Artois & Fosseux. House near church.

Geneviève Delacourt
3 rue de l'Église,
62810 Fosseux, Pas-de-Calais
tel (0)3 21 48 40 13
fax (0)3 21 48 40 13

They are wonderful in their unexpected town farmyard! A retired couple of real farmers, he silently earthy, tending his garden, she comfortably maternal, delighting in her freedom to discover the rest of the world at last. Their typical farmers' house is old-fashioned, pretty and stuffed with china, glass, copper and pewter while the genuine *chambres d'hôtes* are family-furnished and draped with all sorts and conditions of crochet. Street at the front, fields at the back, farmyard and creeper-covered old house in between – and such a friendly welcome. You are perfectly placed for the 20th-century battlefields of France.

rooms	2: 1 double, 1 triple, each with shower or bath, sharing wc.
price	€32 for two.
dinner	€12 with wine, by arrangement.
closed	Rarely.
directions	A26 from Calais, exit Aix-Noulette for Liévin. Head for 'centre ville'; for Givenchy. House 300m past little park.

M & Mme François Dupont
Ferme du Moulin,
58 rue du Quatre Septembre,
62800 Liévin, Pas-de-Calais

tel (0)3 21 44 65 91

map: 2 entry: 8

THE NORTH

After years as a school librarian, Madame has thrown herself into encouraging local tourism: a member of numerous associations – theatre, library, tourism – she loves taking guests on walks and visits, and Monsieur is mayor of the village. Many people drive straight through this area – do take the chance to know it better with people who belong. You enter through the conservatory and every window looks onto flowers and meadows beyond. One room has doors to the garden, the others are upstairs, all are simple but welcoming. Children love it here – farm trips are possible – and you will enjoy some genuine French cooking.

rooms	2: 1 double with shower & separate wc; 1 family suite with bath & wc.
price	€38 for two.
dinner	€16 with wine, by arrangement.
closed	Rarely.
directions	From Calais A26 exit 6 on N41 for St Pol 15km; left D341 to Houdain; left D86 to Magnicourt.

Jacqueline Guillemant
6 rue de l'Europe,
62127 Magnicourt en Comte,
Pas-de-Calais

tel (0)3 21 41 51 00
fax (0)3 21 04 79 76
e-mail Jguillemant@hotmail.com

map: 2 entry: 9

You can see it has character and history and… two dining rooms: one has a unique '1830s-medieval' fireplace, the other is classical French with coffered ceiling, deeply carved door frames, a vast Louis XIII dresser. In an outbuilding, guest rooms are simpler and more modern, each with some old furniture and a neat shower room, one with its own kitchen and garden. Madame loves telling tales of the house and its contents, has a couple of goats in the quiet garden (but weekend racetrack in the valley), will do anything she can to be of service to guests. Both your hosts work constantly on their beloved house – good folk.

rooms	5: 2 doubles, 3 twins, all with shower & wc.
price	€38 for two.
dinner	Restaurants within walking distance; self-catering possible.
closed	Rarely.
directions	From St Pol sur Ternoise, D343 NW for Fruges. Just after entering Gauchin Verloingt, right Rue de Troisvaux; right Rue des Montifaux. House on right.

Marie-Christine & Philippe Vion
Le Loubarré,
550 rue des Montifaux,
62130 Gauchin Verloingt,
Pas-de-Calais

tel	(0)3 21 03 05 05
fax	(0)3 21 41 26 76
e-mail	mcvion.loubarre@wanadoo.fr
web	loubarre.com

map: 1 entry: 10

THE NORTH

The excitement starts in the monumental tower living room (1750): it is crammed with 1000 things, from armoured reminders of the Battle of Agincourt (1415) to hats, statues and teddy bears. You may be bowled over, you may hear the clanking of swords and see medieval knights passing – that's just your hosts on their way to re-enact a battle. Passionate about local history and tales of ghosts, archers and horses, they are also exceedingly generous hosts. The atmospheric bedrooms, dark-beamed, heavy-draped, are in an even older outbuilding with a log-fired dayroom. Huge theatrical fun, a wonderful place for a real change.

rooms	4: 3 doubles, 1 triple, all with shower & wc (1 behind curtain).
price	€46 for two.
dinner	Restaurant 1km; choice 6-15km.
closed	Rarely.
directions	From St Omer D928 for Abbeville. At Ruisseauville 3rd left for Blangy-Tramecourt; at next x-roads, left for Tramecourt; house 100m along.

Patrick & Marie-Josée Fenet
La Gacogne,
62310 Azincourt, Pas-de-Calais

tel	(0)3 21 04 45 61
fax	(0)3 21 04 45 61

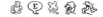

map: 1 entry: 11

Bedrooms round the pretty courtyard have wonky timbers, cream tiled floors, pastel colours and modern bathrooms – a joint effort: Madame's ideas executed by Monsieur. The Garrels left lively Lille for the calm of the country, exchanging staying in B&Bs for running their own. They love meeting guests, both young and old, and children from the village play in their yard. The family room snugly holds all you'll need with, toys, books and twin beds tucked beneath eaves – a dream den. Walk in the hills and woods behind – one of the delightful donkeys will happily accompany you.

rooms	3: 1 double, 1 suite for 4, both with shower, wc & kitchenette; 1 double with shower & wc.
price	€42 for two; €61 for four.
dinner	Restaurants 3-4km; self-catering possible; BBQ.
closed	Rarely.
directions	From Hesdin D928 for St Omer; 1st left D913 through Huby St Leu to Guisy; signs.

Martine & Marc-Willam Garrel
La Hotoire,
2 place de la Mairie,
62140 Guisy, Pas-de-Calais

tel	(0)3 21 81 00 31
fax	(0)3 21 81 00 31
e-mail	a.la.hotoire@wanadoo.fr
web	perso.wanadoo.fr/a.la.hotoire/

THE NORTH

After many years travelling around France, your hosts, an interesting couple, retired and at last had time for gardening, their favourite pastime. Then Monsieur converted the attic into two bedrooms with bathrooms and a cosy sitting room complete with kitchen corner. Weather permitting, breakfast is in the conservatory: the traditional baguette and croissants come with yogurt, cheese, and eggs from their own hens which share a meadow beyond the super garden with a small flock of sheep. For riding, swimming or sand yachting on miles of beach, Le Touquet is just over the bridge from the little port of Étaples.

rooms	2 doubles, each with shower & separate wc.
price	€45 for two.
dinner	Choice of restaurants Montreuil & Le Touquet, 7km.
closed	Rarely.
directions	From A16 exit 26 for Montreuil 1km; over railway; left for Tubersent; house on right.

Paulette Leprêtre Glatigny
La Silexeraie,
62 route d'Hodicq,
62170 Bréxent Énocq,
Pas-de-Calais

tel	(0)3 21 86 76 97
fax	(0)3 21 86 76 97
e-mail	Lasilexeraie@aol.com

A modern bungalow with the heart of traditional French country life. When your hosts handed the family farm on to the next generation, they wanted to go on doing B&B in their new house. The road is at the front, big windows let in the green that wraps the land at the back and it has a real family feel: photos and mementos everywhere, in the comfortable guest rooms too, with their good, pretty bathrooms. Madame, clearly a natural at grandmothering, might even mind your baby if you want to go off to sample the bright lights of Montreuil. Friendly and impeccable, it is excellent value and an ideal stopover.

rooms	2: 1 double with bath & wc; 1 quadruple with shower & wc.
price	€40-€43 for two.
dinner	Good choice of restaurants in Montreuil, 3km.
closed	Rarely.
directions	From A16 exit Montreuil sur Mer N1 for Le Touquet/Boulogne; at lights right to Neuville; right D113 for 200m; house on right.

Hubert & Christiane Fourdinier
30 rue de la Chartreuse,
62170 Neuville sous Montreuil,
Pas-de-Calais

tel	(0)3 21 81 95 05
fax	(0)3 21 81 95 05
e-mail	chfourdinier@wanadoo.fr
web	perso.wanadoo.fr/christiane.fourdinier

THE NORTH

Readers have called *La Saule's* breakfast cakes and compote their best in France. And we know that the Trunnets' smiles are genuine, their delight in your company unfeigned, their converted outbuilding handsome and perfectly finished (down to mosquito nets on windows), if a touch characterless, the beds excellent and the dayroom proud of its beautiful *armoire*. Monsieur is only too happy to show you the flax production process (it's fascinating), while Madame will be baking yet another superb cake for tomorrow's breakfast. Proclaimed "the best cowshed I've ever stayed in" by one happy guest.

rooms	4: 1 double, 3 triples, all with shower & wc.
price	€46 for two.
dinner	Restaurants in Montreuil, 6km.
closed	Rarely.
directions	From A16 exit Montreuil; just before town right at lights; left D349 to Brimeux; left at junction, pass church, house on right, sign. But from N39 exit Campagne les Hesdin.

M & Mme Germain Trunnet
Ferme du Saule,
20 rue de l'Église,
62170 Brimeux, Pas-de-Calais

tel	(0)3 21 06 01 28
fax	(0)3 21 81 40 14

Behind the pretty face hides the wonder of an extraordinary free-standing wooden staircase, a local speciality in the 17th century. Two gracious rooms up here: high ceilings, parquet floors, space and no clutter – the primrose and moss twin over the street has elegant original cupboards; the custard and wine double over the back is cosily alcoved. Families will like the privacy of the snugger room across the yard: pretty blue head cushions and duvet-clothed bunks. Your hosts used to run a bistro and Madame is the jolliest, laughingest hostess we know.

rooms	3: 1 twin with corner bath & wc; 1 double, 1 family room, both with bath & wc.
price	€50 for two.
dinner	Choice of restaurants on doorstep.
closed	Rarely.
directions	In Montreuil, drive to top, Place Darnétal; house on right facing square.

M & Mme Louchez
77 rue Pierre Ledent,
62170 Montreuil sur Mer,
Pas-de-Calais
tel (0)3 21 81 54 68
e-mail louchez.anne@wanadoo.fr

map: 1 entry: 16

THE NORTH

In the walled garden, the ancient dovecote sings with life; perfectly restored for lovers of the soberly authentic, the house feels almost Gothic on a dark night in its bare, white-stoned simplicity. The vaulted oak and stone dining room is a great rarity; bedrooms and bathrooms have huge artistic personality: lit candles, old mirrors, bits of bronze and brass, rich tapestry and patchwork fabrics – unusual yet utterly inviting. Madame is flexible and helpful, breakfasts are full of light, space and home-made jams, her passions include rescuing animals and 1900s dress-dummies. A fine balance of sobriety and fantasy.

rooms	3: 2 doubles, 1 suite for 4, all with bath & wc.
price	€50 for two.
dinner	Wide choice of restaurants 5km.
closed	Rarely.
directions	From Montreuil D901 to Neuville; on sharp bend, D113 past La Chartreuse to Marles/Canche; 2km to village centre; on right at x-roads after tight bend; go slowly!

Mme Dominique Leroy
Manoir Francis,
62170 Marles sur Canche,
Pas-de-Calais
tel (0)3 21 81 38 80
fax (0)3 21 81 38 56

map: 1 entry: 17

Very grand for a farm – the 200-year-old house, outbuildings and courtyard are immaculate. Étienne and Véronique and their family are delightful, warm and generous; they grow cereals, keep cows and may offer you a guided tour of the place. You'll sleep well in your converted cowshed; rooms are white-walled, parquet-floored, spotless. The twin is particularly pretty with its pale beams and fresh blue and white furnishings. The old rampart town of Montreuil sur Mer is minutes away for shops, restaurants and "astonishing points of view". Ancient peace, lovely people and fields as far as the eye can see.

rooms	2: 1 double, 1 twin, both with shower & wc.
price	€43 for two.
dinner	Choice of restaurants nearby.
closed	Rarely.
directions	From Montreuil, arriving in Neuville, right opp. antique shop, 1.5km; left at roadside cross; signs.

Étienne & Véronique Bernard
Le Vert Bois,
62170 Neuville sous Montreuil,
Pas-de-Calais

tel	(0)3 21 06 09 41
fax	(0)3 21 06 09 41
e-mail	etienne.bernard6@wanadoo.fr
web	gite.montreuil.online.fr

map: 1 entry: 18

A calm unaffected welcome and not even a cockerel to disturb the peace. Madame is as kindly and down-to-earth as you would expect of someone who brought up nine children on the farm. The farmhouse, "built in 1724 by Lovergne", has a natural family feel. Rooms are simple: the twin in the main house has country fabrics and a wooden floor; the double off the little rose garden is darker, more intimate. Breakfast can include cheese and home-made jam on fresh baguettes and croissants. Madame is a fount of local knowledge and loves getting to know her guests properly, so do stay on.

rooms	2: 1 double, 1 twin, both with shower & wc.
price	€40-€45 for two.
dinner	Restaurants in Montreuil sur Mer 3km.
closed	December-February.
directions	From A16 exit 26 to Montreuil; D349 for Hesdin; through Beaumerie St Martin; 1st right at signpost.

Francis & Jeanne-Marie Locqueville
L'Overgne,
62170 Beaumerie St Martin,
Pas-de-Calais

tel	(0)3 21 81 81 87
e-mail	jmarie.locqueville@wanadoo.fr

map: 1 entry: 19

On a former English polo pitch sits this neat house in a fabulous garden: curly iron chairs, overflowing pots, quiet glades and tame wild rabbits – the perfect place to retire with a favourite book. Inside, the entire length of a gnarled trunk stretches across the ceiling, English florals and comfy sofas jostle with ethnic rugs and terracotta tiles, bedrooms are warm peaches and cream, ivory and tidy baby-blue stripes with old pine, cream carpets, lacy cotton cushions. Lucie is an attentive hostess who looks after her guests with easy-going elegance, though Nixon the golden Labrador will steal any show.

rooms	4: 2 doubles, 1 family suite, all with private bathrooms; 1 double with bath & wc.
price	€46–€50 for two.
dinner	Restaurants Le Touquet 1.5km.
closed	Rarely.
directions	From A16 exit Le Touquet/Étaples for Le Touquet; across bridge, over big r'bout (McDonalds) then left at 2nd lights; drive 150m down on left.

Lucie & Serge Bournoville
Le Polo,
Allée des Pâquerettes,
62520 Le Touquet, Pas-de-Calais

tel	(0)3 21 05 18 14
fax	(0)3 21 05 36 98
e-mail	bournovilles@minitel.net

THE NORTH

These two are fabulously alive and attentive, cultivated and communicative. Georges is an Orson-Wellesian figure, well able to talk at the same time as gentle but determined Marie… a sort of irresistible double act. The well-proportioned house is an architectural flourish, the contents a pleasing mix of antique and modern. Guest rooms, with their own entrances, have pretty bedding, the odd antique and good bathrooms. The only possible drawback is the Holiday Inn opposite but it's a quiet hotel, the sea is just 10 minutes away through the trees and there's stacks to do locally. Perfect for children, lots of talk and fun.

rooms	2: 1 double, 1 suite both with bath & wc.
price	€60 for two.
dinner	Wide choice of restaurants within walking distance.
closed	Rarely.
directions	From A16 Le Touquet exit; through Étaples; follow signs for Le Touquet centre. After 4th lights, 2nd right for Holiday Inn. 2nd house on right opp. telephone box.

Georges & Marie Versmée
Birdy Land,
Avenue du Maréchal Foch,
62520 Le Touquet, Pas-de-Calais

tel	(0)3 21 05 31 46/(0)3 27 46 39 41
fax	(0)3 21 05 95 07

The tufted dunes whisper in the westerly sea breeze or the easterly road hum: walk out and join others on the path to the beach. Guests have the whole top floor here: dark, dynamic Élena brings breakfast to the flame-covered table in the bright living room or the dune-view veranda. Her décor is pretty with modernistic touches (viz. the bendy wire clock), sofas round a log stove for chilly evenings and snug, individual bedrooms (minimal storage space). Plus sand-yachting and fashionable resort life at your feet. *Entire apartment also available to rent.*

rooms	4: 2 doubles, 1 triple, 1 twin, with 3 bathrooms either shared, or private for a supplement.
price	€50-€55 for two.
dinner	Restaurants in Le Touquet.
closed	Rarely.
directions	At entrance of Le Touquet head for 'Base Nautique Sud'; for Rue de Paris; head straight for dunes. Villa on top of hill.

Élena Desprez
La Crête des Dunes,
Avenue Blériot,
62520 Le Touquet, Pas-de-Calais

tel	(0)3 21 05 04 98
fax	(0)3 21 05 04 98
e-mail	contact@bnbletouquet.com
web	www.bnbletouquet.com

map: 1 entry: 22

THE NORTH

The wheel has to be repaired, so no more milling, but the lake is there and it's good to throw open your window and watch the ducks. This is a classically French B&B with massive new black leather sofas in the sitting room, a padded velvet chair or two in the bedrooms and a painted white table against blue or pink and white striped walls. The dining room has old cherry-wood pieces. All very neat and comfortable in this big, square handsome old house, built in 1855. Christine is reserved and friendly – a comfortable welcome. Utterly reliable and great value.

rooms	2 doubles, both with shower & wc.
price	€43-€45 for two.
dinner	Restaurants 5km.
closed	Rarely.
directions	A16 exit Neufchâtel Hardelot/ Ste Cécile; D940 for Boulogne & Le Touquet; house near church on entering Dannes.

Christine Lécaille
Le Moulin,
40 rue du Centre,
62187 Dannes, Pas-de-Calais

tel	(0)3 21 33 74 74
fax	(0)3 21 33 74 74

map: 1 entry: 23

This fabulous set of buildings was a Cistercian farm and the 13th-century barn – a 'harvest cathedral' – is worth the detour alone. Old arches spring, the brickwork dazzles, the courtyard focuses properly on its duckpond, the guest quarters – bedrooms, log-fired dayroom with separate tables, garden with its furniture – are in a beamy outbuilding and the place still breathes monastic peace. Your hosts work hard to maintain their precious legacy, breeding pheasants as well as caring attentively for guests. Madame loves decorating the cosy, harmonious rooms and has plenty of time to chat over breakfast.

rooms	6: 4 doubles, 2 twins, all with bath or shower & wc.
price	€52 for two.
dinner	Restaurants nearby.
closed	Rarely.
directions	From Calais A16 for Amiens; exit 28, N1 for Montreuil; right for Longvillers; signposted.

Anne & Jean-Philippe Delaporte
La Longue Roye,
62630 Longvillers, Pas-de-Calais
tel (0)3 21 86 70 65
fax (0)3 21 86 71 32
e-mail longue-roye@longue-roye.com
web www.la-longue-roye.com

map: 1 entry: 24

Behind its flat face, the house unfolds round the courtyard, over the porch, into an unexpectedly lovely garden. It is a generous *notaire's* house (the shield signals his office) with original mouldings, tiles and fireplaces. Big, prettily traditional French rooms have antiques, good rugs on wooden floors, modern bathrooms and there's a gloriously original attic *salon* for guests with all the furniture gathered in the centre. Breakfast includes *clafoutis* if you're lucky. The village is genuinely unspoilt and your hosts have a similarly well-bred, olde-worlde air.

rooms	3: 2 twins, 1 family room, all with bath or shower & wc.
price	€40-€45 for two.
dinner	Good restaurant 5km.
closed	Rarely.
directions	From Boulogne N1 S for St Léonard & Montreuil approx. 15km. In Samer, take road that goes down to right of church; house on left, near top of hill.

Joëlle Maucotel
127 rue du Breuil,
62830 Samer, Pas-de-Calais
tel (0)3 21 87 64 19
fax (0)3 21 87 64 19

map: 1 entry: 25

The golden stone of the old farmhouse is easy on the eye as you arrive, flowers flourish to the front, the big garden and orchard go down to the river behind, but there are only a few horses in the stables now; the main stud farm is further away. Madame is lively and fun when relaxed although your hosts have a busy life and may be a little preoccupied. The bedrooms, in a self-contained outbuilding which looks out onto the courtyard and wooded hills, have plain, modern décor (the new double has a canopied bed) and the living room is similarly straightforward. A good family stopover. *Gîte space for 9 people.*

rooms	4: 2 doubles, 1 twin, all with shower & wc; 1 double with bath & wc.
price	€42-€49 for two.
dinner	Auberge in village.
closed	Christmas & New Year.
directions	From Boulogne D940 to St Léonard; at 2nd lights, left on small road to Echingen (no sign); in village centre, left in tiny street immed. after sharp bend; left 1st gateway.

Jacqueline & Jean-Pierre Boussemaere
Rue de l'Église,
62360 Echinghen, Pas-de-Calais

tel	(0)3 21 91 14 34
fax	(0)3 21 91 06 41
e-mail	jp-boussemaere@wanadoo.fr

THE NORTH

Distinction and trust reign: elegant hostess, well-groomed rooms, heavy family furniture, a great floral hall and upright chairs for twelve. Madame, an effervescent animal-lover, says her guests "open the world to her". Fabulous first-floor rooms have a brilliant 1920s bathroom; the top-floor suite is 'Modern Rustic'; the lower room gives onto the patio; all capture the flavour of a particular, lovable kind of France, just below the lovely old walled town of Boulogne.

rooms	3: 1 double with bath & wc; 1 triple with shower & wc on different floor; 1 suite for 4 with shower, sharing wc.
price	€46-€65 for two; €80 for four.
dinner	Wide choice of restaurants within ramparts, walking distance.
closed	January.
directions	Follow signs for 'Vieille Ville'. Rue Flahaut is off Bd Mariette which runs below ramparts on northern side of city past Porte des Dunes.

Simone & Édouard Delabie
26 rue Flahaut,
62200 Boulogne sur Mer,
Pas-de-Calais

tel	(0)3 21 31 88 74

A great place from which to explore the 'Opal Coast', made fashionable by the British in the Thirties, or to spend your first or last night of a trip to France. *Monsieur Hulot's Holiday* is a perfect image of the little seaside town and this ravishingly exuberant house on the front. Mary's décor is soberly luxurious, in keeping with the period: white linen, wooden floors, carefully-chosen fabrics and furniture, lots of books. She speaks excellent English and may offer you tea in the beautiful room looking out to sea. Her huge, delicious breakfast takes place here too. One room is tiny and only two have sea views.

rooms	4: 2 doubles, 2 twins, all with bath or shower & wc.
price	€60-€96 for two.
dinner	€29 with wine, by arrangement.
closed	Rarely.
directions	From A16 exit 3 to Wimereux. There, go to sea front. House about halfway along promenade, 100m left of Hôtel Atlantic (with your back to sea).

Mary Avot
La Goélette,
13 Digue de Mer,
62930 Wimereux, Pas-de-Calais

tel	(0)3 21 32 62 44
fax	(0)3 21 33 77 54
e-mail	lagoelette@nordnet.fr
web	www.lagoelette.com

THE NORTH

Your dark, lively hostess will flash her quick smile and lead you into her house of surprises. The little low frontage opens onto a most unexpected open-plan, double-height living space where modern and family pieces – a superb heavy table made from a pair of convent doors, a baby grand piano, an immensely high carved bridal *armoire* (the French girl's bottom drawer) – sit comfortably together and a picture window brings the garden indoors for breakfast. Upstairs, a gallery leads to the pretty, attic bedrooms where rafters frame dormer windows and crochet bedcovers create that old French country atmosphere.

rooms	3: 1 double, 1 triple, 1 suite for 4, all with shower or bath & wc.
price	€49 for two.
dinner	Good restaurants 3-5km.
closed	Christmas & New Year.
directions	From A16 Calais-Boulogne, exit 9 for Hervelinghen on D244. There, house on right before church.

Catherine & Jean-Marc Petitprez
La Leulène,
708 rue Principale,
62179 Hervelinghen, Pas-de-Calais

tel	(0)3 21 82 47 30
e-mail	laleulene@aol.com
web	catherine.petitprez.free.fr

You could spend hours exploring the woods and meadows that surround this place, there's a sheltered spot for picnics, barbecues and garden games (to share with the owners' three children if you like) and guest rooms are relatively independent – ideal for families. Madame, a warm, naturally outgoing person, teaches part-time so her kindly husband serves your generous breakfast in the converted stables where the huge fireplace is so very warm and welcoming. The bedrooms are plainer with great dark beams, white walls and traditional French country décor – florals and twiddly bits. And it's all marvellously quiet.

rooms	2 family suites for 3, both with shower & wc, 1 with kitchenette.
price	€39 for two.
dinner	Restaurant 3km. Self-catering in one suite.
closed	Rarely.
directions	From Boulogne N42 for St Omer; right D206 for Henneveux; left D253 for Desvres; left D253E2 for Brunembert; through wood, at top, house on left.

	Philippe & Marie-Christine Fastrez
	60 impasse de Bouillets,
	Route des Communes,
	62142 Henneveux, Pas-de-Calais
tel	(0)3 21 83 97 31
fax	(0)3 21 83 97 31
e-mail	mcfastrez@aol.com
web	www.lehautchamp.com

THE NORTH

Sylvie is restoring her old house, painstakingly and very well. Built in 1839 and known in the village as 'le château', it's not really big but, with so many original details intact, it's an architectural historian's delight. Stained glass, marble fireplaces, trompe l'œil wall paintings on the stairs, superb green and white tiling in the kitchen, original colours. The feel is French-traditional, wooden-floored and some of the bedrooms have spectacular carved wardrobes and beds. This is a comfortable house with a great atmosphere, good *table d'hôtes* and a delightful young family at the helm.

rooms	5: 3 doubles, 1 triple, 1 suite for 4, all with bath & wc.
price	€54 for two; €78 for four.
dinner	€23 with wine, by arrangement.
closed	Rarely.
directions	From A26 exit 2; left D217 for Zouafques, Tournehem then Bonningues; house on right just after entering village.

	Sylvie & Pierre Breemersch
	Le Manoir,
	40 route de Licques,
	62890 Bonningues lès Ardres,
	Pas-de-Calais
tel	(0)3 21 82 69 05
fax	(0)3 21 82 69 05
e-mail	pierre.breemersch@wanadoo.fr
web	www.lemanoirdebonningues.com

Madame Breton is irreplaceable: a lovely old lady in a genuine old farmhouse, she talks lots, in French, and otherwise relies on radio and telly for company. Hers is an intriguing, piecemeal family house with good, comfortable old furniture, masses of photographs (a tribe of grandchildren) and very steep stairs. Rooms are country attractive: simple décor, good beds and windows to fields of peace. Madame loves cooking delicious country dishes for visitors and many readers have praised her natural hospitality. Ask to see the exquisite vaulted stables – built for cows and carthorses, fit for thoroughbreds and prizewinners.

rooms	2: 1 double, 1 family room, both with shower & wc.
price	€32 for two.
dinner	€14 with wine, by arrangement.
closed	November-March.
directions	From A26 exit 2 for Tournehem, over N43, follow to Muncq Nieurlet, on for Ruminghem. House on left, about 1.5km after leaving Muncq Nieurlet, at sign.

Mme Françoise Breton
La Motte Obin,
62890 Muncq Nieurlet,
Pas-de-Calais
tel (0)3 21 82 79 63

THE NORTH

Yes, it's new, brand new. So is the garden, bare new. But Madame, a long-standing B&B owner, will soon bring her new house to life, inside and out. Quiet and confident, she simply loves having guests. You have the run of the upper floor, where all three rooms look long and far over green hills, are fairly minimalist in décor with white walls and clothes racks, and share a big spanking bathroom. Downstairs, there's a conservatory for a good friendly breakfast and the rooms are full of light. It's excellent value, so come and watch as the trees begin to grow and the house learns to breathe under Madame's ministrations.

rooms	1 family suite for 2-6 with shower & wc.
price	€39 for two.
dinner	Choice of restaurants 5-10km.
closed	Rarely.
directions	From Calais A26 for Paris; exit Licques; right for Zouafques & Clerques; right opp. church in Clerques for La Chapelle St Louis 500m; house with columns.

Christiane Devines
27 route de Guémy,
Le Hamel,
62890 Clerques, Pas-de-Calais
tel (0)3 21 82 40 65
fax (0)3 21 82 40 65

This organic dairy farm is run with passion by your hosts who receive you in their square old house at the end of the tree-lined drive and ply you with organic-based food. Lut, from Belgium, is a quiet, sensitive and unpretentiously warm mother of two boys – her genuine welcome will touch you. Your rather minimalist double-aspect room spreads comfort with its finely friezed walls and there's a tiny room off it with a refrigerator. It is reached from the recently refurnished sitting room – not used by the family when guests are here – and the romantic garden is great with its rose bowers and little formal hedges.

rooms	1 double with shower & wc.
price	€43 for two.
dinner	€17 with wine, by arrangement.
closed	Rarely.
directions	From A26 exit 2 for Licques; through Tournehem & Bonningues lès Ardres; left after village to farm.

Lut & Jean-Michel Louf-Degrauwe
La Ferme de Beaupré,
129 rue de Licques,
62890 Bonningues lès Ardres,
Pas-de-Calais

tel	(0)3 21 35 14 44
fax	(0)3 21 35 57 35
e-mail	degrauwelut@minitel.net

The 'Cloths of Gold' has been an inn since 1640 and Christine's open, joyful welcome fits the tradition – she will receive you like old friends. She uses colour well too: the warm, bright little guest dayroom is a reflection of her dynamic personality; the bedrooms – blue, yellow, green and red – are equally fresh and bright, with good modern furniture and some pretty fabric effects. Three of them give onto the street but Ardres, a delightful little town, is extremely quiet at night while the green and gentle garden gives a country feel at the back.

rooms	3: 1 twin, 2 doubles, all with shower & separate wc; extra twin for children.
price	€48 for two.
dinner	Restaurants within walking distance.
closed	Rarely.
directions	From Calais A16, exit 17; N43 to Ardres; right after church; house on corner on left.

Christine & François Borel
Les Draps d'Or,
152 rue Lambert d'Ardres,
62610 Ardres, Pas-de-Calais

tel	(0)3 21 82 20 44
fax	(0)3 21 82 20 44
e-mail	christine@drapsdor.com
web	www.drapsdor.com

The softly impressive park belonged to Jean-Jacques' grandfather's château, destroyed in the war – the lake, old trees, sheep and peacocks hug both farmhouse and separate guesthouse. All is straightforward and simple, breakfast is in your own quarters (or the family kitchen for very early starts), where basic pine furniture and slatting grace the smallish rooms and some windows give onto the garden. The closeness to ferry ports is seductive, though the nearby main road may disturb some people, and the open intelligent family, who do wine-tastings and will sell you wine and honey, are delightful.

rooms 3: 2 triples, both with shower, sharing wc on floor below; 1 quadruple with shower & wc.
price €35-€39 for two.
dinner Restaurants nearby.
closed Rarely.
directions From A26 exit 2 onto N43 for Calais. Wolphus on left 1km after junction, with woods beside road. Be careful turning in.

Jean-Jacques Behaghel
La Ferme de Wolphus,
62890 Zouafques, Pas-de-Calais
tel (0)3 21 35 61 61
fax (0)3 21 35 61 61
e-mail ferme.de.wolphus@wanadoo.fr
web perso.wanadoo.fr/ferme-wolphus

THE NORTH

Extrovert Sonia loves music, painting, cooking and spoiling her guests. White walls, dark wooden doors, floors and beams, solid, good-looking furniture – it's 'French rustique'. The bedroom under the eaves is prettily decorated in red *toile de Jouy* and looks onto the garden; the suite, in stylish white and grey with a good big bathroom, is in a separate building and perfect for a family (but watch the stairs). You'll love the garden, bursting with life, full of secret corners. This is walking and pony-trekking country and if you'd like to trade car for horse, Sonia's daughter will happily organise rides.

rooms 3: 2 doubles, 1 family room, all with bath, shower & wc.
price €45-€48 for two.
dinner €18 with wine, by arrangement.
closed Rarely.
directions From A26 exit 2 for Ardres; N43; 1st left for Zutkerque - Château de Cocove; signposted.

Sonia Benoît
La Bohême,
1947 rue de Grasse Payelle,
62370 Zutkerque, Pas-de-Calais
tel (0)3 21 35 70 25
fax (0)3 21 35 70 25

A warm, eager couple, she the artist, he the earthy do-er, and an unusually characterful house: a big converted stable block, a glass and brick screen, a 'little house' (two rooms prettily independent here) and the creeper-covered stable walls (horses can share with the children's ponies) enclose the garden and old stone pond in an embrace of bricks, arches and columns – a deliciously other-worldly feel. The house has space and interesting 1930s furniture; plants, pictures and objects abound; bedrooms, decorated with Françoise's stencils and hand-painted furniture, are fresh and welcoming. It's a delight to be here.

rooms	4: 2 twins, 1 suite, each with shower and wc; 1 triple with shower; wc on floor below.
price	€52 for two.
dinner	Occasionally available €18, with wine; restaurants 1km.
closed	Rarely.
directions	From Calais A16, exit 17 for St Omer N43. Pass Les Attaques, Pont d'Ardres, 1st r'bout at Bois en Ardres; before 2nd r'bout left Rue de St Quentin for 1km; green gate.

	Françoise & Thierry Roger Le Manoir de Bois en Ardres, 1530 rue de St Quentin, 62610 Ardres, Pas-de-Calais
tel	(0)3 21 85 97 78
fax	(0)3 21 36 48 07
e-mail	roger@aumanoir.com
web	www.aumanoir.com

THE NORTH

Tranquil Meldick, a gorgeous 1930s house, is extremely smart behind its electronic gates. The long dining room windows look across the empty garden to pond and fields – hard to imagine that two terrible wars were waged here but one of Madame's fascinating treasures is a real collection of wartime medals and badges. She has huge energy, colour-codes each of her big, panelled, beamed bedrooms for flower names, arranges her many pictures and *objets* with artistic care – you could admire them for hours – and really appreciates guests who respond to this level of chic, this mix of warm home and personal museum.

rooms	5: 2 doubles, 2 twins, 1 quadruple, all with bath or shower & wc.
price	€52 for two.
dinner	Good restaurant 5km.
closed	Rarely.
directions	From A16 exit 19 for Marck; 2nd roundabout exit Le Fort Vert; through Marck; right D119; house 1km on right.

	Jean & Danièle Houzet Manoir du Meldick, 2528 avenue du Général de Gaulle, Le Fort Vert, 62730 Marck, Pas-de-Calais
tel	(0)3 21 85 74 34
fax	(0)3 21 85 74 34
e-mail	jeandaniele.houzet@free.fr

You will receive a marvellous welcome and be treated with immense care by the competent, smiling owners of this fine old house and its opulent garden. The marble-floored hall strikes you first, then the sober breakfast room, the multitudinous stuffed animals in the dining room and another stylish room with painted panelling. Bedrooms are big and most inviting and all is impeccably clean, orderly and utterly French. An elegant, genteel stop for those going to and from the ferry, it is just two to three minutes' stroll from the town centre and is excellent value.

rooms	2 doubles, both with shower & wc.
price	€42 for two.
dinner	Good restaurant 100m.
closed	Rarely.
directions	From Calais A16 E exit 23 into Bourbourg. From Place de l'Hôtel de Ville, Rue des Martyrs (aka Rue de l'Hôtel de Ville) is left of town hall as you face it.

Marilou & Jacques Van de Walle
25 rue des Martyrs de la Résistance,
59630 Bourbourg, Nord

tel (0)3 28 22 21 41
e-mail jacques.van-de-walle@wanadoo.fr

THE NORTH

Helped by the innate character of the solid old house (the original frieze in the hall is superb), Béatrice has applied her artist's imagination and talent to wonderful effect in the four guest rooms. One has Roman ruins on the walls and columns for bedside tables; another is all mahogany; all are light and harmonious with marble fireplaces, hand-painted furniture and big shower rooms. Roger is as friendly and helpful as his wife; their three teenagers are well-mannered; their dinners are based on real Flemish specialities and this very Flemish-minded area is probably the most interesting in northern France. *Gîte space for 9 people.*

rooms	4: 1 twin, 3 doubles, all with shower & wc.
price	€60 for two.
dinner	€25 with wine, by arrangement.
closed	Rarely.
directions	From A25 exit 28 on N225/A25 for Lille; exit 13 on D948 for Poperinghe; immed. right to Goderwaersveld; D139 to Boeschepe; house next to windmill.

Roger & Béatrice Maerten
340 rue de la Gare,
59299 Boeschepe, Nord

tel (0)3 28 49 45 73
fax (0)3 28 49 45 73
e-mail info@boeschepe.com
web www.boeschepe.com

Chantal is a charming hostess, her welcome more than compensates for an unremarkable modern house on a city street. And there's a lovely surprise: the picture window in the uncluttered living room gives onto a garden full of flowers where you can relax after exploring the treasures of Lille. The bedrooms are small, pleasing, cosily-carpeted, and there's a little kitchen for guests. Chantal, bright, energetic and typically French, used to teach English, and speaks it perfectly, then she adapted her house especially to receive guests. Yves has good English too and will dine with you – they both enjoy having an open house.

rooms	3: 2 doubles, both with shower & wc; 1 twin with bath & wc.
price	€35-€45 for two.
dinner	€15 with wine, by arrangement.
closed	Rarely.
directions	From Calais/Dunkerque A25 for Lille exit 4 1.5km; right at lights to Wattignies; straight on 3km; left for C.R.E.P.S/village centre; pass church on left, house on right.

Yves & Chantal Le Bot
59 rue Faidherbe,
59139 Wattignies, Nord
tel (0)3 20 60 24 51
e-mail lebot.yves@wanadoo.fr

map: 2 entry: 42

THE NORTH

Lille is a richly interesting city where plain façades often hide unsuspected beauties. Jeannine Hulin's townhouse reflects her personality: warm and artistic – kitchen and *salon* show masterly use of colour – and she loves having guests. You breakfast at a tiled table in the bright kitchen or in the flower-filled conservatory above the garden. Original floor tiles, stripped pine doors and masses of plants add atmosphere. The big bedroom is lovely with matching sleigh bed, wardrobe and desk, antique white linen and mirrors, and your delightful bathroom has a claw-footed bath. *Happy to collect from railway station.*

rooms	2: 1 double with private bath, 1 twin with shower, both sharing wc on floor below.
price	€42-€45 for two.
dinner	Choice of restaurants in town.
closed	Rarely.
directions	From A1 exit 20 on D917 for Fâches Ronchin/Lille for 4km. At lights (Boulangerie Paul on corner) left; 1st right is Rue des Hannetons.

Jeannine Hulin
28 rue des Hannetons,
59000 Lille, Nord
tel (0)3 20 53 46 12
fax (0)3 20 53 46 12
e-mail jeanninehulin@altern.org

map: 2 entry: 43

The 17th-century archway leads into a typical enclosed farmyard where you feel sheltered and welcomed. Guest rooms in the old stables, where the fairly standard conversion job includes a kitchen, are in simple cottagey style with careful colour matches and very wide showers. Another wing houses the Pollets' new venture, a little country restaurant open at weekends; on weekdays, guests may join them for simple, family meals at home. These attentive, caring dairy farmers love having guests, including children – they have three of their own – and are interesting people to talk to. An ideal family base, it's real value.

rooms	4: 1 double, 1 twin, 1 triple, 1 family, all with shower & wc.
price	€40 for two.
dinner	€13 with wine, by arrangement.
closed	Rarely.
directions	From A1 for Lille onto A22 for Valenciennes exit 'Cité Scientifique' for Cysoing. In Sainghin follow Chambres d'Hôtes signs.

Dominique & Nelly Pollet
Ferme de la Noyelle,
832 rue Pasteur,
59262 Sainghin en Mélantois, Nord

tel	(0)3 20 41 29 82
fax	(0)3 20 79 06 99
e-mail	dominique-nelly.pollet@wanadoo.fr

Behind the low façade are many riches: all is just so, rather like a doll's house – Madame's perfect plaything. The impression is of character and antiques with some modern bits. The big living room has pink walls, beams, marble floor and fireplace and there is an almost overwhelmingly pretty breakfast room: *objets trouvés*, plants and a Thai howdah sofa. The two first-floor rooms, one reached by an outside staircase, can communicate if you want a suite. Smart and mostly pink, they have lovely linen, good bathrooms, beams and views over church and garden. And Monsieur has lots of interesting stories to tell.

rooms	2 double/triples, both with shower & wc.
price	€57 for two.
dinner	Choice of restaurants 5km.
closed	Rarely.
directions	From Paris A16 exit 24 (25 from Calais); N1 for Montreuil 25km; in Vron left to Villers; right Rue de l'Église (opp. café); at end of road, left unpaved lane; house on left.

Pierre & Sabine Singer de Wazières
La Bergerie,
80120 Villers sur Authie, Somme

tel	(0)3 22 29 21 74
fax	(0)3 22 29 39 58

Through the gate and into a vast other world of green and watery peace beside the Authie. The superlative modern house marches round an astonishing courtyard of 'giant bonsais' and sculpted creatures. Living is done in a huge fan-beamed room with marble floor, rich rugs, super antiques and doors to the veranda for breakfast. Sleeping is done upstairs in the guest wing: original rooms, great use of colour, wood and exotica, fine bathrooms. One fishing lake, one bird-breeding lake, two rowing boats, paddocks and woods. Your hosts are lively, interesting and fun – so is Shogun their canine PR agent. *Pets by arrangement.*

rooms	5; 3 doubles, 2 suites, all with shower & wc.
price	€80-€90 for two.
dinner	€30 with wine, by arrangement. Restaurants 300m-5km.
closed	Rarely.
directions	From A16 exit 24 N1 to Vron; right D175 to Argoules; left D192 for Nempont; in Valloires Abbey car park: Chemin des Moines; gate 150m on left.

Michèle Harfaux
La Vallée Saint Pierre,
Chemin des Moines, Valloires,
80120 Argoules, Somme

tel	(0)3 22 29 86 41
fax	(0)3 22 29 86 48
e-mail	michele@vallee-st-pierre.com
web	www.vallee-st-pierre.com

map: 1 entry: 46

PICARDY

A glamorous, welcoming couple, your hosts have restored their fine brick house with respectful imagination, a lesson in that deceptively simple sobriety that turns every patch of colour, every rare object into a rich reward. Basics are white, ivory, sand; floors are pine with ethnic rugs by big new beds; blue, ginger or red details shine out, the setting sun may fill a round window, and great-grandfather's Flemish oil paintings are perfect finishing touches. Drink in the white-panelled, open-hearthed, brown-leather sitting room, revel in the pale, uncluttered dining room – and Claudine's good food. Games room and *pétanque* too. *Gîte space for 6 people.*

rooms	4: 3 doubles, 1 suite for 4, all with shower or bath & wc.
price	€76-€97 for two.
dinner	€25, wine €7-€32.
closed	Rarely.
directions	From A16 exit 24 for Boulogne through Bernay en Ponthieu then 1st left; through Arry; 1km beyond, left to Le Thurel after great barn.

Claudine & Patrick van Bree-Leclef
Le Thurel,
Relais de Campagne,
80120 Rue, Somme

tel	(0)3 22 25 04 44
fax	(0)3 22 25 79 69
e-mail	lethurel.relais@libertysurf.fr
web	www.lethurel.com

map: 1 entry: 47

Enchanting: from its knoll, the house looks down the lush garden, across the front and out to the shimmering bay. Madame is a delight too, happy to impart her deep knowledge of this area to visitors; light and refined like herself, her cooking is locally inspired and it's a privilege to dine in her antique-furnished room beneath the modern tapestry. Up the steep stairs, the big room, full of ocean light, is pale and attractive with lots of pine and a perfect little shower room. The pretty, smaller room across the landing has blue-quilted nesting beds. *Madame happy to babysit. Gîte space for 4 people.*

rooms	2: 1 double, 1 twin/double sharing shower & wc.
price	€54 for two.
dinner	€19, with wine; restaurants in village.
closed	January.
directions	From A16 exit Rue for Le Crotoy 10km; at r'bout follow to 'La Plage' to end; left Rue Jean Vadicocq; No 19 on right after playground.

Micheline Knecht
19 rue Jean Vadicocq,
80550 Le Crotoy, Somme

tel	(0)3 22 27 80 15
fax	(0)3 22 27 80 15

Joanna is amazing: founder of a tribe of 33, she is no ordinary granny. Her little old house, an 18th-century townsman's weekend house in a pretty village, displays a highly original flair for interior décor – daring colour combinations, strong wallpapers, highly modern bathrooms, antiques and modern pieces, crochet, plush and wickerwork – and her artistic gift with clay. It all works brilliantly and she has a great sense of fun. Her ancient garden stretches away from formal box to wild grass and the hills. Breakfast on organic jams in the conservatory among the artworks. One delicious bedroom is reached through the kitchen.

rooms	3: 1 double, 1 suite for 3, 1 suite for 5, all with shower or bath & wc.
price	€45-€50 for two.
dinner	BBQ available; choice of restaurants in Abbeville and in village (150m).
closed	Christmas.
directions	From Boulogne A16, Abbeville/St Riquier exit. At 1st r'bout, to Vauchelles lès Quesnoy. House on main square opp. church.

Mme Joanna Crépelle
Place de l'Église,
80132 Vauchelles lès Quesnoy,
Somme

tel	(0)3 22 24 18 17
fax	(0)3 22 24 18 17
e-mail	joanna_crepelle@yahoo.fr

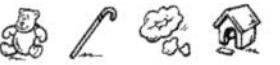

An exquisite horn of plenty: the potager gives artichokes, asparagus, peaches and pears, the farmyard chickens, the fields lamb, the woods game… and Élisabeth makes her own cider. The château, in the family since the Revolution, was gutted by fire but is being properly restored… elegant guest rooms will soon be reached via a 16th-century tower. Rooms in the cottage are modern, low-ceilinged, fresh with pine, softly lit; both have kitchenettes; the suite has sitting room and log fire. Dense trees protect from distant motorway hum; dinners, shared in the château with your charming, self-assured hosts, are a treat. *Gîte space for 5.*

rooms	3: 1 family suite with bath, shower & wc; 2 doubles with bath & wc.
price	€50 for two.
dinner	€20 with wine, by arrangement.
closed	Rarely.
directions	From Calais A16 for Abbeville onto A28 for Rouen 4km; exit Monts Caubert D3; right at Stop sign; D928 to Croisettes; right for Les Alleux NOT Béhen

René-François & Élisabeth de Fontanges
Château des Alleux,
Les Alleux,
80870 Béhen, Somme

tel	(0)3 22 31 64 88
fax	(0)3 22 31 64 88

map: 6 entry: 50

A genuine northern château, but above all a family house. Madame, mother of four lovely-mannered children and lover of things outdoor – dogs, horses, gardening – reigns with energy and a refreshingly natural attitude: what matter if a little mud walks into the hall? In pleasing contrast is the formal dining room with its fabulous patterned parquet floor, vast table, family silver and chandeliers, and excellent food. Up the brilliant ginger-clothed staircase, the comfortable rooms may seem slightly worn: they are gradually being rejuvenated. Come for lively hospitality not smart château bedrooms. *Gîte space for 20 people.*

rooms	4: 1 double, 1 suite for 4, both with bath or shower & wc; 2 doubles sharing bathroom.
price	€54-€61 for two.
dinner	€17, wine €10.
closed	Rarely.
directions	From Abbeville N28 for Rouen. At St Maxent, D29 to Oisemont; D25 for Sénarpont. Sign on edge of Foucaucourt.

Mme Élisabeth de Rocquigny
Château de Foucaucourt,
Foucaucourt Hors Nesle,
80140 Oisemont, Somme

tel	(0)3 22 25 12 58
fax	(0)3 22 25 15 58
e-mail	chateau.defoucaucourt@wanadoo.fr
web	www.chateaudefoucaucourt.com

map: 6 entry: 51

These calm, hospitable people were the first in the Somme to open their house for B&B – a very fine building with an extraordinary staircase. Monsieur, who is Dutch, grows several thousand tulips in serried ranks, makes honey, cider and calvados (ask to see the vaulted cellars) and keeps that supremely French animal, a *trotteur* mare. Madame was mayor of the village for 24 years. Big bedrooms (smaller on the second floor) are comfortable and uncluttered, views are peaceful, the panelled dining room a proper setting for a good breakfast. A great place to stay, and fishing on the lake. *Gîte space for 13.*

rooms	4: 1 double with shower & wc; 3 triples, all with shower & basin, sharing wc.
price	€39-€42 for two.
dinner	BBQ & guest kitchen available; good restaurants 12km.
closed	Rarely.
directions	From Abbeville A28 for Rouen, 28km, exit 5; left at Bouttencourt D1015 to Sénarpont; D211 for Le Mazis, 4.5km; follow Chambres d'Hôtes signs.

Dorette & Aart Onder de Linden
3 rue d'Inval,
80430 Le Mazis, Somme
tel (0)3 22 25 90 88
fax (0)3 22 25 76 04

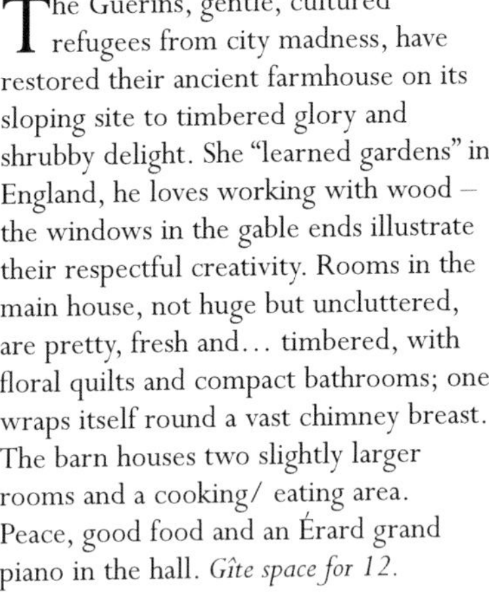

The Guérins, gentle, cultured refugees from city madness, have restored their ancient farmhouse on its sloping site to timbered glory and shrubby delight. She "learned gardens" in England, he loves working with wood – the windows in the gable ends illustrate their respectful creativity. Rooms in the main house, not huge but uncluttered, are pretty, fresh and… timbered, with floral quilts and compact bathrooms; one wraps itself round a vast chimney breast. The barn houses two slightly larger rooms and a cooking/ eating area. Peace, good food and an Érard grand piano in the hall. *Gîte space for 12.*

rooms	4: 2 triples, 1 double, 1 twin, all with bath or shower & wc.
price	€44-€46 for two.
dinner	€15 with wine, by arrangement.
closed	Rarely.
directions	From A16 exit 18 to Quévauvillers; right on D38 & D51 through Bussy lès Poix. Last house on left.

Francis & Françoise Guérin
1 rue de l'Église,
80290 Bussy lès Poix, Somme
tel (0)3 22 90 06 73
e-mail guerin.francis@free.fr

The Richoux love horses, the place's roots go back 1,000 years to the age of myths – so they call it *La Licorne* (the unicorn). Relaxed and likeable, they know their local history and hiking in depth. You sleep in the former chapel, also a *gîte d'étape* (no B&B when groups are here); there's a kitchen, a curious free-standing fireplace and a massive dining/snooker table. Breakfast comes to you here; you can light a fire, play snooker, use the kitchen, lounge in the garden. Under the rafters, one of the smallish bedrooms has the loo in the room. Nearby are water sports, fishing and Amiens' Gothic Cathedral. *Gîte space for 12 people.*

rooms	2: 1 double, 1 triple, both with bath & wc.
price	€35 for two.
dinner	Self-catering available; restaurants 4km.
closed	Rarely.
directions	From Amiens N1 for Beauvais, 15km. Between St Sauflieu & Essertaux, right D153 to Lœuilly; signposted.

Claudine & Bernard Richoux
Route de Conty,
80160 Lœuilly, Somme

tel	(0)3 22 38 15 19
fax	(0)3 22 38 15 19
e-mail	richouxclaudine@aol.com

Madame's welcome is typically, warmly northern. Once a social worker, she is at ease with all sorts and has the most infectious laugh. Monsieur, a big-hearted, genuine, chatty countryman, is good company too, though they don't dine with guests. Bedrooms, each with separate entrance, have been recently redecorated and are furnished with panache, personality and all necessary modernities including good kitchenettes and bathrooms. Ask for the big room in the *grenier* (loft) – it's splendid. The lush green garden at the back has wrought iron furniture, a lily pond and hens scratching in a large pen behind the flowers.

rooms	2 triples, each with shower, wc & kitchenette.
price	€39-€44 for two.
dinner	€15, bottle of wine €10-€12; many good restaurants in Amiens.
closed	November-April, except by arrangement.
directions	From Amiens N1 S to Hébécourt 8km. Opp. church follow Chambre d'Hôtes signs to Plachy Buyon.

Mme Jacqueline Pillon
L'Herbe de Grâce,
Hameau de Buyon,
80160 Plachy Buyon, Somme

tel	(0)3 22 42 12 22
fax	(0)3 22 42 04 42

A handsome old farmstead this, with guest rooms and dayroom in a well-converted barn that gives onto the courtyard. They are fairly blandly furnished with a mix of old and new, pleasing pine-slatted ceilings, fresh flowers in summer and good double-glazing against winter chill and noise from the nearby main road. If you arrive at a sensible time you may be offered a glass of home-made cider in the owners' lofty living room at their impressive coffee table: a giant slice of fallen elm. Breakfast by the vast fireplace here is a home-made feast and there's a very rare holly tree in the garden by the stables.

rooms	4: 1 double, 1 twin, 1 triple, 1 suite, all with bath or shower & wc.
price	€56-€60 for two.
dinner	From €15 with wine, by arrangement. Good restaurants in Amiens.
closed	Rarely.
directions	From A16 Dury exit onto N1 S for Breteuil & Paris. Arriving in Dury, left at traffic lights. House is first on right.

Alain & Maryse Saguez
2 rue Grimaux,
80480 Dury, Somme

tel	(0)3 22 95 29 52
fax	(0)3 22 95 29 52
e-mail	alain.saguez@libertysurf.fr
web	perso.libertysurf.fr/saguez/dury.html

PICARDY

The ground-floor room, straight off the lovely garden – with bantams all about – is white all over with pools of colour in the bed hangings, soft kilim rugs, dark polished antiques, old oils, gilt-framed prints; white doors open to a gorgeous bathroom (antique basin and taps) and a tiny sitting alcove. The upstairs room, soberly cosy, is softly clothed in grey-blue with a perfect little shower room. Madame is a painter, gives a friendly yet unintrusive welcome, and pops a little flask of port in your room. Breakfast, served in a delightful room in the main house, is a most happy affair. *Gîte space for 2-4 people.*

rooms	2 doubles, with bath or shower & wc.
price	€49-€58 for two.
dinner	Restaurant 5km; choice 8km.
closed	November-March.
directions	From Amiens, N29 for Poix; left on D162 to Creuse; signs.

Mme Monique Lemaître
26 rue Principale,
80480 Creuse, Somme

tel	(0)3 22 38 91 50
fax	(0)3 22 38 91 50

The emphasis here is on country family hospitality and Madame, uncomplicated and several times a grandmother, gives guests a wonderful welcome. The rambling garden has stone love-seats and two ponds, swings and a playhouse – a paradise for children – while the old manor house has the feel of an adventure story. Your quarters are nicely independent beyond the hall and your living room leads down to the bedroom; there's plenty of space, a draped bed, and big square French pillows. Most of European history is at your doorstep, from Gothic Amiens to the battlefields of the First World War.
Gîte space for 7-8 people.

rooms	2: 1 suite for 2-4 with bath & wc.
price	€50 for two, €65 for family of 4.
dinner	Auberge 6km.
closed	December-March.
directions	From Amiens D929 for Albert. At Pont Noyelles, D115 left for Contay; signs in Bavelincourt.

M & Mme Noël Valengin
Les Aulnaies,
15 Grande Rue,
80260 Bavelincourt, Somme
tel (0)3 22 40 51 51

PICARDY

A dazzling house whose hill-shaped roof becomes a timbered vault way above swathes of natural stone floor. The Picardy sky pours in and fills the vast minimally-furnished living space and your hostess shows shy pleasure at your amazement... then serves you superb food and intelligent conversation. Bedrooms are pure too: white walls, patches of colour, stone floors, excellent beds and bathrooms, 1930s antiques and touches of fun. Gourmet weekends can be arranged, and modern European history and the First World War battlefields are at your door. An exceptional place.

rooms	5: 2 twins, 1 family, all with bath & wc; 1 suite for 4: 2 bedrooms, 1 bathroom & 1 shower room.
price	€46 for two.
dinner	€19-€21 with wine, by arrangement.
closed	Rarely.
directions	From A1 exit 13 on N29 for St Quentin; in Villers-Carbonnel, right at lights on N17 for 5km to Fresnes Mazancourt; house next to church.

Martine Warlop
1 rue Génermont,
80320 Fresnes Mazancourt, Somme
tel (0)3 22 85 49 49
fax (0)3 22 85 49 59
e-mail martine.warlop@wanadoo.fr

The warm, enthusiastic Verhoevens live in an old farmhouse in an idyllic village of handsome houses surrounded by rolling farmland and green woods. Cows graze in the field and apples grow in the small orchard. Furniture and décor are in various colours, textures and styles, all carefully chosen and placed. Guest rooms in the modern extension have good repro pieces too, and new mattresses. Monsieur is proud to have been a proper 'natural' farmer and Madame is every inch the chatty, friendly, elderly farmer's wife. She is also a charming hostess who loves tending her orchard and kitchen garden... and her guests.

rooms	2 doubles, both with shower, bath & wc.
price	€40 for two.
dinner	3 restaurants within 2km.
closed	Rarely.
directions	From Beauvais for Le Tréport to Troissereux; D133 to Songeons; D143 for Gournay en Bray. 1st village on leaving forest is Buicourt; house near church.

Eddy & Jacqueline Verhoeven
3 rue de la Mare,
60380 Buicourt, Oise
tel (0)3 44 82 31 15

map: 6 entry: 60

PICARDY

In a tiny brick hamlet, this listed courtyard farmhouse, owned by a sophisticated artist/journalist couple, has a sculpture garden and a thrillingly personal interior. Pascal has sculpted all the metallically beautiful furniture, from superb beds to amusing loo-roll holders, giving the plain-coloured bedrooms an air of playful austerity. The old stable timbers show through, floors are coolly tiled, shower rooms are warmly ochre; the high white room is stunning. Meals are taken in the attractive living room where old and new (an old cider-press table bears Pascal's standard lamp) are a foil to Brigitte's fine cooking.

rooms	3: 1 double, 1 triple, 1 quadruple, all with shower & wc.
price	€41 for two.
dinner	€14 with wine, by arrangement.
closed	January.
directions	From Gournay en Bray D930 for 8km; left for Bellefontaine. Number 13 near end of hamlet.

Brigitte & Pascal Bruandet
13 hameau de Bellefontaine,
60650 Hannaches, Oise
tel (0)3 44 82 46 63
fax (0)3 44 82 46 63
e-mail bellefontaine@free.fr
web bellefontaine.free.fr

map: 6 entry: 61

In this rose-climbed former bakery, you sleep in big welcoming rooms with simple furniture, Indian cotton throws, magnificent roof timbers and sober carpets. There are two pretty breakfast rooms where beams, character and vast bread oven still reign. Your farmer hosts have taste and humour; their small farmhouse has a lovely open-plan, timber-frame living room where you may dine with them in all simplicity and soak up the warm, natural atmosphere. *Gîte space for 13 people.*

rooms	4: 2 doubles, 1 triple, 1 quadruple, all with shower & wc.
price	€39 for two.
dinner	€13 with wine, by arrangement.
closed	Rarely.
directions	From Beauvais N31 for Rouen. Leaving Beauvais follow to Savignies. Farm in village, 50m from church.

Annick & Jean-Claude Leturque
La Ferme du Colombier,
60650 Savignies, Oise
tel (0)3 44 82 18 49
fax (0)3 44 82 53 70
e-mail ferme.colombier@wanadoo.fr

PICARDY

Close the garden door and feel yourself secluded in this walled garden with grape-laden vine bower and a green corner for guests. Up an outside stair into your room: the old hayloft, brilliantly converted with originality and red cushions on butter-yellow bedcover on a platform by the little window. The timbers glow their 300 years, there's space, shapeliness and a super little shower room; fridge and dining table too. The separate single is snug and pretty. Dine with your informative hosts by the old farm fireplace – he quietly acts as cook while she keeps you jolly company. A private place of peace, close to Paris.

rooms	2: 1 double, 1 single, both with shower & wc.
price	€46 for two.
dinner	€19 with wine, by arrangement.
closed	Rarely.
directions	From A16 exit 13 for Gisors & Chaumont en Vexin about 20km; after Fleury left to Fay les Étangs; 2nd left; house on left.

Philippe & Chantal Vermeire
Le Clos,
3 rue du Chêne Noir,
60240 Fay les Étangs, Oise
tel (0)3 44 49 92 38
fax (0)3 44 49 92 38
e-mail philippe.vermeire@wanadoo.fr

King of concrete in 1927, Auguste Perret added a piece of design history to a pretty 18th-century house: an immense living room of squares in squares – panels, shelving, tiles, table; above is the green and puce Perret-panelled bedroom with a flourish of columns, super 1930s furniture, terrace and vast view. Other rooms have lovely ethnic fabrics, much light, sophisticated bathrooms. Madame, who is Scottish, loves her house and enjoys sharing its delights. Monsieur is mad about horses; their pasture is part of the sweeping view. And the train can carry you straight from the village to Paris... and back again.

rooms	3: 1 double, 1 triple, 1 quadruple, all with bath or shower & wc.
price	€50 for two.
dinner	€25 with wine, by arrangement.
closed	Rarely.
directions	From Calais A16 exit 13 (Méru) for Chaumont en Vexin. In Loconville, left to Liancourt St Pierre; right to post office & follow left into Rue du Donjon (no through road); high gate on left.

Fiona & Luc Gallot
La Pointe,
10 rue du Donjon,
60240 Liancourt St Pierre, Oise

tel	(0)3 44 49 32 08
fax	(0)3 44 49 32 08
e-mail	lucgallot@aol.com
web	www.la-pointe.com

PICARDY

The soft grandeur of 16th-century brick, the classic contrast of little four-part formal garden and great landscaped park fading into wooded hillside (with railway) behind, exquisite French manners and Irish warmth: Fosseuse mixes things perfectly. The grandest room, up the fine, terrifically worn stone staircase, has a vast, nobly canopied bed and a brand new bathroom; the sweetest is the double hidden over the library/breakfast room: open the panelling to find the secret stair; all have big windows over the park. Your deeply cultured hosts labour on to save their family home and genuinely enjoy sharing it with visitors.

rooms	3: 1 suite, 1 double, all with bath & wc; 1 triple with shower & wc.
price	€70-€75 for two; suite €110 for four.
dinner	Good choice of restaurants 2-10km.
closed	Rarely.
directions	From A16 exit 13 for Esches D923; in Fosseuse, château gate on right at traffic lights.

Shirley & Jean-Louis Marro
Le Château de Fosseuse,
60540 Fosseuse, Oise

tel	(0)3 44 08 47 66
fax	(0)3 44 08 47 66
e-mail	info@chateau-de-fosseuse.com
web	www.chateau-de-fosseuse.com

Down from the rather dingy station road, the modern house, astonishing in its shiny black and red interior, turns through vast windows towards the peace of the Japanese-style garden. There your little studio-nest awaits you: a hideaway under the trees, all white paint, pine slats and restful natural fabrics with just a bright red door (and relatively little traffic noise). Breakfast on a red stool at the black bar with your charming and interesting cosmopolitan hosts – Croatian architect and Anglo-French airport executive – or have it on your own front patio with the birds. Great for Chantilly and Paris.

rooms	1 twin/double with shower, wc & kitchen (studio).
price	€63 for two.
dinner	Self-catering available.
closed	Rarely.
directions	From A1 exit Survilliers to N17 to Chantilly; left at château; at r'bout left again; under railway bridge & Rue Victor Hugo next right.

Sylviane Lokmer
30c rue Victor Hugo,
60500 Chantilly, Oise
tel (0)3 44 57 63 91
fax (0)3 44 57 63 91
e-mail miro.lokmer@wanadoo.fr
web www.vrbo.com/vrbo/2531.htm

PICARDY

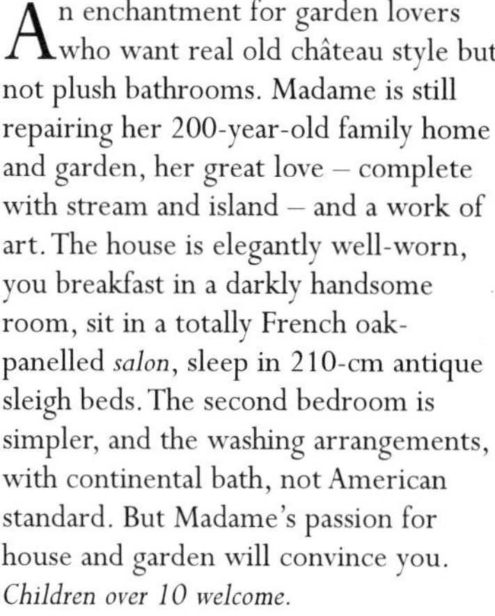

An enchantment for garden lovers who want real old château style but not plush bathrooms. Madame is still repairing her 200-year-old family home and garden, her great love – complete with stream and island – and a work of art. The house is elegantly well-worn, you breakfast in a darkly handsome room, sit in a totally French oak-panelled *salon*, sleep in 210-cm antique sleigh beds. The second bedroom is simpler, and the washing arrangements, with continental bath, not American standard. But Madame's passion for house and garden will convince you. *Children over 10 welcome.*

rooms	Suite: 1 twin with bath & wc, 1 twin with basin & wc, sharing bathroom. Child's room available.
price	€92 for two.
dinner	Good auberge 3km; Senlis 8km.
closed	15 October-15 May.
directions	From Senlis D330 for Borest/Nanteuil for 8km; right at cemetery; 1st right; across Place du Tissard towards big farm; left Rue de la Ferme; gates at bottom: No 1.

Hélène Merlotti
Château de Saint Vincent,
1 rue Élisabeth Roussel,
60300 Borest, Oise
tel (0)3 44 54 21 52
fax (0)3 44 54 21 52

Fear not! Behind the brick walls and imposing archway is a secret garden with goldfish pond, lots of intriguing mementos and a laughing, fun-loving lady, a retired chemist who loves her dogs, travelling and contact with visitors. In the original house, the mellow, beamed, fireplaced rooms are like drawing rooms with old pieces and soft fabrics (and kettle etc); Madame lives in the brilliantly converted barn; all is harmony and warmth among the family antiques. Drink in the atmosphere and her talk of France, the French and the rest of the world. Rest in peace, rouse to the dawn chorus, and enjoy breakfast in the sunshine.

rooms	2: 1 double with bath & basin, 1 twin with shower & basin, sharing wc.
price	€50 for two.
dinner	Restaurants 4-6km.
closed	Rarely, please book ahead.
directions	From A1 exit 10 for Compiègne, 4km. By caravan yard right at small turning for Jaux. 1st right to Varanval, over hill. House on right opp. château gates.

Françoise Gaxotte
La Gaxottière,
60880 Jaux Varanval, Oise
tel (0)3 44 83 22 41
fax (0)3 44 83 22 41

Ressons is a big, active farm out in the wilds, with an unspoilt house among rolling hills and champagne vineyards. Your hosts are hard-working, dynamic and good, even exciting, company; they also hunt. Madame, an architect, works from home, brings up three children *and* nurtures her guests. The deeply-carved Henri III furniture is an admirable family heirloom; rooms are colour-co-ordinated, beds are beautiful, views are stunning, dinners cooked with home-grown produce are excellent; bring rod and permit and you can fish in the pond. Arms are open for you in this civilised household. *Gîte space for 12 people.*

rooms	5: 1 double, 1 twin, both with bath, sharing wc; 2 doubles, 1 twin, sharing bath & 2 wcs.
price	€39-€46 for two.
dinner	€16, wine€13, champagne €18.
closed	Rarely.
directions	From Fismes D967 for Fère en Tardenois & Château Thierry 4km. Don't go to Mont St Martin, cont. 800m beyond turning; white house on left.

Valérie & Jean-Paul Ferry
Ferme de Ressons,
02220 Mont St Martin, Aisne
tel (0)3 23 74 71 00
fax (0)3 23 74 28 88

Longing to sleep in a castle tower? This one is octagonal, in a delicious *troubadour* château, its wonderful great double room and child's room across the landing imaginatively set in the space, all airy and chintzily minimalist. The family have been here for five generations and are likely to remain, given your hosts' tribe of exquisitely behaved children. Shrubs hug the feet of the château, the garden slips into meadow, summer breakfast and dinner (book ahead) are in the enchanting orangery. The old family home, faded and weary, timeless and romantic, is well loved and lived in by these delightful people.

rooms	1 suite for 3, with shower & wc.
price	€46 for two.
dinner	€18 with good wine, by arrangement.
closed	Rarely.
directions	From A26 exit 13 for Laon; Laon bypass for Soissons; N2 approx 15km; left D423; through Nanteuil for La Quincy; château on right outside village.

Jacques & Marie-Catherine Cornu-Langy
La Quincy,
02880 Nanteuil la Fosse, Aisne
tel (0)3 23 54 67 76
fax (0)3 23 54 72 63
e-mail laquincy@caramail.com

PICARDY

Authentic country hospitality and generosity are yours in the big old house. It's welcoming and warmly tatty with mix 'n' not-match wallpapers, funny old prints in bedrooms, comforting clutter in the living room by the old family furniture and grandfather clock. The energetic owners are great fun and love their dinner parties where Monsieur is MC as guests of all nations communicate and the wine flows. They wouldn't dream of changing a thing for the sake of modern sanitising fashions – may they prosper! The rooms are simple and good; one has a ship's shower room, another a Louis XVI bed, all look onto green pastures.

rooms	7: 2 suites for 4, 2 doubles, 1 twin, all with bath or shower & wc; 1 double, 1 twin with basins, sharing bathroom.
price	€34-€48 for two.
dinner	€18 with wine, by arrangement.
closed	20 October-February, except by arrangement.
directions	From A26-E17 exit 13 on N2 for Laon; 2nd left to Athies sur Laon; D516 to Bruyères & M. 7km; left D967 for Fismes; Chérêt sign leaving Bruyères; house on left entering Chérêt.

Mme Monique Simonnot
Le Clos,
02860 Chérêt, Aisne
tel (0)3 23 24 80 64
e-mail leclos.cheret@club-internet.fr

CHAMPAGNE · ARDENNE

The angel of Reims smiles stonily, evenly,
on the king anointed in his cathedral
and on the uncomprehending soldier
slain in the killing fields below.
And the ephemeral bubbles rise and
burst into nonsense, as ever.

The Harlauts are great company, love entertaining and are keen to provide good value and, even though they produce their own marque of champagne and bottles are for sale, it is for the first-class food and the atmosphere that guests return. Dinner *en famille* is either in the dining room or on the terrace overlooking the garden. There are steep narrow stairs up to the warm, wood-floored, uncluttered guest rooms, two of which share a loo – a minor concern as everything is spotless and they make a good family suite. Great views over the plains of Reims, and you must try the champagne cakes.

rooms	3: 1 double, 1 suite for 2-4, all with shower & wc; 1 family room with shower, wc & kitchenette.
price	€41.50-€44.50 for two.
dinner	€20 with wine, by arrangement.
closed	January & Easter.
directions	From A26 exit 15 (Reims La Neuvillette) onto N44 for Laon 2km; left to St Thierry; house in village.

Évelyne & Remi Harlaut
5 rue du Paradis,
51220 St Thierry, Marne

tel	(0)3 26 03 13 75
fax	(0)3 26 03 03 65
e-mail	contact@champagne-harlaut.fr
web	www.champagne-harlaut.fr

Independent champagne growers, the Aristons delight in showing guests round vineyards and cellars (tastings included). Indeed Madame, a wonderful person, started doing B&B for champagne buyers who did not want to leave after tasting! Through the flower-filled courtyard and up a private stair to lovely, light, airy, attic bedrooms with fresh white walls, beams, matching curtains and covers; one has its own kitchenette. Breakfast is served in the characterful old family house with fine jams made by Madame. Guests have use of a fridge and freezer – great for picnics. *Latest bookings taken at 7pm. Gîte space for 6 people.*

rooms	4: 1 double, with bath & wc; 2 doubles with shower & wc; 1 family room with shower, wc & kitchenette.
price	€42-€46 for two; €75 for three.
dinner	Choice of restaurants in Fismes, 11km.
closed	3rd week in August.
directions	From A4 exit 22 on N31 Fismes to Jonchery sur Vesle; left D28 to Savigny sur Ardres; right D386 to Crugny 3km; left D23 to Brouillet; house on right, sign.

Remi & Marie Ariston
Champagne Ariston Fils,
4 & 8 Grande Rue,
51170 Brouillet, Marne
tel (0)3 26 97 43 46
fax (0)3 26 97 49 34
e-mail contact@champagne-aristonfils.com
web www.champagne-aristonfils.com

A neat and utterly French-pretty place, the old family farmhouse, rebuilt in the 1920s after war destruction, has guest rooms and a deep terrace round the quiet courtyard: you can't hear the road, only the two running springs, so sleep till 11 if you like – that's the latest Nathalie serves fresh fruit juice and croissants in her country-furnished living room or on the terrace in summer. Each big, plain-walled, flower- or geometry-draped bedroom is blessed with a sitting area and all have shining modern shower rooms. With their three teenagers, the Lelarges are a delightful young family, welcoming, available and friendly.

rooms	4 suites for 3-4, all with shower & wc.
price	€46 for two; €70 for four.
dinner	Restaurant in village.
closed	January-February.
directions	From Reims D980 SW to Ville en Tardenois 20km; house in town centre opp. Crédit Agricole bank.

Nathalie & Éric Lelarge
Ferme du Grand Clos,
51170 Ville en Tardenois, Marne
tel (0)3 26 61 83 78
fax (0)3 26 50 01 32

A wonderful woman who really understands hospitality and good food will welcome you to this impressive 17th-century farm with its two courtyards: it is all simple and real. In the converted stables: a living room with original mangers, log fire and kitchenette, then steep stairs up to two simply decorated, warmly-carpeted, roof-lit rooms. In the main house: the third room, bigger and cosier with old furniture and a view of the pond. You breakfast next to the kitchen but dine at the big old table in the family *salon* on home-produced vegetables, eggs, poultry and fruit. Fabulous walks to be had in the great Forêt du Gault nearby.

rooms	2: 1 double, 1 twin, each with shower or bath & wc.
price	€37 for two.
dinner	€19 with wine, by arrangement.
closed	Rarely.
directions	From Calais A26 to St Quentin; D1 to Montmirail; D373 for Sézanne, 7km. On leaving Le Gault left at silo; sign.

Famille Boutour
Ferme de Désiré,
51210 Le Gault Soigny, Marne
tel (0)3 26 81 60 09
fax (0)3 26 81 67 95
e-mail domaine_de_desire@yahoo.fr

CHAMPAGNE · ARDENNE

Bannay bustles with hens, ducks, guinea fowl, turkeys, donkey, sheep, cows, goats... the chatter starts at 6am. Children love this working farm with its friendly animals, and love the higgledy-piggledy buildings too; school groups come to visit. The house brims with beams, the rooms dance in swags, flowers and antique bits; the piano swarms with candles and photographs and one bathroom is behind a curtain. Our readers have loved the house, the family and the food. Little English is spoken but the welcome is so exceptional, the generosity so genuine, that communication is easy. Superb outings in the area for all.

rooms	3 doubles, all with bath & wc (1 curtained off);1 suite with shower & wc.
price	€44-€53 for two.
dinner	€23 with wine, €26 with champagne.
closed	Rarely.
directions	From Épernay D51 for Sézanne; at Baye, just before church, right D343; at Bannay right; farm before small bridge.

Muguette & Jean-Pierre Curfs
Ferme de Bannay,
51270 Bannay, Marne
tel (0)3 26 52 80 49
fax (0)3 26 59 47 78

Perched on the side of a hill with views of the garden and champagne vineyards to one side and the sleepy village to the other, Sylvie and Éric's house began life as two winegrowers' cottages. The thoughtfully furnished bedroom, with a desk as well as a round table, is large, and white, has polished floors and furniture and overlooks the garden. Breakfast is a tempting affair with ham, crêpes, *croquignolles* – local pink biscuits – and sometimes home-made cake. Your hosts have four teenage children, she paints, he makes things, both smile a lot and enjoy a good chat.

rooms	1 double, with private bath & wc.
price	€47-€52 for two.
dinner	Choice of restaurants nearby.
closed	Rarely.
directions	From Place de la République in Épernay head towards Châlons; at Chouilly r'about, right for Aivze; cont. 500m; 1st right for Cramant.

Sylvie & Éric Charbonnier
189 rue Ferdinand Moret,
51530 Cramant, Marne
tel (0)3 26 57 95 34
fax (0)3 26 51 60 23
e-mail sylvie.cramant@wanadoo.fr

CHAMPAGNE · ARDENNE

Behind the sober façade is a beautiful, generously hospitable marriage of old and new, French and English. Didier, house-restorer supreme, makes champagne. Imogen, warm, relaxed and informed, has designed, bound books, taught… and now runs two small children and this fine house. They have done the bedrooms brilliantly: two have space, light and luxurious sitting/bathrooms; the smaller has a richly canopied bed, a green and pink oriental atmosphere, a superb claw-footed bath. Work continues on the ground floor, Imogen is an excellent cook, champagne comes with dinner. You'll want to stay for ever. *Gîte space for 4.*

rooms	3: 2 doubles, 1 twin, each with bath & wc.
price	€47-€52 for two.
dinner	€25 with wine, by arrangement.
closed	2 weeks in September & Christmas.
directions	From Calais A26 to Reims; N51 to Épernay; follow for Châlons en Champagne then to Avize; head for Lycée Viticole, house opp. lycée.

Imogen & Didier Pierson Whitaker
Le Vieux Cèdre,
14 route d'Oger,
51190 Avize, Marne
tel (0)3 26 57 77 04
fax (0)3 26 57 97 97
e-mail champagnepiersonwhitaker@club-internet.fr

The quiet is so deep that the grandfather clock inside and the doves cooing in the trees outside can seem deafening. A timeless feel wafts through the new house from that clock, the pretty, traditionally decorated bedrooms (sleigh beds and Louis Philippe furniture), the piano and a lovely old sideboard. Huguette and her husband, who runs the dairy farm, are generous hosts offering traditional unpretentious farmhouse hospitality. You can opt for champagne from their son-in-law's nearby vineyard, with a meal to match the quality of the wine and the welcome. *Gîte space for 14 people.*

rooms	3: 2 doubles, 1 triple, all with bath or shower & wc.
price	€43 for two.
dinner	€19, with wine; €27 with champagne.
closed	Rarely.
directions	From Châlons en Champagne D933 to Bergères (29km); right D9 through Vertus; left, follow signs to La Madeleine 3km.

Huguette Charageat
La Madeleine,
51130 Vertus, Marne

tel	(0)3 26 52 11 29
fax	(0)3 26 59 22 09

CHAMPAGNE · ARDENNE

Your hosts are happy in the converted stables, their son runs the farm, cows still graze, grandchildren come and go easily. Two rooms have their own ground-floor entrance, the third is upstairs in the owners' 'wing'; all three are done in brave contemporary colours that set off the mix of old and new furniture perfectly: bright and pleasing with lovely linen, good mattresses, clean-cut bathrooms. Madame: fun and an excellent cook (lots of organic and farm-grown ingredients), Monsieur: a whizz on local history; both: proud of their country heritage, wonderful with children, deeply committed to 'real B&B'. Great value.

rooms	3: 1 double, 1 suite for 4, 1 quadruple, all with shower & wc.
price	€38 for two.
dinner	€13 with wine, by arrangement.
closed	Rarely.
directions	From A4 exit Ste Menehould D982 (382 on some maps) to Givry en Argonne; left D54 to Les Charmontois (9km).

M & Mme Bernard Patizel
5 rue St Bernard,
51330 Les Charmontois, Marne

tel	(0)3 26 60 39 53
fax	(0)3 26 60 39 53
e-mail	nicole.patizel@wanadoo.fr
web	www.chez.com/patizel

The secluded old mill buildings house two owner families, a fish-tasting restaurant, several guest rooms and 50 tons of live fish – it's a fish farm! On Sundays 500 fishers may gather to catch trout in the spring water that feeds the ponds. Breakfast and *table d'hôtes* are shared with your enthusiastic hosts, who created this place from nothing 40 years ago, in the big beamy restaurant; groups come for speciality lunches. Bedrooms under the eaves are compact, small-windowed, simply furnished, prettily decorated in rustic or granny style, the larger annexe rooms are more modern. Great fun for children. Good English spoken.

rooms	6: 2 doubles, 1 twin, 1 triple, 2 family, all with bath & wc.
price	€55-€65.50 for two.
dinner	€17.55 with wine, by arrangement.
closed	Rarely.
directions	From Paris A5 exit 19 on N60 to Estissac; right on to Rue Pierre Brossolette; mill at end of lane.

Édouard-Jean & Chantal Mesley
Domaine du Moulin d'Eguebaude,
10190 Estissac, Aube
tel (0)3 25 40 42 18
fax (0)3 25 40 40 92

Madame, French-speaking from Quebec, is a busy, chatty young mother of teenagers with a farming husband and parents-in-law "through the wall": sterile hygiene counts less here than a warm atmosphere. She has the key to the fascinating church. It's a lovely setting and her house, built in 1087 with two ancient towers, was the old priory, now with a superb pool. Rooms vary; if you can, take the enormous one on the ground floor with huge stone fireplace, two queen-size beds, wattle walls in great timbers, more beams above, a simple bathroom; others are modern. Breakfast can be a sociable affair and do ask for Madame's crêpes.

rooms	5: 2 quadruples, 2 triples, 1 family room, all with bath or shower & wc.
price	€35-€45 for two.
dinner	Restaurant 10 minutes' walk.
closed	Rarely.
directions	From Troyes N71 SE for 22km. In Fouchères left D81 for Poligny; house just behind church.

Gilles & Sylvie Berthelin
Le Prieuré,
Place de l'Église,
10260 Fouchères, Aube
tel (0)3 25 40 98 09
fax (0)3 25 40 98 09

This was the château family's summer house for two centuries and has been their main house for one: Madame will show you the family books, lovely old furniture and mementos and tell you the stories (of Louis XIV's envoy to Peter the Great who was an ancestor…) in incredibly fast French. She has a wealth of information, a deep love of books (does her own bookbinding), a garden full of roses, each introduced by name, and a couple of horses in the paddock (there are racehorses elsewhere). She is hyperactive and loves to talk – it's great fun and deeply interesting, a fascinating trip back in time.

rooms 1 triple with shower & wc.

price €40 for two.

dinner €16, with wine, children under 12 free.

closed Rarely.

directions A26 to junc. 22 (Troyes); N19 to Bar sur Aube; D384 to Ville sur Terre. Follow for Fuligny. House on long main street.

Nicole Georges-Fougerolle
Les Épeires,
17 rue des Écuyers,
10200 Fuligny, Aube
tel (0)3 25 92 77 11
fax (0)3 25 92 77 11

CHAMPAGNE · ARDENNE

This large and splendid farmhouse is irresistible. For fishermen there's a river, for bird-watchers a fine park full of wildlife (come for the cranes in spring or autumn); for architecture buffs, the half-timbered churches are among the "100 most beautiful attractions in France". Bedrooms are comfortable and attractive; afternoon tea is served in the elegant panelled *salon*; dinner, possibly home-raised boar or carp, is eaten communally or separately but not with your hosts, delightful as they are: they live in another wing and prefer to concentrate on their good *cuisine maison*. *Children over 7 welcome.*

rooms 5: 2 doubles, 2 twins, 1 suite, all with bath or shower & wc.

price €50-€57 for two.

dinner €23 with wine, by arrangement.

closed Rarely.

directions From Troyes D960 to Brienne; D400 for St Dizier; at Louze D182 to Longeville; D174 for Boulancourt; house on left at 1st crossroads, sign 'Le Désert'.

Philippe & Christine Viel-Cazal
Domaine de Boulancourt,
Le Désert, Longeville sur la Laines,
52220 Montier en Der,
Haute-Marne
tel (0)3 25 04 60 18
fax (0)3 25 04 60 18

Here is a typical sleepy French village, a place for getting out and about in several modes: there is riding (and space for 15 guest horses), pony-trapping, walking, mountain-biking, archery, orienteering and a bit of gentle ping-pong. It's a friendly place, simple and easy, with breakfast of home-made jams, fresh brioche and lots of coffee available until midday. Beyond the separate guest entrance, the basic but pretty rooms are right for the price, warmly carpeted (after the corridor upstairs with its 'artexed' walls and 'lino' floor), thinly walled and have good storage space. *Gîte space for 19 people.*

rooms	2: 1 double, 1 triple, sharing shower & wc.
price	€30 for two.
dinner	Restaurant 5km.
closed	Rarely.
directions	From Langres N19 for Vesoul 30km, left D460 for Bourbonne 8km; right D34; 3rd left to Velles; through village to grass triangle; on left.

	Alain & Christine Rousselot
	Les Randonnées du Pré Cheny,
	52500 Velles, Haute-Marne
tel	(0)3 25 88 85 93
fax	(0)3 25 88 85 93
e-mail	randoprecheny@wanadoo.fr

CHAMPAGNE · ARDENNE

While restoring the old house, the Poopes were enchanted to 'meet' the former owners in the shape of faded old photographs in the attic. These inspired the décor of each splendid room – and one has an antique bread trough too. Évelyne and Michel adore doing B&B and do all they can to make you feel at home. Breakfast is deeply local: yogurt from the farm, honey from the village and Évelyne's home-made jam, while dinner may include such delicacies as Langres cheese tart with artichokes or flamed turkey; Michel is chief pastry-cook. He also paints very nicely while Évelyne does floral compositions.

rooms	5: 1 double, 1 twin, both with shower, sharing wc; 2 triples, 1 suite, all with shower & wc.
price	€34-€46 for two.
dinner	€12 with wine, by arrangement.
closed	Christmas.
directions	From A31 exit 7 to north Langres; N19 for Vesoul for 30km. Right at Chambres d'Hôtes sign to Pressigny; just after pond on left.

	Évelyne & Michel Poope
	Maison Perrette,
	24 rue Augustin Massin,
	52500 Pressigny, Haute-Marne
tel	(0)3 25 88 80 50
fax	(0)3 25 88 80 49
e-mail	poopemichel@net-up.com

Vast views across lakes, woods and hills surround 'Grandma's Fields'. The house is a 1960s chalet, tiled downstairs, carpeted up, spotless throughout. Here, it's bed and breakfast plus afternoon tea and cake… and apparently the cakes are to die for. This is a quiet, bookish house (no telly), the perfect spot for a holiday of walking, swimming with the trout in the pond near the house, or reading. In autumn and spring you can go mushrooming and cook your catch in Madame's cosy kitchen. Breakfast, which can be French, German or English, to taste, is warmly in the kitchen too. Supremely peaceful house, place and person.

LORRAINE · ALSACE · FRANCHE COMTÉ

Storks still build their messy nests on the chimney pots of breweries and biscuit factories where working women once wore that giant bow as their traditional head-dress.

rooms	2 doubles, sharing bath & wc.
price	€53.50 for two.
dinner	Good restaurant nearby.
closed	Rarely.
directions	From Strasbourg A352/N420 to St Blaise la Roche 45km; right D424 14km to La Petite Raon; right after church for Moussey; left after café; then left, left & left to house.

Judith Lott
Les Champs Grandmère,
Thiamont,
88210 La Petite Raon, Vosges

tel	(0)3 29 57 68 08
fax	(0)3 29 57 68 83
e-mail	judelott@aol.com

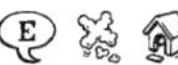

A triumph! Monsieur's seemingly endless restoration of these venerable buildings – one house 400, the other 300 years old – is finished, and very nicely too: fine woodwork, stylish furniture, an intriguing gas chandelier (*gasolier*) in the dining room, elegant terraces and a super garden with a children's play area. Madame is charmingly lively, her attractive rooms have goodnight chocolates, kettle kits, smallish shower rooms and lots of religion on view (bedside Bibles are French Catholic, not American Gideon). Hers is a genuine welcome, breakfast is a highlight and traffic noise seems minimal.

rooms	2: 1 double, 1 twin, each with shower & wc.
price	€43-€54 for two.
dinner	Restaurants 200m; self-catering possible.
closed	Rarely.
directions	From A4 exit Ste Menehould; N3 for Verdun-Chalons; sign in La Vignette, hamlet before Les Islettes; 1st building on left.

M & Mme Léopold Christiaens
Villa des Roses,
La Vignette, Les Islettes,
55120 Clermont en Argonne, Meuse

tel	(0)3 26 60 81 91
fax	(0)3 26 60 23 09
e-mail	gites-christiaens@wanadoo.fr

map: 7 entry: 88

The lively, dynamic owners are justifiably proud of their deeply-adapted stables, built two centuries ago in local stone. Out with the horses, in with the big, plush guest rooms: the suite even has its own telly and phone. They are all done with taste and quality, and there's a new sauna. Dinner is superb, a chance to sample some of the region's best dishes, course after course, wine after wine; Madame will join you for dessert and a chat. In the forest, an 'artist's path' to explore; in the garden, a golf practice area. An excellent stopover in a pretty, peaceful village between the ferries and Germany.

rooms	3: 2 triples, both with shower & wc; 1 suite with bath, shower & wc.
price	€64-€84 for two.
dinner	€25 with wine, by arrangement.
closed	Rarely.
directions	From Reims A4 exit 'Voie Sacrée' N35 for Bar le Duc; at Chaumont sur Aire D902 left to Longchamps sur Aire; D121 left to Thillombois; house next to château.

Lise Tanchon
Le Clos du Pausa,
Rue du Château,
55260 Thillombois, Meuse

tel	(0)3 29 75 07 85
fax	(0)3 29 75 00 72

map: 7 entry: 89

History weighs heavy in these ancient stones: the tower was part of the 13th-century defensive ring around Metz. It is now a typical farmhouse with 110 acres of cereal fields. Brigitte relishes her role as hostess, does it with great talent, makes friends easily and keeps goats, rabbits, a donkey and a dog. The bedrooms are in a separate building, filled with her paintings and beautiful hand-painted furniture. There is a handsome breakfast room with great beams. A wonderful family and a friendly peaceful village, despite the by-pass being built for 2004, as discreetly as possible in a cutting on the other side of the river.

rooms	3: 1 double, 1 triple, both with bath & wc; 1 twin with shower & wc.
price	€46 for two.
dinner	Restaurants 4km.
closed	November-March.
directions	From A31 exit 29 for Féy; right at junction; cont. for Cuvry; farm on edge of village past Mairie; signs.

Brigitte & Jean-François Morhain
Ferme de Haute-Rive,
57420 Cuvry, Moselle
tel (0)3 87 52 50 08
fax (0)3 87 52 60 20

LORRAINE

A most interesting, unpretentious couple, they are passionate about the environment and keen to chat over dinner. He, a retired French architect, has won a prize for this brilliant conversion, she's Polish and paints (work in progress on the easel), patchworks (her work adorns your bed) and dances. It is good news, too, for vegetarians who like a change: Alina is a 'veggie' and will rustle up a hot *borsch* or a dish of *pierogi* (vegetable ravioli), though her talent stretches to delicious meaty things too. An excellent and friendly house with lovely rooms.

rooms	2 triples with shower & wc.
price	€45-€48 for two.
dinner	€18 (meat or fish) or €15 (vegetarian) with wine, by arrangement.
closed	Rarely.
directions	From Metz D3 NE for Bouzonville approx. 21km; right on D53a to Burtoncourt. On left in main street.

Alina & Gérard Cahen
51 rue Lorraine,
57220 Burtoncourt, Moselle
tel (0)3 87 35 72 65
fax (0)3 87 35 72 65
e-mail ag.cahen@wanadoo.fr

A genuine family château where rooms, not big – apart from the twin – have the patina of long history in their antiques (carved *armoires*, Voltaire armchairs, pretty writing desks) and the softness of bygone days in bedhead draperies, pastel fabrics and plush. The real style is in the utterly French many-chaired *salon* and the dining room – reached through halls and hunting trophies – with its huge square table. Here you may share splendid meals with your lively, intelligent hosts: Monsieur a mine of local history, Madame skilfully attentive to all. And always fresh flowers. *Gîte space for 2 people.*

rooms	6: 3 doubles, 3 twins, all with bath & wc.
price	€68-€91 for two.
dinner	€31-€38.50, wine €10.
closed	15 October-15 April.
directions	From Nancy N74 for Sarreguemines/ Château Salins. At Burthecourt x-roads D38 to Dieuze; D999 south 5km; left on D199F; right D199G to château.

Livier & Marie Barthélémy
Château d'Alteville,
Tarquimpol,
57260 Dieuze, Moselle

tel	(0)3 87 86 92 40
fax	(0)3 87 86 02 05
e-mail	chateau.alteville@caramail.com

A real old Alsatian farmhouse in the wine-growing area where you can be in a bustling village street one minute and your own peaceful little world the next. It is on a fairly busy main road but bedrooms, in the separate guest wing, are at the back; they are simple, small, yet comfortable. Your friendly hosts retired from milk and wine production to enjoy having more time for guests. Marie-Claire still teaches German; Paul serves breakfast in the garden or in the dining room. A great place to know at the start of the *Route des Vins*: so close to gorgeous, expensive Strasbourg, it is great value. *Gîte space for 6 people.*

rooms	3 doubles, all with shower & wc.
price	€32-€35 for two.
dinner	Traditional restaurant 200m.
closed	Rarely.
directions	From Saverne A4, exit 45 onto N404/N4 for Strasbourg, 16km. Farm in middle of Marlenheim on left, before post office.

Paul & Marie-Claire Goetz
86 rue du Général de Gaulle,
67520 Marlenheim, Bas-Rhin

tel	(0)3 88 87 52 94

An ingenious conversion of old barns into neat sleeping spaces finished with pretty patchworks, carved stairs, delicately painted eaves – Monsieur works his wood brilliantly – plus a couple of real ponies, a quiet courtyard garden walled off from the busy road, breakfast of fresh juice and home-made cake at the long table with your host or hostess, a welcoming, gentle-mannered couple who live in another house. English speaker home between 8pm and 10pm. *Gîte space for 11 people.*

rooms	5: 3 doubles, 2 family rooms, all with shower (1 behind curtain) & wc.
price	€39-€48 for two.
dinner	Restaurants Pfettisheim 2-3km; self-catering in family rooms.
closed	Rarely.
directions	From A4 exit 48; N63 for Vendenheim/Strasbourg; D64 for Lampertheim to Pfulgriesheim; right D31 to Pfettisheim. In village follow main road; signs.

Marie-Célestine Gass
La Maison du Charron,
15 rue Principale,
67370 Pfettisheim, Bas-Rhin
tel (0)3 88 69 60 35
fax (0)3 88 69 85 45
e-mail maisonducharron@proveis.com
web www.proveis.com/lamaisonducharron

ALSACE

At the centre of a working vineyard in gorgeous old Dambach is a typical, geranium-dripping Alsatian house, built by the first Ruhlmann wine-grower in 1688. Wine buffs enjoy visiting the wine cellar and non-drinkers can taste the sweet water springing from the Vosges hills. The charming rooms, in the guest wing under the sloping roof, have new carpets and old family furniture (there are two less exciting overflow rooms); breakfast is served in the huge relic-filled guest dayroom: a wine press, a grape basket, a superb ceramic stove. Your friendly hostess speaks excellent English.

rooms	2 doubles, both with shower, sharing wc.
price	€38 for two.
dinner	6 restaurants within walking distance.
closed	December-March.
directions	From Sélestat N on D35, 8km. House in village centre, about equidistant between town gates on main road.

Jean-Charles & Laurence Ruhlmann
34 rue Maréchal Foch,
67650 Dambach la Ville, Bas-Rhin
tel (0)3 88 92 41 86
fax (0)3 88 92 61 81
e-mail vins@ruhlmann-schutz.fr
web www.ruhlmann-schutz.fr

ALSACE

Young Madame Engel-Geiger, who really loves receiving guests, will greet you with the warmest welcome and the finest Alsace cooking. The peaceful chalet, with breathtaking views of the mountains and forests, is just the place to enjoy both. All you need to do is breathe deeply, forget everything – and relax. The rooms are simply comfortable with signs of Monsieur's upholstering skills, geraniums cascading from every window, the views pouring in and a guest entrance. Breakfast tables are laden with goodies – try the home-made organic fruit jams and *kougelopf* (Alsace cake to the uninitiated).

rooms	3: 2 doubles, 1 twin, all with shower & wc.
price	€48–€50 for two.
dinner	Choice of restaurants nearby.
closed	Rarely.
directions	From Colmar A35 & N83 Sélestat (exit 11); N59 & D424 to Villé; D697 to Dieffenbach au Val. Careful: ask for exact address as two other Engels do B&B!

Doris Engel-Geiger
Maison Fleurie,
19 route de Neuve Église,
Dieffenbach au Val,
67220 Villé, Bas-Rhin

tel	(0)3 88 85 60 48
fax	(0)3 88 85 60 48
e-mail	infos@lamaisonfleurie.com
web	www.lamaisonfleurie.com

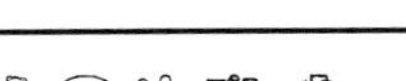

map: 8 entry: 96

FRANCHE COMTÉ

The house is a gallery for Madame's hand-painted stencils (she'll teach you if you like). She and her artistic daughter often paint quietly on the landing. The top-floor pine-clad sitting room is a delight – you feel you are in a boat; bedrooms are big and cosy, the suite in a separate building. Dinner with your hosts and possibly their grown children is a model of conviviality… and Madame should charge extra for her conversation! "Lucky is the traveller who stops here," said one reader. The garden leads out to forest, deer, red squirrels; nearby are golf, skiing and the *Ballons des Vosges* Regional Park.

rooms	2: 1 double, 1 suite for 4, both with shower & wc.
price	€46.50 for two; suite €69.50 for four.
dinner	€20 with wine, by arrangement.
closed	Rarely.
directions	From A36 exit 14 N83 for Mulhouse; in Les Errues left for Anjoutey & Étueffont; at r'bout right for Rougemont; left at 1st bend; house at end.

Astride & Daniel Elbert
Le Montanjus,
8 rue de la Chapelle,
90170 Étueffont,
Territoire-de-Belfort

tel	(0)3 84 54 68 63
e-mail	daniel.elbert@wanadoo.fr
web	www.amiesenfranchecomte.com

map: 8 entry: 97

As part of its vast 100m² suite, this château has one of the most extraordinary bathrooms this side of the Saône, panels hung with old engravings, a sunken bath and an Italian chandelier making an atmosphere of exceptionally elegant luxury; bedroom and sitting room are just as amazing. All this and a family feel. Antiques, attention to detail, a charming hostess with an easy laugh, make it a very special place. Dinner, carefully chosen to suit guests' tastes (if you want snails, you'll have to ask), is exquisitely presented on Gien porcelain, on the terrace in summer. Untouched 18th-century living. *Gîte space for one.*

rooms	1 suite for 3, with bathroom.
price	€66 for two.
dinner	€16, with wine; light supper €8.
closed	September-mid-May.
directions	From A36 exit 3 D67 to Gray 35km; entering Gray right D474; fork left D13 to Beaujeu & Motey sur Saône; left to Mercey; signs in village.

Bernadette Jantet
Le Château,
70130 Mercey sur Saône,
Territoire-de-Belfort
tel (0)3 84 67 07 84

FRANCHE COMTÉ

Here, in a tiny village, stands a mansion where fine materials and craftsmanship breathe elegance and loving care. Gentle light and glowing old floors, delicate mouldings and superb taste make the generous spaces utterly seductive. Roland combs the auctions for lovely rugs, little bronzes, old mirrors and modern paintings; Fabienne puts thick curtains, pretty desks, solid oak or carved walnut *armoires* and soft sofas in vast pale-walled bedrooms. He gardens passionately, she cooks brilliantly – remarkable hosts, interior designers of much flair, they are fun and excellent company. With super-luxy bathrooms to boot, this is value indeed.

rooms	3: 1 double/quadruple, 2 suites (2nd double in each is a sofabed), all with bath or shower & wc.
price	€65 for two.
dinner	€23 with wine, by arrangement.
closed	Rarely.
directions	From Troyes A31 exit 6 Langres-Sud through Longeau; D67 through Gray for Besançon. Cult on right 21km after Gray; signs in village.

Mme Fabienne Lego-Deiber
Les Egrignes,
70150 Cult, Haute-Saône
tel (0)3 84 31 92 06
fax (0)3 84 31 92 06
e-mail lesegrignes@wanadoo.fr

The gaunt exterior, part of the town's 15th-century fortress, imposes – but wait. Guy, novelist, traveller and collector, bought the two-metre-thick walls and, with an architect's help, built a house within them – his pride and joy. The huge ground-floor rooms, open to the public, are gorgeous; the breakfast room is suspended from the ceiling of the *salon*; bedrooms, all differently, artistically marvellous, have luxy bathrooms and great views – it's like sleeping in a modern palace. It could be overwhelming but Guy and Lydie are such a super couple that it is, in fact, unforgettably moving. *Children over 5 welcome.*

rooms	6: 4 doubles, 1 twin, 1 triple, all with bath or shower & wc.
price	€68.50 for two.
dinner	Restaurants 2 minutes' walk.
closed	Mid-October-mid-March.
directions	From A36 exit 2 onto D475 to Pesmes, 20km. House at top of village on left.

M & Mme Guy Hoyet
La Maison Royale,
70140 Pesmes, Haute-Saône
tel (0)3 84 31 23 23
fax (0)3 84 31 23 23

map: 12 entry: 100

FRANCHE COMTÉ

The gentlest, most generous couple live here with all the time in the world for you and a delightful art gallery in their ancient vaulted basement: Madame embroiders but shows other artists' paintings and their son holds wine-tasting sessions. It's a fairly average old wine merchant's house but that welcome, the rooms under the roof, a lovely view of orchards and meadows, a brook to sing you to sleep after a fine family-style meal, make it special. Plus a splendid dresser carved with the lion of Franche-Comté, a tempting garden where a play house awaits children, a piano anyone may play – or golf just down the road.

rooms	2: 1 twin, 1 suite for 4, both with shower & wc.
price	€45 for two.
dinner	€12; wine €6-€11 a bottle.
closed	Rarely.
directions	In Lons le Saunier for Chalon; right before SNCF station D117 for Macournay; D41 to Vernantois; left before houses & follow signs.

Monique & Michel Ryon
Rose Art,
8 rue Lacuzon,
39570 Vernantois, Jura
tel (0)3 84 47 17 28
fax (0)3 84 47 17 28
e-mail rose.art@wanadoo.fr

map: 12 entry: 101

BURGUNDY

In St Claude, they make the prince of pipes; in Dijon, Canon Kir mixes his inimitable vine-fruit nectar; in Beaune, the heady wines fetch fabulous sums in the quiet courtyards – and the fat snail creeps unknowingly to his marriage with parsley and garlic: à table!

Such fun. Everything about this 17th-century royal hunting lodge has an air of exaggeration: a fantastic ceramic stove as big as two men dominates the panelled, stuccoed breakfast room, the huntsman weather vane tells you what the day's weather will be, the stairs are almost too generous, the double windows ingenious, the décor highly voluptuous with total Frenchness of florality and embroidery in the magnificent bedrooms, the tiled bathrooms (one whirlpool) and stained-glass panels are 1930s. Marie, who knows everyone in wine growing, will help you all she can over another cigarette. And Burgundy has so much else to offer.

rooms	5: 1 double, 1 twin sharing shower & wc; 1 twin with bath & wc; 1 triple, 1 twin sharing bath & wc.
price	€61-€76 for two; suite €122-€140 for four.
dinner	€24 with wine, by arrangement.
closed	Rarely.
directions	From Chalon sur Saône N80 for Montceau les Mines 9km; exit 31 on D981 for Givry; follow Complexe Sportif signs; 2nd on right.

Marie & Daniel Lacroix-Mollaret
Manoir du Clos de Vauvry,
3 rue des Faussillons,
71640 Givry Poncey, Saône-et-Loire

tel	(0)3 85 44 40 83
fax	(0)3 85 44 40 83
e-mail	closdevauvry@lycos.fr
web	www.multimania.com/closdevauvry

The guest rooms of this former abbey are in the 17th-century pigeon tower: those hollows are where the original occupants roosted. Ring at the wrought iron gates for your young hosts, the easiest of people who make it all pleasingly eccentric and fun. You have a ground-floor sitting room with a twin room off it – ideal for children – and in the tower itself is that amazing bathroom with the main bedroom on a mezzanine above. Breakfast, a relaxed family affair, is a short walk through the park to the château kitchen; dinner may be in the graciously faded dining room. *Gîte space for 5 people.*

rooms	1 quadruple with bath & wc.
price	€61 for two; €91 for four.
dinner	Restaurant 6-8km.
closed	Rarely.
directions	From A6 exit Chalon south, N6 for Varrennes le Grand; D6 for Le Lac de Laives to La Ferté; at crossroads marked La Ferté, press intercom at large iron gates.

Jacques & Virginie Thenard
Abbaye de la Ferté,
71240 St Ambreuil, Saône-et-Loire
tel (0)3 85 44 17 96
fax (0)3 85 44 17 96
e-mail abbayedelaferte@aol.com
web www.abbayeferte.com

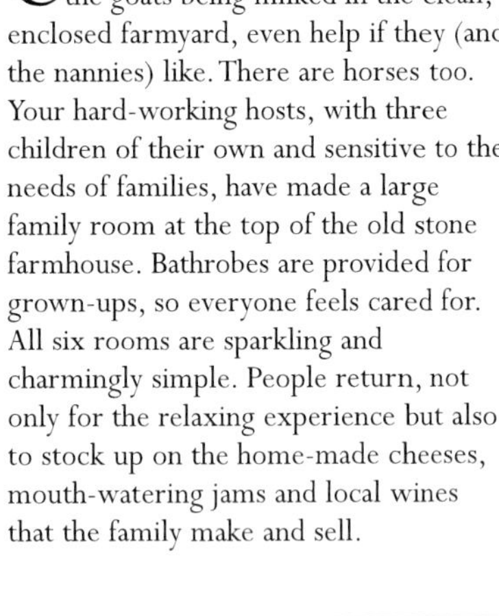

Children love it here: they can watch the goats being milked in the clean, enclosed farmyard, even help if they (and the nannies) like. There are horses too. Your hard-working hosts, with three children of their own and sensitive to the needs of families, have made a large family room at the top of the old stone farmhouse. Bathrobes are provided for grown-ups, so everyone feels cared for. All six rooms are sparkling and charmingly simple. People return, not only for the relaxing experience but also to stock up on the home-made cheeses, mouth-watering jams and local wines that the family make and sell.

rooms	6: 2 doubles sharing shower & wc; 2 twins with shower & wc; 2 family suites with shower, wc & kitchen.
price	€50-€56 for two.
dinner	Self-catering in two rooms; restaurant nearby.
closed	Rarely.
directions	From Tournus D14 for Cluny. At Chapaize, D314 to Bissy sous Uxelles. House next to church.

Pascale & Dominique de La Bussière
La Ferme,
71460 Bissy sous Uxelles,
Saône-et-Loire
tel (0)3 85 50 15 03
fax (0)3 85 50 15 03
e-mail dominique.de-la-bussiere@wanadoo.f
web www.m-fjsolutions.com/BB/

A place to die for – oceans of history behind it (a prehistoric *menhir* stands in the grounds) and charming owners bursting with more restoration ideas who they are passionate about it. Monsieur cultivates the vines and the wine: wine production started here in the 10th century. The bedrooms, in a renovated building near the main 13th-15th-century château, are fresh and unfussy in the stylish way so many are in France – the bigger one is a gem, with its superb beams, vast mezzanine, little veranda, huge new bath. Breakfast is in the château, a delightfully lived-in listed monument. Irresistible.

rooms	2: 1 triple, 1 family room, both with bath or shower & wc.
price	€73 for two.
dinner	5 restaurants within 5km.
closed	November-March.
directions	From Tournus D14 for Cormatin. Passing Brancion on right cont. on main road for 1.5km. Towers opposite on bend.

Bertrand & Françoise de Cherisey
Château de Nobles,
71700 La Chapelle sous Brancion,
Saône-et-Loire
tel (0)3 85 51 00 55

BURGUNDY

A 13th-century wine-growing château with beautiful gardens, tours of the cellars and the *Route des Vins*. Monsieur is the cellar master, Madame manages the B&B and gîtes with charming efficiency. Aperitifs in the cellar are part of the evening ritual and Monsieur may surprise you with an enormous bottle of cognac after a dinner of regional dishes made with home-grown vegetables. The excellent guest rooms are in the beautifully rustic old vine workers' cottages or, more period-style (and more expensive), in the château. A most welcoming if somewhat business-like place with lots of people. *Gîte space for 16 people.*

rooms	4: 2 twins, 1 double/twin, 1 triple, all with bath & wc.
price	€77-€130 for two.
dinner	€20, wine €5.
closed	January.
directions	From A6 exit to Tournus; in centre right on D14. Château on left of D14 between Ozenay & Martailly, 9km from Tournus.

Marie-Laurence Fachon
Château de Messey,
71700 Ozenay, Saône-et-Loire
tel (0)3 85 51 16 11
fax (0)3 85 32 57 30
e-mail chateau@demessey.com
web www.demessey.com

Open-minded and wise after years abroad, a man of many parts and full of mirth who punctuates his phrases with a bemused chuckle and a puff of tobacco, Monsieur is so thoughtful he reads your unspoken wishes. He cannot put enough out for breakfast. In deep wine-growing country, his traditional *Mâconnais* house, thrown open for conviviality, appears to wear typical French décor, then you notice the contemporary paintings, tapestries, pottery, antique African sculpture – fascinating. Guest rooms have the same heart-warming mix of ancient, modern and attention to detail. And the village church is a Romanesque gem.

rooms	2 doubles, both with shower or bath & wc.
price	€44 for two.
dinner	Excellent restaurant nearby, 5km.
closed	Rarely.
directions	From Tournus D14 for Cormatin 12km; left D163 for Grévilly 200m; right to Grévilly; across T-junct.; house 100m on left, outside village, just below church.

Claude Depreay
Le Pré Ménot,
71700 Grévilly, Saône-et-Loire
tel (0)3 85 33 29 92
fax (0)3 85 33 02 79

map: 12 entry: 107

BURGUNDY

Come backstage. Jean-Paul runs a theatre company, *La Mère Folle*, with the local actor-winegrowers and he and Régine, a musician, combine their farmhouse B&B with a thriving summer theatre and permanent art gallery. Busy, artistic people who live in the main house, they create an atmosphere of relaxed energy, take their B&B very seriously and offer attractive, cosy rooms in the converted tithe barn over the theatre and gallery: good beds, original beams, modern pale wood décor and, generously, *Grand-père's* excellent Cubist paintings. A friendly welcome at all times and theatrical novelty in June and July.

rooms	5: 4 doubles, 1 twin, all with bath or shower & wc.
price	€45-€46 for two.
dinner	Bistro 2km, restaurants 6km.
closed	November-February.
directions	From A6 exit Tournus; D56 for Lugny. 3km after Chardonnay right on D463 & follow signs to Chambres d'Hôtes & Théâtre Champvent.

Régine & Jean-Paul Rullière
Le Tinailler,
Manoir de Champvent,
71700 Chardonnay, Saône-et-Loire
tel (0)3 85 40 50 23
fax (0)3 85 40 50 18

map: 12 entry: 108

The lovely stones and cascading geraniums outside, the silk flowers, frilly lampshades and polished furniture inside have an old-world charm. The breakfast room is cosily stuffed with bric-à-brac, bedrooms are family-simple. Madame was a florist: she arranges her rooms as if they were bouquets, is always refreshing them and might put a paper heart on your pillow wishing you *bonne nuit*. She doesn't refuse children but may well be happier if you arrive with a little dog under your arm. She or her husband can do winery visits for non-French speakers. Ask for one of the larger rooms; the smallest feels cramped.

rooms	3 doubles, all with bath or shower & wc.
price	€38-€46 for two.
dinner	Choice of restaurants 3-5km.
closed	Sundays in winter.
directions	From N79 exit La Roche Vineuse. Left to Charnay & Mâcon; after 500m left at r'bout for Sommeré (not into Roche Vineuse); up hill follow EH signs, house at top on left, bell by gate.

Éliane Heinen
Le Tinailler d'Aléane,
Sommeré,
71960 La Roche Vineuse,
Saône-et-Loire
tel (0)3 85 37 80 68
fax (0)3 85 37 80 68

BURGUNDY

There's immense personality in the authentically worn old manor and Madame, with her unorthodox sense of humour, is quite a character too – and a dab hand at woodcuts. She enjoys the contrast between the place's 19th-century *parvenu* origins and artistic present – so should you. Be active (walk, cycle, ride) or contemplative (mountain scenery to imbibe, Érard baby grand to play, local guides and histories to peruse in the library). Super if smallish old-decorated bedrooms, fine modern bathrooms. Give Madame time to come to the door: she may be deep in the garden. *Gîte space for 10 people.*

rooms	2: 1 double with bath, shower & wc; 1 suite for 5 with shower, wc & kitchen.
price	€38-€40 for two.
dinner	Self-catering in suite; restaurant 5km.
closed	Rarely.
directions	From Mâcon N79 for Cluny; at Berzé le Châtel N79-D987 for Charolles exit Clermain, Matour, Trambly; D987 to Trambly; left past church; house on left.

François & Florence Gauthier
Les Charrières,
71520 Trambly, Saône-et-Loire
tel (0)3 85 50 43 17
fax (0)3 85 50 49 28
e-mail gauthierflorence@minitel.net

The Loire at the bottom of the garden: it's a beautiful spot; Monsieur has retired to give more time to his house and his guests: he's a fascinating host. His English nanny made him for ever at home with the English language and culture and he talks passionately over dinner about the region, its history and architecture, his print and corkscrew collections, cooking, wine, art... The entirely lived-in 18th-century château has no end of family furniture and treasures, a boat for guests' use and the Pilgrims Path (GR 13) nearby. A chance to sample the pleasing, unaffected lifestyle of the French provincial aristocracy.

rooms	5: 3 doubles, 1 twin, 1 suite for 4, all with bath & wc.
price	€55-€80 for two.
dinner	€23 with wine, by arrangement.
closed	January-March.
directions	From Digoin D979 for Bourbon Lancy for 25km. In St Aubin, 1st left at sign Les Lambeys; on right.

Michèle & Étienne de Bussierre
Les Lambeys,
71140 St Aubin sur Loire,
Saône-et-Loire

tel	(0)3 85 53 92 76
fax	(0)3 85 53 92 76

The Perreaus are wonderful folk, full of *joie de vivre*, who may even greet you with a glass of something special. They breed cattle and horses and summer foals dance in the buttercup meadows – a lovely backdrop to the terrace and swimming pool. They also have a sideline in organic vegetables – Madame, who is a delight, loves her big potager, you will love its fruits. You stay in the big loft of the old farmhouse where bright, finely furnished bedrooms share a large sitting room and a sweet little breakfast room. A tremendous place for enjoying the good things in life. *Gîte space for 10 people.*

rooms	5: 2 twins, 2 doubles, sharing 2 showers & separate wcs; 1 double with shower & wc.
price	€50 for two.
dinner	€20 with wine, by arrangement.
closed	Rarely.
directions	From Nevers D978 towards Château Chinon. 3km before Châtillon right on D10 for Alluy. In St Gratien left on C3 to La Marquise; 800m on right.

Huguette & Noël Perreau
La Marquise,
58340 St Gratien Savigny, Nièvre

tel	(0)3 86 50 01 02
fax	(0)3 86 50 07 14
e-mail	hcollot@aol.fr
web	perso.wanadoo.fr/la-marquise

This modest, friendly couple clearly enjoy sharing their fine old 1690s house and its great park, dovecote and all; in sunflower season, it's surrounded by them for ever and beyond. Inside the immaculately restored house are a big antique-filled sitting room, a cheery breakfast room with antique plates and small tables, elegant bedrooms with plenty of interesting wallpaper and stupendously curtained bathrooms. Your hosts are happy to advise on local châteaux, lovely canalside walks, pony rides. And Monsieur is keen to flex his English-language muscles with any willing talkers – he has an impressive Burgundy accent!

rooms	3 doubles, all with bath or shower & wc.
price	€46-€56 for two.
dinner	Self-catering possible; restaurant 5km.
closed	Rarely.
directions	From Château Chinon D978 through Châtillon en Bazois for Nevers 4km (not to Alluy); after service station, right D112 for Bernière 1.5km; house on left.

Colette & André Lejault
Bouteuille,
58110 Alluy, Nièvre

tel	(0)3 86 84 06 65
fax	(0)3 86 84 03 41
e-mail	lejault.c@wanadoo.fr
web	perso.wanadoo.fr/bouteuille

map: 11 entry: 113

The peace is palpable as the sun sets over sweeping garden and still lake. Next day, borrow the owners' small boat and row, fish, canoe or windsurf, there's a private beach you can swim from – perfect for children. Breakfast at the scrubbed farmhouse table includes home-grown honey; big, bright, unpretentious rooms have that inimitable French air of gilt-framed mirrors, round tables in modern bathrooms and 'French Rustic' wallpaper. Your lovely hosts, she level-headed, he quietly cheerful, create a relaxed family atmosphere. Madame is learning English but her genuine welcome transcends any language barrier. *Gîte space for 10 people.*

rooms	3: 1 double, 2 triples, all with bath or shower & wc.
price	€43-€46 for two.
dinner	Self-catering possible; restaurants nearby.
closed	Rarely.
directions	From Nevers D978 to Rouy; D132 to Tintury, right on D112 to Fleury (aka Fertrève); 1st right after village, up to lake, turn right; signs.

Michel & Marie-France Guény
Fleury La Tour,
58110 Tintury, Nièvre

tel	(0)3 86 84 12 42
fax	(0)3 86 84 12 42
e-mail	fleurylatour@wanadoo.fr
web	perso.wanadoo.fr/fleurylatour

map: 11 entry: 114

Deep in real country where nothing disturbs the rural peace, here is a place of tremendous hospitality and remarkable views out to the Morvan hills. Inside are open fires, antique beds with antique monogrammed bedclothes, sympathetic period decorations, a sense of old-style secluded comfort and super modern showers. A baronial double staircase leads down to the kempt lawn and the ha-ha where, rather endearingly, chickens may be roaming. Madame Bürgi's fully organic home-made cakes and jams are incomparable – if only breakfast could be more than once a day! *Minimum 3 nights. Gîte space for 2 people.*

rooms	5 doubles/twins, all with bath or shower & wc.
price	€68-€85 for two.
dinner	Restaurant in village, 300m.
closed	November-March.
directions	From Nevers, D977 to Prémery. D977 bis for Corbigny; St Révérien 15km; signposted.

Bernadette Bürgi
& Florent de Beer
La Villa des Prés,
58420 St Révérien, Nièvre

tel	(0)3 86 29 04 57
fax	(0)3 86 29 65 22
e-mail	contact@villa-des-pres.com
web	www.villa-des-pres.com

map: 11 entry: 115

BURGUNDY

You can do a day's canoeing on the Loire and disembark at the bottom of the garden for aperitifs and *boules* beneath the plane trees – pretty classy. Your hosts leave you the run of their fine French garden – box hedges and central pond – and classically symmetrical house with its unusual double stairway. Casually elegant and a whizz at interior decorating, Madame first came from Switzerland to study fine art and loves living here. Bedrooms are light and airy, one of them with a dreamy river view and a step-down bathroom disguised as a cupboard. Breakfast is in the super kitchen, decorated with Monsieur's printed teacloths.

rooms	2 suites, each with bath/shower & wc.
price	€60-€75 for two.
dinner	€20 with wine, by arrangement.
closed	Rarely.
directions	From Cosne sur Loire for Bourges; at r'bout in front of bridge for Nevers (do not cross river); after 3km road turns to left; follow wall on right; gate on right.

Marianne & Daniel Perrier
Habitation BeauvilliersPort Aubry,
58200 Cosne sur Loire, Nièvre

tel	(0)3 86 28 41 37
e-mail	habitationbeauvilliers@hotmail.com

map: 11 entry: 116

Language no obstacle, the Duchets are easy communicators and such natural hosts. Their engagingly cottagey old farmhouse is full of character and space beneath its sweeping roof – exposed beams and old tiles are part of Monsieur's fine renovation job. Madame, who is Portuguese, is a charming, enthusiastic hostess, keen to provide her guests with authentic country hospitality. Breakfast (home-made jams) and dinner are eaten with the family and Madame will make her national specialities if asked – a real treat. Rooms, traditionally decorated and comfortable, include a pleasant living room with books and games.

rooms	2 doubles, both with shower & wc.
price	€48 for two.
dinner	€20, with wine.
closed	November-Easter.
directions	From Cosne sur Loire, D114 towards St Loup; left on D114; Chauffour between St Loup & St Vérain; follow Musée de la Machine Agricole then Chambres d'Hôtes signs.

Elvire & René Duchet
Chez Elvire,
Chauffour,
58200 St Loup, Nièvre
tel (0)3 86 26 20 22

BURGUNDY

Tarperon is uniquely French and an ageless charm breathes from the ancient turrets, fine antiques, paintings and prints. Soisick is modern and good fun, with her sense of humour and her unstuffy formality – if you can't find her, walk in and make yourself at home, she's not far. The rooms are full of family furniture in an utterly uncontrived, fadedly elegant, lived-in décor; the bathrooms are family style, with lots of unusual bits. Dinner, superbly cooked by Claudine and Soisick, is a treat. Also: lovely gardens, fly-fishing, painting courses – stay two or three days to enjoy it all properly. *Minimum 2 nights.*

rooms	5: 3 doubles, 1 twin, 1 triple, all with bath or shower & wc.
price	€60-€65 for two.
dinner	€23 with wine, by arrangement.
closed	2 November-March.
directions	From Dijon N71 for Châtillon sur Seine, 62km; right D901 for Aignay. Tarperon sign on D901.

Soisick de Champsavin
Manoir de Tarperon,
21510 Aignay le Duc, Côte-d'Or
tel (0)3 80 93 83 74
fax (0)3 80 93 83 74
e-mail manoir.de.tarperon@wanadoo.fr
web www.tarperon.com

Genuine French country hospitality by the bucket, meals you will remember for ever (people copy Madame's recipes), a sun trap by the summer house for your own barbecue, stupendous valley views over historic Alésia where Caesar fought Vercingétorix in 52 BC (brush up your Asterix), great walks, medieval villages and a modern house set among bright tulips, terraced features and birdsong. Inside, beyond the Alpine mural, you find spotless rooms, good mattresses and bathrooms, a colourful chintzy décor – all endearingly French. But above all, you will remember these generous, honest and open people.

rooms	2: 1 double, 1 twin, both with curtained shower, sharing wc.
price	€35 for two.
dinner	€15 with wine, by arrangement.
closed	November-Easter, except by arrangement.
directions	From Dijon N71 for Châtillon sur Seine; after Courceau D6 left & follow signs; house on D19A near junction with D6. (50km from Dijon.)

Claude & Huguette Gounand
Villa le Clos,
Route de la Villeneuve,
21150 Darcey, Côte-d'Or

tel	(0)3 80 96 23 20
fax	(0)3 80 96 23 20
e-mail	claude.gounand@libertysurf.fr
web	perso.wanadoo.fr/claude.gounand/

BURGUNDY

You cannot forget the lifeblood of Burgundy: wine buffs will love the twisting drive along the *Route des Vins* into the gravelled courtyard of this fine old wine-grower's house. Your courteous host knows a lot about wine and loves to practise his English, so sample an aperitif in his atmospheric stone-arched cellar, (if you're not a wine fan there are locally-pressed fruit juices too). The house has a classic stone staircase and generous windows, the comfortable and homely bedrooms are reached by outside steps, the breakfast room has flagstones and ochre-coloured walls. In summer, breakfast is in the well-kept, willow-draped garden.

rooms	3: 1 double, 1 twin, 1 family room, all with shower & wc.
price	€50-€56 for two.
dinner	Excellent restaurant 300m.
closed	Rarely.
directions	From Lyon N on A6 exit Nuits St Georges; N74 for Dijon. After approx. 13km left to Marsannay.

Jean-Charles & Brigitte Viennet
34 rue de Mazy,
21160 Marsannay la Côte,
Côte-d'Or

tel	(0)3 80 59 83 63
fax	(0)3 80 59 83 28
e-mail	viennet.jean-charles@wanadoo.fr
web	perso.wanadoo.fr/gite.marsannay

Do pancakes or gingerbread for breakfast sound tempting? Traditionalists can stick to fresh bread and home-made jam. Supper might be *pot-au-feu*, with chicken from the farm next door, followed by cheese and a freshly-baked tart. Françoise will be happy to chat as she makes it, she is passionate about history, antiques and cooking and enjoys seeing her guests happy and relaxed. She is doing up La Monastille herself. It's old, built in 1750 as a wealthy farmhouse. Bedrooms are a soothing mix of muted walls, dark old furniture and crisp yellow and white, or perhaps flowery pink bed covers. Delightful.

rooms	4 doubles, all with shower.
price	€55 for two.
dinner	€23 with wine, by arrangement.
closed	Rarely.
directions	From Beaune D970 to Bligny sur Ouche; after village left to Écutigny; right to Thomirey; house with yellow flower pots by church.

Françoise Moine
La Monastille,
21360 Thomirey, Côte-d'Or

tel	(0)3 80 20 00 80
fax	(0)3 80 20 00 80
e-mail	moine.francoise@wanadoo.fr
web	www.chez.com/thomirey

map: 12 entry: 121

BURGUNDY

The generous warmth of the ochre-tinted, green-shuttered façade reaches indoors, too, where a beautiful Alsatian ceramic stove stands proud beside huge plants in the sunny breakfast room and the double-aspect guest rooms are airy and florally friezed. Interesting prints on the walls too. Your hosts are chatty and friendly. Monsieur teaches economics, Madame gave up a high-powered marketing job to care for two small children and the visitors she so enjoys receiving. The entrance to the fine gardens and house may seem narrow but don't get it wrong: you are very welcome and can always leave the car outside.

rooms	5: 1 triple, 1 twin, 2 doubles, 1 family suite, all with bath, shower, wc & kitchen.
price	€70-€85 for two.
dinner	Restaurant 1km.
closed	Rarely.
directions	From A31 exit Nuits St Georges; N74 for Dijon; at Vougeot r'bout head for Gilly centre; 1st right after station.

André & Sandrine Lanaud
La Closerie de Gilly,
16 avenue du Recteur Bouchard,
Gilly lès Cîteaux,
21640 Vougeot, Côte-d'Or

tel	(0)3 80 62 87 74
fax	(0)3 80 62 87 74
e-mail	informations@closerie-gilly.com
web	www.closerie-gilly.com

map: 12 entry: 122

Ancient rafters, white-swathed roof windows, little florals – the bedrooms, one with a ladder up to the children's mezzanine, are sweetly charming, just like the wide rose-bordered terrace where breakfast is served on fine days. The Dufouleur wine is pretty good too – they are one of the old wine-growing families. This house stands on the remains of the Duke of Burgundy's 13th-century castle (he was Hugues de Quincey) and the little church is floodlit at night. Perfect for peace and wine-lovers. *Children over 12 welcome.*

rooms	3: 2 doubles with shower & wc; 1 triple with bath & wc; loft for children.
price	€60 for two.
dinner	Choice of restaurants 2-3km.
closed	Rarely.
directions	From A31 exit Nuits St Georges for Gerland-Seurre 3km; right to Quincey; house opposite church.

Chantal Dufouleur
Place de l'Église,
21700 Quincey, Côte-d'Or

tel	(0)3 80 61 13 23
fax	(0)3 80 61 13 23
e-mail	dufouleurchantal@wanadoo.fr
web	perso.wanadoo.fr/gite.nuits-saint-georges/

BURGUNDY

A pretty old Burgundian hunting lodge, 'Copper Beeches' stands in a walled garden full of flowers and centenarian trees and has an unexpected air of Provence inside: beautifully judged colour schemes (Madame paints and knows about colour), fine furniture, numerous *objets* and the odd sprig of flowers make a soothing and reviving environment. Your hosts extend a warm, genuine yet ungushing welcome to the weary traveller – lots of towels, superb bed linen, breakfast that has the savour of yesteryear: yogurt, fresh bread and home-made jam. The cottage is a deliciously independent blue hideaway with a working fireplace.

rooms	3: 1 double, 2 twins, all with bath & wc.
price	€82-€173 for two.
dinner	Wide choice of restaurants 10km.
closed	Rarely.
directions	From A31 exit 1 on D35 for Seurre 3km; right to Quincey then Antilly, 4km. House on right.

Jean-François & Christiane Bugnet
Les Hêtres Rouges,
Antilly,
21700 Argilly, Côte-d'Or

tel	(0)3 80 62 53 98
fax	(0)3 80 62 54 85
e-mail	leshetresrouges2@wanadoo.fr
web	www.leshetresrouges.com

If you find yourself in the Mecca of Wine, surely you should stay with a famous family of winegrowers like the Bouchards – and sip your aperitif in the courtyard looking out over the vineyards of the Côtes de Beaune. Then a private wine-tasting? Cécile can arrange it. Her newly refurbished townhouse looks rather 18th-century colonial from the outside; inside all is spotless but in no way sterile. The craftsmanship of the new oak and stone, the quiet good taste of the plain white paint, the space in the comfortable bedrooms and the fittings in the bathrooms – they all beat most three-star hotels into a cocked hat.

rooms	2: 1 double, 1 twin, each with bath & wc.
price	€90 for two.
dinner	Restaurants 100m.
closed	January-February.
directions	On one-way road round ramparts of Beaune, 200m after War Memorial, right at 2nd traffic light; Rue Sylvestre Chauvelot starts at Peugeot garage.

Christophe & Cécile Bouchard
Les Planchottes,
8 rue Sylvestre Chauvelot,
21200 Beaune, Côte-d'Or

tel	(0)3 80 22 83 67
fax	(0)3 80 22 83 67
e-mail	lesplanchottes@voila.fr
web	lesplanchottes.free.fr

map: 12 entry: 125

BURGUNDY

If your French is imperfect but you fancy becoming fluent in the lore of Burgundy – the region and its wine – this is the place for you. Indeed, Jonathan and Susie have worked in practically every wine-growing region of France over the past 20 years. Just outside the ramparts of the old town, peeping over high walls, the house has two creeper-clad wings joined by a tower. Once inside, guests have their own door up to the bedroom overlooking the flower-filled courtyard but will be welcomed on arrival with a glass (or two) of something local. The walled garden behind has a child-safe pool.

rooms	1 double with bath & wc; children's room available.
price	€75-€90 for two.
dinner	Restaurants within walking distance.
closed	Rarely.
directions	On one-way road round ramparts of Beaune, exit for Auxerre (RN, not m'way); house on right after 200m, big white gates.

Jonathan & Susie Lyddon
14 avenue Charles Jaffelin,
Route de Bouze,
21200 Beaune, Côte-d'Or

tel	(0)3 80 22 38 89
fax	(0)3 80 22 38 89

map: 12 entry: 126

Jaquot is as authentically 12th-century as Madame can make it – she's passionate about the place and loves sharing her passion with like-minded visitors. The medieval flavour, called variously fascinating, stagey, strange, hits you as you enter: atmospherically low lighting, objects and artefacts, some as old as the Crusades, jostling for attention, medieval dinners served in the candlelit baronial kitchen. Climb the winding stone turret stair, push the big oak door, choose your four-poster, wallow in the ingenious Gothicky bathroom, admire the brilliant bed hangings. A stylish, romantic retreat for convinced medievalists.

rooms	1 quadruple (2 four-posters) with bathroom.
price	€90 for two.
dinner	€30-€55, with wine (state your budget).
closed	Rarely.
directions	From Avallon N6 for Saulieu. On entering Ste Magnance, 1st house on right, continue up drive.

Martine Costaille
Château Jaquot,
2 route d'Avallon,
89420 Ste Magnance, Yonne
tel (0)3 86 33 00 22

BURGUNDY

Ancient and atmospheric is the pilgrims' hospice beneath the revered Basilica. A gallery of tempting objects and a much-loved coffee shop occupy the 12th-century vaulted hall but guests have the vast fireplace to themselves at breakfast. Rooms are simple, authentic, with good beds. Eccentric, Swiss and slightly shuffling, Monsieur is a gentleman with a sense of humour; Madame is a welcoming artist; both are vividly creative. An exceptional, inimitable house.

rooms	4: 2 doubles, both with shower & wc; 2 doubles, both with shower, sharing wcs.
price	€58-€75 for two.
dinner	€20 with wine, by arrangement.
closed	Rarely.
directions	In Vézelay centre take main street up to Basilica. Park, walk down main street, ring at 2nd door on right.

M Cabalus
Cabalus,
Rue Saint Pierre,
89450 Vézelay, Yonne
tel (0)3 86 33 20 66
fax (0)3 86 33 38 03
e-mail contact@cabalus.com
web www.cabalus.com

The centuries lie weighty and spiritual in the stones and timbers of this simple, totally French house and, to a lesser degree, on its furnishings. Up that turret, a steep stone spiral leads to the bedrooms; the double has a (rather battered) terrace onto the sublime Basilica; both have unpretentious character. Madame, easy, unintrusive and a passionate rider (come on horseback?), serves breakfast in her dining room with its huge fireplace. Pilgrims still climb 'the eternal hill', 600 years on, and there are maps and advice for hikers and cyclists here too. *Gîte space for 4 people.*

rooms	2: 1 double, 1 twin, sharing bath & wc.
price	€45 for two.
dinner	Good restaurants in Vézelay.
closed	Rarely.
directions	From Avallon D957 to Vézelay; up towards 'Basilique' (Rue St Étienne becomes Rue St Pierre); turreted house 100m from 'Basilique'

Monique & Bertrand Ginisty
La Tour Gaillon,
Rue Saint Pierre,
89450 Vézelay, Yonne
tel (0)3 86 33 25 74
e-mail b.ginisty@wanadoo.fr

BURGUNDY

A picture of a place. Different architectural periods are joined by three big staircases and several small ones (not for the stiff-limbed, although one bedroom is in the stable block), giving a real sense of history. Parts are 14th century: it was once fortified, and most of the moat remains; Louis XIV's cousin declined to stay long "because of the ghost". Madame is direct and knowledgeable, her big, old-fashioned guest rooms are idiosyncratic rather than luxurious, the heated swimming pool is tucked away in the three-hectare park. A very special, unpretentious place. *Can be tricky to find: ring for help if lost.*

rooms	3: 2 doubles, 1 twin, all with bath or shower & wc.
price	€65-€76 for two.
dinner	Restaurants nearby.
closed	Rarely.
directions	From Mezilles D965 for St Fargeau 3.5km; small road on right for Dannery, up to white fencing; tree-lined drive to manor house.

Mme Couiteas
Dannery,
89170 St Fargeau, Yonne
tel (0)3 86 74 09 01
fax (0)3 86 74 09 01

Dog lovers are ecstatic about the 40-odd pedigree Schnauzers here. Despite the daunting gates, it's easy to share this genuine and slightly crumbling château with the delightful, unprententious Septiers and their little girl. Downstairs, the thick-walled, vaulted dining and sitting rooms carry antique oak tables and modern leather sofas and support the rest of the house, an impressive and original alternative to deep foundations. An oak staircase leads up to the charming, period-furnished rooms with views over roofs and woods. Meals come with home-grown veg and good wine from the Septiers' cellar.
Gîte space for 5 people.

rooms	4: 2 doubles, both with shower & basin; 2 doubles, sharing 2 bathrooms & wc in corridor.
price	€60 for two.
dinner	€30 with wine, by arrangement.
closed	Rarely.
directions	From A6 exit Auxerre Nord for Auxerre 500m; right D158 for Perrigny, St Georges, Villefargeau; at Relais de la Vallée restaurant, left twice, château at end of road, after riding school.

Jacky & Marianne Septier
1 allée du Château,
89240 Villefargeau, Yonne
tel (0)3 86 41 37 38
fax (0)3 86 41 27 25
e-mail marianne.septier@wanadoo.fr
web perso.wanadoo.fr/marianne.septier/

BURGUNDY

The buildings are quite beautiful: this 16th-century fortified farm complete with towered château is where the owners live; in the converted barn, the sizey guest rooms are simply decorated with some interesting old furniture and sparklingly clean, tiled bathrooms. Your host, who is something of a jam expert, prepares breakfast – and possibly keeps his distance – in the salon/breakfast room with its tearoom-style round tables, open fire and courtyard view. In lovely countryside, it's only 10 minutes' walk from the pretty village with its gourmet restaurant and a healthy bike ride from Auxerre.

rooms	5 doubles/twins with shower or bath & wc.
price	€57-€65 for two.
dinner	Restaurants in village or 3km.
closed	Rarely.
directions	From A6 exit 19 Auxerre Nord on N6 for Auxerre; right for St Georges; straight across all r'bouts to lights. In Chevannes 1st left; last house on leaving village.

Claude & Marie-Claude Brodard
Château de Ribourdin,
89240 Chevannes, Yonne
tel (0)3 86 41 23 16
fax (0)3 86 41 23 16

The handsome millhouse, completely surrounded by a rushing river, is reached via a narrow, private bridge. Wander the beautiful grounds or settle yourself in the most inviting sitting room, complete with roaring log fire when it's cold. Leigh and Cinda are relaxed and easy hosts who delight in sharing their watery world. There's a canoe and a lake where Leigh has sunk a brilliant natural-looking swimming pool; and balloon flights can be arranged. The big, light bedrooms are freshly decorated with good bathrooms and the mill race is generally noisier than the road. Absolutely wonderful. *Gîte space for 4 people.*

rooms	6: 4 doubles, 1 twin, 1 suite for 4, all with bath/shower & wc.
price	€45-€70 for two.
dinner	Restaurants close by.
closed	Rarely.
directions	From Auxerre N6 for Avallon, 22km; just before Vermenton village sign, sharp right, double back & cross bridge.

Leigh Wootton & Cinda Tarasoff
Le Moulinot,
89270 Vermenton, Yonne
tel (0)3 86 81 60 42
fax (0)3 86 81 62 25
e-mail lemoulinot@aol.com

BURGUNDY

These young owners have brought vitality to their handsome old house with a clever conversion that lets in stacks of light – perfect for exhibiting local artists' work: water colours, oils and sculptures. Corinne has decorated each bedroom as if it were her own, they are all comfortable and colourful with co-ordinated headboards and bedspreads and good bathrooms. She loves her flower and vegetable garden too, meals are definitely worth booking – she also runs courses for groups interested in traditional French cooking – and you may choose from Pascal's excellent cellar of Yonne wines.

rooms	4: 2 doubles, 1 twin, 1 family room, all with shower or bath & wc.
price	€52 for two.
dinner	€20, wine €12-€25.
closed	Rarely.
directions	From A6 exit Nitry for Tonnerre for 7km, right at x-roads sign Chambres d'Hotes 1.5km; left for Môlay to Arton; house opposite 'lavoir' (wash hut).

Corinne & Pascal Collin
Le Calounier,
5 rue de la Fontaine-Arton,
89310 Môlay, Yonne
tel (0)3 86 82 67 81
fax (0)3 86 82 67 81
e-mail info@lecalounier.fr
web www.lecalounier.fr

Those ogival windows, which give this fine, château-style house its intriguing personality, fill the uncluttered bedrooms with light. Up two floors, simply furnished, pastel-hued, they have sloping ceilings, ancient rafters and not one common wall. Simplicity and attention to detail are Madame's keynotes: hers is a warm, friendly house with 'Victorian' panelling and superb old tiled floors. Breakfast by the old bread oven before learning to 'grow' truffles, consulting Monsieur on estate wine to take home (the cellar is under the house), or exploring Chablis. A child-friendly house belonging to the nicest possible people.

rooms 5: 4 doubles, 1 suite for 4, all with bath or shower & wc.
price €46-€57 for two.
dinner Restaurant 2km; Auxerre or Chablis 10km.
closed December-February.
directions From A6 exit 20 on D965 for Chablis for 3km; house on right. Do not go to Venoy.

François & Françoise Choné
Domaine de Montpierreux,
89290 Venoy, Yonne
tel (0)3 86 40 20 91
fax (0)3 86 40 28 00

BURGUNDY

On each floor, eight tall windows look down on the fine mature garden that shelters Aviler from noise. At the back is the Yonne where barges peacefully ply. The house was originally a workhouse – destitution in 18th-century France had its compensations. The Barrés were interior decorators by trade and are collectors by instinct, so expect a riot of sumptuous colour in your bedroom and advice on the best local auctions. Monsieur will even help you bid – he's eager and good fun. Sens has a memorable cathedral, a tempting market and botanical gardens – the shops and restaurants of this lovely town simply yell 'quality'.

rooms 3: 2 doubles, both with bath & wc; 1 twin with shower and wc.
price €66-€77 for two.
dinner Restaurants in Sens.
closed Rarely.
directions From A19 exit St Denis lès Sens; at river Yonne, follow road on right bank to No. 43.

Bernard Barré
La Maison d'Aviler,
43 quai du Petit Hameau,
89100 Sens, Yonne
tel (0)3 86 95 49 25
e-mail daviler@online.fr
web www.daviler.online.fr

PARIS · ÎLE DE FRANCE

"He who sits at a pavement café in Paris will see the whole world go by" – under the all-seeing eye of the long-aproned, world-weary waiter who loves his City of Light but will never let you know it.

Several centuries shaped this old hunting lodge, then it was determinedly 'modernised' in the 1920s Art Deco style: high-windowed, fully-panelled dining room with extraordinary dressers, unbelievably moustachioed grandfather, fabulous bathroom fittings. It is exuberantly sober and shapely with Versailles parquet and fine fireplaces as well. Tae, from Chile, uses her perfect sense of style and colour to include these respected elements in her décor alongside richly baroque Chinese chairs and lots of South American pieces and paintings. Quiet spot, vast natural garden, joyous hosts, perfect for Chartres, Paris, Versailles.

rooms	2 suites for 5, both with bath & wc.
price	€69 for two; €99 for four.
dinner	Good restaurant 200m.
closed	Rarely.
directions	From A10 exit 10 to toll gate, right after toll; right again on D27 to St Cyr; continue for Arpajon; 1st house on left.

Claude & Tae Dabasse
Le Logis d'Arnières,
1 rue du Pont-Rué,
91410 St Cyr sous Dourdan,
Essonne

tel	(0)1 64 59 14 89
fax	(0)1 64 59 07 46
e-mail	taedabasse@aol.com

Madame's delightful serenity must be fed by the natural air of farm life wafting in from the great wheat fields. Tractors come and go, the old horse grazes in the meadow, the children play in the sandpit, the dog dances in its pen. The Desforges have done an excellent barn conversion. You climb the steep stairs to the lofty raftered dayroom where breakfast is served (tea-making equipment, an old dresser, a comfortable sofa), and the simply pretty, good-size bedrooms. One is furnished with grandmother's richly carved, if short-bedded, Breton bridal suite, one with grandfather's brass bed; wardrobes are old, mattresses new.

rooms 5: 3 doubles, 2 twins, all with shower & wc.
price €40 for two.
dinner Choice of restaurants in Milly, 3km; picnic possible.
closed Mid-December-January.
directions From A6 exit Cély en Bière for Milly La Forêt. At Milly, 1st r'bout for Étampes; next r'bout, for Gironville, right. Farm 2km on right.

Sophie & Jean-Charles Desforges
Ferme de la Grange Rouge,
91490 Milly la Forêt, Essonne
tel (0)1 64 98 94 21
fax (0)1 64 98 99 91

map: 6 entry: 138

PARIS · ÎLE DE FRANCE

Cocooned behind the garden walls and beneath the fruit trees, your ivy-hugged hideaway leads straight off the garden. The uncluttered, open-plan room is fresh and bright in its cool cream floors, nautical stripes and pale walls. There's a curtain to divide it if needed and a huge new shower. Stretch out on the flower-freckled lawn or curl up in front of the open fire. You can use the kitchenette if you want to be independent or simply cross the garden and join your relaxed, interesting and chatty hosts for dinner – they know about martial arts, among other things.

rooms 1 suite for 2-4, with shower & wc.
price €51 for two.
dinner €18.20 with wine, by arrangement.
closed Rarely.
directions From A5 exit 17 on D210 for Provins 2km; right D133 1km; left for Gardeloup. Left to Grand Buisson.

Florence & Georges Manulelis
L'Atalante,
8 rue Grande du Buisson,
Le Grand Buisson,
77148 Laval en Brie,
Seine-et-Marne
tel (0)1 45 82 94 02
fax (0)1 45 82 94 02
e-mail florence.manulelis@worldonline.fr
web latalante.free.fr

map: 6 entry: 139

Cereals and beets grow in wide fields and show-jumpers add a definite touch of elegance to the landscape. A generous farmyard surrounded by beautiful warm stone buildings encloses utter quiet and a genuine welcome from hosts and Labradors alike, out here where Monsieur's family has come hunting for 200 years (his great-grandfather was a surgeon with Napoleon's army). Family furniture (the 1900s ensemble is most intriguing) in light-filled rooms, spotless mod cons and a vast sitting room for guests with piano and billiard table. Your hosts are excellent tour advisers who can direct you to little-known treasures. *Gîte space for 4.*

rooms	1 + 1 apartment: 1 triple with shower & wc; 1 apartment for 4 with mini-kitchen, shower & wc.
price	€47 for two.
dinner	Auberge in village (3 Michelin stars).
closed	Christmas week.
directions	From A5 exit 15 on N36 towards Meaux, 200m; 2nd right to Crisenoy after TGV bridge, through village for 'Tennis/Salle des Fêtes'; 1.5km to farm.

	Philippe & Jeanne Mauban
	Ferme de Vert Saint-Père,
	77390 Crisenoy, Seine-et-Marne
tel	(0)1 64 38 83 51
fax	(0)1 64 38 83 52
e-mail	mauban.vert@wanadoo.fr
web	vert.saint.pere.free.fr

PARIS · ÎLE DE FRANCE

The high blue doors open onto a pair of long, low stone buildings round a narrow courtyard, the apse of the medieval church looking benignly over the wall and a charming garden at the back. The Laurents are friendly, straightforward, gentle people (the marble bathroom is not their doing!) with ever a new project on the boil. They have two children who adopt stray cats, keep miniature ponies and will do all they can to make your stay peaceful and fruitful, including organising walks and making vegetarian meals (by arrangement) in the heavily-beamed, 1930s-furnished guest dining room.

rooms	4: 1 triple, 2 suites for 5-6, all with shower & wc; 1 suite for 4 with kitchen, 2 showers & 2 wcs.
price	€55-€65 for two.
dinner	Restaurants 2km.
closed	Rarely.
directions	From A4 exit 13 to Villeneuve le Comte; right on D96 through Neufmoutiers to Châtres. House in village centre to left of church.

	Dominique & Pierre Laurent
	Le Portail Bleu,
	2 route de Fontenay,
	77610 Châtres, Seine-et-Marne
tel	(0)1 64 25 84 94
fax	(0)1 64 25 84 94
e-mail	leportailbleu@voila.fr
web	perso.wanadoo.fr/leportailbleu/

The big informal garden merges into fields: don't worry about those new houses, there's green space for everyone. Space in the high-beamed dayroom too, and at the fabulous table made of great old oak beams. Upstairs, the simple, white-walled, softly-coloured rooms, each with two beds on a mezzanine, are ideal for families. An old mirror, table or desk adds character and new shower rooms are cleverly designed. Isabelle has made the two larger, temptingly independent lodges most attractive. She and Patrick, with all the time in the world for their guests, are wonderful hosts. And there's Disney, *bien sûr*! *Gîte space for 8 people.*

rooms	5: 1 triple, 4 quadruples, all with shower & wc.
price	€50-€65 for two.
dinner	Restaurants 4km.
closed	Rarely.
directions	From A4 exit 13 to Villeneuve le Comte; follow signs to Neufmoutiers en Brie then Chambres d'Hôtes signs.

Isabelle & Patrick Galpin
Bellevue,
77610 Neufmoutiers en Brie,
Seine-et-Marne

tel	(0)1 64 07 11 05
fax	(0)1 64 07 19 27
e-mail	bellevue@fr.st
web	www.bellevue.fr.st

An 'Anglo-Norman' face veneered onto a concrete skull concealing an unspoilt 1920s interior: a sort of architectural cuckoo. Fascinating (great arched windows, red and black crested tiles), elegant ('Versailles' parquet), comfortable, beautifully furnished. The guest suite is as untouched as the blue-green panelled *salon*: stone walls, more parquet, marble fireplace and a delicious round sitting corner in the tower. Big breakfasts appear at the long dining table; in good English, your retired hosts will tell the history of grandfather's hunting lodge (they still organise shoots); their welcome is warmly French.

rooms	1 suite with bathroom & wc.
price	€120 for two.
dinner	Variety of restaurants nearby.
closed	Rarely.
directions	From A4 exit 13 to Villeneuve le C.; right D96 for Tournan; after Neufmoutiers, 1st left small road 1.5km, white gates on left.

Hubert & Francine Charpentier
Manoir de Beaumarchais,
77610 Les Chapelles Bourbon,
Seine-et-Marne

tel	(0)1 64 07 11 08
fax	(0)1 64 07 14 48
e-mail	hubert.charpentier@wanadoo.fr
web	www.le-manoir-de-beaumarchais.com

A gorgeous setting: green swards flowing down to a barge-carrying river, a cosmopolitan hostess perfectly tuned to her animal and plant companions. Quietly, intelligently attentive, she loves people too and wants you to enjoy her old family house, once home to the local tax collector/inn keeper (and the neo-Gothic goblin-guarded fireplace belonged to Alexandre Dumas). Her lamp collection is fascinating, her rooms unostentatiously friendly with well-loved old furniture and the big balcony suite looks way out to the hills beyond the River Marne. Keen walkers can follow the Canal de l'Ourcq all the way to Paris.

rooms	2: 1 suite for 3 with shower & wc; 1 suite for 5 with bath & wc.
price	€44-€59 for two.
dinner	Two good restaurants nearby.
closed	November-February.
directions	From A4 exit 18 N3 for Paris through St Jean; 1st right to Armentières; straight on at junction, past church; house last but one on right.

Denise Woehrlé
44 rue du Chef de Ville,
77440 Armentières en Brie,
Seine-et-Marne

tel	(0)1 64 35 51 22
fax	(0)1 64 35 42 95
e-mail	dverlet@aol.com

map: 6 entry: 144

A great mixture: 20 minutes from high-tech CDG airport with a national hiking path (GR1) leading to forests just behind the house; 1990s deluxe bathrooms in a 13th-century farmhouse; a fluting Pan lording it over the manicured profusion of a prize-winning garden. Nothing is left to chance by your well-travelled, graciously caring hostess. Royal breakfasts on rose-patterned porcelain in the peach-panelled *salon*; thirsty bathrobes to wear until changing for dinner, delivered to your room under silver cloches; interesting conversation in several languages. A form of perfection.
A short train ride to Paris.

rooms	2 suites for two, all with bath & wc.
price	€136 for two.
dinner	Restaurants 2-5km.
closed	2 weeks in February.
directions	From A1 exit 'Soissons' A104 for Marne la Vallée; N2 for Soissons 12km; exit Othis; D13 through Othis; at traffic light left to Beaumarchais. In village right after 1st speed bump.

Françoise Montrozier
12 rue des Suisses,
Beaumarchais,
77280 Othis, Seine-et-Marne

tel	(0)1 60 03 33 98
fax	(0)1 60 03 56 71

map: 6 entry: 145

A city home of charm and elegance in an old Parisian building in a quiet back street between the Seine and the Rue de Rivoli – the owners managed to salvage some ancient timbers from the renovator's clean sweep and live happily among signs of great architectural age. It is beautifully done, like a warm soft nest, antique-furnished, lots of greenery, interesting artwork. Madame greatly enjoys her guests and is full of good tips on Paris. Monsieur is a university professor. The compact guest quarters down the corridor are nicely private with good storage space, pretty quilts and lots of light. *Minimum stay 2 nights.*

rooms	1 twin with small bath/shower & wc.
price	€76 for two.
dinner	This is Paris!
closed	Summer holidays.
directions	**Metro** Châtelet (1, 4, 7, 11) or Pont-Neuf (7) (between Louvre & Notre-Dame). **Parking** Conforama car park, via Rue du Pont Neuf then Rue Boucher. Lift to 3rd floor.

Mme Mona Pierrot
Châtelet district
75001 Paris
tel (0)1 42 36 50 65

PARIS · ÎLE DE FRANCE

Coffee in a silver pot on fine linen before the roofs and domes of Paris: Madame treats her guests properly. The compact living room also houses two deep sofas, an upright piano and a collection of curiosities – well worth investigating. Bedrooms are simpler and perfectly comfortable with yet more interesting pictures and new beds. This is a trendy area with the Mosque, the colourful Rue Mouffetard and the quieter Jardin des Plantes, home of the Natural History Museum. Madame is quiet, a little shy, and most helpful. She also has a self-contained one-room apartment to let near Place de la République. *Minimum 2 nights.*

rooms	2: 1 double sharing bathroom; 1 triple with shower; both sharing wc.
price	€68-€83 for two.
dinner	This is Paris!
closed	Rarely.
directions	**Metro** Austerlitz (5, 10). **Parking** Rue Censier. Lift to 8th floor.

Mme Lélia Cohen-Scali
Latin Quarter
75005 Paris
tel (0)1 43 36 51 62
fax (0)1 45 87 94 16
e-mail lelia1@noos.fr

The river, the island, the vast ancientness of Notre Dame, her Gothic buttresses flying through centuries of history in the setting sun, are at the end of the quiet little street. Through a great 17th-century doorway and up the fine old stone staircase, your room, a high-windowed, fireplaced, unpretentiously family room with a mezzanine, looks onto an unexpected garden – a "bowl of air" as they say, a huge privilege in Paris – and you breakfast on the landing by a spiral staircase. Madame is polyglot, active in the city, shyly welcoming and eager to help – she enjoys her guests and the variety of contact they bring.

rooms	1 room for 2-4 with bath & wc.
price	€76 for two.
dinner	Many restaurants nearby.
closed	Rarely.
directions	**Metro** Maubert-Mutualité (10). **RER/Metro** St Michel-Notre Dame. **Parking** Lagrange.

Mme Brigitte Chatignoux
Notre Dame district
75005 Paris

tel	(0)1 43 25 27 20
fax	(0)1 43 25 27 20
e-mail	brichati@hotmail.com

PARIS · ÎLE DE FRANCE

Anna offers the super self-contained studio flat next to hers for B&B or self-catering – a wonderful way to live, however briefly, as Parisians in Paris. The ochre-walled living room has a big blue sofa and comfy chairs on the original herringbone parquet and some wonderful paintings by a once-starving, now-famous Cypriot artist whom Anna befriended. And all this is right in the student-crammed hustle-bustle of the Latin Quarter with its bookshops, cafés, museums and pavement life. And moreover… you are given an aperitif when you dine at her husband's excellent Italian restaurant downstairs. *Le service!*

rooms	1 suite with shower, wc & kitchenette.
price	€75 for two.
dinner	Paris is on your doorstep.
closed	Occasionally.
directions	**Metro** Maubert Mutualité (10), St Michel (4). **RER** St Michel. **Parking** Place Maubert, Pantheon.

Anna Sartori
Latin Quarter
75005 Paris

tel	(0)1 43 25 85 57
fax	(0)1 43 25 85 57
e-mail	stefsart@clubinternet.fr

map: 6 entry: 149

Smart Left Bank outside, intelligence, sobriety and genuine style inside. Madame takes you into her vast, serene apartment: no modern gadgets or over-restored antiques, just a few good pieces, much space and light-flooded parquet floors. Beyond the dining room, the smaller, cosy guest room gives onto the big, silent, arcaded courtyard. Your multilingual hosts have lived all over the world; Monsieur, a retired engineer, spends his days studying or teaching. Madame, as stylish and genuine as her surroundings, enjoys renovating her old mill near Chartres and the company of like-minded visitors – she is worth getting to know.

rooms	1 twin with bath & wc.
price	€80 for two.
dinner	Choice of restaurants within 5 minutes' walk; St Germain des Prés 10 minutes away.
closed	Rarely.
directions	**Metro** Solférino (12), Assemblée Nationale (12) or Invalides (8). **Parking** Invalides. Lift to 2nd floor.

Mme Élisabeth Marchal
National Assembly /
Invalides district
75007 Paris
tel (0)1 47 05 70 21/(0)2 37 23 38 19

PARIS · ÎLE DE FRANCE

Within walking distance of the Luxembourg Gardens is the Monbrisons' intimate little flat, filled with books, paintings and objects from all over the world. Their guest room is quiet, sunny, snug with a king-size bed and its own bathroom. Lively American Cynthia, an art-lover, and quintessentially French Christian, knowledgeable about history, wine and cattle-breeding, offer great hospitality and will take guests on special evening tours to historical landmarks. Twice a week, the street market brings the real food of France to your doorstep and the neighbourhood is always alive with shops, cafés and restaurants.

rooms	1 double/twin with bath/shower & wc.
price	€75 for two.
dinner	Occasionally, by arrangement, varying prices.
closed	August.
directions	**Metro** Edgar Quinet (6) or Montparnasse (4, 6, 12, 13). **Airport buses** from Orly & Charles de Gaulle to Montparnasse (5 minutes' walk).

Christian & Cynthia de Monbrison
Montparnasse district
75014 Paris
tel (0)1 45 38 68 72
fax (0)1 45 38 68 72

A little white blue-shuttered house in a cobbled alley? Just behind Montparnasse? No, it's not a dream and Janine, a fascinating live-wire cinema journalist who has lived in Canada, will welcome you of an evening to her pretty wood-ceilinged kitchen/diner (she's a night bird so breakfast will be laid for you to do your own). The guest room across the book-lined hall is a good, square room with a highly pleasing eclectic mix of warm fabrics, honeycomb tiles, white walls, old chest and contemporary paintings. The new white and pine bathroom has space, all mod cons and good cupboards. Ideal. *German spoken. Min. 2 nights.*

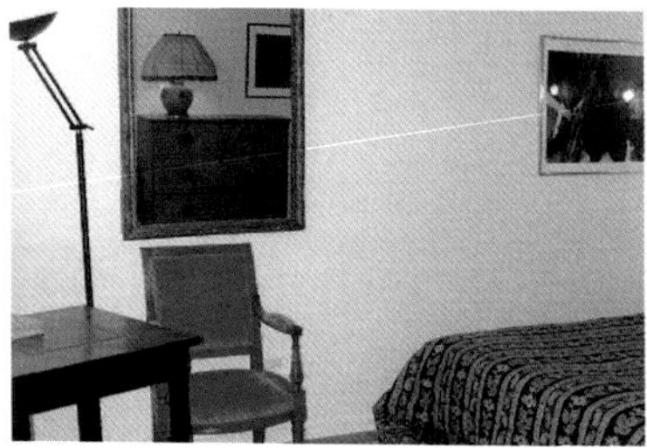

rooms	1 double with bath & wc.
price	€54 for two.
dinner	This is Paris!
closed	July-September.
directions	**Metro** Gaîté (13). **RER** Denfert-Rochereau; airport buses nearby. **Bus routes** 28, 58.

Janine Euvrard
Montparnasse district
75014 Paris
tel (0)1 43 27 19 43
fax (0)1 43 27 19 43
e-mail euvrard@club-internet.fr

PARIS · ÎLE DE FRANCE

On the sixth floor of a fine 1930s building with superb views across the Seine to the new André Citröen park, this well-proportioned flat has big rooms, old family pieces, mementos from distant lands and a well-loved, lived-in patina. The guest room: big, unfussy, with that great view, two narrow single beds; the shower: endearingly old-fashioned tiling; the loo: down the passage. With the window open, you hear the traffic humming. Madame still travels after all these years, has lots of time for guests and lends a very attentive, gracious ear to their travellers' tales. *Repeat your telephone number on answer machine please.*

rooms	1 double/twin with shower & basin, sharing wc.
price	€53 for two.
dinner	Choice of restaurants within walking distance.
closed	July-mid-September.
directions	**Metro** Mirabeau (10), Église d'Auteuil (10), Exelmans (9). **Bus** 72, 22, Petite Ceinture. Lift to 6th floor.

Mme Bargeton
Auteuil district
75016 Paris
tel (0)1 42 88 87 66

The rooms of this magnificent 1890s townhouse are so pure they don't even have wardrobes, just restful white, beige and grey tones, finely subtle fabrics, good bedding, bright white showers – and one loo for three rooms. Touches of humour lighten the great living space: a very rustic oak cupboard on such graceful parquet, a couple of fairly amateur oils hung beneath nobly high ceilings. And the wonderful Parisian rarity of a real terrace and garden for summer breakfast with scrumptious things from the local bakery; your young hostess is intelligently attentive and anxious to please.

rooms	2: 1 double, 1 suite, each with shower & sharing private wc.
price	€ 100 for two.
dinner	Many restaurants in the area.
closed	Occasionally.
directions	**Metro** Pereire (3). **Bus** 84, 92.

Sophie & Damien Vandewynckele
Port Champerret district
75017 Paris
tel (0)1 40 54 83 89

PARIS · ÎLE DE FRANCE

A typical little Paris flat in a proudly moulded and bracketed 1900s building within walking distance of Montmartre but far enough for you not to be harassed by charcoal-waving portraitists. The wooden fireplace, the floorboards, the plasterwork are original; the décor is as young and lively as Françoise and Hervé themselves: theatrical bits and pieces, a flowery balcony, a dry garden inside with grasses and nests, gnomes, puppets and dollies. They love their foreign guests and are happy to share their knowledge of Paris, French food and wine with you. You will like their youth, their spontaneity, their sense of fun.

rooms	1 double sharing shower, wc.
price	€65-€85 for two.
dinner	Plenty of good restaurants nearby.
closed	Rarely.
directions	**Metro** Guy Moquet (13). Directions given when you book.

Françoise & Hervé
Montmartre district
75018 Paris
fax (0)1 44 85 06 14
e-mail fforet@noos.fr

The street throbs with a motley, multicultural crowd but from the top of this clean modern block you can stretch your eyes across Paris to the scintillating towers of La Défense or the Parc de Belleville, a surprising green hillside above the city. Your pretty room lets in fabulous sunsets over the Eiffel Tower and no noise. The flat is all white walls, modern parquet floors and fine old family furniture, lots from Provence where your very proper elderly hosts once lived. Madame serves fresh pastries at breakfast and tells you all about everything while Monsieur twinkles shyly. *Some Spanish spoken. 2 nights minimum.*

rooms	1 double with shower & wc.
price	€64 for two.
dinner	Wide choice of restaurants on the doorstep.
closed	Rarely.
directions	**Metro** Belleville (2, 11) 200m: 15 mins to centre. **Parking** & directions ask owners. Lift to 9th floor.

	Danièle & Bernard de La Brosse
	Belleville district
	75019 Paris
tel	(0)1 42 41 99 59
fax	(0)1 42 41 99 59
e-mail	daniele.delabrosse@libertysurf.fr

map: 6 entry: 156

In a totally Parisian area, your kindly artist hosts live calmly between two tiny gardens and a tall house. The simple guest room, with good double bed and new divan, quietly gentle colours and fabrics, old-fashioned bathroom and welcome tea-maker, shares a building with Sabine's studio. Healthfoody breakfast is in the cosy family room in the main house or outside under the birdsung tree. Jules makes the organic bread and big, beautiful Janto, his guide dog, loves people.

rooms	1 triple with bath & wc.
price	€60 for two.
dinner	Choice of restaurants within walking distance.
closed	July-August.
directions	**Metro** Jourdain (11) or Place des Fêtes (11). **Parking** Place des Fêtes.

	Sabine & Jules Aïm
	Belleville district
	75019 Paris
tel	(0)1 42 08 23 71
fax	(0)1 42 40 56 04
e-mail	jules.aim@wanadoo.fr

map: 6 entry: 157

A smart suburb, a mild woman, a powerful brush. Come share Ruth's atmospheric space, her studio is in the super eclectic living room: worn antique chairs, modern red table, abstracts, collages, books; even follow a work in progress. Your simple, smallish room over the quiet garden has it all: desk, kettle, storage, live art and a snug little shower. One bed tucks under the other, the curtain is leopard-skin voile, the painting leaps off the wall. It's different – and real.

rooms	1 twin/double with shower & wc.
price	€55 for two.
dinner	Restaurants nearby.
closed	Rarely.
directions	Metro Pont de Neuilly (1) or Pont de Levallois (3) and 10 mins' walk. Bus 174, 163, 164, 93, 82.

Ruth Himmelfarb
53 boulevard Victor Hugo,
92200 Neuilly sur Seine,
Hauts-de-Seine
tel (0)1 46 37 37 28
fax (0)1 46 37 37 28

You can be close to the centre of Paris but still relax in a sweet, gnomy garden under the gazebo. Cecilia is Anglo-French and loves having people to stay in her comfortable 1950s suburban house. She enjoys a chat over the breakfast table, helping you plan the day ahead. Green is clearly her favourite colour. Rooms open directly to the garden and are light and airy with replica tapestry wall hangings, chintzy curtains with net drapes, onyx figurine bedside lamps, potted plants and, I need hardly say, green carpets. *You may subtract your breakfast & do your own. Italian spoken. 6 minutes from centre of Paris by train.*

rooms	2 triples, both with shower, wc & kitchenette.
price	€68 for two; €88 for three.
dinner	Self-catering possible; restaurants nearby.
closed	Occasionally.
directions	From Paris Bd Périphérique exit Porte d'Asnières through Levallois, across Seine. Ask for map. Train: from St Lazare, *Banlieue* direct train to Bécon Les Bruyères.

M & Mme Bobrie
10 rue Denfert Rochereau,
92600 Asnières sur Seine,
Hauts-de-Seine
tel (0)1 47 93 53 60
fax (0)1 47 93 53 60
e-mail ceciliasguesthouse@hotmail.com

Wind up the handsome staircase and push open the attic door. Your sitting room has sunny walls, mustard sofas and ethnic rugs on polished floors. Slim, arched bedrooms are blue or vanilla and orange, with family furniture and windows that peep over the rooftops. Meals are in the elegant dining room – Françoise likes to take you on a culinary tour of France – or on the terrace; marble steps, rescued from a local demolition, sweep down to a huge, immaculate lawn, a curtain of trees shields you from the suburbs – all is peace and calm yet only 20 minutes from the centre of Paris.

rooms	2 doubles, both with shower & wc.
price	€76 for two.
dinner	€23 with wine, by arrangement.
closed	Rarely.
directions	From Paris A4; exit 5 for Pont de Nogent; at exit keep left, don't take tunnel; along viaduct; at 2nd lights under bridge; Av. L. Rollin for Le Perreux centre; next lights straight on; 2nd left 200m.

Françoise Marcoz
9 allée Victor Basch,
94170 Le Perreux sur Marne,
Val-de-Marne

tel	(0)1 48 72 91 88
fax	(0)1 43 24 93 79
e-mail	francoisemarcoz@hotmail.com
web	www.chambresdhotes.fr.fm

map: 6 entry: 160

PARIS · ÎLE DE FRANCE

Versailles-grand, human-warm, Maye is a generous mansion whose intelligent, much-travelled owners – your gracious, welcoming hosts – hang powerful modern paintings above classic curly consoles and clean-limbed iron light fittings from original moulded ceilings. Luscious home-made breakfast (fruit salad, pastries) in the elegant dining room, or the orchid-filled conservatory under the black torch-bearer's kindly eye, or the quiet green garden with the blackbirds. Sleep under the fluffiest duvet in a big soft gentle-hued room graced with antiques. Supremely comfortable house, intriguing art, good conversation, fine food.

rooms	5 doubles, all with bath or shower & wc.
price	€170-€210 for two.
dinner	Restaurants walking distance.
closed	Rarely.
directions	From A13 exit 6 'St Germain & Versailles' for Versailles 4km; at Place de la Loi (monument) left Av. Leclerc; right at lights Av. Debasseux into Av. de la Maye; house at end on right. 20 mins. train to Paris.

M & Mme Hourdry
Pavillon de la Maye,
16 avenue de la Maye,
78000 Versailles, Yvelines

tel	(0)1 39 23 21 00
fax	(0)1 39 23 21 01
e-mail	pavillondelamaye@wanadoo.fr
web	www.pavillon-de-la-maye.com

map: 6 entry: 161

Behind the modest façade is a generous and lovely interior where Madame's very interesting paintings – she's an art teacher and an artist – stand in pleasing contrast to elegant antiques and soft plush furnishings. Picture windows let the garden in and the wooded hillside rises beyond. The larger guest room is superb in blue draperies, fur bedcover and big bathroom; the smaller one with skylight and its own bathroom across the landing is excellent value. Madame, active and communicative, sings as well as she paints and enjoys cooking refined dinners for attentive guests; she is very good company. A short drive from Paris.

rooms	2 doubles (1 large, 1 small), both with bath & wc.
price	€45-€60 for two.
dinner	€15 with wine, by arrangement.
closed	Rarely.
directions	From Paris A13 on A12 for St Quentin en Yvelines; exit N12 for Dreux; exit to Plaisir Centre; 1st exit off r'bout for Plaisir Les Gâtines, 1st left for 400m; right into Domaine des Gâtines; consult roadside plan.

Mme Hélène Castelnau
7 rue Gustave Courbet,
Domaine des Gâtines,
78370 Plaisir, Yvelines
tel (0)1 30 54 05 15
fax (0)1 30 54 05 15
e-mail hcastelnau@club-internet.fr

PARIS · ÎLE DE FRANCE

From Indonesia, Morocco and reddest America, this great traveller has amassed carvings great and small, artefacts ancient and modern, inlays and filigrees in brass, lacquer and wood, and filled his family mansion. Here is love of life and beautiful things and bedrooms are an exuberant feast: the Coca Cola room is devastatingly... Coke, the Indonesian bed overwhelmingly rich. Your host is very good company and on weekdays his delightful assistant Taïeb will take excellent care of you. There is also a loo/library and a three-legged cat, exotic fowl, stone boars... and a vast number of honeys and jams for breakfast.

rooms	6: 5 doubles, all with shower & wc; 1 suite for 5 with shower & wc.
price	€54-€63 for two.
dinner	3 restaurants in village.
closed	Rarely.
directions	From N10 north of Rambouillet D937; D936 for Poigny la Forêt, 5km; left on D107 to Poigny; left up road by church; house on right.

François Le Bret
Château de Poigny,
2 rue de l'Église,
78125 Poigny la Forêt, Yvelines
tel (0)1 34 84 73 42
fax (0)1 34 84 74 38
e-mail lechateaudepoigny@wanadoo.fr

A few land miles from Paris, centuries away in feel, this unspoilt stone village, in a dip in the gentle Vexin Nature Park, hides a creeper-clad house and its little cottage where Christine, laughing all the way, has spread the colours of Provence and her flair with ancient newspapers to make a perfect guest nest: a little round-tabled living room onto the garden, two pretty country bedrooms upstairs, good shower rooms and simple old furniture of character. Your hosts, both teachers, will lead you brilliantly through the corridors of French culture and language. Great walking, good talking, peaceful nights.

rooms	2 doubles, both with bath or shower & wc.
price	€50 for two.
dinner	Choice 5km.
closed	Rarely.
directions	From Paris/La Défense D392 32km; A15 NW into N14; 2nd junction left to Théméricourt; in village follow 'Restaurant': house opposite; ring at blue gates and enter.

Christian & Christine Dumaux
5 rue du Moulin,
95450 Théméricourt, Val-d'Oise

tel	(0)1 30 39 28 89
fax	(0)1 30 39 28 89
e-mail	dumaux@freesurf.fr

PARIS · ÎLE DE FRANCE

Utterly original, a meld of brimming creativity and scholarship, Hazeville dazzles. Your artist host uses his fine château-farm, dated 1400s to 1600s, as a living show of his talents: huge abstract paintings, hand-painted plates and tiles, a stunning 'Egyptian' reception room (and loos) and now, photography. The old stables house hi-tech artisans. Beautifully finished guest rooms in the *pigeonnier* are deeply luxurious; generous breakfasts come on china hand-painted by Monsieur to match the wall covering; he also knows the secret treasures of the Vexin. *Well-behaved children over 7 welcome. Hot-air ballooning possible.*

rooms	2: 1 double, 1 twin, both with bath, shower & wc.
price	€115 for two.
dinner	Wide choice of restaurants within 5-10km.
closed	Weekdays & school term time.
directions	From Rouen N14 for Paris. 20km before Pontoise, at Magny en Vexin, right D983 to Arthies; left D81 through Enfer; château on left.

Guy & Monique Deneck
Château d'Hazeville,
95420 Wy dit Joli Village,
Val-d'Oise

tel	(0)1 34 67 06 17/(0)1 42 88 67 00
fax	(0)1 34 67 17 82
e-mail	hazeville.events@airshow.fr

A straightforward welcome, an unpretentious house with that friendly, lived-in air – what matter if sometimes it's just the oilcloth on the table. The Maréchals are amiable, down-to-earth farmers who lead a sociable life and love having their grandchildren around. Low-beamed bedrooms are modest but comfortable with imitation parquet floors and pretty bedcovers. In summer, meals can be taken under canvas in the flower-filled courtyard. Readers have told of hilarious evenings in approximate French and English over honest, family meals, often made with home-grown, chemical-free vegetables. *Gîte space for 18 people.*

rooms	2 doubles, both with bath or shower & wc.
price	€41 for two.
dinner	€15 with wine, by arrangement.
closed	Rarely.
directions	From Dreux N12 to Broué; D305 to La Musse (La Musse between Boutigny & Prouais); 'Chambres d'Hôtes' signs.

Serge & Jeanne-Marie Maréchal
La Ferme des Tourelles,
11 rue des Tourelles, La Musse,
28410 Boutigny Prouais,
Eure-et-Loir
tel (0)2 37 65 18 74
fax (0)2 37 65 18 74
e-mail la-ferme.des-tourelles@wanadoo.fr

PARIS · ÎLE DE FRANCE

Horses and clubs share the quiet style of the Simons' converted farmhouse behind its high gates: Jean-Marc teaches golf to all ages and levels; Catherine has the friendliest mare imaginable and a horse-blanket laundry service. She is full of infectious enthusiasm and advice for visitors. They, their son and two big sloppy dogs receive you with alacrity in the old beamed kitchen then send you up steep barn stairs to simple white rooms where patches of bright colour – cushions, lampshades, towels – punctuate the space. The two lovely new rooms, bigger, higher and more luxurious in fabric and fitting, are good for families.

rooms	5: 1 double, 2 twins, 2 family rooms, all with bath & wc.
price	€58-€76 for two; €108 family room for four.
dinner	Restaurants in Nogent le Roi & Maintenon.
closed	Rarely.
directions	From Paris A13, A12, N12, exit Gambais for Nogent le Roi. Entering Coulombs, left at lights for Chandelles; left at x-roads 1.5km; house on right.

Catherine & Jean-Marc Simon
Les Chandelles,
19 rue des Sablons, Chandelles,
28130 Villiers le Morhier,
Eure-et-Loir
tel (0)2 37 82 71 59
fax (0)2 37 82 71 59
e-mail info@chandelles-golf.com
web www.chandelles-golf.com

Your hosts are delightful: Virginie beautifully French, Richard a gentle Europeanised American and their two young sons. Down a long wooded drive and set in a big leafy garden, the old family house has tall windows, fine proportions and the air of a properly lived-in château: elegance and deep comfortable armchairs by the marble fireplace under crystal chandeliers. The top floor has been converted into five good rooms with sound-proofing, big beds, masses of hot water, rich, bright colour schemes... and just the right amount of family memorabilia: oils, engravings, lamps, old dishes. It feels easy, fun and intelligent.

rooms	5: 4 doubles, 1 triple, all with shower & wc.
price	€55-€65 for two.
dinner	Restaurants 5km.
closed	November-February.
directions	From A11 exit Ablis on N10 for Chartres. At Essars, right to St Symphorien, Bleury & Ecrosnes. There right & immed. left to Jonvilliers, 2.5km. White château gates straight ahead.

Virginie & Richard Thompson
Château de Jonvilliers,
17 rue d'Épernon,
28320 Jonvilliers, Eure-et-Loir
tel (0)2 37 31 41 26
fax (0)2 37 31 56 74
e-mail information@chateaudejonvilliers.com
web www.chateaudejonvilliers.com

NORMANDY

Fierce pagan Vikings came sailing warlike up the Seine in their long battle-boats... then settled docilely into the luscious pastures to breed Christians for the abbeys and milk cows for Camembert.

In the old hunting lodge: a vast, boar- and stag's-headed dayroom with log fire, chandelier and rooms for seven – ideal for parties; in the main house: the huge room for four; from the garden: wide hilltop views. Monsieur manages the Port and is a mine of local knowledge, Madame tends house, garden and guests, masterfully. Proud of their region, they are keen to advise on explorations: nature, hiking, historical visits, wet days, dry days... A delightful, welcoming couple of natural generosity, elegance and manners and an open-minded approach to all. Legend has it that Queen Victoria 'stopped' at this very gracious house. *Gîte space for 4 people.*

rooms	2 + 1 apartment: 1 double, 1 triple, 1 apartment for 5, all with shower & wc.
price	€45 for two.
dinner	In Eu 2km, Le Tréport 4km; self-catering in apartment.
closed	Rarely.
directions	Take D49 to Eu. Before Eu left for Forest of Eu & Route de Beaumont. House 3km on right.

Catherine & Jean-Marie Demarquet
Manoir de Beaumont,
76260 Eu, Seine-Maritime
tel (0)2 35 50 91 91
e-mail cd@fnac.net
web www.demarquet.com

Built in 1850 as part of the Château d'Eu, one of Louis Philippe's residences, this is where all the king's horses and all the king's men were stabled and lodged. Guests are in a creeper-clad 'L' enclosing a courtyard with the other 'L', where Romain was born and he and Nicole live. Bedrooms are elegant with strong colours and bold flowers that are most definitely French. At breakfast, guests from each room have their own table, their own flowers and their own coffee machine. You can walk into Le Tréport along the towpath but in the garden of Sainte Croix you could well be in deep country.

rooms	5: 4 doubles, 1 twin, all with bath or shower & wc.
price	€42-€54 for two.
dinner	Restaurants in Le Tréport, 2km.
closed	Rarely.
directions	From Dieppe D925 for Le Tréport; at Étalondes left at r'bout for Le Tréport; at 2nd r'bout 1st right; 100m, signs.

Romain & Nicole Carton
Prieuré Sainte Croix,
76470 Le Tréport, Seine-Maritime
tel (0)2 35 86 14 77
fax (0)2 35 86 14 77

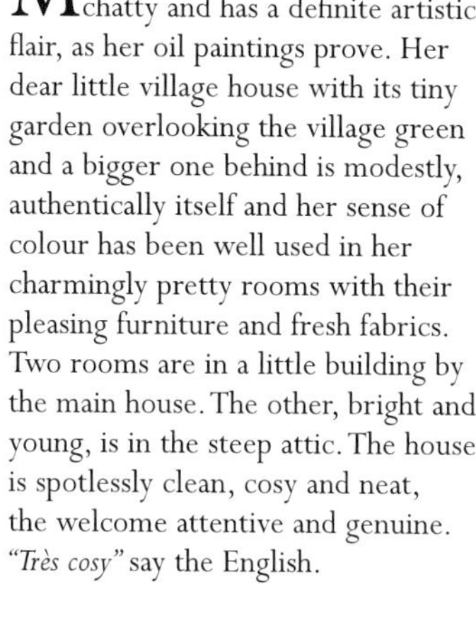

Madame is smart, stylish and chatty and has a definite artistic flair, as her oil paintings prove. Her dear little village house with its tiny garden overlooking the village green and a bigger one behind is modestly, authentically itself and her sense of colour has been well used in her charmingly pretty rooms with their pleasing furniture and fresh fabrics. Two rooms are in a little building by the main house. The other, bright and young, is in the steep attic. The house is spotlessly clean, cosy and neat, the welcome attentive and genuine. *"Très cosy"* say the English.

rooms	3 doubles, all with shower & wc.
price	€40 for two.
dinner	Restaurant in village.
closed	Rarely.
directions	From Le Tréport D925 for Dieppe 15km; in Biville sur Mer right Rue de l'Église, No. 14 faces you in middle of fork in road.

Marie-José Klaes
Le Clos Mélise,
14 rue de l'Église,
76630 Biville sur Mer,
Seine-Maritime
tel (0)2 35 83 14 71
e-mail closmelise@wanadoo.fr

Golfers love it here: the house is hard by the third green. Green comes inside too, thanks to the exotic palms where a parrot may lurk. The light, modern house is a refreshing change, definitely creature-comfortable and it copes well with the transition between '80s-daring and '90s-pleasing. Each room has space (terrace or mezzanine), television and plush modern décor with softening accessories from eastern worlds; no two bedrooms have walls in common. Your hosts are naturally friendly, interesting people and Madame is happy to give you a relaxing yoga lesson. You will feel cocooned here.

rooms: 3: 1 double, 1 triple, 1 suite for 4, all with bath or shower & wc.
price: €59-€94 for two.
dinner: Restaurants 1.5km.
closed: Rarely.
directions: From Dieppe D75 (Route du Littoral) W along coast for Pourville; at golf course, 1st left, 3rd house on right (signs).

Alain & Danièle Noël
La Villa Florida,
24 chemin du Golf,
76200 Dieppe, Seine-Maritime
tel (0)2 35 84 40 37
fax (0)2 35 84 32 51
e-mail adn@lavillaflorida.com
web www.lavillaflorida.com

Informal elegance, old French charm from 1864, a dose of American antiques and masses of warmly impressionistic paintings: Boston-born Daniel adopted France, married Virginie, a chiropractor from Chinon, had three children and chose these two houses, one for B&B, one for the family, in an area they both love; then his mother, a prolific painter, joined them. They put books everywhere and create a youthful, easy atmosphere. The guest-house dining, sitting and music rooms are grand: superb floors, high ceilings, views to the delicious period garden (tennis court too); bedrooms are generous and work progresses on the details.

rooms: 4 doubles, all with bath or shower & wc.
price: €46-€53 for two.
dinner: Good bistro-épicerie in village.
closed: Rarely.
directions: From Dieppe D925 for St Valéry en Caux; 3.5km after Le Bourg Dun, left for La Chapelle sur Dun, opp. church, left at café go to end; enter on left.

Daniel Westhead
Chalet du Bel Évent,
76740 La Chapelle sur Dun,
Seine-Maritime
tel (0)2 35 57 08 44
e-mail dwesthead@yahoo.com
web www.chaletdubelevent.com

Simply irresistible. This gloriously restored and listed 17th-century château is surrounded by formal gardens designed by a pupil of Lenôtre's with beech maze, lime tree avenues and 2,000 varieties of rose. The Prince (Syrian father, French mother) knows each one of them and the special attention it requires. The Princess makes rose-petal jelly for breakfast in the elegant dining room and also loves to prepare authentic 18th-century dishes from old recipes she has unearthed. The panelled bedrooms are delightfully cosy with canopied beds, proper bed linen, fluffy duvets, sweet-smelling bathrooms and heavenly views of roses.

rooms	5: 2 doubles, 1 twin, 2 suites, all with bath & shower & wc.
price	€78.40-€133.40 for two.
dinner	€42 with wine, by arrangement.
closed	Rarely.
directions	From A13 exit 25 Pont de Bretonne & Yvetot. Through Yvetot for St Valéry en Caux. 2km after Ste Colombe, right for Houdetot. Château 2km on left.

Prince & Princesse Kayali
Château du Mesnil Geoffroy,
76740 Ermenouville,
Seine-Maritime
tel (0)2 35 57 12 77
fax (0)2 35 57 10 24
e-mail contact@chateau-mesnil-geoffroy.com
web www.chateau-mesnil-geoffroy.com

NORMANDY

The lush immaculate garden shelters fantails, ducks, bantams, frilly black swans, sleek cats and a phenomenal variety of shrubs and flowering plants. While Monsieur works in town, Madame tends all this, and her guests, with proper respect for everyone's privacy, guidance as to hiking or fishing nearby and tennis down the road. An intelligent, active and graceful person, her bedrooms are cosily colourful, her bathrooms big and luxurious, her breakfast richly varied. After a jaunt, you can read their books, relax among their lovely antiques or make tea in their breakfast room. And the cliffs at Étretat are 20 minutes away. *Gîte space for 7.*

rooms	2: 1 triple with bath & wc; 1 suite with bath, shower & wc.
price	€90 for two.
dinner	Restaurants in Valmont, 1km.
closed	Rarely.
directions	From Dieppe D925 W for Fécamp 60km; left D17 to Valmont centre; left D150 for Ourville 1.2km; right Chemin du Vivier; house 2nd entrance on right (no. 4).

Dominique Cachera & François Greverie
Le Clos du Vivier,
4-6 chemin du Vivier,
76540 Valmont, Seine-Maritime
tel (0)2 35 29 90 95
fax (0)2 35 27 44 49
e-mail dc@le-clos-du-vivier.com
web www.le-clos-du-vivier.com

The 300-year-old house stands in a classic, poplar-sheltered Seine-Maritime farmyard, its worn old stones and bricks and the less worn flints bearing witness to its age, as does the fine timberwork inside. Otherwise it has been fairly deeply modernised, but your retired farmer hosts and the long lace-clothed breakfast table before the log fire – in winter – are most welcoming. Madame was born here, has a winning smile and loves to talk – in French. Her pleasant rooms are in good, rural French style and the only sounds are the occasional lowing of the herd and the shushing of the poplars. *Gîte space for 10 people.*

rooms	4: 1 double with shower & wc; 2 doubles sharing shower & wc, 1 triple with bath & wc.
price	€38 for two.
dinner	Auberge 1km.
closed	Rarely.
directions	From Dieppe N27 for Rouen 29km; right N29 through Yerville, cont. 4.5km; left D20 to Motteville; right to Flamanville. Rue Verte behind church. Farm 300m on left; signs.

Yves & Béatrice Quevilly Baret
La Ferme de la Rue Verte,
76970 Flamanville, Seine-Maritime
tel (0)2 35 96 81 27

NORMANDY

The colourful, flowerful garden, Monsieur's triumph, Madame's great love, is a wonder in almost any season, a hillside oasis of tumbling vegetation in the town (the road is all right at night). A blithe soul, "on holiday all year", Madame will give you a terrific welcome – nothing is too much trouble. Her rooms, cosy, frilly and artificial-flowered, reflect the history of the old place and her collectionitis. Breakfast is in the pretty family dining room. A very French house, full of character, cats and clutter, excellent value and a good base for exploring the myriad local churches and villages. *Gîte space for 4 people.*

rooms	4: 2 doubles, 1 triple, 1 quadruple, all with shower & wc.
price	€47 for two.
dinner	Good restaurant 500m.
closed	Rarely.
directions	In Caudebec, in front of Tourist Office, take Rue de la République (D131) for Yvetot; No.68 is 500m on right.

Christiane Villamaux
Les Poules Vertes,
68 rue de la République,
76490 Caudebec en Caux,
Seine-Maritime
tel (0)2 35 96 10 15
fax (0)2 35 96 75 25
e-mail christiane.villamaux@libertysurf.fr
web villamaux.ifrance.com

The solid-fronted, black-doored face hides a light, stylish interior with soul-lifting views across old Rouen to the spires of the Cathedral. Dominique, a keen and cultured Egyptologist, has a flair for refined decoration – as her paintings, coverings and country furniture declare. Oriental rugs on parquet floor, French windows to balcony and garden, feminine, unfrilly bedrooms, a stupendous orange bathroom. Nothing standard, nothing too studied, a very personal home and a lovely spot for a leisurely feast at her flower-decked breakfast table and a talk with her (her English is excellent) about her latest digs in Egypt.

rooms	3: 1 double with bath & wc; 2 doubles, both with bath, sharing wc.
price	€45-€49 for two.
dinner	€18 with wine, by arrangement.
closed	October-November.
directions	In Rouen follow Gare SNCF signs; Rue Rochefoucault right of station; left Rue des Champs des Oiseaux; over 2 traffic lights into Rue Vigné; fork left Rue Hénault; black door on left.

Dominique Gogny
22 rue Hénault,
76130 Mont St Aignan,
Seine-Maritime

tel	(0)2 35 70 26 95
fax	(0)2 35 52 03 52
e-mail	chambreavecvue@online.fr
web	chambreavecvue.online.fr

NORMANDY

In the historic centre of lovely old Rouen, on an ancient street 100m from the cathedral, stands this 17th-century family home. Monsieur enjoys sharing, in English, German or Norman and with much wry humour, the history of Rouen and the comfort of his lovely quiet townhouse. It is a treasure-trove of curios, with huge beams, big windows and Norman antiques. Bathrooms are a bit old-fashioned, breakfast generous and your reception generally cheerful. *Car park a short walk from house. Gîte space for 8 people.*

rooms	4: 2 doubles, 1 twin, both with bathrooms (can be a suite with kitchen); 1 single, sharing bathroom.
price	€50 for two.
dinner	Vast choice of restaurants on the spot.
closed	Rarely.
directions	On Cathedral-side embankment: at Théâtre des Arts, take Rue Jeanne d'Arc; Rue aux Ours 2nd on right but NO parking: leave car in Bourse or Pucelle car park & walk.

Philippe & Annick Aunay-Stanguennec
45 rue aux Ours,
76000 Rouen, Seine-Maritime

tel	(0)2 35 70 99 68

Patricia has happy childhood holiday memories of this 17th-century manor house and the atmosphere is palpable. She and Jérôme moved here ten years ago to be with her grandmother, who had been living alone in a few rooms for 20 years. A long path flanked by willows leads down to the Seine: perfect for an evening stroll. One set of rooms is on the ground floor, in coral and cream with windows opening to the walled garden, while the family apartment is under the eaves. Breakfast is whenever it takes your fancy: brioche, walnuts and fresh fruit in a pretty green-panelled room. Ask Patricia about the Abbey.

rooms	1: 1 suite for 2 with kitchenette & shower & wc.
price	€64 for two.
dinner	Choice of restaurants 8km.
closed	Rarely.
directions	From A13 exit 24 'Maison Brulée' for La Bouille-Bas to Sahurs; left for St Martin de Boscherville; after Quevillon, 2nd left for Le Brécy; signposted.

Jérôme & Patricia Lanquest
Le Brécy,
72 route de Brécy,
76840 St Martin de Boscherville,
Seine-Maritime
tel (0)2 35 32 69 92
fax (0)2 35 32 00 30
web membres.lycos.fr/lebrecy

NORMANDY

A huge place that breathes comfort – and a huge challenge for the young Caffins: half the château's 65 rooms have yet to be restored. They live in one wing, you in another, a museum sits in between. The handsome guest suite is pale-panelled and red-brocaded, the double elegantly and creamily draped; the twin is less grand, with an enormous bathroom, the guest sitting room serenely sage. There are stylish lawns to the front and majestic trees; stables for the show-jumpers and a maize-fashioned maze for the visitors. Breakfast is at a vast table in a kitchen hung with a tapestry and a hundred copper pans. *Magnifique.*

rooms	2: 1 double, 1 family room, both with bath, shower & wc.
price	€61 for two; €107 for family room for four.
dinner	Choice of restaurants 6km.
closed	Rarely.
directions	From Gournay en Bray N31 for Rouen 17km; left D921 to Lyons la Forêt; D6 for Étrépagny, 1st left for Château de Fleury; left at fork; 5km, house on right, signs.

Kristina Caffin
Château de Fleury la Forêt,
27480 Lyons la Forêt, Eure
tel (0)2 32 49 63 91
fax (0)2 32 49 71 67

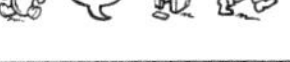

The cottagey garden runs down to the clean, cool River Epte which Monet diverted at nearby Giverny for his famous *Nymphéa* ponds – it bestows the same serenity here. The old house is beautifully furnished with family antiques and Madame, a strong, intelligent and inherently elegant person, willingly shares her great knowledge of all things Norman, including food. She has even devised her own detailed tourist circuits. Rooms are stylish and quiet; one has a majestic Art Deco brass bed designed by *Grand-père* and a hand-painted carved *armoire*, both have original paintings and total individuality. So civilised.

rooms	2 doubles, both with shower or bath & wc.
price	€55-€60 for two.
dinner	€20 with wine, by arrangement.
closed	16 December-14 March.
directions	From Dieppe D915 to Gisors. Cross Gisors; D10 for Vernon. In Dangu, Rue du Gué is beside River Epte.

Nicole de Saint Père
Les Ombelles,
4 rue du Gué,
27720 Dangu, Eure

tel	(0)2 32 55 04 95
fax	(0)2 32 55 59 87
e-mail	vextour@aol.com
web	vextour.ifrance.com

map: 6 entry: 182

NORMANDY

Gorgeous!... and, despite the grand billiard room, without a whiff of pretension. The Brunets, as delightful as their house, have the lightness of touch to combine the fresh best of modern French taste with an eye for authenticity – in a brand new house. There is light flooding in through recycled château windows on both sides of this classically narrow *maison de campagne*, eye-catching stretches of pine-floored corridor, beamed ceilings, big beds, handsome rugs, a brave mix of old and modern furniture and massive comfort. Wild deer, too, visit this exquisite place.

rooms	5: 2 doubles, 3 twins, all with bath or shower & wc.
price	€90-€150 for two.
dinner	Restaurants 1.5km-4km.
closed	December-March, except by arrangement.
directions	From A13 exit 16 to Giverny; left Rue Claude Monet; after church & Hotel Baudy, 1st left Rue Blanche Hoshedé Monet 1.2km; left on white arrow, immed. right on track 800m, left to house.

Didier & Marie Lorraine Brunet
La Réserve,
27620 Giverny, Eure

tel	(0)2 32 21 99 09
fax	(0)2 32 21 99 09
e-mail	ml1reserve@aol.com
web	www.giverny.org/hotels/brunet/

map: 5 entry: 183

Michel and Éliane invested seven years, great care and much good taste in restoring this lovely 19th-century farmhouse in a particularly pretty village. You stay in a self-contained part of the house with your own dayroom and breakfast area where there's lots of space to spread your legs in front of the fire. Bedrooms are spotless with *toile de Jouy* fabrics, beamed ceilings and polished floorboards. Outside, sweeping lawns run down to a pretty stream that meanders beneath high wooded cliffs. Éliane is passionate about her garden and loves to chat about it, pointing out the rich and the rare.

rooms	2: 1 double, 1 twin, both with bath & wc.
price	€45 for two.
dinner	Choice of restaurants nearby.
closed	Rarely.
directions	A13 exit 16 for Cocherel; after 10km to Chambray; left at monument; left after 100m to Fontaine sous Jouy. In centre right Rue de l'Ancienne Forge for 800m; Rue de l'Aulnaie on right.

Éliane & Michel Philippe
L'Aulnaie,
29 rue de l'Aulnaie,
27120 Fontaine sous Jouy, Eure

tel	(0)2 32 36 89 05
fax	(0)2 32 36 89 05
e-mail	emi.philippe@worldonline.fr
web	perso.worldonline.fr/chambre-fontaine/

Handsomely carved Colombian furniture, strong colours and interesting prints create an unusual atmosphere inside this 18th-century manor with its 'Norman cottage' face and surprising turret. Your charming Franco-Spanish hosts spent over 20 years and raised five children in South America before renovating their French home – it vibrates with echoes of faraway places. Bedrooms aren't huge but are solidly comfortable with immaculate bathrooms. There are fresh breads and home-made jams at the huge Andean cedar breakfast table, a quiet, pretty garden and good conversation in English, French, Italian, Spanish or Catalan.

rooms	3: 1 double, 1 family room, 1 suite for 2, all with bath or shower & wc.
price	€45-€55 for two; €65 for four.
dinner	Auberges 6km.
closed	Rarely.
directions	From A13 exit 17 for Gaillon D316 for Évreux through Autheuil, St Vigor & up hill 11km; right to Reuilly; house on road, 200m past Mairie on right.

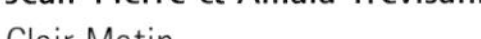

Jean-Pierre & Amaia Trevisani
Clair Matin,
19 rue de l'Église,
27930 Reuilly, Eure

tel	(0)2 32 34 71 47
fax	(0)2 32 34 97 64
e-mail	clair_matin@compuserve.com

Madame cooks great Norman dishes with home-grown ingredients served on good china; also, remarkable tomato and banana jam for breakfast – be brave, it's worth trying. She has been doing B&B for years, is well organised and still enjoys meeting new people when she's not too busy. Guest quarters, independent of the house, have pretty French-style rooms, good bedding and excellent tiled shower rooms while the caringly-restored, listed 15th-century farmhouse, the duck pond, the peacocks and the furniture – each item carefully chosen, some tenderly hand-painted – all give it character. And it's excellent value. *Games room.*

rooms	5: 1 triple, 2 doubles, 2 twins, all with shower & wc.
price	€42 for two; €54 for three.
dinner	€17, with cider.
closed	Rarely.
directions	From Rouen N15 for Paris 40km; at Gaillon right D10 for La Croix St Leufroy about 7km; in La Boissaye, Chambres d'Hôtes signs.

Clotilde & Gérard Sénécal
Manoir de la Boissière,
Hameau la Boissaye,
27490 La Croix St Leufroy, Eure
tel (0)2 32 67 70 85
fax (0)2 32 67 03 18

NORMANDY

The big garden runs down to the banks of the Eure: peace reigns in this privileged spot. Smiley Bernard keeps lawns mown and borders clipped; sweet Madeleine devotes herself to home and guests. The old farmhouse is as neat as a new pin, bedrooms soberly pretty and inviting. The parquet-floored double has French windows to the garden; the suite, papered and friezed in pale green, has a sitting area under the eaves. Refined breakfast is served on antique lace in a dining room with garden views. Woods and water for walking, canoeing, fishing; gentle people; Giverny and Rouen a half-hour drive. A form of perfection.

rooms	2: 1 double with shower & wc; 1 suite for 3 with shower & wc.
price	€45–€51 for two.
dinner	Choice of restaurants 5km.
closed	Rarely.
directions	A13 exit 19 for Louviers/Évreux; 2nd exit N154 to Acquigny; D71 through Heudreville for Cailly to La Londe; left; house on right.

Madeleine & Bernard Gossent
4 sente de l'Abreuvoir,
La Londe,
27400 Heudreville sur Eure, Eure
tel (0)2 32 40 36 89
e-mail madeleine.gossent@online.fr
web www.lalonde.online.fr

Your hostess is a French lady of classic style. Strong, intelligent and gracious, she still bubbles with enthusiasm and energy. The 80m² yellow-tinted living room of her very French house has giant old beams, a huge Turkey rug on antique tiles and some choice relics from her time in Africa; the staircase is beautifully sculpted and the garden goes down to the river. Relaxing, impeccable bedrooms are thoroughly carpeted and she is rightly proud of her breakfast table with its pewter, intricately folded napkins and home-made delights. A most comforting place, halfway between the wonders of Giverny and Rouen. *Gîte space for 4 people.*

rooms 2: 1 double/twin, 1 suite for 5, both with bath & wc.
price €40-€44 for two.
dinner In village or 6km.
closed Rarely.
directions From Paris A13 for Rouen; exit Louviers N154 for Évreux; exit Heudreville D71 to village. House in cul-de-sac opposite church.

Mme Janine Bourgeois
La Ferme,
4 rue de l'Ancienne Poste,
27400 Heudreville sur Eure, Eure
tel (0)2 32 50 20 69
fax (0)2 32 50 20 69

NORMANDY

They are full of character and terribly French, this artist owner and her crooked house marked by the slings and arrows of 500 years: bare floorboards, bathrooms among the beams, old and new furnishings, cultural references (Saint-Exupéry, author of the immortal *Petit Prince* and a friend of Madame's father, stayed here) and a sensuous garden full of old favourites: lilac and honeysuckle, luscious shrubs and fruit trees. Set in the middle of the village, the quiet old house has an atmosphere that inspires ease and rest. Madame, a good, generous soul, used to be an antique dealer so breakfast is served on old silver. *Gîte space for 12.*

rooms 4: 2 doubles, 1 triple, 1 quadruple (in cottage), all with shower & wc.
price €43 for two.
dinner €14; wine list.
closed Rarely.
directions From A13 exit 19 to Louviers; D313 for Elbeuf 11km; left on D60 to St Didier des Bois. House with white iron gate opp. church.

Annick Auzoux
1 place de l'Église,
27370 St Didier des Bois, Eure
tel (0)2 32 50 60 93
fax (0)2 32 25 41 83

The sedately old-French panelled rooms with refreshing colours, good antiques and windows to the gentle world outside are up the grand staircase of this 16th-century house where brick and sandstone sit in peace by birdy orchard, pastoral meadows and spreading lake. Madame is a most welcoming hostess, full of spontaneous smiles, who puts flowers everywhere and whose family has owned the house for 100 years. She also organises seminars (not when B&B guests are here), cares for two teenagers and gardens brilliantly: trees are being planted to Napoleonic plans discovered in the archives... *Gîte space for 34 people.*

rooms	2: 1 quadruple with bath & wc; 1 triple with shower & wc.
price	€42-€58 for two.
dinner	Choice of restaurants 2-8km.
closed	Rarely.
directions	From A13 exit Maison Brulée N138 for Bourgthéroulde & Brionne. 8km after Bourgthéroulde D83 left to Le Gros Theil; enter village, sharp right D92 & follow signs for 2km.

Béatrice & Patrice Noël-Windsor
Manoir d'Hermos,
27800 St Éloi de Fourques, Eure

tel	(0)2 32 35 51 32
fax	(0)2 32 35 51 32
e-mail	manoirhermos@lemel.fr
web	www.members.aol.com/hermos1/hermosfr.htm

NORMANDY

That lovely timber frame embraces a heart-warming antique clutter spread with great taste over original bricks, beams, tiles and carved family furniture. Guests share this marvellous space as family, Madame smiles, welcomes and cooks with brio using her own vegetables – she also tends the intimate paradise of a garden whence views glide over forested hills – while Monsieur smiles, charms and mends everything. The delicious bedrooms are subtly lit by dormer windows, country furnished, pastel hued and comfortably bathroomed; the suite has steep rafters and a smart new shower room. A dream of a place, they deserve a medal.

rooms	3: 2 doubles/twins, 1 suite for 4, all with bath or shower & wc.
price	€48-€50 for two.
dinner	€20 with wine, by arrangement.
closed	October-March, except by arrangement.
directions	From Paris A13 exit 26 for Pont Audemer D89; at 'Médine' r'bout. cont. for Évreux/ Appeville-Annebault 4km; left immed. after Les Marettes sign, follow Chambres d'Hôtes signs.

Françoise & Yves Closson Maze
Les Aubépines,
Aux Chauffourniers,
27290 Appeville dit Annebault,
Eure

tel	(0)2 32 56 14 25
fax	(0)2 32 56 14 25
e-mail	clossonmaze@wanadoo.fr
web	perso.wanadoo.fr/lesaubepines

This charming couple run food-and-wine breaks and cookery courses – a natural development from *table d'hôtes* as they are fabulously knowledgeable and inspiring about the subject. Nicky is English and a *Cordon Bleu* cook, Régis is French with great taste in all departments. There's still nothing nicer than waking up in one of the attractive antique- or ethnic-furnished rooms of their superbly renovated farmhouse (great bathrooms too) and the stylish new dining room is a great success. The grounds just get prettier, strutted by poultry and overseen by black-headed sheep. Come and indulge. *Min. 2 nights.*

rooms	5: 2 doubles, 1 twin, 1 triple, 1 quadruple, all with bath or shower & wc.
price	Half-board €107 for two.
dinner	Breakfast & dinner included.
closed	Rarely.
directions	In Fourmetot turn for Corneville by church for 1km; 50m after small crossroads left through 2 round brick pillars.

Régis & Nicky Dussartre
L'Aufragère,
La Croisée,
27500 Fourmetot, Eure

tel	(0)2 32 56 91 92
fax	(0)2 32 57 75 34
e-mail	regis@laufragere.com
web	www.laufragere.com

map: 5 entry: 192

NORMANDY

Some sort of perfection? It is picture-perfect deepest Normandy, from the fine old timbered cider-press building, built during the French Revolution and beautifully restored, to Monsieur's ship-shape garden (he was a naval man) groaning with flowers and fruit trees, to the soft, lacy, cottagey rooms – Madame's labour of love where her cut and dried flowers peek from every corner. Old lace, antique country beds, wardrobes and dressers from family treasure stores, the scent of beeswax hanging in the air, a gentle, civilised atmosphere. And local specialities with cider for (superb) dinner. *Children over 10 welcome.*

rooms	2 doubles, both with shower & wc.
price	€54 for two.
dinner	€22, with wine; restaurants nearby.
closed	Rarely.
directions	From Le Havre A131 for Paris; cross Pont de Tancarville; D810 right, through Pont Audemer, onto D87 through St Germain village; right on CV19 to Tricqueville; signs (about 50km total).

Gaston & Michelle Le Pleux
La Clé des Champs,
27500 Tricqueville, Eure

tel	(0)2 32 41 37 99
e-mail	redmoon45@aol.com

map: 5 entry: 193

A brightly-coloured tanker is liable to appear from behind the trees heading for the Channel, or the great annual armada to come sailing past – such is the magic of this site on the banks of the Seine just below Rouen. The Laurents' garden goes down to the water's edge and they lend binoculars for bird-watching, maps and books for trail-exploring – it is a Panda (WWF) house. The big house is for guests, the owners have the thatched cottage next door. There are beams and panelling, antiques and windows onto that stunning view, a kitchen/diner, a very comfortable sitting room and Madame has all the time in the world for you. *Gîte space for 14.*

rooms	4: 2 suites for 3, 2 quadruples, all with bath or shower & wc.
price	€47 for two.
dinner	€15, wine €10.50-€12.50, cider €4.50; self-catering possible.
closed	Rarely.
directions	From Pont Audemer D139 NE for 10km to Bourneville & cont. D139 to Aizier. There, left at Mairie for Vieux Port, D95; on right.

Yves & Marie-Thérèse Laurent
Les Sources Bleues,
Le Bourg,
27500 Aizier, Eure
tel (0)2 32 57 26 68
fax (0)2 32 57 42 25

NORMANDY

Ten years ago, this was a low-lying cottage in need of love and affection. Jean-Marc, with boundless energy, transformed it into a floral, country gem to stay, meet, eat – and have fun in. It's a mix of the sober and the frivolous – old and modern pieces, rustic revival and leather, contemporary art and *brocante*. The garden will become exuberant too, as it matures. The bedrooms stand out in their uncomplicated good taste and plain fabrics but it's Jean-Marc who makes the place: candlelit dinners and sporting events, strawberry soup and laughter, home-made bread and jam, flowers in your room. Amazing.

rooms	5: 1 twin with shower & wc; 1 double, 1 triple, 2 family, all with bath & wc.
price	€50 for two.
dinner	€19, with wine; picnic possible.
closed	Rarely.
directions	From Pont Audemer D810 for Bernay 12km; right through St Siméon; up hill for Selles; house on left at top.

Jean-Marc Drumel
Le Coquerel,
27560 St Siméon, Eure
tel (0)2 32 56 56 08
fax (0)2 32 56 56 08
e-mail moreau-drumel@wanadoo.fr
web perso.wanadoo.fr/chambreshotes/

No great château but a family house with old photos on the grand staircase and the farm office downstairs. The yellow bedroom has superb views, all are big and beautifully decorated – Madame did all the wallpapering herself, *merci Madame!*. Tall, sophisticated and immaculate, she is naturally relaxed and welcoming and finds it normal that everyone sit at the same big table in the ochre and scarlet breakfast room. There's a family-friendly common room with billiards, table tennis, picnic table, refrigerator. No finery, a touch of faded grandeur and all-pervasive warmth characterise this splendid house of friendship.

rooms	4: 1 double, 1 twin, 2 family rooms, all with bath or shower & wc.
price	€46 for two.
dinner	Choice of restaurants in Orbec.
closed	Rarely.
directions	From Lisieux N13 for Évreux 18km to Thiberville; D145 for Orbec 10km. On right about 50m after sign 'Le Grand Bus'.

Bruno & Laurence de Préaumont
Château du Grand Bus,
Saint Germain la Campagne,
27230 Thiberville, Eure
tel (0)2 32 44 71 14
fax (0)2 32 46 45 81
e-mail chambrepreaumont@libertysurf.fr
web perso.libertysurf.fr/depreaumont

map: 5 entry: 196

One of the most delicious houses we know in Normandy, it is the new-found delight of your ex-Parisian hosts. It stands in a lush mature garden, overgrown here, tamed there, where typical timber-frame characters peer from the bushes, roses seek the sky and a stupendous walnut tree triumphs behind. Inside, Marie-Hélène, bright-eyed and eager, has used Jouy cloth and elegant colours to dress the marble fireplaces and polished floors with sober intelligence. In the quietly orange dining room, by the prettiest floral-fantasy tiled stove alcove, you will enjoy good food with a courteous gentleman and his happy wife.

rooms	4: 2 twins, 2 doubles, all with shower & wc.
price	€54 for two.
dinner	€19 with wine, by arrangement.
closed	Rarely.
directions	From Évreux N13 for Lisieux 50km; entering Duranville right D41 for St Aubin de S. 2.5km; drive on right.

Marie-Hélène François
La Charterie,
27230 St Aubin de Scellon, Eure
tel (0)2 32 45 46 52/(0)6 20 39 08 63

map: 5 entry: 197

The ancient fortress is 40 years old and the rickety old rail-less bridge over the moat is made of 1960s sleepers. Impeccably classic bedrooms have starched linen and lacy bedcovers and downstairs is a collector's clutter of pictures, porcelain and old shoes. Madame, extraordinary and bohemian, changes from scatty gardener to lady-at-gracious-candlelit-dinner – enjoy antique silver and deeply informed conversation about the arts illuminated with flashes of outrageous humour. Just one loo between three bedrooms is surely a small price to pay for time with this entertaining and cultured person, alone on her tiny island.

rooms	3: 2 doubles, 1 twin, all with bath or shower, sharing wc.
price	€61 for two.
dinner	€20 with wine, by arrangement.
closed	January-February.
directions	From Breteuil D141 for Rugles; through forest; at Bémécourt, left 300m after lights into Allée du Vieux Château.

Mme Maryvonne Lallemand-Legras
Le Vieux Château,
27160 Bémécourt, Eure
tel (0)2 32 29 90 47

NORMANDY

Trompe-l'œil marble and Wedgwood mouldings inherited from an Adam-inspired ancestor; chamber music in the big, log-fired drawing room; breakfast in the dining room wrapped in oak panelling inlaid with precious woods; elegant, alcoved bedrooms full of antiques, books, ancestral portraits, much soft comfort and a loo in a tower: it's a fascinating, human place. And the delightful Longcamps are a civilised, friendly couple, she vivaciously cultured and musical, he a top-class camembert-maker who mows his acres on Sundays. Come and belong briefly to this wonderful world. Good walks start 2km away.

rooms	3: 1 twin, 2 doubles, all with bath & wc.
price	€90–€105 for two.
dinner	2 good restaurants within 5km.
closed	December-March, except by arrangement.
directions	From Verneuil sur Avre, N12 SW 24km to Carrefour Ste Anne. Left D918 for Longny au Perche for 4.5km; left D289 for Moulicent. House 800m on right.

Jacques & Pascale de Longcamp
Château de la Grande Noë,
61290 Moulicent, Orne
tel (0)2 33 73 63 30
fax (0)2 33 83 62 92
e-mail grandenoe@wanadoo.fr
web www.chateaudelagrandenoe.com

Your English hosts take great care of you in the old Percheron farmhouse they have rescued and restored – and enjoy sharing their enthusiasm for exploring this beautiful and undiscovered area of undulating forest famous for the heavy Percheron horses that were bred to haul logs. Feel free to potter on their land or venture further afield and come back to a friendly cup of tea or a delicious supper *en famille* in the farmhouse kitchen. Rex and Helen are wonderful company, natural and full of fun. Books, maps and easy chairs for you in the sitting room; comfortable beds in the big, beamy rooms. A super place.

rooms	2: 1 twin, 1 triple, both with bath & wc.
price	From €46 for two.
dinner	€23, with wine; restaurants within 10km.
closed	December.
directions	From Mortagne au Perche D931 for Mamers for 8km; right on D650 for Coulimer at small x-roads. House 800m on left, last of small group of houses.

Rex & Helen Barr
La Simondrière,
61360 Coulimer, Orne
tel (0)2 33 25 55 34
fax (0)2 33 25 49 01
e-mail prima@wanadoo.fr

map: 5 entry: 200

NORMANDY

This is Barbara's "corner of paradise" and her delight is contagious. In utter peace among the cattle-dotted Norman pastures, here is one brave, outspoken woman, her horses, dogs and cats in a low-lying farmhouse, beautifully rebuilt "from a pile of stones", where old and new mix easily and flowers rampage all around. The lovely sloping garden is all her own work too – she appears to have endless energy. The pastel guest rooms, one upstairs, one on the ground floor with doors to the garden, are pleasantly floral. Come by horse, or walk. Beautiful country and a sociable, interesting, horse-loving woman to welcome you.

rooms	2: 1 double, 1 twin, both with bath or shower & wc.
price	€50 for two.
dinner	Restaurant in village, 1.5km.
closed	Rarely.
directions	From Courtomer, past Mairie right after last building for Tellières. Left at crossroads for Le Marnis. 2nd lane on right.

Barbara Goff
Le Marnis,
Tellières le Plessis,
61390 Courtomer, Orne
tel (0)2 33 27 47 55
e-mail barbaragoff@minitel.net

map: 5 entry: 201

It's angular inside too, the staircase elbowing its way right up to the top, guest-room, floor where the sky rushes in. *Grand-mère's* hobby-camel stands here in its 1905 skin: the house was built by her parents in 1910 in open-plan American style. Sliding glass partitions give grandly generous dining and sitting rooms; bedrooms are excellent, much-windowed, soft-coloured and -bedded, marble-fireplaced, old-mirrored. Impeccable and full of personality, the house is the pride and joy of your alert, intelligent hostess who laughs easily and manages her home, four children and guests expertly. *Please don't arrive before 6pm.*

rooms	2: 1 twin with bath & wc; 1 suite for 4 with shower & wc.
price	€53 for two.
dinner	€22.50 with wine, by arrangement.
closed	December-February.
directions	From Argentan N26 E for 37km. Entrance 4km after Planches on right by small crucifix; long lime-bordered drive.

Antoine & Nathalie Le Brethon
La Bussière,
61370 Ste Gauburge Ste Colombe,
Orne

tel (0)2 33 34 05 23
fax (0)2 33 34 71 47

map: 5 entry: 202

There's home-made elderflower cordial if you arrive on a hot day or a wonderful smell of hot bread may greet you: this converted manor farm with its pigeon tower and duck stream has a lived-in family atmosphere. Your hosts have 800 sheep, 300 apple trees (*Normandie oblige!*), work hard and are thoroughly integrated, as are their daughters. Bedrooms in the old dairy are light, soberly furnished with touches of *fantaisie* and Diana's very decorative stencils. Breakfast is superb, dinner should be an occasion to linger over and remember; both happen under the pergola in fine weather. Watch the steep stairs.

rooms	3: 1 double, 1 twin, 1 triple, all with bath or shower & wc.
price	€50-€55 for two.
dinner	€25 with wine, by arrangement.
closed	December-February.
directions	From Vimoutiers D916 for Argentan. Just outside Vimoutiers fork left D16 for Exmes; D26 for Survie & Exmes.

Diana & Christopher Wordsworth
Les Gains,
Survie,
61310 Exmes, Orne

tel (0)2 33 36 05 56
fax (0)2 33 35 03 65
e-mail christopher.wordsworth@libertysurf.fr
web www.respublica.fr/lesgains

map: 5 entry: 203

Debbie and Daniel, artistic young landscape gardeners fairly new to the world of B&B, are thoroughly enthusiastic about it all – welcoming their guests to their pretty, unfussy rooms, improving the bathrooms, devising and preparing vegetarian menus that look and taste wonderful, redesigning the mature garden with its great old trees to include areas for scent, colour and feel, developing the organic vegetable patch (free-range hens too). They have decorated the place with creative good taste, provide varied, healthy breakfasts and dinners and will take great care of your comfort and well-being.

rooms	3 doubles, all with shower & wc.
price	€57-€63 for two.
dinner	€25 with wine, by arrangement.
closed	Rarely.
directions	D579 from Lisieux to Vimoutiers; D979 for Alençon for 5km; left D12 for L'Aigle. In Ticheville, left opp. church, house 20m on right.

Debbie & Daniel Armitage
La Maison du Vert,
Le Bourg,
61120 Ticheville, Orne

tel	(0)2 33 36 95 84
fax	(0)2 33 36 95 84
e-mail	mail@maisonduvert.com
web	www.maisonduvert.com

map: 5 entry: 204

NORMANDY

With a flurry of colours and styles, from dark autumnal to tiger-print jungle, the Four Seasons guest rooms have old country charm, family furniture, colour-themed linen in florals or checks and old-fashioned bathrooms. Your hosts, caring, generous, sensitive farmers, enjoy contact and share their quiet sense of humour with each other, their guests and their teenage children. Madame spoils you at breakfast with local honey and her home-made jam repertoire includes dandelion-flower and apple. The sitting room, playroom and kitchen facilities are a bonus in this warmly unpretentious rural home.

rooms	4: 2 doubles, 1 triple, 1 quadruple, all with shower & wc.
price	€38 for two.
dinner	Restaurant 4km.
closed	Rarely.
directions	From Argentan, N26 for L'Aigle & Paris. Left at Silly en Gouffern. At Ste Eugénie, last farm on left.

Pierre & Ghislaine Maurice
La Grande Ferme,
Sainte Eugénie,
61160 Aubry en Exmes, Orne

tel	(0)2 33 36 82 36
fax	(0)2 33 36 99 52
e-mail	ghis.p.maurice@wanadoo.fr

map: 5 entry: 205

There are fresh flowers everywhere and your hosts, retired farmers, offer good country hospitality. Peace is the norm not the exception in this deeply rural spot, racehorses graze in the pasture and you are unhesitatingly received into a warm and lively family. Two rooms are in a converted outbuilding and have an appropriately rustic air with beams, old wardrobes and mini-kitchens. The upstairs room is bigger and lighter, the ground-floor room has a little private garden. The suite, ideal for families, is in the main house. Breakfast is at the family table. Children are welcome to visit their son's farm next door.

rooms	3: 2 doubles, both with shower, wc & kitchenette; 1 suite for 4 with bath & wc.
price	€38 for two.
dinner	Restaurant 5km; self-catering in 2 rooms.
closed	Rarely.
directions	From Argentan N158 for Caen; after sign 'Moulin sur Orne', left; house 800m on left; sign (3.5km from Argentan).

Janine & Rémy Laignel
Le Mesnil,
61200 Occagnes, Orne
tel (0)2 33 67 11 12

NORMANDY

Built in 1870, La Maigraire stands in pretty grounds and has its own fishing. Jean and his cousin François bought it in 1998 and did a brilliant restoration, carefully preserving the right atmosphere. Jean studied at the Louvre and worked as an interior designer and antique dealer before falling for La Maigraire. Luckily he had kept a little cache of pieces which look perfectly at home here. These attentive hosts will make you feel very welcome, providing delicious home-made jam for breakfast and perhaps even playing the piano while you have tea in the *grand salon*.

rooms	2: 1 double, 1 suite for 2-3, both with bath or shower & wc.
price	€72-€95 for two.
dinner	Several good restaurants in the area.
closed	Rarely.
directions	From D962, between Flers & Domfront, D260 for Forges de Varennes & Champsecret for 1.5km; left into La Maigraire hamlet.

Jean Fischer
Château de La Maigraire,
61700 St Bômer les Forges, Orne
tel (0)2 33 38 09 52
fax (0)2 33 38 09 52

England's last conqueror lived in Falaise until he left in 1066 to cross the water, but this typical house in its quiet little Norman village is young, only built in the 1600s. Monsieur's family have owned it for 100 years: he was born here and married a local girl who is now mayor. They are a sweet couple, quietly and unobtrusively attentive, and you will feel well tended, like the much-loved garden with its flowery bower holding a stone table. The pretty dining room has some superb family furniture, country French at its best; the pastel bedrooms have more antiques, crinkly pink lights and little bits of *brocante*.

rooms	2: 1 double/triple, 1 suite for 4, both with shower & wc.
price	€35 for two.
dinner	Restaurants Falaise, 3km; BBQ & picnic possible.
closed	Rarely.
directions	From Falaise D63 for Trun, 2km; 2nd left for Villy lez Falaise 1km; in village, farm 1st on left after stop sign.

Alice & Gilbert Thomas
Ferme la Croix,
14700 Villy lez Falaise, Calvados
tel (0)2 31 90 19 98/(0)6 74 46 84 92

NORMANDY

Such very special people, quietly, uncomplicatedly intelligent: what the house lacks in years is made up for tenfold by their timeless, earth-genuine and heartfelt Norman hospitality. Close to all things natural, they plough their big veg patch with the cob in harness, share organic dinners made to old forgotten recipes, offer good rooms where you wake to soul-lifting views over the hushed hills of *La Suisse Normande*. Nothing gushy or corny, these are independent, strong, comforting people who take you to their bosom and genuinely care for your well-being and that of the land.

rooms	3: 1 double, 1 twin, 1 suite, all with shower & wc.
price	€35 for two.
dinner	€13, with cider.
closed	Rarely.
directions	From Caen D562 for Flers, 35km; at Le Fresne D1 for Falaise, 4km; house on right, sign.

Roland & Claudine Lebatard
Arclais,
14690 Pont d'Ouilly, Calvados
tel (0)2 31 69 81 65
fax (0)2 31 69 81 65

A solid, elegant Norman mansion with walled garden and summer house, billiards and *two* dining rooms. Andrew receives you in relaxed style, dynamic Elizabeth is present at weekends. On the airy first floor, your sleeping and sitting rooms have generous light, glowing parquet, French and English antiques against pale walls. Downstairs, the sandy and creamy-white dining room is unusually frescoed and the oak-panelled, many-windowed dining room is beamed and fireplaced; both have seriously big tables. Andrew continues his restoration in excellent taste and it is all most comfortable and welcoming. *Gîte space for 7 people.*

rooms	5: 2 doubles, 2 family rooms, 1 single, all with bath or shower & wc.
price	€60-€65 for two.
dinner	€21 with wine, by arrangement.
closed	Christmas & New Year.
directions	From Caen ring road exit 13 for Falaise; 9km, right to Bretteville sur Laize; continue to Barbery. House behind field on right, with high, green gates.

Elizabeth & Andrew Bamford
Les Fontaines,
Barbery,
14220 Bretteville sur Laize,
Calvados

tel	(0)2 31 78 24 48
fax	(0)2 31 78 24 49
e-mail	lesfontaines@free.fr
web	lesfontaines.free.fr

map: 5 entry: 210

NORMANDY

Built in 1850 on the foundations of one of William the Conqueror's outposts, the square-set château stands handsome still as the park recovers from the devastation of the 1999 storm. It's a place to taste the "world's best cider" (says Monsieur), admire yourself in innumerable gilt-framed mirrors, luxuriate in a jacuzzi or bare your chest to a power shower, play the piano, appreciate Madame's superb cooking, and lie at last in an antique, new-mattressed bed in one of the enormous, deep-tinted bedrooms. Period ceilings, tapestries and furniture make it a real château experience; the people make it very human.

rooms	4: 2 doubles, 2 suites, all with bath or shower & wc.
price	€95-€145 for two.
dinner	€40, with wine & calvados.
closed	Rarely.
directions	From Caen N158 for Falaise; at La Jalousie, right D23; right D235 just before Bretteville; signs.

Anne-Marie & Alain Cantel
Château des Riffets,
14680 Bretteville sur Laize,
Calvados

tel	(0)2 31 23 53 21
fax	(0)2 31 23 75 14
e-mail	acantel@free.fr
web	www.jeanluc.de/riffets

map: 5 entry: 211

It may have a make-believe face, among the smooth green curves of racehorse country, but it is genuine early 1600s. Inside is an equally astounding dining room built by one Mr Swann and resplendently carved, panelled and painted. Two big rooms – *Jaune* and *Verte* – see the sun rise, but *Saumon* is even better with its heavenly sunset prospect; one has a splendid old-style bath and tiling, all are incredible value. Madame, a beautiful Swedish lady, made all the curtains and covers. She and her diplomat husband are well-travelled, polyglot, cultured and make their B&B doubly special.

rooms	3: 2 doubles, 1 twin, all with bath or shower & wc.
price	€45-€55 for two.
dinner	Restaurant 1km.
closed	15 November-February.
directions	From Caen N13 for Lisieux 25km; at Carrefour St Jean, D50 (virtually straight on) for Cambremer; 5km from junc., house on right; sign.

Christine & Arnauld Gherrak
Manoir de Cantepie,
Le Cadran,
14340 Cambremer, Calvados
tel (0)2 31 62 87 27
fax (0)2 31 62 87 27

map: 5 entry: 212

Views from this anciently, beautifully Norman house, a festival of timbers and stones, are pastoral bliss. Ancient layout too: it has two narrow staircases, two bathrooms for four bedrooms, one on another floor. Such super Anglo-Canadian hosts – much travelled and cultured – who cook and talk easily and well, such a personal dining room where Julia has hand-painted the beams, laid out her willow pattern china and hung her friends' paintings. Special bedrooms mix baroque, contemporary and cottage with velvet and quilt, floorboards and rugs. A quite lovely house in a rural cider-making spot a stone's throw from Honfleur.

rooms	4 twins with 2 separate bathrooms (2 baths, 2 wcs & 2 showers).
price	€50 for two.
dinner	€25, with cider.
closed	Rarely.
directions	From Pont l'Évêque D579 for Lisieux; at Fierville les Parcs left to Blangy; right on hairpin for Norolles/Lisieux; 1st left for Les Batailles; house on right.

Julia Mclean
Domaine des Leudets,
Blangy le Château,
14130 Pont l'Évêque, Calvados
tel (0)2 31 64 61 79

map: 5 entry: 213

Françoise and Michel have been doing B&B for years, in one house or another, and are ever ready to welcome guests to their typically Norman house where space is well organised and you won't feel crowded in. Françoise will produce an excellent dinner for you, likely to centre around *confit de canard* and apple or plum tart, depending on the time of year. The rooms are not large but they are comfortably cheerful and look out onto a very pretty garden. The loudest sound you might hear is the odd lawnmower. *Apartment for 4-5.*

rooms	2: 1 double, 1 triple, both with bath or shower & wc.
price	€60-€68 for two.
dinner	€23 with wine, by arrangement.
closed	Rarely.
directions	From Pont l'Évêque D579 for Lisieux. At Le Breuil en Auge r'bout D264 to Le Torquesne. 1st right after church, Chemin des Toutains. House 500m on.

Françoise Valle
Clos St Hymer,
14130 Le Torquesne, Calvados
tel (0)2 31 61 99 15
fax (0)2 31 61 99 36

NORMANDY

Your hosts, a charmingly poised Belgian couple, love their perfect little Normandy manor, built just 20 years ago in typical 'Calvados Cottage' style with timbers inside and out, dormers and sloping atticky ceilings – and Madame adores cooking for her guests. The prettily feminine bedrooms are bright and colourful with stripped pine wardrobes, just enough lacy bits and big, luxurious bathrooms. The living room, the hub of life at Reinette, cleverly mixes contemporary ideas with olde-worlde wood – it's smart yet seductive. And the sea is a ten-minute walk away. *Children over 6 welcome: unfenced pool.*

rooms	3 doubles, all with bath & wc.
price	€53-€60 for two.
dinner	€22 with wine, by arrangement.
closed	Rarely.
directions	From Caen A13 for Paris; exit 29 for Cabourg D400 for Dives sur Mer; D513 for Villers sur Mer; signs for town centre; house up a long lane.

Micheline & Claude Verbelen
Pomme Reinette,
56 avenue de la Brigade Piron,
14640 Villers sur Mer, Calvados
tel (0)2 31 81 17 88
fax (0)2 31 81 17 88
e-mail pomme.reinette@wanadoo.fr
web www.pommereinette.com

Your young hosts have done a great renovation job on their intriguing 18th-century house, preserving old stonework and beams, installing modern showers and decent beds and decorating in 'Contemporary Rustic' style. Mylène has brought pretty Provençal fabrics from her native Drôme, Christian is Norman and trained as a chef, both are friendly, relaxed and keen that their guests get a good glimpse of French country life. There's a wide choice of local and home-made breads and jams at breakfast, a barbecue and refrigerator you can use, table tennis for immediate exercise and a couple of bikes for further exploration.

rooms	2: 1 double, 1 suite for 3, both with shower & wc.
price	€47-€64 for two; suite €76 for three.
dinner	€22 with wine, by arrangement.
closed	Rarely, please book ahead.
directions	From Caen D7 for Douvres 8km; left D404 5.5km; D79 to Courseulles sur Mer; D514 to Ver sur Mer; at village entrance 1st left Av. Provence; 1st right; 1st left cul-de-sac; at end on right.

Christian Mériel & Mylène Gilles
Le Mas Normand,
8 impasse de la Rivière,
14114 Ver sur Mer, Calvados

tel	(0)2 31 21 97 75
fax	(0)2 31 21 97 75
e-mail	lemasnormand@wanadoo.fr
web	pro.wanadoo.fr/lemasnormand

map: 5 entry: 216

NORMANDY

It's just plain lovely, this little group of stone buildings with pretty bridge and terraces by the rushing stream. There's the age-old converted mill for the family and the 'hunting lodge' for guests, where Madame's talented decoration marries nostalgic past (antiques, old prints, photographs) and designer-hued present. You have your own dining room and kitchen, the blue, yellow and green garden, the woods for nut-gathering, beaches nearby, the stream for entertainment on the spot. Your hosts are sweet and love having families. *Italian spoken. Gîte space for 6 people.*

rooms	3: 1 double with shower & wc; 1 double, 1 twin sharing shower & wc.
price	€48 for two.
dinner	Restaurants 2-3km; self-catering possible.
closed	Rarely.
directions	From Ouistreham D35 through Douvres & Tailleville; over D404; right at r'bout entering Reviers; 2nd Chambres d'Hôtes on left.

Patricia & Jean-Michel Blanlot
La Malposte,
15 rue des Moulins,
14470 Reviers, Calvados

tel	(0)2 31 37 51 29
fax	(0)2 31 37 51 29

map: 5 entry: 217

Come and stay on this many-feathered farm for free-range eggs, bucolic walks through the quiet Norman copses and meadows (itineraries provided), or bungee-jumping… and spit-roast dinners in winter. You are warmly greeted by your friendly hosts, the atmosphere is easy and if the big bedrooms are unremarkable – though the triple upstairs is now furnished with a handsome 1920s set – they are clean and peaceful with their own entrance, kitchen and sitting room. Children are welcome: there are cots, games and bikes for them. A useful stopover. *Gîte space for 7 people.*

rooms	2 triples (1 on ground floor), both with shower & wc.
price	€35 for two.
dinner	€14 with wine, by arrangement.
closed	December-February.
directions	From Caen A84 for Avranches; exit to St Martin des Besaces on D53; left D165 for Brémoy; house on right 4km from St Martin.

Jacqueline & Gilbert Lalleman
Carrefour des Fosses,
14260 Brémoy, Calvados
tel (0)2 31 77 83 22
e-mail jg_lalleman@yahoo.fr

NORMANDY

Up the drive, across the cleanest ever farmyard to this totally French house to be met by a charmingly hospitable owner. She delights in gardening and cooking while her husband runs the dairy farm. Beyond the dinky little hall, the *salon*, with its high-backed chairs, beams and antimacassars, is a good place for a quiet read. The big sunny bedrooms are cosily frilly with quantities of lace, country furniture and gentle morning views over the garden dropping down to the pond. Special extras are the pond for fishing, paths for walking, home-made yogurt and cider – and pillows for the asking. *Small dogs welcome.*

rooms	3: 2 doubles, 1 suite, all with shower & wc.
price	€40 for two.
dinner	€19 with wine, by arrangement.
closed	Rarely.
directions	From Caen A13 for Cherbourg, exit Carpiquet & Caumont l'Éventé; 500m before Caumont, left at Chambres d'Hôtes sign.

Alain & Françoise Petiton
La Suhardière,
14240 Livry, Calvados
tel (0)2 31 77 51 02
fax (0)2 31 77 51 02

You could scarcely find easier, friendlier hosts than Joseph and Marie-Thé who have quantities of local lore and advice to communicate, will join you for a farm supper at the long table in the fresh-flowered guests' dayroom, with its log fire in winter, and create a generally fun-loving, relaxed atmosphere. There are animals for children, table football and volleyball for teenagers, *pétanque* for all. They are simple, genuine people, as are their gently-hued rooms and their welcome. This is superb value and far enough from the road not to suffer from much traffic noise.

rooms	4: 1 double, 3 suites for 3-4, all with bath or shower & wc, 1 with kitchen.
price	€34-€35 for two.
dinner	€14, with wine.
closed	Rarely.
directions	From A84/E401 exit 42 on N175 for Cahagnes 2km; right & follow Chambres d'Hôtes signs to farm.

Joseph & Marie-Thé Guilbert
Le Mesnil de Benneville,
14240 Cahagnes, Calvados
tel (0)2 31 77 58 05
fax (0)2 31 77 37 84

NORMANDY

Come through the wood and across the stream and with that timeless quality of solid country dwellers, the Ameys will wrap you in blue-eyed smiles – their unpretentious welcome is full of comfort and warmth. You find simple country furnishings, bar two superb Norman *armoires*; walls are pastel, curtains lace, bathroom pink, towels small. Breakfast brings incomparably good farm milk and butter; dinner is a rare treat of pure, unadulterated Norman fare with home-brewed *pommeau* and cider; the wisteria blooms. The simplest, friendliest place you could imagine: lovely people, excellent value. *Gîte space for 6 people.*

rooms	3 doubles, all with basin, sharing bathroom & separate wc.
price	€33-€35 for two.
dinner	€14, with cider.
closed	Rarely.
directions	From Caen A84 for Mt St Michel, exit 46 'Noyers Bocage'. Right D83 for Cheux 1.5km; left to Tessel; signs.

Paul & Éliane Amey
La Londe,
14250 Tessel, Calvados
tel (0)2 31 80 81 12
fax (0)2 31 80 81 57
e-mail paul.amey@wanadoo.fr

Back to our roots. A Celtic chieftain was buried here 2,100 years ago; then the Romans stayed a bit; the present house is 11th century, rebuilt in 1801. Its brass-railed staircase and *salon* are gracious but the dining room, relaxed in its yellow and green garb with huge fireplace and modern bar, is the hub of life where a warm, jolly family take you naturally into their circle. Madame uses colour and style well, mixing bright with soft, antiques with artificial flowers. The comfortable, fluffy bedrooms, raftered in the attic, fireplaced below, look onto wide fields and the 'Norman' dinners have been praised to the skies.

rooms	4 doubles, all with shower or bath & wc.
price	€45 for two.
dinner	€21.50 with wine, by arrangement.
closed	Rarely.
directions	From Bayeux for Cherbourg 4km; at r'bout to Tour en Bessin; through village, left D100 for Crouay 1km; house on right.

	Catherine & Bertrand Girard Le Relais de la Vignette, Route de Crouay, Tour en Bessin, 14400 Bayeux, Calvados
tel	(0)2 31 21 52 83
fax	(0)2 31 21 52 83
e-mail	relais.vignette@wanadoo.fr
web	perso.wanadoo.fr/relais.vignette/

This delicious couple, who are among our favourite B&B owners, she softly-spoken and twinkling, he jovial and talkative, have retired from farming and moved into Bayeux – you can glimpse the cathedral spires from their creamy-coloured townhouse which was probably part of the former bishop's palace. Beyond the wisteria, the door opens onto a lofty beamed living room rejoicing in good antiques and a monumental fireplace – through (yes) another is the kitchen. Upstairs, the pretty guest rooms, with excellent new bedding and pastel-tiled bathrooms, look quietly over the pocket-handkerchief back garden. An ideal town address.

rooms	3: 2 doubles, 1 twin, all with shower & wc.
price	€53 for two.
dinner	Restaurants 150m.
closed	Rarely.
directions	From Caen N13 to Bayeux; for Gare SNCF; right after traffic lights; over 1st crossroads & traffic lights, park on left; house 50m on right, signs.

	Louis & Annick Fauvel 13 rue au Coq, 14400 Bayeux, Calvados
tel	(0)2 31 22 52 32

The lovely old house of golden stone is the warmly natural home of interesting people: a fascinating military historian who takes battlefield tours (don't be daunted, you'll learn lots) and willingly shares his passion for the dramas that took place here, and his gentle lady who directs things masterfully and serves her own jams for breakfast. Stone stairs lead to big, comfortably casual guest rooms and good, clean bathrooms – nothing flashy. The courtyard houses several tribes of animal and a games room. Here is space and a genuine family-friendly welcome just 15 minutes' walk from the Cathedral. *Gîte space for 6 people.*

rooms	3: 1 double, 2 triples, all with shower & wc.
price	€50–€55 for two.
dinner	Choice of restaurants in Bayeux, 1km.
closed	Rarely.
directions	On Bayeux bypass, at Campanile Hotel D572 for St Lô; 2nd right; follow signs to arched gateway.

Lt-Col & Mrs Chilcott
Manoir des Doyens,
Saint Loup Hors,
14400 Bayeux, Calvados

tel	(0)2 31 22 39 09
fax	(0)2 31 21 97 84
e-mail	chilcott@mail.cpod.fr

map: 5 entry: 224

NORMANDY

A charming couple, she natural, strong and brave, he softly spoken and communicative, with three courteous, smiling sons, they have been enjoying B&B for 20 years now as well as running a large dairy herd. Their 300-year-old farmhouse contains two of the guest rooms; the family room is in the more recent extension with the breakfast room that leads onto the pretty patio. There's also a largish grassy area for run-around children. Rooms are floral, shiny floorboarded and have excellent beds and shower rooms. This is a good, reliable place to stay with a delightful family. *Gîte space for 14 people.*

rooms	3: 1 double, 1 triple, 1 suite for 4, all with shower & wc.
price	€40–€43 for two; suite €61–€70 for four.
dinner	Restaurants St Laurent sur Mer, 4km.
closed	Rarely.
directions	From Cherbourg N13 S 76km; exit Formigny for St Laurent sur Mer; after church right 800m: entrance on left.

Odile & Jean-Claude Lenourichel
Le Mouchel,
14710 Formigny, Calvados

tel	(0)2 31 22 53 79
fax	(0)2 31 21 56 55
e-mail	odile.lenourichel@libertysurf.fr

map: 4 entry: 225

It's all utterly rural. Madame is a quiet, kindly woman who creates an easy family atmosphere. Her son bakes delicious bread in the 18th-century oven he has restored and may produce cakes and pâtisseries of all sorts for tea. Rooms are simple country style. *La Chambre Ancienne*, definitely the best, has a low ceiling, antique beds and planked floor; shower rooms are rather old-fashioned. You might be able to fish on Madame's trout-stuffed pond nearby and they'll organise a boat ride across the bird-full *Marais* for you. There is a small camping site on the farm.

rooms	3: 2 twins, 1 triple, all with shower & wc.
price	€37 for two.
dinner	Ferme-auberge 3km.
closed	Rarely.
directions	From Bayeux D5 W through Le Molay-Littry for Bernesq & Briqueville; right just before Bernesq; house on this road, sign.

Marcelle Marie
Le Ruppaley,
14710 Bernesq, Calvados
tel (0)2 31 22 54 44

map: 4 entry: 226

NORMANDY

A round pigeon tower and a private chapel complete the picture of this charming fortified working farm, parts of which are 15th century. Rooms are big with high beamed ceilings and there's a fine walled garden. The whole place has been carefully restored and it all feels unpretentiously stylish with a friendly, relaxed atmosphere. The bedrooms have been decorated quite beautifully, each with its own theme, mostly traditional variations with antique furniture and flowery fabrics, one in navy blue and white with nautical pictures. The sea is just a short walk away.

rooms	4: 1 double, 1 twin, 1 suite, 1 family room, all with shower & wc.
price	€50 for two.
dinner	Choice of restaurants in Grandcamp Maisy.
closed	November-March.
directions	From Bayeux N13 30km west; exit on D514 to Osmanville & on for Grandcamp 4km; left D199a for Géfosse Fontenay 400m; follow yellow signs on right.

François & Agnès Lemarié
L'Hermerel,
14230 Géfosse Fontenay, Calvados
tel (0)2 31 22 64 12
fax (0)2 31 22 76 37
e-mail lemariehermerel@aol.com

map: 4 entry: 227

Breakfast by the massive fireplace may be candle- or oil-lamp-lit on dark mornings in this ancient fortress of a farm. It also has a stupendous tithe barn and a little watchtower turned into a perfect gîte for two. Madame is proud of her family home, its flagstones worn smooth with age, its fine country antiques so suited to the sober, immensely high second-floor rooms – one has a shower in a tower, another looks over the calving field. Her energy is boundless and she is ever redecorating, cooking imaginative Norman cuisine, improving her rooms, much supported by her cattle-farmer husband – a great team. *Gîte space for 6 people.*

rooms	3: 2 triples, 1 double, all with shower & wc.
price	€50 for two.
dinner	€20, with cider.
closed	Rarely.
directions	From Bayeux N13 30km west; exit on D514 to Osmanville & on for Grandchamp, 5km; left for Géfosse Fontenay; house 800m on left before church.

	Gérard & Isabelle Leharivel Ferme-Manoir de la Rivière, 14230 Géfosse Fontenay, Calvados
tel	(0)2 31 22 64 45
fax	(0)2 31 22 01 18
e-mail	manoirdelariviere@mageos.com
web	www.chez.com/manoirdelariviere

NORMANDY

The solid beauty of the old fortified farmhouse and the serenity of the *Marais* lapping at the lawn make this place near-perfect. Your amiable and generous hosts have been receiving guests for years and love transmitting their deep knowledge of local history and wildlife: theirs is a WWF *Gîte Panda* with nature guides and binoculars on loan. Stretch your eyes across a luminous landscape of marshes and fields, watch storks nesting, the heron fishing in the pond, then negotiate the stone, rope-handled spiral up to big, comfortably simple rooms and sleep in bliss.

rooms	3: 1 double, 1 twin, 1 suite for 5, all with bath or shower & wc.
price	€43 for two.
dinner	Available locally.
closed	October-Easter.
directions	From Bayeux N13 to La Cambe, D113 south. After 1km, D124 to St Germain du Pert, 1.5km.

	Paulette & Hervé Marie Ferme de la Rivière, 14230 St Germain du Pert, Calvados
tel	(0)2 31 22 72 92
fax	(0)2 31 22 01 63

Previously renovated in the 16th and 18th centuries… the glorified farm has 30 rooms with fabulous tiled and parquet floors and classic French décor. At its centre, the grand panelled dining room has sun pouring in from both sides and views across the moat, over the formal garden with its swings and myriad plants, down to the orangery. Breakfast is at separate tables here. The whole house is littered with woodcarvings and furniture made by Monsieur's father and bedrooms are, of course, splendidly, classically French. Madame is a gracious and outgoing hostess. *Pets by arrangement.*

rooms	5 doubles, all with bath & wc.
price	€60-€70 for two.
dinner	Choice of restaurants 7-12km.
closed	December-March.
directions	From Cherbourg N13 to Isigny; right D5 for Le Molay; left near Vouilly church; château on right.

Marie-José & James Hamel
Château de Vouilly,
Vouilly,
14230 Isigny sur Mer, Calvados
tel (0)2 31 22 08 59
fax (0)2 31 22 90 58
e-mail chateau.vouilly@wanadoo.fr

map: 4 entry: 230

NORMANDY

Lush lawns, myriad flowers and white geese soften Nature's wildness here where great swaying pines and a wild coast have stood guard for over 800 years – the English burnt the first castle in 1346. The 16th-century manor's stern granite face hides a warm, elegant welcome in rooms with good beds, superb fireplaces, big windows to let in the light and utterly personal decoration: pictures, antiques and books (breakfast is in the library). Madame, charming and knowledgeable, will enthrall you with tales of Norman history and has detailed maps for hikers; Monsieur is a jovial ex-teacher. Bask in it all. *Gîte space for 6 people.*

rooms	2: 1 double, 1 suite for 3, both with shower & wc.
price	€55-€60 for two; suite €80 for three.
dinner	Auberge walking distance.
closed	Rarely.
directions	From Cherbourg D901 to Barfleur; D1 for St Vaast. After end of Barfleur sign, 2nd right, 1st left.

Mme Claudette Gabroy
Le Manoir,
50760 Montfarville, Manche
tel (0)2 33 23 14 21

map: 4 entry: 231

One of our very best. Your blithe, beautiful, energetic hostess is a delight. Her shyly chatty ex-farmer husband now breeds racehorses while she indulges her passion for interior decoration: her impeccable rooms are a festival of colours, textures, antiques, embroidered linen. It's a heart-warming experience to stay in this wonderful old building where they love having guests; the great granite hearth is always lit for the delicious breakfast which includes local specialities on elegant china; there is a richly-carved 'throne' at the head of the long table. A stupendous place, very special people. *Gîte space for 10 people.*

rooms	3: 2 doubles, all with shower & wc; 1 twin with bath & wc; children's room available.
price	€55-€67 for two.
dinner	Good choice of restaurants in Barfleur, 3km.
closed	Rarely.
directions	From Cherbourg D901; after Tocqueville right, D10; 1st left.

Marie-France & Maurice Caillet
La Fèvrerie,
50760 Ste Geneviève, Manche
tel (0)2 33 54 33 53
fax (0)2 33 22 12 50

NORMANDY

Standing on the Normandy coastal hiking path, the old stone manor looks proudly across the town and out to sea. It is spotless, not over-modernised and furnished in pure French formal style – all velvet, floral linen and marble-topped chests. Retired from farming, the sociable Guérards welcome guests with French courtesy and happily point them towards the cliff walks, the nearby blue-green granite Château of Ravalet and other hidden sights. You are in quiet country, just six kilometres from the ferries and the separate room with its own outside entrance is ideal for early ferry-catchers. *Gîte space for 7 people.*

rooms	3: 1 double, 1 twin, both with bath & wc; outside stairs to 1 triple with shower & wc.
price	€42-€47 for two.
dinner	Restaurants 3km.
closed	Rarely.
directions	From Cherbourg D901 to Tourlaville & for St Pierre Église. Right at lights for Chât. Ravalet/Ham. St Jean; up hill to 'Centre Aéré', follow Ch. d'Hôtes signs (3km from lights).

Mme Guérard
Manoir Saint Jean,
50110 Tourlaville, Manche
tel (0)2 33 22 00 86

Old-fashioned hospitality in a modern house. You are just a mile from the (often) glittering sea and Michel, who makes submarines, is happy to share his passion for sailing and might even take you coast-hopping. His shipbuilding skill is evident here: the attic space has been cleverly used to make two snug rooms with showers and kitchenettes for evening meals; the landing makes a pleasant sitting area. A brilliantly quiet position, simple décor, spotless rooms and an open, chatty hostess who will rise early for dawn ferry-catchers make it ideal for beach holidays and channel crossing alike. *Gîte space for 5-6 people.*

rooms	2 doubles, both with shower & wc.
price	€37 for two.
dinner	Two restaurants within 2km; self-catering.
closed	Rarely.
directions	From Cherbourg D901 then D45 W 13km to Urville Nacqueville; 1st left by Hôtel Le Beau Rivage; up hill D22 for 2km; 2nd left; sign.

Michel & Éliane Thomas
Eudal de Bas,
50460 Urville Nacqueville, Manche

tel	(0)2 33 03 58 16
fax	(0)2 33 03 58 16
e-mail	thomas.eudal@wanadoo.fr
web	www.chez.com/lahague/hebergem/hote/urville1.htm

map: 4 entry: 234

NORMANDY

This engagingly ugly, ramshackle, even dilapidated château houses a delightful couple, their family and all the guests (33 when the gîtes are full) who come to share the vastly relaxed – some would find over-casual – atmosphere. There is a big garden to explore and variegated rooms with old-fashioned bathing spaces. Cavernous *Mussolini* has the balcony with views across the heart-shaped lawn; *Colonial* has pith-helmets and mementos. The Berridges do energetic themed weekends and there's a great value dinner deal for guests at the local bar. A special place but definitely not for the posh-seeker. *Gîte space for 20 people.*

rooms	5: 2 doubles, 1 twin, all with bath & wc (1 screened off); 1 quadruple, 1 triple sharing a bathroom.
price	€40-€50 for two.
dinner	Simple restaurant 2km.
closed	January-February & August.
directions	From Cherbourg N13 for Valognes 12km; right D119 for Ruffosses; cross motorway bridge; follow blue & white signs, 2km.

Mark & Fiona Berridge
Château Mont Épinguet,
50700 Brix, Manche

tel	(0)2 33 41 96 31
fax	(0)2 33 41 98 77
e-mail	epinguet@aol.com

map: 4 entry: 235

The amazingly wonderful granite château with fairy-tale towers, crinkly walls and perfect outbuildings round the courtyard has spanned the centuries as wild breakers crashed on the endless beach 1km away. No wonder its owners worship it! Hosts and furnishings are irreproachably French and civilised – books, fine china, panelling, gilt mirrors, plush chairs, engravings. Your suite has ancient floor tiles, new bedding, a loo in a tower. Stay a while, make your own breakfast with home-made jam and fresh eggs and you may use the grand dining room, and get to know your literary *châtelaine. Gîte space for 8 people.*

rooms	1 suite for 2-4 with shower & wc.
price	€76 for two; €115 for four.
dinner	Restaurants 2-3km.
closed	Rarely.
directions	From Cherbourg D904 for Coutances; 3km after Les Pieux, right D62 to Le Rozel; right D117 into village; house just beyond village; signs.

Josiane & Jean-Claude Grandchamp
Le Château,
50340 Le Rozel, Manche
tel (0)2 33 52 95 08
fax (0)2 33 52 95 08

NORMANDY

A laughing, talkative couple with taste and manners, your hosts give you "the best of France, the best of England" in their fabulous old Norman house: antiques from both countries and English china inside, wild French hares, kestrels and owls outside. The twin is smallish, the studio room under the eaves is big and full of light, both have deep comfort, good bathrooms, soft towels. Seductive dining, sitting and reading rooms, too. Linda varies her menus, napkin colours and china; Ted, an expert on the Second World War, will take you round the landing beaches. They create a tremendous atmosphere of friendship and goodwill.

rooms	3: 2 doubles, both with bath & wc; 1 twin with shower & wc.
price	€54-€62 for two.
dinner	€19, with wine; picnics by arrangement.
closed	Rarely.
directions	From Cherbourg S for Caen; D900 to Bricquebec via Le Pont; cont. for Valognes, past Intermarché, left at T-junc., left after 'Sapeurs Pompiers' for Les Grosmonts; on right after 400m.

Ted & Linda Malindine
La Lande,
Les Grosmonts,
50260 Bricquebec, Manche
tel (0)2 33 52 24 78
fax (0)2 33 52 24 78
e-mail la.lande@wanadoo.fr

Madame is the same honest, open character as ever and Monsieur, now retired, has time to spread his modest farmer's joviality. Two of our favourite owners, they have carefully restored an old *longère* on the edge of this pretty little fishing town – spanking new lime-washed walls, bedding and floral prints. Your side of the house has its own entrance, dayroom with vast old fireplace, good furniture and little kitchen. Old beams and family photographs flourish – all over. The two rooms up the steepish outside stairs are small but welcoming, the ground-floor room is larger – and these people are remarkable hosts.

rooms	3: 1 twin, 1 double, 1 triple, all with shower & wc.
price	€40 for two; €48 for three.
dinner	Choice of restaurants 500m; self-catering possible.
closed	Rarely.
directions	From St Sauveur le Vicomte D15 to Portbail; right just before church Rue R. Asselin; over old railway; house 250m on right.

Bernadette Vasselin
La Roque de Gouey,
Rue Gilles Poërier,
50580 Portbail, Manche
tel (0)2 33 04 80 27

map: 4 entry: 238

NORMANDY

The simple, authentic charm of the Clays' welcome is in quiet harmony with the soft marshes of the Regional Park where their *Gîte Panda* provides full information on the wildlife here and an excellent circular walk runs from the house. In the well-converted farmhouse you climb the handsome stone stairs to big, beamed or raftered, beautifully furnished, peaceful rooms (even 7am church bells are in keeping). The Clays put everyone at their ease, share their television, serve great breakfasts (home-made jams, own eggs), make their own cider. And children love the goats, ducks and rabbits. *Gîte space for 12 people.*

rooms	2 doubles, both with bath or shower & wc.
price	€38 for two.
dinner	Restaurants 5-15km.
closed	Rarely.
directions	From La Haye du Puits, D903 for Barneville Carteret. At Bolleville, right on D127 to St Nicolas; left before church; house on right after cemetery.

Richard & Jay Clay
La Ferme de l'Église,
50250 St Nicolas de Pierrepont,
Manche
tel (0)2 33 45 53 40
fax (0)2 33 45 53 40
e-mail theclays@wanadoo.fr
web perso.wanadoo.fr/normandie-cottages-bed-and-breakfast

map: 4 entry: 239

Up a twisty stone staircase, along a creaky corridor, is one of the finest B&B suites we know: canopies, carved fireplaces, a boudoir, rugs, prints and antiques, a claw-footed bath, and windows onto lush gardens with ancient trees. A stately 16th-century manor where the vast panelled dining room fills with light, the tiled, be-rugged guest sitting room is grand yet welcoming and your hosts are lively, cultured and fun. Belgian Yves is a busy and dynamic young retired businessman and English Lynne offers wonderful aromatherapy sessions and has created splendours in the gardens and by the two lakes.

rooms	2: 1 apartment with 1 double, 1 twin (+ child's bed), bath & wc.
price	€76-€109 for two.
dinner	Restaurants 6-15km.
closed	December-February.
directions	From Carentan D903 for La Haye du Puits; at Baupte (5km) right D69 to Appeville & on for Houtteville; 2nd lane on right; house on left.

Yves Lejour & Lynne Wooster
Le Manoir d'Ozeville,
Appeville,
50500 Carentan, Manche
tel (0)2 33 71 55 98
fax (0)2 33 42 17 79
e-mail ozeville@aol.com

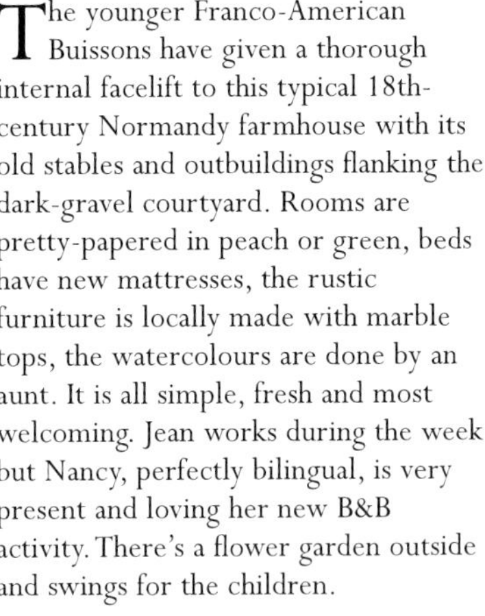

The younger Franco-American Buissons have given a thorough internal facelift to this typical 18th-century Normandy farmhouse with its old stables and outbuildings flanking the dark-gravel courtyard. Rooms are pretty-papered in peach or green, beds have new mattresses, the rustic furniture is locally made with marble tops, the watercolours are done by an aunt. It is all simple, fresh and most welcoming. Jean works during the week but Nancy, perfectly bilingual, is very present and loving her new B&B activity. There's a flower garden outside and swings for the children.

rooms	2 doubles, both with bath & wc.
price	€34 for two.
dinner	Restaurants in St Lô 5km.
closed	Rarely.
directions	From Cherbourg, N13 & N174 to St Lô. At St Georges-Montcocq, D191 to Villiers Fossard. In village, right on C7; house is 800m on right.

Jean & Nancy Buisson
Le Suppey,
50680 Villiers Fossard, Manche
tel (0)2 33 57 30 23
e-mail nancy.buisson@wanadoo.fr

The totally French farmhouse is colourful, neat and immaculate; one room is pink-flavoured, the other blue, with bits of crochet, a Norman wardrobe or a brass bed and a clean, compact shower room each; the gloriously ostentatious blue bathroom is also yours for the asking – giant tub and plants rampaging. But most special of all is the charming, elegant Madame Lepoittevin – she's full of smiles and laughter, has an abundant collection of dolls and she and her husband rejoice in *la convivialité* of B&B. You can picnic in the garden or cook your own on the barbecue.

rooms	2: 1 double with shower & separate wc; 1 double with shower & wc.
price	€38 for two.
dinner	Choice of restaurants 4-10km.
closed	1st two weeks of March.
directions	From St Lô D972 for Coutances, through St Gilles; house sign on left, 4km after St Gilles, on D972.

Jean & Micheline Lepoittevin
Saint Léger,
50570 Quibou, Manche
tel (0)2 33 57 18 41
fax (0)2 33 57 18 41

map: 4 entry: 242

NORMANDY

The place is so French: rich carpeting on floors and walls, highly floral linen, masses of toiletries. Monsieur breeds horses and riding is possible for very experienced riders; the less horsey can enjoy visiting the stables which have produced some great show jumpers. Madame cooks all the food, including her own bread and croissants, and meals are served in the brownly-beamed kitchen/diner. She and her husband are attentive hosts, it is all snug and homey (one room up steep wooden stairs), the setting is charming, among hills, woods and fields. It's a delightful place for a winter visit, too. *Gîte space for 6 people.*

rooms	3: 1 double, 2 twins, all with shower & wc.
price	€32 for two.
dinner	€16 with wine, by arrangement.
closed	Rarely.
directions	From Coutances D971 for Granville; fork quickly left D7 for Gavray for 1.5km; left D27 to Nicorps; through village; 1st right; house on left, signposted.

M & Mme Posloux
Les Hauts Champs,
La Moinerie de Haut,
50200 Nicorps, Manche
tel (0)2 33 45 30 56
fax (0)2 33 07 60 21

map: 4 entry: 243

Here is old-style, down-to-earth, French country hospitality. Madame, an elderly live wire, full of smiles, humorous chat and spontaneous welcome, plays the organ in the village church. Monsieur, a retired farmer, is quietly interested. Their bedrooms have old family furniture (admire *grand-mère's* elaborately crocheted bedcover), really good mattresses, simple washing arrangements. It is all spotless and guests have a biggish, colourful dayroom with massive beams, lots of plants and a kitchen in the old cider press – the great stone is now a flower feature outside.

rooms	3: 1 double with shower & wc; 1 twin, 1 double, both with shower, sharing 2 wcs.
price	€38.50 for two.
dinner	Restaurant 1km; choice St Lô 4km; self-catering possible.
closed	Rarely.
directions	From St Lô D999 for Villedieu 3km; right D38 for Canisy. House 1km along on right.

Marie-Thérèse & Roger Osmond
La Rhétorerie,
Route de Canisy,
50750 St Ébremond de Bonfossé,
Manche
tel (0)2 33 56 62 98

NORMANDY

Deep in the Norman lushness, this ancient farmhouse, originally a sentinel post to the Torigny château, sheltered pilgrims on their journey to Santiago de Compostela. Today's travellers can also rest their weary bones at L'Orgerie – it is superbly welcoming. The dogs greet you as you sip your *pommeau* aperitif and share intelligent conversation with delightful hosts, then dinner is taken in the towering dining room with its gallery and massive granite fireplace. The house is invitingly dark and cosy with age, the bedrooms are snug and few will mind the loo being down the corridor. Amazing value.

rooms	1 family suite: 1 double, 1 twin, sharing shower & separate wc.
price	€30 for two.
dinner	€12 with wine, by arrangement.
closed	Rarely.
directions	From Caen N175 SW for Rennes & Villedieu. At Pont Farcy left on D52 for Vire 3km; house signposted on right (DON'T turn to St Vigor).

Jacques & Jacqueline Goude
L'Orgerie,
50420 St Vigor des Monts, Manche
tel (0)2 31 68 85 58

Madame's pride and joy is her garden, bursting with flowers and light as she is bursting to tell you all about gardening and medicinal plants – while you spy on the squirrels in the lime tree and indulge in a sinfully-laden breakfast table (dare ask for the *kousmine*, a muesli-type concoction to keep you energised all day). Three rooms are in a converted outbuilding, two in the enchanting main house. Beds are brass or carved wood; there are lace and pink and granny-style touches in keeping with an old farmhouse, plus some fine furniture. *Gîte space for 2 people.*

rooms	4: 2 doubles, 1 twin, 1 family room, all with shower & wc.
price	€40-€45 for two.
dinner	Restaurant in village, 1.5km.
closed	1 week in January & September.
directions	From A84 exit 38 to Percy; D58 for Hambye; immed left D98 for Sourdeval, 1.5km. Signposted on right.

Daniel & Maryclaude Duchemin
Le Cottage de la Voisinière,
Route de Sourdeval,
50410 Percy, Manche
tel (0)2 33 61 18 47
fax (0)2 33 61 43 47
e-mail cottage.voisiniere@wanadoo.fr
web perso.wanadoo.fr/cottagedelavoisiniere

NORMANDY

These solid, earthy, farming folk are deeply part of rural France. Monsieur was born in this 200-year-old house; Madame, who is a bit shy, has a lovely sunny smile. She keeps lots of poultry and always encourages guests to visit Sourdeval on Tuesdays to see the cattle market in full swing. Their rooms are unpretentiously simple with candlewick bedcovers, old floor tiles, wooden wardrobes and views of the farmyard or the valley. The family room has a mezzanine for children and a modern bathroom. Guests breakfast at one long table and are welcome to watch the milking. Real people, real value. *Gîte space for 2 people.*

rooms	2 + cottage: Main house: 1 triple, 1 double sharing shower & separate wc. Cottage: family room for 5, shower & wc.
price	€30 for two.
dinner	Choice of restaurants 5km.
closed	Rarely.
directions	From Sourdeval D977 for Vire 6km. Just before 'end of Manche' sign right for Le Val. 2km on right.

Jeanne & Raymond Desdoits
Le Val,
Vengeons,
50150 Sourdeval, Manche
tel (0)2 33 59 64 16
fax (0)2 33 69 36 99

There is space and grandeur in this mixed-period château and Madame and her Dutch partner have bravely taken up the colour challenge: the red and cream sitting room is vast, bedrooms have big colourful paintings and strong plain walls alongside old wooden floors and fireplaces – it's almost minimalist yet great fun and the views sail out of those great windows across copses and woods for miles. Your hostess, a strong, easy-going, independent woman with a fine sense of humour, adores meeting new people and hearing about their lives, her four teenagers are a delight and her meals delicious.

rooms 3 doubles, all with bath or shower & wc.
price €50-€60 for two.
dinner €15, wine €10.
closed Christmas & New Year.
directions From Villedieu les P. N175 /D524 for Vire 1.5km; right D999 for Brécey. After Chérencé le H. left through St Martin B. to sawmill; follow signs to Loges sur Brécey; house 2km, 2nd left after wood.

Nathalie de Drouas
Château des Boulais,
Loges sur Brécey,
50800 St Martin le Bouillant,
Manche
tel (0)2 33 60 32 20
fax (0)2 33 60 45 20

NORMANDY

Generous, artistic and young in spirit, the Champagnacs are a privilege to meet. Their 18th-century *longère* bathes in a floral wonderland: roses climb and tumble, narrow paths meander and a kitchen garden grows your breakfast – wander and revel or settle down in a shady spot. Inside, bedrooms are cosy with handsome antiques, pretty bed linen and polished floors or modern with pale wood and bucolic views. The honey-coloured breakfast room is all timber and exposed stone – pots of home-made jam roost between the beams. *Gîte space for 4.*

rooms 2 + 1 apartment: 2 doubles, both with shower & wc; 1 apartment with 1 double & 1 twin sharing bathroom & wc.
price €78-€120 for two.
dinner Good restaurants 5-25km.
closed November-March.
directions From Avranches D973 for Granville & Sartilly; left at end of village D61 for Carolles; 800m house on left.

Édith Champagnac
La Haute Gilberdière,
50530 Sartilly, Manche
tel (0)2 33 60 17 44
e-mail champagnac@libertysurf.fr
web www.champagnac-farmhouse.com

They say there are as many horses as inhabitants in the area: your hosts train racehorses and are also bringing up five children in this deep country spot by the sea – Mont St Michel can be seen from the roof windows. They are energetic and sociable, have lots of time for guests and really enjoy doing B&B. Your rooms and bathrooms are refreshingly minimalist in their white paint and duvets with simple country or wicker furniture. In the morning, you go through a huge, immaculate kitchen to the simply furnished yellow and blue dining room for a very generous breakfast. *Gîte space for 3 people.*

rooms	2: 1 double, 1 twin, both with bath & wc.
price	€55 for two.
dinner	Restaurants 3km.
closed	Rarely.
directions	From A13/N176 exit Avranches for Granville; over bridge; left D911 for Jullouville; in Dragey right before petrol station 1km; left for Dragey l'Église; house 800m on left.

Florence & Olivier Brasme
Belleville,
Route de Saint Marc,
Dragey l'Église,
50530 Sartilly, Manche

tel	(0)2 33 48 93 96
fax	(0)2 33 48 59 75
e-mail	belleville@mt-st-michel.net
web	www.mt-st-michel.net

map: 4 entry: 250

The extension to the lovely old stone farmhouse, with great windows to luscious views of garden and lake, is for guests on rainy days but the generous continental farmhouse breakfast is served by your bright, chatty hostess at a long table in the inviting, country-furnished living room where obscure farm antiquities parade. Good, fresh and simple bedrooms, three with that lovely view. Your hard-working hosts – dairy herd and show jumpers – are good company and, although there may be 60 cows in the cowshed, six horses in the paddock and a motorway over the hill, you could hear a kitten dance, the peace is so complete.

rooms	4: 2 doubles, 1 triple, 1 family room, all with shower & wc.
price	€39-€42 for two; €59 for four.
dinner	Ferme-auberge 3km.
closed	Rarely.
directions	From A84 or N175 exit 34 for Mt St Michel 800m; left D998 for Juilley 4.2km; D566 for Ferme du Grand Rouet; signs.

Christian & Isabelle Fardin
Le Grand Rouet,
50220 Juilley, Manche

tel	(0)2 33 60 65 25
fax	(0)2 33 60 02 70
e-mail	c.fardin@wanadoo.fr
web	perso.wanadoo.fr/christian.fardin

map: 4 entry: 251

Monsieur, a joyous fellow, formerly a senior fire officer, is proud of his restoration of the old farm (the B&B is his project, Madame works in town). He is an attentive, positive host, full of smiles and jokes. And has done a good job. Old granite glints as you pass the softly-curtained entrance to the duplex where the whirlpool bath is reached via a staircase banistered with oak manger rails; the airy triple has antique beds and brightly-coloured curtains; the white breakfast room with its welcoming granite fireplace is simple and good and the fields around are open to all so no need to worry about the road at the front.

rooms	3: 1 family room, 1 suite, both with shower & wc; 1 triple with bath & wc.
price	€58 for two.
dinner	Restaurants in St James, 6km.
closed	Rarely.
directions	From A84 exit 33; right at r'bout & uphill for about 300m to next r'bout; left then left again D998 for St James; house on right after 5km.

Laurence & Jean-Malo Tizon
Les Blotteries,
50220 Juilley, Manche
tel (0)2 33 60 84 95
fax (0)2 33 60 84 95
e-mail bb@les-blotteries.com
web www.les-blotteries.com

NORMANDY

Madame is smiling and eager to please, not too reserved, not gushing – the sweetest old lady. Hers is a typical, 19th-century village house. Pleasant, country-style bedrooms have floral wallpapers and mats on polished wood floors. There's an inviting, armchaired reading corner on the landing plus a big dayroom with a fireplace. Breakfast is served here at the long 10-seater table. There are (free) tennis courts, a swimming pool and restaurants close at hand and the proximity to Mont Saint Michel is a natural advantage. (When calling, better to have a French speaker to hand.)

rooms	3: 1 double, 1 triple, sharing bath & wc; 1 twin with private shower & wc.
price	€32-€35 for two.
dinner	Gourmet auberge next door.
closed	Rarely.
directions	From Avranches N175 for Pontorson; 3km after Précey, right to Servon.

Mme Marie-Thérése Lesénéchal
Le Bourg,
6 rue du Pont Morin,
50170 Servon, Manche
tel (0)2 33 48 92 13
fax (0)2 33 58 69 52

Three big rooms and a dayroom – at the other end of the farmhouse from two others – face Mont St Michel! And that view is definitely worth the detour; you can walk to the Mount in two hours, or cycle in under one – borrow the bikes. The Gédouins keep cows and pigs; Annick, who used to teach, makes delicious jams; Jean is Mayor – the council meets in his kitchen. Rooms are in pastel, country-floral style and one now has wheelchair access. In the courtyard are passion fruit and figs. All is rural peace in this tiny village by the marshes and there is a warm and kindly welcome from both generations of Gédouins.

rooms	5: 1 double, 1 twin, both with bath & wc; 1 triple, 2 family rooms, all with shower & wc.
price	€35-€44 for two.
dinner	Restaurants 500m-2km.
closed	Rarely.
directions	From A84 exit 33 for St Malo & Pontorson on N175 for 9km; right to Servon; at church right for 500m; farm on left.

Annick, Jean & Valérie Gédouin
Le Petit Manoir,
21 rue de la Pierre du Tertre,
50170 Servon, Manche
tel (0)2 33 60 03 44
fax (0)2 33 60 17 79

map: 4 entry: 254

NORMANDY

Masses of flowers sweeten the air but this is definitely a working farm with 800 pigs and a high-tech milking shed that attracts interest from far and wide; you can watch too. The young owners enjoy contact with visitors and Madame pays special attention to breakfast – her apple tart is delicious. Then you can walk directly out into the lovely countryside to see the little chapel or the local château. The guest rooms, one in the house, the other with its own entrance, are simple and good. This place is as real, unpretentious and comfortable as ever. *Gîte space for 14 people.*

rooms	2 doubles, both with shower & wc.
price	€30 for two.
dinner	Good choice of restaurants 5km.
closed	Rarely.
directions	From Pontorson, N175 to Aucey la Plaine; follow signs to Chambres d'Hôtes La Provostière for 3km. Between Pontorson & Vessey.

Maryvonne & René Feuvrier
La Provostière,
50170 Aucey la Plaine, Manche
tel (0)2 33 60 33 67
fax (0)2 33 60 37 00

map: 4 entry: 255

The old granite stable block, built in 1622, was modernised in the 1970s: polished floors and easy furnishings, cots in the attic rooms and a kitchenette – ideal for families. It is all clean and comfortable, in solid farmhouse style, and guests may use the beamy, antique-furnished sitting room. The *Balcon* room is in a league of its own with exposed timbers and… a (glassed-in) balcony. Madame is quietly friendly, "makes a superb soufflé" and mouthwatering Norman cuisine – she loves it. The poetically-named but perfectly ordinary Two Estuaries motorway now provides quick access 1km away. *Gîte space for 6 people.*

rooms	4: 1 double, 1 twin, 1 triple, 1 quadruple, all with bath or shower & wc.
price	€38 for two.
dinner	€14 with wine, by arrangement.
closed	Rarely.
directions	From A84 exit 32 at St James then D12, following signs for Super U store for Antrain, 900m. On right.

François & Catherine Tiffaine
La Gautrais,
50240 St James, Manche
tel (0)2 33 48 31 86
fax (0)2 33 48 58 17

map: 4 entry: 256

NORMANDY

An authentic farm B&B in a glorious setting. Ivy on walls, beamed attic bedrooms with fresh flowers, woodland walks, lake and château across the way – and an authentic farming family. Jean-Paul and Brigitte are a friendly, interesting couple, travel a lot and talk well. He is a dairy farmer and arbitrator, she is on the council. Meals (they are absolutely delicious) are taken in the lovely dining room with its huge fireplace. A splendid staircase leads you up to the good, snug, cottagey yet unfussy guest rooms. Children love it too – there are games galore and it is a working farm.

rooms	4: 2 doubles, 2 family rooms, all with bath or shower & wc.
price	€40-€42 for two.
dinner	€15 with wine, by arrangement.
closed	Rarely.
directions	From Cherbourg A84 exit 34 for Mt St Michel & St Malo 600m; exit for Mt St Michel & Rennes D43 for Rennes. At r'bout D40 for Rennes, 5.5km; D308 left; signs.

Jean-Paul & Brigitte Gavard
La Ferme de l'Étang,
Boucéel, Vergoncey,
50240 St James, Manche
tel (0)2 33 48 34 68
fax (0)2 33 48 48 53
e-mail jpgavard@club-internet.fr

map: 4 entry: 257

What a treat to stay in this gently grand, gracious château where the Count's family have lived since it was built in 1763. He and the Countess have lived in Paris and Chicago – theirs is an elegant, unstuffy lifestyle in which you are welcome to join. Bedrooms are beautifully furnished and decorated with personal touches, family portraits and embroidered linen sheets. Breakfast, including home-made jams and tarts served on fine china, is taken in the lovely, round, panelled and mirrored dining room. Its French windows give onto the grounds which come complete with lake and private chapel. *Spanish spoken. Gîte space for 6 people.*

rooms	4: 2 doubles, 2 suites, all with bath & shower & wc.
price	€115-€140 for two.
dinner	Restaurants 7-15km.
closed	Rarely.
directions	From Avranches for Mont St Michel exit 34; N175 exit D40 St Michel/Antrain; left for Antrain; left D308 for St Senier de Beuvron: château entrance 800m.

Régis & Nicole de Roquefeuil-Cahuzac
Château de Boucéel,
50240 Vergoncey, Manche

tel	(0)2 33 48 34 61
fax	(0)2 33 48 16 26
e-mail	chateaudebouceel@wanadoo.fr
web	www.chateaudebouceel.com

BOOKING AND CANCELLING

DINNER

Do remember that table d'hôtes is a fixed-price set menu that has to be booked. Very few owners offer dinner every day. Once you have booked dinner, it is a question of common courtesy to turn up and partake of the meal prepared for you. Dining in can be a wonderful opportunity to experience both food and company in an authentic French family atmosphere. Or it may be more formal and still utterly French. Some owners no longer eat with their guests for reasons of diet and waistline.

ROOMS

We have heard of chambres d'hôtes hopefuls arriving unannounced at 7pm and being devastated to learn that the house was full. For your own sake and your hosts', do ring ahead: if they can't have you, owners can usually suggest other places nearby. But arriving without warning at the end of the day is asking for disappointment.

CANCELLING

As soon as you realise you are not going to take up a booking, even late in the day, please telephone immediately. The owners may still be able to let the room for that night and at least won't stay up wondering whether you've had an accident and when they can give up and go to bed.

By the same token, if you find you're going to arrive later than planned, let your hosts know so that they won't worry unnecessrily or… let your room to someone else.

Watercolourist and photographer, the brave, artistic Ruans have launched with passionate enthusiasm into renovating a small château with its ruined chapel, stables and thrilling atmosphere. Their sense of space and colour will triumph. The original staircase curves up to the 'literary' guest rooms: mauve/silver *Proust*, ochre/gold *George Sand*, theatrical suite *Victor & Juliette*; each shower is behind a great rafter; the vastly magnificent drawing/billiard room wears rich reds – it's all brilliant, and great fun. Your gentle hosts love cooking – then sharing dinner and stimulating talk with you.

BRITTANY

rooms	3: 1 twin, 2 family suites for 4, all with bath/shower & wc.
price	€50-€55 for two.
dinner	€21 with wine, by arrangement.
closed	Rarely.
directions	From Rennes N12 west to Bédée 23km; D72 to Montfort sur Meu; D125 for St Méen le Grand; château 4km on left.

The sea! The rocks! Fear not fisherfolk – if the lighthouse cannot save you from wrecking on the reefs, the carved calvaries on shore will send up prayers for your water-logged souls.

Catherine & Luc Ruan
Le Château du Pin,
35370 Iffendic près de Montfort,
Ille-et-Vilaine

tel	(0)2 99 09 34 05
fax	(0)2 99 09 34 05
e-mail	luc.ruan@wanadoo.fr

A place for real intimacy: dinner by the fire in your own room – and breakfast next morning, too. Each room has its own mini-garden with potted shrubs and front door, that private meals service and relatively little contact. So, although they are a caring but busy couple, the atmosphere is not particularly *familiale*. However, Madame's passion for *brocante* and embroidery brings much individuality to the bedrooms and in her mini-boutique you can sit and read on an antique chair, then buy it as you leave. It is in a tiny hamlet and very peaceful.

rooms	3: 1 suite for 5, 1 triple, both with shower & wc. Cottage also available.
price	€50-€55 for two; lovers' night (dinner, champagne & wine) €125.
dinner	€16 with wine, by arrangement.
closed	Rarely.
directions	From Rennes D163/D41 S to Janzé; right D92 for La Couyère about 6km; house on right in La Tremblais: yellow gate & sign. Park behind.

Claudine & Raymond Gomis
La Raimonderie,
La Tremblais,
35320 La Couyère, Ille-et-Vilaine

tel	(0)2 99 43 14 39
fax	(0)2 99 43 14 39
e-mail	la-raimonderie@wanadoo.fr
web	www.la-raimonderie.com

map: 4 entry: 260

BRITTANY

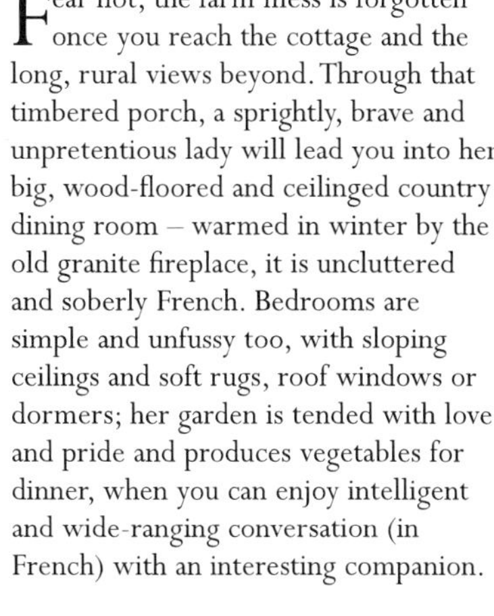

Fear not, the farm mess is forgotten once you reach the cottage and the long, rural views beyond. Through that timbered porch, a sprightly, brave and unpretentious lady will lead you into her big, wood-floored and ceilinged country dining room – warmed in winter by the old granite fireplace, it is uncluttered and soberly French. Bedrooms are simple and unfussy too, with sloping ceilings and soft rugs, roof windows or dormers; her garden is tended with love and pride and produces vegetables for dinner, when you can enjoy intelligent and wide-ranging conversation (in French) with an interesting companion.

rooms	3: 1 triple with shower & wc; 1 double, 1 single sharing continental bath & separate wc.
price	€41 for two; €53 for three.
dinner	€14, wine €9.50.
closed	Rarely.
directions	From Rennes N137 S exit Poligné D47 for Bourg des Comptes for 4km; left to L'Aubrais; right into & across farmyard, down lane 20m, cottage on right.

Yvette Guillopé
Épineu,
35890 Bourg des Comptes,
Ille-et-Vilaine

tel	(0)2 99 52 16 84

map: 4 entry: 261

Here be a genuine welcome and… wizards. Brocéliande Forest, just 500m away, was Merlin's home. His presence is peaceful, the enchantment continues. The suite has two real little round windows and some magic ones in the amazing, soft-coloured murals. Madame's good taste and new ideas in handling her lovely big old manor house give it huge originality; old it is, mainly 1760s with some 15th-century bits, rambling organically round the courtyard. Comfortable but not lavish rooms, beautiful woodwork, fresh juice in the log-warmed breakfast room, a most unusual, interesting companion – one feels at home here.

rooms	3: 2 doubles, 1 suite for 4, all with bath or shower & wc.
price	From €46 for two.
dinner	Choice of restaurants 1-5km.
closed	Rarely.
directions	From Rennes N24 to Plélan le Gr.; right at church D59 for St Malon sur M.; 1st left: Ch. des Châteaux 1km; house on top of small hill, entrance behind on left.

Mme Christine Hermenier
Manoir de la Ruisselée,
35380 Paimpont, Ille-et-Vilaine
tel (0)2 99 06 85 94

map: 4 entry: 262

Two fascinating generations of an ancient Breton family welcome you open-armed to their inimitable house where history, atmosphere and silence rule: private chapel, fishing pond and rare trees outside, monumental oak staircase, Italian mosaic floor, 1900s wallpaper, about 30 rooms inside. Madame Mère sparkles and tells you myriad tales of ancestors (one royalist exile is buried near Waterloo Station); Anne plies you with home-made delights or teaches you wickerwork; Alfred builds organs (there may be piano recitals…). The bathroom has a claw-footed bath and bedrooms are properly old-fashioned. Exceptional.

rooms	3: 2 doubles, 1 triple, all with basin, sharing bathroom & 3 separate wcs. Kitchen available.
price	€40-€50 for two.
dinner	Simple dinner possible. Choice of restaurants 1.5-4km.
closed	Rarely.
directions	From N12 for St Brieuc exit at Bédée D72 to Irodouer; 1st right before church; château entrance 600m on left, signs.

Anne & Alfred du Crest de Lorgerie
Château du Quengo,
35850 Irodouer, Ille-et-Vilaine
tel (0)2 99 39 81 47
fax (0)2 99 39 81 47
e-mail lequengo@hotmail.com

map: 4 entry: 263

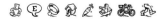

A woman of talent and refined taste, Monique loves people, bakes cakes for breakfast and can guide you round Caradeuc Park or beautiful old Bécherel. She and her husband are warmly natural hosts. On the fine market square, this the oldest house in the 'City of Books', has an elegant living room, a cosy kitchen and long country views. Guest rooms are in the 17th-century weaver's house across the patio: one romantic, in cool blue and warm ochre, has a huge stone fireplace; one feminine and rosy, is pretty pink with pine furniture and garden view; the third has a fascinating antique needlework theme. Delicious.

rooms	2: 1 double/triple, 1 suite for 4, each with bath or shower & wc.
price	€50-€70 for two; €100 for four.
dinner	Crêperie in village, good restaurant 8km.
closed	November-Easter.
directions	From St Malo N137 S for Rennes 43km. At Tinténiac exit, right D20 to Bécherel. House on main square near church.

Monique Lecourtois-Canet
Le Logis de la Filanderie,
3 rue de la Filanderie,
35190 Bécherel, Ille-et-Vilaine
tel (0)2 99 66 73 17
fax (0)2 99 66 79 07
e-mail filanderie@aol.com
web www.filanderie.com

BRITTANY

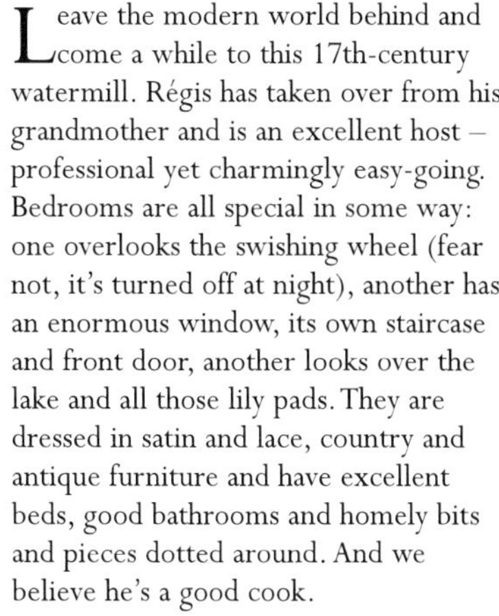

Leave the modern world behind and come a while to this 17th-century watermill. Régis has taken over from his grandmother and is an excellent host – professional yet charmingly easy-going. Bedrooms are all special in some way: one overlooks the swishing wheel (fear not, it's turned off at night), another has an enormous window, its own staircase and front door, another looks over the lake and all those lily pads. They are dressed in satin and lace, country and antique furniture and have excellent beds, good bathrooms and homely bits and pieces dotted around. And we believe he's a good cook.

rooms	4: 2 doubles, 2 triples, all with bath or shower & wc.
price	€60-€63 for two.
dinner	€23 with wine, by arrangement.
closed	Rarely.
directions	From Rennes-St Malo N137, exit St Pierre de Plesguen; D10 for Lanhélin: right for 2.5km; signs.

Régis Maillard
Le Petit Moulin du Rouvre,
35720 St Pierre de Plesguen,
Ille-et-Vilaine
tel (0)2 99 73 85 84
fax (0)2 99 73 71 06
e-mail maillard.regis@aumoulindurouvre.com
web www.aumoulindurouvre.com

The little lakeside house is a dream, in the old bakery, far enough from the main house to feel secluded, snugly romantic and utterly seductive. The new, split-level room in the big house is larger and just as pretty. The whole place is idyllic, bucolic – the beauty of the setting takes you by surprise. You can fish or observe all sorts of water-dwelling folk. If your need for intimacy is deep, then Catherine will deliver breakfast and dinner (course by course, and delicious) to your hideaway. But nicer still to join them at table; they are young and delightful and we have received nothing but praise for them.

rooms	2: 1 double/quadruple in split-level room with *salon*, shower & wc; 1 double/quadruple in cottage with *salon*, shower & wc.
price	€43-€54 for two.
dinner	€16 with wine, by arrangement.
closed	Rarely.
directions	From St Malo N137 to St Pierre de Plesguen; by church D10 for Lanhelin 1.5km; signs on right.

Catherine & François Grosset
Le Pont Ricoul,
35720 St Pierre de Plesguen,
Ille-et-Vilaine

tel	(0)2 99 73 92 65
fax	(0)2 99 73 94 17
e-mail	pontricoul@aol.com
web	www.pontricoul.com

map: 4 entry: 266

BRITTANY

Old bones: the largest mammoth skeleton ever discovered in Europe was found at Mont Dol; old stones: Mont St Michel is so close. But it's Marie-Madeleine who makes this place special: up before breakfast to lay the fire and, in summer, giving her all to garden and orchard. Gentle, bright-eyed Jean says that, tied to the farm, he "travels through his guests". Of course the wear and tear of returning guests shows in some of the linen – so what? Rooms are good, the fireplace huge, your hosts know and love their region intimately and the sea is just 3km away. *Stays of 2 nights or more preferred.*

rooms	3: 1 double, 2 quadruples, all with shower or bath & wc.
price	€40 for two.
dinner	Choice of restaurants in Dol de Bretagne 4km.
closed	Rarely.
directions	From St Malo N137 for Rennes 15km; exit N176 for Mt St Michel 12km. At Dol de Bretagne D80 for St Broládre 3km; left D85 for Cherrueix; house sign on right before 3rd little bridge.

Jean & Marie-Madeleine Glémot
La Hamelinais,
35120 Cherrueix, Ille-et-Vilaine

tel	(0)2 99 48 95 26
fax	(0)2 99 48 89 23

map: 4 entry: 267

House and owner are imbued with the calm of a balmy summer's morning, whatever the weather – timeless simplicity reigns inside, modernity bustles on the village street outside the front door. Isabelle's talent seems to touch the very air that fills her old family house. There is nothing superfluous: simple carved pine furniture, an antique wrought iron cot, dhurries on scrubbed plank floors, palest yellow or mauve walls to reflect the ocean-borne light, harmonious striped or gingham curtains. Starfish and many-splendoured pebbles keep the house sea-connected. The unspoilt seaside village is worth the trip too.

rooms 5: 2 doubles, 1 twin, all with bath & wc; 2 doubles, both with shower & wc.

price €46 for two.

dinner Choice of restaurants in village.

closed Rarely.

directions From St Malo, N137 for Rennes. 6km after St Malo, right on D117 to St Suliac (3km from N137 exit to village entrance). Road leads to Grande Rue down to port; house at top on right.

Isabelle Rouvrais
Les Mouettes,
17 Grande Rue,
35430 St Suliac, Ille-et-Vilaine
tel (0)2 99 58 30 41
fax (0)2 99 58 39 41

BRITTANY

Such a privilege to stay in this amazing, artistic house where the traditional and the esoteric, the antique and the contemporary rub happy shoulders – a deeply aesthetic atmosphere, yet utterly without pretension, as is your hostess. She is warm and talented and has gathered some wonderful wooden artefacts; her husband is a brain scientist and they keep a quietly civilised, cultured house which like-minded guests will revel in. The guest rooms, all different, are beautifully furnished, full of interest and space and have good bathrooms.

rooms 2: 1 double, 1 triple, all with bath, shower & wc.

price €70-€75 for two.

dinner Wide choice of good restaurants nearby.

closed Rarely.

directions From St Malo D155/D76 for Rennes; right at 'Irrigation' building before La Gouesnière; house 2nd on right (black gates).

Mme Marie-Antoinette Duriez
La Haute Barbotais,
35350 St Méloir des Ondes,
Ille-et-Vilaine
tel (0)2 99 89 15 42
e-mail maduriez@wanadoo.fr

Sheer delight for lovers of the utterly personal, even eccentric. In this miniature museum of a house where the stunningly-draped orange dining room leads to an elegant yellow *salon*, the infectiously vibrant Rhona will introduce you to her wiggly Chinese sofa, her husband's regimental drum, an 18th-century looking-glass (one of a remarkable collection) and other cherished household gods. A home like no other, unsurpassed hospitality, a remarkable garden (climb up to the second terrace with a book), a comfortable bed (one has a glass door onto its fine bathroom), a generous and elegant breakfast. Unforgettable.

rooms	2 doubles, both with bath, shower & wc.
price	€54-€60 for two.
dinner	Wide choice of restaurants close by.
closed	Occasionally.
directions	From Dinan central square, Rue de Lehon, through Porte St Louis, follow down, bear left below ramparts, straight across Rue de Coëtquen.

Rhona Lockwood
53/55 rue de Coëtquen,
22100 Dinan, Côtes-d'Armor
tel (0)2 96 85 23 49
fax (0)2 96 87 51 44

BRITTANY

The grand old family house, a 15th-century Breton *longère*, has a cosy, farm atmosphere, utterly delightful owners who are generous with their time and talk, plus a nine-hole golf course and all the trappings (clubhouse, lessons, socialising), carp ponds for those with rods and imaginative decoration. Madame, who paints, has a flair for interiors and uses velvet and florals, plants, paintings, sculptures and photographs – her rooms are appealingly personal and very comfortable. The old Breton bread oven is working again for the baking of bread and the birds cavort in the trees.

rooms	4: 2 doubles, 2 twins, all with bath or shower & wc.
price	€48 for two.
dinner	Restaurant 5km.
closed	Rarely.
directions	From Dinan N176 for St Brieuc; at Plélan le Petit D19 right to St Michel de Plélan; 1km after village, follow golf sign to left.

Odile & Henri Beaupère
La Corbinais,
22980 St Michel de Plélan,
Côtes-d'Armor
tel (0)2 96 27 64 81
fax (0)2 96 27 68 45
e-mail corbinais@corbinais.com
web www.corbinais.com

The everyday becomes remarkable in these people's hands: we seldom consider recent houses but sensitively-designed Malik sailed in. Clad in red cedar, open-plan to provide space for six children, its wood, metal and glass are in perfect harmony, with only the best materials used and every tiny detail taken care of: plain white covers on beds, Eastern-style cushions and wall hangings on plain walls, superb beds and towels, shower pressure just right. Breakfast, beautiful and *un peu brunch*, is as carefully thought out as the house. Lovely people and an exquisite, serene house that seems to hug its garden to its heart.

rooms	2: 1 suite for 2 with *salon*, 1 suite for 4 (2 bedrooms), both with shower & wc.
price	€54 for two.
dinner	Restaurants within walking distance.
closed	December-March.
directions	From Dinan N176 W for St Brieuc for about 12km. Exit right to Plélan le Petit. Follow signs to Centre/ Mairie; at Mairie right for St Maudez then 2nd right.

Martine & Hubert Viannay
Malik,
Chemin de l'Étoupe,
22980 Plélan le Petit,
Côtes-d'Armor

tel	(0)2 96 27 62 71
e-mail	martineviannay@nomade.fr
web	perso.infonie.fr/malikhotes

map: 4 entry: 272

BRITTANY

Here is a long, low Breton house built on hard Breton granite, guarded by a soft Breton spaniel and kept by a relaxed and friendly Breton woman whose family has owned it for generations and who lives in the little house. Old wood is everywhere – ceilings, wardrobes, beams, beds; there are fabrics and fancies: gingham cloths, floral curtains, lace cushions. Breakfasts and evening meals (which must be booked ahead) are cooked on a wood-fired range and served on attractive rough pottery at separate tables in the guests' dining room.

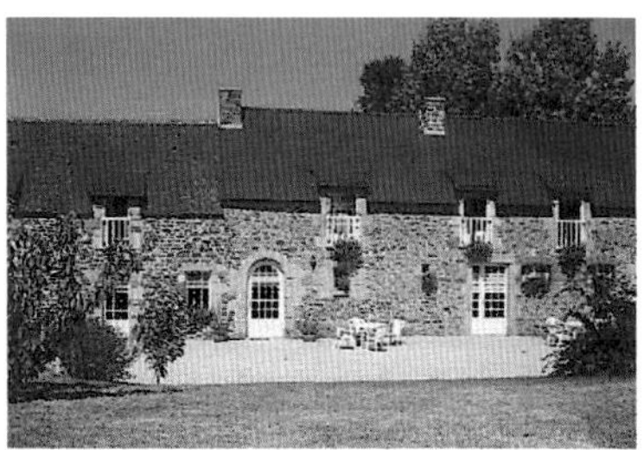

rooms	6: 3 doubles, 1 twin, 1 triple, 1 double & bunks, all with bath or shower & wc.
price	€40-€42 for two.
dinner	€15.50 with wine, by arrangement.
closed	Rarely.
directions	From Dinard, D168 to Ploubalay & D768 to Plancoët; D19 to St Lormel; left opp. school at far end of village; follow signs for 1.5km.

Évelyne Ledé
La Pastourelle,
Saint Lormel,
22130 Plancoët, Côtes-d'Armor

tel	(0)2 96 84 03 77
fax	(0)2 96 84 03 77

map: 4 entry: 273

New to B&B, your shy eager hostess plans to put generous, Breton dishes in your plate and her husband, who works in town, to pour good organic wines (his passion) – they create a welcoming atmosphere in their stone farmhouse. The stylish, very French rooms in the converted stables are enlivened by colourful primitive West Indian paintings and there's yet more colour and garden lushery along the long slow steps through the rockery to the terrace outside your windows. Great bathrooms, a small guest sitting room, real peace in this quiet hamlet just 2km from the coast and a stone's throw from Mont St Michel.

rooms	3 + 1 apartment: 2 doubles, 1 twin, 1 apartment for 4-5, all with bath/shower & wc.
price	€55 for two.
dinner	€20, with wine; good restaurants 4km.
closed	January.
directions	From St Malo D168 for St Brieuc. At 1st r'bout after Ploubalay D26 for Plessix Balisson for 4km to hamlet; house on right, signposted.

	Brigitte & Patrick Noël
	Le Clos Saint Cadreuc,
	22650 Ploubalay, Côtes-d'Armor
tel	(0)2 96 27 32 43
fax	(0)2 96 27 32 43
e-mail	clos-saint-cadreuc@wanadoo.fr

BRITTANY

A working dairy farm, a big traditional dining room, Breton pancakes for breakfast. As well as tending her immaculate garden and her contented guests, Madame does the milking. West-facing, sun-flooded bedrooms have carved mirror-fronted wardrobes, country colours, firm, comfortable beds, polished wood floors and modern bathrooms. There's also a super kitchen annexe for self-catering, climbing frames for children in the front field and bikes. You will feel well looked after in this quiet country place with direct, genuine farming folk – it's excellent value.
Gîte space for 26 people.

rooms	3: 2 doubles, 1 triple, all with bath or shower & wc.
price	€37 for two.
dinner	Choice of restaurants in Yffiniac 4km; self-catering possible.
closed	Rarely.
directions	From N12 exit La Baie (N01 Yffiniac Gare) into village. Go 1km; left for Plédran, through La Croix Orin; house down hill on left, 3.5km from Yffiniac centre.

	Marie-Reine & Fernand Loquin
	Le Grenier,
	22120 Yffiniac, Côtes-d'Armor
tel	(0)2 96 72 64 55
fax	(0)2 96 72 68 74
e-mail	le.grenier@wanadoo.fr
web	www.le.grenier.com

Exceptional: an old château, built in 1373 by the Viscount's ancestor, the sea at the bottom of the drive, vastly wonderful bedrooms, a lively, lovable couple of aristocratic hosts bent on riding, hunting and entertaining you – do come on horseback. Breakfast is in your room or in the dining room with the family silver and antiques. Madame is using her energy and taste to renovating some of the 30 rooms. One suite is pink, another blue and yellow. Beds are draped, windows tall, portraits ancestral, rugs cotton, chapel 18th century, roses myriad – atmosphere unreal yet utterly alive. *Gîte space for 4 people.*

rooms	3: 2 suites, 1 double, all with bath or shower & wc.
price	€80-€125 for two.
dinner	Good choice of restaurants 5km.
closed	October-Easter.
directions	From St Brieuc N12 for Lamballe, exit Yffigniac-Hillion; left D80 to Hillion; D34 for Morieux, 200m to roadside cross on left by château gates.

Vicomtesse Louis du Fou de Kerdaniel
Château de Bonabry,
22120 Hillion, Côtes-d'Armor
tel (0)2 96 32 21 06
fax (0)2 96 32 21 06

BRITTANY

An art teacher in her other life, Julie takes people out painting while Jez, who once ran a vegetarian restaurant, does cook-ins where guests learn what to do with finds from the local markets. Have breakfast sitting on a slab of granite in the courtyard of this traditional Breton cottage just listening to the birds going about their business or planning an expedition. What are these *allées couvertes* you are directed to follow? Ancient burial chambers. There are also standing stones, badgers and wild boar on the moors behind. Civilisation is a short drive away but you'd never need to know it. *Gîte space for 15 people.*

rooms	1 double with shower & wc.
price	€43 for two.
dinner	€15 with wine, by arrangement.
closed	Rarely.
directions	From N164 D44 for Gorges du Daoulas; left at junction for Allées Couvertes; past lay-by on right; Toul Bleïz next track on right.

Julie & Jez Rooke
Toul Bleïz,
22570 Laniscat, Côtes-d'Armor
tel (0)2 96 36 98 34
e-mail jezrooke@hotmail.com
web www.phoneinsick.co.uk

A very special place, aristocratic Kermezen has been in the family for 600 years and feels as if it will stand for ever in its granite certainty. Its 17th-19th-century 'modernisation' is a masterpiece of understated elegance: high ceilings, generous windows, a granite-hearthed, tapestried guest sitting room where old books and family portraits remind you this is "just an ordinary family house". Madame, dynamic and adorable, loves her visitors. All the bedrooms, from traditional to timber-strewn to yellow-panelled, are fascinating. Plus lovely garden, private chapel, old mill... Worth every penny. *Gîte space for 10 people.*

rooms	5: 3 doubles, 2 twins, all with bath, shower & wc.
price	€81–€100 for two.
dinner	Crêperie in village; excellent restaurant nearby.
closed	Rarely.
directions	From St Brieuc N12 to Guingamp; D8 for Tréguier; at Pommerit Jaudy left at lights; signs.

Comte & Comtesse de Kermel
Château de Kermezen,
22450 Pommerit Jaudy,
Côtes-d'Armor

tel	(0)2 96 91 35 75
fax	(0)2 96 91 35 75
e-mail	micheldekermel@kermezen.com

BRITTANY

The 15th-century manor house, only a few minutes' drive from the fishing ports, rocky headlands and long sandy beaches of the coast, is cocooned in noiseless countryside. Wrapped in a rich fluffy towel, gaze out of your lavishly-furnished bedroom onto the lawns below and know your privilege. You may hear the crackling of the log fire in the vast stone hearth downstairs, lit by your perfectionist host, the splash and laughter of guests in the swimming pool, the crack of billiard balls echoing upwards to the tower. But the games room for the younger is in a separate building in the grounds. *Gosford Park* à la Bretonne.

rooms	3: 1 double, 1 suite for 4, 1 suite for 3, each with bath & wc.
price	€80–€90 for two.
dinner	€25, wine €15. Restaurants nearby.
closed	Mid-September-April.
directions	From Paimpol for Lézardrieux; after bridge left to Pleudaniel, right for Pouldouran; through Prat Collet & Passe Porte to sign for Croas Guezou; left; 1st track right 800m.

Christian de Rouffignac
Manoir de Coat Gueno,
Coat Gueno,
22740 Pleudaniel, Côtes-d'Armor

tel	(0)2 96 20 10 98
e-mail	coatguen@aol.com
web	mapage.noos.fr/coatgueno

Enter and you will understand why we chose this modernised house: the ever-changing light of the great bay shimmers in through vast swathes of glass. In guest rooms too you can sit in your armchair and gaze as boats go by. Or take 10 minutes and walk to the beach. Guy chose the house so he could see his small ship at anchor out there (lucky guests may be taken for a sail) and Marie-Clo has enlivened the interior with her talented patchwork and embroidery. It is calm, light, bright; they are attentive and generous and breakfast is seriously good. *Gîte space for 4 people.*

rooms	2 doubles, both with sitting area, shower & wc.
price	€50 for two.
dinner	Lots of restaurants in Perros Guirec.
closed	Rarely.
directions	From Lannion D788 N to Perros Guirec; follow signs to Port; coastal road round bay for approx. 1km; left at sign. (Will fax map or collect you from railway station.)

Marie-Clo & Guy Biarnès
41 rue de la Petite Corniche,
BP 24,
22700 Perros Guirec, Côtes-d'Armor

tel	(0)2 96 23 28 08
fax	(0)2 96 23 28 23
e-mail	guy.biarnes@wanadoo.fr
web	perso.wanadoo.fr/corniche/

map: 3 entry: 280

Such wonderful, gracious hosts with a nice sense of humour: you feel you are at a house party; such age and history in the gloriously asymmetrical château: tower, turrets, vast fireplaces, low doors, ancestral portraits, fine furniture; such a lovely garden, Madame's own work. Once you have managed the worn spiral staircase you find bedrooms with space, taste, arched doors, a lovely window seat to do your tapestry in, good bathrooms; and the great Breton breakfast can be brought up if you wish. An elegant welcome, intelligent conversation, delightful house – and their son breeds racehorses on the estate. *Min. 2 nights.*

rooms	2 twins, both with bath & wc.
price	€85 for two.
dinner	Choice of restaurants 7-10km.
closed	November-Easter
directions	From N12 exit Bégard/Plouaret (bet. Guingamp & Morlaix) to Plouaret; D11 for Lannion to Kerauzern; D30 left for St Michel en G./Ploumilliau, over railway, cont. 3km; left at sign 100m, left again to end.

M & Mme Gérard de Bellefon
Manoir de Kerguéréon,
Ploubezre,
22300 Lannion, Côtes-d'Armor

tel	(0)2 96 38 91 46

map: 3 entry: 281

Inside an enclosed courtyard, it is a charming 17th-century grey stone presbytery. Walled gardens and an orchard for picnics complete the peaceful, private mood. The comfy, lived-in rooms have lots of personal touches, particularly the biggest which is high and stylish and has an amazing, 1950s-deco bathroom. The cosy, cottagey, low-beamed attic rooms have very small shower rooms. Madame knows the area "like her pocket" and has itineraries for your deeper discovery of secret delights (two or three days?). You may eat here but make sure your dinner booking is firm. *Gîte space for 6 people.*

rooms	3: 1 double, 2 twins, all with bath or shower & wc.
price	€50 for two.
dinner	€20 with wine, by arrangement.
closed	Rarely.
directions	From Guingamp N12 for Morlaix, exit Louargat. From Louargat church, D33 to Tregrom (7km). House in village centre opp. church (blue door in wall).

Nicole de Morchoven
L'Ancien Presbytère,
Tregrom,
22420 Plouaret, Côtes-d'Armor
tel (0)2 96 47 94 15
fax (0)2 96 47 94 15

Yolande is a smiling, helpful mother of five, Charlick the most sociable workaholic you could find. Having beautifully renovated their old Breton weaver's house, they are converting other ruins as well as running the small auberge that serves traditional dishes and meats grilled on the open fire. They are active, artistic (he paints) and fun. The rooms have clever layouts, colour schemes and fabrics and brilliant use of wood, all informed by an artist's creative imagination; they are superb in their rustic elegance. All is gentle and soft and there are animals and swings for children's delight. A very special place. *Minimum 2 nights in summer.*

rooms	5: 3 quadruples, 2 doubles, all with bath or shower & wc.
price	€42-€60 for two.
dinner	€17; wine €9-€14.
closed	Christmas-New Year.
directions	From St Brieuc N12 for Morlaix, exit 'Plouigneau' to Plougonven; continue for Plourin lès Morlaix 5km. House on right, sign.

Charlick & Yolande de Ternay
La Grange de Coatélan,
29640 Plougonven, Finistère
tel (0)2 98 72 60 16

Above ancient Breton rocks, sea and pines, it's a modern house with fine old pieces, family trees and ancestors. Your hosts, a great mix of French aristocracy and American academe, are cultured, polyglot, eager to share their love of Brittany. Bedrooms, cosily clothed in plush, patchwork and good furniture, hung with unusual pictures (worth asking about), have a colourful bathroom each; one on a different floor, one containing two bunk beds! (An independent wc and basin allow parents to ablute while offspring sleep.) The big, light, blue and yellow kitchen is a warm place for meals; garden and sea beckon from the door. *Gîte space for 8 people.*

rooms	3: 1 double, 1 twin, 1 suite, all with bath & wc.
price	€62-€70 for two.
dinner	€20-€23 with wine, by arrangement.
closed	Mid-October-Easter, open winter by arrangement.
directions	From Morlaix D64 for 'Lannion par la Côte'; Locquirec 21km from Morlaix, 22km from Lannion. In village, towards 'Sables Blancs'. House on this road.

Comte & Comtesse Hubert de Germiny
Villa Germiny,
11 rue de Keraël,
29241 Locquirec, Finistère

tel	(0)2 98 67 47 11
fax	(0)2 98 67 47 11
e-mail	lorraine-de-germiny@wanadoo.fr

BRITTANY

Crow's Rock Manor: sounds wild? It is wonderfully civilised. Built in the 1840s and admirably restored by your young and sociable hosts, who have three young children, it breathes an air of old-style, refined yet understated luxury in big, lofty-ceilinged, antiqued and chandeliered rooms with superb views of the generous grounds. The drawing-room parquet alone is worth the visit; bed linen is exceptionally luxurious; from one super bathroom you can gaze out to the fields or into a vast mirror; another has tapestries of... baths. Breakfast may include local specialities and fresh fruit salad. *Horse riding possible.*

rooms	2 doubles, both with bath & wc.
price	€57-€67 for two.
dinner	Restaurants nearby.
closed	Rarely.
directions	From Port Morlaix follow right bank of river N for Le Dourduff; 2nd right at Ploujean sign (hairpin bend) 500m. Right for Ploujean; house 3rd on right.

Étienne & Armelle Delaisi
Manoir de Roch ar Brini,
29600 Morlaix Ploujean, Finistère

tel	(0)2 98 72 01 44
fax	(0)2 98 88 04 49
e-mail	rochbrini@aol.com
web	www.brittanyguesthouse.com

Squarely planted in its Breton soil, this is totally a family house open to guests, not a purpose-converted affair. The children run the farm and the Gralls, genuine Breton-speaking Bretons, have time for visitors. After a blissful night – rooms have warm traditional décor, excellent mattresses, neat modern bathrooms – and a bucolic awakening to birdsong in the fields, come down to Madame's home-made crêpes or Breton cake at their square Breton table beside the deeply-carved sideboard. She's an expansive soul, gentle and chatty. Family antiques, family warmth, peace and unity that reassure and relax.

rooms	2: 1 twin, 1 family room, each with shower & wc.
price	€40 for two.
dinner	Restaurant 2.5km.
closed	Rarely.
directions	From St Pol de Léon D10 W to Cléder. Arriving in Cléder, take road to sea for 2km; left following signs to Ferme de Kernévez.

François & Marceline Grall
Kernévez,
29233 Cléder, Finistère
tel (0)2 98 69 41 14
web www.kernevez.fr.fm

In a tiny Breton hamlet on the fascinating, blasted heath that is the Monts d'Arée National Park stands Kreisker, a sensitive, utterly Breton conversion, all local stone, slate roofs and giant slabs of schist from the old floors. Inside is more dark stone, scrubbed wood, ethnic rugs, fresh cotton and pretty china. The independent guest room has a lovely blue-grey brass bed and a fine bathroom. After the feast that is breakfast, your ears ringing with Madame's knowledgeable talk of Breton culture, go and explore this ancient land and blow away your cobwebs.

Children welcome if you bring a child's bed. Gîte space for 8 people.

rooms	1 double with bath & wc.
price	€40 for two.
dinner	Crêperies & restaurants 2.5-7km; book ahead.
closed	Rarely.
directions	From Morlaix, D785 for Quimper. At La Croix Cassée, D42 to Botmeur. 200m after town hall for Feuillée; 1st right.

Marie-Thérèse & Jean-Bernard Solliec
Kreisker,
29690 Botmeur, Finistère
tel (0)2 98 99 63 02
fax (0)2 98 99 63 02
e-mail msol@club-internet.fr

The two most memorable things here are Marie-Christine's smile as she talks about her native Brittany and the sympathetic use of wood on floor, ceilings and walls. Guest rooms are in the old cider-press – pretty and fresh with skylight windows and handsome antiques. Breakfast, perhaps with Breton music in the background (to make the Breton costumes dance?), is prepared in the guest dayroom and eaten at the long refectory table there, with views of the garden and books all around. It is quiet and comfortable and you can be quite independent. *Dinner with Madame's daughter can be arranged. Gîte space for 14 people.*

rooms	2: 1 double, 1 triple, both with shower & wc.
price	€41 for two.
dinner	€14, with wine; restaurants nearby.
closed	Rarely.
directions	From Morlaix D785 for Quimper, approx. 35km. 800m before Brasparts, right (on bend) & follow signs.

Marie-Christine Chaussy
Domaine de Rugornou Uras,
Garz ar Bik,
29190 Brasparts, Finistère
tel (0)2 98 81 47 14/(0)2 98 81 46 27
fax (0)2 98 81 47 99

BRITTANY

Guilfuiffin is a powerful, unforgettable experience. The bewitching name of the warring first baron (1010), the splendidness of the place, its opulent, ancestor-hung, Chinese-potted rooms and magnificent grounds, are utterly seductive. Built with stones from the 11th-century fortress, it is a jewel of an 18th-century château, inside and out. Passionate about furniture and buildings, especially his ancient family seat, your host applies his intelligent energy to restoring his estate, nurturing thousands of plants and, with Madame's help, converting visitors to his views. Deeply interesting and unusual. *Gîte space for 5 people.*

rooms	6: 4 doubles, 2 suites, all with bath or shower & wc.
price	€115-€140 for two; suite €170-€200.
dinner	Choice of restaurants nearby.
closed	Rarely; book ahead in winter.
directions	From Quimper D765 W for 5km; left D784 for Landudec 13km; left & follow signs.

Philippe Davy
Domaine du Guilguiffin,
29710 Landudec, Finistère
tel (0)2 98 91 52 11
fax (0)2 98 91 52 52
e-mail chateau@guilguiffin.com
web www.guilguiffin.com

Madame is a darling: quiet, serene and immensely kind, she really treats her guests as friends. The long, low, granite house has been in the family for all of its 300 years, enjoying the peace of this wind-blown, bird-sung spot just five minutes from the sea and that gorgeous coastal path. And standing stones in the garden! Most of the building is gîtes; the *chambres d'hôtes* are tucked into the far end – small, impeccably simple, like the dining room, with some handsome Breton furniture. With charming Port Manech and good beaches nearby, it is a wonderful holiday spot. *Gîte space for 14 people.*

rooms	4: 2 doubles, 2 twins, all with shower & wc.
price	€41 for two.
dinner	In village, within walking distance.
closed	Rarely.
directions	From Pont Aven, D77 for Port Manech; right just before sign Port Manech; 1st left. Follow Chambres d'Hôtes signs.

Yveline Gourlaouen
Kerambris,
Port Manech,
29920 Nevez, Finistère
tel (0)2 98 06 83 82
fax (0)2 98 06 83 82

The view from all six rooms across fields and wooded hills is perfectly wonderful. In a stone outbuilding separate from the owners' house, each small, neatly modern room, each identically impeccable, has a double-glazed French window onto the long terrace where chairs await. Breakfast, with crêpes or croissants, is in a big modern veranda room where a richly-carved Breton wardrobe takes pride of place. Madame is efficient, full of information about Breton culture, and very purposeful. *Only suitable for older children who can sleep alone. Small pets welcome.*

rooms	6: 4 doubles, 2 twins, all with shower & wc.
price	€41 for two.
dinner	Choice of restaurants, 10km.
closed	Rarely.
directions	From Quimper D765 for Rosporden. At St Yvi left to Kervren; to end of lane (2.5km).

Odile Le Gall
Kervren,
29140 St Yvi, Finistère
tel (0)2 98 94 70 34
fax (0)2 98 94 81 19

Here is a Breton house with naturally hospitable Breton owners, Breton furniture and a huge Breton brass pot once used for mixing crêpes. Madame is welcoming and chatty (in French), Monsieur has a reassuring earthy calmness; they love having children to stay. The large, light, country-style rooms are all merrily painted in sunny yellow, fresh green, orange or pink. Copious breakfasts include those crêpes (though not mixed in the brass pot) and home-grown kiwi fruit in season. An authentic rural haven between *Armor*, the land by the sea and *Argoat*, the land of the woods. *Gîte space for 8 people.*

rooms	4: 3 doubles, 1 twin, all with shower & wc.
price	€40 for two.
dinner	Restaurant 4km.
closed	Occasionally.
directions	From Scaër, D50 for Coray Briec; after 3km, left at 'Ty Ru' & follow signs for Kerloaï.

	Louis & Thérèse Penn
	Kerloaï,
	29390 Scaër, Finistère
tel	(0)2 98 59 42 60
fax	(0)2 98 59 05 67
e-mail	ti.penn@skaer.com

BRITTANY

Meadows of wild flowers and woods surround the enchanting old farmhouse – it feels miles from anywhere. Bare stonework rubs shoulders with whitewashed walls, potted plants and dried flowers throng. The open-plan living room, warmly beamed and berugged, has comfy sofas round an open fire, all shared with your attentive hosts who love dining here with guests. Steep stairs – go carefully – lead to simply-decorated rooms where bright fabrics set off stone walls under sloping rafters. If not relaxing in the garden or strolling the fields, you can play ping-pong, badminton or croquet, go fishing or paddle a canoe. *Gîte space for 5 people.*

rooms	3: 2 doubles, 1 twin, all with shower & wc.
price	€38 for two.
dinner	€14 with wine, by arrangement.
closed	Rarely.
directions	From Pontivy D768 S for 12km; exit for St Nicolas des Eaux then Talvern Nenez; follow for Golf de Rimaison 5km; right opp. golf course for 1km; left & follow signs.

	Marie-Thérèse Vannier
	La Baratte,
	Lelfaux,
	56310 Bieuzy les Eaux, Morbihan
tel	(0)2 97 27 74 11
e-mail	vannier.labaratte@libertysurf.fr

A heavenly place, cradled in a quiet hamlet 200 yards from the river in a very lovely corner of Brittany. Delightful people: Martine looks after old folk and young Melissa, Philippe pots and teaches aikido; both have lots of time for guests. In an outbuilding, you have your own sitting/breakfast room and kitchen and two big, superbly converted, uncluttered attic rooms, decorated with flair in subtle pastels and fitted with good shower rooms. Birds sing; the cat is one of the best ever; the dog will love you. A genuine welcome and possibly a different kind of cake for breakfast every day. Readers' letters are full of praise.

rooms	2 twins, both with shower & wc.
price	€38 for two.
dinner	Wide choice of restaurants in St Nicolas 3km; self-catering.
closed	November-Easter, except by arrangement.
directions	From Pontivy D768 S for 12km; exit to St Nicolas des Eaux; right immed. after bridge; follow signs for Chambres d'Hôtes & Poterie for 3km.

Martine Maignan & Philippe Boivin
Lezerhy,
56310 Bieuzy les Eaux, Morbihan

tel	(0)2 97 27 74 59
fax	(0)2 97 27 74 59
e-mail	boivinp@wanadoo.fr
web	perso.wanadoo.fr/poterie-de-lezerhy/

BRITTANY

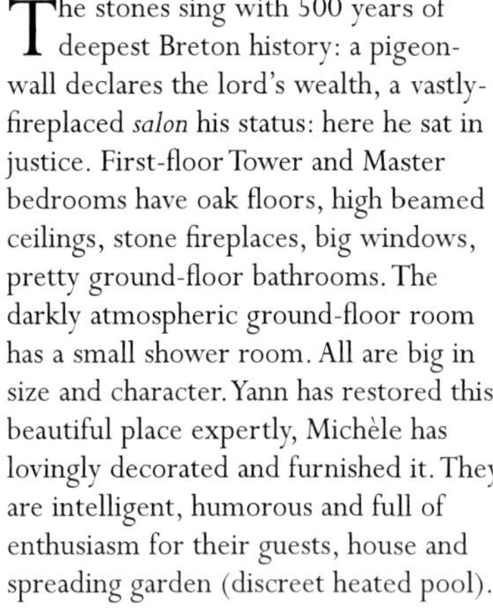

The stones sing with 500 years of deepest Breton history: a pigeon-wall declares the lord's wealth, a vastly-fireplaced *salon* his status: here he sat in justice. First-floor Tower and Master bedrooms have oak floors, high beamed ceilings, stone fireplaces, big windows, pretty ground-floor bathrooms. The darkly atmospheric ground-floor room has a small shower room. All are big in size and character. Yann has restored this beautiful place expertly, Michèle has lovingly decorated and furnished it. They are intelligent, humorous and full of enthusiasm for their guests, house and spreading garden (discreet heated pool).

rooms	3: 1 double, 1 triple, 1 quadruple, all with shower or bath & wc.
price	€58-€69 for two.
dinner	Choice of restaurants in Josselin, 3km.
closed	Rarely.
directions	From Josselin D126 for Guégon. Take 4th right AFTER Guégon turning. House 150m up, on left.

Yann Bourdin & Michèle Robic
Manoir du Val aux Houx,
56120 Guégon, Morbihan

tel	(0)2 97 22 24 32
fax	(0)2 97 75 42 65
e-mail	yann.bourdin@wanadoo.fr

Dreams drift over Keraubert, the pond mirrors the dragonflies' precious dance, a semi-tropical Breton gardens luxuriates. Your hosts create a welcoming, relaxed atmosphere, Bernard's paintings grace many walls and he and Jacqueline quickly convey their refreshing optimism and warm delight in the place. Each pretty but untwee guest room has a garden door with iron table and chairs for two. The deeply pink room is small and cosy with garden views; the thoroughly blue room is bigger, in revived 1930s style, with less view. It is unashamedly romantic with an authentic homey feel and the owners are a lovely couple.

rooms	2 doubles, both with shower & wc.
price	€45 for two.
dinner	Restaurants 6km.
closed	Rarely.
directions	From Rennes N24 for Lorient, exit Baud/Auray; D768 for Vannes 4km; D24 right for Landevant 10km; entrance on right between Lambel & Malachappe.

Bernard & Jacqueline Belin
Keraubert,
56330 Pluvigner, Morbihan
tel (0)2 97 24 93 10
fax (0)2 97 24 93 10

BRITTANY

Gérard loves his cooking, garden and house passionately and shares them generously. The B&B is all his, Nelly works in town. Once a chef for the wealthy and the deprived (château-hotels, then schools for troubled youth), he has revived the old bread oven in the deliciously lush little garden and renovated the 'cottage' with flair and faithfulness, naming the rooms after Breton fairies – they are enchanting. He is quietly welcoming and the whole family is deeply Breton, doing an annual *Fest-Noz* with costumes, dances, pipes and songs, plus a dash of exotic in the odd moonlit game of boules or darts. A super place.

rooms	5: 4 doubles, 1 twin, all with bath or shower & wc.
price	€46-€50 for two.
dinner	€17, with wine or cider.
closed	Rarely.
directions	From Lorient N165 E 39km; exit D24 N 8km; left at sign Chaumière de Kerreo: thatched house, fuschia paintwork at hamlet crossroads.

Gérard Grevès & Nelly Le Glehuir
Chaumière de Kerreo,
56330 Pluvigner, Morbihan
tel (0)2 97 50 90 48
fax (0)2 97 50 90 69

The standing stones of Carnac are minutes away, beaches and coastal pathways close by. Kerimel is a handsome group of granite farm buildings in a perfect setting among the fields. The bedrooms are beauties: plain walls, some panelling, patchwork bedcovers and pale blue curtains, old stones and beams, sparkling shower rooms and fluffy towels. The dining room is cottage perfection: dried flowers hanging from beams over wooden table, tiled floor, vast blackened chimney, stone walls. Gentle, generous, elegant people… "We talked of flowers", wrote one guest.

rooms	4 doubles/twins, all with shower & wc.
price	€60–€68 for two.
dinner	Good restaurants 3km.
closed	Rarely.
directions	From N165 exit for Quiberon/Carnac on D768, 4km; right to Ploemel; D105 W for Erdeven; sign on right, 1.5km.

Babeth & Pierre Malherbe
Kerimel,
56400 Ploemel (Carnac), Morbihan

tel	(0)2 97 56 84 72
fax	(0)2 97 56 84 72
e-mail	elisabeth.malherbe@wanadoo.fr
web	kerimel.free.fr

map: 3 entry: 298

BRITTANY

Bang there on the quayside, an oyster farm! Bedrooms touch the view – you may want to stay and capture that lovely, limpid light on canvas while drinking coffee on the balcony, smelling the sea and listening to the chugging of fishing boats. Madame worked in England, Germany and the USA before coming to Brittany to help François farm oysters – she never looked back. He'll take you out there too, if you ask. Hospitable and generous, alert and chatty, she hangs interesting paintings in her rooms, lights a fire on cool days and serves a good French breakfast. Unusual and very welcoming. *Gîte space for 10.*

rooms	2 + 1 apartment: 1 twin, 1 triple, 1 apartment for 3, all with shower & wc.
price	€46–€61 for two.
dinner	Restaurant 500m.
closed	Rarely.
directions	From Auray D28/D781 to Crach & Trinité sur M.; right at lights before bridge for La Trinité; house 400m along on left, sign 'François Gouzer'.

Christine & François Gouzer
Kernivilit,
St Philibert,
56470 La Trinité sur Mer, Morbihan

tel	(0)2 97 55 17 78
fax	(0)2 97 30 04 11
e-mail	fgouzer@club-internet.fr
web	www.geocities.com/thetropics/cabana/8913/

map: 3 entry: 299

A gem of a setting: the modern house looks over the ever-changing blue-green gulf and its islands. The three well-furnished garden-level rooms have eyes to the sea and loos in the corridor. A carved four-poster reigns imposingly in the room upstairs that leads to an even more startling dayroom with billiard table, books galore, oak altar, 1950s juke box, telescope, baby Louis XV armchair – all neatly arranged as if in a stately home – and the loo. Madame, brisk and practical, has a style that features marked contrasts – you will warm to her – and there's a little beach at the end of the garden for shallow bathing.

rooms	4: 1 double with bath; 3 doubles with basin & bidet sharing 2 showers; all sharing 6 wcs.
price	€48–€55 for two.
dinner	Restaurants in Larmor Baden, 1.5km.
closed	Mid-July & August.
directions	From Auray D101 S for Baden; D316 S for Larmor Baden; through village N/NE for Locqueltas; sign on right, house 10m on right.

Mme M. C. Hecker
Locqueltas
56870 Larmor Baden, Morbihan
tel (0)2 97 57 05 85
fax (0)2 97 57 25 02

WESTERN LOIRE

These are the sweetest people, even if their somewhat kitschy taste is not everyone's cup of tea! They really do "treat their guests as friends". Madame, bright and sparkling, is proud to show you her decorated books, musical scores and hats with the dried flower and gold spray touch; Monsieur is a retired farmer, less chatty, equally friendly. The house is warm (log fire in winter), cosily country-furnished, the smallish rooms are welcoming (mind your head on the way up) with much attention to detail and there's a summer kitchen. Breakfast is served in pretty little baskets at the long table. *Gîte space for 3 people.*

The great waterway moves slowly seawards through lands where Catholic Royalists battled bitterly against the Revolution while the precious, hand-harvested salt travelled upstream in flat, flop-sailed gabares.

rooms	3: 2 triples, each with shower & wc; 1 family room with bath & separate wc.
price	€45 for two; €55 for three.
dinner	Good restaurant 3km; self-catering in summer.
closed	Rarely.
directions	From Rennes N137 for Nantes 63km. Exit at Nozay N171 for Blain 8km. At bottom of hill, left at roadside cross; sign.

Yvonne & Marcel Pineau
La Mercerais,
44130 Blain, Loire-Atlantique
tel (0)2 40 79 04 30

Come for a taste of life with the French country aristocracy – it's getting hard to find. Properly, endearingly, formal – breakfast at 9am sharp, a touch of old-fashioned primness about table manners – your graceful, cultured hosts are excellent company, create a relaxed atmosphere and always dine with you: dress for it and enjoy the hand-painted china and fine glassware, then perhaps a game of billiards. Magnificent bedrooms, of course; and there's a lake and 100 hectares of superb parkland… all within the Brière Regional Park where water and land are inextricably mingled and wildlife abounds. *Gîte space for 10 people.*

rooms	3: 2 doubles, 1 twin, all with bath or shower & wc.
price	€85-€95 for two.
dinner	€40, with wine; excellent auberges nearby.
closed	Rarely.
directions	From N165, exit 15 D774 for La Baule to Herbignac, 10km; fork left D47 for St Lyphard for 4km; house on right.

François & Cécile de La Monneraye
Château de Coët Caret,
44410 Herbignac, Loire-Atlantique

tel	(0)2 40 91 41 20
fax	(0)2 40 91 37 46
e-mail	coetcaret@free.fr
web	coetcaret.free.fr

This is a new family venture. Jean-Philippe, his mother and sister, are engaging hosts, friendly and attentive, providing not only robes but drinks beside the pool. Early-bird and sleeper-in will both be happy: breakfast, complete with eggs and bacon as well as local choices, is served from really early (6am) till pretty late (11am). You can see the sea from upstairs where bedrooms are colourful without being overpowering – Jean-Philippe went to art school and has an eye for detail. Plenty to see and do nearby but children will love just mucking around in the big garden.

rooms	2 + 1 cottage: 1 double, 1 family suite, each with shower & private wc; cottage for 4 with shower, wc & kitchen.
price	€54-€84 for two.
dinner	Restaurants nearby.
closed	Rarely.
directions	From Guérande for La Turballe; just before town D333 right; at x-roads 'Café des 4 Routes' straight on; house 600m on right.

Jean-Philippe Meyran
Le Manoir des Quatre Saisons,
744 bd de Lauvergnac,
44420 La Turballe, Loire-Atlantique

tel	(0)2 40 11 76 16
fax	(0)2 40 11 76 16

Backed against the fortifications of beautiful, medieval Guérande, this Breton house with original mosaic and parquet floors, huge granite fireplace and wide wooden staircase feels older than its 140 years. Valérie's superb sense of colour, choice of fabrics and fine attention to detail blend its traditional solidity with contemporary lightness – her bedrooms are breathtaking. In the green and tranquil garden, breakfast in the company of 100-year-old trees and entertaining modern sculpture. Smiling and friendly, Valérie, who lives mostly in another house, sells local produce and crafts from a shop on the ground floor.

rooms	6: 4 doubles, 1 triple, 1 suite for 4, all with bath or shower & wc.
price	€70-€97 for two.
dinner	Good restaurants within walking distance.
closed	Rarely.
directions	From Nantes/Vannes follow signs to Guérande; enter through La Porte Vannetaise (north town gate), 1st house on right.

Valérie Lauvray
La Guérandière,
5 porte Vannetaise,
44350 Guérande, Loire-Atlantique

tel	(0)2 40 62 17 15
fax	(0)2 51 73 04 17
e-mail	valerie.lauvray@laguerandiere.com
web	www.laguerandiere.com

Local rumour has it that this is not a house at all but a less salubrious, if honourable, retreat for those in dire need to commune with Nature – as the English so coyly put it. However, the truth is less prosaic: the owner travelled in exotic places and was much taken by the Chinese fishing nets of Fort Cochin in Kerala and the 'outhouses' of Vanuatu in the Solomon Islands. This astonishing little B&B is the result, an architectural fusion that is a world first. Beyond that, your breakfast is fresh from the river, your air fresh from all sides, you will be undisturbed and your own sandy beach is a drop away. Impeccable authenticity.

rooms	One communal, all-purpose space with front and rear 'balcony' areas, sharing open-floored facilities.
price	A certain amount of bravery.
dinner	Fishing available off end of living room (high tide only).
closed	Never, but sometimes inaccessible.
directions	From end of coast road, follow coastal path on foot until you encounter a strut.

Allon Maillône
Maison Longues Jambes,
Les Sables sur Mer,
543210 Une Plage Trop Loin,
Loire-Atlantique

tel	zéro
fax	non
e-mail	sorry-gone_fishing@sea
web	www... can't remember the rest.

Looks impressive? The gutsy Scherers bought a "challenge in ruins" five years ago: the work they have done on the old château and its fabulous 19th-century-listed park (myriad camellias, 100 types of geranium, great pond, miles of woodland walks) is impressive too and the whole village worships in the chapel twice a year. Inside, there's space and more space: for guests to have their own entrance, log-fired sitting room, billiard room, stuccoed breakfast room, big parquet-floored bedrooms done for family-style comfort with some antiques and Madame's paintings, photographs and stencilling. Great people – may they flourish.

rooms	3: 1 double with bath/shower & wc; 1 family suite (1 double, 1 twin) with bath/shower & wc.
price	€75 for two.
dinner	Restaurant 3km.
closed	Rarely.
directions	From Nantes D723 for Paimbœuf; near Frossay left following signs to château.

Catherine Scherer
Château de La Rousselière,
44320 Frossay, Loire-Atlantique
tel (0)2 40 39 79 59
fax (0)2 40 39 77 78
e-mail larouss@club-internet.fr
web www.larousseliere.com

WESTERN LOIRE

A palm tree grows in the courtyard, a grassy garden big enough to satisfy the liveliest child stretches endlessly across vineyards of crisp Muscadet grapes. Madame is as full of fun and energy as ever and Monsieur, who is shyer and a retired baker, provides delicious cakes for breakfast on the terrace. The guest rooms in the main house are comfortable and very French with their fine carved *armoires* and fabric flowers. The other two, up steep outside stone stairs, are bright and cheerful, one a daring pink and yellow, the other bright blue, each with a kitchenette and sparkling bathroom. *Gîte space for 5 people.*

rooms	5: 4 doubles, 1 twin, all with shower & wc.
price	€40 for two.
dinner	Choice of restaurants 6km; self-catering in annexe.
closed	Rarely.
directions	From Nantes N249 for Poitiers, exit Vallet for Loroux Bottereau & Le Landreau, 5km; 600m before Le Landreau right; signs to La Rinière.

Françoise & Louis Lebarillier
Le Relais de La Rinière,
44430 Le Landreau,
Loire-Atlantique
tel (0)2 40 06 41 44
fax (0)2 51 13 10 52
e-mail riniere@netcourrier.com
web www.riniere.com

The lofty dining room has massive beams, a massive table, massive old flags; the panelling took 500 hours to restore, fine period furniture gleams – Monsieur, a wine merchant, is passionate about buildings and an avid auction-goer (he buys old wells!) – and an air of Renaissance nobility pervades, except in the bathrooms, which are reassuringly modern and white. Madame seems charmingly eccentric and, under daughter Gaëlle's management, the estate produces a Muscadet from the surrounding vineyards that is served as an aperitif at about seven, before you sally forth for dinner. *Gîte space for 10.*

rooms	5 doubles, all with bath or shower & wc.
price	€75-€105 for two.
dinner	Wide choice of restaurants within 5 minutes.
closed	November-March, except by arrangement.
directions	From Nantes N249 for Poitiers; right N149 for Le Pallet; 1km before Le Pallet D7 right to Monnières; left for Gorges; château 1km on left.

	Annick & Didier Calonne
	Château Plessis-Brezot,
	44690 Monnières, Loire-Atlantique
tel	(0)2 40 54 63 24
fax	(0)2 40 54 66 07
e-mail	a.calonne@online.fr
web	www.chateauplessisbrezot.com

When she was expecting her twins, Anna drew the house of her dreams and this is it: a small 18th-century château in a 12-hectare park where she has created an unusually beautiful, harmonious home. Walls are white or red-ochre, ceilings beamed, bathrooms a perfect blend of old and new. There's a delightful attention to detail – a pewter jug of old roses by a mirror, a contemporary wicker chair on an ancient, exquisite terracotta floor. You have your own entrance and the run of the sitting room, log-fired in winter. Anna serves real hot chocolate at breakfast, and maybe a glass of Muscadet on arrival. A dream of a place.

rooms	3 doubles, all with bath or shower & wc.
price	€74-€100 for two.
dinner	Choice of restaurants in Clisson.
closed	Last week in January.
directions	From Nantes N249 for Poitiers; 2nd exit N149 for le Pallet; through village, 1st right, signposted.

	Anne Cannaferina
	Château de la Sébinière,
	44330 Le Pallet, Loire-Atlantique
tel	(0)2 40 80 49 25
e-mail	la.sebiniere@libertysurf.fr

History-loaded Le Plessis belonged to the Roche family who crossed with William in 1066. The Belordes had it in 1632, kept it for centuries, lost it, bought in back 30 years ago. Pure château, it has velvet curtains and high-backed chairs in the *salon*; silver coffee pots and fresh orange juice at breakfast; 3,000 rosebushes in the garden and bedrooms of huge antique personality. Madame's father was in London with de Gaulle and she loves the English, enjoys cosmopolitan conversation and offers candlelit champagne dinners. Expensive but special – you are in another world. *Gîte space for 4 people.*

rooms	3: 1 double, 1 twin/quadruple, 1 suite for 5, all with bath & wc.
price	€100-€150 for two.
dinner	€50-€62.50, with wine; €75 with champagne.
closed	Rarely.
directions	From Nantes leave A83 ringroad on D85 past airport. At T-junc. at Champ de Foire left through Pont St Martin & follow signs to Le Plessis.

M & Mme Belorde
Château du Plessis-Atlantique,
44860 Pont St Martin,
Loire-Atlantique

tel	(0)2 40 26 81 72
fax	(0)2 40 32 76 67
e-mail	ecolebuissonniere@wanadoo.fr

WESTERN LOIRE

Monsieur's parents bought this old *logis Vendéen* when he was six. Years later, researching the history of the house, he found his family first owned it in 1670! Madame's family tree, framed in the hall, goes back to the 14th century. But they are both warm and welcoming, not at all grand, and the house is full of personal touches: Madame painted the breakfast china and embroidered the beautiful tablecloth. Bedrooms are vast, with peaceful views and lots of fresh and dried flowers. The suite, and huge grounds, would be ideal for a family but very small children would need watching near the two pretty ponds.

rooms	3: 2 doubles, 1 suite for 5, all with bath or shower & wc.
price	€53-€60 for two.
dinner	Restaurants in nearby village.
closed	Rarely.
directions	From Nantes through le Bourg for Challans & Machecoul; on leaving Bourg left after restaurant le Paradis; Logis 150m left.

Mme de Ternay
Logis de Richebonne,
44650 Legé, Loire-Atlantique

tel	(0)2 40 04 90 41
fax	(0)2 40 04 90 41
e-mail	adeternay@wanadoo.fr

The friendly, unobtrusive Desbrosses particularly enjoy the company of foreign visitors to their typical long low 18th-century house. In the guest wing, you may choose one of their many books and withdraw to a deep leather chair by the monumental drawing room fireplace. Guest rooms and bathrooms are frilly and old-fashioned – so are some of the beds. The excellent breakfast and occasional dinner are served on matching blue and yellow plates in the blue and yellow dining room – Madame is a delightful potter and the strong colours are her own, successful choice. A lovely setting for a quiet escape.

rooms	2: 1 double, 1 suite, both with bath & wc.
price	€51 for two.
dinner	€22 with wine, by arrangement.
closed	November-February.
directions	From Nantes D937 for La Roche sur Yon; at Rocheservière D753 to Legé centre, for Touvois; left after Le Paradis restaurant; signs.

Christine & Gérard Desbrosses
La Mozardière,
Richebonne,
44650 Legé, Loire-Atlantique

tel	(0)2 40 04 98 51
fax	(0)2 40 26 31 61
e-mail	christine@lamozardiere.com
web	www.lamozardiere.com

WESTERN LOIRE

Annick has been running this old stone farmhouse as a B&B for a few years now, after restoring it inch by inch. Her years as an Accident & Emergency nurse stand her in good stead: everything is immaculate, even the vegetable garden, but she still finds time to make you feel at home and is happy to chat while she cooks. One room is up steep steps, both are bright, with colourful bed linen and interesting windows. Both the main house and the guest rooms have exposed stone walls, polished wood floors and rugs. Children are very welcome – Annick's are teenagers but definitely not the growly kind.

rooms	2: 1 double, 1 triple, both with shower & wc.
price	€37 for two.
dinner	€14 with wine, by arrangement.
closed	Rarely.
directions	From Montaigu D763 for Cugand 8.5km; D77 for La Bernardière; left after railway crossing; signposted.

Annick & Marc Broux
La Bérangeraie,
85610 Cugand, Vendée

tel	(0)2 51 43 62 02
e-mail	annick.broux@wanadoo.fr
web	perso.wanadoo.fr/laberangeraievendee

Hurry! Here is a lovely, quiet family with cows that they know by name and a love of the land that is becoming rare. Michelle does the B&B, Gérard and their son run the farm. The hub is the huge living room where you all relax after a gorgeous dinner of regional dishes made with their own produce (guest sitting room upstairs too). Bedrooms are not large but comfortable in French country style, the two in the separate old sheepfold ideal for a family; the big garden has games for children and an immaculate potager. Come for these wonderful, kind hosts and her superb cooking rather than the rooms.

rooms	5: 2 doubles, 2 triples, all with shower & wc; 1 family room with bath & wc.
price	€42 for two.
dinner	Restaurants in St Christophe.
closed	November-April.
directions	From Challans D948 to St Christophe du Ligneron; opposite baker's right D2 for Palluau for 4km; left at sign for house.

Michelle & Gérard Loizeau
L'Hubertière,
85670 St Christophe du Ligneron,
Vendée

tel	(0)2 51 35 06 41
fax	(0)2 51 49 87 43
e-mail	michelle.loizeau@terre-net.fr
web	www.vendee.com/hubertiere

WESTERN LOIRE

The lovely, lively Pikes and their two sets of identical twin teenage sons (*la fraternité*) brim with optimism and pleasure in their adopted country where they grow game birds. Their simple, old-fashioned, easily-renovated 1900s farmhouse has a big garden where children play and adults barbecue; then, up the outside stairs in the former apple loft are two fresh, comfortable rooms for restful seclusion, all details cared for. Ian manages the farm, Janty helps with the eggs, they all love guests and will point you towards the hidden treasures of the area they have come to love.
Gîte space for 8 people.

rooms	2: 1 double with bath, shower & wc; 1 twin with shower & wc.
price	€40 for two.
dinner	Good restaurant 3km.
closed	Mid-September-mid-June, unless booked ahead.
directions	From La Roche sur Yon D948 25km through Aizenay; 4km after lake, D94 left for Commequiers, 1km (signs to La Fraternité); left for Maché, house immed. on right.

Janty & Ian Pike
La Fraternité,
Maché,
85190 Aizenay, Vendée

tel	(0)2 51 55 42 58
fax	(0)2 51 60 16 01
e-mail	janet.pike@wanadoo.fr
web	www.chez.com/lafraternite/

Eleanor of Aquitaine was born across the road in the exquisitely cloistered Abbey – something of the serenity and simplicity of the convent permeates the pretty, immaculate bedrooms. The largest is in a splendidly converted loft with the original massive oak door, timbered ceiling, terracotta-tiled floor and simple red-checked fabrics. The breakfast room is the old stable, complete with manger, while the old laundry, with vast stone wash-tub, is now a sitting room. Guests can picnic in the walled garden, overlooked by the Abbey. It's a family affair and when Christine is busy with her twins, her parents look after guests.

rooms	4: 1 double, 1 twin, 2 triples, all with shower & wc.
price	€44-€47 for two.
dinner	Restaurant & crêperie 100m.
closed	October-April.
directions	From Niort N148 for Fontenay le Comte 20km (or A83 exit 9); after Oulmes right to Nieul sur l'Autise to Abbey: house just beyond on left.

Christine Chastain-Poupin
Le Rosier Sauvage,
1 rue de l'Abbaye,
85240 Nieul sur l'Autise, Vendée
tel (0)2 51 52 49 39
fax (0)2 51 52 49 46
e-mail rosier.sauvage1@tiscali.fr

WESTERN LOIRE

A stone's throw from the house, the River Vendée winds sleepily through this secret valley. The steep sloping garden, where hoopoes nest, is full of hidden shady corners to linger in. For rainy days there is a sunny sitting room with videos and books about this unique marshy corner of France known as "the Green Venice". The comfortable, immaculate bedrooms are beautifully decorated in a stylish mix of old and new. Marie-Françoise, an attentive and intelligent hostess, makes delicious and unusual jams from garden fruit and flowers, and Jean-Claude teaches cabinet-making. A perfect place to unwind.

rooms	2: 1 double, 1 family room, both with shower & wc.
price	€43 for two.
dinner	Choice of restaurants 3-10km.
closed	November-March.
directions	From A83 exit Fontenay le Comte D938ter for La Rochelle 6km; right at small sign to Massigny; 1st house on left entering hamlet.

Marie-Françoise & Jean-Claude Neau
Massigny,
85770 Velluire, Vendée
tel (0)2 51 52 30 32
fax (0)2 51 52 30 32

Pure serendipity: Madame's laughing eyes and infectious enthusiasm will lift the spirits of the world-weariest as she steps through the door. Choose from the old rocking chair in the conservatory, the chess set, books and a long monastery table in the sitting room, the vast garden where nature and man live happily side by side – mulberry trees, a wisteria-hung pergola, a punt to drift you into the mysterious *Marais*. Bedrooms are traditionally furnished with creaky polished parquet and fine family furniture, one with a four-poster bed, and the pretty garden room is in the converted hen-house. *Gîte Panda*.

rooms	5: 3 doubles, 1 triple, 1 twin, all with bath or shower & wc.
price	€61 for two.
dinner	Restaurants in village.
closed	Rarely.
directions	From Fontenay le Comte N148 for Niort 9km; right D15 to Maillezais; follow signs for Abbaye; house on left, sign.

Mme Liliane Bonnet
69 rue de l'Abbaye,
85420 Maillezais, Vendée

tel	(0)2 51 87 23 00
fax	(0)2 51 00 72 44
e-mail	liliane.bonnet@wanadoo.fr
web	www.marais-poitevin.com/heberg-ch/bonnet/bonnet.html

map: 9 entry: 318

WESTERN LOIRE

The Migons, who couldn't be nicer, have expertly renovated their unusual, long-faced, narrow-waisted house with its barn-enclosed courtyard, two towers and covered terrace. Big, north-facing bedrooms are elegant and comfortable behind their shutters. There's a good mix in the reception rooms: contemporary leather sofas and a suit of armour; blue and green painted beams over antique dining-room furniture; two billiard tables, a piano, a set of drums in the games room. Monsieur collects veteran cars and plays bass guitar – promises of entertaining evenings. Superb grounds with a fishing pond and an 'aperitif gazebo'.

rooms	6: 5 doubles, 1 suite for 4, all with bath or shower & wc.
price	€70-€100 for two.
dinner	€25 with wine, by arrangement.
closed	Rarely.
directions	From A11 exit 20 on D923. Cross Loire to Liré on D763; right D751 to Drain; left D154 for St Laurent des Autels. In Drain, house 3.5km after church on left.

Brigitte & Gérard Migon
Le Mésangeau,
49530 Drain, Maine-et-Loire

tel	(0)2 40 98 21 57
fax	(0)2 40 98 28 62
e-mail	le.mesangeau@wanadoo.fr
web	www.anjou-et-loire.com/mesangeau

map: 9 entry: 319

Your hosts are lovely people, interesting, amusing and educated. Bernard likes to cook dinner for guests occasionally, with the emphasis on simple recipes using the best local ingredients. Facing the big garden with its swimming pool, the main house has a friendly family kitchen and a dining room with stacks of books and a pianola in the fireplace. The duplex guest rooms in a converted outbuilding are well but simply furnished and the old chapel, where the great playwright Racine, put there by an uncle, once officiated as prior, is now a garden room for breakfast. His life changed too, when he was removed by the bishop.

rooms	3: 1 suite for 2 with bath & wc; 2 suites for 4-5, both with bath & 2 wcs.
price	€65 for two.
dinner	€25 with wine, by arrangement.
closed	15 September-April.
directions	From Angers N23 for Nantes 13km; through St Georges; cont. 1.5km; left after garage. Pass château: house on left. Park outside, walk through gate.

Bernard & Geneviève Gaultier
Prieuré de l'Épinay,
49170 St Georges sur Loire,
Maine-et-Loire

tel	(0)2 41 39 14 44
fax	(0)2 41 39 14 44
e-mail	bgaultier@compuserve.com

map: 9 entry: 320

WESTERN LOIRE

A rare survivor of Cholet's imperial past, when the whole town flourished on making handkerchiefs, this elegant townhouse was the orangery of a long-gone château. Nothing imperial about Édith though, who loves to make guests feel at home. The bedrooms are light and beautiful with fine period furniture and gleaming modern bathrooms. Two give onto the quiet street, the suite looks over the rose-filled, tree-shaded garden. There are two pretty *salons* and a glass-roofed dining room in the sunken courtyard – excellent dinners here. French style and hospitality at its best.

rooms	3: 2 doubles, 1 suite, all with shower or bath & wc.
price	€61-€76 for two; suite €120 for four.
dinner	€23, with wine; restaurants 50m.
closed	Rarely.
directions	Rue Nationale is one-way street through Cholet centre. No.28 200m down on right.

Édith & Jean-René Duchesne
Demeure l'Impériale,
28 rue Nationale,
49300 Cholet, Maine-et-Loire

tel	(0)2 41 58 84 84
fax	(0)2 41 63 17 03
e-mail	demeure.imperiale@wanadoo.fr
web	demeure-imperiale.com

map: 9 entry: 321

The whole place sings this lovely lady's independent, artistic and nature-loving personality and her sensitive approach to interiors domestic and human. The suite is superb in dramatic red, white and blue, the children's room deeply child-friendly, the bathroom fetchingly jungly. The light pours in and you bask in the harmony of warm, authentic comfort: stripped woodwork, richly-clothed walls (all Madame's work), old but not wealthy furniture. Outside the rambling 19th-century château lies a lush magical haven, a 10-acre oasis of semi-wild vegetation where endangered flora and fauna take refuge. Out of this world.

rooms	3: 2 doubles, 1 suite for 5, all with bath or shower & wc.
price	€65-€90 for two; suite €150 for five.
dinner	Good restaurants in Saumur, 9km.
closed	In winter, except by arrangement.
directions	From Saumur N147 for Longué to La Ronde; D767 for Vernantes; left D129 for Neuillé; 1km before Neuillé follow Fontaine Suzon; signposted.

Mme Monique Calot
Château du Goupillon,
49680 Neuillé, Maine-et-Loire

tel	(0)2 41 52 51 89
fax	(0)2 41 52 51 89

map: 10 entry: 322

This highly-sculpted neo-Gothic folly is home to a couple of charming, unselfconscious aristocrats and lots of cheerful children. The baronial hall is properly dark and spooky, the reception rooms formal with plush, gilt and ancestors on the walls. In the vast 'suite' room you will find a sitting area and a library corner in an alcove. The smaller double has the shower in a turret, the loo in another, outside. Both are elegantly, unfussily decorated with period French pieces and some modern fabrics. The park is huge, wild boar roam, spring boarlets scamper. Madame plays the piano and holds concerts. An amazing experience. *Gîte space for 7.*

rooms	1 suite for 2-5 with bath & wc.
price	€75-€200 for two; €305 for 5 for five.
dinner	€50; wine €18-€26.
closed	Rarely.
directions	From A85 exit 'Saumur' on D767 for Le Lude. After 1km, left on D129 to Neuillé. Signposted.

Monica Le Pelletier de Glatigny
Château de Salvert,
Salvert,
49680 Neuillé, Maine-et-Loire

tel	(0)2 41 52 55 89
fax	(0)2 41 52 56 14
e-mail	info@salvert.com
web	www.salvert.com

map: 10 entry: 323

How can it be so peaceful? Despite having five children under 12, doing all the restoration, running the B&B and even planning to open as a hotel in due course, Caroline and Philippe are unfailingly relaxed and welcoming. Perhaps their secret is that they want everyone to fall in love with La Paleine, just as they did. One room is white and simple, the family suite is cheery in yellow and green. On the edge of an interesting village with an auberge just down the road for supper, you will find a great family atmosphere, home-made jam and yogurt for breakfast and a bag of walnuts to take home. *Gîte space for 5.*

rooms	2: 1 double with shower & wc; 1 suite for 4 with bath & wc.
price	€46 for two.
dinner	Good auberge 200m (closed wednesdays).
closed	Rarely.
directions	From A11 onto A85 exit Saumur for Poitiers; N147 exit Le Puy; 2nd right (Toutes Directions); house opp. Stop sign.

Caroline & Philippe Wadoux
Château la Paleine,
10 place Jules Raimbault,
49260 Le Puy Notre Dame,
Maine-et-Loire

tel	(0)2 41 38 28 25
e-mail	p.wadoux@libertysurf.fr
web	www.france-bonjour.com/chateau-la-paleine/

map: 10 entry: 324

History speaks from every cranny: from 16th-century convent to courtier's residence to police station, it became a B&B, keeping its superb stone staircases. The *Suite Blanche* is orange and white and has beams, tiles, mirrors, fireplaces, carved *armoires*. Other rooms are big too, and inviting. It's a bit like staying in a beloved granny's house. The glorious living room with its mystifying high-level old bread oven, beamed ceiling and original built-in cupboards is worth the visit by itself. Monsieur restored antiques – his house speaks well of his skill; Madame is gentle and efficient; renovation continues.

rooms	3: 2 suites, 1 triple (with kitchenette), all with bath or shower & wc (very occasionally sharing).
price	€55 for two.
dinner	Choice of restaurants in town or self-catering.
closed	November-February.
directions	From Saumur, D147 for Poitiers. In Montreuil Bellay, follow signs to Les Petits Augustins la Joie Vivante; entrance to house near chapel; left at Café Marcel.

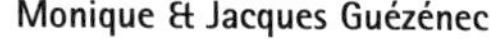

Monique & Jacques Guézénec
Demeure des Petits Augustins,
Place des Augustins,
49260 Montreuil Bellay,
Maine-et-Loire

tel	(0)2 41 52 33 88
fax	(0)2 41 52 33 88
e-mail	moniqueguezenecbb@minitel.net

map: 10 entry: 325

Deep inside old Saumur, this miniature medieval 'palace', with courtyard balcony worthy of a lover's lament, is a superb blend of old and new, a rare surprise achieved by its inspired architect owner and quietly enjoyed by Madame: bedroom beams, shutters and fabrics of highly original colour and design; sitting room fireplace, furniture, pictures and tapestries of huge quality and interest. Juliets and their Romeos won't easily forget this place of rich welcoming intimacy.

rooms	1 suite for 2 with shower & wc.
price	€100 for two.
dinner	Samur is full of restaurants.
closed	November-March.
directions	From Tourist Office to Église St Pierre; in Place St Pierre, Rue Hte St Pierre on right opp. church.

Marie & Marc Ganuchaud
La Mascaron,
6 rue Haute St Pierre,
49400 Saumur, Maine-et-Loire
tel (0)2 41 67 42 91

WESTERN LOIRE

Two vast rooms in an old, castle-like tower, the cream and blue bold-striped one big enough for four, the third, smaller room in the house overlooking the garden. Christian is the "artist in the kitchen", makes things just right for guests and looks after their little girl while Sophie works. Breakfast is in the tower or on your own terrace; the garden is enclosed and perfect for children, though you can hear some cars; history and sights jostle for attention outside.

rooms	3: 1 double, 1 triple, 1 quadruple, all with bath or shower & wc.
price	€49-€55 for two; €69-€77 for four.
dinner	€15-€20, wine €8.
closed	Rarely.
directions	From Saumur tourist office, D947 for Montsoreau, 5km; house on right, signs.

Christian & Sophie Pommery
Le Petit Hureau,
540 route de Montsoreau,
49400 Dampierre sur Loire,
Maine-et-Loire
tel (0)2 41 67 92 51
e-mail petithureau@loire-saumur.com
web www.loire-saumur.com/petithureau

The flattish countryside round the traditional farmhouse gives little inkling that under your feet are quarries and caves, transformed by Carole and Michel into a maze of terraced gardens and courtyards. One cave is now a kitchen for guests and another a gallery for Carole's stained-glass works. Three bedrooms open onto the sunny, Mediterranean-style courtyard, the others look down onto a sunken garden. All are simply, attractively decorated, while mouthwateringly vibrant colours give an exotic feel to the dining room. Delightful young artist hosts – a fascinating place. *Children over 7 welcome.*

rooms	4: 3 doubles, 1 suite, all with shower & wc.
price	€48-€58 for two.
dinner	Use of kitchen extra; restaurants 3-13km.
closed	Rarely.
directions	From Saumur D960 to Doué la Fontaine; 1st right D214 to Forges. Through village; fork left at crucifix. House on left, sign.

Carole Berréhar & Michel Tribondeau
L'Estaminet de la Fosse,
La Fosse,
49700 Forges, Meigné sous Doué,
Maine-et-Loire

tel	(0)2 41 50 90 09
e-mail	info@chambrehote.com
web	www.chambrehote.com

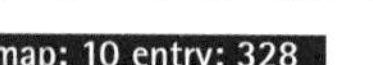

map: 10 entry: 328

WESTERN LOIRE

The solid old manor on the edge of town is a real French family house, loved and lived in by these energetic health-food shop owners, and their four children. Not renovated beyond recognition or period-furnished up to the eyeballs, it just has some inherited antiques in the well-proportioned reception rooms and the occasional quaint touch in the unfrilly, slightly faded guest rooms. Otherwise they are simple and unpretentious, though the easy, welcoming Bastids are constantly improving. The big bosky garden is a good barrier against the road and all diets can be catered for at breakfast, on request. *Gîte space for 2-5 people.*

rooms	3: 1 double, 1 triple, 1 suite, all with bath or shower & wc.
price	€46-€57 for two.
dinner	Wide choice of restaurants in Saumur
closed	Rarely.
directions	From Saumur Tourist Office N147 for Angers; over Loire (2 bridges) & railway; straight on 500m; left Av. des Maraîchers; 400m, right Rue Grange Couronne; 1st on right.

Catherine & Emmanuel Bastid
La Bouère Salée,
Rue Grange Couronne,
49400
St Lambert des Levées, Saumur,
Maine-et-Loire

tel	(0)2 41 67 38 85/(0)2 41 51 12 52
fax	(0)2 41 67 38 85/(0)2 41 51 12 52
e-mail	manubastid@aol.com
web	www.ifrance.com/labouere/

map: 10 entry: 329

Nothing pretentious about this quiet village house but a genuine welcome from nature-loving Carmen, a sprightly retired English teacher, and ex-chef Hervé who cooks excellent traditional French dinners. Bedrooms in the old farmhouse in the shady courtyard, two of them with their own entrances, are simply but pleasantly decorated with small shower rooms. One has a magnificent stone fireplace. Another, up outside stairs, has old beams, stone walls and pretty yellow and white fabrics. Trees almost engulf the house and the sunny conservatory dining room looks over a bosky garden. *Gîte space for 4 people.*

rooms	3: 2 doubles, 1 triple, all with private shower or bath & wc.
price	€40-€43 for two.
dinner	€19.50 with wine, by arrangement.
closed	Rarely.
directions	From A85 exit 2 (Longué); then N147 for Saumur; at Super U r'bout D53 to St Philbert. House on right on entering village.

Carmen & Hervé Taté
La Closerie,
Le Bourg,
49160 St Philbert du Peuple,
Maine-et-Loire
tel (0)2 41 52 62 69
e-mail carmenhervetate@aol.com

WESTERN LOIRE

House and hostess achieve the perfect balance of refinement and relaxed welcome. Once the servants' quarters of the château (they housed their servants grandly in those days...), it is in a deep, secluded valley, right on the GR3 long-distance path and the Loire Valley Walk. The bedrooms are under the high exposed roof beams, elegantly and discreetly done with good antiques, matching wallpaper and flowery English-style fabrics, impeccable bathrooms and loos. Breakfast is beautifully served – linen table napkins and silver teapot – and you can picnic in the garden later if you wish. *Gîte space for 4 people.*

rooms	2: 1 twin/triple, 1 suite for 4, both with shower & wc.
price	€61 for two.
dinner	Choice of restaurants 1km.
closed	Rarely.
directions	From Saumur D751 W 15km. In Gennes D69 for Doué la Fontaine, up hill, past church & police station. At r'bout take road past Super U; drive to house is 500m along on left.

Annick & Jean-Baptiste Boisset
Le Haut Joreau,
49350 Gennes, Maine-et-Loire
tel (0)2 41 38 02 58
fax (0)2 41 38 15 02
e-mail joreau@fr.st
web www.joreau.fr.st

Serenity and rural peace are the hallmarks here. Not the most spectacular countryside but the house is tranquil in its hamlet and for excitement Monsieur will guide beginners in the art of billiards. Quiet and kind, Madame is spontaneously welcoming and properly proud of her house. The lovely sitting room, dominated by the hearth beneath the old beams, mixes comfort and antiques; immaculate, unfussy bedrooms have pastel colours, tiled floors and oriental rugs between old rafters and stones; country-fresh breakfast can be in the garden on fine mornings. You can picnic there too or bicycle down to the banks of the Loire.

rooms	3: 2 doubles, 1 triple, all with shower & wc.
price	€44 for two, €57 for three.
dinner	€20 with wine, by arrangement.
closed	Rarely.
directions	From Angers N761 for Brissac & Doué. At Les Alleuds left on D90 for Chemellier. Hamlet 3km on left. Sign on right, house immed. left.

Éliette Edon
Chambres d'Hôtes,
49320 Maunit Chemellier,
Maine-et-Loire
tel (0)2 41 45 59 50
fax (0)2 41 45 01 44

WESTERN LOIRE

Martine, young, dynamic and very likeable, knows what B&B lovers really want. She cherishes the character of the fine old farm and there's virtually no farm mess to spoil its arched symmetry though the family work hard growing lupin, hollyhock and thyme seeds – the air is heady with the scent. Your hosts' wing (other family members live in other wings) has been done with simple good taste: the vast new ground-floor room is superb in its old tiled floor, subtle lighting, big double bed; each comfortable room has a personal touch; there are landing chairs for guests to watch farmyard life go by – in peace. *Gîte space for 18 people.*

rooms	4: 2 doubles, both with shower & wc; 1 double, 1 twin, both with shower, sharing 2 wcs (showers behind curtains).
price	€40-€50 for two.
dinner	Good restaurants 3-7km.
closed	Rarely.
directions	From Angers, N260 for Cholet; D748 for Poitiers. After Brissac, D761 for Poitiers. House signposted on left after 2km, at end of avenue of chestnut trees.

Jean-Claude & Martine Colibet
La Pichonnière,
Charcé Saint Ellier,
49320 Brissac Quincé,
Maine-et-Loire
tel (0)2 41 91 29 37 (mealtimes)
fax (0)2 41 91 96 85
e-mail gite-brissac@wanadoo.fr
web www.gite-brissac.com

From the old cobbles climb the mysterious steps into the house: the formal 19th-century dining room cannot prepare you for Claudine's bold bright explosion upstairs. Each stunning bedroom, lively green, daffodil-yellow or butterflies, is a statement of her vibrant, confident personality. Two have unbeatable views of the mighty Loire, the others – two secluded in the old stable block – look onto the fine garden and its superb trees. Claudine does weekends with mystery tours, old Loire songs or story-telling – a lovely woman. Good for families too: safe garden, kids' pizzas in the old bread oven, small prison, games room.

rooms	6: 2 doubles, 1 twin, 2 triples, 1 suite for 4, all with shower & wc; 2 with kitchenettes.
price	€55-€63 for two.
dinner	€24-€26 with wine, by arrangement.
closed	Rarely.
directions	From Angers D952 for Saumur. Entering St Mathurin, house on left-hand side (signposted).

Mme Claudine Pinier
La Bouquetterie,
118 rue du Roi René,
49250 St Mathurin sur Loire,
Maine-et-Loire

tel	(0)2 41 57 02 00
fax	(0)2 41 57 31 90
e-mail	cpinier@aol.com
web	www.anjou-et-loire.com/bouquetterie

map: 10 entry: 334

WESTERN LOIRE

This conversion of farm and outbuildings is impeccably done and Mireille's sense of style and attention to detail are everywhere: perfectly co-ordinated colour schemes with her own stencilling, new beds, good linen, nice big towels and a living area with refrigerator and microwave for guests – meals are served here or outside. The Métiviers want you to be comfortable and relaxed; they love to chat and are fascinating about local history and the environment; but they'll fully understand if you prefer to eat alone. A lovely garden too – all utterly restful. *Children under two free.*

rooms	2 doubles with extra single bed, both with shower & wc, 1 wc separate.
price	€47.50 for two.
dinner	€14 with wine, by arrangement.
closed	2 weeks in summer.
directions	From Angers N147 for Saumur; 3km after Corné D61 left for Baugé for 2km past dairy & agricultural co-op; 2nd left at sign. House 1st on right.

Mireille & Michel Métivier
Le Haut Pouillé,
La Buissonnière,
49630 Mazé, Maine-et-Loire

tel	(0)2 41 45 13 72
fax	(0)2 41 45 19 02
e-mail	labuissonniere@mageos.com
web	www.labuissonniere.fr.st

map: 10 entry: 335

It's a charming 16th-century house complete with the old *pigeonnier* and its resident owl. He may woo you in from his impressive quarters next to the huge guest dining room: they are about three feet across with a ceiling which can be pulled back to show the ancient carpentry. Your smiley, generous hosts converted the stables leaving its original beauties, some fine brickwork and tiled floors, exposed for admiration. Antique French country pieces that they restored themselves are buoyed up by colourful furnishings. Stay for dinner, then take a stroll around the fairy-tale woodland garden. Enchanting.

rooms	4: 1 double, 1 twin, 1 triple, 1 suite for five, each with bath or shower & wc.
price	€48-€53 for two.
dinner	€18 with wine, by arrangement.
closed	Rarely.
directions	From Saumur N147 for Longué; right D938 for Baugé; in Jumelles left at church for Brion; signs.

Patricia & Gilles Patrice
La Chouannière,
Domaine des Hayes,
49250 Brion, Maine-et-Loire

tel	(0)2 41 80 21 74
fax	(0)2 41 80 21 74
e-mail	chouanniere@loire-passion.com
web	www.loire-passion.com

A refreshingly enthusiastic young family and Madame an imaginative cook with a fine sense of humour – dinner with them in the vast converted stable is a joyous daily event. Monsieur restores houses – very well: simple bright guest rooms, separate from the main house and each with its own entrance, wear lovingly-restored 18th-century beams and honeycomb tiles, perfect foils for old *armoires* and bedheads. Steep stairs lead up to the children's mezzanine rooms, everything is in unpretentious good taste and the old *pressoir* (wine press) is now pool house, ping-pong and bird-watching spot (binoculars on loan).

rooms	5: 1 double, 1 twin, 1 triple, 2 suites, all with bath or shower & wc.
price	€49-59 for two.
dinner	€20 with wine, by arrangement.
closed	2 weeks in January.
directions	From Saumur N147 N/NW 15km past Longué; D938 right for Baugé 2.5km; left to Brion; signposted in village opp. church.

Anne & Jean-Marc Le Foulgocq
Le Logis du Pressoir,
Villeneuve,
49250 Brion, Maine-et-Loire

tel	(0)2 41 57 27 33
fax	(0)2 41 57 27 33
e-mail	lepressoir@wanadoo.fr
web	www.lepressoir.fr.st

Unusual. alternative and great for the informal. Joyce, a quietly relaxed, welcoming aromatherapist, grows organic veg, cooks good veggie food, receives art, yoga and meditation workshops in her lovely meditation room and shares her comforting, lived-in space with easy generosity. Beams spring everywhere in the 500-year-old farmhouse – take care going to bed. One room has steps to the courtyard, the other looks over the pond where otters may be playing, both are earthy-coloured, in harmony with the old wood and stone. Old rural it feels, mature alternative it sings. Small camping site, lots of animals. *Gîte space for 6 people.*

rooms	2: 1 double, 1 twin, sharing bath & wc.
price	€46 for two.
dinner	Vegetarian dinner €15 with wine, by arrangement.
closed	Rarely.
directions	From Le Mans N23 to La Flèche; D37 to Fougeré; D217 for Baugé, 1.5km. House on left.

Joyce Rimell
La Besnardière,
Route de Baugé,
49150 Fougeré, Maine-et-Loire
tel (0)2 41 90 15 20
fax (0)2 41 90 15 20

WESTERN LOIRE

Artistic, relaxed, convivial; Madame is huge fun and loves decorating her wonderful mansion with intriguing, unusual touches; Monsieur is an artist, his hand visible everywhere. In the quiet woods, the house is a Victorian extravaganza with older tower and dovecote. Inside it's a study in disorganised elegance, masses of antiques, *brocante* and modernities – sophisticated and entertaining. There are relaxation sessions, billiards, piano, and coffee-roasting, a sense of magic in the park, the odd statue peering from the bushes, a pond fed by a reputedly miraculous spring. Good food, too.

rooms	5: 4 doubles, 1 suite for 4, all with bath & wc.
price	€68.50-€70 for two.
dinner	€22.50 with wine, by arrangement.
closed	January-February.
directions	From A11 left on A85 for Tours. Exit at Longué on D938 for Baugé 5km. Right on D62 for Mouliherne. House 5km along on right.

Françoise & Michel Toutain
Le Prieuré de Vendanger,
49150 Le Guédeniau,
Maine-et-Loire
tel (0)2 41 67 82 37
fax (0)2 41 67 82 43
e-mail info@vendanger.fr
web www.vendanger.fr

Michael and Jill are good talkers, good listeners and great fun; their two lively children, their guinea pigs, cats, chickens and ponies bring young cheer to the old French house. Bedrooms are big, bright and comfortable: the double, up characterfully creaky stairs, has a green 'marbled' fireplace, garden views and two deep armchairs from which to survey the scene; the quadruple, under the beamed roof and with rugs on parquet floors, has those same views through low windows, a large sofa and a small shower room. Everything is clean and tidy without being oppressively so. *Gîte space for 4 people.*

rooms	2: 1 double with private bath & wc, 1 family room with shower & wc.
price	€50 for two.
dinner	Very good restaurants 2.5km.
closed	1 week in February & July.
directions	From La Flèche D308/D938 to Baugé; follow signs for Tours & Saumur; right at lights on D61 to Le Vieil Baugé. Sign after 2km.

Michael & Jill Coyle
La Chalopinière,
49150 Le Vieil Baugé,
Maine-et-Loire

tel	(0)2 41 89 04 38
fax	(0)2 41 89 04 38
e-mail	rigbycoyle@aol.com

map: 5 entry: 340

WESTERN LOIRE

Down-to-earth, fun-loving and decent, Madame is a splendid woman and hers is authentic farmhouse hospitality. Breakfast is in the cosy, farmhouse living room, alive with the desire to please. The attic has become three well-finished, honest guest rooms and a children's room with a fascinating original enclosed bed. Great old roof timbers share the space with new beds and inherited *armoires*. It is simple and clean-cut with discreet plastic flooring, pastel walls, sparkling new showers. Your hosts are delighted to show you their exclusively grass-fed brown oxen, have two lively kids and provide toys, games and swings for yours.

rooms	3: 1 double, 1 twin, 1 triple, all with shower & wc; 1 children's room.
price	€40 for two.
dinner	Choice of restaurants 5km.
closed	Rarely.
directions	From Angers N23 to Seiches sur le Loir; right D766 Tours, 9km; right into Jarzé D59 for Beaufort en Vallé. On left 700m after Jarzé.

Véronique & Vincent Papiau
Le Point du Jour,
49140 Jarzé, Maine-et-Loire

tel	(0)2 41 95 46 04
fax	(0)2 41 95 46 04

map: 5 entry: 341

An 1840s neo-Gothic delight in a stork-nested, deer-roamed park, a river for swimming and rowing and a film set of an interior; the sitting room is splendidly 'medieval', the panelled *salon* pure 18th century, taken whole from a château, with superb hangings and immensely high doors. This was once a self-sufficient country estate with its own chapel, dovecote and mill (remains still visible). And a Bishop's Room, of course, where you can sleep. The corner room has a fine four-poster; all are a mixture of old and new with super river views. Your hosts are gracious and humorous, fascinating to listen to and utterly French.

rooms	4: 1 triple, 3 doubles, all with bath or shower & wc.
price	€65-€75 for two.
dinner	€25 with wine, by arrangement.
closed	November-Easter.
directions	From Angers N23 to Seiches sur Loir; D74 for Châteauneuf sur Sarthe 5.5km. Château on right as you leave Montreuil village.

Jacques & Marie Bailliou
Château de Montreuil,
49140 Montreuil sur Loir,
Maine-et-Loire

tel	(0)2 41 76 21 03
e-mail	chateau.montreuil@anjou-et-loire.com
web	www.anjou-et-loire.com/chateau

The park will explode your senses: the big lake with its resident heron, the formal sculpted bits, borders of fruit and flowers, astounding squash bowers (yes!). Equally magnificent is the 15th-century château, carefully tended by the same family for 300 years. Heirs Régis and Nicole are bringing fresh energy to the house along with a passion for gardening. A very old stone staircase illuminated by a stained-glass chapel window leads to the properly formal bedrooms whose bold blues and oranges were interior-design flavour of the period; the wooden floors, thick rugs and antiques are only slightly younger. Remarkable.

rooms	3: 1 double with bath & wc; 1 double with bath, wc & kitchen; 1 suite for 4 with bath, wc & kitchen.
price	€69-€83 for two; suite €121 for four.
dinner	Choice of restaurants nearby.
closed	Rarely.
directions	From A11 exit 14; D52 for Châteauneuf sur Sarthe 16km; at Tiercé left D74 through Écuillé for Sceaux d'Anjou; cross D768; château sign 1km on left.

Régis & Nicole de Loture
Château de Montriou,
49460 Feneu, Maine-et-Loire

tel	(0)2 41 93 30 11
fax	(0)2 41 93 15 63
e-mail	chateau-de-montriou@wanadoo.fr
web	www.chateau-de-montriou.com

Age-old peace and youthful freshness breathe from the old farmhouse, transformed from tumbledown dereliction to rural idyll for this cultured, artistic, unpretentious couple and their four children. Rooms are decorated with flair and simplicity with strong, warm colours, seagrass flooring and good fabrics. Wonderful meals – Regina's regional recipes are very sought after. A perfect retreat too for music, art and nature lovers. This is the family estate: join the Tuesday choir practice at the château, take singing lessons with Patrice's sister. And fish, boat or walk in the unspoilt countryside. A special place.

rooms	3: 1 double, 1 twin, 1 triple, all with bath or shower & wc.
price	€58 for two.
dinner	€23 with wine, by arrangement.
closed	Rarely.
directions	From Angers for Lion d'Angers. At Montreuil Juigné right on D768 for Champigné. 500m after x-roads at La Croix de Beauvais right up drive to La Roche & Malvoisine.

Patrice & Regina de La Bastille
Malvoisine,
49460 Écuillé, Maine-et-Loire
tel (0)2 41 93 34 44
fax (0)2 41 93 34 44
e-mail bastille-pr@wanadoo.fr
web www.malvoisine-bastille.com

You cannot fail to warm to Madame's easy vivacity and infectious laugh. She virtually lives in her beloved garden or in her kitchen in the house opposite, making pastries and bread in the old bread oven. The typical, lovingly-preserved Segré farmhouse with its deep roof and curious *outeau* openings (some would have put in modern dormers) has great beams, a big fireplace, exposed stone and new country furniture. Attic bedrooms are deliciously rustic: crochet, terracotta, pine, with bathrooms cunningly sneaked in among the rafters. The woods are full of birdlife and cows graze peacefully under the children's window.

rooms	3: 1 double, 2 quadruples, all with bath or shower & wc.
price	€34-€36 for two.
dinner	Choice of restaurants 2-5km; kitchen available; picnic in garden possible.
closed	Rarely.
directions	From Angers N162 to Lion d'Angers; cont. for Rennes/Segré on D863 3km; left at Chambres d'Hôtes sign; 1km along on left.

Jocelyne & François Vivier
Les Travaillères,
49220 Le Lion d'Angers,
Maine-et-Loire
tel (0)2 41 61 33 56/(0)6 77 86 24 33

Through the door in the wall, under the tunnel of greenery and lo! a fine presbytery rises from the lawns, fairly well sheltered from the road. The Ruches have done their classic French house in thoughtful, unusual fashion: a taffeta theme throughout with draperies and florals, collections of glass, china, dolls (the Indian puppets on the dining room walls are a joy) and modern paintings under high beautifully-beamed ceilings, a piano by the great sitting-room fireplace and a convivial refectory table for breakfast. These are fun, generous people (he's a pilot) with a talent for interior design and a desire to please.

rooms	4 doubles, all with bath or shower & wc.
price	€60-€115 for two.
dinner	€20 with wine, by arrangement. Restaurants in village.
closed	Rarely.
directions	From Le Mans A11 exit 11; D859 for Châteauneuf sur Sarthe; D89 for Contigné; left at lights, house opp. church, signposted.

Carole & Oliver Ruche
La Ruchelière,
6 place Jacques Ledoyen,
49330 Contigné, Maine-et-Loire

tel (0)2 41 32 74 86
fax (0)2 41 32 74 86
e-mail webmaster@anjou-bnb.com
web www.anjou-bnb.com

map: 5 entry: 346

WESTERN LOIRE

Sprightly red squirrels decorate the stone balustrade, the wide river flows slowly past the lush garden: it feels like deep country yet this handsome manor has urban elegance in its very stones. Panelling, mouldings, subtly-muted floor tiles bring grace; traditional French florals add softness. It looks fairly formal but Madame, energetic, relaxed and communicative, adores having guests and pampers them, in their own quarters, with luxury. Monsieur is jovial, makes wine and jam and loves fishing! Plush, lacy-feminine, sunny bedrooms, three with river views, all with superb bathrooms. Walking and cycling paths are marked.

rooms	4: 2 doubles, 2 twins, all with bath/shower & wc.
price	€65-€75 for two.
dinner	€25, wine €10. Crêperie 50m.
closed	Rarely.
directions	From Angers N162 for Lion d'Angers 20km to Grieul; right D291 to Grez Neuville. At church, Rue de l'Écluse towards river on left.

Jacqueline & Auguste Bahuaud
La Croix d'Étain,
2 rue de l'Écluse,
49220 Grez Neuville,
Maine-et-Loire

tel (0)2 41 95 68 49
fax (0)2 41 18 02 72
e-mail croix.etain@anjou-et-loire.com
web www.anjou-et-loire.com/croix

map: 4 entry: 347

The original 18th-century townhouse was "cloned" by a 19th-century owner for his daughter! The austere topiaried spinning-tops flanking the drive belie the warm, quietly elegant, sunny rooms ahead. Richard has a book shop in Angers, Florence paints and runs art courses at home, the house breathes books, art and music. Built on the ramparts of the old fortified village, it has wonderful views over open countryside from the pretty 'hanging' garden and two of the delightfully decorated bedrooms, while sunny yellow and lime green fabrics and hand-painted butterflies brighten up the north-facing room. Very special.

rooms	4: 1 double, 2 twins, 1 suite for 4, all with bath & wc.
price	€46 for two; suite €69 for four.
dinner	€17 with wine, by arrangement.
closed	Rarely.
directions	From Angers N162 to Le Lion d'Angers; D863 to Segré; D923; left D863 to l'Hôtellerie de Flée; D180 to Châtelais. 1st left on entering village.

Richard & Florence Sence
Le Frêne,
22 rue Saint Sauveur,
49520 Châtelais, Maine-et-Loire
tel (0)2 41 61 16 45
fax (0)2 41 61 16 45
e-mail lefrene@hotmail.com

WESTERN LOIRE

Here beside the luminous fast-flowing river reigns the easy atmosphere of genuine class – you are welcomed by Madame's gentle intelligence and Monsieur's boundless energy. The house has been much added to since the family arrived 400 years ago but each object, antique and picture has a tale to tell. The first-floor double and big light bathroom are full of interest and comfort; the second-floor suite is ideal for families with its four-poster double and choice of other rooms. The large, formal sitting room is pure 'château' while across the hall/piano room there's an elegant dining room with separate tables for breakfast.

rooms	3: 1 double, 1 twin, 1 suite, all with bath & wc.
price	€76 for two.
dinner	Restaurants nearby.
closed	Rarely.
directions	In Château Gontier N162 N for Laval. Entrance on left 50m after last r'bout as you leave town.

Brigitte & François d' Ambrières
Château de Mirvault-Azé,
53200 Château Gontier, Mayenne
tel (0)2 43 07 10 82
fax (0)2 43 07 10 82
e-mail chateau.mirvault@worldonline.fr

Prize-winning cows in the fields, prize-winning owners in the house. They are an exceptionally engaging, relaxed couple and their conversation is the heart and soul of this marvellous place. At dinner, everything from pâté to *potage* to pâtisserie is home-made *Normand* and attractively presented. Breakfast is a feast at which you help yourself to eggs, cheese and lashings of coffee. The refurbished, Japanese grass-papered bedrooms have a few antiquey bits and bobs and pretty window boxes. Good rooms, creative cooking, excellent people.

rooms — 3: 1 double, 1 twin, 1 triple, all with shower or bath & wc.
price — €45 for two.
dinner — Good choice of restaurants nearby.
closed — December-March.
directions — From Fougères N12 east for Laval 25km; farm sign on right.

Maurice & Thérèse Trihan
La Rouaudière,
Mégaudais,
53500 Ernée, Mayenne
tel (0)2 43 05 13 57
fax (0)2 43 05 71 15

WESTERN LOIRE

The old stairs wind up through the subtly-lit interior to fairly sophisticated rooms with lovely furniture, beams and low doorways, plenty of sitting areas, rooms off for your children or your butler. The French-Irish Drions' beautiful restoration of this ancient priory, mostly 14th and 15th century, is a marvel (famous people get married in the chapel). They are friendly and humorous, horse and hunting enthusiasts who greatly enjoy their B&B activity. The huge grounds lead to open country unspoilt by 20th-century wonders, that big pond is full of carp for keen fishers and there's a tennis court.

rooms — 4: 1 double, 2 family rooms, all with bath & wc; 1 double with shower & wc.
price — €55-€90 for two.
dinner — €23 with wine, by arrangement.
closed — 16 October-April.
directions — From Château Gontier D28 for Grez en Bouère; at Gennes right D15 for Bierné; in St Aignan right before church; house 2km on left.

Ghislain & Françoise Drion
La Gilardière,
53200 Gennes sur Glaize, Mayenne
tel (0)2 43 70 93 03
fax (0)2 43 70 93 03
e-mail ghislain.drion@wanadoo.fr

Monsieur le Comte is the sprightly patriarch of this very close and welcoming family; it will extend to include you, too. Loïk and Hélène, the younger generation, create a wonderfully relaxed atmosphere for their guests. An exceptional place, Craon has innumerable expressions of history, taste and personality: oval windows, canopied beds, sunken marble bath, children's room, lift to bathroom, ancient oaks, bread oven, ice house, endless reception rooms, magnificent stone staircase, pool like a 'mini-Versailles'. Teresa Berganza stayed and practised at the grand piano – she too enjoyed that gracious and natural sense of hospitality.

rooms	6: 2 doubles, 1 twin, 2 singles, 1 suite for 2, all with bath or shower & wc. Extra space for children.
price	€140 for two; suite €240 for two.
dinner	Restaurants in village.
closed	Mid-December-mid-January.
directions	From Château Gontier, N171 to Craon; clear signs as you enter town. 30km south of Laval.

Comte Louis de Guébriant,
Loïk & Hélène de Guébriant
Château de Craon,
53400 Craon, Mayenne

tel	(0)2 43 06 11 02
fax	(0)2 43 06 05 18
e-mail	guebriant@club-internet.fr
web	www.chateaudecraon.com

map: 4 entry: 352

WESTERN LOIRE

All who stay at the Logis du Ray are sure to be wonderfully looked after – the dozen or so fine draught horses by Jacques, B&B guests by Martine. From their previous life in Paris as antique dealers comes a love of beautiful things to add to their natural hospitality, but if you can tear yourself away from the lovely welcoming bedrooms, the homely sitting room or the delightful cottage garden, there are riverside walks and unspoilt countryside to explore on foot or by pony and trap (your hosts run a carriage-driving school). Our readers love it.

rooms	3: 1 double, 2 triples, all with shower & wc.
price	€58-€65 for two; €90 for three.
dinner	Good restaurants in village.
closed	Rarely.
directions	From Sablé sur Sarthe D309/D27 for Angers; entering St Denis, 1st left at 'Renov' Cuir' sign. House 100m along; signs.

Martine & Jacques Lefebvre
Le Logis du Ray,
53290 St Denis d'Anjou, Mayenne

tel	(0)2 43 70 64 10
fax	(0)2 43 70 65 53

map: 5 entry: 353

Of vast age and character – and with an amazing oak staircase – this farmhouse is home to a delightful couple who skillfully and humorously juggle cattle, children and guests, with their iron man and secret *grog flambé* recipe as reminders of ancestral traditions. In the big, soft rooms, every bed is canopied except the single box-bed which is carved and curtained to a tee. There are nooks, crannies, crooked lines and angles; terracotta floors, half-timbered walls, antiques – and pretty shower rooms. Ducks paddle in the enchanting pond, cows graze in the fields, apples become cider – bucolic peace. *Gîte space for 8 people.*

rooms	4: 2 doubles, 1 triple, 1 family room, all with shower/small bath & wc.
price	€40-€44.50 for two.
dinner	€13, wine €7.50.
closed	Rarely.
directions	From Laval N162 for Château Gontier 14km; right through Villiers Charlemagne to Ruille Froid Fonds; left C4 for Bignon 1km. Signs.

Christophe & Christine Davenel
Villeprouvé,
53170 Ruille Froid Fonds, Mayenne
tel (0)2 43 07 71 62
fax (0)2 43 07 71 62

WESTERN LOIRE

Here are *chambres d'hôtes* on the grandest of scales in the heart of the town: a splendid mansion, a fine park with its formal French box garden and romantic 'English' landscaped section – and exquisitely courteous hosts (Monsieur speaks perfect English). The magnificently châteauesque rooms are large and light, each in individual inimitably French style. There's an easy mix of luxury and comfort in the cavernous bathrooms, marble fireplaces and beautiful panelling, some of it delicate blue against striking yellow curtains and bedcovers. Exceptional position, style and attention to detail.

rooms	4: 3 doubles, 1 suite, all with bath & shower & wc.
price	€90-€100 for two.
dinner	Good choice of restaurants in Laval.
closed	December-January.
directions	In Laval follow signs to Mairie then brown signs to Le Bas du Gast – opp. 'Salle Polyvalente' & 'Bibliothèque' (1km from Mairie).

M & Mme François Williot
Le Bas du Gast,
6 rue de la Halle aux Toiles,
53000 Laval, Mayenne
tel (0)2 43 49 22 79
fax (0)2 43 56 44 71
e-mail chateaubasdugast@wanadoo.fr

This unusual and proudly restored 15th-century manor has a staircase tower to the upstairs bedroom to lend an air of mystery. Downstairs are the bread oven and a fine dining room where breakfast is served to the chiming of the church clock. The Nays' old family home is well lived in and they love sharing it with guests. Rooms are elegant with antiques and decent bathrooms. Your welcoming and unintrusive hosts can teach you French, weave baskets or make music. A wonderful atmosphere in delectable countryside – readers have loved the "real character of the place".

rooms	2: 1 double, 1 triple, both with bath or shower & wc.
price	€38 for two.
dinner	Restaurants in village or 3km.
closed	Rarely.
directions	From Laval N157 for Le Mans; at Soulgé sur Ouette D20 left to Evron; D7 for Mayenne. Signs in Mézangers.

Léopold & Marie-Thérèse Nay
Le Cruchet,
53600 Mézangers, Mayenne
tel (0)2 43 90 65 55
e-mail bandb.lecruchet@wanadoo.fr

WESTERN LOIRE

The owners are Franco-British, the breakfast sometimes 'Scandinavian', the house indisputably French. In this haven of quiet, Denis will fill you with tales of their days as foreign correspondents. Patricia has plenty of stories too and is a passionate gardener: wonderful flowers and a sward of green. For you, there are good beds in country décor, a cosy sitting room with the old bread oven, a complete kitchen, a lovely path down to the stream, even red squirrels on the lawn. After visiting villages, walking the trails, dreaming in the rolling country, return to good conversation and real hospitality.

rooms	2 doubles/twins, both with bath & wc.
price	€52 for two.
dinner	Auberge in village; good restaurants nearby; guest kitchen available.
closed	November-Easter.
directions	From Mayenne N12 for Alençon 5km; left D34 for Lassay. In Montreuil Poulay, left D160; house 700m along.

Denis & Patricia Legras-Wood
Le Vieux Presbytère,
53640 Montreuil Poulay, Mayenne
tel (0)2 43 00 86 32
fax (0)2 43 00 81 42
e-mail 101512.245@compuserve.com

The door stands open to welcome all comers or for waving excitedly to the little steam train. This happy, active couple run three teenagers and a farm and keep a truly hospitable house, he the handyman, she the decorator and mosaic-layer (superb pool in a converted barn). Dinner is a lengthy, gregarious, joyful affair – wonderful for lovers of French family cooking. The endearingly French guest quarters in the outbuildings may show signs of the passing of time, and of the family cats... but you will like the Langlais a lot. And Madame's 150 egg cups. *Well-behaved pets with watchful owners only. Gîte space for 6 people.*

rooms	5: 2 doubles, 1 twin, 1 triple, plus 1 suite in 'La Petite Maison', all with shower & wc.
price	€44-€46 for two.
dinner	€18, with wine or cider.
closed	One week at Christmas.
directions	From Alençon N138 S for 4km; left D55 through Champfleur for Bourg le Roi; farm sign 1km after Champfleur.

Denis & Christine Langlais
Garencière,
72610 Champfleur, Sarthe
tel (0)2 33 31 75 84
fax (0)2 33 27 42 09
e-mail denislanglais@wanadoo.fr

WESTERN LOIRE

Parts of this old French farmhouse can be traced back to the 11th century but until recently Claude and Ginette spent 20 years rearing 20th-century chickens for the local market. They now cook delicious meals for their guests, *poulet à l'estragon* being one of Claude's specialities. The bedrooms, which have sloping ceilings and exposed beams, are comfortable, attractively decorated and furnished. One has a fine white iron bedstead, another a tiny window at floor level. But what beats everything is the view from the dining room – the surrounding countryside is luscious. *Gîte space for 4 people.*

rooms	3 doubles, all with shower & separate wc.
price	€43 for two.
dinner	€19.50 with wine, by arrangement.
closed	Rarely.
directions	From Mamers D311 for Alençon 7km; right D116 for Villaines la Carelle; enter village towards St Longis. Sign on left.

Claude & Ginette Pelletier
Le Fay,
72600 Villaines la Carelle, Sarthe
tel (0)2 43 97 73 40
web assoc.wanadoo.fr/bunia/lefay/

Your hosts are the nicest, easiest of aristocrats, determined to keep the ancestral home alive in a dignified manner – 19 generations on. A jewel set in rolling parkland, sheep grazing under mature trees, horses in the paddock, swans on a bit of the moat, peacock, deer, boar... it has antiques on parquet floors and modern beds; bathrooms and loos in turrets, cupboards, alcoves; an elegant dining room with family silver, a sitting room with log fire, family portraits, a small book-lined library – and do ask to see the chapel upstairs. Hunting trophies, timeless tranquillity, genuine, lovely people.

rooms	6: 4 doubles, 1 twin, 1 suite for 3, all with bath or shower & wc.
price	€89–€134 for two.
dinner	€37 with wine, by arrangement.
closed	Rarely.
directions	From Alençon N138 S for Le Mans about 14km; at La Hutte left D310 for 10km; right D19 through Courgains; left D132 to Monhoudou; signs.

Michel & Marie-Christine de Monhoudou
Château de Monhoudou,
72260 Monhoudou, Sarthe
tel (0)2 43 97 40 05
fax (0)2 43 33 11 58
e-mail monhoudou@aol.com
web www.monhoudou.com

WESTERN LOIRE

You may think yourself as lucky to stay in this relaxedly luxurious place as the owner and his young family are to have inherited it, so fine and genuine inside and out. Pure 17th century with a magnificent avenue of trees, moat, lofty beamed ceilings and three *salons* for guests, it brims with antiques, books and atmosphere yet never overwhelms. First-floor rooms are proper château stuff, upstairs they are cosier, less grand, sharing the loo and those pretty oval mansard windows. If you choose the gourmet dinner, your host will set out the family silver and Wedgwood as well as unforgettable food. Wholly delightful. *Gîte space for 10.*

rooms	6: 4 doubles, 2 suites, all with bath or shower & wc.
price	€75–€150 for two.
dinner	€25 with wine, by arrangement.
closed	Rarely.
directions	From A11 exit 8, N157 for Laval; D28 for La Quinte; left by church for Coulans; 1km, wayside cross, fork right & Éporcé entrance on left.

Rémy de Scitivaux
Éporcé,
72550 La Quinte, Sarthe
tel (0)2 43 27 70 22
fax (0)2 43 27 89 29
e-mail eporce@wanadoo.fr

Following her family's tradition, Marie is a good, helpful hostess while Laurent is in motor racing: buffs flock for Le Mans. Theirs is so French a château, not overwhelming, just peaceful loveliness with farmland and woods beyond. Some rooms look onto an amazing 400-year-old cedar, others have gorgeous garden views, all have interesting furniture and are being redone (50 windows to replace!). The long panelled sitting room feels like the inside of an old ship and it is all unpretentious with some gratifyingly untidy corners, small, pretty shower rooms and much unselfconscious good taste. Wonderful. *Gîte space for 6 people.*

rooms	5: 2 double/triples, 3 suites for 4-5, all with bath or shower & wc; 2 separate wcs.
price	€52-€58 for two.
dinner	€19 with wine, by arrangement.
closed	Occasionally, please book ahead.
directions	From Le Mans N23 for La Flèche to Cérans Foulletourte; D31 to Oizé; left on D32; sign to right.

Laurent Sénéchal & Marie David
Château de Montaupin,
72330 Oizé, Sarthe
tel (0)2 43 87 81 70
fax (0)2 43 87 26 25
e-mail chateaudemontaupin@oreka.com

WESTERN LOIRE

A happy house, part farm, part *maison bourgeoise*, where the smell of baking may greet you and the delicious results be on the table in the morning: fabulous pastries, breads and cakes. Your easy, funny hosts have three young children – yours are welcome too and there's space indoors for little ones to run their socks off when they tire of the garden. Then it's up the spiral staircase to a cassis and orange bedroom (it works); or try the purple room in the old farmhouse kitchen. All very rural and river-viewed, yet pretty Malicorne, with its château and *faienceries*, market and restaurants, is a few minutes' meander.

rooms	2: 1 double, 1 triple for 4, both with bath or shower & wc.
price	€46 for two.
dinner	Excellent restaurants in Malicorne, 800m.
closed	Rarely.
directions	From Le Mans N23 for La Flèche; at Fontaine St Martin, D8 for Malicorne sur Sarthe; D23 for Le Mans; house last on left, signs.

Catherine & Jean Paul Beuvier
Le Perceau,
72270 Malicorne, Sarthe
tel (0)2 43 45 74 40
e-mail leperceau@libertysurf.fr

The plain face on the street hides another world behind. A beautifully decorated 17th-century house; guest rooms with personality in a 14th-century outbuilding round a lily-pond courtyard; a garden with 300 trees; a concealed pool. Once in the garden, you'll scarcely know you're in town. The rooms are nicely independent – the suite, in a building of its own, even has kitchenette and washing machine – while convivial meals are shared in the dining room. Monsieur, a good cook, prides himself on his choice of wines, all from small, unpublicised wine-growers. Charming house, host and region.
Gîte space for 4 people.

rooms	3: 1 double, 1 triple, 1 suite for 4-5 with small kitchen, all with shower & wc.
price	€46-€56 for two.
dinner	Restaurant 200m.
closed	Rarely.
directions	From Le Mans D147 to Arnage; D307 to Pontvallain; house in town centre; signs.

Guy Vieillet
Place Jean Graffin,
72510 Pontvallain, Sarthe
tel (0)2 43 46 36 70
fax (0)2 43 46 36 70

WESTERN LOIRE

Bushels of history pour from the beams and vaulted ceilings of the moated priory, snug beneath its old church: built in the 12th, extended in the 16th, it had monks into the 20th century. Christophe loves telling the history, Marie-France does the decorating, brilliantly in keeping with the elegant old house: oriental rugs on old tiled floors, pale-painted beams over stone fireplaces, fine old paintings on plain walls and good modern beds under soft-coloured covers. They are attentive, intelligent hosts, happy to share their vaulted dining room, antique furniture and peaceful garden, and the road is not an inconvenience.

rooms	4: 1 twin, 2 doubles, 1 suite, all with bath, shower & wc.
price	€84-€99 for two; suite €114 for three.
dinner	Auberge opposite & restaurants nearby.
closed	November-February, unless booked in advance.
directions	From Le Mans A28 for Tours; exit Ecommoy; N138 to Dissay sous Courcillon; signs in village.

Christophe & Marie-France Calla
Le Prieuré,
1 rue de la Gare,
72500 Dissay sous Courcillon, Sarthe
tel (0)2 43 44 09 09
fax (0)2 43 44 09 09
e-mail ccalla@club-internet.fr

It's a brilliantly converted old watermill, this couple's labour of love, down to the smooth cogwheels that turn in the great kitchen where you breakfast at the huge oak table. Marie-Claire is so relaxed, such good company, such fun and unflappably efficient that it's hard to believe she has four children under 10 – other kids love it here. The double-height sitting room bursts with books and videos for all; simple, attractive rooms have good beds, old tiled floors, bare stone walls. The atmosphere embraces you; the country sounds of stream, cockerel and Angelus prayer bells soothe; the unsung area brims with interest.

rooms	3: 2 doubles, 1 family room, all with bath or shower & wc. Studio available.
price	€45 for two.
dinner	Restaurant opposite.
closed	Rarely.
directions	From Tours N138 for Le Mans 35km to Dissay sous C.; left at lights; mill just past church.

Marie-Claire Bretonneau
Le Moulin du Prieuré,
3 rue de la Gare,
72500 Dissay sous Courcillon,
Sarthe
tel (0)2 43 44 59 79

What a picture: a three-acre pond full of mirrored trees, fish, frogs and exotic fowl, quietly low buildings, views to a hilltop village, space for all. There are games (croquet, table tennis, boules), a boat, even a sauna. Smallish rooms have well-worn modern and old furnishings and separate entrances: a degree of independence somewhat at the price of homeliness, perhaps. Madame loves feeding guests and chatting; Monsieur twinkles and gets on with the garden – they are a charming, caring couple. Breakfast includes cheese and cold meats. Dinner is an important event, so indulge! And it's heaven for children, of course.

rooms	5: 2 doubles, 1 twin, 2 triples, all with shower & wc.
price	€43 for two; €53 for three.
dinner	€14 with wine, by arrangement.
closed	15 November-February.
directions	From Le Mans D304 to Grand Lucé & La Chartre; left D305 through Pont de Braye; left D303 to Lavenay & follow signs (2km).

Monique & Jacques Déage
Le Patis du Vergas,
72310 Lavenay, Sarthe
tel (0)2 43 35 38 18
fax (0)2 43 35 38 18

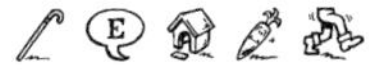

This was Roger and Dagmar's country cottage until they left Paris 10 years ago to live here. He's a retired chef, she left her native Germany and adopted France many moons ago. They are friendly and hospitable and will probably join you for breakfast where there will be hot croissants – or you could make it a huge meal, with ham, smoked salmon and cheese. If you time it right, the walls are covered with roses: it looks a cosy place to stay, even from the outside. One bedroom is wood-panelled, the other more typical with sloping rafters; fabrics are flowered and the varnished wooden floors are symmetrically rugged.

LOIRE VALLEY

rooms	2: 1 double, 1 suite for 3, both with bath & wc.
price	€43-€51 for two.
dinner	€19 with wine, by arrangement.
closed	January-February.
directions	From Verneuil sur Avre D939 for Chartres; in Maillebois left on D20 to Blévy; follow signs to Chambres d'Hôtes.

Oh gentle living that was here – and deep, dark intrigue – when the Renaissance blossomed by the banks of France's mightiest river and kings and courtiers rode out to hunt the noble stag.

	Roger Parmentier
	2 route des Champarts,
	28170 Blévy, Eure-et-Loir
tel	(0)2 37 48 01 21
fax	(0)2 37 48 01 21
e-mail	parti@club-internet.fr
web	www.bab-blevy.com

The soaring glory of bustling Chartres is just 15 minutes away but the house is wrapped about by fields worked single-handedly by Bruno. No typical farmer, he went to the Lycée Français in London, so conversation can be in either language, and Nathalie loves to chat, in French. Rooms are blissfully quiet with fresh colour schemes and a satisfying mix of old-fashioned and modern. Dinner is generally good – try Nathalie's goat's cheese starter – but the family do tend to be over-stretched at harvest time. Simple sitting/dining room, a delightful donkey and dog act, genuine, hard-working people.

rooms	3: 2 doubles, 1 twin, all with bath or shower & wc.
price	€55 for two.
dinner	€15 with wine, by arrangement.
closed	Rarely.
directions	In Chartres N154 N for Dreux; after Chartres left D133 for Fresnay; D134 for Bailleau l'Evêque; signs.

Nathalie & Bruno Vasseur
Ferme du Château,
Levéville,
28300 Bailleau l'Évêque,
Eure-et-Loir
tel (0)2 37 22 97 02
fax (0)2 37 22 97 02

The whole world comes to enjoy this gentle, polyglot family and the serene vibes of their old Chartrain house. Up two steep spirals to the attic, across the family's little prayer room (your sitting room), past the stained-glass window, the lovely bedroom feels a bit like a chapel with beds. Lots of books; reminders of pilgrimage – properly so, just beneath the great Cathedral; perfect hosts: Madame knowledgeably friendly, Monsieur a charmer who enjoys a chuckle, their children, genuinely interested in your travels; they're all happy to sit and talk when you get back. An unusual and welcoming place in a timeless spot.

rooms	1 twin with private shower & wc on floor below.
price	€44 for two.
dinner	Choice of restaurants on your doorstep.
closed	Rarely.
directions	Arriving in Chartres follow signs for IBIS Centre; park by Hotel IBIS (Place Drouaise); walk 20m along Rue de la Porte Drouaise to Rue Muret (approx. 100m car to house).

Jean-Loup & Nathalie Cuisiniez
Maison JLN,
80 rue Muret,
28000 Chartres, Eure-et-Loir
tel (0)2 37 21 98 36
fax (0)2 37 21 98 36
e-mail jln.cuisiniez@wanadoo.fr

A beautiful painted sign points to the well-restored yet somewhat quaint old house. Madame is matronly and trusting and the house has a warm, family, lived-in air, with old pieces of furniture and pets ensconced on sofas. The three cosy white guest rooms and one very large ground-floor room have excellent bedding. Birdsong soothes your ear – your hosts know all about the various bird species – and wheat fields rest your eye as you sit in the pretty garden. Eulogies for these people have reached us. *Bookings not confirmed by 5pm on day of arrival may be re-allocated. Swimming pool for children available.*

rooms	4: 1 double, 1 triple, 2 quadruples, all with shower & wc (some on landing).
price	€42 for two.
dinner	Choice of restaurants 7km.
closed	Rarely.
directions	From A11 exit Thivars; N10 for Châteaudun, 15km; left to Moriers; D153 to Pré St Martin; signs.

Bernadette & Jean-Baptiste Violette
Le Carcotage Beauceron,
8 rue Saint Martin,
28800 Pré St Martin, Eure-et-Loir
tel (0)2 37 47 27 21
fax (0)2 37 47 38 09
e-mail carcotage.beauceron@wanadoo.fr
web www.carcotage.com

LOIRE VALLEY

Michel is a farmer with a difference and has a rare expertise of which he is very proud: he grows poppies for use in pharmaceuticals. Géraldine's lively manner and easy welcome into her delightful family relieve the dreariness of the ever-flat Beauce. The farm is set round a quiet, tidy courtyard where rabbits and hens lead their short lives, the good guest rooms are light and pleasantly if simply furnished, the bathrooms pristine. "Remarkable value, real people," said one reader, but don't expect designer décor or gourmet food at these amazing prices – it's just gentle and genuine. *Gîte space for 5 people.*

rooms	4: 2 doubles, 1 twin, all with shower & wc.
price	€33 for two.
dinner	€11, with wine, by arrangement only.
closed	Rarely.
directions	From A10 exit Allaines on D927 for Châteaudun to La Maladrerie; D39 to Loigny. Sign opp. church.

Géraldine & Michel Nivet
8 rue Chanzy,
28140 Loigny la Bataille,
Eure-et-Loir
tel (0)2 37 99 70 71
fax (0)2 37 99 70 71

Here is a taste of real French provincial aristocratic style, with much horsiness: the suite is over the stables, other rooms are full of equine reminders, including Toulouse-Lautrec lithographs. You sleep in great comfort under period rafters, dine *en famille* by candlelight (outside in summer), and breakfast whenever you like – "people are on holiday", says Madame generously. Both your hosts were members of the French national carriage-driving team and offer rides in their prize-winning equipage. Lots of other outdoor activities are to be found in the huge forest which surrounds the quietly elegant building.

rooms	4: 3 doubles, 1 suite, all with bath & wc.
price	€115 for two.
dinner	€35 with wine, by arrangement.
closed	Rarely.
directions	From Montargis N7 for Paris 6km; right through forest to Paucourt; enter village, 1st right Route Grotte aux Loups for 200m; house on left, ivy on wall.

Émmanuelle & Antoine de Jessé Charleval
Domaine de Bel Ébat,
45200 Paucourt, Loiret

tel	(0)2 38 98 38 47
fax	(0)2 38 85 66 43
e-mail	belebat@wanadoo.fr

LOIRE VALLEY

This elegant 18th-century canalside townhouse has inherited an expansive atmosphere from its wine merchant builders. They were loading their wine onto barges on the canal which flows under the windows until the 1930s. So much for the past. For the present: you will dine with your refined hosts in the antique-furnished, chandeliered dining room, sleep in good, very individual rooms, breakfast off ravishing Gien china with fruit from the garden, meet Lucia the black Labrador who helps her owner welcome guests over a glass of local white wine. Madame is happy to arrange visits to wine growers.

rooms	1 + 2 apartments: 1 triple, 1 apartment for 4, both with bath & wc; 1 apartment for 5 with bath & wc downstairs.
price	€50 for two.
dinner	€25 with wine, by arrangement.
closed	Rarely.
directions	From Orléans N60 E for Montargis & Nevers, exit to Fay aux Loges; through Fay, cross canal, left D709; house 1st on left arriving in Donnery.

Nicole & Jacques Sicot
Les Charmettes,
45450 Donnery, Loiret

tel	(0)2 38 59 22 50
fax	(0)2 38 59 55 67
e-mail	nsicot@club-internet.fr

The original 16th-century house huddles up to a cluster of only slightly younger siblings: the result is a charmingly higgledy-piggledy family, mothered by your delightful, easy-going and unintrusive hostess. Since the Moutons arrived here 30 years ago, the outskirts of Orléans have crept out to meet them but the country sounds still win through. Crunch along the drive to the split-level suite with masses of books and a bright new sofabed, sleep beneath the steeply-pitched roof and under Provençal fabrics, then repair to the huge breakfast room with its massive fireplace and the bust of a moustachioed *grand-père*.

rooms 2: 1 double with shower & wc; 1 suite with shower & wc.
price €38-€55 for two.
dinner Plenty of restaurants nearby.
closed 1 November-31 March.
directions In Chaingy N152; left at lights from Blois; right at light from Orléans, Rue des Fourneaux 300m; left Rue de la Grolle. Signs.

Ursula Mouton
18 rue de la Grolle,
45380 Chaingy, Loiret
tel (0)2 38 80 65 68
e-mail u.mouton@Free.fr
web titmar.free.fr/Chambreshotes.htm

LOIRE VALLEY

Life-size boars guard this typical brick and stone Solognote house. The plains of Sologne were the hunting ground of kings and your elegant, chatty hostess is keen on hunting and horses (and golf). Hunting prints and antlers preside over her open living area with its great beams and flagstones; jazz plays, the telly chats. Guest rooms in the house are cosy, yet chic, with sloping ceilings and historic fabrics. The big suite has its own entrance and kitchen – ideal for families, as is the pool and peaceful garden. Madame will happily drive you to and from the restaurants in nearby Vannes. Do stay more than one night.

rooms 2: 1 double, 1 suite for 4, both with bath or shower & wc.
price €54-€77 for two.
dinner 2 auberges 1km; self-catering possible.
closed Christmas & New Year.
directions From Orléans N60 E to Jargeau; over bridge through town centre; left on D951 for Tigy; D83 through Vannes; house about 2km on right.

Agnès Célèrier
Domaine de Sainte-Hélène,
Route d'Isdes,
45510 Vannes sur Cosson, Loiret
tel (0)2 38 58 04 55
fax (0)2 38 58 28 38
e-mail celerierloiret@hotmail.com

A vast estate by the Loire, a house for guests, another for family, exotic pheasants and peacocks strutting around the splendid garden; there's even a private hunting reserve (long-stay guests may visit it). Your welcoming young hosts – he is a busy vet, she looks after the house, their small children and you with natural elegance – make it feel friendly despite the grand appearance. The rooms are carefully decorated with high ceilings and lovely old furnishings. Breakfast is in the *salon*, where the games and hi-fi live, or on the flowered terrace. *Gîte space for 3 people.*

rooms	3: 2 doubles, all with shower or bath & wc; 1 suite for 3 with bathroom & kitchen.
price	€45-€58 for two.
dinner	Good restaurants in Briare or Gien 4km; self-catering in suite.
closed	Rarely.
directions	From A6 onto A77 for Nevers, exit Briare; D952 for Gien. Between Briare & Gien: sign by nurseries.

Mme Bénédicte François
Domaine de la Thiau,
45250 Briare, Loiret

tel	(0)2 38 38 20 92
fax	(0)2 38 67 40 50
e-mail	lathiau@club-internet.fr
web	perso.club-internet.fr/lathiau

map: 6 entry: 377

LOIRE VALLEY

There's a barge restaurant in summer just a stroll from the house and you must see the great 19th-century canal bridge over the Loire at Briare. The canal flows gently past this handsome old village house but you may hear the less gentle road in the morning. Guest rooms are rustic-furnished and good-looking – the suite in the loft in the main house with its exposed beams is particularly handsome – and there are two cosy self-contained cottages with kitchens. Nicole and her husband are kind, well-educated and welcoming and have decorated their breakfast room with lots of pretty, personal knick-knacks. *Gîte space for 4 people.*

rooms	2: 1 double, 1 suite for 3, both with shower & wc.
price	€43 for two.
dinner	Restaurants nearby.
closed	Rarely.
directions	D952 to Gien, cross Loire for Poilly lez Gien; left D951 to Châtillon sur Loire; signs.

Nicole Lefranc
La Giloutière,
13 rue du Port,
45360 Châtillon sur Loire, Loiret

tel	(0)2 38 31 10 61

map: 6 entry: 378

Utter peace... this boxy 1970s farmhouse is cradled in tumbling woodland and wrapped in birdsong. Goats softly bleat on the farm below. Madame is chatty and genuine, she still helps out with the animals and can arrange goaty visits for children. The downstairs double is functional, the upstairs suites are perfect for families: all have stencilled furniture, some good family pieces, tongue-and-groove pine and stacks of colour. Walls, ceilings and doors are filled with fun murals: sunflowers shine, bees bumble and butterflies flutter by. Your tasty breakfast comes with honey from a friend's bees and, of course, goat's cheese.

rooms	3: 1 double with shower & wc; 1 suite for 3-5, 1 suite for 4-6, each with shower & wc.
price	€31 for two; €68 for six.
dinner	Choice of restaurants nearby.
closed	Rarely.
directions	From Sancerre D923 for Jars & Vailly sur Sauldre; 2km before Jars right on track into wood, house at end of track, signposted.

Madeleine & Philippe Jay
La Brissauderie,
18260 Jars, Cher

tel	(0)2 48 58 74 94
fax	(0)2 48 58 74 94
e-mail	madeleine.jay@wanadoo.fr
web	www.pays-sancerre-sologne.com

map: 11 entry: 379

Retreat to this little house in the woods: perfect bedrooms are in a pretty outbuilding, the suite, with an old tiled floor, a wine-walled sitting room and a massive dining table, looks onto the garden; the double has the same tiles underfoot, beams overhead, with a stylish mix of stone, cream and bold *toile de Jouy* and an impressive shower-room. The Count and Countess, who manage their forests, farm and hunt, are relatively new to B&B, are charming and thoroughly hospitable. If you arrange to eat in, you will join them for dinner in the main house. Members of the family run a vineyard in Provence, so do try their wine.

rooms	2: 1 double with shower & wc, 1 suite for 2-4, with bath & wc.
price	€75-€99 for two; €145 for four.
dinner	€15-€28, with wine; self-catering possible.
closed	Rarely.
directions	From Paris A6 to A77 exit 19 for Gien. From Bourges D940 to Chapelle d'Angillon; D12 to Ivoy le Pré. At church left D39 for Blancafort, Oizon, Château de la Verrerie for 2.5km; gate on right.

Étienne & Marie de Saporta
La Verrerie,
18380 Ivoy le Pré, Cher

tel	(0)2 48 58 90 86
fax	(0)2 48 58 92 79
e-mail	m.desaporta@wanadoo.fr

map: 11 entry: 380

A marriage of 18th-century stones and 20th-century design have created ideal guest quarters in the old stables. Pale timber clothes the space with clever architectural features such as the vast staircase leading to the tree-house-like top bedroom. The breakfast/sitting room combines new wood, contemporary artists' work and antiques; bedrooms are all different: Japanese-style doors and shutters, modern fabrics, lacy linen, crocheted covers. The garden, where guests have a terrace, is full of green and flowery things. Meals are delicious – chic, gracious Madame adapts regional dishes to please today's lighter taste.

rooms	5: 3 doubles, 2 twins, all with bath or shower & wc (2 on ground floor).
price	€46 for two.
dinner	€18 with wine, by arrangement.
closed	15 November-February.
directions	From Sancerre D955 for Bourges for 16km; D44 left to Montigny & 5km beyond; signs.

Élisabeth Gressin
La Reculée,
18250 Montigny, Cher

tel	(0)2 48 69 59 18
fax	(0)2 48 69 52 51
e-mail	e.gressin@terre-net.fr

map: 11 entry: 381

Your hosts came to this rustic haven, where the natural garden flows into woods and fields, deer roam and birdlife astounds, to bring up their new family. Jean is a kindly young grandfather, proud of his efforts in converting his outbuildings for *chambres d'hôtes*. Bedrooms reflect his travels to distant places: Indian rugs, Moroccan brasses, a collection of fossils in an old chemist's cabinet and lots of old farmhouse stuff everywhere, nothing too sophisticated. Breakfast is in the main house where family life bustles busily around you. Return after contemplating Bourges to meditate in this corner of God's harmonious garden.

rooms	4: 2 triples, 1 quadruple, all with shower & wc; 1 family room with bath & wc.
price	€40 for two.
dinner	Restaurant 2.5km.
closed	Rarely.
directions	From Bourges D944 for Orléans. In Bourgneuf left at little r'bout; immed. right & follow signs 1.5km.

Jean Malot & Chantal Charlon
La Grande Mouline,
Bourgneuf,
18110 St Éloy de Gy, Cher

tel	(0)2 48 25 40 44
fax	(0)2 48 25 40 44

map: 11 entry: 382

Deepest Berry, the heartland of rural France, where this articulate husband-and-wife team run their beef and cereals farm, taxi their children to school, make their own jam and still have time for their guests. Laurence is vivacious and casually elegant and runs an intelligent, welcoming house. The big, simple yet stylishly attractive bedrooms of her superior 18th-century farmhouse are of pleasing proportions – one of them in an unusual round brick-and-timber tower, others have views over the peaceful park. Guests may use the swimming pool, set discreetly out of sight, at agreed times. *Gîte space for 9 people.*

rooms	5: 2 doubles, 1 twin, 1 triple, 1 quadruple, all with bath or shower & wc.
price	€51-€54 for two.
dinner	Restaurants in village or choice 6km.
closed	Rarely.
directions	From Vierzon N76 for Bourges through Mehun sur Yèvre; D60 right to Berry Bouy & beyond for about 3km; farm on right.

Laurence & Géraud de La Farge
Domaine de l'Ermitage,
18500 Berry Bouy, Cher
tel (0)2 48 26 87 46
fax (0)2 48 26 03 28

LOIRE VALLEY

Cross the leafy, secret, garden courtyard and step into this venerable 15th-century guesthouse. Beyond the dining room, where ancient timbers, and niches have been exposed in all their mixed-up glory, the knight in shining armour beckons you up the staircase. Bedrooms are elegant with antique beds and new mattresses, marble fireplaces and a claw-footed bath. Climb up to the attic, where the pretty double is festooned with beams. Your charming hosts live just across the courtyard with their two small daughters. Add the privilege of sleeping beneath that unsurpassed Cathedral and it feels like a gift from the angels.

rooms	4: 2 suites for 3-4, both with bath & wc; 2 doubles, both with bath/shower & wc.
price	€58-€69 for two.
dinner	Great choice of restaurants within walking distance.
closed	Rarely.
directions	In Bourges towards Cathedral; Rue des 3 Maillets; Rue Bourbonnoux. Park in yard if space permits.

Nathalie Llopis
Les Bonnets Rouges,
3 rue de la Thaumassière,
18000 Bourges, Cher
tel (0)2 48 65 79 92
fax (0)2 48 69 82 05
e-mail bonnets-rouges@bourges.net
web bonnets-rouges.bourges.net

Quiet country folk with tanned faces, clear eyes and much gentle reality, the Chambrins are the most honest, no-fuss, genuinely hospitable couple you could hope for. Special touches, such as great swathes of creeper outside and dried flowers and an old iron cot inside, give character to their simple old farmhouse set among the sunflower fields. The kitchen-cum-breakfast room, with its carved dresser, is small and intimate. Rooms are comfortable, though not huge, and there is a nice guests' sitting area on the landing with well-worn, quilt-thrown sofas, books and games. *Gîte space for 5 people.*

rooms	3: 1 double, 1 twin, 1 triple, all with shower & wc.
price	€35 for two.
dinner	Bistro 1km.
closed	Rarely.
directions	From Bourges, N144 to Levet; D28 for Dun sur Auron. After 2km right. House 300m from junction.

Marie-Jo & Jean Chambrin
Bannay,
18340 St Germain des Bois, Cher
tel (0)2 48 25 31 03
fax (0)2 48 25 31 03

map: 11 entry: 385

LOIRE VALLEY

The beautifully proportioned house in its big shady garden has been in the family for over 200 years. The *salon* is a cool blue-grey symphony, the dining room smart yellow-grey with a rare, remarkable maroon and grey marble table: breakfast is in here, dinner *en famille* in the big beamed kitchen. Each stylishly comfortable room has character and Madame has a fine eye for detail. She is charming, dynamic, casually elegant and genuinely welcoming. Visitors have poured praise: "quite the most beautiful house we've ever stayed in", "a unique experience of French hospitality and taste". *Gîte space for 6 people.*

rooms	3: 1 double with bath & wc; 2 twins, both with bath or shower & private wc.
price	€45-€53 for two.
dinner	€17 with wine, by arrangement.
closed	Rarely.
directions	From A71 exit 8; at r'bout D925 W for Lignières & Châteauroux. Sign 500m on right.

Marie-Claude Dussert
Domaine de la Trolière,
18200 Orval, Cher
tel (0)2 48 96 47 45
fax (0)2 48 96 07 71

map: 11 entry: 386

The two Claudes inspire remarks like: "I learned heaps about Art Deco and gardening", "a wonderful lanky couple full of life, laughter and intelligence", "lovely, artistic, wacky". Conversation flows effortlessly over glass and ashtray. Their 1940s manor is entirely Art Deco with an eclectic collection of modern art. You find original art and good beds in the rooms, can learn how to make a properly formal French garden, have breakfast when you want. Dine until the small hours beneath the huge collage in the congenial, bohemian, fun-loving atmosphere created by your down-to-earth hosts. Out of the ordinary – we love it.

rooms	3: 2 doubles, 1 twin, all with bath, shower, wc.
price	€61-€76 for two.
dinner	€23-€30 with wine, by arrangement.
closed	Rarely.
directions	From St Amand Montrond, D951 for Sancoin & Nevers. At Charenton Laugère, D953 for Dun sur Auron; house 300m on left.

M & Mme Claude Moreau
La Serre,
18210 Charenton Laugère, Cher

tel (0)2 48 60 75 82
fax (0)2 48 60 75 82

LOIRE VALLEY

A gem – grand hunting lodge rather than château, it stands in acres of parkland before a vast private lake (boating and safe swimming). Karin lovingly tends every inch of it, including the vast picture window that seems to bring the lake into the sitting room. A great staircase leads to the 'Austrian baroque' room with its sloping ceilings, gorgeous rugs and super-luxy bathroom. The pretty 'modern' room on the ground floor has yellow walls and masses of cupboards. And nothing is too much trouble for Karin. *German, Spanish and Dutch also spoken. Gîte space for 2 people.*

rooms	2 doubles, with bath or shower & wc.
price	€54 for two.
dinner	€19 with wine, by arrangement.
closed	Rarely.
directions	From Châteauroux D943 to Ardentes; left on D14 for St Août 8km; left at château sign 400m; entrance on right.

Karin Verburgh
Château de la Villette,
Saint Août,
36120 Ardentes, Indre

tel (0)2 54 36 28 46

This brave and endearing young English couple came to farm in France, with their rabbit-eared sheep (they have two children, and cattle, too) and invite you to drive 2km through the woods for a taste of rural French tranquillity with an English flavour. Their house still has some old beams and a stone fireplace. Rooms are big, pale-floored, simply furnished, supremely peaceful: pilgrims to Compostela often stay here. Alison will take good care of you, and Robin may tell you tales of shearing French sheep and settling into this other land, or where to gaze on rare orchids. Argenton, 'Venice of the Indre', is a must.

rooms	4: 1 double with bath & wc; 2 doubles, 1 family room, sharing bathroom & separate wc.
price	€46 for two.
dinner	€15 with wine, by arrangement.
closed	January-March.
directions	From Châteauroux A20 exit 16 to Tendu; 1st left into village. Pass Mairie, fork left at church for Chavin & Pommiers. 2km up track.

Robin & Alison Mitchell
La Chasse,
36200 Tendu, Indre
tel (0)2 54 24 07 76

map: 10 entry: 389

LOIRE VALLEY

One guest comes every year for the dragonflies to this most striking house in its large park where protected species thrive. Your hostess fell in love with it too and renounced her beloved Paris, but she needs lots of people to make it hum. Relaxed and sociable, she prefers doing to tidying, collects egg cups, will treat you as family and may take you to look for deer. The generous rooms have beams and good old French furniture, the ochre-walled hall is a homely clutter of riding gear, the dining room feels definitely lived in and the open view across parkland to the woods beyond is supremely tranquil. *Minimum 2 nights July-August. Gîte space for 4 people.*

rooms	3: 1 double, 1 double/twin, 1 suite for 4, all with bath or shower & wc.
price	€80 for two; €145 for four.
dinner	Restaurants 5km.
closed	November-March.
directions	From Poitiers N151 60km to Le Blanc; right before river D10 to Bélâbre; left D927 for St Gaultier for 5km; house on right.

Aude de La Jonquière-Aymé
Le Grand Ajoux,
36370 Chalais, Indre
tel (0)2 54 37 72 92
fax (0)2 54 37 56 60
e-mail grandajoux@aol.com
web grandajoux.tripod.com

map: 10 entry: 390

Epicurean asceticism from Alain, a musical, artistic craftsman, cultivator of the senses, seeker of harmony, and Isabelle, a lovely, warm, serene person – and superb cook. A fascinating couple. In bedrooms of almost monastic simplicity, nothing distracts from the natural warmth of old tiles and Alain's beautiful local-wood furniture: all is light, space, harmony. The magnificent room under the rafters is used for recitals and furniture display. Isabelle's vegetable garden centres on a lily pond and there's a little path through the 'wild' wood beyond: this house is a meeting of market place and wilderness where people grow.

rooms	4: 1 double, 2 triples, 1 suite for 5-6, all with bath or shower & wc.
price	€40-€45 for two.
dinner	€19 with wine, by arrangement.
closed	November-Easter.
directions	From Le Mans N157 for Orléans 52km; left D921 to Mondoubleau; Carrefour de l'Ormeau is central village junction; house on corner opp. Ford garage.

Alain Gaubert & Isabelle Peyron
Carrefour de l'Ormeau,
41170 Mondoubleau, Loir-et-Cher
tel (0)2 54 80 93 76
fax (0)2 54 80 93 76
e-mail i.peyron1@tiscali.fr

The restoration of this late-15th-century, fairy-tale manor house, complete with Renaissance façade, is almost all Grégoire's doing. The guest rooms, reached via a wonderful turret draped with Indian fabrics, have lofty ceilings, beautiful dusky pink or yellow ochre walls, four-poster beds, antique furniture and interesting *objets* at every turn. Guests also share a perfectly majestic sitting room. It's an enchanting place to stay in the loveliest, most peaceful surroundings: you can breakfast, laze, sketch the Barbary ducks, make friends with the donkey or fish in the grounds – rods are provided.

rooms	2: 1 triple, 1 suite for 6 (2 rooms), both with bath & wc.
price	€45-€48 for two.
dinner	Wide choice of restaurants 5km.
closed	November-Easter.
directions	From Vendôme D917 to Montoire; cross Loir; D10 for Couture sur Loir 1.5km; right at signpost for 2.5km; house 4th on left (with tower).

Grégoire Lucien-Brun
Manoir de la Chevalinière,
41800 St Martin des Bois,
Loir-et-Cher
tel (0)2 54 72 53 94
fax (0)2 54 72 53 94
e-mail gregoirelucienbrun@hotmail.com

Fabienne is a charming, sociable hostess who genuinely wants you to get the most out of your stay. A lot of the decorative detail is hers and the pretty rooms are named after the flowers she loves and tends in her garden. Light floods in through the big windows of the dining room and there's always home-made jam and cake for breakfast. Fabienne may go with you on local walks or bike rides to make sure you don't miss anything. The troglodyte village of Trôo is just 4km away and it's 6km to the craft centre of Poncé where you can watch potters and glass-blowers at work. *Gîte space for 6.*

rooms	3: 1 double with bath & wc; 2 doubles with shower & wc.
price	€35-€38 for two.
dinner	Good restaurant in Pont de Braye, 2km.
closed	November-Easter.
directions	From Vendôme, D917 for Montoire & Trôo. Sougé is 4km after Trôo. House on left at entrance of village.

Fabienne & Alain Partenay
La Mulotière,
10 rue du Bourg Neuf,
41800 Sougé sur Braye,
Loir-et-Cher
tel (0)6 80 33 72 55
fax (0)2 54 72 46 97

LOIRE VALLEY

The history lesson on the old schoolroom ceiling covers the Creation, Noah's Ark, the Kama Sutra. Artists, writers, musicians love this place. Your hosts, both wordsmiths, are articulate and delightfully relaxed: children come and go to *grand-mère's* house via a ladder over the wall; conversations turn on ancestral recipes and climate change. The unspoilt schoolhouse has white rooms and bright paintwork, original paintings and myriad *objets*. Woods and fields lie beyond the semi-wild garden where you can sit in a live willow *gloriette*. Home production is king here: hams, sheepskins, dandelion jelly... *Small dogs welcome.*

rooms	3: 1 double, 1 twin, 1 triple, all with bath or shower, sharing wc.
price	€33 for two.
dinner	€13.50 with wine, by arrangement.
closed	Occasionally.
directions	From Vendôme N10 for Tours 19km; right D71 to Villechauve; in village, house on right just after church.

Claude & Ariane Laballe
La Lune et les Feux,
Le Bourg,
41310 Villechauve, Loir-et-Cher
tel (0)2 54 80 37 80

With its sweeping farmyard, its pond and such a spontaneous welcome, it is, as one reader wrote, "a little gem of a B&B". You can see for miles across fields filled with lark song and cereals. The owners are a smiling couple who give you their time without invading your space but are delighted to show you their immaculate farm, orchard and vegetable garden if you're interested. Their rooms have gentle colours, soft materials and firm mattresses. The furniture is simple and rustic, the bedrooms and bathrooms are deeply raftered, the old farmhouse breathes through its timbers. It is peaceful, pretty and a place for picnics.

rooms	3: 1 double with shower & wc; 2 doubles sharing bath & wc.
price	€35-€41 for two.
dinner	€13, with wine; restaurant 6km.
closed	Rarely.
directions	From Vendôme D957 for Blois 6km. Right to Crucheray & Chambres d'Hôtes. 4km from turning; signposted.

Élisabeth & Guy Tondereau
Les Bordes,
41100 Crucheray, Loir-et-Cher
tel (0)2 54 77 05 43
fax (0)2 54 77 05 43

LOIRE VALLEY

An old townhouse with a country feel, a pretty garden, a majestic towering chestnut and miniature trees at the bottom to screen the outbuildings. Madame will be found in the picture-framing workshop; her jovial husband farms and will serve your breakfast in the dining room among an array of pictures, samplers and *objets*. Up the characterful sloping-treaded stairs, the light, simple rooms are decorated in understated good taste and pale colours. There are beams, polished parquet or tiled floors, billiards in the sitting room and a kitchenette for guests. A lovely place to stay. *Gîte space for 6 people.*

rooms	5: 1 double/twin, 3 triples, 1 suite, all with bath or shower & wc.
price	€45-€65 for two.
dinner	Choice of restaurants in Mer.
closed	January.
directions	From N152 enter Mer & park by church. House is short walk up main street; entrance in picture-framing shop on left. (Car access details on arrival.)

Joëlle & Claude Mormiche
9 rue Dutems,
41500 Mer, Loir-et-Cher
tel (0)2 54 81 17 36
fax (0)2 54 81 70 19
e-mail mormiche@wanadoo.fr
web www.chambres-gites-chambord.com

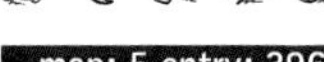

Beyond the security gates, a blissful, informal garden – lakes and bridges, nooks and ducks, even a gingko biloba, the hardiest tree on earth – rambles round the old millhouse (a mill stood here in 1455). Inside, a warmly sensitive atmosphere radiates from beautiful old floor tiles, timbered ceilings, lovely family furniture. Your hosts are gently caring about your well-being. Madame uses her innate feeling for history to advise on visits; Monsieur restored the old mill wheel; there are myriad teas for breakfast – and bedrooms, all different, are big, harmonious in fabric and colour and lit by the garden sky.

rooms	5: 2 doubles, 2 triples, 1 suite, all with bath or shower & wc.
price	€54-€76 for two.
dinner	Excellent choice of restaurants within 7km.
closed	Rarely.
directions	From A10 exit 16 N152 for Blois. 3.5km after Mer, right for Diziers – follow Chambres d'Hôtes signs.

Marie-Françoise & André Seguin
Le Moulin de Choiseaux,
8 rue des Choiseaux,
41500 Suèvres, Loir-et-Cher

tel	(0)2 54 87 85 01
fax	(0)2 54 87 86 44
e-mail	choiseaux@wanadoo.fr
web	www.choiseaux.com

LOIRE VALLEY

A house of style, originality and lovely surprises, with fascinating people. Madame, an art historian, talks exuberantly and creates beauty with her hands – patchwork, sculpture… Monsieur has a great sense of fun too, yet their house hums with serenity. Rooms are period-themed with family pieces: the *1930s* has an old typewriter, a valve radio and an authentic, garish green bathroom; the *1900s* has a splendid carved bed. The romantic garden is a mixture of French geometric and English informal, the house set back enough for the road not to be a problem and the Loire a short step from the garden gate.

rooms	4: 1 double, 1 twin, 1 triple, 1 single, all with bath or shower & wc.
price	€60 for two.
dinner	2 restaurants in village.
closed	November-March, except by arrangement.
directions	From A10 exit 16 for Chambord; cross Loire river at Mer; after bridge right D951; house on right at end of village.

Francis & Béatrice Bonnefoy
L'Échappée Belle,
120 rue Nationale,
41500 St Dyé sur Loire,
Loir-et-Cher

tel	(0)2 54 81 60 01
e-mail	fbonnefoy@libertysurf.fr
web	perso.libertysurf.fr/fbonnefoy

Why the Italian name, the Italianate look? Queen Marie de Médicis used to take the waters here in the 17th century: the fine garden still has a hot spring and the Loire flows regally past behind the huge old trees. Muriel, a flower-loving perfectionist of immaculate taste, has let loose her decorative flair on the interior. It is unmistakably yet adventurously French in its splash of colours, lush fabrics and fine details – fresh flowers too. Carved wardrobes and brass beds grace some rooms. The suite is a great 1930s surprise with a super-smart bathroom. You will be thoroughly coddled in this elegant and stylish house.

rooms	6: 2 doubles, 2 twins, 1 quadruple, 1 suite, all with bath or shower & wc.
price	€66 for two.
dinner	€30 with wine, by arrangement.
closed	In winter, except by arrangement.
directions	Macé is 3km north of Blois along N152 for Orléans. In village follow signs; 500m on right before church.

Muriel Cabin-Saint-Marcel
La Villa Médicis,
Macé,
41000 St Denis sur Loire,
Loir-et-Cher
tel (0)2 54 74 46 38
fax (0)2 54 78 20 27

Sophie, who speaks fluent English, left glamorous theatre management in Paris to devote her energy to her new B&B project where the emphasis is on simple living and organic food (*cuisine bio*). Breakfast bread, from the organic bakery, is made with milk and *fromage blanc* and her imaginative dinner menus, 95% organic too, use home-grown ingredients or stuff from the local organic co-operative. Rooms are attractive and functional with bright bedspreads, original sketches and paintings. She's passionate about British history and particularly loves talking to British guests. *She also speaks some Spanish and German.*

rooms	5: 3 doubles, 1 twin, all with shower & separate wc; 1 twin with shower & wc.
price	€43-€50 for two.
dinner	€16 with wine, by arrangement.
closed	Occasionally.
directions	From Blois D764 to Montrichard for 18km. In Sambin, house up lane between church & grocer's.

Sophie Gélinier
Chambres d'Hôtes du Prieuré,
23 rue de la Fontaine St Urbain,
41120 Sambin, Loir-et-Cher
tel (0)2 54 20 24 95
fax (0)2 54 20 24 95
e-mail sophie.gelinier@libertysurf.fr

A house of endless happy discoveries, an architectural dream marrying 16th-century roots with an ultra-modern, marble-floored open plan and a glass walkway five metres overhead. Easy-going Marie-France and her husband live in an oasis of sophisticated rusticity with a few sheep and hens and egg hunts for children. They love the garden, too. The house has a soft, attractive feel and a gorgeous woodsy valley view. A cylindrical shower amazes in the centre of one room, a billiard table awaits above another, the suite has a full kitchen; a sense of texture and fabric inhabits them all. And your hosts are a great couple.

rooms	3: 2 doubles, 1 family suite for up to 8, all with shower & wc.
price	€64-€84 for two; suite €130 for 5.
dinner	Good restaurants 3-7km.
closed	Rarely, but please book ahead.
directions	From Blois D751 to Candé, left after bridge for Valaire; pass memorial & silo; right at fork; left for Le Chêne Vert; house on left after small bridge.

Marie-France Tohier
Le Chêne Vert,
41120 Monthou sur Bièvre,
Loir-et-Cher

tel	(0)2 54 44 07 28
fax	(0)2 54 44 17 94
e-mail	tohier@sci-le-chene-vert.com
web	www.sci-le-chene-vert.com

LOIRE VALLEY

Down a half-mile tunnel of pines, the garden disappears into fields which disappear into woods – this amazingly quiet place seems impervious to all those wine cellars and châteaux throbbing with visitors (even the 'big house' next door has a moat). Your delightful, dynamic hosts are eager to make their converted 19th-century stables, where horses clearly lived like kings, perfect for you and to share stimulating conversation over Madame's excellent dinners (book ahead). The splendid living room has a fine fireplace; each big, simple, attractive bedroom has its own personality; and the welcome is warmly genuine.

rooms	5: 2 doubles, 1 twin, 2 family, all with bath or shower & wc.
price	€50 for two.
dinner	€21 with wine, by arrangement.
closed	January-March.
directions	From Amboise D23 3km to Souvigny; D30 to Vallières les Grandes; D27/D28 right for Montrichard; lane 2nd left after water tower; house just after manor house.

Annie & Daniel Doyer
Ferme de la Quantinière,
41400 Vallières les Grandes,
Loir-et-Cher

tel	(0)2 54 20 99 53
fax	(0)2 54 20 99 53
e-mail	fermequantiniere@minitel.net
web	www.france-bonjour.com/la-quantiniere/

A delight for the eyes: stunning ancient buildings outside, Madame's decorating flair inside. The 13th-century chapel, still used on the village feast day, and the newer manor house (1500s...), drip with history, 16th-century antiques, tapestries and loveliness – huge sitting and dining rooms, smallish cosy bedrooms. One has a large stone fireplace, painted beams and lovely fabrics. The setting is superb, fine mature trees shade the secluded garden and you can put your horse in the paddock. You can't fail to like your hosts and their estate wine and they can arrange wine tastings for you.

rooms	3: 2 doubles; 1 suite with bath, shower & wc, all with shower & wc.
price	€61-€65 for two; suite for four €137.
dinner	Wide range of restaurants locally.
closed	Rarely.
directions	St Georges is between Chenonceau & Montrichard on N76. In town centre, up hill to 'La Chaise' (signs); cont. up Rue du Prieuré. No. 8 has heavy wooden gates.

Danièle Duret-Therizols
Prieuré de la Chaise,
8 rue du Prieuré,
41400 St Georges sur Cher,
Loir-et-Cher

tel	(0)2 54 32 59 77
fax	(0)2 54 32 69 49
e-mail	prieuredelachaise@yahoo.fr
web	www.prieuredelachaise.com

map: 10 entry: 403

LOIRE VALLEY

The artist's touch and Jean-Lou's wonderful paintings vibrate throughout this house of tradition and originality where you are instantly one of the family: Persian Puss, Hector the gentle giant hound, a bright and friendly little girl, her congenial artist father and her relaxed linguist mother. Rooms – two in the main house, two in the studio house – are subtle-hued with good family furniture and bold bathrooms. An Aubusson tapestry cartoon too, understated elegance in the sitting and dining rooms, a joy of a garden, interesting, fun-loving hosts and a big welcoming table in the evening. *Painting and French courses.*

rooms	4 doubles, all with bath & wc.
price	€54 for two.
dinner	€23 with wine, by arrangement.
closed	Rarely.
directions	From Blois D956 to Contres; D675 to St Aignan; over bridge; D17 right to Mareuil sur Cher. House on left in hamlet Le Moutier (just before cat breeder sign) before main village.

Martine & Jean-Lou Coursaget
Le Moutier,
13 rue de la République,
41110 Mareuil sur Cher,
Loir-et-Cher

tel	(0)2 54 75 20 48
fax	(0)2 54 75 20 48
e-mail	lemoutier.coursaget@wanadoo.fr
web	perso.club-internet.fr/vilain/lemoutier

map: 10 entry: 404

In the romantic intimacy of the Loir valley, the little house in the garden has kitchen and bathroom downstairs, two bedrooms upstairs and its own piece of flowered garden for private breakfasts. Or you can join Madame in her light and cheerful kitchen, baskets hanging from the beams. She is friendly, cultivated, dynamic and an excellent adviser, will cook you refined dinners and is also a great maker of jams. Not luxurious but elegantly homely, quiet and welcoming.

rooms	2 doubles in cottage, sharing bathroom, only let to same group.
price	€46 for two; €80 for four.
dinner	€20 with wine, by arrangement.
closed	November-March.
directions	From Tours/La Membrolle N138 for Le Mans. At Neuillé Pont Pierre D68 to Neuvy le Roi. House on road; blue front door, opp. turning to Louestault.

Ghislaine & Gérard de Couesnongle
20 rue Pilate,
37370 Neuvy le Roi, Indre-et-Loire

tel	(0)2 47 24 41 48
e-mail	de-couesnongle-neuvy@caramail.com

map: 5 entry: 405

Swim in the beautiful pool then carouse over dinner in the lovely old room with its beams and large open fireplace; the meal, very much *en famille*, starts after the evening's milking – this is a working goat farm producing its own delicious cheese. The atmosphere round the table, the unusual and lovely setting and the interesting conversation of your easy, good-natured hosts make the fairly basic rooms out in the converted pighouse utterly acceptable. Bits of the house are 13th century: it was built by a glass-maker, a very superior trade in those days, and overlooks the extraordinary ruins of a large castle.

rooms	4: 2 doubles, 1 twin, 1 family room, all with shower & wc.
price	€41 for two.
dinner	€15 with wine, by arrangement. Good value restaurants 400m.
closed	16 October-March.
directions	From Château la Vallière D34 for Langeais – 1st right, right again, past ruined castle: at top of track.

Gérard & Martine Ribert
Vaujours,
37330 Château la Vallière,
Indre-et-Loire

tel	(0)2 47 24 08 55
fax	(0)2 47 24 19 20
e-mail	rib007@aol.com

map: 5 entry: 406

Simplicity, character and a marvellous welcome make La Louisière very special. Madame clearly delights in her role as hostess; Monsieur, who once rode the horse-drawn combine, tends his many roses and they are both active in their community – a caring and unpretentious couple. The traditional rooms have subtle, well-chosen colour schemes and sparkling bathrooms. Touches of fun, too: a couple of parrots perch in the children's room. Breakfast in the dining room is home-made jams, flaky croissants and crusty bread. Surrounded by chestnut trees, the house backs onto the gardens of the château and is wonderfully quiet.

rooms	3: 1 triple, 1 twin, 1 suite for 5, all with bath or shower & wc.
price	€40-€42 for two.
dinner	Auberge 300m.
closed	Rarely.
directions	From Tours D29 to Beaumont la Ronce. Signs to house in village.

Michel & Andrée Campion
La Louisière,
37360 Beaumont la Ronce,
Indre-et-Loire
tel (0)2 47 24 42 24
fax (0)2 47 24 42 24

LOIRE VALLEY

A smart, almost lavish château with its listed garden (stupendous trees) and an attentive new owner who serves a magnificent breakfast buffet in the new wrought iron conservatory overlooking the garden. Three rooms are in the château (lots of stairs to the top room but what a view), three in the *Closerie*, one with a dramatic oval window onto the setting sun. Superb décor with lovely materials, subtle colours, fine furniture, attention to origins. One 'monastic' room (plain walls, exposed brick and timber) contrasts pleasingly with the classy plushness. And a heated outdoor pool! A treat worth paying for.

rooms	6: 2 doubles, 1 twin, 2 triples, 1 suites for 4, all with bath, shower & wc.
price	€95-€170 for two.
dinner	Restaurant 800m.
closed	Rarely.
directions	From Tours N152 for Blois 4km. Left at St Georges; follow signs 1km to château.

Laurent Gross
Château de Montgouverne,
37210 Rochecorbon, Indre-et-Loire
tel (0)2 47 52 84 59
fax (0)2 47 52 84 61
e-mail info@montgouverne.com
web www.montgouverne.com

High on a cliff above the Loire, it looks over the village, across the vines and the valley to a château. It may be modern imitating old, but we chose it for Madame's superb, generous, five-star hospitality. The house is immaculate and meticulously kept; one room is repro Louis XIV, plus orangey carpet and flowery paper. There is a big living area with tiled floor and rugs, an insert fireplace and views over the large sloping garden; the oldest bit, a troglodyte dwelling, lies beneath the lawn! Mountain bikes to borrow, giant breakfasts, wonderful welcome – great value for the Loire.

rooms	3: 2 doubles, 1 suite, all with bath & wc.
price	€49 for two; suite €78 for four.
dinner	Several restaurants in village, 1km.
closed	Rarely.
directions	From Tours A10 for Paris; cross Loire; exit 20 to Rochecorbon. In village left at lights & right up steep narrow lane; signs.

Mme Jacqueline Gay
7 chemin de Bois Soleil,
37210 Rochecorbon, Indre-et-Loire

tel	(0)2 47 52 88 08
fax	(0)2 47 52 85 90
e-mail	jacqueline.gay2@wanadoo.fr
web	perso.wanadoo.fr/hautes-gatinieres

LOIRE VALLEY

All this in one place? There are 14 hectares of heron and duck, wild boar and deer – and three tame mallards; plus a 9-hole golf course. Mark, a gallicised Englishman, and Katia, an anglicised French woman, great travellers come to rest, are so enthusiastic about their new life here. The old farmhouse is done, naturally, with a mix of English and French: pleasing antiques, crisp bright bedrooms beneath old beams, dinners of fresh seasonal things such as gentle local asparagus. And the splendours of the Loire just down the road. *Golf, 9 holes.*

rooms	3 doubles, all with shower & wc; 1 with bath, too.
price	€55-€75 for two.
dinner	€25 with wine, by arrangement.
closed	December-January.
directions	From A10 exit 18 on D31 for Amboise to Autrèche; left D55 to Dame Marie les Bois; right D74; 1st house on left after woods.

Mark & Katia Foster
Le Clos du Golf,
Fleuray,
37530 Cangey, Amboise,
Indre-et-Loire

tel	(0)2 47 56 07 07
fax	(0)2 47 56 82 12
e-mail	closdugolf@wanadoo.fr

Even the pool is special: a 'Roman' bath hewn out of the hillside with a fountain and two columns, set on one of several garden levels that rise to the crowning glory of vines where chemical-free grapes are grown by natural methods. The new young owners brim with enthusiasm for their elegant, history-laden château, built in 1518 to gaze across the Loire at Amboise. Every detail has been treated with taste and discretion. Rooms, two in the main house, one smaller in a charming, old *pavillon*, are light and fresh, and there's a troglodyte suite, new this year. Fine dinners with a hint of Italian finish the picture.

rooms	4: 1 troglodyte suite for 4 with 2 baths & wc; 2 doubles with bath & wc; 1 double with shower & wc.
price	€90-€105 for two.
dinner	Choice of restaurants in Amboise.
closed	Christmas Day & New Year's Day.
directions	From A10 exit 18 for Amboise 12km; right D1 to Pocé/Cisse & Nazelles Négron; in village centre, narrow Rue Tue la Soif between Mairie & La Poste.

Véronique & Olivier Fructus
Château de Nazelles,
16 rue Tue la Soif,
37530 Nazelles, Indre-et-Loire
tel (0)2 47 30 53 79
fax (0)2 47 30 53 79
e-mail info@chateau-nazelles.com
web www.chateau-nazelles.com

LOIRE VALLEY

Your 17th-century manor sits in blissfully secluded grounds yet you can walk into the centre of old Amboise. Annick has bags of energy and enthusiasm for her new-found role as *chambres d'hôtes* hostess and gives you two comfortable, fine-sized bedrooms in a converted outbuilding. The downstairs room is tiled and beamed with a small patio overlooking the garden; the upstairs one, under the eaves, is charming, beamy and reached via an outdoor spiral stair. The carefully landscaped young garden is full of promise and bursting with roses and irises. Look out for the 16th-century pigeon loft – a historical rarity.

rooms	2 doubles, both with bath & wc.
price	€70 for two.
dinner	Choice of restaurants in Amboise.
closed	Rarely.
directions	From Place du Château in Amboise for Clos Lucé; round park; straight on at 1st stop sign, right at 2nd stop sign, 2nd left. Signs.

Annick Delécheneau
Manoir de la Maison Blanche,
18 rue de l'Épinetterie,
37400 Amboise, Indre-et-Loire
tel (0)2 47 23 16 14
e-mail annick.delecheneau@wanadoo.fr
web www.lamaisonblanche-fr.com

A narrow meandering track leads you through a gorgeous 'lost valley' to this light and airy house where the lawns run down to the banks of the Cher with not a neighbour in sight. The whole place is being beautifully restored by the present owners, refugees from the Parisian bustle. Using traditional paler-than-pale *tuffeau* stone, typical of the region, they have created a magnificent dining room. The garden-level bedroom has an African theme with terracotta tiling; another, at the top of the house, has an enormous full tester bed which looks big enough to sleep four.

rooms	3: 1 double, 2 triples, all with bath & wc.
price	€46-€62 for two.
dinner	2 restaurants 4km.
closed	Rarely.
directions	From Tours N76 for Bléré; pass sign for Athée sur Cher, continue to Granlay; immed. left to Vallet.

Denise & Augustin Chaudière
Le Pavillon de Vallet,
4 rue de l'Acqueduc,
37270 Athée sur Cher,
Indre-et-Loire
tel (0)2 47 50 67 83
fax (0)2 47 50 68 31
e-mail pavillon.vallet@wanadoo.fr
web www.multimania.com/lepavillon

LOIRE VALLEY

From plain street to stately courtyard magnolia to extraordinary marble-walled spiral staircase with dome atop – it's a *Monument Historique*, a miniature Bagatelle Palace, a bachelor's folly with a circular *salon*. The light, airy, fadingly elegant rooms, small and perfectly proportioned, are soft pink and grey; lean out and pluck a grape from the vine-clad pergola. Monsieur was a pilot and still flys vintage aircraft. Madame was an air hostess and English teacher and is casually sophisticated and articulate about her love of fine things, places and buildings. Wonderful, and a stone's throw from Chenonceaux.

rooms	2: 1 double, 1 suite for 4, both with shower & wc.
price	€61-€76 for two.
dinner	Good restaurant opposite, book ahead.
closed	Rarely.
directions	From Amboise D31 to Bléré through Croix en Touraine; over bridge (Rue des Déportés opp. is 1-way): left, immed. right, 1st right, right again. OR collection from private airport 5km.

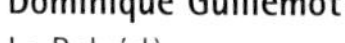

Dominique Guillemot
Le Belvédère,
24 rue des Déportés,
37150 Bléré, Indre-et-Loire
tel (0)2 47 30 30 25
fax (0)2 47 30 30 25
e-mail jr.guillemot@wanadoo.fr
web www.multimania.com/lebelvedere

Pure magic for all *Wind in the Willows* and other watermill fans. Three old mills side by side on a great sweep of the Indre, a boat for just messing about in, wooden bridges to cross from one secluded bank to another, a ship-stern view of the river from the terrace as you share a civilised dinner with your amusing, well-travelled hosts. The airy, elegant, uncluttered rooms have stunning river views (fear not – the sound of rushing water is limited to a gentle murmur at night), in styles to suit a Lieutenant, a Colonel and a Prior (in ascending order!).

rooms	3: 2 doubles, both with shower & separate wc; 1 twin with bath & wc.
price	€85-€100 for two.
dinner	€30 with wine, by arrangement.
closed	Occasionally.
directions	From Tours N143 for Loches for 12km; 500m after Esso garage, right D17 for 1.3km; left to Vontes; left to Bas-Vontes. At end of road.

Odile & Jean-Jacques Degail
Les Moulins de Vontes,
37320 Esvres sur Indre,
Indre-et-Loire
tel (0)2 47 26 45 72
fax (0)2 47 26 45 35
e-mail info@moulinsdevontes.com
web www.moulinsdevontes.com

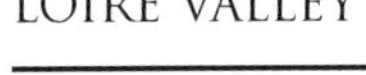

Once home to people called *Boher* who trained knights for medieval jousting tournaments, this is now a peaceful, flowery place – Madame really loves flowers and her summer garden is glorious. She is relaxed and keen to make you feel at home in her pretty farmhouse among the sunflower fields. Rooms, predictably flower-themed and fresh-flower decorated, are smallish but bright and cheerful, the guests' dayroom opens onto the terrace and the family dining room is most welcoming. And how about enjoying a spot of billiards practice before dinner?

rooms	5: 2 doubles, 1 twin, 2 triples, all with bath or shower & wc.
price	€40-€43 for two.
dinner	Restaurant 4km.
closed	Rarely.
directions	From Tours N143 for Loches; 10km after Cormery, left at Massy-Ferguson garage for Azay sur Indre & Chambres d'Hôtes; house 700m, signs.

Marie-Agnès Bouin
La Bihourderie,
37310 Azay sur Indre,
Indre-et-Loire
tel (0)2 47 92 58 58
fax (0)2 47 92 22 19
e-mail mignes.bouin@freesbee.fr

Follaine is a particularly tranquil place – it feels as old as the hills (actually the Middle Ages), with the fortified farm in the background that was used as a hunting lodge by Lafayette. Ornamental geese and ducks adorn the lake, the neatly-tended garden has places to sit, read or paint in, brightly-decorated bedrooms blend well with antique furniture and lake views. Amazingly, the old milling machinery in the breakfast area still works – ask and Monsieur will turn it on for you – and there are other relics from the old days, including original flour sacks from Azay. Fascinating. *Gîte space for 6 people.*

rooms	4: 2 doubles, 2 suites, all with bath & wc.
price	€59 for two.
dinner	Good auberge in village, 500m.
closed	Rarely.
directions	From Tours N143 for Loches; left D58 to Reignac; D17 to Azay sur Indre; left opp. restaurant; at fork, left (over 2 bridges); mill below fortified farm on right.

Mme Danie Lignelet
Moulin de la Follaine,
37310 Azay sur Indre,
Indre-et-Loire
tel (0)2 47 92 57 91
fax (0)2 47 92 57 91
e-mail moulindelafollaine@wanadoo.fr
web www.moulindefollaine.fr.st

LOIRE VALLEY

Do you dream of living in a watermill? Your charming young hosts have converted theirs, near the magnificent château of Montrésor, in properly stylish and simple good taste: a wooden staircase leading to the coconut-matted landing, super colours, good linen. It's welcoming, very warm, with lots of original features… and quiet flows the water over the wheel beneath the glass panel in the dining room – wonderful! Madame is cultured and well-travelled, her family has had the château for 200 years but no-one stands on ceremony and there's a sense of timeless peace here, miles from anywhere.

rooms	4: 1 double, 1 twin, 2 triples, all with bath or shower & wc.
price	€50-€55 for two; under 4s free.
dinner	Choice of restaurants within 5km.
closed	Rarely.
directions	From Loches D760 to Montrésor; left for Chemillé; mill on left; signs.

Sophie & Alain Willems de Ladersous
Le Moulin de Montrésor,
37460 Montrésor, Indre-et-Loire
tel (0)2 47 92 68 20
fax (0)2 47 92 74 65
e-mail alain.willems@wanadoo.fr

The Anglo-French Mievilles, who have also lived in Spain and are fascinated by all things cross-cultural, have turned their lovely 15th-century watermill into a cosy, colourful home full of flowers and scatter cushions. Guest rooms, on three floors of one wing, are freshly, crisply decorated and your sitting room is lovely with its books and open fire. The original machinery still occupies the terracotta-tiled mill room where you have breakfast. With its millpond, flowing stream and little island, the garden is gorgeous: birds, flowers, lots of shade for those hot summer days and public footpaths close by. *Spanish spoken.*

rooms	4: 2 doubles, 2 triples, all with bath & wc.
price	€55-€58 for two.
dinner	Restaurant within walking distance.
closed	November-March.
directions	From Blois D764 through Montrichard for Genillé-Loches. Just before Genillé, D10 right for St Quentin sur Indrois. Mill on left.

Josette & Clive Mieville
Le Moulin de la Roche,
37460 Genillé, Indre-et-Loire
tel (0)2 47 59 56 58
fax (0)2 47 59 59 62
e-mail clive.mieville@wanadoo.fr
web www.moulin-de-la-roche.com

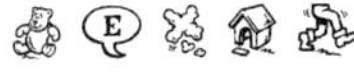

A delicious island setting, a lovely interior, but it's the people who make it. Sue is champion hostess, Andrew an inspired cook, his humour spot on – such fun. The restored mill is all ups and downs and nooks, big rooms and small, character and variety with perfect *brocanterie* and Sue's stencils. Plus shady garden, heated pool, yards of paperbacks – and an atmospheric green dining room with more water in its fish pond. *Not for young children: unfenced water.*

rooms	5: 2 doubles, 2 twins, 1 triple, all with bath or shower & wc.
price	€60-€65 for two.
dinner	€25 with wine, by arrangement.
closed	December-February.
directions	From Loches N143 for Châteauroux; pass Perusson; left at sign to St Jean; house is last over 1st bridge on left.

Andrew & Sue Page
Le Moulin,
Saint Jean Saint Germain,
37600 Loches, Indre-et-Loire
tel (0)2 47 94 70 12
fax (0)2 47 94 77 98
e-mail millstjean@aol.com
web lemoulinstjean.com

Monsieur grew up in a château and some fine family pieces have followed him here, including a rare Napoleon III billiard table, one of only two in France. The small 16th-century farmhouse has been beautifully extended to incorporate an old barn for guest rooms, each one bright and airy with private access to a patio and a bank of pink roses. Your hosts, charming and friendly, are proud of their finely comfortable house with its tranquil garden and pool. The estate stretches as far as the eye can see and has its own lake. Help yourself to boats and fishing rods or visit the cathedral and market of medieval Loches.

rooms	2 doubles, both with shower & wc.
price	€48 for two.
dinner	€15 with wine, by arrangement.
closed	Rarely.
directions	From Loches D760 for Ste Maure de Touraine; left D95 for Vou; 1st right at sign 'La Métairie des Bois'.

M & Mme Jean-Claude Baillou
La Métairie des Bois,
37240 Vou, Indre-et-Loire
tel (0)2 47 92 36 46
fax (0)2 47 92 36 46
e-mail baillou@wanadoo.fr

LOIRE VALLEY

In unspectacular countryside where her quiet, affable husband has his family goat's cheese business, Natacha, a busy, bubbly, intelligent young mother, runs her unassuming B&B with sweet, attentive care. The fairly basic, French cheap 'n' cheerful bedrooms are in a separate wing with a good sitting space and real disabled facilities in one room. You can visit the farm and its 200 goats 3km away; Le Grand Pressigny and its superb museum of prehistory 10km away; the tiny Petit Pressigny and its Dallais Restaurant with one whole Michelin star – on your doorstep! (The village has a more modest eating house too.)

rooms	4 doubles, all with shower & wc.
price	€40 for two.
dinner	In village, 1 restaurant Michelin starred, 1 simple 'family'.
closed	Rarely.
directions	From Châtellerault D725 through La Roche Posay & Preuilly sur Claise. 1km after Preuilly left on D50/D41 to Le Petit Pressigny. In centre opp. Restaurant Dallais.

Bernard & Natacha Limouzin
La Pressignoise,
37350 Le Petit Pressigny,
Indre-et-Loire
tel (0)2 47 91 06 06
e-mail natacha.limouzin@wanadoo.fr

When a diplomat's wife with impeccable taste and a flair for interior design is let loose on an austere 18th-century townhouse, the result is a treat. The family's antique furniture blends with pieces of art, sculpture and rugs from Africa and the Middle East; tall windows, storied terracotta floors and an oval oak staircase are the grand backdrop; bedrooms are traditional and sumptuous, overlooking, via window and balcony, a walled formal garden which ends in a semi-wild area of bamboo. All is peace: even the fine chime of the church clock over the wall falls bashfully silent at night. *The* house in Richelieu? Yes.

rooms	4: 2 doubles, 2 twins, all with bath & wc.
price	€80 for two.
dinner	Ask Mme for recommendations.
closed	Mid-October-mid-April
directions	From A10, exit Ste Maure de Touraine; left D760 for Noyant; left D58 for Richelieu; in town, cross over la Place des Religieuses, 1st left, signs.

Mme Michèle Couvrat-Desvergnes
La Maison,
6 rue Henri Proust,
37120 Richelieu, Indre-et-Loire

tel	(0)2 47 58 29 40
fax	(0)2 47 58 29 40
e-mail	lamaisondemichele@yahoo.com
web	www.lamaisondemichele.com

LOIRE VALLEY

Down in a valley where time has stood still, Anne's house is camouflaged under its blanket of creeper and roses. The two pretty and freshly redecorated guest rooms (one with a fine old carved wedding bed) are just across the courtyard looking out onto the hillside garden – a magical blend of the work of (wo)man and nature. Gutsy, green-fingered Anne is a great source of wisdom about things to see and do in this bounteous corner of Touraine, and will show the way to walk in the footsteps of Eleanor of Aquitaine up the valley and through the forest to the nearby Abbey of Fontevraud.

rooms	2 doubles, both with shower & wc.
price	€44 for two.
dinner	Wide choice of restaurants within 5km.
closed	November-March.
directions	From Saumur D947 for Chinon to Montsoreau; D751 through Candes & St Germain sur Vienne. 500m after church, at Goujon Frétillant restaurant, right; follow signs for 1.5km.

Anne Dubarry
7 La Vallée des Grottes,
37500 St Germain sur Vienne,
Indre-et-Loire

tel	(0)2 47 95 96 45

This solid wine-grower's house sings in a subtle harmony of traditional charm and contemporary chic under thoroughly modern Martine's touch. Terracotta sponged walls, creamy beams and colourful modern fabrics breathe new life into rooms with old tiled floors and stone fireplaces. Windows are flung open to let in the light and the stresses of city living are forgotten in cheerful, easy conversations with your hostess. There is a baby grand piano in the elegant sitting room for the musical, a pool for the energetic and wine-tastings at the vineyard next door. A great place.

rooms	3: 2 doubles, 1 suite, all with bath & wc.
price	€80 for two.
dinner	€25 with wine, by arrangement.
closed	Rarely.
directions	From Chinon D749 for Richelieu; 1km after r'bout D115 right for 'Ligré par le vignoble' 5km; left to Le Rouilly; left at Dozon warehouse; house 800m on left.

	Martine Descamps
	Le Clos de Ligré,
	Le Rouilly,
	37500 Ligré, Indre-et-Loire
tel	(0)2 47 93 95 59
fax	(0)2 47 93 06 31
e-mail	martinedescamps@hotmail.com

map: 10 entry: 425

This low, gloriously-proportioned 17th-century stable block has all the elegance of a château with none of the pomposity; the same goes for your youthful hosts! They moved recently from Paris with sundry children and pets and have lovingly and sensitively restored the house to reveal its innate glory of stone and timber-work. Guests are immediately made to feel at home yet well-protected from the hurly-burly of family life. The unusual half-timbered bedrooms are decorated with stylish simplicity and a copious breakfast is served in the sunny dining room with its enormous double-bread-ovened fireplace. A great place.

rooms	4: 2 doubles, 1 twin, 1 family suite, all with bath/shower & wc.
price	€75-€100 for two.
dinner	Choice of restaurants nearby; cold supper €15.
closed	Rarely.
directions	From A85 exit Bourgueil for Chinon; just before Chinon right at r'about for Loudun; at La Roche Clermault right D24 through Lerné; at end of road on leaving village.

	Marie-Claire & André Geoffroy
	La Renaudière,
	Domaine du Château de Chavigny,
	37500 Lerné, Indre-et-Loire
tel	(0)2 47 95 91 77
fax	(0)2 47 95 91 77
e-mail	larenaudiere@wanadoo.fr

map: 10 entry: 426

A tree-shaded garden shields this charming old white-stone walnut farmer's house, now an antique dealer's. A cornucopia of exotica mingles with traditional antique furniture in splendid oak-beamed, book- and stone-clad rooms. Immaculate bedrooms are a good size, one bathroom big enough to dance in; the suite has its own large sitting room downstairs with a huge open fireplace. And if you find your antique carved bedhead irresistible, you may be able to buy it! Barbara, articulate and efficient, believes in mollycoddling her guests: hand-embroidered linen sheets on the beds, sumptuous breakfasts served on the best china.

rooms	2 doubles, both with bath & wc.
price	€80-€90 for two.
dinner	Auberge in village; good choice in Chinon, 12km.
closed	Rarely.
directions	From Tours D751 to Chinon; D21 to Cravant les Côteaux. House is approx. 1.5km after village on right, at sign 'Bernard Chauveau – Antiquaire'.

Barbara Chauveau
Domaine de Pallus,
37500 Cravant les Côteaux,
Indre-et-Loire
tel (0)2 47 93 08 94
fax (0)2 47 98 43 00
e-mail bcpallus@club-internet.fr

LOIRE VALLEY

The ochre and maroon sitting room – deep chairs round gleaming brass coffee table – calls for intelligent, convivial conversation; the dining alcove brings gasps of delight; the bedrooms have huge beautiful personalities, each detail lovingly chosen to honour this 19th-century townhouse by the stately River Vienne – *Iris*: her name and blue and yellow décor inspired by turret windows; *Loriette*: essential pink married to creamy quilt and magnificent old writing desk. Jean sings in the choir, Jany does ceramics, they are an articulate, music-, cat-, art-loving couple and the nicest possible, most caring hosts.

rooms	3: 1 double with shower, bath & wc; 1 double with shower & wc; 1 single with shower & wc.
price	€53-€61 for two; single €38.
dinner	Good choice of restaurants within walking distance.
closed	15 October-March.
directions	Entering Chinon on D751 from Tours, along river past bridge & Rabelais statue. House just after Post Office.

Jany & Jean Grosset
84 quai Jeanne d'Arc,
37500 Chinon, Indre-et-Loire
tel (0)2 47 98 42 78
fax (0)2 47 98 42 78

Dug into the hillside with the engulfing forest behind and a panorama of vines, fields and sky in front, venerable oak beams gnawed by generations of woodworm inside and stone cut by troglodyte stonemasons, this 'traditional' wine-grower's manor successfully pretends it was built in the 1800s rather than the 1980s. Bedroom furniture is antique too: superb carved wooden bedheads, big puffy eiderdowns, old prints. Only the pool, elegant bathrooms and guests' functional sitting and utility rooms show the owners' thoroughly contemporary concern for luxury and comfort. And there is wine to taste and buy. *Gîte space for 4 people.*

rooms	3: 1 suite for 3-4 in main house, 2 doubles in pool-side cabin, all with bath or shower & wc.
price	€61-€77 for two.
dinner	Choice of restaurants 5km.
closed	Rarely.
directions	From Chinon, D21 to Cravant les Côteaux. On towards Panzoult; house on left after 2km.

Marie-Claude Chauveau
Domaine de Beauséjour,
37220 Panzoult, Indre-et-Loire
tel (0)2 47 58 64 64
fax (0)2 47 95 27 13
e-mail info@domainedebeausejour.com
web www.domainedebeausejour.com

LOIRE VALLEY

A most welcoming, enthusiastic hostess, Éliane loves talking to people about their interests and her own. New to B&B, she is constantly looking for ideas to improve her rooms, the pink, mezzanined quadruple in her pretty old farmhouse and the other larger triple in a converted outbuilding. Parts of the house are 17th century with massive beams, good mixes of new and old furniture, wild and dried flowers, colours and fabrics. A goose wanders about the little garden and it is all deliciously cosy.

rooms	2 quadruples, both with shower & wc.
price	€38-€42 for two.
dinner	Auberge nearby.
closed	Rarely.
directions	From A10 exit Ste Maure de Touraine; N10 for Tours 6km; right to Ste Catherine de Fierbois; D1 for Bossé – house 3km.

Mme Éliane Pelluard
La Tinellière,
37800 Ste Catherine de Fierbois,
Indre-et-Loire
tel (0)2 47 65 61 80

The Scarlet Pimpernel would feel at home here, it's so elegantly 18th century. In front: the formal courtyard with fountain playing; on either side: 15th-century outhouses where guests stay; behind: swimming pool, informal garden, barbecue. Madame has decorated the rooms with easy-going chic and charm, converting their artisan origins into the luxury of warm yellow fabrics, prints and tiles. The suite has corridors, alcoves, stained-glass windows and a tiny oratory – the peace of the convent here. And over your welcome drink, your hostess will regale you with tales of her world travels (Scarlet Pimpernel, you said?).

rooms	3: 2 doubles, 1 suite, all with bath or shower & wc.
price	€80-€88 for two.
dinner	Auberge in village. Restaurants in Chinon, 8km.
closed	Rarely.
directions	From D751 north of Chinon D16 to Huismes; 1st left on entering village, sign 'L'Étui'; house ahead on small junction.

Anne-Claude Berthelot
La Chancellerie,
37420 Huismes, Indre-et-Loire

tel	(0)2 47 95 46 76
fax	(0)2 47 95 54 08
web	www.lachancellerie.com

map: 10 entry: 431

LOIRE VALLEY

These two will take huge care of you in their genuine old French family house: they love having guests and opening doors onto Loire secrets, Monsieur will take you to see his favourite wine growers and craftsmen, Madame is properly proud of her fine linen and pretty rooms. *Oncle Vincent* has two big single beds, one made for Vincent with matching wardrobe and chest of drawers, the other, brass-knobbed and not matching the cane chair… *Tante Angèle* did the samplers in *her* room, while the Gardener's Cottage breathes rustic charm in the lovely big garden.

rooms	2 + 1 cottage: 1 double with bath, 1 twin with shower, sharing wc. Cottage for 3.
price	€37-€48 for two.
dinner	Auberge 50m, choice of restaurants 7km.
closed	Christmas Day.
directions	From Chinon, D16 to Huismes. Under arch between church & large house, 1st left; house 2nd on right.

Anne & Jean-Marc Bureau
Le Clos de l'Ormeau,
4 rue du Presbytère,
37420 Huismes, Indre-et-Loire

tel	(0)2 47 95 41 54
fax	(0)2 47 95 41 54
e-mail	bureau.jm@wanadoo.fr

map: 10 entry: 432

Antoinette indulges two loves, bringing people together and caring for nature, in her old vine-surrounded farmhouse on this environmentally-sensitive spit of land. Loire and Vienne meet nearby and the air tingles with watery prisms, spring flowers fill the meadow behind the house, shady trees and tall hollyhocks provide private corners in the large walled courtyard. There are delicious home-made jams for breakfast in the cool, stone-walled, low-beamed dining room with its huge 15th-century fireplace and there is a well-equipped kitchen for guests' use. Pleasant, comfortable rooms complete the picture.

rooms	5: 3 doubles, 1 twin, 1 suite for 3, all with bath or shower & wc.
price	€42-€56 for two.
dinner	Good restaurants nearby.
closed	January.
directions	From Chinon D749 for Bourgueil; Beaumont r'bout 3rd exit for La Roche Honneur; left at sign to Grézille & continue to house.

Antoinette Degrémont
La Balastière,
Hameau de Grézille,
37420 Beaumont en Veron,
Indre-et-Loire
tel (0)2 47 58 87 93
fax (0)2 47 58 82 41
e-mail balastiere@infonie.fr
web perso.infonie.fr/balastiere

Guests at Cheviré stay in the well-converted stable block of an elegant stone house in a quiet little village, all a-shimmer in the Loire's inimitable limpid light – welcome to the protected wetlands between the rivers Loire and Vienne. Your quarters have ancient beams, stone walls, new floors, space to sit or cook, a little terrace. The uncluttered, sizeable rooms show the same happy mix of old and new with some fine pieces. Your hospitable, gentle hosts, proud of their house and area, will direct you to less obvious places of interest. "Very clean, very friendly, very good food", say our readers. *Dinner must be booked.*

rooms	3: 2 triples, both with bath & wc; 1 double with shower & wc.
price	€36-€43 for two.
dinner	€16 with wine, by arrangement. Self-catering possible.
closed	15 December-15 January.
directions	From Chinon D749 for Bourgueil 6km; left to Savigny en Véron; in village follow 'Camping'; house 1km after campsite on right.

Marie-Françoise & Michel Chauvelin
Cheviré,
11 rue Basse,
37420 Savigny en Véron,
Indre-et-Loire
tel (0)2 47 58 42 49
fax (0)2 47 58 42 49

Monsieur, a man of many talents – wine grower, antique dealer, genial host – and Madame, delightfully down-to-earth, speak excellent English and organise memorable gourmet and wine-tasting evenings involving a ritual aperitif and game of boules before a five-course dinner round a jolly family table in their country kitchen (booking essential). Simple bedrooms, some larger than others, are light and cheerful with old features such as marble fireplaces, floor tiles, the odd antique; the guest sitting room is endearingly lived-in with comfortable sofas and books and the whole feel is utterly welcoming.
Gite space for 10.

rooms	6: 2 doubles, 3 triples, 1 family room, all with bath, shower & wc.
price	€45-€52 for two.
dinner	€20, wine €7.
closed	November-March.
directions	From Langeais N152 for Saumur 7km; right D35 for Bourgeuil 5km; in Ingrandes right D71 Rue de l'Ouche d'or; 2nd right Rue St André.

Michèle & Michel Pinçon
Le Clos Saint André,
37140 Ingrandes de Touraine,
Indre-et-Loire

tel	(0)2 47 96 90 81
fax	(0)2 47 96 90 81
e-mail	mmpincon@club-internet.fr

map: 10 entry: 435

LOIRE VALLEY

The brook next to the old miller's house gently flows and soothes – so relaxing. Myriam and Jean-Claude are interesting and energetic and have renovated their house with a blend of styles: original stonework, beams and terracotta floors and some funky modern furniture. The Moroccan tiled table with wrought iron legs works well with the old stone fireplace in the dining room. Simple, pleasantly decorated bedrooms have parquet floors, good bedding and stylish modern lighting. The garden is a delight with its wide-planked bridge, fruit trees and dessert grapes and Jean-Claude is happy to arrange visits to local wine-growers.

rooms	5: 1 double with shower & wc; 3 doubles/twins, 1 triple, each with bath & wc.
price	€46-€53 for two.
dinner	€15 with wine, by arrangement.
closed	Mid-December-mid-January.
directions	From A85 exit Saumur; D10/D35 to Bourgueil; at r'bout on Bourgueil ringroad (north), D749 for Gizeux 4km; right immed. after restaurant; 200m on left.

Myriam & Jean-Claude Marchand
3 rue du Moulin de Touvois,
37140 Bourgeuil, Indre-et-Loire

tel	(0)2 47 97 87 70
fax	(0)2 47 97 87 70
e-mail	moulindetouvois@wanadoo.fr
web	www.moulindetouvois.com

map: 10 entry: 436

Surrounded by forest, standing in a big 'English' garden (Madame is passionate about her flowers, both inside and out), this imposing lodge has a harmonious feel despite being built so recently… in 17th-century Angevin style with old materials from the château next door. An unusual and refreshingly natural place, it reflects the family's plan to return to country simplicity. They are gentle, caring, cultivated and creative, as proved by the carefully designed and decorated bedrooms. There's a lovely new 'pigeon loft' room with half-timbered walls and a round window – very enticing. *Children over 10 welcome.*

rooms	3: 1 double, 2 twins, all with shower (1 behind curtain) & wc.
price	€55 for two.
dinner	Restaurants 2-5km.
closed	20 December-5 January.
directions	From Tours N152 for Saumur to St Patrice; D35 to Bourgueil; D749 to Gizeux; D15 to Continvoir; left on D64; signs.

Michel & Claudette Bodet
La Butte de l'Épine,
37340 Continvoir, Indre-et-Loire
tel (0)2 47 96 62 25
fax (0)2 47 96 07 36

An energetic, artistic anglophile with a sense of fun and a real interest in people, Éric delights in his superb garden and the beautifully finished details of his house: he's just the person to consult on buying antiques. Four bedrooms have stone beams, fireplaces and their own terraces; upstairs, the gentle grey and white room has a big balcony, the other is full of powerful florals; all have classy bathrooms and a stylish use of colour. Hall and dining room are splendiferous in their 18th-century elegance; there's a cosy sitting room, and billiards too. The whole place is a haven of history, culture, peace – magical.

rooms	6: 2 doubles, 1 twin, 1 suite (1 double & 1 twin), 2 triples, all with bath or shower & wc.
price	€95 for two.
dinner	Cold meals available.
closed	December-February.
directions	From Tours D7 for Savonnières; there, left at Hôtel Faisan D7 for Ballan Miré; up hill about 1km. House on left; signs.

Éric & Christine Salmon
Prieuré des Granges,
15 rue des Fontaines,
37510 Savonnières, Indre-et-Loire
tel (0)2 47 50 09 67
fax (0)2 47 50 06 43
e-mail salmon.eric@wanadoo.fr
web prieuredesgranges.com

Intriguing, this thoroughly contemporary mansion on the old château foundations: in the Garden of France, the wisteria will soon grow to soften its new face as the (sculpted) sheep graze the lawn and the superb trees – giant cedars, age-old sequoias – stalk the splendid grounds. Humour, intelligence and love of fine things inhabit this welcoming family and their guest wing is unostentatiously luxurious in rich fabrics, oriental and modern furniture, good pictures and lovely, scented cedar-lined bathrooms. Ground-floor rooms have a private terrace each, upstairs rooms have direct access to the roof garden.

rooms	4: 1 double, 2 twins, 1 suite for 3, all with bath, shower & wc.
price	€90 for two.
dinner	Good choice of restaurants locally.
closed	Rarely.
directions	From Tours D7 for Savonnières; 3km before village left after 'Les Cèdres' restaurant, 800m on left.

Marie-Laurence Jallet
Les Mazeraies,
Route des Mazeraies,
37510 Savonnières, Indre-et-Loire

tel	(0)2 47 67 85 35
e-mail	lesmazeraies@wanadoo.fr
web	www.lesmazeraies.com

LOIRE VALLEY

Traditional materials – soft Touraine stone, lime render, wood – and old furniture, pale colours and lots of light make the old slate-topped house a welcoming haven by the Cher where the birdsong drowns out the trains. Here live Anne, Éric, their four children and various animals. They have lots of local lore for you, and concoct wonders from their mini-Villandry flower and vegetable garden. Anne adores looking for new recipes, new bits of antiquery (your bedhead in the lovely guest room is an adapted Breton *lit clos*) and attends lovingly to every detail. *Spanish spoken.*

rooms	1 family room with shower & wc.
price	€52 for two, €90 for four.
dinner	€18 with wine, by arrangement.
closed	Rarely.
directions	From Tours D7 to Savonnières; right across bridge; left for 3.8km; on right.

Anne & Éric Gaudouin
Le Chat Courant,
37510 Villandry, Indre-et-Loire

tel	(0)2 47 50 06 94
e-mail	lechatcourant@netcourrier.com
web	www.le-chat-courant.com

Philosopher Bruno and Titian-haired Nancy, engaging parents of four, have turned his family château into a delightful refuge for the world-weary traveller. The demands of children to be taken to dancing lessons and guests needing intellectual and physical sustenance are met with quiet composure and good humour. Generations of sliding young have polished the banisters on the stairs leading to the large, light bedrooms, freshly decorated round splendid brass bedsteads and family memorabilia. On fine summer evenings, you can take a supper tray to picnic *à la* Glyndebourne in a favourite corner of the vast grounds.

rooms	4: 3 doubles, 1 triple, all with bath/shower & wc.
price	€95 for two.
dinner	€20-€38 with wine, by arrangement.
closed	Occasionally.
directions	From Tours D751 for Chinonr 5km. In Ballan Miré, right at lights before level crossing. Signs; entrance opp. golf course.

Bruno & Nancy Clément
Château du Vau,
37510 Ballan Miré, Indre-et-Loire
tel (0)2 47 67 84 04
fax (0)2 47 67 55 77
e-mail chateauduvau@chez.com
web www.chez.com/chateauduvau

SOME FALSE FRIENDS

Biologique and Organic

If you want organically-grown, chemical-free food in France, ask for items *de culture biologique*, called *bio* for short. If you talk about *organique*, people may think you're having trouble with your organs.

Donjon: medieval keep, all above ground, unlike an English dungeon.
Compote: Stewed fruit.
Marmelade: Well-stewed fruit.
Marmalade: *Confiture d'oranges amères* (bitter-orange jam).
Mousse (la): Mousse, as in lemon; or foam, lather, froth, as on sea, soap, beer; or foam rubber; or moss; or (*le mousse*) ship's boy.
Offrir: To give (for free), to offer; *offert*: free.
Prune: Plum; *pruneau*: prune.
Pomme de pin: fircone. Pineapple: *ananas*. *Pamplemousse*: grapefruit.
Grappe: bunch, cluster – *Grappe de raisins*: bunch of grapes.
Raisin: Generic term for the fruit of the vine: 'grapes'; one grape is *un grain de raisin*.
Raisins de Corinthe: currants; *raisins de Smyrne*: sultanas; *raisins secs*: raisins!
Une pie: Magpie – *La Pie Voleuse*: The Thieving Magpie; *une pie volante*: a flying magpie.
Tourte: a savoury pie with pastry on top.
Un pis (pronounced like pie): udder of any milking animal.
Scotch: Whisky or adhesive tape – context will tell...
Soldes: Sales, i.e. reduced-price goods, not yet sold.
Tartine: Usually half a baguette sliced lengthwise and buttered; *tartine grillée*: the same, toasted before being buttered.
Trouble: Cloudy, murky (liquid, story) – you can send that bottle back.
Troublé: Troubled, disturbed.
À la manière de... In the manner of...

POITOU · CHARENTES

That heady golden liquid is distilled near ancient wetlands where for centuries fugitives have hidden from tyranny, flat-bottoms have carried hunters and waterfowl have risen wild.

Set proudly at the end of its drive, the finely-proportioned 18th-century manor is a genuine farming family's house, not at all imposing. Five generations of Picards have lived here serenely, where Madame, intelligent, feisty and down-to-earth, will welcome you as family. Overlooking the chestnut-treed garden, the generous bedrooms have handsome wardrobes, good firm mattresses and slightly faded wallpapers. Sunlight streams onto the well-matched beams, white walls and terracotta floor of the huge sitting room, breakfast is in the yellow dining room or on the leafy terrace and there are simple cooking facilities for guests.

rooms	2: 1 double with shower & wc; 1 suite with shower, bath & wc.
price	€43 for two.
dinner	600m, self-catering possible.
closed	Rarely.
directions	From Richelieu D7 towards Loudun for 4km; right into drive lined with lime trees.

Jean & Marie-Christine Picard
Le Bois Goulu,
86200 Pouant, Vienne
tel (0)5 49 22 52 05
fax (0)5 49 22 52 05

After 20-odd years of B&B, your hosts still enjoy their guests enormously so come and experience daily life in a small hilltop village with a fine 12th-century church. He, a jovial retired farmer (their son now runs the farm), who knows his local lore; she smiling quietly and getting on with her cooking in the big homely kitchen – they are the salt of the earth. Up the superb old solid oak staircase, bedrooms are clean and bright with good beds, curtained-off showers and separate loos. A warm and generous welcome is guaranteed plus masses of things to do and see.

rooms	3 doubles, 1 with extra bed for child, all with shower & wc.
price	€38 for two.
dinner	€15 with wine, by arrangement.
closed	Rarely.
directions	From Loudun for Thouars; D60 for Moncontour. From Mouterre Silly church, house 50m for Silly, signposted 'Chambres d'Hôtes'.

Agnès & Henri Brémaud
Le Bourg,
86200 Mouterre Silly, Vienne
tel (0)5 49 98 09 72
fax (0)5 49 98 09 72

POITOU · CHARENTES

You will be mollycoddled by these delightful, good-humoured people. One room in a converted woodshed has beams, pretty curtains, blue and yellow tiled floor and view over the large, rambling garden with its meandering frog pond (hence *Grenouillère*); all show remarkable attention to detail. Two rooms are upstairs in a house across the courtyard where Madame's mother, a charming lady, lives and makes a phenomenal collection of jams. Pleasant, comfortable rooms, a most attractive group of buildings, meals on the shaded terrace in summer and messing about in the small rowing boat.

rooms	5: 3 doubles, 2 triples, all with bath or shower & wc.
price	€42–€45 for two.
dinner	€18 with wine, by arrangement.
closed	Rarely.
directions	From Tours N10 S for Châtellerault 55km. In Dangé St Romain, right at 3rd traffic lights, cross river, keep left on little square. House 200m along on left; signs.

Annie & Noël Braguier
La Grenouillère,
17 rue de la Grenouillère,
86220 Dangé St Romain, Vienne
tel (0)5 49 86 48 68
fax (0)5 49 86 46 56

Nothing austere about this imposing, lovingly-restored, 15th-century fortified castle. A wide spiral stone staircase leads to the beautifully decorated, comfortable rooms where old family furniture, vast stone fireplaces and beds with richly textured canopies, finely stitched by your talented hostess, preserve the medieval flavour, while bathrooms are state-of-the-art. There is an elegant dining room and a huge, high-ceilinged, light-filled sitting room for enlightened conversation with your cultured and charming hosts. *Gîte space for 8 people.*

rooms	4: 1 twin, 1 triple, 2 suites all with bath & wc.
price	€65-€110 for two.
dinner	€23 with wine, by arrangement.
closed	Rarely.
directions	From Paris A10 exit Châtellerault Nord; at r'bout after toll for Usseau 5km; D749 for Richelieu; D75 to Usseau.

	Jean-Marie & Marie-Andrée Bardin
	Château de la Motte,
	86230 Usseau, Vienne
tel	(0)5 49 85 88 25
fax	(0)5 49 85 89 85
e-mail	j-marie.bardin@wanadoo.fr
web	www.chateau-de-la-motte.net

POITOU · CHARENTES

A "passionate gardener" is how Martine describes herself, with a soft spot for old-fashioned roses: they ramble through the wisteria on the walls and gather in beautifully tended beds. The 'L' of the house shelters a very decent pool while furniture is arranged in a welcoming spot for picnics. Martine works but will see you for breakfast or in the evening: she's the one with the big smile. A peaceful, welcoming retreat with the Futuroscope literally minutes away. You can hire bikes nearby, or play tennis, and there's a huge range of day trips to choose from.

rooms	3: 2 doubles, 1 triple, all with shower/bath & wc.
price	€43-€45 for two; €55-€57 for three.
dinner	Several restaurants 3km.
closed	Rarely.
directions	From Châtellerault D749 for Chauvigny & Limoges about 13km (through Vouneuil); follow sign on left 750m; left, house down track.

	Michel & Martine Poussard
	La Pocterie,
	86210 Vouneuil sur Vienne, Vienne
tel	(0)5 49 85 11 96

This charming young couple, frank, sociable and good company, will spend time with guests after dinner when their young children allow. They have converted a fine big barn into guest quarters – older than the main house, it has been well done, muted colour schemes harmonising with ethnic rugs in dark and pleasant rooms, a good dayroom with an open fireplace, a superb cobbled terrace inviting you to sit on balmy evenings and gaze across the wide landscape while the wind plays in the poplars. With a nature reserve on the doorstep – dragonflies a speciality – here is a little-known corner waiting to be discovered.

rooms	2: 1 double, 1 triple, both with bath & wc.
price	€46 for two.
dinner	€16 with wine, by arrangement.
closed	Rarely.
directions	From Châtellerault D749 to Vouneuil sur Vienne; left in church square & follow Chambres d'Hôtes signs. Last house on right in hamlet of Chabonne.

Florence & Antoine Penot
Chabonne,
86210 Vouneuil sur Vienne, Vienne

tel	(0)5 49 85 28 25
fax	(0)5 49 85 22 75

map: 10 entry: 447

POITOU · CHARENTES

A great couple in their genuine family château of fading grandeur – mainly 17th century, it has a properly aged face. From the dramatic dark-panelled, orange-walled hall up the superbly bannistered staircase, through a carved screen, you reach the *salon* gallery that runs majestically through the house. Here you may sit, read, dream of benevolent ghosts. Bedrooms burst with personality and wonderful old beds. Madame's hand-painted tiles adorn a shower, her laughter accompanies your breakfast in the splendid family living room; Monsieur tends his trees and is a fund of local wisdom. A warm, authentic place.

rooms	3: 2 twins, 1 suite, all with bath or shower & wc. Extra children's room.
price	€61-€69 for two.
dinner	Auberge nearby; good choice 10km.
closed	Rarely.
directions	From A10 Futuroscope exit D62 to Quatre Vents r'bout; D757 to Vendeuvre; left D15 through Chéneché. Labarom 800m on right after leaving Chéneché.

Éric & Henriette Le Gallais
Château de Labarom,
86380 Chéneché, Vienne

tel	(0)5 49 51 24 22
fax	(0)5 49 51 47 38
e-mail	chateau.de.labarom@wanadoo.fr

map: 10 entry: 448

An utterly delightful couple who cannot do enough for you. Monsieur once resuscitated cars – he now takes far more pleasure in reviving tired travellers; Madame cares for every detail. Their house is on the old ramparts and the pretty garden looks directly over the boulevard below where you would expect a moat (quiet enough at night). Two neat rooms with good beds and old *armoires*: one has bold, big-flower wallpaper, the smaller is plain blue; both have space and the shower room has been prettily retiled. You have breakfast in high-backed chairs at the long table in the converted stables beneath the old hay rack.

rooms	2 twins, both with shower or bath & wc.
price	€38 for two.
dinner	Restaurants in village.
closed	Rarely.
directions	From Châtellerault D725 for Parthenay 30km. In Mirebeau, left immed after Gendarmerie traffic lights; No.19 about 50m on right.

Jacques & Annette Jeannin
19 rue Jacquard,
86110 Mirebeau, Vienne
tel (0)5 49 50 54 06
fax (0)5 49 50 54 06

POITOU · CHARENTES

Madame, vivacious and dynamic, is delighted for you to enjoy her simple, pretty rooms in the converted outbuilding and hugely generous breakfast in the creeper-clad patio or dining room (you can ask for doggy bags). The two rooms sharing kitchen and sitting room are traditional French-furnished. Off the games room, the duplex has two smaller, more 'rustic' rooms and an intriguing window layout. So close to lovely old Poitiers, even closer to the high-tech Futuroscope, yet only the ping-pong of a little white ball or the splish-splosh of swimmers disturbs the hush of the tiny village. Excellent value and a big garden.

rooms	3: 1 double, 1 triple, 1 suite for 4-5, all with bath or shower & wc.
price	€42-€45 for two.
dinner	Choice of restaurants 3km; self-catering in double & triple.
closed	Rarely.
directions	From A10 exit 28 on D18 for Avanton 2km. Signs in hamlet of Martigny.

Annie & Didier Arrondeau
La Ferme du Château de Martigny,
86170 Avanton, Vienne
tel (0)5 49 51 04 57
fax (0)5 49 51 04 57
e-mail annie.arrondeau@libertysurf.fr
web www.lafermeduchateau.fr

A quiet village, a fine 18th-century coaching inn, a charming courtyard, large garden and mature trees: an oasis of green peace. Attractively restored by Monsieur Flambeau and his vivaciously welcoming English/French wife, the rooms are immaculate: Spring – very French with its old cherrywood bed; Summer – brass four-poster; Winter – snow-white canopied bed; Four Seasons – almost English with old-style pine furniture and pretty children's room; and a peach-pink double. All have beautifully tiled bathrooms to match and guests have a sitting room in the old stables. Good food, too. *Baby-sitting available.*

rooms	5: 1 suite for 5, 3 triples, 1 double, all with bath or shower & wc.
price	€46-€56 for two.
dinner	€23 with wine, by arrangement.
closed	Mid-November-February.
directions	From Poitiers N149 W for Nantes 14km; at Vouillé left D62 to Latillé. (24km total.) House is largest in main village square.

Yvonne Flambeau
La Demeure de Latillé,
1 place Robert Gerbier,
86190 Latillé, Vienne
tel (0)5 49 51 54 74
fax (0)5 49 51 56 32
e-mail latille@chez.com
web www.chez.com/latille

POITOU · CHARENTES

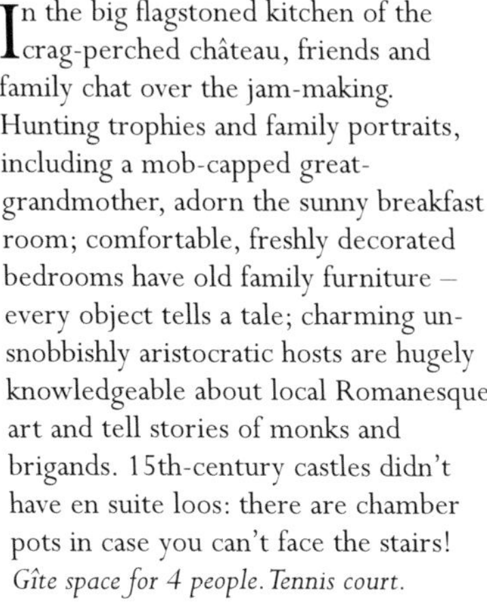

In the big flagstoned kitchen of the crag-perched château, friends and family chat over the jam-making. Hunting trophies and family portraits, including a mob-capped great-grandmother, adorn the sunny breakfast room; comfortable, freshly decorated bedrooms have old family furniture – every object tells a tale; charming un-snobbishly aristocratic hosts are hugely knowledgeable about local Romanesque art and tell stories of monks and brigands. 15th-century castles didn't have en suite loos: there are chamber pots in case you can't face the stairs! *Gîte space for 4 people. Tennis court.*

rooms	3: 1 double/twin, 1 double, 1 suite, all with shower or bath & wc.
price	€61 for two.
dinner	Restaurants 3km.
closed	Rarely.
directions	From A10 exit Poitiers Nord N149 for Nantes 12km; at bottom of hill left for Masseuil.

Alain & Claude Gail
Château de Masseuil,
86190 Quinçay, Vienne
tel (0)5 49 60 42 15
fax (0)5 49 60 70 15

In the generous château outbuildings are the guest quarters, decorated with a wonderful flair for fabrics and colours – mats and tablecloths match crockery, and bathrooms match bedrooms. It's smart yet utterly welcoming, as befits a converted château bakery. The largest room, finely renovated with exposed beams, stones and thick white curtains, holds the old bread oven. Your hosts are well-travelled, sociable people who will happily chat – Monsieur in perfect English – in the pleasant sitting area, and they know everything there is to know about the cultural treasure-chest that is the Poitou region.

rooms	6: 2 doubles, 2 twins, 2 family rooms, all with bath, shower & wc.
price	€54-€68 for two.
dinner	Restaurants 2-8km; self-catering possible.
closed	Rarely.
directions	From A10 exit 29 Rocade Est (ring road) for Limoges & Châteauroux 5km; exit left D3 for Montamisé 3km; right D18 for 2.5km. Château on right.

Daniel & Agnès Vaucamp
Château de Vaumoret,
Rue du Breuil Mingot,
86000 Poitiers, Vienne
tel (0)5 49 61 32 11
fax (0)5 49 01 04 54

POITOU · CHARENTES

Naturally, unstiltedly, aristocratically French, owners and house are full of stories and character: a fine jumble of ten French chairs, bits of ancient furniture, pictures, heirlooms, lamps in the stone-flagged *salon*, a properly elegant dining room; there are statues indoors and out; large bedrooms bursting with personality; bathrooms too. Monsieur's interests are history and his family, Madame's are art and life – they are a delightful combination of unselfconscious class and flashes of Mediterranean non-conformism. You are very much part of family life in this people- and dog-friendly house.

rooms	4: 2 doubles, 1 twin, 1 suite, all with bathrooms (1 on separate floor).
price	€61 for two.
dinner	€16 with wine, by arrangement.
closed	Rarely.
directions	From A10 exit Poitiers Nord, N10 for Limoges 7km; left to Bignoux; follow signs to Bois Dousset.

Vicomte & Vicomtesse Hilaire de Villoutreys de Brignac
Logis du Château du Bois Doucet,
86800 Lavoux, Vienne
tel (0)5 49 44 20 26
fax (0)5 49 44 20 26

A dream place of sophisticated, simple luxury, this ravishing château is full of air and light. Michel, with his lawyer's charm and gift of the gab, will welcome and guide you; if Monique seems distant, she may be 'seeing' you, seeking inspiration for your perfect candlelit dinner, often of local or home-grown produce. She's also a superb interior designer: from the imposing staircase lined with all sorts and positions of antique dolls to the stunning rooms where contemporary and traditional mix in uncluttered serenity, all is style and comfort with the odd dab of drama. And the 'honeymoon' room is worth every penny.

rooms	4: 2 doubles, 1 twin, 1 family room, all with bath & wc.
price	€90-€120 for two.
dinner	€30 with wine, by arrangement.
closed	November-April.
directions	From Poitiers N147 for Limoges; first left for Savigny l'Évescault; D89 continue 5km; 1st right on entering village.

	Monique & Michel Tabau
	Château de la Touche,
	86800 Savigny l'Évescault, Vienne
tel	(0)5 49 01 10 38
fax	(0)5 49 56 47 82
e-mail	infos@chateaudelatouche.com
web	www.chateaudelatouche.com

map: 10 entry: 455

POITOU · CHARENTES

A bee farm! The humble bee reigns royal here where honeys and other bee products are made – the small shop is a hive of activity. Jacky does the bee-tending while vivacious Charline welcomes you with a genuine smile. She is excellent at explaining (in French) the ancient complicity between man and insect over breakfast in the separate guest building. Two bedrooms are in the converted pigsty; downstairs has ivy-framed windows, upstairs has big skylights, colourful décor and plenty of space. The third room is behind the main house – smallish and cosy with its own tiny garden. Great for children too.

rooms	3: 2 doubles, 1 twin, all with bath or shower & wc.
price	€40 for two.
dinner	Restaurant in St Savin. BBQ available.
closed	15 October-February.
directions	From Chauvigny, N151 for St Savin. 2km before St Savin, left to Siouvre; signs.

	Charline & Jacky Barbarin
	Siouvre,
	86310 St Savin, Vienne
tel	(0)5 49 48 10 19
fax	(0)5 49 48 46 89
e-mail	charline.barbarin@wanadoo.fr
web	www.lafermeapicole.fr.st

map: 10 entry: 456

This delightful farming family are rooted in village life, including the local drama group. Monsieur also shares his time with mayoral duties and his dream of restoring the 12th-century Villesalem priory. Madame, somewhat shyer, embroidered the exquisite samplers. Both enjoy sharing their simple, stylish, much-loved house with cultured, like-minded guests. The suite is in the old coach house, its kitchen in the bread oven. All three finely decorated rooms blend with the garden and woodlands (golden orioles, hoopoes, wild orchids...). You may visit the goats, watch the cheese-making, fish in their big lake.

rooms	3: 2 doubles, 1 suite for 4-5 with kitchen/diner, all with bath or shower & wc. Extra room for children.
price	€44 for two.
dinner	€16 with wine, by arrangement.
closed	Rarely.
directions	From Poitiers N147 SE to Lussac les Châteaux; D727 E for 21km; left D121 to Journet. There, N for Haims; house 1km on left.

Jacques & Chantal Cochin
Le Haut Peu,
86290 Journet, Vienne
tel (0)5 49 91 62 02
fax (0)5 49 91 59 71

POITOU · CHARENTES

The Salvaudons are educated, intelligent farmers, he energetic and down-to-earth, she gentle and smiling, who are committed to the natural way, like swapping travellers' tales and sharing simple, lasting values while providing decent guest rooms in a relaxed and genuine house. There is indeed "more here than the Futuroscope". The farm is fully organic: don't miss Madame's Limousin specialities – lamb, chicken cooked in honey, vegetable pies – round the family table. The sheep pastures lie in rolling, stream-run country beloved of fisherfolk and Monsieur will take children to meet the animals. *Gîte space for 6 people.*

rooms	2 doubles, both with shower & basin, sharing wc.
price	€31 for two.
dinner	€13 with wine, by arrangement.
closed	Rarely.
directions	From Poitiers D741 to Civray; D148 east & D34 to Availles; D100 for Mauprévoir, 3km; signs.

Pierre & Line Salvaudon
Les Écots,
86460 Availles Limousine, Vienne
tel (0)5 49 48 59 17
fax (0)5 49 48 59 17
e-mail pierre.salvaudon@wanadoo.fr

Approaching by the long tree-lined drive, you can't imagine that this typical Poitevin farmhouse is plumb in the middle of the village, its original front door on the main street, but Jean-Louis, a genial twinkly man, really used to farm here. He now sticks to vegetables, chickens and a role in local events. Geneviève is a keen artist with an eye for colour and detail. Her bedrooms are freshly French-decorated, furniture is suitably old, sheets are embroidered linen, the canopy over one bed was made for her great-grandmother's wedding. A genuine, comforting place. *Heated Pool.*

rooms	2: 1 twin with shower & separate wc; 1 quadruple with shower & wc.
price	€44-€46 for two.
dinner	€11.50-€15 with wine, by arrangement.
closed	Rarely.
directions	From A10 exit Poitiers Sud N10 for Angoulême to Vivonne; 2nd exit D4 to Champagne St H. & Sommières du C.; right D1 for Civray 8km; left to Champniers; signs.

Geneviève & Jean-Louis Fazilleau
Le Bourg,
86400 Champniers, Vienne

tel	(0)5 49 87 19 04
fax	(0)5 49 87 96 94
e-mail	jeanlouis.fazilleau@free.fr
web	chambres-hotes-poitou-charente.ifrance.com

A stream winds through the quiet tree-shaded garden of this fine 15th-century house, passed down through the female line of the same family for 200 years; portraits in the *salon* show women of great character. The current first lady is no exception – gauloise-smoking, husky-voiced and a splendid cook while Monsieur is a charming and genial host. The bedrooms are real family rooms, witnesses to the passage of time: one very big, with old family furniture, a huge bathroom and grand views of the garden; the atmospheric tower room almost circular, lit by one long narrow window. Delightfully, aristocratically eccentric.

rooms	3: 1 double with shower, sharing wc; 1 triple with bath, shower & wc; 1 triple sharing shower & wc; 2 children's rooms.
price	€38-€61 for two.
dinner	€23 with wine, by arrangement.
closed	Rarely.
directions	From Poitiers N10 for Angoulême 3km; N11 for Niort; at Lusignan D950 3km; after Melle right D301 through St Romans; house in valley just before church.

M & Mme Rabany
Le Logis,
79500 St Romans lès Melle,
Deux Sèvres

tel	(0)5 49 27 04 15
fax	(0)5 49 29 18 37

Conversation is easy with your engaging hosts as you linger over home-made rosemary wine and dinner prepared by Michel – a Father Christmas look-alike whose speciality is pigeon (he used to breed them), while Marie-Claude teaches English at a local school. The fine creeper-clad house is in a rambling churchless village (but with a museum of Protestantism: this was the heart of Huguenot country). The second-floor suite is a happy mix of contemporary and traditional ideas; the two duplex apartments in a converted barn are simply but stylishly decorated; each has its own kitchen and sitting room and can be self-catering.

rooms	3: 2 suites for 4, 1 triple, all with shower & wc.
price	€41 for two.
dinner	€15 with wine, by arrangement.
closed	Rarely.
directions	From A10 exit Niort Centre or A83 Niort Est for La Mothe St Héray 8km; right for Prailles. Sign on left entering village; continue & then left to house.

Michel & Marie-Claude Duvallon
5 rue des Petites Justices,
79370 Prailles, Deux Sèvres
tel (0)5 49 32 84 43
e-mail m_c_d@club-internet.fr

POITOU · CHARENTES

Moat, drawbridge, dreams: it's all real. Two stone spirals to "the biggest bedroom in France": granite windowsills, giant hearth, canopied bed, shower snug in the old *garde-robe*; high in the keep, the stunning medieval family room: vast timbers, arrow slits and real windows. Furniture is sober and fires are always laid, as in olden times, and you breakfast under the guardroom vault, feet on 14th-century flagstones. Indeed, the whole place is brilliantly authentic, the magnificent gardens glow from loving care and Pippa is eager and attentive – flowers, bubbly, fishing in the moat, all on the house! *Gîte space for 5 people.*

rooms	2: 1 double, 1 suite for 2-4, all with shower & wc.
price	€110-€135 for two.
dinner	Restaurant 4km; choice 9km.
closed	Christmas-New Year.
directions	From A10 exit 29 on N147; N149 W to Parthenay; round Parthenay northbound; cont. N149 for Bressuire; 7km north of Parthenay right at sign for château.

Nicholas & Philippa Freeland
Château de Tennessus,
79350 Amailloux, Deux Sèvres
tel (0)5 49 95 50 60
fax (0)5 49 95 50 62
e-mail tennessus@csi.com
web www.tennessus.com

Madame is very proud of her pretty breakfast table and the old family house down by the riverside where she was born. Monsieur, who is most knowledgeable about the utterly fascinating *Marais* area, will take you out in his boat (at reasonable rates). Once the trippers have gone, the evening peace descends and the charming old-world atmosphere of house and garden takes over. Rooms are crammed with a lifetime's collection of objects, solid repro furniture and Madame's own tapestries. Your hosts are fun with a dry sense of humour but no English. Families welcome, preferably without toddlers (unfenced water). Real value.

rooms	2: 1 double, 1 triple, both with shower & wc.
price	€40-€45 for two.
dinner	Restaurants within walking distance.
closed	Rarely.
directions	From Coulon centre, D23 for Irleau. At end of village, immed. left along bank of River Sèvre which is Rue Élise Lucas.

Ginette & Michel Chollet
68 rue Élise Lucas,
79510 Coulon, Deux Sèvres
tel (0)5 49 35 91 55/42 59

POITOU · CHARENTES

The old farmhouse, lovingly restored and decorated, is simple, pristine, with biggish, comfortable rooms overlooking a pretty garden where you may picnic (there's a useful guest kitchen too). They are an interesting couple of anglophiles. Madame knows about nutrition and serves generous breakfasts with home-made jam, cheese, yogurt and cereals, all on local pottery. Monsieur teaches engineering in beautiful historic La Rochelle: follow his hints and discover the lesser-known treasures there. They love children of any age – there's some baby kit, table tennis and country peace. Good value.
No pets in rooms.

rooms	2: 1 room for 2-4, 1 suite for 6, all with bath or shower & wc.
price	€45-€50.50 for two.
dinner	Occasionally available €18.50, with wine; restaurants within 5 minutes' drive.
closed	Rarely, but please book ahead.
directions	From La Rochelle N11 E for 11km; north on D112 to Longèves; in village, right at 'Alimentation', 1st left, past Mairie; 700m on left.

Marie-Christine Prou
43 rue du Marais,
17230 Longèves,
Charente-Maritime
tel (0)5 46 37 11 15
fax (0)5 46 37 11 15
e-mail mcprou@wanadoo.fr
web perso.wanadoo.fr/17longeves

In this lovingly-restored grand old 16th-century house lives a lively young family: three children to entertain young visitors, sophisticated parents, who are avid and cosmopolitan collectors, to decorate with elegance and eclectic flair, cook with exotic inspiration and organics, and talk with passion. Old and modern rub happy shoulders: traditional *armoires* and new beds, a collection of scales and disabled facilities in the newer-style cottage, antique treasures and a tennis court. The air is full of warm smiles, harmony breathes from walls and woodwork, your hosts are endlessly thoughtful, families are positively welcome.

rooms	2 + 1 cottage: 1 triple, 1 suite for 6. Cottage for 5, all with bath or shower & wc.
price	€60 for two.
dinner	€23 with wine, by arrangement.
closed	Rarely.
directions	From Surgères Gendarmerie & fire station, D115 for Marans & Puyravault 5km, following signs.

Brigitte & Patrick François
Le Clos de la Garenne,
9 rue de la Garenne,
17700 Puyravault,
Charente-Maritime
tel (0)5 62 08 97 61
fax (0)5 46 35 47 91
e-mail info@closdelagarenne.com
web www.closdelagarenne.com

POITOU · CHARENTES

Behind its modest, wisteria-covered mask, this 17th-century former wine-grower's house hides such a pretty face and a magnificent garden that flows through orchard and potager into the countryside – freshest fruit and veg for your five-course dinner. Outstanding bedrooms too: light, airy and immaculate, every detail just so, they are beautifully done with luxurious bathrooms. The room for disabled guests is the best we have ever seen. Your hosts, recently retired from jobs in agriculture and tourism, have given their all to make house and garden as near perfect as possible and you will find them wonderfully attentive.

rooms	3: 2 doubles, 1 suite for 4, all with bath, shower & wc.
price	€45-€50 for two.
dinner	€15 with wine, by arrangement.
closed	Rarely.
directions	From A10 exit 34 on D739 to Tonnay Boutonne; left D114 to Archingeay; left for Les Nouillers; house just after turning.

Marie-Thérèse & Jean-Pierre Jacques
Chambres d'Hôtes,
17380 Archingeay,
Charente-Maritime
tel (0)5 46 97 85 70
fax (0)5 46 97 61 89
e-mail jpmt.jacques@wanadoo.fr

Part of a lovely sleepy village in the heart of *pineau* and cognac country, this farm once produced *pineau*, a Charentes wine distilled with cognac. You have your own entrance here you and can be as private as you like – but Valérie and Nicolas are generous hosts and happy for you to have the run of the house. Bedrooms, with views onto a young garden, are large, light and catch the morning sun. Décor is French-traditional; mattresses and sheets top-of-the-range. There's space to roam, an outdoor pool and dinners are relaxed, four-course affairs full of merriment and conversation. A real find for families.

rooms	2: 1 double, 1 suite for 4, both with bath & wc.
price	€46 for two.
dinner	€18 with wine, by arrangement.
closed	Rarely.
directions	From A10 exit 33 E601 to Mauzé sur le Mignon; D911 to Surgères; D939 12km, right to Chervettes; behind iron gates.

Valérie & Nicolas Godebout
Les Grands Vents,
17380 Chervettes,
Charente-Maritime

tel	(0)5 46 35 92 21
fax	(0)5 46 35 92 21
e-mail	godebout@club-internet.fr
web	www.les-grands-vents.com

map: 9 entry: 467

POITOU · CHARENTES

A wonderful old house and sure-footed hosts who grow endives – what more could one ask? Built in 1600, renovated in 1720, the house stands in a garden of mature trees reaching to the River Boutonne (lovely for swimming). In clean, fresh bedrooms you find good beds and big *armoires*; in the huge guest sitting room, antiques, armchairs and a French billiard table. Indeed, the whole place has a totally French country feel to it: you might be staying with your favourite granny, though Monsieur has a wicked sense of humour. There are good bike trails to spin off on and fabulous Romanesque churches to visit.

rooms	2: 1 double/twin with shower & wc; 1 suite for 4 with bath & wc.
price	€44 for two.
dinner	€16 with wine, by arrangement.
closed	Rarely.
directions	From Gendarmerie in St Jean d'Angély, D127 NE for Dampierre, 8km. In Antezant, 1st right.

Pierre & Marie-Claude Fallelour
Les Moulins,
17400 Antezant,
Charente-Maritime

tel	(0)5 46 59 94 52
fax	(0)5 46 59 94 52

map: 10 entry: 468

Your hostess brazenly indulges her passion for old buildings in this area of vast architectural wealth. She'll teach you stone-wall restoration, the intricacies of the Romanesque style or how to garden beautifully – the creamy local stone is a perfect foil for flowers and the veg is organic. In the old cognac press, the cool, light garden bedrooms are big and uncluttered, effective in their pale colours with a few well-chosen pieces each and exquisite bathrooms. Cognac nearby, the island beaches not too far and such a delightful, intelligent couple, full of fun and sparkle, make this a very special place to stay. *Gîte space for 4 people.*

rooms	3: 2 doubles, both with bath or shower & wc, 1 twin to make family suite with double.
price	€47 for two.
dinner	€17 with wine, by arrangement.
closed	Rarely.
directions	From A10 exit 34 for St Jean d'Angély. E on D939 to Matha (20km); right for Thors; left before entering Thors; Le Goulet on right.

Frédérique Thill-Toussaint
Le Clos du Plantis,
1 rue du Pont, Le Goulet,
17160 Sonnac, Charente-Maritime

tel	(0)5 46 25 07 91
fax	(0)5 46 25 07 91
e-mail	auplantis@wanadoo.fr

POITOU · CHARENTES

A totally French house, a thoroughly English couple. Jenny gardens and writes, with pleasure; John builds his boat for crossing the Atlantic, with dedication; together they have caringly restored their *Charentais* farmhouse and delight in creating a welcoming atmosphere. Feel free to go your own way, too: you have a separate guest entrance. The beautifully landscaped garden with its pretty windmill (let separately) and croquet lawn has an English feel – but the 'sense of place' remains unmistakably French. And St Savinien is a painter's delight – this really is a lovely part of the country. *Gîte space for 2 people.*

rooms	1 room for 2-4 with bath & wc.
price	€43-€49 for two.
dinner	By arrangement, €16, with wine; restaurants 3-10km.
closed	Christmas.
directions	From St Savinien bridge D114 along river, under railway, left D124 for Bords 2km; 2nd left after Le Pontreau sign; 200m on right.

John & Jenny Elmes
Le Moulin de la Quine,
17350 St Savinien,
Charente-Maritime

tel	(0)5 46 90 19 31
fax	(0)5 46 90 19 31
e-mail	elmes@club-internet.fr

It's an enormous, intriguing old château with dark walls, weapons on the walls, fabulous antiques – and lots of light: it's just one room thick. Your hostess, a beautiful, laughing extrovert, has lived here for decades, knows the history deeply and is addicted to receiving guests. Appropriately old-fashioned bedrooms are furnished with taste and flair (plumbing a bit old-fashioned too) and the open-fired original kitchen, where you step over and under priceless objects, is a gem, ideal for cold-weather breakfast. Artists and musicians love the long thin house and its fine gardens; Madame is unforgettable for all.

rooms	4: 1 double, 1 triple, both with shower & wc; 2 twins, sharing shower & wc.
price	€53-€60 for two.
dinner	At neighbouring farm; restaurants 5-12km; picnic possible.
closed	November-March.
directions	From Saintes N137 for La Rochelle 10km; D119 to Plassay; house on right on entering village, signs.

Alix Charrier
Le Logis de l'Épine,
17250 Plassay, Charente-Maritime
tel (0)5 46 93 91 66

POITOU · CHARENTES

Arrive at La Jaquetterie and step back in time: the old virtues of having time for people and living at a gentler pace are here in this well-furnished, old-fashioned house, and it is so comfortable. These kindly farmers are really worth getting to know: Madame keeps a good home-produced table; Monsieur organises outings to distilleries and quarries; both enjoy their guests, especially those who help catch escaping rabbits. Great old *armoires* loom in the bedrooms, lace covers lovely antique sleigh beds, and one of the bathrooms is highly modern-smart. An authentic country experience with genuinely good, kind people.

rooms	2: 1 triple on ground floor, 1 suite for 2-4, both with shower & wc.
price	€46 for two.
dinner	€15 with wine, by arrangement.
closed	Rarely.
directions	From A10 exit Saintes N137 for Rochefort & La Rochelle, 11km; D119 to Plassay. House on left on entering village.

Michelle & Jacques Louradour
La Jaquetterie,
17250 Plassay, Charente-Maritime
tel (0)5 46 93 91 88
fax (0)5 46 93 48 09

A sense of immense age swells as your eyes soar to the high barn roof with its intricate timbers. You are in the guest house on the converted farm: a sitting space for all with log fire, billiards, rocking chairs and the *Picardie* bedroom downstairs (with doors to the garden); off the gallery: *Pearl Buck*, who's oriental, of course, and two more; all have books, lace and warm comfort. If you want to know what the guides don't tell you about local history and sites, ask Monsieur Trouvé. He and his wife bubble with delight in their visitors and pile on the home-made cakes for breakfast. *Gîte space for 5 people.*

rooms	4: 3 doubles, 1 twin, all with shower & wc.
price	€43.50 for two.
dinner	Restaurants 2.5-7km.
closed	Mid-November-April.
directions	From Saintes N137 for Rochefort 6km; left D127 to St Georges. Rue de l'Église in village centre, house on left.

Anne & Dominique Trouvé
5 rue de l'Église,
17810 St Georges des Coteaux,
Charente-Maritime

tel	(0)5 46 92 96 66
fax	(0)5 46 92 96 66
e-mail	adtrouve@yahoo.fr

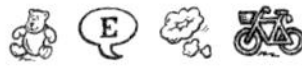

POITOU · CHARENTES

Your hosts have lavished care, money and time on their superb farmhouse since settling here after years in Morocco – you can tell they love it. They are a delightful couple: Anne-Marie is a talented artist whose stylish painted furniture, patchwork, painstakingly-constructed rag rugs and co-ordinated colour schemes adorn the house; her husband is mayor of the village; they share good breakfasts and dinners with their guests in the dining room or by the swimming pool. Their gardens are landscaped and terrace paved, flowers blooming and bedrooms big. *Quiet children over 6 welcome.*

rooms	4 doubles, all with bath & wc.
price	€63 for two.
dinner	€23 with wine, by arrangement.
closed	Rarely.
directions	From Saintes N150 W for 5km; fork right N728 for 29km; right D118 to St Sornin. In centre, Rue du Petit Moulin opposite church door.

Anne-Marie Pinel-Peschardière
La Caussolière,
10 rue du Petit Moulin,
17600 St Sornin,
Charente-Maritime

tel	(0)5 46 85 44 62
fax	(0)5 46 85 44 62
e-mail	caussoliere@wanadoo.fr
web	www.caussoliere.com

Sue's talent for watercolours springs from the same sense of style and colour she has brought to revitalising this handsome farmhouse – prettily decorated bedrooms, bright and fresh and furnished with French antique-style pieces; new shower rooms with sensibly big towels. There's plenty of choice at breakfast and if you've arranged dinner there will be home-grown vegetables, or there's a barbecue for you to do your own. Beyond the large garden are vineyards and, in summer, fields of sunflowers. This is good walking and cycling country and it's a 20-minute drive to the beach and to Cognac.

rooms	3: 2 doubles, 1 twin, all with bathroom & wc.
price	€55 for two.
dinner	€20 with wine, by arrangement.
closed	Occasionally.
directions	From A10 exit 36 for Pons; after toll bear right; right for Gémozac 1.5km; left for Tanzac & Givrezac; centre of Givrezac left at garage; last on left.

Sue & Phillip Capstick
La Belle Maison,
Route de Belluire,
17260 Givrezac, Charente-Maritime

tel	(0)5 46 49 06 66
fax	(0)5 46 49 06 66
e-mail	capstickphillip@online.fr

map: 9 entry: 475

The grand house lords it over a tiny hamlet surrounded by superb walking country and tantalising views. Dinah is English and tends a beautiful garden; Claude's ravishing collection of ornaments and antiques is on display in every room. Big bedrooms, one of which has a fabulous ormolu wardrobe, are magnificently decorated and scattered with oriental rugs. The huge hall and staircase give a great feeling of space. Look at the floor tiles in the *salon*: they were left to dry outside in the woods where they collected imprints of the feet of foxes, badgers and birds, before being laid in a church. Wonderful stuff.

rooms	4: 2 doubles, 1 twin, 1 family suite, all with bath, shower & wc.
price	€63-€70 for two.
dinner	€23, with wine, by arrangement.
closed	Occasionally.
directions	From A10 exit 37 for Mirambeau. At r'bout pass 'Marché U'; D254 1st right to St Georges des Agoûts; right at church D146; 1st junc. left & follow Chambres d'Hôtes signs.

Dinah & Claude Teulet
Les Hauts de Font Moure,
17150 St Georges des Agoûts,
Charente-Maritime

tel	(0)5 46 86 04 41
fax	(0)5 46 49 67 18
e-mail	cteulet@aol.com
web	www.fontmoure.com

map: 9 entry: 476

Protected by a magnificent park, yet in the town centre, here are the genuine château works: gilt, marble, mouldings and period furniture to match the 1850s building. House and garden are being brilliantly restored. Designer and art historian, Monsieur has a natural feel for colour and fabric; he loves arches too – there's one over each bath; large, finely-proportioned rooms overlook the park where guests can picnic and admire the botanical wonders. It is all superb, as are his fascinating talk about resuscitating the château and his candlelit dinners of traditional regional dishes in a most congenial, civilised atmosphere.

rooms	3: 2 doubles, 1 twin, all with bath, shower & wc.
price	€75-€85 for two.
dinner	€35 with wine, by arrangement.
closed	Occasionally.
directions	From A10 exit 37 to Mirambeau Centre. Av. de la République is after & opp. Tourist Office & swimming pool, behind trees on your right.

René Ventola
Le Parc Casamène,
95 avenue de la République,
17150 Mirambeau,
Charente-Maritime
tel (0)5 46 49 74 38
fax (0)5 46 49 74 38
e-mail parc.casamene@wanadoo.fr

POITOU · CHARENTES

Both former market researchers, Londoner Gordon and Parisienne Laure thoroughly enjoy people. Laure cooks because she loves it and breakfast is a spread. The two big, spotlessly clean rooms in the annexe are pretty and welcoming with tea-making stuff and plenty of stone and wood. Everyone can sit by the hosts' sitting-room fire or out by the pool and the kitchen door is always open. Once a modest inn for train travellers, the house still overlooks the old station, now another house, and there's a pond with thousands of frogs behind. As the owners say, La Font Bétou is not a place that pretends to be anything, it just is.

rooms	2: 1 split-level double, 1 twin, both with shower & wc + sitting space downstairs.
price	€55 for two.
dinner	€23 with wine, by arrangement.
closed	January.
directions	From Angoulême N10 S for 45km; left D730 for Montguyon. 1km after Orignolles, right to house, signposted.

Laure Tarrou & Gordon Flude
La Font Bétou,
17210 Orignolles,
Charente-Maritime
tel (0)5 46 04 02 52
fax (0)5 46 04 02 52
e-mail tarrou@club-internet.fr
web www.fontbetou.com

This is a gem of a place, both grand and intimate. Béatrice inherited the exquisitely French neo-Gothic château and she lovingly protects it from the worst of modernisation (though the hurricane took its toll in the garden and trees have had to be replanted). Sleep between old linen sheets, sit in handsome old chairs and wallow in a superb bathroom. The sitting room has that unusual quirk, a window over the fireplace, the dining room a panelled ceiling studded with plates. Béatrice, a teacher, and Christopher, a lecturer in philosophy, are interesting, cultured hosts who enjoy eating with their guests.

rooms	4: 2 doubles, 1 twin, 1 family suite, all with bath or shower, sharing 2 wcs on guest room floor & 1 downstairs.
price	€46 for two.
dinner	€12 with wine, by arrangement.
closed	Rarely.
directions	From A10 exit 36 to Pons, Archiac & Barbezieux; D731 for Chalais 12km. After Passirac, 1st right at roadside cross; up leafy drive.

Mme Béatrice de Castelbajac
Le Chatelard,
Passirac,
16480 Brossac, Charente
tel (0)5 45 98 71 03
fax (0)5 45 98 71 03
e-mail c.macann@wanadoo.fr

POITOU · CHARENTES

There's an old-fashioned, well-lived-in, much-loved air to this interesting house. The bedrooms have parquet floors, old-style wallpapers, pretty old beds with new mattresses; bathrooms have been modernised. Madame's regional cooking is highly appreciated and dinner is worth coming back for. A conservatory has been built to seat more people round a bigger table where your hosts stay and chat if not too busy serving you. They'll also show you the fascinating old cognac still and on winter weekends you may be able to help with the distilling process. A blissful spot. *Camping possible.*

rooms	6: 2 doubles, 1 twin, 2 triples, 1 family suite for 4, all with shower & wc.
price	€37 for two; suite €68 for four.
dinner	€13 with wine, by arrangement.
closed	Rarely.
directions	From A10 Pons exit D700 for Barbezieux Archiac. After Echebrune D148 (1st left) for Lonzac-Celles; right D151 & follow signs.

Micheline & Jacky Chainier
Le Chiron,
16130 Salles d'Angles, Charente
tel (0)5 45 83 72 79
fax (0)5 45 83 64 80
e-mail mchainier@voila.fr

Loyal to its wealthy roots as a cognac-grower's mansion, this superb place has all the trappings of classic French elegance: imposing arched entrance, tall windows, marble floors, ornate fireplaces, and the old still is a treat. The Fordhams found it in a sad state – and lavished all their energy and flair to create a striking yellow hall, bedrooms that are big, light and beautifully furnished, sheer English comfort in the sitting room, one roofless barn for the lovely pool, another as a small theatre for summer sketches (Jenny acts with the local group). The lime trees smile again. *Minimum 2 nights at weekends.*

rooms	3 doubles, all with shower & wc.
price	€66 for two.
dinner	Good choice of restaurants nearby.
closed	Rarely.
directions	From Angoulême N141 for Cognac/La Rochelle 16km; left for Mouliders/Vibrac; house on right after 1.5km.

Jenny & Derek Fordham
Les Tilleuls,
Chez Quillet,
16290 Moulidars, Charente
tel (0)5 45 21 59 00
fax (0)5 45 21 59 01
e-mail derek@les-tilleuls.fr
web www.les-tilleuls.fr

POITOU · CHARENTES

Breakfast is in bed for *les amoureux*, so settle those map-reading arguments before you arrive. Elegant and down-to-earth, willing to chase eggs in the chicken-run dressed to kill, Madame is an interior decorator and has done it all beautifully. A lovely wooden staircase takes you to the first-floor rooms, all gorgeous with fine fabrics, linen and towels. One gargantuan bathroom has chairs and dressing table. There are huge rooms to explore downstairs and you'll find peace and quiet in the music room. The two hectares of grounds hide an old tower and a bamboo grove to disappear into with a book.

rooms	4: 2 doubles, 1 triple, 1 suite for 4, all with bath or shower & wc.
price	€107 for two.
dinner	€39 with wine, by arrangement.
closed	Rarely.
directions	From Paris A10 for Bordeaux, exit Poitiers & Cognac; N10 for Angoulême; D699 for Magnac sur Touve, signs.

Mme Joly
Château de Maumont,
4 rue Aristide Briand,
16600 Magnac sur Touvre,
Charente
tel (0)5 45 90 81 10
e-mail hiram.deco@wanadoo.fr
web perso.wanadoo.fr/chateau.maumont

Do look up as you enter the guest house in the old stables: the hall ceiling is marvellous. Breakfast is served here if it isn't fine enough to sit outside. Rooms are good too: white paint and exposed stone make a stunning setting for fine antiques and old beds fitted with new mattresses. Madame, busy breeding horses (gorgeous foals in summer), is full of smiles and always has time to help arrange cognac-distillery visits or invite you to relax in a hammock after a bit of badminton. Monsieur may offer a local aperitif to guests of an evening.
A peaceful wooded spot in a very special corner of France. *Gîte space for 8 people.*

rooms	2: 1 double, 1 twin, both with shower & wc.
price	€46 for two.
dinner	Good restaurant at St Adjutory.
closed	Rarely.
directions	From Angoulême, N141 to La Rochefoucauld; right at 3rd traffic light on D162 to St Adjutory; in village 2nd right & follow signs.

Sylviane & Vincent Casper
La Grenouille,
16310 St Adjutory, Charente
tel (0)5 45 62 00 34
fax (0)5 45 63 06 41

map: 10 entry: 483

POITOU · CHARENTES

What an interesting, unexpected place – a paradise for children. Pretty, fresh guest rooms, one large, one smaller, are in a converted outbuilding – from the front window you see deer by the lake, from the back door, llamas and wallabies. Sitting on the ostrich-skin sofa you will be offered a chilled glass of delicious, local *pineau des Charentes*. Alex left hectic London for French farming with a difference and is thoroughly enjoying his new life. Hélène loves pergolas, so there are plenty of spots to sit and enjoy the fascinating surroundings. Fun and hugely welcoming. *Gîte space for 4 people.*

rooms	2: 1 quadruple, 1 triple, both with bath or shower & wc.
price	€40 for two.
dinner	€16, wine€8; auberge 2km.
closed	Rarely.
directions	From Poitiers D741 S for Confolens 50km. 10km after Pressac, left on D168 for St Germain de Confolens; sign after 2km.

Alex & Hélène Everitt
Le Pit,
Lessac,
16500 Confolens, Charente
tel (0)5 45 84 27 65
fax (0)5 45 85 41 34
e-mail everitt16@aol.com

map: 10 entry: 484

Young English farmers, their bilingual children, family antiques and friendly dogs occupy this house and all its original delights. From the high, soft-coloured, panelled dining hall a splendid staircase rises to airy, plainly-furnished rooms, one if them rather romantic with stained-glass and claw-footed bath. Your hosts are busy but still happy to sit round the big table at informal, family meals. Real value and an excellent base for a few days exploring *en famille*.

rooms	4: 2 doubles, both with bath & wc; 1 double with shower & sharing wc; 1 twin with shower & wc.
price	€40 for two.
dinner	€14, with wine; choice of restaurants Confolens.
closed	Rarely.
directions	From Confolens, D948 for Limoges for 4km; sign on road.

Stephen & Polly Hoare
Lesterie,
Saint Maurice des Lions,
16500 Confolens, Charente
tel (0)5 45 84 18 33
fax (0)5 45 84 01 45
e-mail polly.hoare@libertysurf.fr
web www.lesterie.com

REGIONAL FOOD STYLES

À l'Alsacienne: With sauerkraut and sausage.
À l'Américaine: A corruption of à l'Armoricaine from Armor, Celtic for Britanny – with shallots and tomatoes (see also Bretonne).
À l'Anglaise: Plain boiled.
À l'Ardennaise: With juniper berries.
À l'Auvergnate: With cabbage and bacon bits.
À la Basquaise: With onions, rice, sweet peppers and possibly Bayonne cured ham.
À la Bretonne: With leeks, celery, beans (see also Américaine).
À la Dauphinoise: With cream, garlic and sometimes cheese.
À la Dijonnaise: With mustard sauce.
À la Flamande: Flemish – cooked in beer or vinegar.
À la Lyonnaise: With onions, wine, vinegar and often sausage.
À la Niçoise: With anchovies and olives.
À la Normande: With cream.
À la Périgourdine: With goose liver and truffles.
À la Provençale: With tomatoes, garlic, olive oil.
À la Savoyarde: With cream and cheese.

And four supra-regional manners:

À la Bonne Femme: Good Woman style – with white wine, shallots and mushrooms.
À la Bourgeoise: Townswoman style – with a carrot, onion and bacon sauce.
À la Ménagère: Housewife style – with onions, carrots, turnips, peas.
À la Paysanne: Peasant/Country Woman style – with vegetables!

From Brazil, New Zealand, the New Hebrides, the Sahara, Michèle came home to the hacienda-style house built when her family's old wine-growing farm crumbled away. The imitation zebra and tiger skins in the living room fit strangely well with all the memorabilia and African sculptures; bedrooms are good traditional, with fine views across oceans of vines. It is relaxed and exotic and Michèle, lively and intelligent, knows all there is to know about this area (ask her about the roses planted at the ends of the vines) and its great wines. Their own wine comes with dinner and the nearby ferry comes from Blaye and Royan.

rooms	2: 1 double with bath & wc; 1 twin with shower & wc.
price	€50-€55 for two.
dinner	€25 with wine, by arrangement.
closed	Rarely.
directions	From Bordeaux bypass exit 7 on D1 to Castelnau; N215 through St Laurent; 4km, D104 to Vertheuil; abbey on right, over level crossing, house 1km on left.

Our very first artists painted their powerful magic underground; then stilted shepherds led their flocks through the swamplands; then pines were planted to drain the swamps – so stilts are now seen only when dancing for foreigners at high-class wine fairs.

Michèle Tardat
Cantemerle,
9 rue des Châtaigniers,
33180 Vertheuil Médoc, Gironde

tel	(0)5 56 41 96 24
fax	(0)5 56 41 96 24
e-mail	micheletardat@minitel.net
web	www.bbfrance.com

These people take extraordinary trouble to make each guest feel at home, so forget the suburban environment and enjoy delightful Philippe's deep wine knowledge and lively Monika's eagerness to please. She is German, once nursed in Vietnam and loves filling her space with crochet, danglers and soft toys; he's a retired cellar master who will prepare visits for individual guests. They are urbane, well-travelled polyglots who can obtain entry to most big wine châteaux for you. The mature trees and large fish-and-lily pond add a note of serenity. And the beach is just 20 minutes away. *Gîte space for 4.*

rooms	3: 1 double/twin, 1 double, 1 suite, all with bath or shower & wc.
price	€42-€62 for two.
dinner	Three restaurants 7km.
closed	Rarely.
directions	From Bordeaux ring road exit 7 N215/D1 41km; right D104 to Cissac; right at War Memorial Rue du Luc; house 1km on left, after water tower.

Philippe & Monika Achener
Le Luc,
6 route de Larrivaux,
33250 Cissac Médoc, Gironde
tel (0)5 56 59 52 90
fax (0)5 56 59 51 84
e-mail achener@gmx.net
web www.achener.com

AQUITAINE

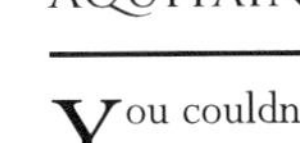

You couldn't be deeper into wine country than this. Alain is a wine broker and although he doesn't bring his work home, he could probably be persuaded to talk wine of an evening. Natalie's father was born in this house and it is very much a family home, despite its size. Alain and Natalie enjoy having an aperitif and a chat with their guests so they can plan the most congenial seating arrangement at dinner. The house is set back from the village road in a large garden with a big and very interesting pool: jets can be set so it feels like swimming against the current.

rooms	6: 5 double/twins, 1 suite for 4, all with bath or shower & wc.
price	€45-€140 for two.
dinner	€25 with wine, by arrangement.
closed	Rarely.
directions	From Bordeaux A630 exit 7; D1 for Le Verdon sur Soulac; skirt around Castelnau; N215 for St Laurent 1km to Bouqueyran. Sign on left.

Alain & Natalie Genestine
Domaine les Sapins,
33480 Moulis en Médoc, Gironde
tel (0)5 56 58 18 26
fax (0)5 56 58 28 45
e-mail domaine-les-sapins@wanadoo.fr
web www.domainelessapins.com

Here you will find three good and very big bedrooms, a stone entrance hall, a wrought iron balcony terrace for a glass of the Bassereaus' own dry white Semillon wine, and decorative bantams all over the garden. They are a hard-working young couple in an 18th-century château without quite enough money to make it over-stylish, thank heavens. It is relaxed and easy – even busy – with three young children, and deer in the woods. Breakfast is on the terrace, wine-tasting in the magnificent *salle de dégustation*. The small pool is for evening dippers rather than sun-worshippers.

rooms	3: 1 family room with bath, shower & wc; 2 triples, both with shower & wc.
price	€53 for two; €91.50 for four.
dinner	Choice of restaurants in Bourg.
closed	February & 1 week in August.
directions	From A10 exit 40a or 40b through St André de Cubzac; D669 through Bourg for Blaye; quickly right D251 for Berson for 1km; sign on right up lane.

M & Mme Bassereau
Château de la Grave,
33710 Bourg sur Gironde, Gironde
tel (0)5 57 68 41 49
fax (0)5 57 68 49 26
e-mail reservation@chateaudelagrave.com
web www.chateaudelagrave.com

AQUITAINE

Old tiles, a fine stone staircase, light colours, long windows, modern bathrooms and the joy of big bedrooms with plenty of space: to stow your luggage, sit in comfort, lounge on big beds (with new mattresses) and dream up your next move. The relaxed, welcoming Heftres have done a huge amount, from shifting stone to hunting antiques to running up curtains, and are proud of the results – the place feels loved but not over-smart. Ask Monsieur if you may play the piano; he does, and also occasionally leads tours of this rich wine-producing area. A fine old manor house, in unspoilt countryside – with a covered swimming pool.

rooms	3: 2 doubles, both with bath & wc; 1 triple with shower & wc.
price	€55–€65 for two.
dinner	Choice of restaurants 1.5-4km.
closed	Rarely.
directions	From Coutras D10 towards Guitres; over river Dronne, 1.1km; second house on right.

M & Mme Heftre
Château le Baudou,
33230 Coutras, Gironde
tel (0)5 57 49 16 33
fax (0)5 57 49 16 33
e-mail le.baudou@wanadoo.fr

Perfect for those who want to 'do' Bordeaux, a *maison vigneronne* 10km from St Émilion, presided over by viticulturist Monsieur (do taste the wines) and his wife, the delightful Marie-Christine. Your rooms are in two attractive 17th-century stone cottages and have top-quality furnishings, excellent showers, books, maps, magazines, space. Downstairs, a kitchen with washing and ironing room, *salon*, woodburner, table for cards and games. The garden is full of shady corners and window boxes are beautifully tended. It's polished, professional, friendly, and very French.

rooms	4: 2 doubles, 1 twin, 1 family, all with shower & wc.
price	€69 for two.
dinner	Choice of restaurants 3km.
closed	Rarely.
directions	From A10, exit 40 for St André de Cubzac; D670 for Libourne; in St Michel de Fronsac, at post office, follow signs for Lariveau, 1.5km; signposted.

Marie-Christine Aguerre
Clos Saint Michel,
1 Lariveau,
33126 St Michel de Fronsac,
Gironde

tel	(0)5 57 24 95 81
fax	(0)5 57 24 95 30
e-mail	clos.saint.michel@wanadoo.fr

map: 10 entry: 491

AQUITAINE

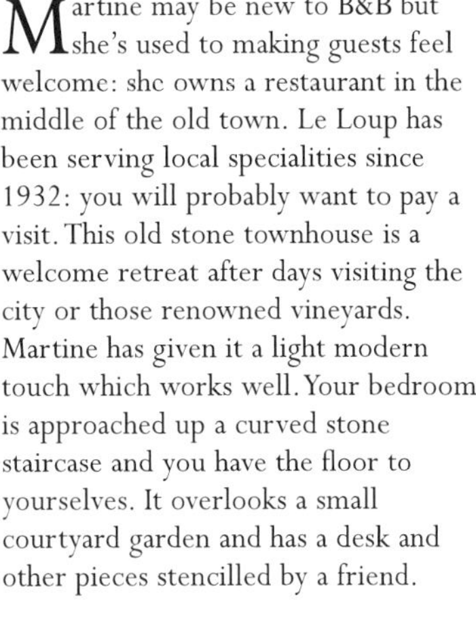

Martine may be new to B&B but she's used to making guests feel welcome: she owns a restaurant in the middle of the old town. Le Loup has been serving local specialities since 1932: you will probably want to pay a visit. This old stone townhouse is a welcome retreat after days visiting the city or those renowned vineyards. Martine has given it a light modern touch which works well. Your bedroom is approached up a curved stone staircase and you have the floor to yourselves. It overlooks a small courtyard garden and has a desk and other pieces stencilled by a friend.

rooms	1 double/twin with shower & wc.
price	€60 for two.
dinner	Madame's restaurant near Cathedral.
closed	August.
directions	Take Les Boulevards to Barrière de Pessac; 100m, 1st right, right again onto Rue de Patay.

Martine Peiffer
83 rue de Patay,
33000 Bordeaux, Gironde

tel	(0)5 56 99 41 74
fax	(0)5 56 48 20 21
e-mail	martine.peiffer@wanadoo.fr

map: 9 entry: 492

Arrive, soak up the serenity, and time will cease to matter – pilgrims have rested at this hospitable priory for 800 years. Lie in a hammock under the walnut tree, let the fantails coo you into a blissful siesta, the nightingales serenade your dawn. Susie, a cultured, interesting aromatherapist with a good sense of humour, simply loves her old stone house and rambling gardens and provides big inviting rooms done with a sophisticated combination of antique and modern pieces. In summer, there may be a friendly *al fresco* supper with other guests. Lovely pool, too. *Gîte space for 6 people. 2 nights minimum July-August.*

rooms	2 + 1 apartment: 2 doubles with shower, bath & wc, 1 apartment with 2 doubles, sitting room & kitchenette.
price	€91 for two; apartment €129 for two-four.
dinner	€15-€20; restaurants 3-7km.
closed	Rarely.
directions	From Bordeaux D936 for Bergerac; exactly 1km after St Quentin de Baron, sign on right, house at end of lane.

Susie de Castilho
Le Prieuré,
33750 St Quentin de Baron, Gironde

tel	(0)5 57 24 16 75
fax	(0)5 57 24 13 80
e-mail	stay@stayfrance.net
web	www.stayfrance.net

You appreciate good wine? Believe you can absorb the knowledge by osmosis? Then you will enjoy this coolly restrained, very beautiful manor among the vines. It has been in the family for nine generations, though the owners live in another Grand Cru château leaving nephew and pleasantly relaxed manager to run this one. They come every day and will invite you to taste the goods in the cellars – an easy if busy couple. Rooms, with plain sandstone or painted walls and simple antiques, offer sober quiet and the shrubby garden has an arch of trees that gives dappled shade as you walk towards the distant statue.

rooms	2: 5 doubles, 1 twin, 1 family room, all with shower & wc.
price	€61-€115 for two.
dinner	Restaurants nearby.
closed	Rarely.
directions	From A10 exit St André de Cubzac through Libourne for Bergerac; 3km after Bigaroux left D234E for St Laurent; right before railway for St Hippolyte; house on left.

Bernard & Béatrice Rivals
Château Monlot Capet,
St Hippolyte,
33330 St Émilion, Gironde

tel	(0)5 57 74 49 47
fax	(0)5 57 24 62 33
e-mail	mussetrivals@belair-monlot.com
web	www.belair-monlot.com

Tradition has deep, proud roots here. Monsieur is a kind, gentle man, his big farmhouse has stood for three centuries, his vines, now tended by the next generation, are mature, his wine superb; the lovely linen, patchwork and lace are family heirlooms and the family has a strong, lively presence. The country-style, stone-walled, old-furnished bedrooms and their small bathrooms are immaculate, though great beams and attic ceilings may reduce your space. You have your own living room and kitchen (ideal if you're daunted by local restaurant prices). Superb breakfasts are served in the cosy family dining room.

rooms	5: 2 doubles, 2 twins, 1 triple, all with bath or shower & wc.
price	€46-€49 for two.
dinner	Choice of restaurants St Émillion; self-catering possible.
closed	15 January-15 February.
directions	From Libourne D243 for St Émilion; pass Château Girard Bassail on right; 3km before St Émilion left D245 towards Pomerol; house 300m on right.

Claude Brieux
Château Millaud-Montlabert,
33330 St Émilion, Gironde

tel (0)5 57 24 71 85
fax (0)5 57 24 62 78

map: 10 entry: 495

AQUITAINE

Utterly quiet in its large walled garden where the shutters match the oleander flowers, the elegant townhouse has properly classy furnishings – superb antiques set off by unfussy fabric or grasspaper walls, beautiful rugs on polished floors, lustrous chests, paintings and prints of real quality and an astounding quantity of tapestry work done by Monsieur himself. The smallest (cheapest) room is fine enough, the others are sheer luxury. Your hosts, smart and highly hospitable retired professionals, know the local winegrowers and can guide you round. A high-class house in an amazing, historic town.

rooms	3: 1 twin, 1 suite, both with shower & wc; 1 double with private bathroom.
price	€60-€90 for two.
dinner	€30 with wine, by arrangement.
closed	Christmas & New Year.
directions	From Libourne D243 to St Émilion; r'bout right to Hôtel de Ville. Park in square: Rue Abbé Bergey leads off this.

François & Élisabeth Musset
3 rue Abbé Bergey,
33330 St Émilion, Gironde

tel (0)5 57 24 70 12
fax (0)5 57 24 70 12

map: 10 entry: 496

Monsieur has lived all round the world – there are quantities of fascinating souvenirs to tell the tale, but this immaculate and comfortable 1750s farmhouse was his family holiday home for years; Madame, pleasant and houseproud, is an artist who used to be a nursery school teacher; their combined conversation is stimulating. She does much to please her guests and we were naturally offered tea and cake on the terrace. Beautiful bedrooms, simple yet not stark, have white or clean stone walls, the suite has a bathroom big enough to hold a decent party in and the whole place is full of peace. *Minimum 2 nights. Gîte space for 2-4.*

rooms	3: 1 double/twin, 1 suite for 2/4, both with bath & wc.
price	€52 for two.
dinner	Restaurants nearby.
closed	Rarely.
directions	From Bordeaux D936 E for 36km; 4km after Branne right D670 for Agen 1km; at Lavagnac left after 'Boucherie-Charcuterie'; 2nd house on left.

France Prat
Le Refuge du Peintre,
3 chemin de Courbestey, Lavagnac,
33350 Ste Terre, Gironde

tel	(0)5 57 47 13 74
e-mail	france.prat@wanadoo.fr
web	perso.wanadoo.fr/france.prat

map: 10 entry: 497

AQUITAINE

Food and wine buffs love it here with these kind, courteous people: Madame is an excellent cook who can cater for special diets (with advance warning), Monsieur is a wine expert – enjoy it all in the Art Deco dining room. Set among fields and vineyards, the farmhouse is attractively furnished and the beamed, wallpapered guest rooms are big and comfortable. The family room is particularly lovely: it has a more contemporary feel with its mezzanine and sitting area overlooking the garden. Your hosts offer wine courses and vineyard trails all over the Bordelais, and you can buy their preserves.

rooms	3: 1 double, 1 triple, 1 family room, all with bath, shower & wc.
price	€53 for two.
dinner	By arrangement €20-€32; good wine list.
closed	16 October-December.
directions	From Libourne D670 S for 31km; left D230 to Rimons; at sawmill on right, 1st left; signs.

Dominique & Patrick Lévy
Le Grand Boucaud,
Rimons,
33580 Monségur, Gironde

tel	(0)5 56 71 88 57
fax	(0)5 56 61 43 77
e-mail	grandboucaud@free.fr
web	grandboucaud.free.fr

map: 15 entry: 498

Think it looks modest? Don't be fooled – go through the main buildings and splendour strikes. Discover delightful gardens and a great pool enclosed by charming guest quarters: your dynamic hosts, both full-time doctors, have converted the old stables brilliantly, keeping much of the original dark wood, adding elegant antiques and artefacts to each of the large, individual bedrooms, *armoires* lined with sophisticated fabrics matching curtains and wallpaper, good bathrooms. Superb breakfasts may be served by the housekeeper as your hosts are out by 9am. Good value. *Gîte space for 6 people.*

rooms	3: 2 doubles, 1 twin, all with bath or shower & wc.
price	€70 for two.
dinner	Restaurant 300m.
closed	Rarely.
directions	From Libourne D670 S 45km to La Réole; left N113 for Agen; house on left on edge of town opp. Automobile & Train Museum.

Christian & Danielle Henry
Les Charmettes,
Henry's Lodge,
33190 La Réole, Gironde
tel (0)5 56 71 09 23
fax (0)5 56 71 25 13

map: 15 entry: 499

AQUITAINE

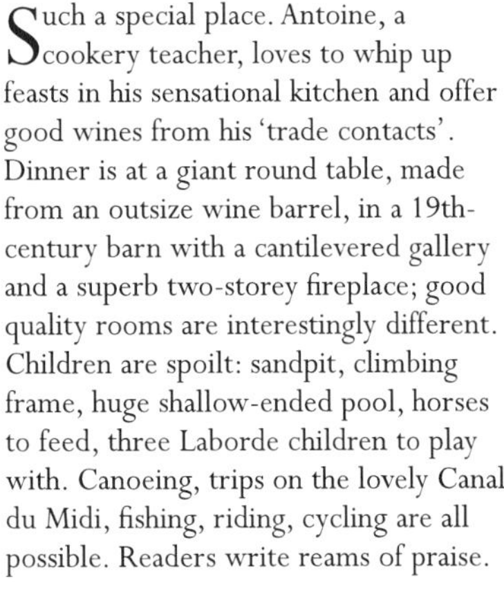

Such a special place. Antoine, a cookery teacher, loves to whip up feasts in his sensational kitchen and offer good wines from his 'trade contacts'. Dinner is at a giant round table, made from an outsize wine barrel, in a 19th-century barn with a cantilevered gallery and a superb two-storey fireplace; good quality rooms are interestingly different. Children are spoilt: sandpit, climbing frame, huge shallow-ended pool, horses to feed, three Laborde children to play with. Canoeing, trips on the lovely Canal du Midi, fishing, riding, cycling are all possible. Readers write reams of praise.

rooms	5; 3 doubles, 1 triple, 1 twin, all with bath and/or shower & wc.
price	€55 for two.
dinner	€22 with wine, by arrangement.
closed	Occasionally.
directions	From A62 exit 4 onto D9; left for Bazas-Grignols; over m'way bridge; 1st left, 250m after bridge; follow signs Chambres d'Hôtes 3km.

Claire & Antoine Laborde
La Tuilerie,
33190 Noaillac, Gironde
tel (0)5 56 71 05 51
fax (0)5 56 71 05 51
e-mail claire.laborde@libertysurf.fr

map: 15 entry: 500

A house to satisfy your soul: lost in a forest, its windows onto endless oaks and pines with duck pond and river beyond. Madame, a lovable person, teaches yoga (for guests too); her artist son's hand-painted decoration (marbling, stencilling, trompe-l'œil) brings originality without offence to old stone and brickwork; grandchildren live next door, all in harmony with nature, and summer walks yield wildflower treasures. The simple rooms are not large but there is real family space at the piano or around the huge kitchen fireplace during delicious dinners.
German spoken too.

rooms	3: 1 double, 1 twin, 1 triple, all with shower & wc.
price	€34–€39 for two.
dinner	€12.50 with wine, by arrangement.
closed	Rarely.
directions	From Mont de Marsan N134 NW to Garein; left D57 for Ygos & Tartas; follow signs: 1km of lane to house.

Mme Liliane Jehl
Moulin Vieux,
40420 Garein, Landes
tel (0)5 58 51 61 43
fax (0)5 58 51 61 43

map: 14 entry: 501

AQUITAINE

Light, birdsong and ocean breezes whisper round this seductive modern house and its balmy garden so don't be daunted by the residential area or the steep drive. Up and down go the pale wooden decks connecting living spaces and levels – is it an earthbound ship or a luxurious Californian beach house? Waves of light wash over super contemporary furniture, natural colours, finishes and fabrics that are gentle on the eye and Madame's exotic pieces from Africa and the Far East. Straightforward and unpretentious, she revels in her house and guests' appreciation of their soft, cleancut rooms and *al fresco* breakfasts.

rooms	2 + 1 apartment: 1 double, with bath & wc, 1 twin with shower & wc; 1 apartment for 4 with bath & wc.
price	€60–€75 for two; apartment €110–€140.
dinner	Choice of restaurants nearby.
closed	Rarely.
directions	From A63 exit 8 for St Vincent de Tyrosse & Seignosse; cont. for Golf 3km; over r'about, 800m; left into Av. de Morfontaine, 200m, blue house, signs.

Jean-Luc & Noëllie Annic
Villa Ty Gias,
1 avenue Hilton Head,
40510 Seignosse, Landes
tel (0)5 58 41 64 29
fax (0)5 58 41 64 29
e-mail tygias@wanadoo.fr
web perso.wanadoo.fr/tygias

map: 14 entry: 502

The miniature château in its secluded setting rejoices in a fine chestnut staircase with iron banister, a veranda paved with rare Bidache stone, high ceilings, old prints, a glimpse of the Pyrenees and the call of a peacock. Madame is a gem, gracious and charming – she teaches yoga, paints, is a long-distance walker and a committed vegetarian; her husband is gently reserved; Braco the dog loves company. Children can roam the 20 hectares of parkland freely – they love it. The rooms, large and properly decorated, have gorgeous parquet floors and relatively little 'château' furniture. We think the smaller ones give better value.

rooms	3: 2 doubles, 1 twin, all with shower or bath & wc.
price	€46-€77 for two.
dinner	Good restaurant in village.
closed	November-March, except by arrangement.
directions	From A10 or A63 exit St Geours de Maremne to Orist. Or, from A64 exit Peyrehorade to Dax. In both cases, 10km to Monbet.

M & Mme Hubert de Lataillade
Château de Monbet,
40300 St Lon les Mines, Landes

tel	(0)5 58 57 80 68
fax	(0)5 58 57 89 29
e-mail	chateau.de.monbet@wanadoo.fr

AQUITAINE

Astounding furniture, captivating house, brilliant décor. "The whole place is stunning, inside and out!" Our inspector was obviously moved by this house with prodigious original panelling (1610), whose contents have been accumulated by Colette's family for 14 generations: portraits from the 12th century onwards; spectacular bedrooms with canopied antique beds, strong colours, wonderful furniture; three with open fireplaces. Dining room and *salon* are handsome, too: more antiques, terracotta tiles and a huge stone fireplace. Colette is elegant, attentive, helpful and hugely resourceful. An exceptional place.

rooms	4 doubles, all with bath or shower & wc.
price	€43-€56.50 for two.
dinner	€17 with wine, by arrangement.
closed	Rarely.
directions	From Dax D947 for Pau/Orthez; from r'about at end of town cont 10km; at crossroads on D947 ignore sign for Mimbaste; take NEXT right C16; follow discreet yellow signs for 1km.

Colette Dufourcet-Alberca
Maison Capcazal de Pachioü,
40350 Mimbaste, Landes

tel	(0)5 58 55 30 54
fax	(0)5 58 55 30 54

An atmosphere of dream-like tranquillity wafts over this grand and appealing old French country house and its original oak floors. Just outside the park gates is the beautiful River Adour, rich in bird and wildlife – every 10 years or so it comes and kisses the terrace steps. The two south-facing bedrooms overlook the river and a great spread of communal meadows where animals graze freely. There is a vast choice for 'flexitime' breakfast on the terrace or in the dining room. Madame, an attractively energetic and interesting hostess, was a publisher in Paris for many years. *Spanish spoken.*

rooms	3 doubles, all with bath or shower & wc.
price	€60 for two.
dinner	Wide choice of restaurants 2-5km.
closed	Rarely.
directions	From A63 exit 8 to St Geours de Maremne; D17 S for 5km to Saubusse; right just before bridge; château 800m on right.

Claude Dourlet
Château de Bezincam,
Route de l'Adour,
Saubusse les Bains,
40180 Dax, Landes
tel (0)5 58 57 70 27
fax (0)5 58 57 70 27

map: 14 entry: 505

AQUITAINE

A place of contrasts, this beautiful Basque farmhouse on a golf course has 17th-century timbers and old stones outside, minibars and cleancut minimalist décor inside: pastel sponged rooms, rustic headboards softly stained to match, simple, practical furniture on polished floorboards. Philippe is a journalist. Deeply patriotic, he knows every Basque detail, every good eatery and can arrange golf and spa deals for guests. In his tidy, clean house, rooms have independent entrances yet you are treated like family with typical, unintrusive Basque hospitality. Plus rolling green views and the sea just 400m away. *4km from Biarritz airport.*

rooms	5: 3 doubles, 2 twins, all with bath/shower & wc.
price	€91.20-€137.20 for two.
dinner	Wide choice nearby.
closed	Rarely.
directions	On A64 exit Biarritz; N10 south for Bidart. Right at r'bout by supermarket. House on left 600m after lights & after Auberge d'Ilbarritz.

Philippe Etcheverry
La Ferme Irigoian,
Avenue de Biarritz, Ilbarritz,
64210 Bidart, Pyrénées-Atlantiques
tel (0)5 59 43 83 00
e-mail irigoian@wanadoo.fr
web www.irigoian.com

map: 14 entry: 506

The house cornerstone, the magnificent magnolia, the towering pines were all planted on one day in 1881. The Mallor family's welcome is as generous as they: an enchanting couple with teenage children who have lived and fished in southern seas. Their deeply sensitive restoration includes a Blue Marlin room, canopied pine beds, modern fittings and respect for the original chestnut panelling. They know about good food and wine too: Krystel ran a restaurant, Philippe's cellar is brilliant – do dine with them. There's great walking, a sauna for afterwards and lots more. *Spanish spoken.*

rooms	5: 3 doubles, 2 triples, all with shower & wc.
price	€65-€70 for two.
dinner	€23, with wine; restaurants 700m.
closed	Rarely.
directions	From A63 exit on D932, on through Ustaritz & Cambo les Bains; left into Louhossoa; straight over crossroads. House 800m on left.

	Krystel & Philippe Mallor
	Domaine de Silencenia,
	64250 Louhossoa,
	Pyrénées-Atlantiques
tel	(0)5 59 93 35 60
fax	(0)5 59 93 35 60
e-mail	silencenia@aol.com
web	www.domaine-de-silencenia.fr.st

map: 14 entry: 507

AQUITAINE

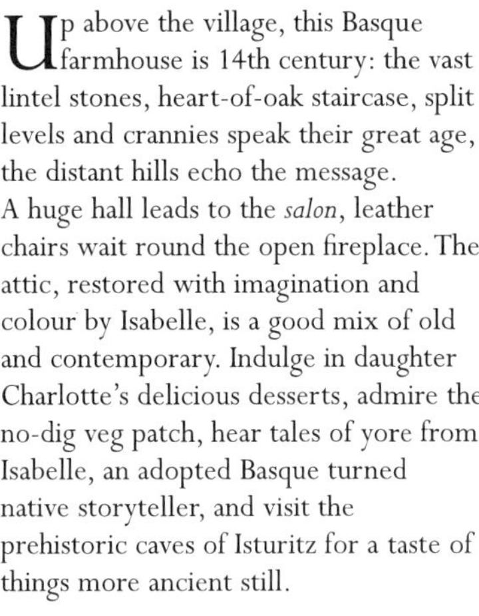

Up above the village, this Basque farmhouse is 14th century: the vast lintel stones, heart-of-oak staircase, split levels and crannies speak their great age, the distant hills echo the message.
A huge hall leads to the *salon*, leather chairs wait round the open fireplace. The attic, restored with imagination and colour by Isabelle, is a good mix of old and contemporary. Indulge in daughter Charlotte's delicious desserts, admire the no-dig veg patch, hear tales of yore from Isabelle, an adopted Basque turned native storyteller, and visit the prehistoric caves of Isturitz for a taste of things more ancient still.

rooms	5: 2 doubles, 3 triples, all with shower & wc.
price	€53-€62 for two; €67-€74 for three.
dinner	€20 with wine, by arrangement.
closed	February.
directions	From A64 Briscous exit D21 to Hasparren; left D10 for Labastide Clairence for 3km; right D251 through Ayherre to Isturitz. Signposted.

	Isabelle & Charlotte Airoldi
	Urruti Zaharria,
	64240 Isturitz,
	Pyrénées-Atlantiques
tel	(0)5 59 29 45 98
e-mail	urruti.zaharria@wanadoo.fr
web	www.urruti-zaharria.fr

map: 14 entry: 508

A lovely face among all the lovely faces of this superb listed village, the 16th-century Basque farmhouse, resuscitated by its French/Irish owners, is run with well-organised informality. Dinners around the great oak table are lively; local dishes excellent. Rooms are big, light, well-decorated with hand-stencilling and pretty fabrics, beams and exposed wafer bricks, country antiques and thoughtful 'extras' such as good books and bottled water. Breakfast is on the terrace in warm weather. And Gilbert will laugh and teach you *la pelote basque*.

rooms	3 doubles, all with bath or shower & wc.
price	€50-€62 for two.
dinner	€22 with wine, by arrangement.
closed	Occasionally.
directions	From A64 junc. 4 for Urt & Bidache; right on D123 to La Bastide Clairence. House on main street, opp. bakery.

Valerie & Gilbert Foix
Maison Marchand,
Rue Notre Dame,
64240 La Bastide Clairence,
Pyrénées-Atlantiques

tel	(0)5 59 29 18 27
fax	(0)5 59 29 14 97
e-mail	valerie.et.gilbert.foix@wanadoo.fr
web	perso.wanadoo.fr/maison.marchand

AQUITAINE

Sylvianne lives on a hill in a typical old Basque farmhouse full of timbers, pictures, carved country furniture and her own skillfully orchestrated patches of colour – she loves colour! Up the twisty old staircase, each super room has its strong chromatic vibration: *Pamplona* rippling blue and yellow with an open timber frame in the middle; *Seville* vigorously orange and green; *Cordoue* fresh blue and acid green; bits and bobs, bouquets and bows finish the effects and bathrooms are good. Downstairs, you will be generously received by your smilingly bright young hostess who knows the area and cooks very well.

rooms	4: 1 quadruple, 3 triples, both with shower & wc
price	€53-€56 for two.
dinner	€20.50 with wine, by arrangement.
closed	Rarely.
directions	From A64 exit 4 for Urt; right D123; through Labastide Clairence for St Palais for 3km. House on left on top of hill; signposted.

Sylvianne Darritchon
Lacroisade,
64240 La Bastide Clairence,
Pyrénées-Atlantiques

tel	(0)5 59 29 68 22
fax	(0)5 54 29 62 99
e-mail	lacroisade@aol.com

Guilhat is one of those sturdy Béarn houses with solid old furniture and traditional décor to which Marie-Christine has added her own decorative touches over the years – colourful bedroom wallpapers, small, modern bathrooms – and everything is immaculate. She is elegant and energetic, doing nearly all the work here herself and longing to show you her remarkable garden. It has huge old trees, magnolia, azalea, rhododendron, with benches discreetly placed for quiet reading... and the Pyrenees as a backdrop. There's table tennis and the new spa centre in Salies is good for swimming all year. *Gîte space for 10.*

rooms	3: 1 double, 1 twin, 1 suite, all with bath or shower & wc.
price	€47-€54 for two.
dinner	€17 with wine, by arrangement.
closed	Rarely.
directions	From A64 exit 7; right for Salies '

	Marie-Christine Potiron
	La Closerie du Guilhat,
	64270 Salies de Béarn,
	Pyrénées-Atlantiques
tel	(0)5 59 38 08 80
fax	(0)5 59 38 08 80
e-mail	guilhat@club-internet.fr

map: 14 entry: 511

AQUITAINE

The Desbonnets completely renovated their grand 18th-century village house after finding it and this sleepy village in the Pyrenean foothills: both house and owners are quiet, elegant, sophisticated and full of interest, the furniture a feast for the eyes. Dinner is a chance to pick their well-stocked brains about the region and do delve into their tempting library (she binds books). The light, airy bedrooms have more interesting furniture on lovely wooden floors. *La Rose* is very chic, *La Verte* is a dream – enormous and boldly coloured with views of the mountains and a 'waltz-in' bathroom.

rooms	2 doubles, both with shower or bath & wc.
price	€50 for two.
dinner	€20 with wine, by arrangement.
closed	Rarely.
directions	From Navarrenx D2 for Monein to Jasses; right D27 for Oloron Ste Marie; in Lay-Lamidou, left, 1st right, 2nd house on right.

	Marie-France Desbonnet
	Maison L'Aubèle,
	4 rue de la Hauti,
	64190 Lay-Lamidou,
	Pyrénées-Atlantiques
tel	(0)5 59 66 00 44
fax	(0)5 59 66 00 44
e-mail	desbonnet.bmf@infonie.fr
web	www.ifrance.com/chambrehote/

map: 14 entry: 512

This exceptional couple, Heather, warmly communicative, Desmond, ex-architect with a great sense of fun, have brilliantly restored Agnos (and do all the cooking). There are high ceilings framing remarkable mirrors, paintings set into panelling, fine period furniture, a black marble dining room fountain, a medieval kitchen, an old prison… François I is said to have escaped by a (still secret) tunnel. Bedrooms are great: *Henri IV* has antique gilt beds, *François I's* black and white bathroom has an antique cast-iron bath. It's huge and you will feel completely at home. *Children over 12 welcome. Gîte space for 14 people.*

rooms	5: 1 double, 1 twin, 3 suites, all with bath and/or shower & wc.
price	€60–€120 for two.
dinner	€18.50, wine €10.
closed	2 weeks in February & November.
directions	From Pau N134 for 35km to Oloron Ste Marie; through town; N134 towards Zaragoza 1km. In Bidos, right for Agnos.

Heather & Desmond Nears-Crouch
Château d'Agnos,
64400 Agnos, Pyrénées-Atlantiques

tel	(0)5 59 36 12 52
fax	(0)5 59 36 13 69
e-mail	chateaudagnos@wanadoo.fr

map: 14 entry: 513

AQUITAINE

Landscape painters love this haven. From terrace and pool you can see for ever into the high Pyrenees – sunlit snowy in winter, all the greens in summer. Beside their 1700s farmhouse, the Brownes' remarkable barn conversion shelters refined, beamed and stone-walled bedrooms and a superb dining room – Isabelle's trompe-l'œil floor, huge carved table: an eclectic style reflecting their multinational origins (Polish, French, South African). They are a happy, relaxed and thoroughly integrated family. It is informal, easily friendly and, on windless, balmy, summer evenings, the food is deliciously garden-aromatic.

rooms	5: 1 double, 2 double/triples, 1 twin, 1 family room; all with bath or shower & wc.
price	€48–€60 for two.
dinner	€25 with wine, by arrangement.
closed	Rarely.
directions	From Pau N134 S for Saragosse to Gan; right at lights after chemist, D24 for Lasseube 9km; left D324. Follow Chambres d'Hôtes signs; cross 2 small bridges; house on left up hill.

Simon & Isabelle Browne
Maison Rancesamy,
Quartier Rey,
64290 Lasseube,
Pyrénées-Atlantiques

tel	(0)5 59 04 26 37
fax	(0)5 59 04 26 37
e-mail	missbrowne@wanadoo.fr
web	www.missbrowne.com

map: 14 entry: 514

Quintessentially French B&B is yours at this down-to-earth 17th-century manor-farm. Old pillared gates, smooth grass, glimpses of farm life – barns, thousands of ranging hens, tractors, sheep: it is instantly, warmly real. Your animated, extrovert hostess leads you, in good English, to big unflouncy bedrooms done in best French provincial style with opulent but unostentatious white bathrooms and views of meadows and woods. The family take you to their bosom: dine at their big dining table, swim in their lovely pool, play billiards, table tennis, croquet and, of course, boules and… eat their eggs for breakfast.

rooms	3: 1 double, 2 twins, all with shower & wc.
price	€55–€68 for two; suite €98 for four.
dinner	€22, with wine by arrangement.
closed	Rarely.
directions	From Marmande D933 S for Casteljaloux 10km. Château signposted on right opposite D289.

M & Mme de La Raitrie
Château de Cantet,
Samazan,
47250 Bouglon, Lot-et-Garonne
tel (0)5 53 20 60 60
fax (0)5 53 89 63 53
e-mail tdelaraitrie@hotmail.com

AQUITAINE

Walk through the entrance hall into the handsome country kitchen and thence onto the lawns that roll towards those views. Or stay there and dine: it has a big fireplace, pottery pieces, sculpture, and a lot of flowers. In the sitting room, terracotta tiles and kilim rugs, a fireplace and grand piano give a comfortably smart air. Adriana is Swiss-Italian, Jocelyn South African, and they tend to do things well. Relatively new to B&B, they are hugely committed, creating lush bedrooms with a touch of luxury in the bathrooms. The abiding memory will be of terracotta tiles, attention to detail and great food. *Gîte space for 8 people.*

rooms	1 suite with bathroom & wc.
price	€67–€82 for two.
dinner	€18 with wine, by arrangement.
closed	Rarely
directions	From A10 exit St André de Cubzac to Ste Foy La Grande; D708 to Duras; 4km after Duras left C1 to St Pierre.

Jocelyn & Adriana Cloete
Manoir de Levignac,
Saint Pierre sur Dropt,
47120 Duras, Lot-et-Garonne
tel (0)5 53 83 68 11
fax (0)5 53 93 98 63
e-mail cloete@wanadoo.fr

On the old market place of an unspoilt village: 18th-century elegance, a walled garden and a terrace with breathtaking country views. Fiona, an inspired cook, is Scottish, Leif, a wonderful raconteur, is Danish; their background: cosmopolitan in film and design; their house: full of paintings, antiques, props from film and theatre productions; the feel: beige and white luxury of white-painted floors, sumptuous raw linen fabrics, fine furniture. *Gîte space for 8 people.*

rooms	3: 1 double, 2 twins, all with bath or shower & wc.
price	€60-€80 for two.
dinner	€30, with wine; picnic basket possible.
closed	Rarely.
directions	From Marmande D708 for Duras 17km to Lévignac; bear left; head for Centre Ville; house on left behind market hall: two bay trees & white front door.

Leif & Fiona Pedersen
La Maison de la Halle,
47120 Lévignac de Guyenne,
Lot-et-Garonne

tel	(0)5 53 94 37 61
fax	(0)5 53 94 37 66
e-mail	maison.de.la.halle@wanadoo.fr
web	www.lamaisondelahalle.com

AQUITAINE

Having lived vibrantly on the Riviera, the Peyres moved here in search of rural peace, then longed to share their love of the place: why not do B&B? The huge twin room has rugs on the original wood floor and carved beds in proper French country-house style. French windows to their own terrace and splendid valley and lake views bring space into the smallish double rooms. Then there's the vast yellow-tiled kitchen, the glorious main rooms, the stunning furniture – a remarkable solid brass candelabra, a piano, handmade carpets… the list goes on. Highly civilised casualness in both house and owners. *Gîte space for 4 people.*

rooms	3: 2 doubles, 1 twin, all with shower & wc.
price	€65-€85 for two.
dinner	€19 with wine, by arrangement.
closed	November-March.
directions	From Bergerac D933 for Marmande. 1.5km after Eymet left C1 for Agnac-Mairie; 500m on left.

Françoise & Henri Peyre
Château de Péchalbet,
47800 Agnac, Lot-et-Garonne

tel	(0)5 53 83 04 70
fax	(0)5 53 83 04 70
e-mail	pechalbet@caramail.com
web	pechalbet.free.fr

A many-gloried 17th-century family château with 15 fabulous hectares of garden and woodland: red squirrels and deer cavort, wild orchids glow, the Babers nurture 400 new trees. Their furniture from Scotland sits graciously in the French rooms, white carpeting spreads deep luxury in the lovely suite, family antiques grace the guest sitting room and they love you to share their welcoming manor. Breakfast generously in the huge kitchen or on the terrace then roam, relax or play: there's a carp lake for fishing, a tennis court, a 16-metre child-friendly pool. Great hosts, rooms, local markets, restaurants and wines. *Gîte space for 8 people.*

rooms	3: 2 doubles, 1 family suite, all with bath & wc.
price	€87-€121 for two.
dinner	Several good restaurants in Castillonnès.
closed	Christmas & New Year.
directions	From Bergerac N21 for Villeneuve. 1.5km after Castillonnès, pass 'Terres du Sud' on left. After 50m, sign on right before crest of hill.

James Petley, Patricia & David Baber
Domaine des Rigals,
47330 Castillonnès, Lot-et-Garonne
tel (0)5 53 41 24 21
fax (0)5 53 41 24 79
e-mail babersrig@aol.com

AQUITAINE

With infectious energy and fluent English, Madame tells her love of her house, land and gently cropping horses. Hawks and owls nest outside the old-style *pigeonnier* where one bold-coloured, kempt bedroom sits above the other, plus tiny children's attic, minute kitchen and log-fired living room. Throw open the shutters, smell the freshness, behold the Pannetier empire of paddocks, pool and lake (for fishing and boating) up to distant hills. After breakfast at the family table, on the terrace or in your dayroom, launch into this area's endless riches. Children fully provided for. *Gîte space for 8 people.*

rooms	2: 2 doubles/twins, both with shower & wc, 1 with mini-kitchen.
price	€51 for two.
dinner	€18 with wine; self-catering €9 per day.
closed	Rarely.
directions	From Villeneuve sur Lot D676 to Monflanquin; D272 towards Monpazier. 1.5km beyond x-roads to Dévillac, left before bridge; 3rd house on right.

Michel & Maryse Pannetier
Colombié,
47210 Dévillac, Lot-et-Garonne
tel (0)5 53 36 62 34
fax (0)5 53 36 04 79
e-mail colombie@wanadoo.fr

Paul and Pippa did this triumphant restoration themselves, with two small children and a passionate commitment to the integrity of the ancient building, so brash modernities are hidden (the telephone lurks behind a model ship). It is breathtaking: an elaborate *pisé* floor set in cabalistic patterns and lit only with candles, two stone staircases, patches of fresco, a vast hall with giant fireplace and table – the welcome is to scale. The tower room is unforgettable, so is the pool. This family is veggie-friendly and pro-organic; dinner may feature home-reared lamb and last for hours; people simply love it. *Gîte space for 9 people.*

rooms	5: 3 doubles, 2 suites, all with bath, shower & wc.
price	€70–€100 for two.
dinner	€18 with wine, by arrangement.
closed	Rarely.
directions	From Fumel D102 to Tournon; D656 for Agen 300m; left to Courbiac, past church, right at cross for Montaigu 1km; house on left.

Paul & Pippa Hecquet
Château de Rodié,
47370 Courbiac de Tournon,
Lot-et-Garonne

tel	(0)5 53 40 89 24
fax	(0)5 53 40 89 25
e-mail	Chateau.Rodie@wanadoo.fr

map: 15 entry: 521

AQUITAINE

The overflowing stone plunge-pool in the green, tumbling terraced garden is unforgettable (OK for children too). John and Jane's talent is a restful atmosphere, their conversion a brilliant marriage of cottage simplicity – simple décor with sparks from African throws and good paintings – and contemporary style. Delightful, energetic Jane offers superb, imaginative food in the new veranda or the bright, rustic dining room with its limed walls and ticking chair covers, and early supper for children. And John "is a joy to be with". Lovely people and a house of taste in a tranquil view-drenched spot. *Gîte space for 4 people.*

rooms	5: 2 doubles, 1 twin, all with shower & wc; 1 double, 1 twin sharing bath & wc.
price	€46–€53 for two.
dinner	€17, wine €8.
closed	Rarely.
directions	From Angoulême D939 for Périgueux 29km; right D12 for Ribérac to Verteillac; left D1 for Lisle 5km; right D99 for Celles for 400m; sign to left.

Jane & John Edwards
Pauliac,
Celles,
24600 Ribérac, Dordogne

tel	(0)5 53 91 97 45
fax	(0)5 53 90 43 46
e-mail	pauliac@infonie.fr
web	www.pauliac.fr

map: 10 entry: 522

Long views down the hamlet-studded valley and a graceful restoration by owners who swapped London for deepest Dordogne. They have created three fine bedrooms with big beds, white walls and fresh flowers, coir floors and sylvan views. Two of them share an enchanting lavender-panelled bathroom with a swish shower. Snug up on the landing sofa with a book, seek out a private corner in the elegantly simple garden where the hidden pool is heated to West Indian temperatures – Sue was brought up in Trinidad. Seven hectares for walkers and wild orchids, delightful civilised people, superb food. Worth a proper stay.

rooms	3: 1 double with shower & wc; 2 doubles sharing bathroom & wc.
price	€48 for two.
dinner	€18, wine €8.
closed	Rarely.
directions	From Ribérac D708 for Verteillac; over bridge; D99 right to Celles; through village leaving church on right. House sign 2nd right after Peugeot garage.

Sue & Nick Gild
Le Vignoble,
Celles,
24600 Ribérac, Dordogne

tel	(0)5 53 90 26 60
fax	(0)5 53 90 26 60
e-mail	nsgild@compuserve.com

AQUITAINE

The perfect site, with lovely wide rural views, was carefully chosen to transplant this lovely old barn – once the garden has matured, you'll think it's been here for centuries. Marie-Ange and Philippe's country furniture looks just right on the old floor tiles beneath the old oak beams – all is bright and uncluttered, ancient and modern mix and match, the fresh young bedrooms have views, stylish fabrics and superior mattresses. Sit on the rose-covered terrace and contemplate a spot of fishing – they have their own lake – horse riding or touring; another member of the family runs stables nearby. *Gîte space for 12 people.*

rooms	3: 2 doubles, 1 twin, all with shower & wc.
price	€54 for two.
dinner	Good choice of restaurants 3km.
closed	Rarely.
directions	From Libourne A89 exit Monpon Ménestérol; right D708 for Ste Foy la Grande 8km. Right in St Rémy, opp. Le Pressoir, D33 for St Martin/Villefranche; follow signs.

Marie-Ange Caignard
Domaine de la Mouthe,
24700 St Rémy sur Lidoire,
Dordogne

tel	(0)5 53 82 15 40
fax	(0)5 53 82 15 40
e-mail	lamoutheperigord@wanadoo.fr

The Kieffers did the brave and utterly successful restoration of their old Dordogne mill themselves, their professional gardening past speaks softly in the herb-scented patio and the little brook trembles off past grazing horses to the valley. Inside, levels juggle with space, steep stairs rise to smallish rooms of huge character with wood-lined walls, brilliantly chosen colours, rich rugs and selected antiques. Your sitting room is seductive with its logs on the fire and a forest overhead. Add a relaxedly bubbly welcome, delicious home-grown organic dinners, home-made bread and jams for breakast, and you have excellent value.

rooms	2: 1 double, 1 twin, both with shower & wc; child's room available.
price	€50 for two.
dinner	€16; bottle of wine €9.
closed	November-February.
directions	In Mussidan, at church, for Villamblard 4km; follow blue signs left for St Séverin 2km, blue sign on right.

Jacques & Ginette Kieffer
Le Moulin de Leymonie du Maupas,
24400 Issac, Dordogne
tel (0)5 53 81 24 02

map: 10 entry: 525

AQUITAINE

This deeply united family honours tradition: the recipes for hand crafting pâtés and *foie gras* are their heirlooms, the wiggly roof tiles original, the wallpapers timelessly French. Wonderful Marie-Jeanne shares the B&B tasks with her son, a poultry breeder, and daughter-in-law, a brilliant (non-vegetarian) cook. She'll welcome you with her natural, vigorous humour, settle you into your pure 'French Rustic' room, let you admire the view, then drive you across the Dordogne to her son's lovely old house for a memorable dinner. Exceptionally genuine French country people – all power to them.
Gîte space for 5 people.

rooms	3: 1 double, 1 triple, 1 quadruple, all with shower & wc (1 curtained).
price	€45 for two.
dinner	€18 with wine, by arrangement.
closed	1 November-15 March.
directions	From Bergerac D32 for Ste Alvère for 10km then look for signpost 'Périgord – Bienvenue à la Ferme'.

Marie-Jeanne & Marie-Thérèse Archer
La Barabie,
Lamonzie Montastruc,
24520 Mouleydier, Dordogne
tel (0)5 53 23 22 47
fax (0)5 53 22 81 20
e-mail regis.archer@wanadoo.fr

map: 10 entry: 526

Your Belgian hosts know their adopted region "like their pocket" and are keen that you discover hidden treasures not just the oversubscribed star sights. Their fine set of Périgord buildings sits high on a wooded, hawk-hunted hill and the big, solar-heated pool is a decent distance from the beautifully restored house – the garden is taking shape too. In the biggest room, you sleep under a soaring timber canopy – a hymn to the carpenter's art – supporting a crystal chandelier. Easy décor, good furniture, a friendly welcome and the run of the kitchen. You may even be able to paint your own souvenir tile.
Gîte space for 6 people.

rooms	3: 1 double, 1 triple, 1 quadruple, all with bath & wc.
price	€42-€60 for two.
dinner	Auberge 2km; choice of restaurants in Bergerac, 9km; use of kitchen possible.
closed	Rarely, but please book ahead in winter.
directions	From Bergerac N21 for Périgueux. 4km after Lembras, Les Rocailles sign on right.

Marcel Vanhemelryck
& Nicole Denys
Les Rocailles de la Fourtaunie,
24520 Lamonzie Montastruc,
Dordogne

tel	(0)5 53 58 20 16
fax	(0)5 53 58 20 16
e-mail	rocaille@infonie.fr

map: 10 entry: 527

AQUITAINE

The whole family are involved: Madame has handed the daily management of auberge and B&B to her two daughters, Monsieur runs the mixed farm producing fruit, vegetables, poultry and wine, and they all thrive. The two bedrooms, in Grandmother's old house over the road from the auberge, are simple and good, perfect for two couples travelling together who could have the whole house. People come quite a way to eat here, the food is so good (open every day for lunch – leave time for a siesta afterwards – and dinner). With a brand new pool in the kempt little garden, it's a real bargain.

rooms	2 doubles, both with shower & wc.
price	€38.50 for two.
dinner	€15-€24 with wine.
closed	October-April.
directions	From Périgueux N21 for Bergerac. 4km after Bordas left to St Maime; continue for Vergt & immediately left for Castagnol. Follow Auberge signs.

Laurence & Ghislaine Gay
La Petite Auberge,
Castagnol,
24380 St Maime de Péreyrol,
Dordogne

tel	(0)5 53 04 00 54
fax	(0)5 53 04 00 54

map: 10 entry: 528

Robert or Stuart's greeting is the first line of an ode to hospitality written in warm stone and breathtaking gardens, set to the tune of the little stream hurrying by to the lake. Freshly flowery, the immaculate rooms in the guest barn are comfortingly filled with excellent beds; bathrooms are utter luxury. The breakfast room has pretty tables and tea-making kit: have your succulent fruit salad here or on the vine-shaded terrace. All is lovingly tended, in perfect peace; nearby is unspoilt Paunat with its huge church – the whole place is a delight. *Ask about pets; children must be supervised as there is unfenced water.*

rooms	6 double/twins, all with bath or shower & wc.
price	€75-€79 for two.
dinner	2 good restaurants 5km.
closed	Rarely; winter 3 nights minimum stay.
directions	From Le Bugue D703/D31 through Limeuil. Past viewpoint to x-roads; D2 for Ste Alvère; after 100m fork left; house 2km on left.

Robert Chappell & Stuart Shippey
Le Moulin Neuf,
Paunat,
24510 Ste Alvère, Dordogne
tel (0)5 53 63 30 18
fax (0)5 53 63 30 55
e-mail moulin-neuf@usa.net
web www.francedirect.net/moulin.htm

map: 10 entry: 529

AQUITAINE

Carine, half-Greek, easy-going and helpful, makes you feel very welcome in the sunny kitchen of her restored farmhouse. She enjoys cooking French and international dishes, with local ingredients where possible, and sometimes organises barbecues round the swimming pool. Each new-bedded, newly-decorated, modern-bathroomed bedroom in the converted barn has its own terrace onto the shady garden (the pool is far enough away not to disturb your siesta); the unfussy style relies on exposed stonework and beams, fresh paintwork and local country furniture. Spend two or three nights and get to know the area.

rooms	4: 2 doubles, both with shower & wc; 2 twins, both with bath & wc.
price	€44.50-€47.50 for two.
dinner	€14 with wine, by arrangement.
closed	January.
directions	From Le Bugue go to Ste Alvère; at main x-roads there, D30 for Trémolat. House 2nd right, 500m after sign Le Maine at top of hill.

Carine Someritis
Les Hirondelles,
Le Maine,
24510 Ste Alvère, Dordogne
tel (0)5 53 22 75 40
fax (0)5 53 22 75 40

map: 10 entry: 530

Enter the creeper-climbed courtyard through the old arch: looks a bit sophisticated? Francine and Odile will reassure you – they are funny, extrovert, intelligent, and wonderful company. Browse in their library, seize the chance to share their genuine pleasure in their house and guests. The curvy roof, wafer bricks and ancient timbers may be familiar friends but the long-drop privy is a fascinating rarity. Splendid main rooms combine simplicity and taste, antique and modern; smaller, tempting bedrooms have hand-stencilled doors and the playroom has table tennis, telly and tea kitchen. Marvellous! *Gîte space for 6 people.*

rooms	5: 3 doubles, 1 twin, 1 family suite, all with bath or shower & wc.
price	€55 for two.
dinner	€20 with wine, by arrangement.
closed	Rarely.
directions	From Bergerac D660 for Lalinde & Sarlat; right over R. Dordogne at Pont de Couze (still D660); at Bayac right D27 for Issigeac 2km; house on left at top of hill.

Francine Pillebout & Odile Calmettes
Le Relais de Lavergne,
Lavergne,
24150 Bayac, Dordogne
tel (0)5 53 57 83 16
fax (0)5 53 57 83 16
e-mail relaisdelavergne@wanadoo.fr

AQUITAINE

The intriguing new house opens big eyes to rolling paddocks and woods, the garden slithers past in soft lines and curves, terraces parade before spectacular sunsets. Your enthusiastic hosts have married one of humanity's oldest businesses – breeding horses – to a sure sense of modern design. Travellers hoping for peace and uncluttered style will appreciate the mood created by lots of wood, books, restful fabrics and fine fittings. Rooms face south or onto the terraces. The Simon children only use the pool when you're out and Madame is eager to make you comfortable without invading your privacy. Appealing in all aspects.

rooms	3 doubles, all with bath or shower & wc.
price	€70 for two.
dinner	Choice of restaurants 1.5-5km.
closed	Rarely.
directions	From Bergerac D660 19km to Port Couze; cross Dordogne to Couze; after Mairie left up hill; sharp right; sharp left; past cemetery, house 1st on right.

Anne & Denis Simon
Les Chambres de Toutifaud,
24150 Couze St Front, Dordogne
tel (0)5 53 57 28 55
fax (0)5 53 57 28 55
e-mail contact@chambres-hotes-perigord.com
web www.chambres-hotes-perigord.com

Waltz in the marble halls of this magnificent manor, sophisticate in its fine new bathrooms, go natural with Richard's ark of roaming animals and gorge on his home-grown fruits. He knows his mushrooms too, and can take you there. He and Isabelle, happily out of the tourist industry and fervent B&B believers, will share their imaginative cooking with you if you are a small group (book ahead). Simple white bedrooms with plain beds and Richard's excellent paintings are a calm contrast to the opulence below but the pool area is wickedly tempting. Luxury, enthusiasm, efficiency all make this special. *Gîte space for 5 people.*

rooms	7: 2 doubles, 3 twins, all with shower or bath & wc (2 connect for family use); 2 suites in separate building.
price	€53-€69 for two.
dinner	€16-€23, wine €9-€19.
closed	Rarely.
directions	From Périgueux D710 S for Belvès. At r'bout do NOT fork right to Belvès, stay on D710 500m then left; signs. House 600m on left.

Richard & Isabelle Ginioux
Le Branchat,
24170 Belvès, Dordogne

tel	(0)5 53 28 98 80
fax	(0)5 53 28 90 82
e-mail	lebranchat@lebranchat.com
web	www.lebranchat.com

map: 15 entry: 533

AQUITAINE

Once a wreck, now a village manor again thanks to your hosts' hard labour and touch of easy elegance. In the living room overlooking the sweeping lawn, warm bright colours reflect Madame's sunny, Latin personality and you're welcome to play the piano and read the books. The tower suite and small double have a modern feel, the three other rooms are more traditional, huge and high-ceilinged; all have very good modern comforts. There are children's games, a free beach nearby on the Dordogne, good food (neighbours' produce) if you dine in, plenty of choice out and riding stables next door – altogether delightful.

rooms	5: 3 doubles, 1 double/twin, 1 suite, all with bath or shower & wc.
price	€70-€110 for two.
dinner	€25, with wine; good restaurants nearby.
closed	Rarely.
directions	From Sarlat D57 to Beynac; D703 to St Cyprien; 7km beyond, right to Coux et Bigaroque; through village, left after Mairie; house on right after about 1km, just past wayside cross.

Ghislaine & Marc Oréfice
Manoir de la Brunie,
La Brunie,
24220 Coux et Bigaroque,
Dordogne

tel	(0)5 53 29 61 42
fax	(0)5 53 28 62 35
e-mail	marc.orefice@wanadoo.fr

map: 10 entry: 534

Graham, who's English, has virtually gutted his mid-19th-century elegantly arch-windowed, manor house, saving every original feature possible – panelling, old oak doors, a variation on the theme of the baronial double entrance – and creating four excellent bedrooms as well as the library and sitting room he shares with guests. He is a charmingly outgoing and caring person, always concerned for guests' welfare and with a deep love of the French way of life. The whole place is furnished with good taste and fine antiques and the 150-yard triumphal tree-lined avenue marching up to the 200-year-old plane is a grand sight.

rooms 4: 1 double, 1 twin, both with bath and wc; 2 twins, each with shower & wc.

price €75 for two.

dinner €20 with wine, by arrangement.

closed December-mid-January.

directions From Sarlat D703 for Bergerac; exit for Siorac at r'bout; right over Dordogne; 1st right D703. House 1st on right.

Graham Templeton
Le Hêtre Rouge,
24220 Coux et Bigaroque,
Dordogne
tel (0)5 53 31 14 29
fax (0)5 53 31 27 31
e-mail g.templeton@wanadoo.fr

AQUITAINE

Once a charterhouse, this good-looking Périgord house sits squarely in 10 hectares of parkland and peace, a tribute to the rich, sober taste of the area. Inside reflects outside: the same dark timbers against pale stone and the new owners have redecorated the bedrooms most charmingly. They are gradually replacing the modern furniture with country antiques and the feel is warmly authentic. And moreover, they used to run a restaurant – it's well worth dining here. Sitting at the big table for house guests, you may find other gourmets in the beamed dining room: a few outsiders are occasionally allowed. *Gîte space for 6 people.*

rooms 5: 1 double, 2 twin, 1 triple, 1 quadruple, all with bath or shower & wc.

price €61-€90 for two.

dinner €20, wine €7-€14.

closed 2 November-March.

directions From Sarlat D46 to Cénac St Julien. At end of village on for Fumel. House 3rd turning on right.

Brigitte & Christophe Demassougne
La Guérinière,
Baccas,
24250 Cénac et St Julien, Dordogne
tel (0)5 53 29 91 97
fax (0)5 53 30 23 89
e-mail contact@la-gueriniere-dordogne.com
web www.la-gueriniere-dordogne.com

Neither dream nor museum, Puymartin is a chance to act the aristocrat for a spell, in your own wing, and survey the trippers. The fireplace in the tapestried baronial dining room would take a small tree, painted beams draw the eye, the carved stone staircase asks to be stroked, all the furniture is authentic 17th-century Perigordian, history oozes from every corner (there may be a ghost). Bedrooms are vastly in keeping – twin four-posters, a loo in a turret, thick draperies. The ever-elegant Countess is friendly and very French; her son helps in the château and speaks good English; both are delightful. *Gîte space for 10 people.*

rooms	2: 1 twin, 1 family suite, both with bath, shower & wc.
price	€115 for two.
dinner	Good restaurant 5km; choice in Sarlat.
closed	November-March.
directions	From Sarlat D47 for Les Eyzies 8km. Château signposted regularly.

Comte & Comtesse de Montbron
Château de Puymartin,
24200 Sarlat la Canéda, Dordogne
tel (0)5 53 59 29 97
fax (0)5 53 29 87 52
e-mail xdemontbron@wanadoo.fr

map: 10 entry: 537

AQUITAINE

In a tiny, peaceful hamlet in a particularly lovely area, La Licorne is three old buildings with a stream bounding the pretty courtyard. Claire and Marc are from the Alps – she teaches skiing, he works in tourism and is an experienced cook – and are keen to make their new home a relaxing, easy place to be. Clutter-free rooms, one in the 13th-century barn overlooking the nut trees and garden, are small, white, with modern furniture and the occasional old carved cupboard door. The dining room is superb with its big fireplace and gallery at each end; food is light and vegetable-orientated. *Please arrive after 5pm.*

rooms	3: 2 doubles, 1 suite for 4, all with bath or shower & wc.
price	€54-€57 for two.
dinner	€18, with wine; restaurants 500m-6km.
closed	November-Easter.
directions	From Montignac D65 south for 6km; left on minor road to Valojoulx. House in centre of hamlet, left of Mairie.

Claire & Marc Bosse
La Licorne,
Valojoulx,
24290 Montignac Lascaux,
Dordogne
tel (0)5 53 50 77 77
fax (0)5 53 50 77 77
e-mail licorne.lascaux@wanadoo.fr
web www.licornelascaux.com

map: 10 entry: 538

Fascinating people, they are committed to the rural heritage movement. Their sensitive restoration of this lovely, listed group of ancient buildings, with a shingle-roofed bread oven, illustrates that commitment. Bedrooms, at opposite ends of the long building, have odd layouts: one has the shower in a (big) cupboard next to the fireplace, an antique washbasin that tips straight into the drain (genuine period feature) and a 120-cm brass bed. They founded the local music and dance festival, are very involved in the cultural life of the community and go to Glyndebourne whenever they can.

rooms	2: 1 double with shower & wc; 1 suite for 4 with bath & wc.
price	€53–€56 for two.
dinner	Restaurant 1.5km; picnic possible.
closed	Last 2 weeks of October; Christmas-January.
directions	From Périgueux N21 N to Sarliac sur l'Isle; D705 to Coulaures; right D73 to Tourtoirac. Right after bridge, left D67 for St Orse; house 1km on left.

Danièle & Jean-Pierre Mougin
Bas Portail,
Tourtoirac,
24390 Hautefort, Dordogne
tel (0)5 53 51 14 35
e-mail bestofperigord@perigord.com
web www.best-of-perigord.tm.fr

map: 10 entry: 539

AQUITAINE

A panorama of apple orchards, river, lakes and two châteaux captures the visitor's eye on this 360-hectare estate. In a modernized outbuilding, each stylish bedroom has an original colour scheme, immaculate wooden floors, the odd country antique and a splendid bathroom with 21st-century shower. You will share breakfast, a sumptuous affair, with the Dutch owners or, in their absence, with charming Véronique. There's so much to do you may never leave: a vast heated pool with sauna and bar, three pool tables and an antique juke box in the baronial hall, cycling and fishing on the estate. A magnificent place.

rooms	5: 3 doubles, 2 twins, all with bath or shower & wc.
price	€79–€110 for two.
dinner	€15 with wine, by arrangement.
closed	Rarely.
directions	From Limoges D704 for St Yreix; 60km right on D705 for Excideuil; 1km, house on right.

Ellen & Jeroen Bakker
Domaine d'Essendieras,
24160 St Médard d'Excideuil,
Dordogne
tel (0)5 53 52 81 51
fax (0)5 53 52 89 22
e-mail domaine-essendieras@wanadoo.fr
web www.essendieras.fr

map: 10 entry: 540

David and Alison have created such a pretty garden – you eat, separately from your hosts, under a wooden pergola covered in roses, honeysuckle and vines and the pool looks out over heavenly countryside. Convinced vegetarians, they also produce their own vegetables, eggs, honey and jam. The two large uncluttered bedrooms, with sloping ceilings and massive beams, are in a converted barn where they share a dayroom furnished with pieces made by David, a first-rate carpenter. And it's a great place for children who adore the donkeys, goats, chickens and cats. *German spoken. Gîte space for 8 people.*

rooms	2: 1 double, 1 twin, both with shower & wc.
price	€55 for two.
dinner	Restaurants 12km.
closed	Christmas Day.
directions	From D675 (Nontron to Brantôme), D98 east. La Roche on right about 3km from D675.

David Allison & Alison Coutanche
La Roche,
Quinsac,
24530 Champagnac de Belair,
Dordogne
tel (0)5 53 54 22 91
e-mail allisons@club-internet.fr
web perso.club-internet.fr/allisons/

AQUITAINE

Your hostess, painter, flautist, French teacher, shares her library and, drawing on a long and interesting life, her talent for good conversation. Come to her long-viewed cottage among bird-filled woods and fields for cultural and rural peace. Furnished with interesting Belgian pieces and exceptional paintings, it has a split-level sitting room opening to the terrace, unfussy bedrooms, open fires and a big heated pool. Single visitors are welcome for week-long rest cures or French language immersion and excellent guided tours of the area – enquire about full-board terms. *2 nights minimum. Gîte space for 4 people.*

rooms	2: 1 double, 1 twin, sharing bath, shower & wc (2nd wc on ground floor).
price	€46 for two.
dinner	€15 with wine, by arrangement.
closed	Rarely.
directions	From Angoulême D939 S 29km; right D12/D708 22km to Bertric Burée; D106 for Allemans 3km; right for Chez Marty 1km, left at junction; last house to left at end of lane.

Anne Hart
La Fournière,
Chez Marty,
24320 Bertric Burée, Dordogne
tel (0)5 53 91 93 58
fax (0)5 53 91 93 58

LIMOUSIN

In a leaf-green paradise, ancestral tribes buried their dead beneath great smooth stones; early saints sowed the seeds that grew into Romanesque bell-towers; troubadours sang courtly love into the strong stones and hearts of feudal castles.

The serene 18th-century château stands proud for all to see on the site of an ancient fortification, and the sun sets over the lake. Bedrooms are mostly vast, traditionally furnished, regally wallpapered, modern bathroomed; breakfast is seriously good. Madame, full of energy, charm and enthusiasm, has restored the fine hanging gardens and organises cookery courses. The atmosphere in the spectacular west-facing dining room, with pale blue and yellow panelling, high-backed tapestried chairs and antique table may be informal, but the surroundings do impose civilised dressing for dinner. *Golf courses nearby. Gîte space for 10.*

rooms	4: 3 doubles, 1 twin, all with bath & wc.
price	€ 110 for two.
dinner	€ 25 with wine, by arrangement.
closed	Rarely.
directions	From Poitiers N147 towards Limoges, through Bellac; left D96 for St Junien les Combes. 1st left in village for Rancon approx. 1km.

Comte & Comtesse Aucaigne de Sainte Croix
Château de Sannat,
St Junien les Combes,
87300 Bellac, Haute-Vienne

tel	(0)5 55 68 13 52
fax	(0)5 55 68 13 52
e-mail	labeljack@aol.com
web	www.chateausannat.com

map: 10 entry: 543

Plain, simple and real French value, Thoveyrat is an organic meat farm (sheep and pigs) run by a sweet young couple who delight in their French country cooking, done with home-grown vegetables, lamb, duck, pigeon and rabbit (delicious pâtés). Myriam cares for their baby and guests while Pierre looks after the farm and sees to house improvements. The 18th-century farmhouse has lots of dark old wood – a sturdy great staircase, beams and timber framing – family clutter, fireplaces, peaceful, functional bedrooms and a garden full of toys.

rooms	4: 1 double, 1 triple, 2 family rooms, all with shower & basin, 3 wc in corridor.
price	€32 for two.
dinner	€13 with wine, by arrangement.
closed	November.
directions	In Bellac follow signs to Limoges; just before leaving Bellac D3 right for Blond 4km to Thoveyrat. House sign on left.

Pierre & Myriam Morice
Thoveyrat,
87300 Blond, Haute-Vienne
tel (0)5 55 68 86 86
fax (0)5 55 68 86 86
e-mail chambrehote@freesurf.fr

LIMOUSIN

Among lovely Limousin lakes and woods, here is a nature-loving, chemical-free house where natural materials triumph: wood outside and in (have you strayed into the Alps?), cork insulation, organic food, and they've been doing it for 30 years! The central heating is carried by steam ducts leading from the cooking-pot over the open fire. Lorenzo's paintings decorate the big airy rooms; Édith made all the upholstery, bedheads and patchworks; rooms have soothing, successful colour schemes and more wood. And there are more fabulous colours, and walks, to be found outside. *Minimum 2 nights July-Aug.*

rooms	3: 2 doubles, 1 triple, all with shower & wc.
price	€44-€48 for two.
dinner	€16 with wine, by arrangement.
closed	Rarely.
directions	From A20 exit 25 D44 for St Sylvestre; left D78 for Grandmont & St Léger la Montagne; through Grandmont; right for Les Sauvages, 200m.

Lorenzo & Édith Rappelli
Les Chênes,
Les Sauvages,
87240 St Sylvestre, Haute-Vienne
tel (0)5 55 71 33 12
fax (0)5 55 71 33 12
e-mail les.chenes@wanadoo.fr
web www.haute-vienne.com/chenes.htm

Your own wisteria and rose-clad entrance leads to a kitchen area with stairs up to the appealing bedroom: white walls, off-white carpet, seagrass wallpaper and wide view. The other is a useful overflow bedroom. You have your own rather fine living room too, with an open fire. (It can all be let as a gîte.) The house is lovely, splashed with colour and imaginative gestures, and the big garden makes further demands upon a willing but busy pair of owners. Néline, a gently direct and energetic hostess, will bring your breakfast in a basket if you prefer your own company. *Dutch & German spoken.*

rooms	2: 1 double/twin, 1 twin, sharing shower, wc & small kitchen with dishwasher & washing machine (same group only).
price	€45 for two.
dinner	Self-catering.
closed	Rarely.
directions	From Limoges N141 to St Léonard; D39 for St Priest 5km; right for Lajoumard; 1st left & follow signs.

Mme Néline Jansen de Vomécourt
La Réserve,
Bassoleil,
87400 St Léonard de Noblat,
Haute-Vienne
tel (0)5 55 56 18 39
e-mail vomecourt.jansen1@libertysurf.fr

LIMOUSIN

Exciting yet homely, with Michel's works as artist and handyman everywhere: his sculptures lead you magically through the big, unusual garden; in the old stables, his iron balustrade and carved door frames open onto an abundance of ceiling and bed coverings in generous, painting-hung bedrooms. These are Josette's work, as are the opulent floor-length curtains, wall fabric and tented ceiling in the *salon*. An interesting, likeable couple of ex-Parisians, Michel has a fascinating studio/gallery, Josette loves cooking for vegetarians. In a beautiful forested valley, the people, house and area deserve a lengthy visit.

rooms	2 doubles, both with shower & wc.
price	€47 for two.
dinner	€15 with wine, by arrangement.
closed	January-March.
directions	From Eymoutiers D30 for Chamberet. House in village of La Roche, 7km beyond Eymoutiers.

Michel & Josette Jaubert
La Roche,
87120 Eymoutiers, Haute-Vienne
tel (0)5 55 69 61 88
web clos.arts.free.fr

Run by Madame and her two granddaughters, this 400-year-old jigsaw of a house has been in the family for generations and is definitely different, with a glorious touch of eccentricity. You may share a bath or tiptoe down a floor for the loo, but one room is authentic Charles X and all are deeply evocative. The main house has a spectacular stone staircase with Egyptian vases pillaged from a Pharaoh's tomb, huge bedrooms and modern bathrooms. The great dining hall has wood panelling but breakfast is in a small guest *salon* or in the cottage kitchen. Most unusual. *Gîte space for 6 people.*

rooms	3: 2 doubles, 1 family suite, all with bath, shower & wc.
price	€46-€69 for two.
dinner	€15 with wine, by arrangement.
closed	Rarely.
directions	From Limoges D979 for Eymoutiers; Fougeolles on left just before entering Eymoutiers, Chambres d'Hôtes signs.

Michèle du Montant
Fougeolles,
87120 Eymoutiers, Haute-Vienne
tel (0)5 55 69 11 44

map: 11 entry: 548

LIMOUSIN

Set in four acres of park and garden, here is a 17th-century coaching inn on the Santiago pilgrim trail where two sprightly Englishmen keep up the tradition of welcome and sanctuary. Their conversation wafts all your cares away – they are entertainers as well as good, attentive hosts; their cuisine leaves you in a state of gastronomic rapture; the lavish bedrooms are a treat for eye and limb; the peace of the grounds brings total relaxation. If these two had been around a few hundred years ago and I a pilgrim, I would never have made it to Santiago.

rooms	4 doubles with shower or bath & wc.
price	€65 for two.
dinner	€27 with wine, by arrangement. Restaurant in village.
closed	Rarely.
directions	From A20 exit 35, D979 for Eymoutiers; 24km, right for Châteauneuf la Forêt; left in Neuvic Entier; signs.

Leigh Andrews &
James Humphrey
La Croix du Reh,
Avenue Amédée Tarade,
87130 Châteauneuf la Forêt,
Haute-Vienne
tel (0)5 55 69 75 37
fax (0)5 55 69 75 38
e-mail LaCroixduReh2@aol.com
web www.lacroixdureh.com

map: 10 entry: 549

Magic walking country: the emphasis here is outside, countryside and woods are your garden. With total commitment to the welfare of their region, the land and all life systems, your hosts run a bio-dynamic goat farm and are as self-sufficient as can be – we salute them. The old farmhouse has been modernised inside and the four simple bedrooms, pine clad and functionally furnished, share a living room and kitchen. But do dine with this genuine, unpretentious couple if you can: they are very good company, their food is all home-grown and deliciously nourishing. And children love helping to milk the goats and collect the eggs.

rooms	4: 3 doubles, 1 triple, all with shower & wc.
price	€38 for two.
dinner	€14, with wine, 1 July-15 August only; self-catering possible. Restaurants in village 4km.
closed	Rarely.
directions	From A20 exit 41 to Magnac Bourg; D215 (between Total service station & Brasserie des Sports) SW & follow signs 4km to La Chapelle.

Patrick & Mayder Lespagnol
La Chapelle,
87380 Château Chervix,
Haute-Vienne
tel (0)5 55 00 86 67
fax (0)5 55 00 70 78
e-mail lespagno@club-internet.fr

LIMOUSIN

The nicest possible people, they have done just enough to this proud old building so it looks as it did 200 years ago when it forged cannon balls. The farm is relaxed and natural, they keep animals (including Lusitanian horses), three small children and a super potager, make pâtés and *confits* by the great mill pond and hang the duck breasts and hams to dry over the magnificent hearth in their big stone sitting room with its tatty sofa. Relish the drive up past tree-framed lake (boating possible) and stone outbuildings and the prospect of dining on home-grown ingredients. It's glorious. *Ask about pets when booking.*

rooms	3 doubles, all with shower & wc.
price	€39 for two.
dinner	€17 with wine, by arrangement.
closed	October-15 April; Sundays July-August.
directions	From A20 exit 39 to Pierre Buffière; cross river D15/D19 for St Yrieix for 15km. At Croix d'Hervy left D57 for Coussac Bonneval; mill on left after lake (7km).

Valérie & Renaud Gizardin
Moulin de Marsaguet,
87500 Coussac Bonneval,
Haute-Vienne
tel (0)5 55 75 28 29
fax (0)5 55 75 28 29

The Lardners were born to do B&B: interested in others, they genuinely love having visitors, their enthusiasm for their adopted area is infectious, Anne's cooking is superb – good wine too. The kitchen is a wonderful place, full of farm things and Anne's sunny presence – she delights in texture, smell and colour and her cooking reflects her pleasure. Their house restoration, done under Jim's caring guidance, is a form of perfection. Many local farmers are friends and visits can be arranged, proof of thorough integration among the rolling hills of rural France. Deep peace and really excellent value. *Gîte space for 2 people.*

rooms	2 twins with bath or shower & wc. Extra children's room.
price	€34 for two.
dinner	€17 with wine, by arrangement.
closed	Rarely.
directions	From Argentat N120 for Tulle; left D921 for Brive. Pass sign to Albussac; 300m on; left to Le Prézat; through hamlet; house on right with lawn.

Anne & Jim Lardner
Le Prézat,
19380 Albussac, Corrèze
tel (0)5 55 28 62 36
fax (0)5 55 28 62 36
e-mail jlardner@libertysurf.fr

map: 11 entry: 552

LIMOUSIN

Jacquie, half-French, and Ian, half-Hungarian, are fervent francophiles who know the local people, history, flora and building regs. intimately and will tell you all. Indeed, aperitifs and dinner *en famille*, even breakfast in the separate guest house, are intensely stimulating occasions – not for shrinking violets. A professional chef, Ian serves superb food with a flourish and wines from his cellar. Their clever renovation of the little old village house makes for a communal kitchen, a biggish downstairs room and two cosy rooms under the rafters with Laura Ashley-style décor and some nice furniture.

rooms	3: 2 doubles, 1 twin, all with bath or shower & wc.
price	€31-€34 for two.
dinner	€15 with wine, by arrangement.
closed	Rarely.
directions	From Tulle N120 to Forgès. Left into Place de la Mairie, park in church square behind.

Ian & Jacquie Hoare
La Souvigne,
1 impasse La Fontaine,
19380 Forgès, Corrèze
tel (0)5 55 28 63 99
fax (0)5 55 28 65 62
e-mail la.souvigne@wanadoo.fr
web perso.wanadoo.fr/souvigne

map: 11 entry: 553

Up, up the wild wooded hillsides until suddenly you're on top of the world, miles of it, fabulous for walking and wildlife. Here, clinging to the slope, is the Carvers' big old barn, a brilliant conversion made of space, air and formidable blocks of stone. Guests have a great fireplace in their light bright living area, games, books, a piano and warm hangings. Bedrooms are done in plain, soft colours and understated quality; bathrooms are almost lavish. New to the village and B&B, your easy-going hosts are full of enthusiasm (she sings in the choir) and have a miniature Shetland pony. *Not suitable for children under 8.*

rooms	2: 1 double with bath & wc; 1 double with shower & wc.
price	€45 for two.
dinner	€15 with wine, by arrangement.
closed	Rarely.
directions	From Tulle N120 S 20km to St Charmant; left to St Bonnet; at memorial right to Le Roux; on RH bend after Le Roux, left down track; barn at end on left.

Sue Carver
La Grange,
19380 St Bonnet Elvert, Corrèze
tel (0)5 55 28 38 36
e-mail ceavia@aol.com

map: 11 entry: 554

LIMOUSIN

The delightful Madame Lafond was born in the area and will never move away – you will soon understand why. With rooms in a modern extension, Saulières is no ancient monument but it's a picture of genuine French rural style, blissfully quiet in its conservation area. Ideal for families, it has masses of space, lots of grass for playing on, a guest kitchen and big, log-fired living room with good old armchairs, magazines and games, plus some fabulous places to visit. The superbly 'family, friends and farming' atmosphere created by this highly likeable couple has been much praised. *Gîte space for 2 people.*

rooms	4: 1 quadruple, 1 triple, 1 double, 1 twin, all with shower & wc.
price	€40 for two; €65 for four.
dinner	Self-catering possible; good choice of restaurants, 2km.
closed	Rarely.
directions	From Tulle N120 to Argentat; D12 along R. Dordogne for Beaulieu, past Monceaux to Saulières (6km from Argentat).

Marie-Jo & Jean-Marie Lafond
Saulières,
Monceaux sur Dordogne,
19400 Argentat, Corrèze
tel (0)5 55 28 09 22
fax (0)5 55 28 09 22

map: 11 entry: 555

This pretty converted school has three fresh and simply decorated bedrooms downstairs (one with a mezzanine), sharing a living room and kitchenette. The upstairs suite, more traditional, also has its own living room – the headmistress's study perhaps? A flower-covered loggia leads to the dayroom: it is entirely glazed on one side to let in the beautiful garden, which also produces vegetables for excellent dinners. Béatrice and Henry are delightful, happy to talk in French or English and keen to help you discover their fascinating area. Guided flora and fauna tours and boats for hire too.

rooms	4: 1 double, 1 twin, 1 triple, 1 quadruple, all with shower or bath & wc.
price	€42 for two.
dinner	€14 with wine, by arrangement.
closed	15 December-2 January.
directions	From A20 exit 22 to La Souterraine; D951 through Dun le Palestel; right D15 to La Celle Dunoise; right in front of Auberge des Pecheurs, left after tennis courts for Anzême, about 4km; sign.

Béatrice & Henry Nguyen
L'École Buissonnière,
23800 La Celle Dunoise, Creuse
tel (0)5 55 89 23 49
fax (0)5 55 89 27 62
e-mail ecolebuissonniere@wanadoo.fr
web www.ecole-b.com

LIMOUSIN

Brigitte-Marie's house is a breath of fresh air, a place of organised chaos where paintings by friends old and new, carvings from Borneo, antiques from her native Belgium and Bauhaus steel-and-leather armchairs sing together in artistic harmony: objects of interest are everywhere. Bedrooms are vast, inviting and full of yet more original works – the two scenes of life in Zimbabwe are wonderful. Even the bathrooms are full of stylish character. Brigitte-Marie, a fabric designer, travelled a lot with her husband and is happy to be receiving appreciative guests in this old 1800s wine merchant's house which was the first in a land of cider.

rooms	2 doubles with bath or shower & wc.
price	€40-€46 for two.
dinner	€15 with wine, by arrangement.
closed	Rarely.
directions	From A20 exit 23 to Guéret; N145 to Gouzon; D997 to Boussac; D71 for Clugnat 4km; D13 for Domeyrot; 1.4km left D77. At 'Les Montceaux' on hill, right before chestnut tree. 1st house on right.

Brigitte-Marie Van de Wege
Les Montceaux,
23600 Toulx Ste Croix, Creuse
tel (0)5 55 65 09 55
fax (0)5 55 65 09 55
e-mail brigitte.van-de-wege@wanadoo.fr
web perso.wanadoo.fr/chez.brigitte

This delightful, scatty couple were in *haute couture* so Daniel wears a thimble and Françoise teaches teddy-making. Their quirky, creative house is a collector's treasure chest of bouncy dog, exquisite patchwork and fading wallpaper. See the medieval castle from cluttered terrace and double room; wade through dollies and glassware to good chairs in the lovely *salon*; glory in fine furniture and handmade curtains. Totally French and an ideal touring base. *Gîte space for 7 people.*

rooms	3: 1 double, 1 twin, 1 suite (double + bunk beds), all with bath or shower & wc.
price	€48 for two.
dinner	5 restaurants 500m.
closed	October.
directions	From A71 exit 10 on D94 W for 15km; right D916 to Boussac; in main square, road to left of Mairie; left again at butcher's; on right.

	Françoise Gros & Daniel Colsenet
	La Courtepointe,
	3 rue des Loges,
	23600 Boussac, Creuse
tel	(0)5 55 65 80 09
fax	(0)5 55 65 80 09
e-mail	courtepointe@wanadoo.fr
web	perso.wanadoo.fr/courtepointe

AUVERGNE

On the wild plateau, protected by a multitude of medieval castles, the ancient hardwoods share the land with mild cows, hardy sheep and a few farmers – their ancestors ate those chestnuts, their pigs those acorns.

Thick, thick walls, great old stones and timbers: the immense age of this gloriously isolated house, once a fortified manor, is evident but it has been beautifully restored. Big, cosy, subtly-lit rooms, lovingly decorated with family antiques and memorabilia, are reached by a treat of a spiral staircase. The family's cattle graze safely in the the fields which surround the house – here, you can walk, fish and hunt mushrooms in season. Easy and good-natured, Madame Raucaz opens her heart, her intelligence and her dining table to all (excellent-value dinners); this is really somewhere you can feel at home and relax.

rooms	4: 2 doubles, 1 twin, 1 triple, all with bath or shower & wc.
price	€40-€43 for two.
dinner	€16 with wine, by arrangement.
closed	Rarely.
directions	From Nevers N7 S 22km; right D978a to Le Veudre; D13 then D234 to Pouzy Mésangy. Signs.

Claire Raucaz
Manoir Le Plaix,
Pouzy Mésangy,
03320 Lurcy Levis, Allier

tel (0)4 70 66 24 06
fax (0)4 70 66 25 82

Opulent are those gilded curlicues, marble fireplaces and ornate mirrors; light pours in through the tall *salon* windows, bouncing off the glowing floor; even the games room is panelled. A fine mansion, built by a devout family whose bricks were refused for a church, it is now owned by a descendent of Corot and there's good art in every room as well as a small gallery. Lovely knowledgeable hosts who also have an excellent eye for colour. Their rooms are good enough for the glossies yet it remains an unpretentiously welcoming family house.

rooms	5: 2 doubles, 1 triple, all with shower & wc; 1 triple with bath & wc; 1 suite for 4 with shower & wc.
price	€67-€73 for two.
dinner	€17-€23 with wine, by arrangement.
closed	Rarely.
directions	From Moulins N9 S 20km; in Châtel de Neuvre left to La Ferté Hauterive; house on right.

Jérôme & Annick Lefebvre
Demeure d'Hauterive,
03340 La Ferté Hauterive, Allier
tel (0)4 70 43 04 85
fax (0)4 70 43 00 62
e-mail hauterive@val-de-sioule.com
web www.demeure-hauterive.com

AUVERGNE

The Montaignacs are elegant, immaculate and gracious; like the dining room, with its panelling, breakfast silver and great looming ancestor they are the epitome of Old France. Choose the ground-floor, original-parqueted and fireplaced suite, or glide up the fine stone staircase past more ancestors to the twin room. Both rooms welcome you with antiques, old engravings, personality. Monsieur knows books-worth of fascinating history; Madame is quietly attentive. Peaceful at the end of its long drive, this is a wonderful place, albeit more formal than some.

rooms	2: 1 twin, 1 suite for 2-4 people, both with bath or shower & wc.
price	€93 for two.
dinner	Good choice of restaurants within 9km.
closed	Rarely, but advance bookings only.
directions	From Montluçon, N371 for Chamblet; sign on right.

Yves & Jacqueline de Montaignac de Chauvance
Château du Plaix,
03170 Chamblet, Allier
tel (0)4 70 07 80 56

Billowing hilly pastures surround the hamlet with sensuality. Here, built in 1886 as a rich man's summer place, is a generous, sophisticated house, informed by Madame's broad cultural interests, her father's paintings and her superb Provençal furniture that sits so well by original panelling and wide, modern fireplace. Alone up steep shiny stairs, the guest space is a sweep of pine floor and ceiling; light floods in past royal blue curtains, big pine bed, old chest; a proud tree shades the splendid shower room. Deep rest, super breakfast with wide-ranging conversation, Romanesque jewels to visit – a must. *Not suitable for children.*

rooms	1 double/twin with shower & wc.
price	€60 for two; book ahead.
dinner	Restaurant in village.
closed	November-February.
directions	From A75 exit Gannat to Vichy; over Allier; immed. right Bd JFK, left for Cusset; over r'way; 5 traffic lights, D906 right for Ferrières; right D995 9km; left D121; bear right to Cognet 800m. House with iron gates.

	Bénita Mourges
	Cognet,
	03300 La Chapelle, Allier
tel	(0)4 70 41 88 28
e-mail	andre.mourges@wanadoo.fr

map: 11 entry: 562

A generous and handsome family house: the volcanoes gave their lava for dining room and staircase floor slabs; ancestors gave their names for bedrooms where their faded photographs and intricate samplers hang on the walls. Others left some fine old *objets* and pieces of furniture and built the stupendous brick barns that shelter the garden; Élisabeth applied all her flair to the décor, marrying vital colour harmonies and soft fabrics. She is dynamic, intelligent and full of wry humour, once a trace of shyness has worn off, and serves her deliciously wholesome breakfast in the flower-decked garden in summer.

rooms	3 doubles, all with shower & wc.
price	€52-€58 for two.
dinner	Good restaurants 9km.
closed	November-March, except by arrangement.
directions	From A71, Riom exit, N144 for Combronde & Montluçon. 2.5km after Davayat, right onto D122 to Chaptes.

	Mme Élisabeth Beaujeard
	8 route de la Limagne,
	Chaptes,
	63460 Beauregard Vendon,
	Puy-de-Dôme
tel	(0)4 73 63 35 62

map: 11 entry: 563

Is this real or a fairy tale? Creak along the parquet, pray in the chapel, swan around the *salon*, sleep in one tower, bath in another. It's been in the family for 800 years and room names are as evocative as furnishings are romantic – worthy of the troubadours who surely sang here. Breakfast on home-hive honey, brioche, yogurt, eggs, cheese, get to know your delightfully entertaining hosts, visit the donkey, admire the magnificent trees or, if you're feeling homesick, have a drink in Guy's evocatively vaulted cellar *pub* with its impressive collection of beer mats. A dream of a place. *Gîte space for 5 people.*

rooms	2: 1 double with bath & wc; 1 triple with shower & wc.
price	€50-€70 for two.
dinner	Auberge 3km.
closed	Rarely.
directions	From A72 exit 3 on D7 through Celles sur Durolle to Col du Frissonnet. Château 1st right after Col du Frissonnet.

Guy & Régine Dumas de Vaulx
Château de Vaulx,
63120 Ste Agathe, Puy-de-Dôme
tel (0)4 73 51 50 55
fax (0)4 73 51 50 55

AUVERGNE

Ternant is *grand style* – marble, mouldings, gilt frames – with modern touches to prevent any stiffness, Madame's astoundingly beautiful patchwork hangings to make it utterly personal and the scent of beeswax hovering. All is pure Auvergne: owners, house, original porcelain basins, fabulous breakfasts. Bedrooms have antique beds – brass, carved, delicious 1930s – on polished parquet with good rugs and, of course, Madame's artistic needle. The dining room is elegant, the *salon* sophisticated, the billiard room a library. They are an interesting, sociable, professional couple who have lived in foreign lands and enjoy their guests.

rooms	4: 1 double, 1 twin, 2 suites for 4, all with bath or shower & wc.
price	€79-€83 for two.
dinner	Restaurants in nearby town.
closed	15 November-15 March.
directions	From A71 for Clermont Ferrand; exit Riom for Volvic & Puy de Dôme; at Le Cratère, left for Clermont; right for Chanat, 3km Ternant, signs.

Catherine Piollet
Domaine de Ternant,
Ternant,
63870 Orcines, Puy-de-Dôme
tel (0)4 73 62 11 20
fax (0)4 73 62 29 96
e-mail domaine.ternant@free.fr
web domaine.ternant.free.fr

Perched above Saint Nectaire with views of almost endless forest and mountain, it's the farmhouse in the perfect setting. Inside lives the bubbly Monique, enthusing her guests with descriptions of the Auvergne in perfect English. She does not pretend to provide luxury, just cosy comfort and the feeling of being in a real home. Guests stay in an attached but independent cottage and have a kitchen area of their own. They go for breakfast into Monique and Daniel's large, vaulted dining room, full of exposed beams and stone, to eat copiously and listen to the humour and zest of a couple who were born to hospitality. *Gîte space for 4.*

rooms	1 double with shower & wc.
price	€40 for two.
dinner	Restaurants in St Nectaire. Guests' kitchen available.
closed	December-January.
directions	From A75 exit 6 to St Nectaire; at church D150 for 1.5km; left D643. Last house 300m.

Monique & Daniel Deforge
Sailles,
63710 St Nectaire, Puy-de-Dôme

tel	(0)4 73 88 40 08
e-mail	daniel.deforge@wanadoo.fr

map: 11 entry: 566

AUVERGNE

What is B&B perfection? Spring water running from the taps of a huge walk-in shower? La Closerie, a typical old stone-walled and -shingled house, sits among the ancient volcanoes of Auvergne where great rivers rise and water is pure. Françoise, called Manou, is a delight, sprightly and elegant, as generous with her time as with her scrumptious embroidered-napkin buffet breakfast, served in the impressive dining room or the garden. Bedrooms are perfect, hung with silk, hairdryers hide in bathrooms; in short, every modern comfort against a timeless backdrop of drama and character. *Book ahead. Gîte space for 4-8 people.*

rooms	5: 2 doubles, 1 twin, 2 triples, all with shower & wc.
price	€60-€70 for two.
dinner	Several good restaurants in village.
closed	15 November-February.
directions	From A71/75 exit 2 on D799 to Bordeaux; N189, 23km; left D983 to Le Mont Dore by Col du Gery; in Mont Dore right for Murat le Quaire; pass the Mairie, 3km to Le Genestoux. House signposted.

Françoise Larcher
La Closerie de Manou,
Le Genestoux,
63240 Le Mont Dore, Puy-de-Dôme

tel	(0)4 73 65 26 81
fax	(0)4 73 65 58 34
e-mail	lacloseriedemanou@club-internet.fr
web	www.auvergne.maison-hotes.com

map: 11 entry: 567

The solid reality of this magical tower is deeply moving. Michel's skill in renovation (well, reconstruction from near-ruin), Anita's decorating talent, their passionate dedication, have summoned a rich and sober mood that makes the 15th-century *chastel* throb with authenticity: only 'medieval' materials; magnificent deep-tinted fabrics, many designed by Anita; antique tapestries, panelling and furniture – nothing flashy, all simply true to the density of the place. Spectacular bedrooms, amazing bathrooms of antique-faced modern perfection and a generous breakfast – this is a must. *Minimum 2 nights July-August.*

rooms: 3 doubles, all with bath/shower & wc.
price: €87-€122 for two.
dinner: Auberge & traditional restaurants 1-4km.
closed: January-February.
directions: From A75 exit 6 for St Nectaire; through Champeix to Montaigut le Blanc; follow signs up to château.

Anita & Michel Sauvadet
Le Chastel Montaigu,
63320 Montaigut le Blanc,
Puy-de-Dôme
tel: (0)4 73 96 28 49
fax: (0)4 73 96 21 60
web: www.le-chastel-montaigu.com

AUVERGNE

Whichever of the splendid rooms is yours – we loved the yellow *Louis Philippe* – you will feel grand: here a canopied bed, there an exquisite little dressing room, everywhere shimmering mirrors, fabulous views of acres of parkland, ancient trees, the Puy-de-Dôme. The vast, panelled, period-furnished drawing and dining rooms are quite dramatic. A perfect hostess, Madame makes you feel immediately at ease and helps you plan your day over a delicious breakfast. She will show you the 14th-century vaulted chapel, the walled garden and how to make lace (*dentelle du Puy*). Really very special.

rooms: 5: 3 doubles, 1 twin, 1 suite, all with bath and/or shower & wc.
price: €61-€87 for two.
dinner: Excellent restaurants 2km.
closed: November-March.
directions: From Clermont Ferrand A75 exit 13 to Parentignat; D999 for St Germain l'Herme 6km; sign on right. (8km from A75 exit.)

Henriette Marchand
Château de Pasredon,
63500 St Rémy de Chargnat,
Puy-de-Dôme
tel: (0)4 73 71 00 67
fax: (0)4 73 71 08 72

Pierre is the gardener, Johan the cook and Frederick a brilliant handyman. All South African, your charming hosts left the film and television world for this village in the heart of the Livradois-Forez Regional Park. A few steps from the romantic, private garden, full of roses, ancient fruit trees and well-tended vegetables and herbs, will find you walking some of the most stunning and unspoilt trails through the Massif Central. Rooms have antique beds and Persian carpets and flowers from the garden; a stylish living room is for guests. Arrange to have dinner: you'll enjoy the conversation as much as the *confit de canard*.

rooms	4: 2 doubles, with bath, shower & wc; 1 double & 1 twin, with shower & wc.
price	€46-€53 for two.
dinner	€20 with wine, by arrangement.
closed	Rarely.
directions	From A72 exit 2 for Thiers (west); D906 for Ambert & Le Puy en Velay; 67km, signs on entering Arlanc; close to Roman church on left.

Johan Bernard, Pierre Knoesen & Frederick Bezuidenhout
Ma Cachette,
10 rue du 11 Novembre,
63220 Arlanc, Puy-de-Dôme

tel	(0)4 73 95 04 88
fax	(0)4 73 95 04 88
e-mail	cachette@club-internet.fr
web	www.ma-cachette.com

map: 11 entry: 570

AUVERGNE

Built on the ramparts of the ancient town, just below the medieval Abbey whose August music festival draws thousands, the old house has been lovingly filled with flowers in every fashion and form – carpets, curtains, wallpaper, quilts. It is a soft French boudoir where mother and daughter, quietly attentive, welcome their guests to sleep in cosy, pine-slatted bedrooms with firm-mattressed divan beds and good little bathrooms (some with wonderful views out to the hills) and enjoy true Gallic cuisine enhanced by bone china and bohemian crystal before the huge stone fireplace.

rooms	4: 1 double, 1 twin, 2 triples, all with bath or shower & wc.
price	€49 for two.
dinner	€19 with wine, by arrangement.
closed	Rarely.
directions	From Brioude D19 to La Chaise Dieu. Head for Centre Ville; facing Abbey, right to Place du Monument. Park here; house is off square: bottom right-hand corner then down on left.

Jacqueline & Carole Chailly
La Jacquerolle,
Rue Marchédial,
43160 La Chaise Dieu, Haute-Loire

tel	(0)4 71 00 07 52

map: 11 entry: 571

Simple, unaffected people and keen walkers love Rosa, her somewhat dated décor and her fabulous home-grown, home-made food which oozes genuine natural goodness. A real old soldier, she manages the flock of milk-producing sheep, is surrounded by grandchildren and welcomes all-comers with a 'cup of friendship' before her great granite hearth. The house is warm, the rooms basic but perfectly adequate, the meals good, the hostess unforgettable. And walkers can join a circuit here and walk from B&B to B&B in this superbly unspoilt area; or cross-country ski it in winter.

rooms	3: 1 double, 1 twin, 1 triple, all with shower & wc.
price	€32 for two, €35 for three.
dinner	€10 with wine, by arrangement.
closed	November-February.
directions	From Le Puy en Velay, D589 to Saugues; D585 for Langeac, left onto D32 to Venteuges.

Rosa Dumas
Le Bourg,
43170 Venteuges, Haute-Loire
tel (0)4 71 77 80 66

map: 11 entry: 572

On the southern slope of Europe's largest extinct volcano, where nine valleys radiate for fabulous walking, stands a rustic 18th-century château guarded by an 11th-century tower. Here are two gasp-worthy vaulted bedrooms, one with four-poster. The very elegant twin room has the right furbelows and drapery and in the glorious kitchen – vast inglenook, beams supporting gigantic blocks of lava – Phoebe serves home-smoked ham and veg from her organic garden. She and Michel are cultured, bilingual hosts. You play an instrument? Bring it with you. Bridge? Bring your tricks. And dream on.
Gîte space for 7 people.

rooms	3: 2 doubles, 1 twin, all with bath or shower & wc.
price	€47-€61 for two.
dinner	€23, with wine; super restaurant in Laguiole.
closed	Rarely.
directions	From Clermont Ferrand A75 to St Flour; up to old town; left D921 10km; right D990, through Pierrefort to St Martin. Right for Brezons; château 3km on right.

Michel Couillaud & Phoebe S Verhulst
Château de Lescure,
15230 Pierrefort, Cantal
tel (0)4 71 73 40 91
fax (0)4 71 73 40 91
e-mail michel.couillaud@wanadoo.fr
web www.multimania.com/psvlescure

map: 11 entry: 573

Your young hosts escaped from heaving, stressful Paris to this rural paradise where their brilliant conversion of an old Cantal farmhouse has preserved the original scullery ledge and sink (made of vast slabs of stone), the beams, the inglenook fireplace. They now aim to convert their neighbours to better environmental (get the scrap metal off the hillside) and social (more respect for your woman?) attitudes. The rooms are well and simply done with good colours and fabrics and no unnecessary frippery, the meals are feasts, there's a games room, billiards and books, and the Balleux are a most interesting and happy couple.

rooms	5: 1 double, 1 suite for 2 in house; 2 suites, 1 double in cottage; all with bath or shower & wc.
price	€40-€54 for two; half-board €32-€39.
dinner	€12 with wine, by arrangement.
closed	Rarely.
directions	From Aurillac D920 to Arpajon; left on D990 for 10km (don't go to St Étienne de Carlat); left for Caizac; signposted.

Francine & Jacky Balleux
Lou Ferradou,
Caizac,
15130 St Étienne de Carlat, Cantal

tel	(0)4 71 62 42 37
fax	(0)4 71 62 42 37
e-mail	lou.ferradou@tiscali.fr
web	www.louferradou.com

AUVERGNE

A treat, an experience from another age: the deliciously organic old château in pure Cantal style surveying the panorama has been in the family for ever and is utterly lavish. The courtroom (the lord of the manor was chief justice) panelled and dazzlingly painted; the fine and formal dining room (do dress for dinner); the Aubusson-hung, chandeliered *salon*; the Louis XV guest room with its lovely carved fireplace, the extraordinary four-postered Troubadour room and another painted ceiling, a remarkable Dinky Toy collection, and more. Come and enjoy the company of your gentle, caring hosts. *Gîte space for 2.*

rooms	4: 2 doubles, 1 twin, 1 triple, all with bath & wc.
price	€112 for two.
dinner	€34 with wine, by arrangement.
closed	November-Easter.
directions	From Clermont-Ferrand N89 to Tulle; left D922 to Bort les Orgues; D681 to Mauriac & Ally. Signs.

Bruno & Anne du Fayet de la Tour
Château de la Vigne,
15700 Ally, Cantal

tel	(0)4 71 69 00 20
fax	(0)4 71 69 00 20
e-mail	la.vigne@wanadoo.fr
web	perso.wanadoo.fr/chateau.de.la.vigne

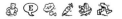

Passionate eager hosts, a refined old manor in an idyllic setting, magnificent rooms, meals cooked by a master (in winter they run an alpine restaurant). Abel and Anna's restoration is caring and sophisticated, rooms and bathrooms are statements of simple luxury, the great kitchen, where cookery demonstrations and meals happen, is a dream, its cooker a wonder to behold, fireplace massive, ceiling vaulted. There is space for togetherness and privacy, your hosts are unintrusively present and Anna can offer a professional massage after Abel's demanding wine-tastings. You get more than you pay for – enjoy it to the hilt.

MIDI · PYRÉNÉES

Wielding the shepherd's favourite Laguiole blade over a shaggy flock beneath the ruins of heaven-seeking Cathar fortresses, the guardian goose must eventually surrender his own fatted liver to the knife.

rooms	4 doubles, all with bath & wc.
price	€92-€120 for two.
dinner	By arrangement €31; good wine list.
closed	Mid-October-May.
directions	A20 exit 53 for Cressensac; left 1st dual carriageway; left immed. for Cuzance & Église de Rignac; right at cemetery & stone cross; house 800m on right.

Anna & Abel Congratel
Manoir de Malagorse,
46600 Cuzance, Lot
tel (0)5 65 27 15 61
e-mail acongratel@manoir-de-malagorse.fr
web www.manoir-de-malagorse.fr

Frogs and kingfishers enchant the pool, a 13th-century mill, brilliantly restored by its generous, welcoming Australian owners, guards a garden of peace and beauty, lily pads and lawns, willows and water – it is ineffably lovely. Coral sings like a bird (garden choir concerts in summer) and cooks like an angel; Bill, former marathon-runner, makes tables and intelligent conversation – do join him for billiards. Big, properly-raftered rooms have cast-iron beds, soft fabrics, antique chests. The dining room is anciently barrel-vaulted but meals are mostly in the glorious garden.
Children over 10 welcome.

rooms	2: 1 double, 1 triple, both with private bathrooms.
price	€55 for two.
dinner	€18 with wine, by arrangement.
closed	Rarely.
directions	From Martel on the N140 D23 for Creysse. After 3km take right fork for Le Goth. Mill is 1st house on right after stone bridge, 1.5km.

	Coral Heath-Kauffman
	Moulin de Goth,
	46600 Creysse, Lot
tel	(0)5 65 32 26 04
fax	(0)5 65 32 26 04
e-mail	coral.heath1@fnac.net

map: 10 entry: 577

The old farmhouse is quaint and inviting with its steep roofs and light-coloured stone: the Bells' restoration has been a labour of love. The original character of beams, old floors and twisty corners has been preserved, furnishing is simple with cast-iron beds, original paintings and, in the huge living-kitchen, an open hearth and a closed stove. It's not smart, just family-comfortable and relaxed. Gavin, an artist and potter, and Lillian, an easy, open person, left South Africa to live with their young son in this quiet place. They'll give you a great welcome – and you can picnic if you want.
Gîte space for 10 people.

rooms	2: 1 double, 1 double & bunks, both with bath or shower & wc.
price	€40 for two.
dinner	Restaurants 2km.
closed	Rarely.
directions	From Brive N20 S 10 km; N140 for Rocamadour; D36 left to Rignac; at church, left then right; D36 for Lavergne 50m; left for Pouch 2km; first house, blue shutters.

	Gavin & Lillian Bell
	Pouch,
	46500 Rignac, Lot
tel	(0)5 65 33 66 84
fax	(0)5 65 33 71 31
e-mail	lilianbel@aol.com
web	www.bellfrance.com

map: 11 entry: 578

The converted 18th-century barn with its great Lot views feels instantly like home. Madame spent years in America, is bilingual, loves ceramics and patchwork, uses her creative touch everywhere, including the garden and terrace – all shrubs and ferns and secluded spots – and is a fount of historical and cultural lore. The open-plan living room, where old skylights deliver splashes of sky, is full of artistic character with oak floors, old stove and pretty antiques beneath paintings of all periods. The airy ground-floor guest room has its own antique writing table, watercolours and a glazed stable door to the garden.

rooms	1 double/twin with private bathroom; extra room for children.
price	€46 for two.
dinner	€16 with wine, by arrangement.
closed	Rarely.
directions	From Gramat N140 for Figeac; left for 'Le Bout du Lieu' after sign for Thémines; house, 200m on left; signposted.

Élisabeth de Lapérouse Coleman
La Buissonnière,
Le Bout du Lieu,
46120 Thémines, Lot
tel (0)5 65 40 88 58
fax (0)5 65 40 88 58

MIDI · PYRÉNÉES

Charles cooks – the huge kitchen/entrance hall is his domain – and meals, French or Franco-Japanese, are memorable. Kako paints – even the wooden coat hangers bear her flowers. The house is French and spotless. All bedrooms, in the older, lower part of the house, have an exceptionally tranquil rolling view, superb mattresses and lush bathrooms; the oldest has an ancient stone fireplace and the original stone sink. They are delightful people, a multi-talented, cosmopolitan couple who keep house here in the summer and live in Japan in the winter. And Figeac is said to be one of the best-renovated towns in Europe.

rooms	3: 2 twins, 1 suite for 3, all with bath or shower & wc.
price	€46 for two.
dinner	€20 with wine, by arrangement.
closed	November-March
directions	From Gramat N140 for Figeac 17km; through Le Bourg, sharp left immed. after small bridge on edge of village. Sign on left, 1km.

Kako & Charles Larroque
Mas de la Feuille,
46120 Le Bourg, Lot
tel (0)5 65 11 00 17
fax (0)5 65 11 00 17
e-mail larroquecharles@club-internet.fr

You will be made hugely welcome at Montsalvy. There are five hectares of garden, a vast swimming pool with a 'summer kitchen' where you can make yourself lunch, a tennis court and swings for children. Guy and Gilou will even play a game of tennis with you if you wish. The beautiful terrace has wonderful views, perfect for warm summer dinners. Everything has been newly done for B&B so the mattresses are good, the comfort is perfect and there's a children's bedroom with two beds and a platform in the *pigeonnier*. *Gîte space for 4 people.*

rooms 2 doubles, both with shower & wc; extra room for children available.
price €46 for two.
dinner €16 with wine, by arrangement.
closed Rarely.
directions From Gourdon D673 for Fumel; left D6 to Dégagnac; follow SNCF signs; after football ground, 2nd right; at top of hill right to house.

Guy & Gilou Nodon
Domaine de Montsalvy,
Montsalvy,
46340 Dégagnac, Lot
tel (0)5 65 41 51 57
fax (0)5 65 41 51 57
e-mail gnodon@aol.com
web domaine-de-montsalvy.com

map: 15 entry: 581

MIDI · PYRÉNÉES

The whole house has a light, happy feel and Gisèle, a much-loved B&B owner (we were flooded with praise for them in their old house), is making guests feel utterly at home again in this brand new, architect-designed house. It is horseshoe-shaped: owners' and guests' wings flank a fine big kitchen/living area with a clever mix of modern and antique furniture, some good Art Deco ornaments and a wall of window onto the pool terrace. Bedrooms, Apricot and Raspberry, are prettily done in pine and comfort with super bathrooms. And Gisèle still cooks with delight, including her organic jams. An exceptional B&B.

rooms 2: 1 twin, 1 suite for 4-5, both with shower & wc.
price €46 for two; €71 for four.
dinner €16 with wine, by arrangement.
closed Rarely.
directions From Gourdon D673 for Fumel; to Salviac; from Crédit Agricole bank straight ahead & follow signs to Bertrand Joly.

Gisèle & Alain Hauchecorne
La Maison Jaune,
Bertrand Joly Haut,
46430 Salviac, Lot
tel (0)5 65 41 48 52
fax (0)5 65 41 48 52
e-mail lamaisonjaune@wanadoo.fr
web perso.wanadoo.fr/lamaison.jaune/

map: 15 entry: 582

The Italian ambassador, homesick for Florence, built this house and its balustraded terrace overlooking the river in 1805. It has a beautiful garden and a swimming pool in a flowery corner of the lawn (for guests in the mornings) but inside, the first word that comes to mind is 'dramatic'. The library is raspberry with a zebra throw over the black leather sofa while the big, white beamed dining room – once the kitchen perhaps? – is dominated by a vast fireplace, bold still-lifes and red and white checks.
A teacher, who loves to talk to people, Claude is due to retire soon and finds B&B the perfect solution.

rooms	2 doubles, all with shower & wc.
price	€50 for two.
dinner	Choice of restaurants nearby.
closed	Rarely.
directions	From Cahors D8 to Pradines; right at roundabout; house 100m down on right through big gates.

Claude Faille
Valrose - Le Poujal,
46090 Pradines, Lot
tel (0)5 65 22 18 52
e-mail claude.faille@libertysurf.fr
web perso.libertysurf.fr/valrose

MIDI · PYRÉNÉES

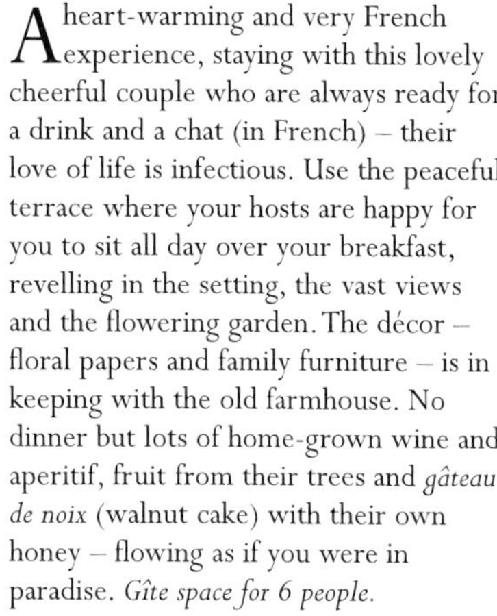

A heart-warming and very French experience, staying with this lovely cheerful couple who are always ready for a drink and a chat (in French) – their love of life is infectious. Use the peaceful terrace where your hosts are happy for you to sit all day over your breakfast, revelling in the setting, the vast views and the flowering garden. The décor – floral papers and family furniture – is in keeping with the old farmhouse. No dinner but lots of home-grown wine and aperitif, fruit from their trees and *gâteau de noix* (walnut cake) with their own honey – flowing as if you were in paradise. *Gîte space for 6 people.*

rooms	1 double with curtained-off shower & wc.
price	€40 for two.
dinner	Good restaurant 2km.
closed	Rarely.
directions	From Cahors D8 for Pradines 8km; at sign for Flaynac, follow Chambres d'Hôtes sign on right, then right & right again.

M & Mme Jean Faydi
Flaynac,
46090 Pradines, Lot
tel (0)5 65 35 33 36

Dr Rouma, a distinguished local figure and Consul General, built the house in the 1850s. It was almost a ruin before the Arnetts found it on their return from Japan and restored it, keeping as much of the original as possible, including the wallpaper in the hall where the winding staircase is such a delight. The décor has an oriental tendency, particularly in the enormous dining room. The setting just couldn't be better; there are stunning views over the river and the pretty old town – famous for its medieval music festival which climaxes, by the way, with the "largest firework display in France".

rooms	3: 2 doubles, 1 twin, all with bath, shower & wc.
price	€46 for two.
dinner	Choice of restaurants nearby.
closed	Rarely.
directions	From Cahors D911 for Fumel & Villeneuve sur Lot. At Puy l'Évêque take Rue du Dr Rouma to bridge: house last on right before bridge.

Bill & Ann Arnett
Maison Rouma,
2 rue du Docteur Rouma,
46700 Puy l'Évêque, Lot
tel (0)5 65 36 59 39
fax (0)5 65 36 59 39
e-mail williamarnett@hotmail.com
web www.puyleveque.com

MIDI · PYRÉNÉES

The golden Lot stone glows, there are stunning views over two valleys, the pool is solar-heated and salt-purified, so what matter if rooms are smallish with limited storage and the atmosphere sometimes a little chaotic. The Scotts labour ever on at their little empire, restoring the 17th-century farmhouse and outbuildings to their original character and adding modern comforts for gîtes and B&B. Zoé will charm you, see you have a good time, serve breakfast at any time. Dinner, sometimes a poolside barbecue, is fun, relaxed and informal and Peter plays the guitar. Pool-house kitchen and fridge for picnic lunches. *Gîte space for 22 people.*

rooms	2: 1 double with bath; 1 suite for 2 with bath & wc.
price	€40–€55 for two.
dinner	€17 with wine, by arrangement.
closed	Rarely, please book ahead.
directions	From Cahors for Toulouse; at r'bout D653 for Agen 16km; at junc. right D656 for 14km; through Villesèque, Sauzet, Bovila; after Bovila, 3rd left; signposted.

Peter & Zoé Scott
Mondounet,
46800 Fargues, Lot
tel (0)5 65 36 96 32
fax (0)5 65 31 84 89
e-mail scotsprops@aol.com

Quiet Gilbert will take you egg-hunting or goose-feeding of a morning. Soft, smiling and big-hearted, Michèle loves doing B&B, has won prizes for her recipes, invents sauces and makes her own aperitif. The quaintly old-fashioned rooms are comfortable (beware waist-low beams) but food is definitely the priority here. Fishing rods on loan for use in the pond; footpaths out from the gate; proper hiking trails a bit further away; the treasures of Moissac, lovely villages, caves, all within easy reach. This is exceptional farm B&B. *Small pets welcome. Gîte space for 4 people.*

rooms	4: 2 doubles, 2 twins, all with bath, shower & wc.
price	€38 for two.
dinner	€14, with wine; restaurant 5km.
closed	Rarely.
directions	From Moissac D7 for Bourg de Visa about 14km; before Brassac, just before bridge, right for Fauroux; farm 2km; signs.

Gilbert & Michèle Dio
La Marquise,
Brassac,
82190 Bourg de Visa,
Tarn-et-Garonne

tel	(0)5 63 94 25 16
fax	(0)5 63 94 25 16
e-mail	mglamarquise@infonie.fr

Warm country people, the Sellars left a big Sussex farm for a smallholding in deepest France to breed sheep, goats and poultry naturally, traditionally: no pesticides, no heavy machines, animals roaming free. Their enthusiasm and guts – it's hard work – have earned them great respect locally and their recipe for a simple, rewarding life includes receiving guests happily under the beams, by the open hearth, in pretty-coloured, country-furnished rooms. Julie will welcome you to her wonderful farmhouse kitchen, the hub of Tondes, where she creates feasts of organic veg and home-made marvels. Even the geese are friendly.

rooms	2: 1 double, 1 family room for 3-4, both with shower & wc.
price	€40 for two.
dinner	€15 with wine, by arrangement.
closed	Rarely.
directions	From A62 exit 8 D953 for Cahors (round Valence d'Agen) 21km; follow Cahors & Lauzerte, just before Fourquet, house sign, 2km.

Julie & Mark Sellars
Tondes,
82400 Castelsagrat,
Tarn-et-Garonne

tel	(0)5 63 94 52 13

As lovingly restored as the dreamy hamlet with its wonderful church, this 19th-century stone farmhouse is owned by a Franco-Dutch couple who enjoy sharing their summers here with guests. Madame teaches Spanish, is extrovert and energetic, Monsieur is calm, diplomatic and in business and they offer delicious dinners at their long, convivial table – regional and exotic dishes and an excellent cheeseboard. The honeysuckled courtyard and tall-treed garden are lovely, the rooms are fresh and light with good prints, local art, old wardrobes, terracotta tiles – a happy marriage of old and new. *Only open July-August. Spanish & Dutch spoken.*

rooms	2: 1 suite for 2-4, 1 double, both with bath & wc.
price	€43 for two.
dinner	€15 with wine, by arrangement.
closed	September-June.
directions	From A62 exit 8 for Gramont; follow signs to Lachapelle; entering village, house on right.

M & Mme Van den Brink
Au Village,
82120 Lachapelle, Tarn-et-Garonne
tel (0)5 63 94 14 10 /(0)1 39 49 07 37
e-mail lachapelle_vdb@hotmail.com
web monsite.wanadoo.fr/lachapelle_vdb

MIDI · PYRÉNÉES

The Gorges de l'Aveyron here are worth a big detour – a paradise of clear water, cliffs, wildlife, canoeing and rugged scenery. Johnny and Véronique, suitably, are sports teachers – all tan and dynamism, they encourage the active-holiday idea with great enthusiasm. They have renovated their house beyond the constraints of its origins – its rooms are simple, modern and functional, with little that is memorable or quintessentially French. But the food is good and generous and so are your friendly hosts. It's great for children – and very busy in summer so don't expect family intimacy then.

rooms	5: 2 doubles, 2 twins, 1 family room, all with bath or shower & wc.
price	€49-€53 for two; €46 for two, out of season.
dinner	€17, with wine; restaurant 2km.
closed	Rarely.
directions	From Cahors, N20 to Caussade; D964 for Gaillac. At Montricoux, D115 for Nègrepelisse; after 500m, signposted.

Johnny & Véronique Antony
Les Brunis,
82800 Nègrepelisse,
Tarn-et-Garonne
tel (0)5 63 67 24 08
fax (0)5 63 67 24 08

Your hosts' enthusiasm still brims here for their new life as B&B owners. Having catered in many places but never in France, they are loving it all: the elegant simplicity of their renovated 13th-15th-century townhouse with its sense of light and space, airy hall and great spiral staircase; the views through to the garden courtyard; the original tiles and stone walls; the big, beautifully-decorated rooms, one with its own terrace; "the delightful guests who have already been to share it all with us", – and little Travis. Seriously into food, they do an excellent *table d'hôtes*, all home-made. A lovely young couple.

rooms	6: 4 doubles, 2 twins, all with bath & wc.
price	€61-€69 for two.
dinner	€21 with wine, by arrangement.
closed	Rarely.
directions	From Montauban N20 22km to Caussade; right D926 for 7km; right D5 to St Antonin Noble Val (12km); follow signs.

Françoise & Richard Green
La Résidence,
37 rue Droite,
82140 St Antonin Noble Val,
Tarn-et-Garonne

tel	(0)5 63 68 21 60
fax	(0)5 63 68 21 60
e-mail	info@laresidence-france.com
web	www.laresidence-france.com

MIDI · PYRÉNÉES

Le Gendre is pure rural Frenchness, a working farm where fowl and pigs roam. Lively and empathetic, these people share their home easily, without fuss: rustic, cluttered living room with a warming open fire; simply furnished, pleasing, spotless bedrooms with slightly old-fashioned patterns and good beds; breakfast coffee in a bowl and, with her lovely smile, Madame taking you in as family. Her dogs and cats are as friendly as she is. Go lightly on lunch: dinner is uncompromisingly, deliciously 'farmhouse' with portions suitable for a hard-working farmer – she loves feeding her guests.

rooms	2: 1 double, 1 suite for 4, both with shower & wc.
price	€37 for two.
dinner	€14 with wine, by arrangement.
closed	Rarely.
directions	N20 S from Cahors to Caussade; left D926 to Septfonds; 3km beyond, left for Gaussou. Farm 1km on; sign.

Françoise & Jean-Louis Zamboni
Ferme du Gendre,
82240 Lavaurette, Tarn-et-Garonne

tel	(0)5 63 31 97 72

Tranquillity itself. The 19th-century house and its wonderful converted barn for guests are enchanting and Colette's garden adds to the magic, a little paradise with every cranny a carefully unmanicured, flower-filled delight. Breakfast in a shady arbour, while away the afternoon in a steamer chair, sink into a deep sofa with a good book before the open fire. Charming, stylish and utterly welcoming, Colette pours as much enthusiasm into looking after her guests as her garden. Inviting, spotless bedrooms, done with refined simple taste, tempt the weary with their garden views. A true find for those seeking perfect peace.

rooms	3 doubles, all with shower & wc.
price	€54 for two.
dinner	Restaurants in Parisot, 2km.
closed	Rarely.
directions	From Caylus D926 for Villefranche de Rouergue; pass Parisot; left for Belvesé; signs.

Mme Colette Norga
La Grange,
Belvésé,
82160 Parisot, Tarn-et-Garonne
tel (0)5 63 67 07 58
fax (0)5 63 67 07 58

map: 16 entry: 593

MIDI · PYRÉNÉES

La Salasse was a 13th-century *salle* (a fortified meeting-house) and overlooks the old Roman road, the Pilgrims Route. Beneath are flower-lined sunken meadows with a fairy-tale château within walking distance. Françoise will welcome you with real warmth. She and Bernard are deeply committed Catholics – though, as he said with a smile, they don't say grace at breakfast – and Françoise is a leading light in the Friends of Santiago de Compostela, helping find accommodation for pilgrims. You'll love the rooms, the beds and vast peaceful grounds, with a safely fenced pool: they have 19 grandchildren! *Gîte space for 4.*

rooms	1 twin with bath & private wc.
price	€50 for two.
dinner	Restaurants 6km.
closed	August & occasionally in winter.
directions	From Lectoure N21 for Agen 5km; left D248 for Castéra-Lectourois; immed. right; house 500m on left.

Françoise & Bernard Migeot
La Salasse,
32700 Lectoure, Gers
tel (0)5 62 68 79 29
fax (0)5 62 68 79 29
e-mail st-jacques-compostelle-gers@club-internet.fr
web www.st-jacques-compostelle-gers.org

map: 15 entry: 594

No splashing, no screaming – no pool! Peace reigns in the big garden; the gently rolling, wooded and brooked countryside beckons; wild orchids and woodpecker thrive in the clean air. Once a professional cook, Rosie still loves cooking, knows about vegetarian as well as local cuisine and uses virtually organic veg and eggs from Sam's fine potager. The late 19th-century house has wood-burning stoves and comfortable, relaxing furniture; bedrooms have polished wooden floors, big windows and impeccable bathrooms. And the area bursts with temptation for the gourmet and the *sportif*.

rooms	3: 1 double, 1 twin, 1 triple, all with shower & wc.
price	€60 for two; special terms for long stays.
dinner	€18 with wine, by arrangement.
closed	Rarely.
directions	From Agen D931 to Condom; D15 to Castelnau; right for 'Centre Village'; right at crossroads D43 for St Pé & Sos about 5km; house on left before bridge.

Rosie & Sam Bennett
Les Colombiers,
Bournic,
32440 Castelnau d'Auzan, Gers
tel (0)5 62 29 24 05
fax (0)5 62 29 24 05
e-mail rabennett@talk21.com

MIDI · PYRÉNÉES

After several years in elegant Marrakech, these two sophisticated, kind-hearted chaps and Jim the Irish setter are now welcoming guests to their adopted Gersois village, sleepy between the pilgrimage towns of Condom and Eauze. From the history-laden stone house – the *salon* used to be the château kitchens, ruined at the Revolution – light airy bedrooms look over the fruit-hung *jardin de curé*. All have luxury beds, travel mementos, good storage; the vast Retro bathroom has a bath big enough to swim in. Jacques may lay out an impromptu picnic by the old *lavoir* while Patrick regales you with historical tales and gossip. Great stuff.

rooms	3: 2 doubles, 1 suite, all with bath or shower & wc.
price	€50-€75 for two.
dinner	Restaurants in village.
closed	November-March.
directions	From Condom D931 for Eauze 12km; after church, right into Rue de Montespan; house on left.

Patrick Turner & Jacques Julia
5 rue Montespan,
32330 Gondrin, Gers
tel (0)5 62 29 12 70

Setzères is an 18th-century Gascon manor, square and generous in its large lush garden – boules, badminton, tranquil pool. Beautifully restored, decorated with English antiques and oriental mementos, breathing charm and peace, it has heart-stopping views to the Pyrenees. Christine is well travelled, her local dishes are made with fresh ingredients and dinner conversation on the star-lit terrace is both cosmopolitan and fun. This is hidden France: old stone hamlets scattered across wide empty countryside, fascinating architecture, fabulous food. A highly civilised place to stay. *Children over 12 welcome. Gîte space for 10 people.*

rooms	3: 1 double, 1 twin, 1 suite for 4, each with bath, shower & wc.
price	€110 for two.
dinner	€40, good wine list.
closed	2 weeks December-January.
directions	From Auch N124 for Vic Fézenac 5km; left D943 to Barran, Montesquiou, Bassoues (32km); D943 left for Marciac, sign for Scieurac & Flourès; in village left by church; house on right.

Christine Furney
Setzères,
Scieurac et Flourès,
32230 Marciac, Gers

tel	(0)5 62 08 21 45
fax	(0)5 62 08 21 45
e-mail	setzeres32@aol.com
web	www.setzeres.com

map: 15 entry: 597

MIDI · PYRÉNÉES

Noailles rejoices in a very French and delightfully secluded setting of hills, crops and pastures. Madame has lived here all her life and her son now runs the busy farm. The house, full of French *paysan* warmth, is as genuine as your kindly hostess. Breakfast is outside or at a long table by a huge open hearth; there's a useful guests' kitchen area too. Bedrooms open onto the balcony overlooking the courtyard, have ancient rickety wooden floors and some endearing features like Granny's wedding furniture (beds are old but have first-class mattresses). It is all down-to-earth and clean with proper country charm.

rooms	3: 1 double, 1 triple, 1 family suite, all with bath & wc.
price	€38 for two.
dinner	Self-catering possible.
closed	Rarely.
directions	From Auch, N21 for Tarbes. 6km after Mirande, sign on left.

Marthe Sabathier
Noailles,
32300 St Maur, Gers

tel	(0)5 62 67 57 98

map: 15 entry: 598

Youthful and enthusiastic, outgoing and warm-hearted, Mireille is an inspired cook and a delight to be with; Olivier is shyer but just as warm a presence and those rolling bird-filled spaces beyond the wooden terrace outside your window are his wheat and sunflower crops. Together, they fill their cosy house with antique plates, prints, pictures and furniture. Their guest room is as family-comfortable, warm-furnished as the rest. Theirs is a relaxed and happy family home with the essential dogs and cats plus a swimming pool by the gîtes. Perfect for children. *Gîte space for 10 people.*

rooms	1 double (+ 1 small room for 1 child) with shower & wc.
price	€44 for two.
dinner	€14 with wine, by arrangement.
closed	Rarely.
directions	From Auch N21 for Tarbes 2km; left D929 for Lannemezan; in Masseube, left for Simorre 4km; left for Bellegarde; 1st left, before church & castle.

Mireille & Olivier Courouble
La Garenne,
Bellegarde,
32140 Masseube, Gers
tel (0)5 62 66 03 61
fax (0)5 62 66 03 61

MIDI · PYRÉNÉES

The sober buildings give no inkling of the explosion inside: 80 years ago, Italian painter Mario Cavaglieri spread his heart and love of form and colour over ceilings and doors. 'His' suite has vast space, fine antiques, a dream of a great bathroom and dazzling paintings. Theresa and Ian fell for the romantically wild house and park and left high-pressure London jobs to save the whole place from dereliction – their enthusiasm and sensitive intelligence show in every room. And in the Italian garden, the waterfall, the wild bit – there's no other place like it. *Gîte space for 21 people with separate pool.*

rooms	2 suites, both with bath & wc.
price	€65-€115 for two.
dinner	€23 with wine, by arrangement.
closed	Rarely.
directions	From Auch N21 south 3km; left D929 for Lannemezan; in Pavie, left after Mairie, cross old bridge, bear right at fork; house 1km on left.

Theresa & Ian Martin
Domaine de Peyloubère,
32550 Pavie, Gers
tel (0)5 62 05 74 97
fax (0)5 62 05 75 39
e-mail martin@peyloubere.com
web www.peyloubere.com

The house, its 'secret' formal garden and wilder great park – places to meander, meditate or hide in – breathe again under the influence of Maria, an Italian architect, Andrew, an English hotelier and their two babes. Tail is their life project, a fabulous exercise in Anglo-Italian taste: two high 19th-century drawing rooms with antiques everywhere; cosily luxurious bedrooms, including three four-posters in elegant Jouy drapes in the outbuildings. Delicious dinners, deeply interesting people, the beautiful Bread Basket of France and Madiran wines to explore (this is more Gers than Pyrenees). A highly affordable luxury.

rooms	4: 1 twin, 1 double, 1 suite, 1 triple, all with bath, shower & wc.
price	€64-€100 for two.
dinner	€24, with wine; restaurant 5km.
closed	Rarely, but booking essential in winter.
directions	From Tarbes D935 N for 40km; left for Castelnau; from village centre, follow signs to Goux.

Andrew & Maria Hedley
Château du Tail,
65700 Castelnau Rivière Basse,
Hautes-Pyrénées

tel	(0)5 62 31 93 75
fax	(0)5 62 31 93 72
e-mail	hosts@chateaudutail.com
web	www.chateaudutail.com

map: 15 entry: 601

Standing in rolling farmland on the Gers border – a wildlife haven an hour from the mountains – this is the most relaxed house you could wish for: 18th-century bones, 20th-century flesh. Dominique's decorative talent runs to cleverly-used bright colours, her own fantasy patchwork and great flair at auction sales. Nick cooks with French, Thai, Latin American flourishes and is a great entertainer. They have three teenage children, are a well-travelled, thoughtful couple, involved in the local music festival, concerned with the countryside – evenings on the terrace can be stimulating. Great walks, super food, easy living.

rooms	3: 2 doubles, 1 triple, all with shower & wc.
price	€50 for two.
dinner	€20 with wine, by arrangement.
closed	Rarely.
directions	From Tarbes D632 to Trie sur Baïse; through village onto D939 for Mirande 1km; house up little road sign on left.

Nick & Dominique Collinson
Jouandassou,
65220 Fontrailles, Hautes-Pyrénées

tel	(0)5 62 35 64 43
fax	(0)5 62 35 66 13
e-mail	dom@collinson.fr
web	www.collinson.fr

map: 15 entry: 602

The Hindu greeting *namaste* is the name; slightly exotic is the feel of this comfortable 18th-century farmhouse. The Fontaines restored it, polished the floors and created a lasting air of harmony. One of the two ground-floor guest rooms has doors onto a semi-secluded corner of the garden and a fine big shower room. The two rooms upstairs are ideal for people doing yoga, dance or art workshops here. In cold weather, enjoy the huge open fire in the comfortable *salon* and make the most of Jean's dinners at the long communal table: he's a dab hand at vegetarian food and likes to use organic ingredients.

rooms	2: 1 quadruple with bath & wc; 1 triple with shower & wc.
price	€43 for two.
dinner	€16 with wine, by arrangement.
closed	Rarely.
directions	From A64 exit 16 on D939 through Lannemezan to Galan; from village square/church, Rue de la Baïse for Recurt; house 500m on left.

Jean & Danielle Fontaine
Namaste,
13 rue de la Baïse,
65330 Galan, Hautes-Pyrénées

tel	(0)5 62 99 77 81
fax	(0)5 62 99 77 81
e-mail	namaste_65@libertysurf.fr
web	www.namaste-pyrenees.com

map: 15 entry: 603

Madame is gracefully down-to-earth and her house and garden an oasis of calm where you may share her delight in playing the piano or golf (3km) and possibly make a lifelong friend. Built in Napoleon's time, her house has an elegant hall, big, airy bedrooms and great bathrooms, while fine furniture and linen sheets reflect her pride in her ancestral home – a combination of uncluttered space and character. The huge quadruple has space to waltz in and the smallest bathroom; a beautifully presented breakfast comes with civilised conversation. Come to unwind – you may never want to leave for this is a remarkable place.

rooms	3: 1 double, 1 triple, 1 quadruple, all with bath & wc.
price	€45 for two.
dinner	Good restaurants 5-7km.
closed	Rarely.
directions	From A64 exit 16 to Lannemezan; there, N117 for Toulouse 5km; at Pinas church D158 for Villeneuve. House on right 1km.

Mme Marie-Sabine Colombier
Domaine de Jean-Pierre,
20 route de Villeneuve,
65300 Pinas, Hautes-Pyrénées

tel	(0)5 62 98 15 08
fax	(0)5 62 98 15 08
e-mail	marie.colombier@wanadoo.fr
web	www.domainedejeanpierre.com

map: 15 entry: 604

You could weep, this valley is so beautiful; so are the house, its story, garden, owners. A doctor built it (see the caduceus on the great newel post), then fostered one Bishop Laurence, who 'proved' Bernardette's miracles and set Lourdes up for glory. Arlette, a miracle of industry and human warmth, sews, decorates, cooks brilliantly (you'll never want to eat out) and still finds plenty of time for guests. Quiet and attentive, Robert will take you hiking and fishing in that gorgeous valley (Pyrenean high-mountain trout are the best, naturally). A very special place.

rooms	4: 3 doubles, 1 triple, with bath or shower & wc.
price	€39-€45 for two.
dinner	€20-€28, with wine; restaurants in Lourdes.
closed	Rarely.
directions	From Lourdes N21 S for 2km; left at bridge; immediately left again D26 to Juncalas; house in village centre on right.

Arlette & Robert Assouère
Maison de L'Évêque,
Impasse Monseigneur Laurence,
65100 Juncalas, Lourdes,
Hautes-Pyrénées
tel (0)5 62 42 02 04
fax (0)5 62 94 13 91

MIDI · PYRÉNÉES

A couple of Basques from either side of the Pyrenees: Henri, whose family have lived here for over 1000 years, is home at weekends, Ione is a gently hospitable mother of two and there's Valdo, the frizzy little dog who smiles. The fine old house with its wonderful four-sided roof and grand staircase looks from its mountain niche over amazing scenery. Family-comfortable pastel bedrooms, one with the balcony, have antique French sheets; the living room, where a fire roars and dinner is served on winter weekends, is a great space to come back to after a day's white-water rafting, skiing, falconing... And really sweet people.

rooms	3: 1 suite for 3, with bath, wc & balcony, 1 suite for 3, with shower & wc, 1 twin, with shower & wc.
price	€45-€54
dinner	November-April €15 with wine, by arrangement. Restaurants 8km.
closed	Rarely.
directions	From Lourdes for Argelès-Gazost; in village left after Total; Beaucens follow Vielle signs.

Henri & Ione Vielle
Eth Berye Petit,
15 route de Vielle,
65400 Beaucens, Hautes-Pyrénées
tel (0)5 62 97 90 02
fax (0)5 62 97 90 02
e-mail contact@beryepetit.com
web www.beryepetit.com

Fabienne and Jean-Luc are working wonders, undoing some rather ruthless decorating left by their predecessors. Rooms are huge and bright, the cheery yellow family room in the house, the other two in the barn, one a restful white and blue, the other pink *toile de Jouy*. Having two little boys of their own, Fabienne and Jean-Luc make children very welcome and give them the run of the walled garden. Fabienne enjoys cooking typical local meals and chatting round the table while Jean-Luc, Pyrenean born and bred, is a source of great mountaineering stories. Don't miss St Bertrand de Comminges, twelve kilometres away.

rooms	3: 2 doubles, 1 quadruple, with bath, shower & wc.
price	€44 for two; €54 for three.
dinner	€15 with wine, by arrangement.
closed	Rarely.
directions	From Toulouse A64, exit 17; D938 west, 7km; signposted. 8km from Lannemezan station.

Fabienne & Jean-Luc Garcia
La Souleillane,
4 rue de l'Ancienne Poste,
65150 St Laurent de Neste,
Hautes-Pyrénées

tel	(0)5 62 39 76 01
e-mail	fjl.garcia@wanadoo.fr
web	www.souleillane.com

MIDI · PYRÉNÉES

From the lovely dining room you see straight across to a great snowy peak, a spectacular view for breakfast. Expressionist André Derain hid here during the war, understandably. Inside are pretty fabrics and your hosts' own works (from July to September they stage a special exhibition). Goan Teresa was educated in England and paints; Alpine-born, Paris-educated Bernard is an expert on water mammals, sculpts and draws. A very special couple. And this tiny village (pop. 60) feels almost Alpine. *Children over five or babies only (ladder to mezzanine). Gîte space for 4 people.*

rooms	2: 1 double, 1 single, both with bath & wc.
price	€42 for two.
dinner	Good restaurants within 5km.
closed	Rarely.
directions	From A64 exit 20 to St Girons; right D618 for Castillon 12km; tiny D404 on left to Cescau. Park below church on left.

Teresa & Bernard Richard
Chambres d'Hôtes,
09800 Cescau, Ariège

tel	(0)5 61 96 74 24
fax	(0)5 61 96 74 24
e-mail	tizirichard@caramail.com

The tiny hamlet has spectacular views up to the mountains and across miles of fields, farms and forests – ineffably lovely. Nick, a fauna and flora guide who really knows his stuff, lists 200 different birds and over 50 orchids; he also cooks a mean fish pie, served with salad from the garden. He and Julie, who's a nurse, are a thoroughly likeable pair, genuinely welcoming, helpful and interesting. Their simple, pretty renovated house has small bedrooms and a big cosy family living room: this is family B&B *par excellence*, where you stay in their house, occupy their sofa, share their lives. Great people, great value.

rooms	3: 1 double, 2 twins, all with shower & wc.
price	€37 for two.
dinner	€13 with wine, by arrangement.
closed	November-April
directions	From St Girons D117 E for 7km; just before fork for Mas d'Azil left at Chambres d'Hôtes sign; up tiny, metalled track for 2km.

Nick & Julie Goldsworthy
La Baquette,
09420 Lescure, Ariège

tel	(0)5 61 96 37 67
fax	(0)5 61 96 37 67
e-mail	goldsnj@aol.com

MIDI · PYRÉNÉES

After years of renovation your delightful weaver hosts have made this rural idyll what it is today. Samples of their work, using only natural dyes from local plants, are everywhere and fit well with the exposed stone and woodwork of the old house. Bedrooms are rustic-warm with good views. Dine *en famille* in a huge living/dining room (village dances were held here!) and share the Loizances' local knowledge. Perfect for summer walking and winter cross-country skiing: the tiny hamlet is perched 900m up on the side of a National Park valley and the valley above is virtually unpopulated.

rooms	5: 4 doubles, 1 triple, all with shower & wc.
price	€40 for two.
dinner	€14 with wine, by arrangement.
closed	Rarely.
directions	From Foix D17 for Col des Marrous 15km; do not follow for Le Bosc on left: 'Hameau de Madranque' sign on right.

Birgit & Jean-Claude Loizance
Madranque,
09000 Le Bosc, Ariège

tel	(0)5 61 02 71 29
fax	(0)5 61 02 71 29
e-mail	birgit.loizance@libertysurf.fr

Once you've reached this typical old stone mountain house, you won't need wheels again: 80km of hiking trails, from easy to tough, lead from the front door into a paradise for botanists, bird-watchers and tree insect fanatics, and your kindly hosts know them intimately. A paradise of rest for the weary heat-drenched traveller too: Layrole's most memorable features are the greenery, the riot of flowers all round the south-facing terrace, the babbling brook. Your room has an immaculate new bed, a mass of books and many personal touches; the Orient Express loo will appeal to train buffs and dinners are good homely fare.

rooms	1 double with shower & sharing wc.
price	€34 for two.
dinner	€14 with wine, by arrangement.
closed	Mid-October-mid-April.
directions	From Foix N20 S to Tarascon; D618 for St Girons; 2.5km after café/bar at Saurat, right up steep road for Cabus; house 700m on right.

Roger & Monique Robert
Route de Cabus,
09400 Saurat, Ariège
tel (0)5 61 05 73 24

MIDI · PYRÉNÉES

Bring your hiking boots to this magical valley where nails were once made. Beds are softer but don't expect silver or lace: it is simple and honest, the room is white and pine with a little sitting corner, the shower small. There's a lovely terrace, two adorable furry-eared donkeys to delight young and old, and rushing water for trout (in season), which will lull you to sleep after that great walk. Your hospitable hosts, who love to chat but don't flutter, will gladly harness a horse for a day in the foothills with a picnic lunch. You have a private kitchen; breakfast is *à la française. Gîte space for 4 people.*

rooms	1 twin with shower & wc. Kitchenette available.
price	€32 for two.
dinner	Good restaurant in St Pierre de Rivière, 2km.
closed	January.
directions	From Foix D21 to Ganac. After 5km take route to Micou 'Les Carcis'; right just after small bridge.

Sylviane & Guy Piednoël-Drouet
Les Carcis,
09000 Ganac, Ariège
tel (0)5 61 02 96 54
fax (0)5 61 02 96 54
e-mail guy.drouet@libertysurf.fr

High up on a remote edge of the world, surrounded by 70 hectares of breathtaking forested Pyrenean foothills, the setting is out of this world, the house has tons of character – local stone, beams, low windows, uneven ceilings, all excellently renovated – and your hosts know what real *chambres d'hôtes* means. They raise horses and Newfoundlands, will let you join their picnics, ride their horses (if you are an experienced rider), live in their space for a while and hear their stories, in several languages, of sailing the Atlantic or the Caribbean: don't miss dining with them. Good rooms and excellent value. *Gîte space for 6 people.*

rooms	5: 2 doubles, 1 twin, 1 triple, 1 quadruple (summer only), all with shower & wc.
price	€40-€46 for two.
dinner	€13-€15 with wine, by arrangement.
closed	November-Easter.
directions	From Foix D17 towards Col de Marrous 9km; in La Mouline left at Chambres d'Hôtes sign for 1.5km, right C6, tiny but easy track, to house.

Bob & Jenny Brogneaux
Le Poulsieu,
Serres sur Arget,
09000 Foix, Ariège
tel (0)5 61 02 77 72
fax (0)5 61 02 77 72
e-mail le_poulsieu@hotmail.com

MIDI · PYRÉNÉES

Down on the Cathar Trail, how about breakfast in a Protestant temple? Well, remains of, turned into a pretty patio by twinkling, down-to-earth John and lively, sociable Lee-anne – Australians restoring this elegant mansion and loving it. Graciously high ceilings, a sweeping spiral staircase, lovely great windows: it's a fine and formal house in an oasis of ancient, stream-kissed oaks made relaxed and welcoming by your hard-working, fun-loving hosts. Guest rooms are generous too, in pastels and just enough antiques; one even has the vast original claw-footed bath.

rooms	5: 1 triple with bath, shower & wc; 3 doubles, 1 suite for 4, all with bath or shower & wc.
price	€61-€76.50 for two; suite €94 for four.
dinner	€20; wine €6-€15; restaurant 200m.
closed	Rarely.
directions	From Toulouse A61 for Montpellier; exit 22 at Bram to Mirepoix on D4; D119; D625 to Lavelanet, 11km; at Aigues-Vives left for Léran D28.

John & Lee-anne Furness
L'Impasse du Temple,
09600 Léran, Ariège
tel (0)5 61 01 50 02
fax (0)5 61 01 50 02
e-mail john.furness@wanadoo.fr
web www.chezroo.com

Enchanting: spectacular setting, fine fireplaces, antique chests, elegant airy bedrooms, good snug bathrooms. Michel, twinkly and teasing, the finest chef around, takes inspiration from the market and loves talking about cooking (try him on the Cathars); he may even let you into his sanctum. Simone is all grace and refinement. Choose your space for thr season: perched glass porch, devouring armchairs, summer dining room with enamelled lava table... And moreover, Unac church next door is an early Romanesque jewel – people fight for the room with the bell-tower view. *Well-behaved children over 5 welcome.*

rooms	2: 1 double, 1 triple, both with bath & wc.
price	€64 for two.
dinner	€28 with wine, by arrangement.
closed	Rarely.
directions	From Foix N20 S 33km through Tarascon to Luzenac; left D2; follow signs to Unac; 2nd entrance to Unac; house just down from church, 100m on right.

Michel & Simone Descat
L'Oustal,
09250 Unac, Ariège
tel (0)5 61 64 48 44

MIDI · PYRÉNÉES

Steve a wonderful cook and Kris a man of the theatre have achieved a splendid restoration of their remote old mill whose stream now feeds their fully-fledged organic smallholding: kitchen garden, sheep, poultry, all for your dinner delight. They are deeply involved in the local environment, preserving trees and wildlife and helping farmers. Inside, the fire roars, French country furniture glows, rugs are oriental, colours simple and they still dream of a turbine to make heat from the river (so rooms may be a little chilly in winter). They are a wonderfully friendly pair, it's great value and the Pyrenees are so near.

rooms	4: 2 triples, both with bath/shower & wc; 1 double, 1 triple sharing shower & wc.
price	€43 for two.
dinner	€15 with wine, by arrangement.
closed	Rarely.
directions	From Toulouse A64 to Boussens, exit 21; D635 to edge of Aurignac; right D8 for Alan 3km; left past Montoulieu to Samouillan D8, 7km; D96; signs.

Stephen Callen & Kris Misselbrook
Le Moulin,
Samouillan,
31420 Aurignac, Haute-Garonne
tel (0)5 61 98 86 92
fax (0)5 61 98 60 77
e-mail kris.steve@free.fr
web www.moulin-vert.net

A quiet lane, a happy family, an old manor decorated in peaceful good taste: it's a delight. Every antique, including cupboard doors, is the right one, bed linen is pretty, most rooms have a gentle blue and white valentine theme; the beautiful new room is in warm yellows, as cheerful as Brigitte's personality and done with her very special feel and an exquisite bathroom. All is soft, mellow, uncluttered; she is smiling, enthusiastic, young; her daughters are adorable and helpful. A dreamy, comfortable, joyful house where you appreciate the skill of Bruno the hard-working kitchen gardener when you sit down to dinner.

rooms	3: 1 double, 1 twin sharing shower & wc; 1 double with shower & wc.
price	€40 for two.
dinner	€14 with wine, by arrangement.
closed	Last week in August & Christmas week.
directions	From Toulouse N117 SW for about 50km; exit S D6 to Cazères; over River Garonne, 1st right D7, right D62; house 2nd left after Camping.

Brigitte & Bruno Lebris
Les Pesques,
31220 Palaminy, Haute-Garonne
tel (0)5 61 97 59 28
fax (0)5 61 98 12 97

Gérard taught philosophy, Chantal taught English and theirs is a well-stocked library. They love music, too. Formerly a working farm, the house still has its hay loft, well and bread oven and you will gape, astounded, at the scale of the inglenook fireplace with all its attendant oak beams plus a nail where *Grand-mère* used to hang her money among the washing. A large terrace overlooks the hills (kites available), a vine-covered pergola gives shade, a grassy courtyard has a barbecue, table tennis and home-made exercise machines. No antiques, but we loved it for its unpretentious simplicity and the intelligent company.

rooms	4: 3 triples, 1 double & bunk, all with bath or shower & wc.
price	€37-€41 for two; €49-€53 for three.
dinner	Restaurants 5-6km.
closed	Rarely.
directions	From A68 exit 3 to Montastruc; D30 for Lavaur for 5km; left D30c to Azas; continue 2km; sign for Garrigue (D22g).

Chantal & Gérard Zabé
En Tristan,
31380 Azas, Haute-Garonne
tel (0)5 61 84 94 88
fax (0)5 61 84 94 88
e-mail gerard.zabe@free.fr
web en.tristan.free.fr

Over the hill and far away… high iron gates open into a stupendous garden where formal rolls into natural. Frenchness indeed. The old manor twists and turns through history, old pictures, books and antiques, into a properly draped and ornamented *salon* in the elegant patina of age, up to fine rich bedrooms, big old bathrooms. Long views and the smell of wax polish are everywhere. Madame's warm and genuine interest in people is manifested with "a mix of the formidable and the lovable, the dignified and the mischievous". Long chatty breakfasts are on the terrace, in the lovely dining room or the snug breakfast room.

rooms	4: 3 doubles, 1 family room, all with bath or shower & wc.
price	€77 for two.
dinner	Restaurant 4km.
closed	Rarely.
directions	From Toulouse A68 for Albi; exit 3 Montastruc 2km; right D30 for Lavaur 4.5km; right D30E for Verfeil & follow for Stoupignan; house 1km on left.

Claudette Fieux
Stoupignan,
31380 Montpitol, Haute-Garonne
tel (0)5 61 84 22 02
fax (0)5 61 84 22 02

map: 16 entry: 619

MIDI · PYRÉNÉES

The magnificent hallway and sweeping staircase carry you with billows of French character to fine, airy rooms that abound in old fireplaces, beams, interesting pictures, super views of Cordes and beautiful furnishings (matt satin and very fitting prints). A gentle couple with a keen dry sense of humour, your hosts warm up over dinner – most of which they'll proudly tell you they produced themselves. Children are welcome: there are games, a little park for picnics, Léonard the beloved donkey and Géant his pony friend. The whole place glows with sensitive, loving care – a small corner of delight beneath the sky.

rooms	5: 2 doubles, 1 twin, 1 triple, 1 quadruple, all with shower & wc.
price	€50-€58 for two.
dinner	€18 with wine, by arrangement.
closed	Rarely.
directions	From Albi D600 to Cordes; there follow signs 'Parking 1 & 2'; signs.

Annie & Christian Rondel
Les Tuileries,
81170 Cordes sur Ciel, Tarn
tel (0)5 63 56 05 93
fax (0)5 63 56 05 93
e-mail christian.rondel@wanadoo.fr

map: 16 entry: 620

You'll know you will love it here as you drive into the crunchy gravel courtyard. Palest stone, topped with sun-mellowed tiles, Les Vents Bleus is as inviting as its name. Isabelle and Laurent have restored the house – and outbuildings as gîtes – so well that nothing looks 'done up'. Rooms are large, airy with lots of cream and white, set off by confident touches of colour. The smell of figs warming in the sun wafts across the courtyard at breakfast, while Isabelle can provide a feast most evenings. Great for children too, with a safe pool, sandpit and huge enclosed garden.

rooms	5: 2 doubles, 2 twins, 1 family room, all with bath & wc.
price	€80-€105 for two.
dinner	€30, with wine, on Saturday, Sunday & Monday only.
closed	November-February
directions	From Gaillac, D622 for Cordes; 5km after Cahuzac sur Vère, right D33 to Donnazac; pass village church, house on left, signposted.

Isabelle & Laurent Philibert
Les Vents Bleus,
Route de Caussade,
81170 Donnazac Cordes sur Ciel,
Tarn

tel	(0)5 63 56 86 11
fax	(0)5 63 56 86 11
e-mail	lesventsbleus@free.fr

MIDI · PYRÉNÉES

Ian & Penelope's good furniture, books and paintings are thoroughly at home now in this seriously old, history-laden house (the watchtower is 13th century) and all is serene and inviting. Each freshly decorated room has its own private entrance, balcony or terrace and stupendous views. The house is on the southern slope of the hilltop village of Cordes (only five minutes from both the top and the bottom), the swimming pool is big enough for real exercise and there's a poolside barbecue, kitchen and dining area. Cosy in winter too. Enough to entice you to stay a while and try the special three-day deal?

rooms	4: 1 double, 3 twins, all with bath or shower & wc.
price	€50-€64 for two.
dinner	Wide choice of restaurants in Cordes, within easy walking distance. BBQ & summer kitchen available.
closed	January-February.
directions	From Albi D600 to Cordes; up 'Cité' road on right of 'Maison de la Presse' for 500m; fork left for Le Bouysset; left at hairpin bend marked Rte de St Jean; house 200m on right.

Ian & Penelope Wanklyn
Aurifat,
81170 Cordes sur Ciel, Tarn

tel	(0)5 63 56 07 03
fax	(0)5 63 56 07 03
e-mail	aurifat@wanadoo.fr
web	www.aurifat.com

A child's dream become an adult's paradise of history, culture and peace: inside those stern walls you climb old stone stairs to the open sentry's gallery, enter your chamber and gasp at the loveliness of the room and the depth of the view. Beyond the fine old timbers and stonework, glowing floor, furniture and fabrics, your eyes flow out over luscious gardens and woods. Alan is a softly-spoken Scot, Laurence a charming Parisienne, both are passionate about their prize-winning restoration – original materials, expert craftsmen – and they hold musical evenings and produce excellent wine. Quite a place. *Gîte space for 3 people.*

rooms 2: 1 double, 1 twin, both with bath, shower & wc.
price €69 for two.
dinner Restaurants within 5km.
closed 20 December-February.
directions From Gaillac D964 for Castelnau de Montmiral; at junc. D15 to Château de Mayragues, signposted.

Laurence & Alan Geddes
Château de Mayragues,
81140 Castelnau de Montmiral,
Tarn
tel (0)5 63 33 94 08
fax (0)5 63 33 98 10
e-mail geddes@chateau-de-mayragues.com
web www.chateau-de-mayragues.com

map: 16 entry: 623

MIDI · PYRÉNÉES

A fantastic base for touring the bastide towns or just basking in the garden beneath stunning hilltop Castelnau – even picnics can be arranged. Catherine runs her 19th-century manor farmhouse with quiet sophistication and gentle humour: she wants you to love this place as much as she does. There's table tennis, *pétanque*, a discreetly hidden pool; immaculate rooms with pretty colours, good bedding, scintillating bathrooms; meals in the bright, pleasant dining room or on the terrace. And outside are fascinating Albi, the Grésigne forest, great walks and the nearby lake complex with all those water sports.

rooms 3: 1 double, 2 triples, all with bath or shower & wc.
price €51 for two.
dinner €18 with wine, by arrangement.
closed Rarely.
directions From Gaillac D964 to Castelnau de Montmiral, right at bottom of village 100m; right at sign Croix du Sud; fork left for Mazars; on left.

Catherine Sordoillet
La Croix du Sud,
Mazars,
81140 Castelnau de Montmiral,
Tarn
tel (0)5 63 33 18 46
fax (0)5 63 33 18 46
e-mail catherine@la-croix-du-sud.com
web www.la-croix-du-sud.com

map: 16 entry: 624

Lots of space with absolutely no clutter; the house is big, solid, bright and sensible, on top of a hill with grand views all around. Nothing is too much trouble for Christine and families would have a marvellous time here. Fred runs photography courses – a great excuse for enjoying this countryside and its famous towns. Wonderful value, both for the food and the house, and a great stopover for cyclists, too. Fred and Christine have been in France for a few years and love it. No frills, lots of informal good cheer, and those views.

rooms	4: 1 twin with shower & wc; 1 triple, 2 family rooms, all with bath & wc.
price	€38 for two.
dinner	€12 with wine, by arrangement.
closed	Mid-October-April.
directions	Take D999 Montauban-Albi. Village is 15km from Gaillac. Signposted.

Fred & Christine Challis
La Maison Rose,
Rue Gérard Roques,
81630 Salvagnac, Tarn

tel	(0)5 63 40 59 22
fax	(0)5 63 40 59 22
e-mail	fchallis@photohols.com
web	www.photohols.com

map: 16 entry: 625

MIDI · PYRÉNÉES

George and Pippa are ideal B&B folk – relaxed, good-natured, enthusiastic about their corner of France, generous-spirited and adding lots of little extras to make you comfortable. Sudre is a warm friendly house with beautiful furniture, shelves full of books, big inviting bedrooms. Wine-tastings can be arranged and there's a large shady garden set in rolling vineyards and farmland where you can sleep off any excesses. The more energetic may leap to the pool, boules, bikes or several sorts of tennis and you are genuinely encouraged to treat the house as your own. *Gîte space for 10 people.*

rooms	4: 2 doubles, 2 twins, all with shower & wc.
price	€60 for two.
dinner	Good choice of restaurants nearby.
closed	Rarely.
directions	From Gaillac for Cordes; over railway; fork imm'ly left D964 for Castelnau de M. 1km; left D18 for Montauban 400m; right D4 1.5km; 1st left, 1st house on right.

Pippa & George Richmond-Brown
Mas de Sudre,
81600 Gaillac, Tarn

tel	(0)5 63 41 01 32
fax	(0)5 63 41 01 32
e-mail	masdesudre@wanadoo.fr

map: 16 entry: 626

Come for an absolutely fabulous French bourgeois experience: huge cool entrance hall, massive stone staircase, trompe l'œil marble alcoves, high ceilings and southern colours – deep blue shutters, white walls. Add the owners' passion for Napoleon III furniture, oil paintings and ornate mirrors and the mood, more formal than family, is unmistakably French. Bedrooms, some with cathedral, some with rooftop views, are antique-furnished and very comfortable; breakfast is on the terrace overlooking the cathedral square. It's good to be in a town with utterly French people. And Madame has a keen sense of humour.

rooms	6: 4 doubles, 1 twin, 1 suite, all with bath or shower & wc.
price	€43-€45 for two.
dinner	Restaurants within walking distance.
closed	Rarely.
directions	In centre of Gaillac, directly opposite St Michel abbey church as you come in across bridge from A68 Toulouse-Albi road.

Lucile Pinon
8 place Saint Michel,
81600 Gaillac, Tarn
tel (0)5 63 57 61 48
fax (0)5 63 41 06 56

Genuine human warmth and refined luxury are the keynotes of this beautifully restored house and its superb gardens. Forty-three big ebony beams (brought from Madagascar in the family's repatriation luggage...) went into the renovation. The atmosphere is happily, humorously family with many traces of those years on exotic shores – in the cooking as well as the bathrooms. The large, pretty bedrooms are immaculate, and the cultured, people-loving owners are most unusual, both refined and down-to-earth, country-comfortable and artistic. A wonderful place. *If they haven't heard from you by 8pm they may re-let the room.*

rooms	2: 1 double, 1 twin, both with bath or shower & wc.
price	€50 for two.
dinner	€18 with wine, by arrangement. Plenty of restaurants in the area.
closed	Mid-December-mid-January.
directions	From Rabastens D12 for Coufouleux; cross River Tarn; left at lights D13 for Loupiac. Just before village right by cemetery; skirt cemetery, fork right, follow signs for La Bonde 1km.

Maurice & Bernadette Crété
La Bonde-Loupiac,
81800 Rabastens, Tarn
tel (0)5 63 33 82 83
fax (0)5 63 33 82 83
web www.labonde81.com

Drive through imposing gates and up the gravel drive. This magnificent house is shamelessly luxurious – wonderful stained-glass windows in the dining room, interesting paintings, pottery and exotic rugs everywhere, each bedroom and bathroom stylishly decorated with unusual attention to detail in superb furnishings and linens, embroidered towels and bathrobes. The sprawling gardens are filled with birdsong, the large swimming pool is discreetly distant, your cosmopolitan hosts generate a lively, relaxed atmosphere.

rooms	4: 2 doubles, 1 twin, 1 suite, all with bath or shower & wc.
price	€65-€84 for two.
dinner	By arrangement €23; good wine list.
closed	Rarely.
directions	From A68 Toulouse-Albi exit 6. At Saint Sulpice D13 for Coufouleux for about 3km. House on left, clearly signed.

Tony & Marianne Silver
Le Manoir de la Maysou,
81800 Coufouleux, Tarn
tel (0)5 63 33 85 92
fax (0)5 63 40 64 24
e-mail tonysilver@compuserve.com
web www.manoir-maysou.8m.com

map: 16 entry: 629

MIDI · PYRÉNÉES

Geneviève moved here from Alsace for more sun and a slower pace of life. As soon as you enter the courtyard and see the mellow old house with little angels guarding the steps you will want to be one of her returning guests, all welcomed as old friends. The chapel in the garden is dedicated to Our Lady of the Angels. One room is soft green with a muslin canopy and more angels round the walls. The family room is white with rosebuds. Both rooms are Geneviève's own work and utterly appealing. Breakfast is on a sunny terrace under the lime trees looking at the garden and fields. Possibly dinner, too.

rooms	2: 1 double, 1 family room, both with shower & wc.
price	€55 for two.
dinner	€15.50 with wine, by arrangement.
closed	Rarely.
directions	From Revel D84; right V10 for Lamothe; follow signs 'Les Abélias'.

Geneviève Millot
Les Abélias,
Lamothe,
81700 Blan, Tarn
tel (0)5 63 75 75 14
fax (0)5 63 75 75 14
e-mail lesabelias@libertysurf.fr
web www.revel-lauragais.com/abelias.html

map: 16 entry: 630

Madame Sallier is delightful, running her family château with boundless energy and infectious *joie de vivre*, serving breakfast in her big kitchen in order to chat more easily to you, loving everyone, especially children. Charming bedrooms still have their original personality – one has rare 1850s wallpaper – and turning walk-in cupboards into showers or loos was a stroke of brilliance; antique-filled sitting rooms are totally French; the little reading room holds hundreds of books; even the fresh roses are old-fashioned. It's all comfortably worn around the edges and you're welcome to use the tennis court.

rooms	4: 1 double, 1 twin, 2 family suites, all with bath or shower & wc.
price	€60-€75 for two.
dinner	€19-€22 with wine, by arrangement.
closed	Rarely.
directions	From Revel D622 for Castres for 9km; left D12 to Lempaut; right D46 for Lescout; house on left.

Monique & Charles Sallier
La Bousquétarié,
81700 Lempaut, Tarn
tel (0)5 63 75 51 09
fax (0)5 63 75 51 09

MIDI · PYRÉNÉES

Davina left Paris to set up her dream *chambres d'hôtes* in this deliciously unspoilt corner of France. She has poured love and energy into the 1860 *maison de maître*, enfolded by gardens and birdsong. The soft furnishings are all handmade, the furniture and linen unearthed from *brocantes*. This is a cool, minimalist haven of cream and white, of stripped wooden floors, muslin, hessian and voile, embellished here and there with a glint of gold in door knob or mirrror. A touch spartan for some, maybe, but Davina loves meeting people and her two young daughters are a delight.

rooms	3 doubles, all with bath & wc.
price	€46-€54 for two.
dinner	€15-€28 with wine, by arrangement.
closed	Rarely.
directions	From Castres D622 for Brassac/Lacaune; 17km then signs for Ferrières & Varbre; house on edge of village, signs.

Davina Doughan
La Ramade,
81260 Ferrières, Tarn
tel (0)5 63 73 47 08
fax (0)5 63 73 47 08
e-mail ddoughan@aol.com

Your Anglo-French hosts welcome guests as friends to their deeply converted farmhouse. The pastel-painted, prettily-stencilled rooms are smallish but beds are good, the hospitality is great and it's a deliciously secluded place to stay and walk or bike out into the country. The Wises grow their own vegetables and summer dinners happen on the terrace overlooking the lovely Tarn valley, a largely undiscovered part of France where birds, bees and sheep will serenade you. Watch the local sheep farmers milking for Roquefort and don't miss Albi, with that fascinating red-brick cathedral.

rooms	3: 1 twin, 1 double, both with shower & wc; 1 twin sharing bathroom.
price	€38 for two.
dinner	€15 with wine, by arrangement.
closed	Rarely.
directions	From Albi D999 for Millau 25km; at La Croix Blanche left to Cambon du Temple, up to La Barthe on D163; right; house on left.

Michèle & Michael Wise
La Barthe,
81430 Villefranche d'Albigeois, Tarn
tel (0)5 63 55 96 21
fax (0)5 63 55 96 21
e-mail labarthe@chezwise.com
web www.chezwise.com

MIDI · PYRÉNÉES

Way off the beaten track, just 30km from Albi; this young couple have recreated the past in their brilliantly authentic restoration of a crumbled old farmhouse. Sylvie's kitchen is a poem: cooking area in the farmer's old fireside bed, shelves groaning with jars of goodies from Pierre's garden. She adores cooking, he loves to chat, has an excellent sense of humour and good English. They have put their heart into their house with its natural garden, intriguing collection of country antiques and sweetly rustic guest rooms full of beams, *armoires*, Provençal prints – plus super modern shower rooms. Exceptional value.

rooms	2: 1 double, 1 triple, both with shower & wc.
price	€40 for two.
dinner	€15 with wine, by arrangement.
closed	Rarely.
directions	From Albi for Ambialet to Valence d'Albigeois; left D53 to Tanus 5.5km; left towards St Marcel for 1.5km; Chambres d'Hôtes sign; opposite church.

Sylvie & Pierre Dumetz-Manesse
Saint Marcel,
Padiès,
81340 Valence d'Albi, Tarn
tel (0)5 63 76 38 47(0)5 63 43 41 23
fax (0)5 63 43 41 23

A gem, both house and garden, in the post-industrial waste of this old mining area. You are received by a lively hostess who, deeply interested in art and furniture, loves decorating her beamy old house with style and poise that reflect her personality, tending her garden of plenty – three secret sitting corners – and gathering the fruit that hangs richly around – yes, you may. A stream runs at the bottom, forests march along the edge, you are æons away from the ugliness down the road. Bedrooms, bearing bookish names, are painted white with colour trimmings and lots of wood (beams, floors, antiques) – delightful.

rooms	3: 1 twin, 2 doubles, all with shower & wc.
price	€43 for two.
dinner	Light supper €10.50, with wine; restaurant 1km.
closed	Rarely.
directions	From A20 or N20, N140 for Figeac & Decazeville; just before Decazeville right to Viviez; over railway; sign.

Mireille Bernard
Joany,
12110 Viviez, Aveyron

tel	(0)5 65 43 42 90
fax	(0)5 65 43 42 90
web	www.joany.org

MIDI · PYRÉNÉES

A mini-hamlet in the calm green Aveyron where there is so much space. Two rooms, in the main house, each with a little terrace, look out over a typical medieval château; the third, in an outbuilding, has a mezzanine; all are welcoming, two have cooking facilities. The garden is full of flowers, the view stupendous, your hosts – he half-American, she French – delightful, solicitous and eager to please. The food is "outstanding and imaginative" – Pierre and Monique used to run a restaurant.
Well-behaved children and pets welcome.
Gîte space for 8 people.

rooms	2 + 2 cottages: 2 doubles, both with bath or shower & wc; 2 cottages for 4.
price	€43-€46 for two.
dinner	€15, with wine; restaurant 1km.
closed	2 weeks in September.
directions	From Villefranche D922 for Albi; at entrance to Sanvensa, follow signs on right to Monteillet Chambres d'Hôtes.

Monique & Pierre Bateson
Monteillet-Sanvensa,
12200 Villefranche de Rouergue,
Aveyron

tel	(0)5 65 29 81 01
fax	(0)5 65 65 89 52
e-mail	pbc.@wanadoo.fr

The ever-welcoming Riebens exchanged a cosy northern village with paddocks for a swathe of southern Auvergne – farmhouse, fields, woods, a lake and… paddocks for Jacques' beloved horses. Views from the terrace merit several hours of gazing; or get out there and discover the walks and the wildlife. House and furniture are properly old-fashioned and quaint (bathrooms are recent) and the décor respects them utterly: stripped wooden floors, original beams, good old beds, soft colours and plenty of little pieces to give it the personal touch. Your hosts love their new home – so will you. *Gîte space for 10 people.*

rooms	2: 1 double, 1 family suite, all with bath & wc.
price	€43 for two; €73 for four.
dinner	Restaurant in village.
closed	Rarely.
directions	From Villefranche de Rouergue for Rodez D911; exit Rieupeyroux for Rodez 2km; right D85 to Tayrac. At La Rode right for La Salvetat Peyralès; towards Montarsès, signs.

Jo & Jacques Rieben
Montarsès de Tayrac,
12440 La Salvetat Peyralès,
Aveyron

tel	(0)5 65 81 46 10
fax	(0)5 65 81 46 10
e-mail	chantelouve@club-internet.fr
web	www.ifrance.com/aveyronvacances

map: 16 entry: 637

MIDI · PYRÉNÉES

An energetic, lovable couple live in this astonishing old place, built on a hillside before a heart-stopping view. You go from level to delightful level: the ancient timber frame holds brilliantly restored rooms done in a simple, contemporary style that makes the old stones glow with pride. The emphasis is on communal living, of course – superb dining and sitting rooms with original paving, huge organic potager, great atmosphere – but there are little terraces and a library for quiet times. Lovely guest rooms are big (except the singles), pale or bright. Exceptional. *Children over 4 welcome. Gîte space for 6 people.*

rooms	7: 5 twins with shower & wc; 2 singles with shower & separate wc.
price	€65 for two.
dinner	€18 with wine, by arrangement.
closed	Rarely.
directions	From Millau D992/D999 for Albi; at St Pierre D902 right for Réquista; 3km after Faveyrolles left through Salelles; signposted.

Hans & Nelleke Versteegen
La Grande Combe,
12480 St Izaire, Aveyron

tel	(0)5 65 99 45 01
fax	(0)5 65 99 48 41
e-mail	grande.combe@wanadoo.fr
web	www.la-grande-combe.nl

map: 16 entry: 638

Vast pastures slope away, a castle towers on a rock: it's ideal for outdoors lovers – orchids to hunt, canoeing, climbing, hang-gliding to practise – though with less of a family feel than some. The 16th-century guest *bergerie* has shiny terracotta floors, old beams and white walls; Jean, your friendly farmer host, made a lot of the pine furniture. There are tapestries and antiques smelling of years of polish in the dining room where Véronique's excellent meals of home-grown organic meat and veg are served. Worth staying some time.

rooms	6: 2 twins, 2 doubles, 1 triple, 1 family room, all with bath or shower & wc.
price	€43 for two.
dinner	€15-€17; good choice of restaurants in Millau.
closed	Mid-November-March.
directions	From Millau N9 to Aguessac; on way out, D547 right to Compeyre; left in village, follow signs for 2km.

Jean & Véronique Lombard-Pratmarty
Quiers,
12520 Compeyre, Aveyron

tel	(0)5 65 59 85 10
fax	(0)5 65 59 80 99
e-mail	quiers@wanadoo.fr
web	www.ifrance.com/quiers

MIDI · PYRÉNÉES

The house is modern and rather dark, the rolling Languedoc hills are wild and very ancient. You can put on your wings and join the paragliders launching off the nearby cliff, or you can watch them from the safety of your breakfast table in the garden, enjoying Madame's *lafloune*, a local sheep's-milk cake. It matters little that she speaks no English: she is kind and welcoming and you can get a long way with smiles and sign language while Monsieur tends his sheep. The immaculate, simply and attractively furnished bedrooms include a suite which is perfect for a family. A simple unpretentious home.

rooms	2: 1 double, 1 suite for 4, both with shower & wc.
price	€37-€40 for two.
dinner	Choice of restaurants Millau, 3km.
closed	Rarely.
directions	From Millau D911 for Cahors. Just after leaving city limits right after 'Auberge' x-roads. Signposted. Follow small road for about 2km.

Mme Henriette Cassan
Montels,
12100 Millau, Aveyron

tel	(0)5 65 60 51 70

Fascinating Quézac: a pilgrimage 'street-village' with a Black Virgin and a lovely old bridge over the Tarn. Amazingly, Marius is a new house: it fits in perfectly with its old stones, beams and doors and its warm, lived-in feel, all light and fresh. Genuine locals, Dany and Pierre adore embellishing their home – delightful country fabrics, hand-painted furniture and murals – and spoiling their guests with home-made and home-grown delicacies from their superb veg patch. Their speciality? *Gâteau de noix* made with their own walnuts. Lovely terrace and rose garden where only birds, water and wind are to be heard.

LANGUEDOC · ROUSSILLON

rooms	5: 4 doubles, 1 family suite, all with shower or bath & wc.
price	€50-€65 for two.
dinner	€25 with wine, by arrangement.
closed	Rarely.
directions	From A75 exit 39 on N88 E for 25km; right N106 for Alès 25km; at Ispagnac right to Quézac; signs in village.

Rugby rouses great passions here, as do corridas and high dramas enacted beneath the Roman arches; down on the coast, traditional water-jousters get less emotional but much wetter.

Danièle Méjean & Pierre Parentini
La Maison de Marius,
8 rue du Pontet,
48320 Quézac, Lozère

tel	(0)4 66 44 25 05
fax	(0)4 66 44 25 05
web	www.chez.com/maisondemarius

Sit in the château's drawing room where a dozen French chairs open their arms. Or wander onto the balcony with panoramic view across river, dramatic viaduct and red-roofed village to terraced hills beyond. The big beautiful bedrooms have a perfect château feel with their strong-coloured walls setting off the family furniture. Madame, one of an old French silk family who have been here for several generations, is as elegant and charming as her house; a good cook, too. She will show you where to find really good walks, exciting canoeing, tennis, riding, interesting wildlife spots and ancient buildings to visit nearby.

rooms	3: 2 doubles, 1 twin, all with bath or shower & wc.
price	€58-€74 for two.
dinner	€22 with wine, by arrangement
closed	Rarely.
directions	From Millau S on N9 for 19km to La Cavalerie; left D7 for Le Vigan about 50km to Bez; before bridge, sign on left.

Françoise du Luc
Château Massal,
Bez et Esparon,
30120 Le Vigan, Gard
tel (0)4 67 81 07 60
fax (0)4 67 81 07 60

LANGUEDOC · ROUSSILLON

John is a charmer: open-minded, fun and generous, he runs a deliciously relaxed house where either B&B guests share the quiet with him or groups meet for yoga and music workshops. It's a beautiful set of buildings that he is still restoring, as well as cooking meals for long, talk-filled, wine-flowed evenings. Rooms are simple and perfect within their white walls, Indian cotton bedcovers for a splash of colour and a mix of French farm antiques and English stripped pine and there's space for all on the various levels of garden. *Studio with piano available. Gîte space for 8 people.*

rooms	4: 1 double, 1 twin sharing shower & wc; 1 triple, 1 family both with shower & wc.
price	€46-€61 for two.
dinner	€15, with wine; restaurants 10km.
closed	Rarely.
directions	From Nîmes D999 to St Hippolyte du Fort; D39 for Lasalle for about 10km; sign on left.

John Macdonald
Domaine de Bagard,
30460 Lasalle, Gard
tel (0)4 66 85 25 51
fax (0)4 66 85 25 51
e-mail johnmacdonald@minitel.net

An 18th-century silkworm farm, the rambling house has old stones, arched terraces, a lovely courtyard and is done in the owners' own friendly, informal image. Delightful Isabelle is an artist, her warm sensitivity evident in her imaginative treatment of space, with African artefacts and original paintings indoors, a lovely orchard and shrubby pool area outside. Delicious breakfast is taken on the shady terrace in summer. You dine here, too, on Isabelle's cosmopolitan creations – meals are good fun (booking essential). This is genuine B&B, nothing hotelly, the three children join in and the road shouldn't impinge.

rooms	4: 2 twins, 1 triple, 1 quadruple, all with shower & wc.
price	€51 for two.
dinner	€18 with wine, by arrangement.
closed	Rarely.
directions	From Alès D16/D579 NE through Barjac for Vallon Pont d'Arc; 300m after Gendarmerie, house on right, arched doorway.

Antoine & Isabelle Agapitos
Le Mas Escombelle,
La Villette,
30430 Barjac, Gard
tel (0)4 66 24 54 77
fax (0)4 66 24 54 77
e-mail mas-escombel@wanadoo.fr
web perso.wanadoo.fr/mas-escombel/

LANGUEDOC · ROUSSILLON

Reached through aromatic banks of thyme, lavender and juniper, set among hills and woods, here is a place for potters and walkers. Monsieur is a talented *potier* – the house is dotted with lovely pieces and there's a little gallery – and runs international pottery courses bringing an informal, creative atmosphere with lots of interesting people. Madame is delightful and an excellent cook. The guest room, separate from the main house, is simply furnished, meals (dinner on request) are served on the terrace or in the log-fired living room and the summer brings masses of festivals and happenings.
Gîte space for 8 people.

rooms	1 double with shower & wc.
price	€45 for two.
dinner	€15 with wine, by arrangement.
closed	Rarely.
directions	From Alès D16 through Le Saut du Loup. 7 km after Le Saut D241 left for St Julien de Cassagnas; sign.

Michel & Françoise Simonot
Mas Cassac,
30500 Allègre, Gard
tel (0)4 66 24 85 65
fax (0)4 66 24 80 55
e-mail mas.cassac@online.fr
web www.ceramique.com/Mas-Cassac

Cassandra's refuge from Switzerland lies in the heart of a delectable 17th-century village. You too may revel in her sheltered courtyard, sunny terrace pergola (where gentle canine Pastis may join you for a glass), cool vaulted dining room and bedrooms with their pure white walls, superb beds and simple, good furniture: Swiss design sense and French atmosphere in perfect balance. Good shower rooms too. You will enjoy her direct vivacity and her ability to respect your privacy.

rooms	3 doubles, all with shower & wc.
price	€54 for two.
dinner	Restaurants within walking distance.
closed	November-February.
directions	From A7 exit Bollène for Pont St Esprit; in Bagnols/Cèze D980 towards Barjac 16km; right to St André; park Place de la Mairie; house 20m away.

Cassandra Branger
Chez Cassandra,
Rue du Four Banal,
30630 St André de Roquepertuis,
Gard

tel	(0)4 66 82 19 21
e-mail	chez.cassandra@wanadoo.fr
web	www.avignon-et-provence.com/bb/cassandra

LANGUEDOC · ROUSSILLON

An ancestor of Madame's built the fine old fortified farmhouse 200 years ago: it still stands, proudly worn, by the Ardèche River and has its own beach. Inside, in sudden contrast, is the magic of imagination and originality. Madame paints furniture, doors, friezes, ceilings, anything, brilliantly; rooms have all been redone; there's the superb stone staircase, the much-painted ruined bridge, the squirrelly, tall-treed park where shade invites summer lingerers. Monsieur can accompany you on canoe trips (you may spot an otter) – they are an attractive, sociable couple who enjoy their guests. *Gîte space for 8 people.*

rooms	5: 2 doubles, 1 twin, 1 triple, 1 quadruple all with shower & wc.
price	€55 for two, €65 for four.
dinner	Good restaurants in village.
closed	Rarely.
directions	From A7 Bollène exit D994 to Pont St Esprit; N86 for Bourg St Andéol; sign before bridge across river.

Mme de Verduzan
Pont d'Ardèche,
30130 Pont St Esprit, Gard

tel	(0)4 66 39 29 80
fax	(0)4 66 39 51 80
e-mail	pontdardeche@aol.com
web	www.pont-dardeche.com

This happy, artistic couple open their arms to welcome guests to their open, light-filled, authentically renovated old Cévenol silk farm, splashed with colour and *objets*. Flashes: pretty ochre-coloured plates, a long wooden table on the uneven stone floor of the huge kitchen, the old stone sink opposite; beams twisting through the house, glimpses of sky through little windows, a ravishing courtyard, big, uncluttered, attractive bedrooms, a roof terrace looking over Provence. Michèle manages tranquilly and adores cooking, Michel knows his wines and the local community, their talk is deeply cultural and enriching.

rooms	3: 2 doubles, 1 suite, all with shower & wc.
price	€50-€55 for two.
dinner	€17 with wine, by arrangement.
closed	Rarely.
directions	From Alès D6 E 27km; left D979 beyond Lussan for Barjac 1km; left D187 to Fons sur Lussan; right at fountain; up on left by church.

Michèle Dassonneville
& Michel Genvrin
La Magnanerie,
Place de l'Horloge,
30580 Fons sur Lussan, Gard
tel (0)4 66 72 81 72
e-mail la-magnanerie@wanadoo.fr

They are a delightfully open couple, in love with their life and their 19th-century *maison de maître*, who welcome guests with exuberant gaiety. John is a joiner with a fine eye for interior design while Michel, quieter, softer, does the cooking. From the classic black and white tiles of the entrance hall to the carefully planned lighting in the bedrooms, every detail counts. A very generous breakfast is served under the chestnut trees or by the pool; afterwards you can wander off to join in lazy Provençal village life or visit Avignon, Uzès or nearby Lussan, the fortified Cévenol village.

rooms	4: 2 doubles, 2 twins, all with bath or shower & wc.
price	€80-€95 for two.
dinner	€30 with wine, by arrangement.
closed	Rarely.
directions	From A9 exit 23 W to Uzès 19km; D979 N 7.5km; right D238 to La Bruguière. House on big square next to Mairie (vast Micocourier tree in front).

John Karavias & Michel Comas
Les Marronniers,
30580 La Bruguière, Gard
tel (0)4 66 72 84 77
fax (0)4 66 72 85 78
e-mail les.marronniers@12stay.co.uk
web www.les.marronniers.12stay.co.uk

Out among the almond trees of the scented *garrigue*, delicate, energetic Sylvie has restored the old sheep and silk farm with flair and sensitivity. The house is full of secret corners – and hearts (*cœurs*), collected over 20 years and discreetly integrated; there are garden spaces for all where a fountain fiddles; her marriage of old stones and colour, beams and wall hangings, simple southern furniture and gentle lighting is one of love and good taste – and then she serves tempting Mediterranean meals on the leafy terrace. She adores people, and also knows where to get superior lavender essence.

rooms	2: 1 suite for 4 with shower & wc; 1 apartment for 3 with mini-kitchen, shower & wc.
price	€76 for two.
dinner	€23, with wine; restaurants 5-10km.
closed	Rarely.
directions	From A9 exit Nîmes Ouest N106 to Alès; right D6 for Bagnols & Cèze 19km; D356 left 2km; left to Saussines; house 1st on right.

Sylvie Sommer
Maison Cœurs,
Saussines,
30580 Bouquet, Gard

tel	(0)4 66 72 97 53
fax	(0)4 66 72 81 86
e-mail	shappy@wanadoo.fr

LANGUEDOC · ROUSSILLON

Yours is the pink-shuttered bit, the owners have yellow. They have restored these lovely old buildings with a very sure touch, white walls a perfect foil for southern-toned fabrics and materials. The little vaulted *Green* room is intimate and alcoved, the big *Red* room smartly 4-postered. The guest house also has a big soft living room, tables on the terrace under the great leafy tree and a lawn sloping down to the river bed – brilliant spots for silent gazing. You'll enjoy the pool in its roofless barn and your charming hosts will have coffee with you after dinner (book ahead). Very pretty in its detachment.

rooms	3 doubles, all with shower & wc.
price	€65-€75 for two.
dinner	By arrangement €25, good wine list.
closed	Rarely.
directions	From Alès, D6 for 12km; right on D7; in St Just, left for Vacquières, pink signs to house.

Thomas & Miriam van Dijke
Mas Vacquières,
Hameau de Vacquières,
30580 St Just et Vacquières, Gard

tel	(0)4 66 83 70 75
fax	(0)4 66 83 74 15
e-mail	info@masvac.com
web	www.masvac.com

A magical, mostly 17th-century moated château (parts are 12th-century) with its very own ghost, *la Dame à la Rose*. Towers overlook the monumental courtyard where Mary Stuart (later Queen of Scots) once walked. Madame runs a cultural centre and stages a summer music festival; this is a château that works. Breakfast is in the courtyard or in the dining room. The vast bedrooms, some with round tower bathrooms, have been renovated with colourful details such as bright new satin canopies. Thoughtfulness like 'no lawn-mowing during siesta-time' is typical of the attitude here.

rooms	6: 3 doubles, 2 quadruples, 1 twin, all with bath & wc.
price	€91 for two.
dinner	Plenty of restaurants nearby.
closed	Rarely.
directions	From Avignon, N580 for Bagnols & Cèze. At junction in L'Ardoise, left D9 for Laudun; signs.

Gisèle & Jean-Louis Bastouil
Château de Lascours,
30290 Laudun, Gard
tel (0)4 66 50 39 61
fax (0)4 66 50 30 08
e-mail chateau.de.lascours@wanadoo.fr

LANGUEDOC · ROUSSILLON

Circles of delight: the Provençe of vines and umbrella pines, a peaceful typical village, high doors, a lovely converted barn and glowing little house, a warm, affectionate couple who genuinely enjoy having guests. Joël paints and Michèle is a keen and good cook. Meal times are flexible, the atmosphere relaxed, the sheltered, well-tended courtyard or cosy dining room conducive to lingering chat. Cottagey, beamed bedrooms have good solid furniture, wooden floors, patchwork, plants and sensible bathrooms. An easy place to be, 10 minutes from Avignon, 20 minutes from Nîmes and in excellent rosé wine, olive and fruit country. *Gîte space for 2.*

rooms	1 double with bath & wc.
price	€46 for two.
dinner	€15 with wine, by arrangement.
closed	Rarely.
directions	From Avignon & Villeneuve N580 for Bagnols & Cèze; right on D377 & D177 to Pujaut. House opp. town hall; large metal door.

Joël & Michèle Rousseau
Les Bambous,
Rue de la Mairie,
30131 Pujaut, Gard
tel (0)4 90 26 46 47
fax (0)4 90 26 46 47
e-mail rousseau.michele@wanadoo.fr

A village or not a village? It feels like one and is a perfect place to stay when Avignon itself is heaving with people. A former stable block, the house is next door to La Chartreuse de Villeneuve, a beautiful 13th-century monastery, now a European Centre for Literature and Theatre. Pascale runs the Écuries as a B&B though in fact you have a fully-equipped studio, so can opt to be independent. But don't think she doesn't want you! She is on hand with breakfast, information and magazines you can borrow, and an aperitif before you head out for the evening.

rooms	3: 2 doubles, 1 suite, all with bath, shower & wc.
price	€60-€84 for two.
dinner	Good choice of restaurants nearby.
closed	Rarely.
directions	From Avignon cross Rhône for Nîmes/Villeneuve lès A. Just after bridge right for Villeneuve centre, Rue de la République. House next to La Chartreuse.

Pascale Letellier
Les Écuries des Chartreux,
66 rue de la République,
30400 Villeneuve lès Avignon, Gard
tel (0)4 90 25 79 93
fax (0)4 90 25 79 93
e-mail ecuries-chartreux@avignon-et-provence.com
web www.avignon-et-provence.com/ecuries-chartreux

LANGUEDOC · ROUSSILLON

Helen and Jacques met in Africa – she a nurse, he an agriculturist – and are an interesting, committed couple (10% of their B&B income goes to development projects). Come and share their simple life in this little old village house with all its stairs, African mementos and pine furniture. There's space in your white-vaulted, red-curtained suite and you won't hear much traffic in enchanting Pujaut. The pretty, peaceful, terraced garden has a summer kitchen for guests but is not really suitable for adventurous toddlers. Super people with whom to share good conversation over delicious suppers and a village worth exploring.

rooms	1 suite for 2 with shower & wc.
price	€40 for two.
dinner	€12.50 with wine, by arrangement.
closed	Rarely.
directions	From Avignon N580 for Bagnols/Cèze; right D377 & D177 to Pujaut. In village head for Mairie; house 300m into old village from Mairie & church.

Helen Thompson
& Jacques Sergent
Saba'ad,
Place des Consuls,
30131 Pujaut, Gard
tel (0)4 90 26 31 68
fax (0)4 90 26 31 68

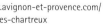

A path through the woods leads from the house to the river by the Pont du Gard, a World Heritage site – the setting is truly wonderful. Indoors, the décor is fulsome, definitely idiosyncratic – a net canopy over one of the beds, hanging hats, splayed fans, silk flowers, etc. The rooms are themed. *La Provençale* has a small connecting room with bunk beds and soft toys for the younger guest. Monsieur works in Nîmes but gives all his remaining time to welcoming and caring for his guests. The swimming pool is an added enticement and bedrooms have air conditioning. *Gîte space for 11.*

rooms	5: 2 doubles, 2 twin, 1 suite, with bath or shower & wc.
price	€90 for two.
dinner	Choice of restaurants within 3km.
closed	October-March.
directions	From Remoulins follow signs for Pont du Gard 'Rive Droite'. Sign on right.

Gérard Cristini
La Terre des Lauriers,
Rive Droite - Pont du Gard,
30210 Remoulins, Gard
tel (0)4 66 37 19 45
fax (0)4 66 37 19 45
e-mail gerard.cristini@laterredeslauriers.com
web www.laterredeslauriers.com

LANGUEDOC · ROUSSILLON

Lovely, long stone buildings enfold the two-tier courtyard, great trees give generous shade, the Cévennes hillsides march away behind. It is enchanting. Your young and welcoming Dutch hosts are still renovating but the garden and lawn around the pool, the glowing old furniture inside are already a triumph. Bedrooms are simple: light and white, very separate from each other round the courtyard. Esther really loves cooking – make the most of good regional dishes outside or in their beautiful dining room. *Minimum 2 nights in winter. Gîte space for 6 people.*

rooms	3 doubles, all with shower & wc.
price	€55-€66 for two.
dinner	€21; wine €5.50-€12.
closed	Rarely.
directions	From Uzès D981 to Montaren for 6km; right on D337 to St Médiers; in village cont. up & around to right. House on left.

Léonard Robberts & Esther Küchler
Mas d'Oléandre,
Hameau St Médiers,
30700 Montaren et St Médiers, Gard
tel (0)4 66 22 63 43
fax (0)4 66 03 14 06
e-mail info@masoleandre.com
web www.masoleandre.com

Christian's flair and human touch have revived the grand old stones with beautiful Indonesian furniture and hangings, soft lighting and a gentle golden sandy colour – he and Pierre are delighted with their new *Maison*. Beneath the daytime chimes of the old church of lovely Blauzac, the lush garden and ancient tower look over wavy red rooftops to blue hills, bedrooms bask in ethnic fabrics and relaxed good taste, the stunning suite has its own roof terrace. Plus masses of books and a long long breakfast table in the library, Pierre's piano and good sofas in the *salon*. Superb. *Children need parental supervision: unfenced water.*

rooms	4: 3 doubles with shower & wc; 1 suite for two, with bath & wc.
price	€95-€160 for two.
dinner	2 bistros in village.
closed	Rarely.
directions	From Nîmes, D979 for Blauzac & Uzès 16km; after Pont St Nicolas, left for Blauzac; enter village, house behind church.

Christian Vaurie
La Maison,
Place de l'Église,
30700 Blauzac, Gard

tel	(0)4 66 81 25 15
fax	(0)4 66 81 02 18
e-mail	lamaisondeblauzac@wanadoo.fr

LANGUEDOC · ROUSSILLON

Fronted by a graceful curve of 1850s balustrade, this hunting lodge became a wine estate and now a gîte-cum-B&B. You are as private as can be yet your hosts are there when you need them – breakfast is brought to the room and Monsieur is ever ready with a chat, a whisky, a cigarette – and tomatoes from the garden. Madame ran a boutique in Paris and has an elegant eye: both the large, lofty rooms have pale green walls, beams and white-painted furniture. Beds are on mezzanines, kitchenettes to the side; bathrooms are spotless and white. The wonderful, peaceful garden with its pool protects you from the midday sun.

rooms	2 doubles, both with bath & wc.
price	€75-€90 for two.
dinner	Choice of restaurants nearby.
closed	Rarely.
directions	From A9 exit Nîmes-Ouest (Le Vigan) to Quissac. At r'bout, left & straight to 3rd r'bout; right then 2nd left then 1st right; house on left after carpark.

M & Mme Ducastel
Château de la Devèze,
710 chemin de la Devèze,
30260 Quissac, Gard

tel	(0)4 66 77 16 15
fax	(0)4 66 77 16 15
e-mail	genevieve.ducastel@wanadoo.fr

At his *hôtel particulier* (private mansion), Philippe receives with warm refinement. Each very private room, named after a different local luminary (including our own Lawrence Durrell), is in traditional Provençal style: polished floors, warm-painted walls, white bedcovers, a different and beautiful wall hanging over each bed, super big bathrooms. The magic secluded terrace garden with gasping views over the roofs of the old town is where you swim; breakfast, which to Philippe is *the* moment of the day, is in the old-style dining room or the gorgeous courtyard. Grand, elegant – and utterly lovable.

rooms	6: 4 doubles, 1 twin, 1 triple, all with bath or shower & wc.
price	€58-€76 for two. Special winter prices.
dinner	€23 with wine, by arrangement.
closed	Rarely.
directions	From Nîmes D40 W 28km to Sommières; from town centre for centre historique; from Post Office follow street up to château; signposted.

Philippe de Frémont
Hôtel de l'Orange,
Chemin du Château Fort,
30250 Sommières, Gard
tel (0)4 66 77 79 94
fax (0)4 66 80 44 87
e-mail hotel.dorange@free.fr
web hotel.delorange.free.fr

LANGUEDOC · ROUSSILLON

A Moorish tang colours Marion's 17th-century townhouse and garden: a fountain in the wall of the deliciously cool walled garden, candlelit dinners that taste of Provence and North Africa, adventurous colours and lovely fabrics, a sunken bath in the open-plan suite, beautiful pieces of furniture and paintings placed just where they enhance the generous proportions. It isn't grand, just simply elegant. This talented lady is a wonderful hostess who adores having guests, serving breakfasts of cold meats, cheese and local *fougasse* (a soft delicate bread) then pointing them to the cultural riches of the area. Very special.

rooms	4: 3 doubles, all with bath or shower & wc; 1 suite with bath & wc.
price	€65-€95 for two.
dinner	€25 with wine, by arrangement.
closed	Rarely.
directions	From A9 exit 26 Aimargues Centre. Cross r'bout with fountain down plane tree lane 300m. Entrance opp. Carli Immo, Rue de la Violette (3 cypresses behind garden wall).

Marion Escarfail
26 boulevard Saint Louis,
30470 Aimargues, Gard
tel (0)4 66 88 52 99
fax (0)4 66 88 52 99
e-mail marionmais@aol.com
web members.aol.com/marionmais

The sun-drenched village street with its arched doorways and shuttered windows leads you to the gates of a fine old house where bull-fighting posters hang in the hall. At the back, your eye leaps to the parallel vines and uneven hills – a festival of flaming colour in autumn. Monsieur is English; Madame is French, an artist and good company. She has done her house with great sympathy for its original spaces and stone floors. Her works are a bonus on the walls. It is a privilege to be her only guests, enjoy the big unfussy bedroom onto the garden and step out into the morning light for home-made fig jam.

rooms	1 double with bath & wc.
price	€57 for two.
dinner	Choice of restaurants 5km.
closed	Rarely.
directions	From A9 exit 27; D34 Sommières; left to St Christol; right of post office for Cave Coop.; left at r'bout (before small bridge) 800m, left Av. des Bruyères; Rue de l'Église.

Monique Sykes-Maillon
La Ciboulette,
221 rue de l'Église,
34400 St Christol, Hérault

tel	(0)4 67 86 81 00
fax	(0)4 67 86 81 00
e-mail	happy@stchristol.com
web	www.stchristol.com

On the edge of a wild, unspoilt forest, in a green oasis flooded with mimosa, hibiscus and iris where 40 tortoises roam freely, it's hard to believe you're just 3km from lively Montpellier. The house is recent, built with old materials, its young vegetation already thick and rich, the swimming pool set among atmospheric stone 'ruins'. You sleep in rooms full of family furniture and colourful fabrics and sharing a very good bathroom. Your hostess, once a city girl in public relations, loves this place and her tortoises passionately (she knows each one by name), talks easily and is excellent company. *Gîte space for 2.*

rooms	2 doubles, sharing shower & separate wc.
price	€68-€91 for two.
dinner	Montpellier 3km.
closed	Rarely.
directions	From Mairie in Castelnau le Lez take Rue Jules Ferry; 5th left Chemin de la Rocheuse; last house on left.

Dominique Carabin-Cailleau
Castle's Cottage,
289 chemin de la Rocheuse,
34170 Castelnau le Lez, Hérault

tel	(0)4 67 72 63 08
fax	(0)4 67 72 63 08
e-mail	dpcc@libertysurf.fr
web	www.multimania.com/castlecottage

A perfect B&B on a superb estate with mulberry-lined drive, hills, vineyards and a real family atmosphere: simplicity, space, peace, fine big rooms and a genuine welcome. The delightful, hard-working owners have four children of their own and run an inn in their beautifully restored old family house. In a separate building, guest rooms have soft-coloured walls, generous mezzanines, pretty shower rooms. The big dining room has old honey-coloured beams – a dream – and gives onto the terrace and rows of vines beyond: just the place to try a glass of estate wine followed by an authentic auberge dinner.

rooms	4 double/quadruples, all with shower or bath & wc.
price	€54 for two.
dinner	€19, with wine; pizzeria & brasserie 3-5km.
closed	Last week in October.
directions	From Gignac east towards Montpellier; at edge of town 'Hérault Cuisines' on right; right & follow signs for 3km.

Isabelle & Baudouin Thillaye de Boullay
Domaine du Pélican,
34150 Gignac, Hérault

tel	(0)4 67 57 68 92
fax	(0)4 67 57 68 92

LANGUEDOC · ROUSSILLON

Madame's work upon the walls (she's an artist and sculptor), Monsieur's fine horse in the paddock – the modern house has lots of atmosphere and your hostess is an open, fun person who loves getting to know you, even teaching you to sculpt (do enquire). Rooms are big and simply furnished, each with a few lovely things, good fabrics and a private outside space onto the green garden with a summer kitchen. All in a fabulous spot protected by umbrella pines by the Salagou Lake, magnificent for sailing and swimming on long, hot summer's days, great biking, walking, riding in winter. Definitely worth staying two nights or more.

rooms	2 doubles, both with bath or shower & wc.
price	€50-€60 for two.
dinner	2 restaurants 3.5km.
closed	Rarely.
directions	A9 exit 34 on D13 N 10km; N9 to Clermont l'Hérault; D156 left for Lac du Salagou 3km; left to Liausson; 700m along last house on right before woods.

M & Mme Neveu
La Genestière,
Route de Liausson,
34800 Clermont l'Hérault, Hérault

tel	(0)4 67 96 30 97/(0)4 67 96 18 46
fax	(0)4 67 96 32 56
web	www.mediatisse.com/Lac-du-Salagou/genestie/genestie.htm

A vast and lovely stone winery is the guest wing on this old family property. Your host's sensitive conversion uses old tiles, doors and beams; high bedrooms are designed for comfort and privacy, each with an excellent shower room, superb bedding and French windows onto the well-caressed garden courtyard. Jean-François and his mother happily share their living space: go through the big hall, hung with some fine prints, to breakfast in the pleasing living room where a cabinet of treasures will intrigue. Outside, a discreet pool glimmers under a vast umbrella pine.

rooms	4 doubles, all with shower & wc.
price	€60-€66 for two.
dinner	Restaurants 3-12km.
closed	Rarely.
directions	From Clermont L'Hérault N9 r'bout D4 for Brignac 3.5km; house on right entering village.

Jean-François Martin
La Missare,
9 route de Clermont,
34800 Brignac, Hérault

tel	(0)4 67 96 07 67
fax	(0)4 67 50 14 11
e-mail	la.missare@free.fr
web	la.missare.free.fr

LANGUEDOC · ROUSSILLON

Start with: "The exotic vegetation matches the anachronism of the architecture adding to the impression of a theatrical décor", then: "Vast, amazing" – the brochure lies not. Towers, turrets, Troubadour style – yet a very simple welcome from Marie-France, a remarkable, courageous woman, and her children. Crystal chandeliers, grand piano, original wallpapers, cavernous rooms with great beamed ceilings, lovely inner courtyard, delightful gardens, defensive walls – it is all 19th century (including some of the summer dust?), has adopted the comforts of the 20th yet clings to old-style hospitality. *Gîte space for 7 people.*

rooms	3: 2 doubles, 1 twin, all with bath & wc.
price	€98-€107 for two; suite €155 for four.
dinner	Restaurant in Chateau grounds.
closed	Rarely.
directions	From A75 exit 35 Béziers N112 NW 10km; right D909 for Bédarieux 17km; right to Grézan.

Mme Marie-France Lanson
Château de Grézan,
34480 Laurens, Hérault

tel	(0)4 67 90 28 03
fax	(0)4 67 90 05 03
e-mail	chateau-grezan.lanson@wanadoo.fr

The château is perched right on top of the town. From the windows, ancient mellow rooftops give way to vineyards and more hills. Soft, plastered walls, honey-coloured floorboards or pale, nearly white stone floors and bleached linen curtains around beds give a wonderful feeling of light – unexpected in such an old building. Breakfast is in an enclosed courtyard, dotted with lemon trees and white oleander and guests can cook supper in their own kitchen. Whether you are interested in wine or the Cathars, want to cycle along the Canal du Midi or swim from a river beach – this is just the place. *Minimum 2 nights.*

rooms	1 double, 2 triples, 1 suite for 3, all with shower & wc.
price	€70 for two.
dinner	Restaurants nearby; self-catering possible.
closed	Rarely.
directions	From A9 exit 35 for Centre Ville; at 1st & 2nd r'bouts: for Bédarieux; 3rd r'bout: for Corneilhan/Murviel; in Murviel centre, next to Mairie.

Yves & Florence Cousquer
Château de Murviel,
1 place Georges Clémenceau,
34490 Murviel lès Béziers, Hérault
tel (0)4 67 32 35 45
fax (0)4 67 32 35 25
e-mail chateaudemurviel@free.fr
web www.murviel.com

LANGUEDOC · ROUSSILLON

The famous, tree-lined, much-cycled Canal du Midi runs through this lovely medieval village and the old townhouse looks pretty grand. Yet nothing prepares you for its château-like interior: ceilings magnificent in their 18th- and 19th-century paintings, walls frescoed with Languedoc scenes. Big, comfortable rooms have power showers and much attention to detail. Your Australian hostess is very welcoming; and you are only 5km from the sea. *Gîte space for two.*

rooms	4: 2 doubles, 2 twins, all with bath or shower & wc.
price	€50 for two.
dinner	€18 with wine, by arrangement.
closed	Rarely.
directions	From A9 exit Béziers Est to Villeneuve; N112 then D37 to town centre; house opp. Hôtel de Ville.

Jennifer-Jane Viner
7 rue de la Fontaine,
34420 Villeneuve lès Béziers,
Hérault
tel (0)4 67 39 87 15
fax (0)4 67 32 00 95
e-mail anges-gardiens@wanadoo.fr
web www.le-guide.com/anges-gardiens

An English photographer, a New Zealand cookery teacher... and a French name! They love France, wine, food, their fine house in this enchanting old village and the dazzling countryside around. The red door opens onto a high cool hall, old stone stairs lead to delicately decorated bedrooms in mainly modern style with new shower rooms and some super views to the hillside. You can walk, ride, climb rocks; swim, canoe in the river; follow Denis's wine trail; visit the unusual succulent garden – and return drunk with exertion and beauty for a superb, civilised meal on the terrace with your delightful hosts. *Gîte space for 4 people.*

rooms	5: 2 doubles, 2 twins, 1 suite, all with shower & wc.
price	€70-€80 for two.
dinner	€27, wine €8-€30.
closed	November.
directions	From Béziers N112 W for St Pons for 1/2km; right D14 through Maraussan, Cazouls lès Béziers, Cessenon to Roquebrun; signposted in village.

Denis & Sarah La Touche
Les Mimosas,
Avenue des Orangers,
34460 Roquebrun, Hérault

tel	(0)4 67 89 61 36
fax	(0)4 67 89 61 36
e-mail	welcome@foodiesinfrance.com
web	www.foodiesinfrance.com

LANGUEDOC · ROUSSILLON

The shyly friendly Dutch owners of the elegant Cerisaie came to visit, fell in love with it and bought it, lock, stock and furniture. Honorah serves a fabulous lunch buffet from 12 till 5pm: catch it early before, or late after a long wild walk. She has also hung lots of her attractive paintings, a personal touch that the classically-proportioned rooms really respond to. A proud old staircase mounts to the bedrooms which are just right – light, roomy, marble-fireplaced, old-furnished, double-glazed against the road (though there is some noise), with super views of hills and the truly lovely garden. *Gîte space for 4 people.*

rooms	6: 3 doubles, 2 twins, 1 suite for 2 with kitchenette, all with bath or shower & wc.
price	€59.50-€74.50 for two.
dinner	€19.50 Wednesdays, wine €10-€17; Lunch à la carte. Good restaurant nearby.
closed	November-Easter
directions	From A9 exit Béziers Ouest; D64; N112 for Castres, Mazamet & St Pons; 1km before St Pons right D908 to Riols; house on left leaving Riols.

Honorah & Albert Jan Karsten
La Cerisaie,
1 avenue de Bédarieux,
34220 Riols, Hérault

tel	(0)4 67 97 03 87
fax	(0)4 67 97 03 88
e-mail	cerisaie@wanadoo.fr
web	www.cerisaie.net

In these superbly wild, pastoral surroundings with great walking and climbing trails, you bathe in simplicity, stream-babble and light. Your hosts, hard-working walnut and chestnut growers, have carefully transformed their barn for guests. Country antiques, old cotton lace curtains, new bedding and soft blue tones relax the eye, and there's a fireplace and a full kitchen too. Monsieur has a real, friendly handshake, Madame is gentle and welcoming – they are lovely people running a genuine B&B despite the separate quarters. Breakfast on the shady terrace includes cheese or walnuts or honey. *Gîte space for 3 people.*

rooms	3: 2 doubles, 1 single, all with bath & wc.
price	€43 for two.
dinner	Self-catering; restaurants nearby.
closed	October-March, except by arrangement.
directions	From A9 exit Béziers Ouest; D64; N112 to Mazamet; N112 for St Pons de Thomières. At Courniou, right to Prouilhe; farm on left.

Éliane & Jean-Louis Lunes
La Métairie Basse,
Hameau de Prouilhe,
34220 Courniou, Hérault
tel (0)4 67 97 21 59
fax (0)4 67 97 21 59

LANGUEDOC · ROUSSILLON

Here, among the twisting lanes of beautiful, medieval Caunes, five centuries of bread was baked. The house's easy, intelligent new American owners have kept the steep narrow stairs and made five cosy guest rooms – antique beds, new mattresses – and a tiny terrace for summer breakfasts. Diminutive ground floor too, but hugely good conversation, an annual exhibition of San Francisco artists (Terry was a reporter there), and all that exploring to do. *Minimum 2 nights.*

rooms	5: 2 doubles with bath, shower & wc; 1 double & 1 triple, sharing shower & wc; 1 family suite with bath & wc.
price	€41.20-€61.20 for two.
dinner	Restaurant opposite.
closed	Christmas.
directions	From Carcassonne D620 to Caunes Minervois; cross river & follow to Mairie; house behind Épicerie opp. Place de la Mairie.

Terry & Lois Link
L'Ancienne Boulangerie,
Rue St Gènes,
11160 Caunes-Minervois, Aude
tel (0)4 68 78 01 32
e-mail ancienneboulangerie@compuserve.com
web www.caunes-minervois.com

Romantics, painters, poets – here be paradise. One room looks onto the lush-wild, magic-exotic park watered by 17th-century monastic hydraulics, the other over the great courtyard, where the donkey may call you, to the ruined Cistercian abbey. Rooms are big, beamy and simply refined in their white cotton and fine old *armoires*. Sisters Renée and Claude, earthy and generous, were born here, are renovating with loving care on a shoestring, will take you to meet each great tree and provide extravagantly elegant dinners with family linen and silver. There are four retired horses... and so much more. It's incomparable.

rooms	2 doubles, with bath & wc.
price	€50 for two.
dinner	€16 with wine, by arrangement. Auberge in village, 100m.
closed	Rarely.
directions	From A61 exit Bram; D4 through Bram & St Martin le Vieil; right on tiny D64 3km to Abbey. Caution: Go to Côté Jardins B&B not the Abbey B&B next door.

Claude Antoine
Abbaye de Villelongue-Côté Jardins,
11170 St Martin le Vieil, Aude
tel (0)4 68 76 09 03
e-mail avillelongue@free.fr
web avillelongue.free.fr

LANGUEDOC · ROUSSILLON

There are space and air galore in this 19th-century gentleman-farmer's house; the freshly decorated bedrooms – with own entrance – are vast, comfortably furnished (plus good mattresses) and impeccably clean, and the restful gardens cover one whole hectare. A generous breakfast is served on the terrace in fine weather. Madame, open and welcoming, willingly chats to guests in her big warm kitchen and enjoys their travellers' tales. You are in the country yet so near the buzz of Carcassonne while the dreamy Canal du Midi and the vineyards offer their seductively parallel alternatives.
Gîte space for 5 people.

rooms	3: 1 double, 1 triple, 1 suite for 5, all with shower & wc.
price	€55-€60 for two.
dinner	Choice of restaurants nearby.
closed	Rarely.
directions	On A61 exit Carcassonne-West to Salvaza airport; stay on D119 for approx. 4km more. Sign on left.

Isabelle Clayette
Domaine des Castelles,
11170 Caux et Sauzens, Aude
tel (0)4 68 72 03 60
fax (0)4 68 72 03 60

Your admirable hosts have saved this utterly romantic place, a near-ruin of an ancestral château, by dint of sheer crusading aristocratic grit, intelligent research and hard manual work. The Viscount, a self-taught master builder, even regilded the lofty baroque ceilings. There are 40 rooms and four ghosts; Madame can recount pre-Revolutionary family lore for hours; every piece of furniture tells a tale, personal, ancestral or just quirky; the cedars are regal, the river peaceful, breakfast luxurious with grandmama's fine silver. Guests have the privilege of the best renovations: two fine *salons*, huge, elegant bedrooms. Exceptional.

rooms	2: 1 double with bath & wc, 1 double with private bath & wc.
price	€115 for two.
dinner	Restaurant 50 metres.
closed	Christmas holidays.
directions	A61 for Carcassone; exit Villefranche de Lauragais for Gardouch; cross Canal du Midi; left D625, 10km. In St Michel left cross bridge; château on left.

Vicomte & Vicomtesse Vincent de La Panouse
Le Château,
1 rue du Pont de l'Hers,
11410 St Michel de Lanès, Aude

tel	(0)4 68 60 31 80
fax	(0)4 68 60 79 73
e-mail	chateausaintmichel@tiscali.fr
web	www.chateausaintmichel.com

LANGUEDOC · ROUSSILLON

Rigby has lovingly renovated the old pharmacy, preserving the elegant oak staircase where theatre posters clothe the red walls, the sitting-room marble fireplace (music scores on these walls), the beautiful wooden fireplace in the warm green dining room. Masses of antiques and works of art, but the house feels very lived in. French windows lead to the oh-so-peaceful garden, a two-part paradise: swimming pool on one side and formal box hedging on the other with deep borders, shingle paths, shady trees and the relaxing sound of running water. Rigby is intelligent, amusing and incredibly artistic – you will enjoy being here.

rooms	4: 1 twin, 3 doubles, all with bath or shower & wc.
price	€55-€60 for two.
dinner	€25, with wine; restaurant 1km.
closed	Rarely.
directions	From A61 exit 22 to Bram. At r'bout follow signs for Centre Ville; right at lights; 200m on right.

Rigby Holmes Field
Le Lierre,
2 avenue Ernest Léotard,
11150 Bram, Aude

tel	(0)4 68 76 52 01
fax	(0)4 68 76 60 30
e-mail	lelierrebram@aol.com
web	www.lelierre.com

There are donkeys and goats roaming around and, as this is definitely Cathar country, the rooms are named after Cathar castles. They are ordered rather than cosy but the cool impression of alarm clocks and televisions is dispelled by the Ropers' warm personal attention and the library of 1,000 books, many on the Cathars, many on cookery. Breakfast is hearty with several types of bread, honey, cheese, home-made cakes and jams. Supper could be grilled salmon with lemon sauce and Madame's crême caramel. Nearby are fortified Carcassonne, medieval Foix and Mirepoix. The setting is wonderful.

rooms	3: 2 doubles, 1 twin, all with shower & wc (& children's room).
price	€56-€59 for two.
dinner	€21 with wine, by arrangement.
closed	Rarely.
directions	From Limoux D620 for Chalabre 7km; fork right D626 for Mirepoix to Peyrefitte. Signs from village.

Jean-Pierre &
Marie-Claire Ropers
Domaine de Couchet,
11230 Peyrefitte du Razès, Aude

tel	(0)4 68 69 55 06
fax	(0)4 68 69 55 06
e-mail	jean.pierre.ropers@fnac.net
web	domainedecouchet.free.fr

LANGUEDOC · ROUSSILLON

Beautifully converted Sauzette, resplendent in huge beams, open fireplace and impeccable taste, has five pretty rooms (one for disabled), utter quiet to relax into and wonderful walks around. A superb hostess, Diana is lively, attentive and a great cook, though meals, served in the enormous dining room or outside, have been known to run late. She and Chris revel in the area, its birdlife, wild flowers, history and wine. They have lovely children (and well-behaved large dogs) and give language courses in winter. And all this just 5km from Carcassonne, 10km from an 18-hole golf course. *Minimum 2 nights May-September.*

rooms	5: 3 doubles, 1 twin, 1 triple, all with bath or shower & wc.
price	€58-€67 for two
dinner	€26 with wine, by arrangement.
closed	January & November.
directions	From Carcassonne D142 to Cazilhac. Left opp. Mairie D56 for Villefloure (bear left at cemetery); right fork at wine bottle for 2km; left at Sauzette sign.

Chris Gibson & Diana Warren
Ferme de la Sauzette,
Route de Villefloure, Cazilhac,
11570 Palaja, Aude

tel	(0)4 68 79 81 32
fax	(0)4 68 79 65 99
e-mail	info@lasauzette.com
web	www.lasauzette.com

The 'House on a Hill' overlooks medieval Carcassonne, just a short kilometre through the vines. A quiet and sumptuous haven from bustling postcard-sellers, ablaze with colour inside and out, full of pictures, lovely old furniture and treasures (hats, handmade pots, straw sandals). The wonderfully festooned bedrooms have bathrooms to match – one with an extra-big shower. Madame is open and generous, serves a fantastic array of home-made jams at breakfast on the terrace and is helped by her daughter who also made the striking coffee table of polished cement and iron. *Gîte space for 4 people.*

rooms	4 + 1 apartment: 4 doubles, 1 apartment for 4, all with shower or bath & wc.
price	€57-€77 for two.
dinner	€25 with wine, by arrangement.
closed	December-February.
directions	Go to Carcassonne Cité main gate, left, pass cemetery on right; follow Chambres d'Hôtes signs for 1km along narrow lane through vineyards. Well signposted.

	Mme Nicole Galinier
	La Maison sur la Colline,
	Sainte Croix,
	11000 Carcassonne, Aude
tel	(0)4 68 47 57 94
fax	(0)4 68 47 57 94
e-mail	nicole.galinier@wanadoo.fr
web	www.lamaisonsurlacolline.com

map: 16 entry: 680

LANGUEDOC · ROUSSILLON

Coming in from the magnificent gardens, you catch a wonderful smell of herbs as you walk through the house. The happy new owners, educated, well-travelled and charming, moved here from east France for a more relaxing way of life and climate. Using exquisite taste, they have combined original 18th-century elegances with new necessities in big bedrooms and bathrooms of pure luxury, each with its own lovely colour scheme. Outside, there are shaded spots for all, a superb 150-year-old cedar, olive trees and a salt-water swimming-pool surrounded by roses with covered terrace for relaxing. A place of great beauty.

rooms	5: 1 twin, 3 doubles, 1 suite for 4, all with bath, shower & wc.
price	€80-€150 for two; 2 nights min. high season.
dinner	Restaurants in Carcassonne.
closed	January-February.
directions	From A61 exit 23 for Mazamet; at r'bout D620 for Villalier; after 1.5km, towards Villedubert; on right, through wrought-iron gates.

	Christophe & Catherine Pariset
	Domaine Saint Pierre de Trapel,
	11620 Villemoustaussou, Aude
tel	(0)4 68 77 00 68
fax	(0)4 68 77 01 68
e-mail	cpariset@trapel.com
web	www.trapel.com

map: 16 entry: 681

With all her energy, Sally has turned her 17th-century coaching inn into a balanced marriage of solid old French base and modern inspiration. Having lived in England and America, where she was an interior designer, she then adopted France and her sense of style permeates the old house in a comfortable mix of antique and contemporary. She is also a superb cook, making delicious Mediterranean-inspired dishes with the best local produce, provides all possible goodies in her big, well-furnished bedrooms and loves to share her passion for, and books on, history and travel. *Children over 12 welcome. 2 nights minimum June-September.*

rooms	3: 2 doubles, 1 suite for 4, all with bath & wc.
price	€69 for two; suite €114.
dinner	€30 with wine, by arrangement.
closed	Rarely.
directions	From Carcassonne N113 to Trèbes; left D610 to Homps; left D910 to Olonzac; follow signs to Pépieux; next to church.

Sally Worthington
Le Vieux Relais,
1 rue de l'Étang,
11700 Pépieux, Aude
tel (0)4 68 91 69 29
fax (0)4 68 91 65 49
e-mail sally.worthington@wanadoo.fr
web perso.wanadoo.fr/carrefourbedbreakfast/

So you want the peace but not the deep countryside? Here you have it. Sheltered behind stone walls, by the château in the middle of this pretty village – a brief drive from the medieval town of Minerve – La Marelle became a school in the 19th century, when the one huge reception room was the old refectory. Nicole and Réné are new to B&B and obviously love it, especially the cooking. Their daughter is away at the École des Beaux Arts but pops home at weekends to make delicious pâtisserie. Most rooms have old terracotta tiles – the family room in palest pink is especially appealing.

rooms	5: 4 doubles, 1 family room, all with bath or shower & wc.
price	€50 for two.
dinner	€19 with wine, by arrangement.
closed	Rarely.
directions	Exit A61 at Carcassone Est; D610 for Marseillette & Puichéric; 23.5km, left for La Redorte; signs.

René & Nicole Bascou
La Marelle,
19 avenue du Minervois,
11700 La Redorte, Aude
tel (0)4 68 91 59 30
fax (0)4 68 91 59 30
e-mail la-marelle11@wanadoo.fr
web perso.wanadoo.fr/lamarelle/

The big inviting bedrooms – called *Syrah*, *Chardonnay*... to reflect Jacques' passion for his wild and wonderful Cathar country and its wines – have a superb feeling of space and light. Divine smells rise from the kitchen where Françoise bakes cakes to be served for tomorrow's breakfast on the stone terrace that leads to the garden. She so clearly loves having guests to cook for and chat to. Wide stone stairs, old pieces of furniture and soothing colours make this house most comfortable and welcoming. "A little corner of Paradise", reported one guest – and excellent value. *Minimum 3 nights July-August. Gîte space for 6 people.*

rooms 5: 4 doubles, 1 twin, with bath or shower & wc.
price €61-€65 for two.
dinner €23 with wine, by arrangement.
closed Rarely.
directions From A61 exit 25 for Lézignan; D212 for Fabrezan (back over A61); D106 to Ferrals les Corbières; D161 to Boutenac; signs in village.

Françoise & Jacques Camel
La Bastide des Corbières,
17 rue de la Révolution,
11200 Boutenac, Aude
tel (0)4 68 27 20 61
fax (0)4 68 27 62 71
e-mail bastide.corbieres@wanadoo.fr
web perso.wanadoo.fr/bastide.corbieres

map: 16 entry: 684

LANGUEDOC · ROUSSILLON

It feels almost Moroccan, this old Catalan house, as it unfolds onto its exposed stone and beams, pine floors and terracotta tiles. Airy, well-equipped bedrooms and the upstairs *salon* (music and books) look out to great wild hills, to the sea, or to the vineyards. Your host, an ex-professional trumpet player, really knows his regional wines, which are served with dinner (he's an excellent cook). It's perfect after the delights of Collioure, cloisters and Cathar castles (Spain, sea and mountains are all 40 minutes away); and there's a pool. *Main house occasionally available to rent. Gîte space for 2-12 people.*

rooms 3: 1 double, 1 twin, 1 suite for 4, all with shower or bath & wc.
price €52.50-€55 for two; suite €85 for 3-4.
dinner €22 with wine, by arrangement.
closed Rarely.
directions From A9 exit 42 on D612 west for Thuir. Just before Thuir D615 south to Fourques; D2 west 11km to Caixas (on right). Next to church.

Ian Mayes
Mas Saint Jacques,
66300 Caixas, Pyrénées-Orientales
tel (0)4 68 38 87 83
fax (0)4 68 38 87 83
e-mail masstjacq@aol.com

map: 16 entry: 685

The Bethells have created a haven of Pyrenean-Scottish hospitality among some of Europe's wildest, remotest landscapes just 15 minutes walk from lively Céret. In the magical, lush garden, the family parrot may flit with you among the intimate sitting areas where views dazzle up to snowy Canigou or down to the sea. Super, romantic rooms have original works of art and bright scatter cushions, two of them even promise the bliss of a private terrace for breakfast, delivered by Kim – a very warm and lovely person. And for dinner, there's the famous Terrasse au Soleil. *Children welcome with parental supervision (pool).*

rooms	6: 3 doubles, 1 twin/double, 2 suites all with shower & wc.
price	€84-€130 for two.
dinner	Excellent restaurant 400m or choice in village; BBQ available.
closed	December-January.
directions	A9 to Spain, last exit before border; into Céret for Centre Ville then for Hôtel La Terrasse au Soleil. House 400m after hotel, on left.

Kim & Gill Bethell
La Châtaigneraie,
Route de Fontfrède,
66400 Céret, Pyrénées-Orientales

tel	(0)4 68 87 21 58
fax	(0)4 68 87 68 16
e-mail	gill&kim@ceret.net
web	www.ceret.net

LANGUEDOC · ROUSSILLON

Hand-painted crockery, local-woven fabrics, hand-made beds, antique farm furniture: every detail has been lovingly thought out, every piece particularly chosen by this young couple who have poured their hearts into a dream place lost among the Pyrenean foothills, the horse-herded meadows before, the Canigou range beyond. Amazing hospitality – and two toddlers – with fabulous Catalan food round the pool (people come from Barcelona for the privilege) as you gaze at the snow-capped mountain tops; old stone walls, bright colours, bathrooms with character inside; and everywhere an incredible sense of space.

rooms	1 double with shower & wc.
price	€46 for two.
dinner	€15 with wine, by arrangement.
closed	July & August.
directions	From A9 exit 43 for 26km; 6km after Arles sur Tech left for St Laurent de Cerdans 6km; D64 right for Serralongue 1km; track on left at sign.

Emmanuelle Prats
& Patrick Duboux
Mas del Faig,
La Forge del Mitg,
66260 St Laurent de Cerdans,
Pyrénées-Orientales

tel	(0)4 68 39 53 91
e-mail	emmanuelle.prats@wanadoo.fr
web	www.masdelfaig.com

A piece of paradise. The climate: Mediterranean. The setting: high, rural, hidden, silent, in the nature-rich Monts d'Ardèche park. The views: long, of mountain peaks, inspiring. The house: of stone, and wood from the surrounding chestnut forests, gently restored, light, open, lovely. Bedrooms: sunny, just right. Food: organic, home-grown, imaginative, lots of honey. Your warm, trusting hosts are quickly your friends. Marie sings; Gil makes beautiful furniture – see their monumental dining table – and keeps bees; cool, clear music plays. There's lots more: come up the long narrow road to walk, talk, and believe us.

RHÔNE VALLEY · ALPS

In the valley where once horn-helmetted Gauls harassed Roman legions, the country's greatest chefs now reign; among the chilly peaks above, the marmot warms his furry cockles with Savoy's richly gooey fondue.

rooms	3: 1 double, 1 triple, 1 suite for 5, all with shower & wc.
price	€48 for two.
dinner	€19 with wine, by arrangement.
closed	Christmas.
directions	From Aubenas N102 for Le Puy 8.5km. At Lalevade left to Jaujac centre. By Café des Loisirs cross river & follow signs 4km along narrow mountain road.

Marie & Gil Florence
Les Roudils,
07380 Jaujac, Ardèche
tel (0)4 75 93 21 11
fax (0)4 75 93 21 11

The high-walled garden is a dream where hibiscus, oleander, mallows and vines rampage, nothing is too kempt and statues can take you by surprise. It has secret corners and a perfect breakfast terrace with splendid pots against the pale stone wall. Indoors, Madame plays soothing classical music so the antics of Ivan the dachshund don't impinge.
A gently friendly hostess, she brought her children up here and creates a family atmosphere. The guest room's fireplace can be lit to make the fine red and blue tiled floor cosier, its antique bookshelves are stuffed with books, the spot of damp is due for repair. A good hideaway.

rooms	1 double with shower & wc.
price	€46 for two.
dinner	€15 with wine, by arrangement. Good auberge in village.
closed	Rarely.
directions	From A7 exit Bollène to Pt St Esprit; N86 for Bourg St Andéol; in St Just, Rue de Versailles opp. church; house with big gates 100m on right.

Jacqueline Crozier
Quartier Versailles,
07700 St Just d'Ardèche, Ardèche
tel (0)4 75 04 60 52

RHÔNE VALLEY · ALPS

Honey and lavender scent this glorious spot; let the wild sun-baked granite and lush little valleys be your playground, or a cradle for total relaxation. Bring boots, bike, canoe – the Gorges de l'Ardèche are five miles away – and watch out for wild boar (a vast trophy adorns the dining room). The splendours are outside; inside, the handsome farmhouse is family plain and simple and each room has the rare privilege of its own terrace. Monsieur has elevated 'home brew' to a new plane, making aperitifs and digestifs to go with his energetic lady's specialities or tapas dinners, eaten *en famille*. Quiet, natural simplicity.

rooms	4: 3 doubles, 1 family room, all with shower & wc.
price	€45 for two.
dinner	€16 with wine, by arrangement.
closed	Rarely.
directions	From Bourg St Andéol D4 for Vallon Pont d'Arc to St Remèze centre; D362 for Gras. Sign on right.

Sylvette & Gérard Mialon
La Martinade,
07700 St Remèze, Ardèche
tel (0)4 75 98 89 42
fax (0)4 75 04 36 30
e-mail sylvetlm@aol.com
web www.angelfire.com/la/lamartinade/

The drive up is spectacular – go gently. Once there, gasp at the view, then stay and unwind among the flower-tumbled terraces. The 400-year-old house, a haven of unpretentious cosmopolitan elegance hugging its courtyard, has super old-new, light-filled, balconied bedrooms, a fine vaulted *salon*, good art on the walls, a small indoor pool, solarium and sauna and fabulous walking. Henri and Jacote have spared nothing to renovate their amazing house; relaxed and interesting hosts who love sharing their space, they provide excellent food – home-made sorbets to die for – with real conversation. Oh, and 20 jams for breakfast.

rooms	6: 2 doubles, 2 twins, 2 family rooms, all with shower & wc.
price	€69-€75 for two.
dinner	€20 with wine, by arrangement.
closed	December-April, except by arrangement.
directions	From Joyeuse D203 for Valgorge. At Pont du Gua cross bridge; narrow paved road up hillside to La Roche (10 hairpins in 3km!).

Henri & Jacote Rouvière
La Petite Cour Verte,
07110 La Roche Beaumont, Ardèche

tel	(0)4 75 39 58 88
fax	(0)4 75 39 43 00
e-mail	henri.rouviere@wanadoo.fr
web	www.lapetitecourverte.com

A charmingly typical Napoleon III manor, square and confident in its five acres of superb parkland and the famous Troisgros restaurant just 8km away make this a place to spend some time. There's a tennis court and great walking (all levels) to create an appetite for the local gastronomy. You are guests in a family home, your antique-furnished bedroom is relaxedly formal, the bath is a claw-footed marvel (plenty of towels and bathrobes go with it) and Madame a gentle, generous widow. She loves sharing a welcome cup and guiding one to the hidden delights of this lovely area. *Ask about pets. Gîte space for 2-3 people.*

rooms	2: 1 double with shower & wc; 1 suite for 3-4 with bath & wc.
price	€72 for two; suite €108.
dinner	Choice of restaurants within 3km; Trois Gros at Roanne, 8km.
closed	15 November-15 March.
directions	From Roanne D53 for 8km. Right into village & follow signs.

Mme Gaume
Domaine de Champfleury,
42155 Lentigny, Loire

tel	(0)4 77 63 31 43
fax	(0)4 77 63 31 43

Once upon a time, kindly Anne-Marie lived in a big town. One day she found her dream house in the Auvergne near deep mysterious woods and singing streams so she left the city, lovingly restored and hand-coloured her house, installed her old family furniture and opened the door so that visitors could share her dream. So, after a delicious supper, before the roaring fire, Anne-Marie may treat you to a fairytale of her own making. (She also offers breathing and relaxation courses.) Thus you will all live happily ever after and never forget this exceptional woman.

rooms	5: 2 triples, 2 twins, 1 double, all with shower & wc.
price	€50-€65 for two.
dinner	€25 with wine, by arrangement.
closed	Rarely.
directions	From A72 exit 4 D53 E to Champoly. D24 E to St Marcel d'Urfé; D20 S for St Martin la Sauveté & follow signs.

Anne-Marie Hauck
Il fut un temps,
Les Gouttes,
42430 St Marcel d'Urfé, Loire

tel	(0)4 77 62 52 19
fax	(0)4 77 62 52 19
e-mail	anne-marie.hauck@wanadoo.fr
web	www.eazyweb.co.uk/ilfut

map: 12 entry: 693

RHÔNE VALLEY · ALPS

It took 150 tons of tiles to restore the two towers and tons of loving care from charming young Emmanuel, whose partner Jean-Luc works in town, to restore the brilliantly intricate parquet floor. One of the bedrooms is panelled in cherrywood; one has a royal blue baldaquin flecked with golden fleur-de-lys; all are generous and uplifting, each with a fireplace and a big jacuzzi bathroom. And just enough of just the right furniture. Built between the 10th and 16th centuries with fairy-tale turrets in a natural clearing and views down the valley, it is so peaceful a place that it might almost be an hallucination.

rooms	4 doubles, all with bath or shower & wc.
price	€100-€115 for two.
dinner	€25 with wine, by arrangement.
closed	Rarely.
directions	From A6 exit Belleville D37 for Beaujeu to St Vincent; left D9 to Quincié, Marchampt, Lamure; at end of Lamure, lane opp. 'terrain de sport' for Pramenoux.

Emmanuel Baudouin & Jean-Luc Plasse
Château de Pramenoux,
69870 Lamure sur Azergues, Rhône

tel	(0)4 74 03 16 43
fax	(0)4 74 03 16 28
e-mail	pramenoux@aol.com
web	www.chateau-de-pramenoux.com

map: 12 entry: 694

Your genuinely charming hosts are new to B&B – Madame used to be a clothes designer, Monsieur a computer expert. Their sandy 15th-century stone house and its four neighbours all have softly pleasing Beaujolais views and super bedrooms with exquisitely embroidered antique bed linen in rich strong colours, plain painted walls and exposed beams. A claw-footed bathtub and double hand basins are an extra luxury. Manon Roland – she who uttered that famous death cry "Oh Liberty, how many crimes have been committed in thy name?" – once lived here. These days the house is a place of peace.

rooms	2 + 1 apartment: 2 doubles with bath or shower & wc; 1 family apartment with shower & wc.
price	€45-€75 for two.
dinner	Good choice of restaurants nearby.
closed	December-February.
directions	From A6 exit 31 at Villefranche D38 for Bagnols; D38e for Theizé; signs.

Stéfanie & Marcel Stantina
La Ferme du Saint,
69620 Theizé, Rhône

tel	(0)4 74 71 15 48
e-mail	lafermedusaint@wanadoo.fr
web	perso.wanadoo.fr/lafermedusaint/

RHÔNE VALLEY · ALPS

Orange trees in the *orangerie*, an obelisk amid the topiary chessmen, two spectacular Lebanon cedars, wine from the estate, beautiful 17th-century beams to guard your sleep… and more. Your hosts, much-travelled, sophisticated and informal, love sharing their enthusiasm for the area and its wines and will organise tastings, including their own. Bedrooms, pure château from pastel to bold with hints of modernity, some with fine carved door frames, are eclectically and elegantly furnished (Olivier's brother is an antique dealer) and dinner is certainly worth booking. If you want to sample *le grand style*, this is for you.

rooms	5: 3 doubles, 2 suites, all with bath & wc.
price	€96-€101 for two.
dinner	€32 with wine, by arrangement.
closed	Rarely.
directions	From north A6 exit 'Belleville'; N6 for Lyon 10km; right D43 to Arnas. Through village; château on right after 1.5km.

Alexandra & Olivier du Mesnil
Les Jardins de Longsard,
Château de Longsard,
69400 Arnas, Rhône

tel	(0)4 74 65 55 12
fax	(0)4 74 65 03 17
e-mail	longsard@wanadoo.fr
web	www.longsard.com

Come and join this family's charming, authentically aristocratic life: no prissiness (two screened-off bathrooms) in their big townhouse, just unselfconscious style. The richly-decorated golden *salon* has a piano, books and open fireplace. The richly-stocked garden has a pool, a summerhouse, a large terrace, 150 species of trees, an organic vegetable garden and a statue of *Grand-père*. Madame is too busy cooking to eat with guests but welcomes company as she's preparing dinner. Children love it – there are toys and the hosts' own children to play with.

rooms 4: 2 doubles, 2 twins, all with bath or shower & wc.
price €65 for two.
dinner €20, wine €12, by arrangement.
closed Rarely.
directions From A6 exit Macon Sud or Belleville; N6 to Romanèche & Lancié. In village for Fleurie into Square Les Pasquiers.

Jacques & Laurence Gandilhon
Les Pasquiers,
69220 Lancié, Rhône
tel (0)4 74 69 86 33
fax (0)4 74 69 86 57
e-mail ganpasq@aol.com

RHÔNE VALLEY · ALPS

An amazing avenue of plane trees takes you to this exceptional house and hostess. Madame is a live wire, laughing, enthusing, giving – unforgettable; her house is as elegantly colourful as she is. Climb the grand stairs to your splendid château-style room, revel in Persian carpets, trompe-l'œil, antiques, fresh flowers. Sitting beside Shakespeare and the candles, Madame pours tea from silver into porcelain and artfully moves the breakfast butter as the sun rises; at night she'll light your bedside lamp, leaving a book open at a carefully chosen page for you to read after a game of (French) Scrabble. Inimitably fine…

rooms 2: 2 doubles both with bath or shower & wc.
price €79 for two.
dinner Good restaurant 3km.
closed Rarely.
directions From Bourg en Bresse N83 towards Lyon. At Servas right D64 towards Condeissiat 5km; left at sign Le Marmont: plane-tree avenue. Don't go to St André.

Geneviève & Henri Guido-Alhéritière
Manoir de Marmont,
01960 St André sur Vieux Jonc, Ain
tel (0)4 74 52 79 74

Anne-Marie, outgoing and a delight to talk to, makes this place – come if you want to bathe in genuine French mountain hospitality. She speaks English, keeps horses, organises treks to the Alpine pastures. The mood here is rustic and characterful; don't expect spick or span. Exceptional walking: you may see chamois and marmots if you go far enough. The chalet has a mini-museum of olden-day Alpine farm life. Dinner (served late to allow you time to settle) is eaten at the long wooden table, with grand-mama's recipes cooked on a wood-fired stove – and the half-board formula includes absolutely everything.

rooms	5: 1 triple with shower & wc; 4 doubles sharing 2 showers & 2 wcs.
price	Half-board only €34.50 per person.
dinner	Dinner with wine included in price.
closed	Rarely.
directions	From Thonon les Bains, D26 for Bellevaux. House 2km before Bellevaux on left; sign.

Anne-Marie Félisaz-Denis
Le Châlet,
La Cressonnière,
74470 Bellevaux, Haute-Savoie
tel (0)4 50 73 70 13
fax (0)4 50 73 70 13

map: 13 entry: 699

RHÔNE VALLEY · ALPS

Jenny came to France from South Africa 40 years ago, fell in love with the place and stayed; a warm, friendly person, she is deliriously happy in her small chalet among the high Alpine meadows and waterfalls. There's walking for all levels in spectacular scenery, white water rafting on the river, excellent cross-country and Alpine skiing, sleepy people-watching with the locals. The bedsitter in the wood-lined lower floor of the chalet has just enough room for a kitchenette, shower, loo and sofabed – all perfectly finished, warm and charming with a little terrace outside its own entrance. *Gîte space for 5 people.*

rooms	2: 1 double (sofabed), 1 single (child) with shower, wc & kitchenette.
price	€49 for two.
dinner	Self-catering possible. Restaurants walking distance.
closed	Rarely.
directions	From Samoëns D907 to Sixt Fer à Cheval; over 2nd bridge D29 opp. War Memorial; after sign 'Maison Neuve', 2nd right; go to end; No. 14 last on right.

Jenny Vanderplank
Chalets de Sixt 14,
Maison Neuve,
74740 Sixt Fer à Cheval,
Haute-Savoie
tel (0)4 50 34 10 55
fax (0)4 50 34 10 55
e-mail jennyvplank@wanadoo.fr
web www.pour-les-vacances.com/shanti

map: 13 entry: 700

Madame has boundless energy, is a great walker, adores her mountain retreat in this lovely valley and cooks very well indeed. Her chalet rooms, all wood-clad of course, are bright and welcoming in blue, white and orange; they have unusually high ceilings, good storage and plenty of space. The open-plan living area looks out of big windows to the small garden and the mixture of old and modern furniture plus bits and pieces of all sorts gives the whole place a comfortable, family feel. With Annecy so close and Geneva just an hour away, it's ideal for a mountain holiday.

rooms	3: 1 double with shower & separate wc; 2 doubles share bath & separate wc.
price	€40 for two.
dinner	€15, with wine; restaurant 800m.
closed	Rarely.
directions	From Annecy D909 to Thones; D12 for Serraval & Manigod; 200m after 'Welcome to Manigod' sign, left at cross; chalet on left.

Josette Barbaud
Proveyroz,
74230 Manigod, Haute-Savoie
tel (0)4 50 44 95 25
fax (0)4 50 44 95 25

map: 13 entry: 701

RHÔNE VALLEY · ALPS

The Brownes have built a hymn to wood, outside and in, plus lovely fabrics and furniture to make their new traditional chalet warm and reassuring. It has panoramic views south across the valley to rising green Alpine pastures and great rocky mountains. Guests have a room with doors to the garden and that fabulous view. Your hosts, retired contented travellers, are great fun, energetic and enthusiastic about their house, the 135km of marked mountain trails and their lovely Labradors, who enjoy the walking too. Delightful Annecy is just two dozen kilometres and a few bends away; Geneva is an hour. And the skiing's great.

rooms	1 twin with shower & wc.
price	€60 for two.
dinner	€20 with wine, by arrangement.
closed	Rarely.
directions	From Annecy D909 to Thônes; D12 for Serraval & Manigod; very shortly after, D16 to Manigod; through village, 1st left past garage; house 4th on right.

Colin & Alyson Browne
Les Murailles,
74230 Manigod, Haute-Savoie
tel (0)4 50 44 95 87
fax (0)4 50 44 95 87
e-mail colin.browne@wanadoo.fr

map: 13 entry: 702

Outside, the terrace is for viewing a land that reaches right across to the Jura peaks. Inside, the bedrooms – blue *Albanaise*, raspberry *Aixoise*, oak-beamed, four-postered *Écossaise* – are for loving the unostentatious luxury of fine fabrics and seductive bathrooms. The dining room is for indulging in a dazzling daily brunch. Warm-hearted and relaxed, Denyse and Bernard delight in entertaining, decorating and cooking: their occasional dinners are never forgotten. Beautiful Annecy with its gleaming lake, Chamonix-Mont Blanc, the towering Alps, swinging Geneva, are all nearby. *Gîte space for 3 people.*

rooms	3: 2 doubles, 1 twin, all with bath or shower & wc.
price	€120 for two.
dinner	€40 with wine, by arrangement.
closed	Rarely.
directions	From A41 exit Alby & Rumilly, N201 for Chambéry. In St Félix D53 at church; 300m past cemetery; left for Mercy to statue, right & immed. left, past farm & through gate.

Denyse & Bernard Betts
Les Bruyères,
Mercy,
74540 St Félix, Haute-Savoie
tel (0)4 50 60 96 53
fax (0)4 50 60 94 65

RHÔNE VALLEY · ALPS

A kind micro-climate reigns here: the mountains attract the clouds so the sun can beat a clear path to the door of the independent guest chalet with its no-frills, almost sparse blue and white rooms and bathrooms – smallish, simple and clean. The relaxed, friendly Martins know their area well and there are fabulous walks to be taken. Breakfast is in the airy dining room and for supper there's a kitchen in the guest chalet, or they can recommend restaurants; they'll babysit too. Outside, the garden is a pleasant surprise with swings and ropes for youngsters. Only 10km from Annecy. *Gîte space for 6 people.*

rooms	2 doubles in cottage, both with shower & wc.
price	€46 for two.
dinner	Self-catering possible.
closed	Rarely.
directions	From A41 exit Annecy Sud for Chambéry; at D16 right for Rumilly 10km; enter Marcellaz Albanais, immed. left D38 for Chapeiry 1km; right for Chaunu; 200m on right.

Claudie & Jean-Louis Martin
Chemin de Chaunu,
74150 Marcellaz Albanais,
Haute-Savoie
tel (0)4 50 69 73 04
fax (0)4 50 69 73 04
e-mail lac@cario.fr

The light, harmonious air in this old Savoyard farmhouse is created by stone and wood, white paint, dried flowers and country antiques – and it matches Madame's delightful, energetic presence. Now virtually retired from farming, Monsieur happily shares his great knowledge of the area, wines and mushrooming; they will do anything for you. Your sitting room has a half-moon window at floor level (the top of the old barn door), your big light bedroom has antique, new-mattressed, lace-covered beds and spotless glass-doored shower. A revelation to those who expect farms to be a bit scruffy.

rooms	3: 1 double, 2 twins, all with shower & wc (1 behind curtain).
price	€58–€59.50 for two.
dinner	Savoyard restaurant 3-4km.
closed	Rarely.
directions	From Annecy N201 for Geneva. 1km after Cruseilles, left D27 through Copponex; left at cemetery; signs to Chambres d'Hôtes Châtillon. House on left.

Suzanne & André Gal
La Bécassière,
Châtillon,
74350 Copponex, Haute-Savoie

tel	(0)4 50 44 08 94
fax	(0)4 50 44 08 94

RHÔNE VALLEY · ALPS

Overlooking the valley, vineyards and distant peaks, the 18th-century house, once the château's cottages and stables, has been a country cottage for years. Simone and Henry did some sensitive renovation, using old materials and recreating an authentic atmosphere, then they started doing B&B. They are still feeling their way, learning how much contact or privacy their guests expect, hunting for little tables and pieces of character to add to their very well-finished, mezzanined guest rooms – each has a small sitting area. Breakfast is in the pretty courtyard garden in summer. Excellent hosts and good value. *Gîte space for 4 people.*

rooms	2: 1 double, 1 twin, both with bath & wc.
price	€69 for two.
dinner	Good choice of restaurants 2-10km.
closed	November-Easter.
directions	A41 exit Aix les Bains D991 to Viuz; D56 right for Ruffieux; at r'bout head for Chessine & Chambres d'Hôtes.

Simone & Henry Collé
Chessine,
73310 Ruffieux, Savoie

tel	(0)4 79 54 52 35
fax	(0)4 79 54 52 35
e-mail	chessine@noealexinfo.com
web	www.chessine.fr.st

Château life is yours, once you have greeted the gentle Giant Danes and taken in the scale of La Terrosière. In the luxuriously converted stable block there are vast antique-furnished bedrooms (you may need a mounting block for the four-poster), brilliant bathrooms, a softly embracing living room with open fire, staff to wait on you and a *châtelaine* of charm and wit to make fine food, bring superb wines from her cellar and keep you company at table. Horses exercise in the school; a tennis court, fishing lake and heated spring-water pool beckon on the 100-acre estate. You won't regret a cent. Oh, and it's brunch, not breakfast.

rooms	3: 1 twin, 2 suites, all with bath and shower & wc. Possible to rent house with kitchenette.
price	€130-€140 for two.
dinner	€55 with wine, by arrangement.
closed	August, October & Christmas, except by arrangement.
directions	From Chambéry N504 N via Le Bourget du Lac through small tunnel to Chevelu; left D921 to St Paul. After r'bout, 1st left. On right about 1km along (large iron gates).

Mme Jeannine Conti
La Terrosière,
73170 St Paul sur Yenne, Savoie
tel (0)4 79 36 81 02
fax (0)4 79 36 81 02

RHÔNE VALLEY · ALPS

Mountains march past Mont Blanc and over into Italy, cows graze in the foreground – La Touvière is perfect for exploring this walkers' paradise. Myriam, bubbly and easy, adores having guests with everyone joining in the lively, lighthearted family atmosphere. In their typical old unsmart farmhouse, the cosy family room is the hub of life. Marcel is part-time home-improver, part-time farmer (just a few cows now). One room has a properly snowy valley view, the other overlooks the owners' second chalet, let as a gîte; both are a decent size, simple but not basic. And it's remarkable value. *Gîte space for 8 people.*

rooms	2 doubles, both with shower & wc.
price	€34 for two.
dinner	€14 with wine, by arrangement.
closed	Rarely.
directions	From Albertville N212 for Megève for 21km; after Flumet, left at Panoramic Hotel & follow signs to La Touvière.

Marcel & Myriam Marin-Cudraz
La Touvière,
73590 Flumet, Savoie
tel (0)4 79 31 70 11

Perched on the edge of a mountain, you have a superb view of peaks above and villages below, be you in your room, in the jacuzzi, or rolling in the snow after your sauna. Blazing fires, natural wood – all pure *Savoyard*. Plus big rooms and luxury bathrooms – such a treat. The televisions and the card phone in the hall give a slight 'hotelly' feel, but what matter? After a hearty breakfast your Franco-American hostess will gladly help you map out your itinerary – mountain-lake fishing in summer, skiing in winter, superb walking all year. *Gîte space for 9 people.*

rooms	6: 3 doubles, 3 suites for 4, all with bath or shower & wc.
price	€110-€160 for two.
dinner	€30 with wine, by arrangement.
closed	October-November; May-June.
directions	From Bourg St Maurice D902 for Val d'Isère through Ste Foy Tarentaise. After La Thuile left for Ste Foy Station & follow signs.

Nancy Tabardel & Jean Marc Fouquet
Yellow Stone Chalet,
Bonconseil Station,
73640 Ste Foy Tarentaise, Savoie

tel	(0)4 79 06 96 06
fax	(0)4 79 06 96 05
e-mail	yellowstone@wanadoo.fr
web	www.yellowstone-chalet.com

map: 13 entry: 709

RHÔNE VALLEY · ALPS

A year-round Alpine dream. In summer it's all flowers, birds and rushing streams… in winter you can ski cross-country, snow-walk or take the ski lift, just 500m away, to the vast ski field of Les Arcs. La Plagne and Val d'Isère are quite close too. Cooking takes place in the outside wood oven and the food is delicious. Your dynamic and friendly young hosts cater for children with early suppers, son Boris and daughter Clémence may be playmates for yours, and Claude will babysit in the evening. Guests have their own comfortable dayroom with a refrigerator. *Discount on ski hire and passes.*

rooms	2: 1 double for 2-3, 1 suite for 4-5, both with shower & wc.
price	€40 for two.
dinner	€14 with wine, by arrangement.
closed	Rarely.
directions	From Albertville N90 to Moutiers; on for Bourg St Maurice. Right D87E to Peisey Nancroix; left to Peisey centre; follow green arrows. 9km from main road to house.

Claude Coutin & Franck Chenal
Maison Coutin,
T12 Peisey,
73210 Peisey Nancroix, Savoie

tel	(0)4 79 07 93 05
fax	(0)4 79 04 29 23
e-mail	maisoncoutin@aol.com
web	www.maison-coutin.fr.st

map: 13 entry: 710

We like to celebrate tradition in our special places, particularly long-held tradition. The most traditional of the lot, this abode has kept its raw, down-to-earth Alpine style for millennia. Secure, snug and authentically stony under the wing of a rocky crag (avalanches have been reported during its long life but it has managed to dodge destruction every time), it is testament to the determined nature of its architects: undaunted by weather, distance, inhospitable geography and poor parking – just as you will need to be to make the most of this confidently unadorned mountain retreat. Bring a friend for extra warmth.

rooms	Two: well, let us call them 'spaces'. Each has a roof; one turfed, the other part-turfed.
price	Free – almost frighteningly so. Beware members of local animal tribes who may wish to share with you.
dinner	Bring your own wine (if you can carry it up the hill). Otherwise, the food here is either wildly vegetarian or comes on a catch-and-kill basis.
closed	Never, not a door in sight.
directions	Just keep going up that hill. It seems endless but, like all good things in life, this destination is well worth the trek.

Pierre du Roc
La Cave sans Vin,
Le Mont du Top,
99999 Les Pics de Granit, Rhône

tel	Pah!
fax	Bof!
e-mail	no-e-for-email@this_place.uc?
web	www.might-be-a.con

RHÔNE VALLEY · ALPS

Although this is not a working farm, it might as well be. The Garniers adore animals. They have seven Camargue horses (for stroking, not riding), ducks, chickens, turkeys, guinea fowl, a pig, two dogs and a cat! Albert is French, Jean-Margaret is English, she loves cooking and grows all her own vegetables. She also has a large collection of dolls from around the world. The classic Dauphinoise house is a thoroughly welcoming family home decorated in French country style with some modern pieces and a pretty garden; all this near a ramblingly attractive old village in rolling wooded countryside.

rooms	3: 2 triples, 1 twin, all with shower & wc.
price	€45 for two.
dinner	€15 with wine, by arrangement.
closed	Rarely.
directions	From A43 exit La Tour du Pin to N6; right at r'bout for Aix les Bains; left at lights at St Clair de la Tour. 3km for Dolomieu; Chambres d'Hotes signs.

Jean-Margaret & Albert Garnier
Le Traversoud,
38110 Faverges de la Tour, Isère

tel	(0)4 74 83 90 40
fax	(0)4 74 83 93 71
e-mail	garnier.traversoud@free.fr

The Barrs are Scottish and Irish but have lived in France for more than 25 years so are pretty well French too. Mary, an easy, relaxed person, loves flowers and helps Greig with his wooden-toy business in winter. They have renovated their old farmhouse to give it an English feel yet preserve its utterly French character: the atmosphere is light, airy and warm as well as solid and reassuring. In the big guest rooms, the beds have excellent mattresses, the views are rural, the bathrooms (one en suite, one on the landing) super with lots of pretty china bits. A very civilised place to stay.

rooms	2 twins/doubles, each with bath & wc.
price	€46-€56 for two.
dinner	€23 with wine, by arrangement.
closed	September-December.
directions	From A43 exit 8, N85 through Nivolas. Left D520 for Succieu. After 2km, left D56 through Succieu for St Victor; 3km; sign for Longeville on right; farm at top of steep hill.

Mary & Greig Barr
Longeville,
38300 Succieu, Isère
tel (0)4 74 27 94 07
fax (0)4 74 92 09 21
e-mail mary.barr@free.fr

RHÔNE VALLEY · ALPS

The most caring and endearing of B&B owners: he, warmly humorous and humble about his excellent cooking abilities; she, generous and outgoing with lots of interesting talk. Built in 1646 as a fort high on a hill beside a spring that still runs through the shrubby garden, their superb old house is wrapped round a big green-clad courtyard. Inside, levels change, staircases abound, vast timbers span the dining room, guest rooms have separate entrances and floral papers, plush chairs and country antiques, impeccable bathrooms – and a bedhead from Hollywood in the best room. A deep country refuge 15 minutes from Lyon.

rooms	4: 3 doubles, 1 suite for 4, all with bath & wc.
price	€91-€119 for two.
dinner	€32 with wine, by arrangement.
closed	Rarely.
directions	From A7, A46 or A47 exit Chasse/Rhône; through large Centre Commercial; under railway; left for Trembas. (Will fax map or guide you to house.)

M & Mme Fleitou
Domaine de Gorneton,
712 chemin de Violans,
38670 Chasse sur Rhône, Isère
tel (0)4 72 24 19 15
fax (0)4 78 07 93 62
e-mail gorneton@wanadoo.fr
web www.gorneton.com

The original (modernised…) 17th-century kitchen complete with wood-fired range, stone sink and cobbled floor on the ground floor of the tower is where Hélène makes her own bread, honey and jams and prepares meals using vegetables from her garden; she even makes her own aperitifs (the *vin d'orange* is superb). And there'll be wine from the Rossis' own vineyard near Montpellier. The château has loads of character – enormous rooms, high heavy-beamed ceilings, large windows overlooking the valley – and the bedrooms are up an ancient stone spiral staircase which sets the imagination reeling.

rooms 5: 2 doubles, 2 twins, 1 family room, all with bath or shower & wc.
price €54 for two.
dinner €17 with wine, by arrangement. Self-catering possible.
closed Rarely.
directions From Grenoble A51 or N75 for Sisteron 25km to r'bout; follow signs to St Martin de la Cluze. Château signs in village.

Jacques & Hélène Rossi
Château de Paquier,
38650 St Martin de la Cluze, Isère
tel (0)4 76 72 77 33
fax (0)4 76 72 77 33
e-mail hrossi@club-internet.fr
web chateau.de.paquier.free.fr

RHÔNE VALLEY · ALPS

Opt for the simple country life at this friendly farm. In the family for over 100 years, it has gone back to using *biologique* (organic) methods. Madame calls this "acupuncture for the land" – she's also interested in feng shui. Meals of regional recipes are served family-style and include home-grown vegetables, fruit and eggs. Monsieur collects old farming artefacts and Madame, although always busy, finds time to chat with guests. The bedrooms are in a separate wing with modern interiors, interesting antique beds, florals, lace and candlewick. At the foot of the Vercors range, the setting is utter peace.

rooms 4: 1 twin, 1 double, 1 triple, 1 family room, all with shower or bath & wc.
price €40-€45 for two.
dinner €15, with wine; restaurants 3km.
closed Rarely.
directions From Romans D538 for Chabeuil. Leaving Alixan left by Boulangerie on D119; left again, Chambres d'Hôtes St Didier signs for 3km; farm on left.

Christiane & Jean-Pierre Imbert
Le Marais,
26300 St Didier de Charpey, Drôme
tel (0)4 75 47 03 50
e-mail imbert.jean-pierre@wanadoo.fr

A good stopover, high above the valley outside Valence, this 1970s villa is in something of a time warp: dark floral paper in hall, stairs and bedrooms, animal skins on floors and sofas, interesting modern sculptures in many corners. Your hostess is chatty (in French), enthusiastic and welcoming, a gift inherited from Armenian parents. Enjoy breakfast with home-made organic jam on the terrace and admire the magnificent chalk escarpments of the Vercors range (beyond less attractive Saint Marcel). Little traffic noise can be heard. *Careful: this is the B&B on the left-hand side of the road.*

rooms	2: 1 twin with shower & wc; 1 double with bath & wc.
price	€45-€51 for two.
dinner	Restaurants in village, 500m.
closed	Rarely.
directions	From A7 exit Valence Nord; through Bourg lès Valence; left N532 for Grenoble; exit to St Marcel; Place de la Mairie left; over Stop, under bridge, up hill (total 400m); house on LEFT round hairpin.

Marie-Jeanne Katchikian
La Pineraie,
383 chemin Bel Air,
26320 St Marcel lès Valence,
Drôme
tel (0)4 75 58 72 25
e-mail marie.katchikian@minitel.net

RHÔNE VALLEY · ALPS

This artistic, caring couple are deeply concerned with social and ecological issues and have renovated their farmhouse with sensitivity, using nothing but authentic materials. Art lovers will enjoy Mado's beautifully-made china dolls – and the summer courses. Guest quarters, in a separate building, have good rooms and handsome carpentry by her son. Organic meals with home-grown vegetables and fruit are served in the vaulted guest dining room or on the terrace. A special house with a very special atmosphere. *Minimum 2 nights. Gîte space for 15 people. Seminars for up to 15 people who may self-cater or be catered for.*

rooms	5: 4 doubles, 1 suite for 4, all with bath or shower & wc.
price	€42-€60 for two.
dinner	€15 with wine, by arrangement.
closed	Rarely.
directions	From Chabeuil, D538 for Crest 5km (ignore signs for Montvendre). Left at sign Maison d'Hôtes Art' Aime; house 700m on right next to Auberge-Restaurant sign.

Mado Goldstein & Bernard Dupont
Les Dourcines,
26120 Montvendre, Drôme
tel (0)4 75 59 24 27
fax (0)4 75 59 24 27

Here is the grandmother we all dream of, a delightful woman who cossets her guests, putting flowers, sweets and fruit in the bedrooms. This old stone farmhouse facing the Vercors mountains is definitely a family home and meals of regional dishes with local wine, prepared by daughter Élisabeth, can be very jolly with family, friends and guests all sharing the long wooden table in the kitchen. And there's a *menu curieux* using ancient forgotten vegetables! The roomy, old-fashioned, much-loved bedrooms have handsome walnut *armoires* breathe a comfortable, informal air. The whole place has a timeless appeal.

rooms	3 triples, both with bath or shower & wc.
price	€40 for two.
dinner	€15 with wine, by arrangement.
closed	Rarely.
directions	From A6 exit Valence Sud on D68 to Chabeuil. There, cross river; left on D154 for Combovin 5km; signs.

Mme Madeleine Cabanes
Les Péris,
D154 - Route de Combovin,
26120 Châteaudouble, Drôme

tel (0)4 75 59 80 51
fax (0)4 75 59 48 78

map: 12 entry: 719

RHÔNE VALLEY · ALPS

Madame's kindliness infuses her home, one that at first glance is coy about its age and charms. Her eventful life has nourished a wicked sense of humour but no bitterness and she is a natural storyteller (she'll show you the photographs too). She alone is worth the detour and the slightly fading carpets and small shower rooms become incidental after a short while. Enjoy, instead, the pretty bedrooms, the peace and birdlife of the lush leafy garden which shelters the house from the road and relish breakfast – organic honeys, home-made jams and cake, cheese – where the table is a picture in itself. *Gîte space for 7 people.*

rooms	3: 2 twins, 1 single/twin, all with shower & wc.
price	€45-€48 for two.
dinner	Restaurants 2-7km.
closed	Rarely.
directions	From A7 Valence Sud exit A49 for Grenoble. Exit 33 right D538a for Beaumont, 2.6km; right at sign Chambres d'Hôtes & Chambedeau; 600m on right, tarmac drive.

Mme Lina de Chivré-Dumond
Chambedeau,
26760 Beaumont lès Valence,
Drôme

tel (0)4 75 59 71 70
fax (0)4 75 59 75 24
e-mail linadechivredumond@minitel.net

map: 12 entry: 720

Francis has renovated the house with huge care, giving new life to old beams and tiles – the stone cross-vaulting in the dining room is absolutely wonderful. He clearly knows about structures and loves his house. Jackie is immediately likeable too, an artist who really goes out of her way to make people feel at home. An organic vegetable garden produces the basics, plus fruit and eggs, for some superb meals. The rooms are perfectly simple, with tiled floors and Provençal print fabrics, and have their own entrance. Lively and charming people living in lovely countryside.

rooms	4: 1 double, 1 twin, 2 triples, all with bath or shower & wc.
price	€52-€60 for two.
dinner	By arrangement €19, good wine list.
closed	Occasionally.
directions	From Montélimar D540 E to La Batie Rolland (10km). In village left onto D134 for 2km for St Gervais; sign on right.

Francis & Jackie Monel
La Joie,
26160 La Batie Rolland, Drôme

tel	(0)4 75 53 81 51
fax	(0)4 75 53 81 51
e-mail	f.monel@infonie.fr
web	www.lajoie.fr

map: 17 entry: 721

Lavender and honey wafting, lawns sloping away to the shade of the woods, the swimming pool mountain-gazing, big rooms filling with light, parquet floors gleaming – a real Drôme treasure. The Pourras' informal style makes for happy meals: open-air breakfasts of home-made breads and jams, possibly *clafoutis maison*, in the shade of superb, mature trees; traditional dinners with local market-fresh ingredients (Madame will share her recipes). And quirky finds from the antiques and*brocante* world: hats, baskets, a tailor's dummy. It all adds up to a healthy lack of grandeur in a classically handsome setting.

rooms	5: 4 doubles, 1 family room, all with bath or shower & wc.
price	€69-€98 for two.
dinner	€22, wine €14.
closed	Rarely.
directions	From A7 exit Montélimar Nord for Dieulefit. House on left as you enter village.

Martine & Dan Pourras
Villa Mary,
16 allée des Promenades,
26220 Dieulefit, Drôme

tel	(0)4 75 46 89 19
fax	(0)4 75 46 30 23
e-mail	daniel.pourras@wanadoo.fr
web	www.guideweb.com/provence/bb/villa-mary

map: 17 entry: 722

So lovely, this ruined old *bergerie*, so beautifully revived: arches and vaults white-plastered, Greek-style, with deep cushions and not a straight line to hurt the eye – it's stylishly simple but not spartan. Madame, open, caring and as restful as her beautiful home, formerly a fashion/textile designer, now plans to teach History of Art and has a very fine feeling for space and light and the contemporary taste for things authentic and high-quality. Young cypresses line the drive, a big, old maple cools the garden and the grounds slope down to a valley of meadows and forests. Blissful and utterly peaceful. *Gîte space for 3.*

rooms	1 triple with bath & separate wc.
price	€70-€80 for two, €100 for four.
dinner	Available locally. Lunch €15 with glass of wine.
closed	During French school terms.
directions	From A7 exit Montélimar Sud; N7 S for 3km; left D133 for Grignan, Nyons 8km; left for Roussas; 1.5km after village, left up small road.

Véronique Guichard Catoire
La Combe de Blayn,
26230 Roussas, Drôme

tel	(0)6 86 81 51 63 (Mon-Fri) (0)4 75 98 62 44 (weekend)
fax	(0)4 78 89 25 76
e-mail	guichardv@aol.com

RHÔNE VALLEY · ALPS

Imaginative splashes of colour over clean modern lines and plenty of space – these bedrooms are great, each with French windows to its little terrace, a king-size bed, an excellent bathroom. The place, swimming pool included, has truly beautiful views over vineyards to Mont Ventoux; breakfast and excellent dinners are served by the pool or in the stylish dining room. Then there's the apartment: same design flair plus its own kitchen/sitting room. Your enormously likeable young Dutch hosts will surely make a huge success of their new venture. Do stay a while – there's stacks of scope for walking, cycling and simply unwinding.

rooms	4 + 1 apartment: 4 doubles, all with bath or shower & wc; 1 apartment for 4 with bath, wc & kitchen.
price	€70-€100 for two.
dinner	By arrangement €23, good wine list.
closed	November-mid-March.
directions	On A7 exit 19 for Bollène; D94 for Nyons; before St Maurice 1st left, 450m; signs.

Marieke & Clemens Colsen
La Fontaine au Loup,
26110 St Maurice sur Eygues,
Drôme

tel	(0)4 75 27 65 19
fax	(0)4 75 27 65 19
e-mail	info@la-fontaine-au-loup.com
web	www.la-fontaine-au-loup.com

If you enjoy people who love country life and are without pretension, then go and stay with this well-educated, relaxed couple in their creeper-clad, wisteria-hung farmhouse in a forgotten corner of the Drôme. Breakfast and dinner include home-made jams, eggs, vegetables from their superb kitchen garden and, in season, truffles hunted in their own secret ways. The Pagis are generous and off-beat, their guest rooms in the next-door barn are simple, the bathroom and kitchen really basic – but it's not the 'facilities' that make this place special, it's the people. And Jean-Jacques plays trumpet in the local salsa band.

rooms	2: 1 double, 1 quadruple, sharing kitchen, bath & wc.
price	€34 for two.
dinner	€12, with wine; self-catering possible.
closed	December-February.
directions	From Vaison la Romaine, D938 for Malaucène 4km. Left on D13 8km. Right on D40 to Montbrun les Bains, right for Sault. House 1km on left.

Jean-Jacques & Agnès Pagis
Le Chavoul,
Reilhanette,
26570 Montbrun les Bains, Drôme
tel (0)4 75 28 80 80
e-mail antoine3@wanadoo.fr

map: 17 entry: 725

RHÔNE VALLEY · ALPS

Ten minutes and a world away from the motorway, this pretty and impressive old building on the main village square, originally a hotel, is now a real family house where guests can share one of Madame's much-praised dinners with their hosts under the lime tree as the evening fades. Bedrooms are big, warm, lightly floral with very French beds, be they brass or sleigh, fine armoires and good bathrooms. Windows look over the walled garden behind or to the square in front; there's space and a sense of old-time comfort. And your friendly hosts have collected quantities of coffee grinders and *carafes* – mind-boggling.

rooms	3: 1 double, 1 twin, with bath or shower & wc; 1 triple with bath, shower & separate wc.
price	€40-€46 for two.
dinner	€17, with wine; restaurants in town.
closed	October-June.
directions	From A72 exit 4 (Noirétable-Les Salles) for Noirétable for 500m; left D73 through St Julien la Vêtre to St Didier – house on main square.

Dany Trapeau
La Closerie,
Le Bourg,
42111 Saint Didier sur Rochefort, Loire
tel (0)4 77 97 91 26
fax (0)4 77 97 91 26

map: 12 entry: 725a

PROVENCE · ALPS · RIVIERA

Keen and knowledgeable walkers, Jean-Max and Jacqueline are quite able to plan a whole walking holiday for you. You can walk – or ski – straight out onto the mountains from this dramatically-set house with its wonderful views over to Italy. Jean-Max, who's a retired architect, designed and built it with its bedrooms snugly beneath the eaves. The self-contained apartment has its own garden; true, the third person does have to sleep in the kitchen/living room, but has sole use of the microwave and that magnificent view. *Advance booking essential.*

The best bouillabaisse *ingredients swim among the white Mediterranean horses; on shore, the native white ponies carry their dashing* gardians *over the Camargue, herding the great black bulls.*

rooms	3 + 1 apartment: 2 doubles, sharing shower & wc; 1 twin with shower & wc; 1 apartment for 2-4 with bath & wc.
price	€50-€64 for two.
dinner	Restaurants in Briançon, 4km.
closed	1 April-24 May; 9 Sept-20 Dec; 5 Jan-2 Feb.
directions	From Gap N94 to Briançon. Entering town, left at 1st traffic light for Puy St André. In village, house 3rd on left.

Jacqueline & Jean-Max Laborie
Le Village,
Puy Saint André,
05100 Briançon, Hautes-Alpes

tel	(0)4 92 21 30 22
fax	(0)4 92 21 30 22
e-mail	jlabalastair@club-internet.fr

Come to ski across country or down hills, hire your snow shoes on the spot, do some exceptional summer walks, hang-glide or just bathe in splendour. Michel, who took a half-ruined farmhouse and turned it into this atmospheric, country-warm house of welcome with small, no-frills rooms that have all you could want, is a burly, good-natured host who loves the convivial evenings around the communal table. Claude's artistry is seen in the décor, her kindness is in the air. Your first taste of the magnificent scenery here is the drive up – you should not be disappointed.

rooms	6: 1 double, 2 twins, 2 quadruples, 1 suite, all with shower & wc.
price	€48 for two. Half-board €38 for one.
dinner	€18 with wine, by arrangement.
closed	Rarely, but please telephone to check.
directions	From Gap N94 E for Briançon; right just before Embrun D40 10km. Follow 'Station des Orres' down hill; house in hamlet, on left just before bridge.

Michel & Claude Hurault
La Jarbelle,
Les Ribes,
05200 Les Orres, Hautes-Alpes
tel (0)4 92 44 11 33
fax (0)4 92 44 11 23
e-mail lajarbelle@wanadoo.fr

PROVENCE · ALPS · RIVIERA

History and mystery ooze from the ancient bits of this village château. Plays based on high spots of 'French history at Montmaur' are enacted on summer Fridays, the exhibition room has a five-metre-high fireplace, the breakfast room – family silver on a magnificent Provençal cloth – has superb old beams and your energetic hostess is kindness itself; she will also give you a guided tour. Guest rooms, not in the château proper, are somewhat dim and cramped with unremarkable furnishings. But romantics at heart come for the ghostly splendour of it all.

rooms	3 triples, all with shower & wc.
price	€76 for two.
dinner	Choice of restaurants, 4-10km.
closed	October-April.
directions	From Gap, D994 for Veynes. 4km before Veynes, D320 for Superdévoluy; Montmaur 2km on, visible from road. Drive along château wall then towards church.

Élise Laurens
Château de Montmaur,
05400 Veynes, Hautes-Alpes
tel (0)4 92 58 11 42
fax (0)4 92 58 11 42
e-mail chateau.de.montmaur@wanadoo.fr

Castellanes built Esparron in the 1400s, both have been pivots of Provençal history. The superb stone stairs lead to vastly luscious bedrooms: plain walls and fresh flowers, tiles and gorgeous fabrics, family antiques with tales to tell. The garden is small but perfect. Slender, apple-blossom Charlotte-Anne and her two beautiful children are pure Gainsborough. She attends to everyone: husband, children, staff, guests. Bernard, a mine of information with suntan and real manners, adds a touch of 1930s glamour. Wonderful family, splendiferous house, vast breakfast in the cavernously cosy kitchen.

rooms	5: 3 doubles, 1 twin, 1 suite, all with bath & wc.
price	€130-€200 for two.
dinner	Restaurant 5 minutes' walk.
closed	November-March.
directions	From Aix en Pr. A51 exit 18 on D907; D82 to Gréoux les Bains; follow on D952 & D315 to Esparron. Stop & ring at gates (once past, it's impossible to turn).

Bernard & Charlotte-Anne de Castellane
Château d'Esparron,
04800 Esparron de Verdon,
Alpes-de-Haute-Provence

tel	(0)4 92 77 12 05
fax	(0)4 92 77 13 10
e-mail	chateau@esparron.com
web	www.esparron.com

map: 18 entry: 729

PROVENCE · ALPS · RIVIERA

Venerable stones in the remote thyme-wafted air of a hillside village: an apparently modest old house unfolds into a place of grandeur with a vast flourish of a dining hall, a tower, a pigeon loft and well-travelled, fascinating hosts who are a fine mix of shyness, extroversion and humour. The courtyard is wisteria-clad, the garden sheltered, the food superb. Two rooms on the 17th-century lower level charm with their simple ancientness, the canopy bed lies in splendour below serried beams; they overflow with character if not with hanging space. And there are two lovely terraces. Divine. *Gîte space for 5-6 people.*

rooms	3: 1 double with shower, bath & wc; 2 doubles with shower & wc.
price	€70 for two.
dinner	€28-€30 with wine, by arrangement.
closed	Rarely.
directions	From Forcalquier N100 for Apt; at 1st r'bout D950 right to Banon; D51 to Montsalier; house at entrance of village beside Mairie; signposted.

Mme Karolyn Kauntze
Montsalier,
04150 Banon,
Alpes-de-Haute-Provence

tel	(0)4 92 73 23 61
fax	(0)4 92 73 23 61
e-mail	montsalier@infonie.fr

map: 17 entry: 730

Come for the view of row upon row of peaks fading into the distance, the walking, the welcome. Hélène and Olivier bought the dilapidated *mas* as a holiday home 17 years ago, restored it with loving care then moved here permanently and began taking guests. Olivier is a walker and can arrange a spectacular circuit, with a donkey carrying your stuff, from one B&B to the next. One bedroom has an ancient brick bread oven in a corner; another was a stable with the manger to prove it. Breakfast and dinner are on the terrace in warm weather or in the fine old wooden barn, and you can use the biggish pool behind the house.

rooms	4: 1 double with shower & wc; 1 triple with bath & wc; 2 suites with shower & wc.
price	€44 for two; €57 for three; €79 for four.
dinner	€15 with wine, by arrangement. Good restaurant 5km.
closed	Mid-November-March.
directions	From Châteauneuf Val St Donat 1.5km for St Étienne les Orgues; house on bend, on right above road; steep 100m drive to house.

Hélène & Olivier Lenoir
Mas Saint Joseph,
04200 Châteauneuf Val St Donat,
Alpes-de-Haute-Provence
tel (0)4 92 62 47 54
e-mail lenoir.st.jo@wanadoo.fr
web provenceweb.fr/04/st-joseph

REGIONAL FOOD STYLES

À l'Alsacienne: With sauerkraut and sausage.
À l'Américaine: A corruption of à l'Armoricaine from Armor, Celtic for Britanny – with shallots and tomatoes (see also Bretonne).
À l'Anglaise: Plain boiled.
À l'Ardennaise: With juniper berries.
À l'Auvergnate: With cabbage and bacon bits.
À la Basquaise: With onions, rice, sweet peppers and possibly Bayonne cured ham.
À la Bretonne: With leeks, celery, beans (see also Américaine).
À la Dauphinoise: With cream, garlic and sometimes cheese.
À la Dijonnaise: With mustard sauce.
À la Flamande: Flemish – cooked in beer or vinegar.
À la Lyonnaise: With onions, wine, vinegar and often sausage.
À la Niçoise: With anchovies and olives.
À la Normande: With cream.
À la Périgourdine: With goose liver and truffles.
À la Provençale: With tomatoes, garlic, olive oil.
À la Savoyarde: With cream and cheese.

And four supra-regional manners:

À la Bonne Femme: Good Woman style – with white wine, shallots and mushrooms.
À la Bourgeoise: Townswoman style – with a carrot, onion and bacon sauce.
À la Ménagère: Housewife style – with onions, carrots, turnips, peas.
À la Paysanne: Peasant/Country Woman style – with vegetables!

Michael still has many plans for this handsome, rambling old house and garden in prime walking and cycling country. The mood inside is relaxed and comfortable: plenty of fresh, bright colours, stripped and be-rugged wooden floors, interesting *brocante* pieces, original fireplaces and the odd period bath and basin. Breakfast at nine, often outside under mature trees with vineyards and distant mountain views, on local bread and home-made jam. Dinner should be good too: Michael is English and an imaginative chef.
Gîte space for 2-3 people.

rooms	4: 3 doubles, 1 suite for 4, all with bath or shower & wc.
price	€70-€73 for two.
dinner	€29 with wine, by arrangement.
closed	November-March.
directions	From Vaison la Romaine D938 N for Nyons, 5km; right on D46 for Buis les Baronnies, 4km. On entering Faucon, house on right at crossroads with D205 (blue gate).

Michael Berry
Les Airs du Temps,
84110 Faucon, Vaucluse
tel (0)4 90 46 44 57
fax (0)4 90 46 44 57
e-mail michaelaberry@hotmail.com

map: 17 entry: 733

PROVENCE · ALPS · RIVIERA

A stone jewel set in southern lushness and miles of green vines and purple hills. Country furniture (a seductive choice of Provençal chairs) is polished with wax and time; big, luminous bedrooms are prettily uncluttered: moss-coloured *Birds* sings to the tune of the aviary outside, *Elephant* has Indian fabric and… elephants, *Camargue*, in the mezzanined old barn, has a balcony and a *gardian's* hat. John rightly calls himself a Provençal Englishman, Monique is warmly welcoming too – theirs is a happy house. *German spoken.*

rooms	3: 1 double with bath & wc; 1 double, 1 family room with shower & wc.
price	€48-€54 for two.
dinner	Restaurant in village. Self-catering possible.
closed	Mid-November-Easter.
directions	From A7 exit Bollène for Nyons D94; D20 right for Vaison & Buisson; cross River Aygues; left for Villedieu & Cave la Vigneronne D51 & D75 for 2.2km.

Monique Alex & John Parsons
L'École Buissonnière,
D75,
84110 Vaison La Romaine, Vaucluse
tel (0)4 90 28 95 19
fax (0)4 90 28 95 19
e-mail ecole.buissonniere@wanadoo.fr
web www.guideweb.com/provence/bb/ecole-buissonniere

map: 17 entry: 734

A great spot for exploring Provence. The big old house, surrounded by its vineyards and within harmless earshot of a road, is very handsome and Madame brings it to life with her special sparkle and enthusiasm for what she has created here. The decoration is all hers – more 'evolved French farmhouse-comfortable' than 'designer-luxurious'. She loves cooking, herbs and flowers; you may be offered her elderflower aperitif and have home-made cakes at breakfast. Nothing is too much trouble – walkers' luggage can be transferred, picnics can be laid on, or wine, or honey tastings…

rooms	5: 2 doubles, 1 triple, 1 suite for 4, 1 suite for 6, all with bath or shower & wc.
price	€84 for two.
dinner	€21 with wine, by arrangement.
closed	Rarely.
directions	A9 exit Bollène for Carpentras 18km; leaving Cairanne, head for Carpentras 1.5km; house on right-hand turn.

Élisabeth & Jerry Para
Domaine du Bois de la Cour,
Route de Carpentras,
84290 Cairanne, Vaucluse

tel	(0)4 90 30 84 68
fax	(0)4 90 30 84 68
e-mail	infos@boisdelacour.com
web	www.boisdelacour.com

map: 17 entry: 735

PROVENCE · ALPS · RIVIERA

Madame and her house both smile gently. It's a simple, authentic Provençal farmhouse that has escaped the vigorous renovator, its courtyard shaded by a lovely lime tree. Madame, who grows chemical-free vegetables and fruit, considers dinners with her guests, in dining room or courtyard, as the best part of B&B – her meals are showcases for local specialities. The interior is a bright version of traditional French country style with old family furniture and tiled floors. Set among vineyards below the Montmirail hills, it has soul-pleasing views across the surrounding country and unspoilt villages.

rooms	4: 1 double, 2 twins, 1 family room, all with shower & wc.
price	€39 for two.
dinner	€13 with wine, by arrangement. Restaurants in village 3km.
closed	November-March.
directions	From Carpentras D7 N through Aubignan & Vacqueyras; fork right (still D7) for Sablet; right 500m after 'Cave Vignerons Gigondas'; signposted.

Sylvette Gras
La Ravigote,
84190 Gigondas, Vaucluse

tel	(0)4 90 65 87 55
fax	(0)4 90 65 87 55

map: 17 entry: 736

Narrow, cobbled streets lead to this fascinating and very beautifully furnished house that was once part of the 17th-century Bishop's Palace. The Verdiers are charming, cultivated people – he an architect/builder, she a teacher – with a keen interest in antiques and modern art. There's an impressive poster collection in the cosy guest sitting room, and the serene bedrooms – whitewashed beamed ceilings, terracotta floors – have a Provençal feel. Well-presented breakfasts on the terrace come complete with French and English newspapers and, best of all, long, magnificent views to the Roman bridge.

rooms	4: 1 double, 2 twins, 1 suite for 3, all with bath or shower & wc.
price	€66-€73 for two; suite €98 for three.
dinner	Good choice of restaurants in Vaison.
closed	2 weeks in November.
directions	From Orange, D975 to Vaison. In town, follow 'Ville Médiévale' signs.

Aude & Jean-Loup Verdier
L'Évêché,
Rue de l'Évêché,
84110 Vaison la Romaine, Vaucluse

tel	(0)4 90 36 13 46
fax	(0)4 90 36 32 43
e-mail	eveche@aol.com
web	www.eveche.com

Sincere, charming, animated hosts: Monsieur is a keen cook and prepares Provençal dishes using local produce and herbs while Madame makes the desserts and also gives Feldenkrais ('conscious movement') sessions. Their 19th-century farmhouse, built around a courtyard shaded by a spreading lime tree, is in great walking country among fields of lavender with vast views. The family living/dining room is homely and warm with a large table and a fireplace for cooler weather. The comfortable, light-filled rooms are carefully decorated in an unpretentious mix of new and old. Stay long enough to taste all these pleasures.

rooms	5: 1 suite for 4, 1 suite for 3, 3 triples, all with bath or shower & wc.
price	€65-€85 for two.
dinner	By arrangement €22; good wine list.
closed	January-February.
directions	From Carpentras, D941/D1 to Sault, 41km; D942 for Aurel. Just before Aurel, left at sign.

Christian & Visnja Michelle
Richarnau,
84390 Aurel, Vaucluse

tel	(0)4 90 64 03 62
fax	(0)4 90 64 03 62
e-mail	richarnau@free.fr
web	richarnau.free.fr

Built on the foundations of a 12th-century watermill, this solid old aristocratic *bastide* has thick stone walls which keep rooms cool in the fiercest heat. Not far from a busy-by-day road but in lovely, tree-filled gardens, the house is full of interesting mementos of the owners' time in various North African countries; bedrooms are traditionally furnished and beds have good mattresses. Families with children will adore the huge pool with its splashing fountains some way from the house. Breakfast includes home-made jam out on the terrace or in the dining room and dinners feature Madame's Provençal specialities.

rooms — 4: 2 doubles, 2 family suites, all with bath or shower & wc.
price — €62 for two.
dinner — €22 with wine, by arrangement.
closed — Rarely.
directions — From Carpentras, D974 for Bédoin/Mont Ventoux; stay on this road, do NOT enter Crillon village. Mill is on left below signpost.

Bernard & Marie-Luce Ricquart
Moulin d'Antelon,
Route de Bédoin,
84410 Crillon le Brave, Vaucluse
tel — (0)4 90 62 44 89
fax — (0)4 90 62 44 90
e-mail — moulin-dantelon@wanadoo.fr

PROVENCE · ALPS · RIVIERA

These are young hosts, with a passion for wine and a great collection of carpets, who've escaped here from their city pasts. Their guest bedrooms in this converted farmhouse are all very different: one white and cream with a blue and white bathroom, a twin with Senegalese bedspreads and a Paris Metro-tiled bathroom; a family room with a big brass double bed and, on a separate floor, three singles. The land here is flat with a high water table so the garden, sheltered by trees and the surrounding tall maize in summer, is always fresh and green – a perfect retreat after a hard day's sight-seeing.
Gîte space for 5 people.

rooms — 3: 1 double, 1 twin, 1 family room, all with bath, shower & wc.
price — €75-€85 for two.
dinner — Choice of restaurants 6km.
closed — November-March, except by arrangement.
directions — From A7 exit 23; after toll right at r'bout for Carpentras/Entraigues; 1st exit to Vedène D6 to St Saturnin lès Avignon; left to Le Thor D28 for 2km; right Chemin du Trentin.

Frédéric & Emmanuelle Westercamp
Le Mas de Miejour,
117 chemin du Trentin,
84250 Le Thor, Vaucluse
tel — (0)4 90 02 13 79
fax — (0)4 90 02 13 03
e-mail — mas.miejour@free.fr
web — mas.miejour.free.fr

Summer evenings are spent beneath the ancient spreading plane tree as the setting sun burnishes the vines beyond the slender cypresses and the old stones of this 17th-century *mas* breathe gold. With the eager help of seven-year-old Marie for any children you may bring, your hosts, simple, smiling and unpretentious, will welcome you happily into their traditional interior: lots of wood, almond-green paintwork, a lavishly yellow and orange dining room, warmly plain farm furniture. Bedrooms are in quietly gentle pastels with pretty bedcovers. And, at the big, convivial table, good Provençal cooking.

rooms	5: 4 doubles, 1 family room, all with bath or shower & wc.
price	€74-€84 for two.
dinner	€24, with wine; restaurants nearby.
closed	Rarely.
directions	From Carpentras D4/39 to St Didier; D28 right for Pernes; house sign on left before Pernes.

Jean-Pierre & Françoise Faure-Brac
Mas Pichony,
1454 Route de St Didier D28,
84210 Pernes les Fontaines,
Vaucluse
tel (0)4 90 61 56 11
fax (0)4 90 61 56 33
e-mail mas-pichony@wanadoo.fr
web www.maspichony.com

The Lawrences couldn't be nicer and thoroughly enjoy their role as hosts – they offer an open-hearted welcome and a real guest room in a real home. The room has its own dressing room, an extra mezzanine single and a newly-tiled shower; guests have use of a fridge and are welcome to picnic. This is a modern house built of old stone in traditional local style and surrounded by hills, woods and vineyards with lovely views across the valley towards Goult and the Lubéron. The Lawrences worked overseas for 40 years and the house is full of attractive *objets* from their travels. *Gîte space for 16 people.*

rooms	1 triple with shower & wc.
price	€46 for two.
dinner	Good choice of restaurants 5km.
closed	Rarely.
directions	From Avignon N100 towards Apt. At Coustellet, D2 for Gordes. After Les Imberts right D207/D148 to St Pantaléon; pass church; D104 for 50m; left small hill; 3rd drive on right.

Pierrette & Charles Lawrence
Villa La Lèbre,
Saint Pantaléon,
84220 Gordes, Vaucluse
tel (0)4 90 72 20 74
fax (0)4 90 72 20 74

Turning a fortress-like face to the Mistral when it tears down the valley, the old house is a blessed refuge from wind or heat. Sunshine yellows and soft greens, fresh flowers and natural stone inside are partnered by a tempting, shade-dotted garden and views of the Lubéron. The Gouins are real Provençal fruit-growers and Madame a renowned cook. Breakfast may see her *galette de pommes*; dinners under the spreading plane tree are outstanding. The apartment (three rooms, jacuzzi!) is ideal for teenage families. Simply arrive, absorb and wonder what on earth you did to deserve this gem. *Children over 12 welcome.*

rooms	5 + 1 apartment: 2 doubles, 2 quadruples, 1 suite, 1 apartment for 6 (2 nights minimum), all with shower & wc.
price	€92-€122 for two; apartment €182.
dinner	€25 with wine, by arrangement.
closed	Rarely.
directions	From Avignon N7 E then D22 for Apt (approx. 29km total). After Le Petit Palais, sign on right.

Isabelle & Rolland Gouin
La Ferme des 3 Figuiers,
Le Petit Jonquier,
84800 Lagnes, Vaucluse
tel (0)4 90 20 23 54
fax (0)4 90 20 25 47
e-mail lestroisfiguiers@wanadoo.fr

A totally revamped 18th-century silkworm farm, it's a handsome building with a clever mix of old and new: big, country-elegant bedrooms, gnarled beams, old stonework and *armoires*, then modern touches such as glass-topped tables, good bedding, linen and bathrooms. In the stylish guest sitting room you can enjoy an open fire, comfy sofa, books, games and bits of Provençalia – bunches of dried lavender, candles... Add feast-like breakfasts and dinners, great views from the pool, a boules court and a terraced garden with a backdrop of cherry trees. Very appealing. *Minimum 2 nights.*

rooms	5: 2 double, 1 twin, 2 triple, all with bath, shower & wc.
price	€75-€85 for two.
dinner	3 Provençal restaurants 6-12km.
closed	15 November-February.
directions	A7 exit Cavaillon for Apt through Robion; D3 right for Ménerbes; at foot of village head for Bonnieux for 3km; house 200m, sign.

Natalie & Vincent Rohart
La Magnanerie,
Le Roucas,
84560 Ménerbes, Vaucluse
tel (0)4 90 72 42 88
fax (0)4 90 72 39 42
e-mail magnanerie@aol.com
web www.magnanerie.com

Stepping into this typical Provençal townhouse from the busy street one enters a magical oasis, a refined, elegant and colourful cocoon of lived-in gentility and old-world charm where period furniture – to each room its style – and a throng of objects create an intrinsically French house, unchanged since Balzac. Affable, attentive and cultured, Madame runs the B&B with her daughter, a fluent English-speaker whose children bring sparkle to the old house. Guest quarters, including breakfast room, are self-contained on the top floor, there's a patio with summer kitchen and a cool, fragrant garden for all below.

rooms	5: 2 doubles, 3 twins, all with bath or shower & wc.
price	€55-€70 for two.
dinner	Restaurants nearby.
closed	Rarely.
directions	From Aix en Provence N96 & D556 to Pertuis; D973 to Cadenet; D943 for Bonnieux to Lourmarin.

Mme Lassallette
Villa Saint Louis,
35 rue Henri de Savornin,
84160 Lourmarin, Vaucluse

tel	(0)4 90 68 39 18
fax	(0)4 90 68 10 07
e-mail	villasaintlouis@wanadoo.fr

PROVENCE · ALPS · RIVIERA

The stones, the light, the colours of Provence! An estate that grows grapes, olives, lavender, a house weathered by five centuries of history, a clutch of bewitchingly decorated bedrooms, all drag-painted and stained-furnitured, with myriad crazy lights, books, pictures, *objets* and small, colourful bathrooms, a travel-filled guest *salon*, a most inviting pool scene, an exotic inner courtyard... From the hub of this vast Aladdin's cave (touches of Alice too) that is the great-tabled dining hall, live-wire, rainbow Anny and her artist daughter Amandine are realising a dream of resurrection and new life. Wine weekends, too.

rooms	4: 2 doubles, 2 suites for 4, all with bath or shower & wc.
price	€74-€119 for two.
dinner	€23, good wine list.
closed	Rarely.
directions	From A7 for Marseille exit Sénas for Aix; at r'bout left for Pertuis; cont. towards Pertuis; exit Puyvert/Lourmarin; 300m left for Puyvert; house 300m on left.

Anny Jeanpierre
Le Mas de Foncaudette,
La Lombarde,
84160 Puyvert, Vaucluse

tel	(0)4 90 08 42 51
fax	(0)4 90 08 42 51
e-mail	foncaudette@yahoo.fr
web	www.foncaudette.com

Stone wolves at the gate, two real ones superbly stuffed in the *salon*, flowers pouring over arch, tower and well: this astounding 17th-century house drips with character, its wealth of history beseiges you, it lacks only the sound of an idly-plucked lute. Artist Véronique's courtesy and culture are enchanting: an ode to the house, a Greek admiral ancestress (*louve des mers?*), a flair for marrying cosmopolitan mementos with local materials, serenely elegant rooms, breakfast exquisitely laid in patio or dining room. An exceptionally atmospheric experience. *Min. 2 nights. Children over 12 welcome.*

rooms	4: 1 double, 1 twin, 2 suites for two, each with bath, shower & wc.
price	€99-€145 for two.
dinner	Wide choice of restaurants.
closed	Rarely.
directions	From A51 exit 15 to Pertuis; left D973 to Lauris r'bout; follow to Puyvert; house on main street opposite Mairie.

Véronique Pfeiffer
La Louveterie,
3 rue des Écoles,
84160 Puyvert, Vaucluse

tel	(0)4 90 08 76 50
fax	(0)4 90 08 76 51
e-mail	info@lalouveterie.com
web	www.lalouveterie.com

PROVENCE · ALPS · RIVIERA

Sophisticated simplicity is here: white walls and fine pale fabrics, old beds and cupboard doors that glow venerably in the sunlight filtering through the greenery outside – Bassette is an ethereal picture of pure Provence. Your hosts are as quiet and charming, gentle and generous as their 15th-century *mas* and its magical great garden where the swimming pool hides among big potted plants and wooden furniture. Big bedrooms are perfect: one picture and one framed text chosen by Marie for each, old terracotta tiles and wicker chairs, thick towels and soap in a basket. Superb value, utter peace.
Air-conditioning in bedrooms.

rooms	2 doubles, both with bath, shower & wc.
price	€75-€95 for two.
dinner	Good restaurants 5-20km.
closed	Rarely.
directions	In Barbentane for Abbaye St Michel du Frigoulet; at windmill for tennis club; house entrance near club; signposted.

Marie & François Veilleux
Mas de Bassette,
13750 Barbentane,
Bouches-du-Rhône

tel	(0)4 90 95 63 85
fax	(0)4 90 95 63 85
e-mail	bassette@club-internet.fr
web	www.masdebassette.com

You may want to share a *grillade* (barbecue) in the garden with this charming, vivid and genuine couple or listen for hours to Monsieur's humorous talk of arcane Provençal traditions and tales. If so, start practising your French now – *Risoulet*, the previous owner's name, means 'smiling man' in patois and is utterly appropriate. The rooms are as colourful as their owners in their flowery, joyous decoration – the sky blue, the almond green, the yellow with its special sunflower-shaped brass beds and little sitting area under the roof. Such authenticity is rare in the area and the traffic does die down at night.

rooms	3: 1 twin, 2 doubles, all with shower & wc.
price	€46-€54 for two.
dinner	Good restaurants 2-5km.
closed	Rarely.
directions	From A7 exit Avignon south for Tarascon 8km; left D34 for La Crau, Eyragues, St Rémy 2km; at La Crau sign on right.

Charly & Colette Bertrand
Le Mas le Risoulet4122 D34,
13160 Châteaurenard,
Bouches-du-Rhône
tel (0)4 90 94 71 38
fax (0)4 90 90 02 92

PROVENCE · ALPS · RIVIERA

The elegant manor is enhanced by Marie-Pierre's refined, pastel, almost baroque décor. She is passionate about art and books, Christian loves music and making furniture, both were journalists travelling the world before settling here and they organise concerts in the barn and painting classes. The stylish, well-furnished bedrooms, one in the tower wing, one with carved mezzanine, all with great personality, have beams and stone walls, fine old *armoires* and polished floors, excellent bathrooms and wonderful views of the Provençal hills beyond. A flower-bordered pool, memorable breakfasts, much peace. *Gîte space for 4 people.*

rooms	4: 2 doubles, 1 triple, 1 suite, all with shower or bath & wc.
price	€85-€105 for two.
dinner	€29 with wine, by arrangement.
closed	Rarely.
directions	From Avignon D570 to Tarascon; leave road to Arles to left; now on D970: under bridge; 2km beyond, left on humpback bridge through white gate.

Marie-Pierre Carretier
& Christian Billmann
Le Mas D'Arvieux,
Route d'Avignon,
13150 Tarascon, Bouches-du-Rhône
tel (0)4 90 90 78 77
fax (0)4 90 90 78 68
e-mail mas@arvieux-provence.com
web www.arvieux-provence.com

On an old cobbled street right in the heart of old Tarascon, this *maison de maître* has ancient origins. It has been beautifully, artistically renovated without losing any of the lovely patina of stone walls and tiles. Built round a typical ochre-hued courtyard where breakfast is served and candles are lit in the evening, it feels ineffably Mediterranean. The impeccable, stylish rooms have fine old furniture and beams, excellent bathrooms and linen. While you can be totally independent, your charming hosts receive guests in the most relaxed, friendly way and thoroughly enjoy the contact. A very lovely, atmospheric place. *Min. 2 nights July-Aug.*

rooms	5: 3 doubles, 2 twin, all with bath or shower & wc.
price	€64-€76 for two.
dinner	Choice of restaurants in town. (€20-€30).
closed	November-20 December, except by arrangement.
directions	In Tarascon centre take Rue du Château opposite château (well signposted). No. 24 is on right.

Yann & Martine Laraison
24 rue du Château,
13150 Tarascon, Bouches-du-Rhône

tel	(0)4 90 91 09 99
fax	(0)4 90 91 10 33
e-mail	ylaraison@wanadoo.fr
web	www.chambres-hotes.com

PROVENCE · ALPS · RIVIERA

This little old stone townhouse, built into the 500-year-old ramparts of history-gorged St Rémy, is Vanessa's new hideaway, a refuge from the West Country, and you are invited to share her pretty Provençal dining room, the tiny two-person courtyard and the cosy sitting room. The high-ceilinged bedrooms are furnished in a satisfying mix of local, ethnic and English and hung with interesting pictures. It all has a secret atmosphere, closed in upon itself inside its exposed stone walls, and the hurly-burly of the lively town seems dim and distant, yet you are within walking distance of all its treasures.

rooms	2: 1 double with bath & wc; 1 twin with bath/shower & wc.
price	€50-€60 for two.
dinner	Restaurants in town.
closed	1 November-1 March open by arrangement only.
directions	One way system in St Rémy town. 7 bd Marceau close to L'Amandier museum on left side of one-way system; before church opp. main square. Car park.

Vanessa Maclennan
7 boulevard Marceau,
13210 St Rémy de Provence,
Bouches-du-Rhône

tel	(0)4 90 92 15 73
e-mail	vanessamaclennan@hotmail.com

A manicured farmhouse whose interior is as southern cool as the welcome from its owners is sincerely Franco-Irish – John is big and relaxed, Christiane is trim and efficient. Natural stone, oak beams, terracotta floors and cool colours give a wonderfully light and airy feel to the house while bedrooms are carefully elegant with small, functional shower rooms. Outside, a delectable garden, centuries-old plane trees, a vine tunnel, three hectares of cypresses and horses (why not head for the Alpilles mountains?) add to the magic. An oft-tinkled piano is there for you to play.

rooms	5: 3 doubles, 2 twins, all with shower & wc.
price	€92-€115 for two.
dinner	Choice of restaurants in St Rémy.
closed	November-Easter.
directions	From St Rémy D571 for Avignon; over 2 r'bouts, left before 2nd bus stop (Lagoy), opp. 2nd yellow Portes Anciennes sign, Chemin de Velleron; house 6th on right.

Christiane & John Walsh
Mas Shamrock,
Chemin de Velleron &
du Prud'homme,
13210 St Rémy de Provence,
Bouches-du-Rhône
tel (0)4 90 92 55 79
fax (0)4 90 92 55 80

PROVENCE · ALPS · RIVIERA

Float in the pool and watch the sun set over the Alpilles before strolling to the large, picture-hung kitchen where Madame's mother may be imparting her knowledge of Provençal food and gardening – there are always home-made cakes. Built by great-grandfather in 1897, up a quiet lane, surrounded by fields and fruit trees, this *mas* blends modern with rustic Provence. Quarry-tiled rooms with colourful local fabrics open onto terrace and garden. Madame, a former teacher, will help you choose the ideal walk or restaurant or you can use the guest kitchen/dining/reading room or the pretty veranda.

rooms	2: 1 double, 1 suite for 4, both with shower & bath.
price	€61-€68 for two; suite €95-€103 for four.
dinner	Good restaurants nearby; self-catering available.
closed	Rarely.
directions	From Avignon, N7 for Aix-Marseille, exit for Plan d'Orgon – Cavaillon. House shortly before church on left (arrow signposts).

Magali Rodet
Mas de la Miougrano,
447 route des Écoles,
13750 Plan d'Orgon,
Bouches-du-Rhône
tel (0)4 90 73 20 01
fax (0)4 90 73 20 01
e-mail lamiougrano@net-up.com
web perso.net-up.com/lamiougrano

Fanfares of lilies at the door, Haydn inside and Michael smiling in his chef's apron. *Rabassière* means 'where truffles are found' and his Epicurean dinners are a must: vintage wines and a sculpted dancer grace his terrace table. Cookery classes with olive oil from his trees, jogging companionship, airport pick-up are all part of his unflagging hospitality, aided by Théri, his serene Pakistani assistant. Big bedrooms and drawing room are classically comfortable in English country-house style: generous beds, erudite bookshelves, a tuned piano, Provençal antiques. Come savour this charmingly generous and individual house.

rooms	2 large doubles, both with bath & wc.
price	€115 for two, €65 for one.
dinner	€30 with wine, by arrangement.
closed	Rarely.
directions	From A54 exit 13 to Grans on D19; right on D16 to St Chamas, just before r'way bridge, left for Cornillon, up hill 2km; house on right before tennis court. Map sent on request.

Michael Frost
Mas de la Rabassière,
Route de Cornillon,
13250 St Chamas,
Bouches-du-Rhône
tel (0)4 90 50 70 40
fax (0)4 90 50 70 40
e-mail michaelfrost@rabassiere.com
web www.rabassiere.com

PROVENCE · ALPS · RIVIERA

An enormous 1850s *bastide aixoise*, decorated in local period style – the ceiling in the huge dining room, painted by Coulange-Lautrec (distant relative of Toulouse?), is remarkable. Monique is quite an expert on Provençal culture, custom and dress. Her special talent is making Nativity cribs and there is a wonderful *crèche* in the sitting room which she redecorates every Christmas. Bedrooms are comfortable, peaceful and simply furnished. Everywhere there are hints of the house's aristocratic past: family portraits, antiques, vases of dried and silk flowers. Fascinating.
Minimum 2 nights.

rooms	3; 2 doubles, both with shower & wc; 1 suite for 4 with bath, shower & wc.
price	€70 for two; suite €110 for four.
dinner	Restaurants in village, 1km.
closed	November-March.
directions	From Aix N8 for Marseille through Luynes; at large r'bout right for Gardanne 600m; D59B right towards Bouc Bel Air. On left about 1.2km after x-roads, 300m back from road.

Monique & Henri Morand
La Lustière,
442 Petit Chemin d'Aix,
13320 Bouc Bel Air,
Bouches-du-Rhône
tel (0)4 42 22 10 07
fax (0)4 42 94 13 42
e-mail morand.m.reservation@wanadoo.fr

On its hilltop on the edge of pretty Peynier, the old *mas* stands in glory: pull the cowbell, pass the wooden doors and the solid red-shuttered mass surges up from beds of roses. Beautifully restored, it once belonged to painter Vincent Roux and memories of Vincent and his friend Cézanne live on. The Roux room (the best) has a delicious garden view, beams, terracotta tiles, a fantastic ochre/green bathroom down the hall. The others are good too, if more functional, and the *salon* is a lovely spot. We have heard much praise for the atmosphere created by your gracious hostess. *Older children welcome.*

rooms	2 doubles, all with bath or shower & wc.
price	€62–€70 for two.
dinner	Restaurants in village; summer kitchen available for lunches.
closed	1st 3 weeks in August.
directions	From Aix on D6, 4km before Trets, right D57 to Peynier; up hill to Trets/Aubagne road; left D908; right between Poste & Pharmacie. House 50m.

Mme Jacqueline Lambert
Mas Sainte Anne,
3 rue Auriol,
13790 Peynier, Bouches-du-Rhône
tel (0)4 42 53 05 32
fax (0)4 42 53 04 28

PROVENCE · ALPS · RIVIERA

The Babeys are relaxed and easy, their modern, Provençal-style house sits above the surrounding vineyards and orchards as if in a Cézanne: the view of the Montagne Sainte Victoire is loaded with breathtaking references. Their cosy, rustically furnished guest cottage or *cabanon* (illustrated), just below, has one large bedroom with mezzanine and a separate kitchen/sitting room with south-facing terrace. There's a fine pool, table tennis, boules, the sea 45 minutes away and lovely old Aix within easy reach. *Check pool availability.*

rooms	Cottage for 4: 1 double/twin on ground floor, 1 double on mezzanine, bathroom & kitchenette.
price	€61 for two.
dinner	Self-catering; restaurants in village, 2km.
closed	Rarely.
directions	From Aix, N7 Nice for approx. 15km; left just after Château Bégude for Puyloubier; Ch. des Prés 20m on right. House at end.

Jean-Pierre & Sophie Babey
Les Bréguières,
Chemin des Prés,
13790 Rousset, Bouches-du-Rhône
tel (0)4 42 29 01 16
fax (0)4 42 29 01 16

Simply welcoming, your hosts were born in this unspoilt part of the Var where beautiful, distant views of the Pre-Alps – and genuine human warmth – await you at their modernised farmhouse (19th-century foundations). The smallish bedrooms have typical Provençal fabrics and antiques and personal touches such as dried-flower arrangements; the bathrooms are kept spotless. Over breakfast of wholemeal bread, local honey and apple juice, brought to you on the private terrace or in the dining room, Madame will happily help you plan your day. She couldn't be kinder and thoroughly enjoys chatting with her guests. *Gîte space for 4 people.*

rooms	3: 1 double, 1 twin, 1 triple, all with shower & wc.
price	€52 for two.
dinner	Restaurants 1-3km. BBQ available.
closed	Rarely.
directions	From Aups, D9 & D30 to Montmeyan; D13 for Quinson. On left of road, 1km along; signs.

Dany & Vincent Gonfond
Mas Saint Maurinet,
Route de Quinson,
83670 Montmeyan, Var
tel (0)4 94 80 78 03
fax (0)4 94 80 78 03

PROVENCE · ALPS · RIVIERA

A taste of genuine Provençal farm life is yours with these happy, civilised people in their anciently rambling *bastide*. Rooms of almost monastic simplicity are in the old tower: exposed stones, old tiles breathing coolness, smart bedcovers glowing, each room its own entrance. Delicious dinners with home-grown fruit and veg are at separate tables in the main dining room or on the terrace. There are bright peacocks doing what peacocks do, friendly dogs, pure-bred Arab ponies (Monsieur's passion) and... active young Romeo. Riding and visits to wine cellars can be arranged. Timelessly restful – with a touch of exotic.

rooms	5: 3 suites for 3, 1 triple, 1 twin, all with bath or shower & wc.
price	€50 for two.
dinner	€18 with wine, by arrangement.
closed	December-March.
directions	From Ginasservis D23 for Rians, 1.5km; left D22 for Esparron, 1km. Sign on left.

Fatia & Michel Lazès
Aubanel,
83560 Ginasservis, Var
tel (0)4 94 80 11 07
fax (0)4 94 80 11 04
e-mail aubanel-lazes@wanadoo.fr

Readers write: "Armelle is wonderful". Breakfast is the highlight of her hospitality: she is full of ideas for excursions while Monsieur, an historian, happily shares his vast knowledge of the area. Theirs is a warm, lively family – a delightful, cultivated couple, four lovely children – and their working vineyard has a timeless feel to it. The first-class, authentically Provençal bedrooms and the breakfast room (with mini-kitchen) are in a separate wing but, weather permitting, breakfast is on the terrace. Peace and privacy in a beautiful old house, superb walking country, seriously good value. *Gîte space for 4.*

rooms	3: 2 twin/doubles, 1 suite for 4, all with bath or shower & wc.
price	€50-€60 for two; suite €76 for four.
dinner	Self-catering; good restaurant 1.6km.
closed	November-March.
directions	From A8 exit St Maximin & Ste Baume D560 to Barjols; cont. D560 2km for Draguignan; entrance opp. D60 turning for Pontevès.

Guillaume & Armelle de Jerphanion
Domaine de Saint Ferréol,
83670 Pontevès, Var
tel (0)4 94 77 10 42
fax (0)4 94 77 19 04
e-mail saint-ferreol@wanadoo.fr

Four years ago, the Muselets said farewell to their toy business, fell in love with this old sheep farm, its 57 tranquil Mediterranean acres of woods, vines and lavender, and started their B&B: five excellent rooms with garden doors, a vast terrace for meals, ancient oaks for shade, exquisite pool.
A charming, discreet couple, they strive for perfection in all they do; three times a week, their *table d'hôtes* is a house-party event with candlelight, delicious food and local wine. The airy, elegant dining room, pale-walled, stone-floored, is the hub of the house and it's a wonderfully relaxing and civilised place to stay.

rooms	5: 3 doubles, 2 twins, all with bath or shower & wc.
price	€64-€83 for two.
dinner	€22 with wine, by arrangement.
closed	Mid-November-mid-February.
directions	Leave A8 exit St Maximin la Ste Baume; D560 for Barjols 8km; right D35 for Bras 3km; left before bridge 1km; signs.

Jean-Patrick & Cécile Muselet
Bastide de la Fave,
83119 Brue Auriac, Var
tel (0)4 94 69 94 43
fax (0)4 94 69 94 43
e-mail bastide-de-la-fave@wanadoo.fr
web bastide-de-la-fave.com

Alain and Jean-Yves have tackled their new careers here with panache, bringing their own inimitable sense of style, their noble black Labrador, two donkeys and some lovely new paintings, furniture and *objets* to an already fine house. There's a bust of Marie-Antoinette in the dining room and freshness in the uncluttered, stylish bedrooms, five of which have private terraces. The gardener cares for the lavender, herbs and organic vegetables in front of the house, and there's a lovely pool. Breakfast can be brought to your room between 8am and midday; dinners are imaginative and delicious. A very special place.

rooms	6: 3 triples, 2 doubles, 1 suite for 4, all with shower & wc.
price	€70 for two.
dinner	Mondays and Saturdays, €23 with wine, by arrangement.
closed	November-December.
directions	In St Maximin D28 for Bras & le Val for 3km to sign on right. Follow narrow road for further 3km.

Alain Van't Hoff
& Jean-Yves Savina
Domaine de Garrade,
Route de Bras,
83470 St Maximin la Ste Baume,
Var

tel	(0)4 94 59 84 32
fax	(0)4 94 59 83 47
e-mail	garrade@aol.com
web	www.provenceweb.fr/83/garrade

map: 18 entry: 763

PROVENCE · ALPS · RIVIERA

Madame lavishes equal amounts of loving care on her guests and her spectacularly beautiful Mediterranean garden with its tall trees, flowering shrubs and manicured lawn. Indeed, the whole place, designed by Monsieur 20 years ago as a big luxurious family villa with thoughtfully concealed pool, is thoroughly manicured. Comfortable Provençal-style rooms have lovely Salernes bathroom tiles; one has its own piece of garden. Monsieur is shyly welcoming, Madame smilingly efficient and the hills full of medieval villages and wine estates to explore. Or make a picnic in the summer kitchen and just laze.
Gîte space for 4 people.

rooms	4: 2 doubles, 1 suite for 4, all with bath or shower & wc.
price	€69 for two.
dinner	Restaurants in village.
closed	Rarely.
directions	From Toulon N8 for Aubagne; in Le Beausset cross 2 r'bouts; right opp. Casino supermarket; immed. left by boulangerie, right Ch. de la Fontaine 1.5km; sign on left.

Charlotte & Marceau Zerbib
Les Cancades,
1195 chemin de la Fontaine,
83330 Le Beausset, Var

tel	(0)4 94 98 76 93
fax	(0)4 94 90 24 63
e-mail	charlotte.zerbib@wanadoo.fr
web	www.les-cancades.com

map: 18 entry: 764

The Poutets' renovation of their 16th-century wine-growing château is stunning: long views over vines and olive-pocked hills, pale old honeycomb-tile floors, luscious family antiques, totally beautiful bedrooms, light-hearted punctuation – snapshot stickerboard, free-standing candelabra – and calm, elegant colour schemes. It's a family affair, designed by Monsieur Poutet, decorated by Madame, run by Sandrine, their charming, capable and energetic daughter-in-law, with her delightful young children. They are new to B&B, full of generosity, flair and energy in a fabulous place – a superb place to stay. *Gîte space for 8 people.*

rooms	5: 2 doubles, 3 twins, all with bath & wc.
price	€84-€100 for two.
dinner	Restaurant in village, 2.5km.
closed	Rarely.
directions	From Toulon-Marseille A50 exit 11 for La Cadière d'Azur; left at yellow sign 'Moulin St Come'; left D266; house 1.5km on right.

Sandrine Michelangeli
& Jacqueline Poutet
Château de Saint Côme,
Chemin des Arnaud,
83740 La Cadière d'Azur, Var

tel	(0)4 94 90 07 71
fax	(0)4 94 90 07 53
e-mail	contact@chateaudestcome.com
web	www.chateaudestcome.com

map: 17 entry: 765

PROVENCE · ALPS · RIVIERA

This young house, informed by the natural charm and taste of an old-established family, stands in a haven of green peace. The three rooms off the cool patio are good, simple and restful (though walls may be rather thin) with a modern feel, the odd antique, excellent showers and little gates onto the lawn. Your host, a former French forestry commissioner, loves all growing things and is laying out a fascinating "botanical walk" in his fine big garden; his seriously kind-hearted wife loves people and… dogs (three live here); they and their daughter, a nurse, will give you an unobtrusively warm family welcome.

rooms	3 twin/doubles, all with shower & wc.
price	€65 for two.
dinner	Restaurants 2-4km.
closed	Rarely.
directions	A50 exit 11 for Le Beausset/La Cadière d'Azur; in Beausset N8 for Toulon; left at 1st r'about; signs for Baro Nuecho.

Élisabeth & Frank
Guibert de Bruet
Le Vallon,
1253 chemin de la Baro Nuecho,
83330 Le Beausset, Var

tel	(0)4 94 98 62 97
fax	(0)4 94 98 62 97
e-mail	le-vallon@beausset.com
web	www.beausset.com

map: 18 entry: 766

The warm-hearted, tireless Didiers seem to have been born to run a happy and hospitable B&B and they do so, enthusiastically, in their quiet 1960s villa with its backdrop of vineyards and hills. Two spotlessly clean bedrooms with real attention to comfort – good cupboards and bedside lights, for example – share the modern shower room and are hung with Amélie's fine paintings. The guest dining room leads to a private outside terrace and thence to the peaceful, beautiful garden; ideal for relaxing after the day's visit, maybe by boat to one of the Îles d'Hyères.

rooms	1 suite of double & twin with bath, shower & wc.
price	€70 for two; €110 for four.
dinner	Simple restaurants nearby; choice in Le Lavandou.
closed	Rarely.
directions	From Le Lavandou D559 E to La Fossette. Arriving in village, left Av. Capitaine Thorel, left again Ch. des Marguerites. If lost, phone for help!

Robert & Amélie Didier
21 chemin des Marguerites,
La Fossette,
83980 Le Lavandou, Var

tel (0)4 94 71 07 82
fax (0)4 94 71 07 82

PROVENCE · ALPS · RIVIERA

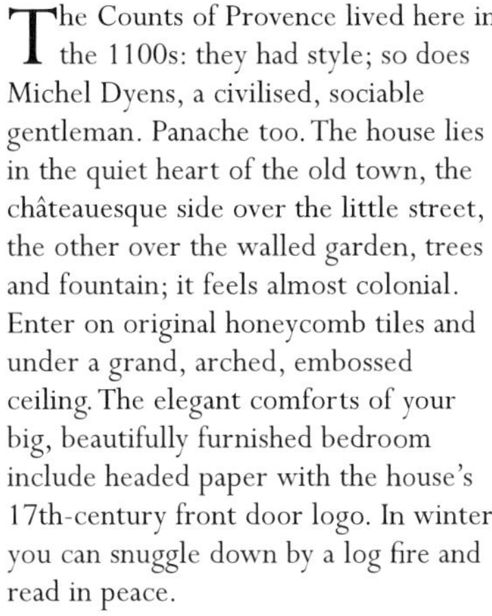

The Counts of Provence lived here in the 1100s: they had style; so does Michel Dyens, a civilised, sociable gentleman. Panache too. The house lies in the quiet heart of the old town, the châteauesque side over the little street, the other over the walled garden, trees and fountain; it feels almost colonial. Enter on original honeycomb tiles and under a grand, arched, embossed ceiling. The elegant comforts of your big, beautifully furnished bedroom include headed paper with the house's 17th-century front door logo. In winter you can snuggle down by a log fire and read in peace.

rooms	5: 3 doubles, 1 twin, 1 triple, all with bath/shower & sep. wc.
price	€62-€91.50 for two.
dinner	€23, with wine; restaurants in Brignoles.
closed	Rarely.
directions	From A8 exit Brignoles; over river for Centre Ville, immed. right for Hôtel de Claviers; round Pl. Palais de Justice; right Av. F. Mistral; Rue des Cordeliers on left.

Michel Dyens
La Cordeline,
14 rue des Cordeliers,
83170 Brignoles, Var

tel (0)4 94 59 18 66
fax (0)4 94 59 00 29
e-mail lacordeline@ifrance.com
web ifrance.com/lacordeline

Bravo Nathalie! The children are growing, the guest rooms refreshed, and she's still in calm, friendly control of this gorgeous, well-restored 18th-century *bastide*. One whole wing is for guests: yours the light, airy, vineyard-view bedrooms, pastel-painted and Provençal-furnished with a happy mix of antique and modern, yours the big bourgeois sitting room (little used: it's too lovely outside), yours a swim in the great spring-fed tank. Gently confident, Jean-François runs the vineyard, the tastings and the wine talk at dinner with sweet-natured ease. Utterly relaxing and very close to perfection, we thought.

rooms	4: 1 double, 1 twin, 1 triple, 1 family room, all with bath or shower & wc.
price	€61 for two.
dinner	€18 with wine, by arrangement.
closed	November-February.
directions	From A8 Brignoles exit north D554 through Le Val; D22 through Montfort sur Argens for Cotignac. 5km along left; sign.

Nathalie & Jean-François Roubaud
Domaine de Nestuby,
83570 Cotignac, Var

tel	(0)4 94 04 60 02
fax	(0)4 94 04 79 22
e-mail	nestuby@wanadoo.fr
web	www.sejours-en-provence.com

map: 18 entry: 769

Built in 1760 as a silkworm farm, this delicious old manor house still has mulberry trees shading the wonderful terrace that gives onto a mature walled garden. Plus a meadow area with children's games, a summer pool and a stupendous view to the distant hills. Inside it is just as authentic: old tiles with good rugs, beams, white walls and simple, comfortable antique furniture. Organised, warm-hearted Nicola cannot be here for every month of the year but has arranged for a friendly, alternative helper to be there for you on the few occasions when she is away. *Minimum 2 nights.*

rooms	4: 1 double, 1 twin, both with shower & wc; 1 double, 1 twin, sharing shower/bath & wc.
price	€93 for two.
dinner	Wide choice of restaurants within walking distance.
closed	Rarely.
directions	From A8 exit 13 on N7 E to Vidauban; left D48 to Lorgues. In main street, post office on right: right, right again; at T-junction left Pl. Arariso. Leave square on left into Rue de la Canal; house on left.

Nicola d'Annunzio
La Canal,
177 rue de La Canal,
Quartier le Grand Jardin,
83510 Lorgues, Var

tel	(0)4 94 67 68 32
fax	(0)4 94 67 68 69
e-mail	lacanallorgues@aol.com

map: 18 entry: 770

Georges is retired and runs the B&B with great efficiency, keeping the house and its surprising touches of colour and imagination immaculately. The bedrooms are indisputably pretty; one, the much larger of the two, has floral curtains on a brass rod, peach-coloured 'dragged' walls and a painted bed. Hard to imagine anyone not liking the look – or the doors onto the private terrace. Half a mile up a rough stony track, it is all immensely peaceful, there's a splendid pool, views across the tree-laden countryside and generous windows to let the Provençal light stream in. *Gîte space for 5 people.*

rooms: 2 doubles, both with shower or bath & wc.
price: €70 for two.
dinner: Good restaurants nearby.
closed: Rarely.
directions: From A8 exit Le Muy for Ste Maxime & St Tropez. About 5km before Ste Maxime right D74 to Plan de la Tour; entering village left D44 for Grimaud.

M & Mme Georges Ponselet
Le Petit Magnan,
Quartier Saint Sébastien,
83120 Plan de la Tour, Var
tel (0)4 94 43 72 00
fax (0)4 94 43 72 00
e-mail lepetitmagnan@worldonline.fr
web www.lepetitmagnan.fr.st

PROVENCE · ALPS · RIVIERA

The sunny breakfast terrace, the pepper trees beside the pool, the joyous welcome from Joanna and her loving Labrador Juno, this 1970s Provençal house near fashionable Grimaud has it all. Choose between two extra-big rooms: close-carpeted comfort upstairs or rustic simplicity and your own patio in the garden studio. Supper parties are held on Sundays; other evenings, wander up to watch the sun set below Grimaud castle, explore watery Port Grimaud or zip into St Tropez. Joanna is bilingual – she's lived here for years – and willingly shares her local knowledge while walking the dog in the lovely Var countryside.

rooms: 2 doubles, each with bath/shower & wc.
price: €75-€85 for two.
dinner: Sunday supper €18 with wine, by arrangement. Restaurants within walking distance. Picnic lunches possible.
closed: 2-3 weeks July-August.
directions: Leaving Grimaud D14 for St Tropez, just after RH bend, small fork left Chemin St Joseph; house 2nd on right, wooden gate "Attention au chien".

Joanna Morris
Les Deux Poivriers,
Chemin St Joseph,
83310 Grimaud, Var
tel (0)4 94 43 66 85
fax (0)4 94 43 16 97

What a view! Sit here, gazing past palms and pool to the plunging sea and enjoying Yvette's speciality of the day (tart, crumble...). She is a wonderful woman, sprightly and endlessly caring; Guy, a gentle and invaluable member of the team, collects the fresh bread and helps you plan your stay; they have travelled lots and simply love people. All three pretty, pastel guest rooms lead off a delightful bright, Moroccan-touched landing – brass lamps, hand-painted mirror – and have lovely Moroccan rugs on honeycomb-tile floors. The biggest room is definitely the best. And a sandy beach is just ten minutes down the cliff.

rooms	3: 1 twin, 1 double, both with shower & wc; 1 double with bath & wc.
price	€75-€105 for two.
dinner	Restaurants in Les Issambres.
closed	October-May.
directions	From Ste Maxime N98 E through San Piere; after Casino supermarket, 4th left Av. Belvédère; right Av. Coteaux; left Corniche Ligure; house on junction.

Yvette & Guy Pons
Les Trois Cyprès,
947 boulevard des Nymphes,
83380 Les Issambres, Var
tel (0)4 98 11 80 31
fax (0)4 98 11 80 32
e-mail gyjpons@mac.com
web homepage.mac.com/gyjpons/TOC.html

PROVENCE · ALPS · RIVIERA

Let the peace and space of Marjolaine envelop you, then believe that your hostess runs a *Hilton pour Chiens* – even the animals are spellbound. Lying languid in the red hills above a valley, the house overlooks an alluringly unspoilt village. Bedrooms are serene and light; the magnificent pool is balm for frayed city nerves; the piano will thrill at your touch. With her infectious smile and natural hospitality, Philippa is a woman of parts: she introduced polo to the area, sings in local choirs, plays the organ. Very integrated and knowledgeable, she will happily let you in on the best-kept local secrets. *Apartment for 2-4 people.*

rooms	3: 2 double, 2 twins sharing 1 bathroom & 2 shower rooms.
price	€77-€110 for two.
dinner	By arrangement but choice of restaurants in village.
closed	Rarely.
directions	From A8 exit 38 D4 to Bagnols, 12km; left D47 for Le Muy; near chapel follow 'Ancienne Route de Fréjus'; 1st left, 2nd sign on left, bell on gate.

Philippa Anderson
Domaine de la Marjolaine,
83600 Bagnols en Forêt, Var
tel (0)4 94 40 61 47
fax (0)4 94 40 61 47
e-mail philippaanderson@aol.com
web www.lamarjolaine.co.uk

On an ancient hillside studded with rows of gnarled, sentry-like olive trees, this generous modern house is an oasis of cool peace between sophisticated Monte Carlo and the wild Verdon gorges. The sheer pleasure your hosts find in giving hospitality fills the serene place and its comfortable new and 'medieval' furnishings. Monsieur will tell you about everything (in French) and may take you walking in the 'red' Esterel hills; Madame is quieter with the sweetest smile; both are wonderfully attentive. The excellent double room – good storage and lighting – shares a big pink shower room with the much smaller twin room.

rooms	2: 1 double, 1 twin, sharing bathroom & wc.
price	€48 for two; €88 for four.
dinner	Restaurant short walk or choice in Montauroux, 4.5km.
closed	Rarely.
directions	From A8 exit 39 on D37 N for 8.5km; cross D562; continue 200m; house on right; signs.

Pierre & Monique Robardet
Chemin de la Fontaine d'Aragon,
Quartier Narbonne,
83440 Montauroux, Var

tel	(0)4 94 47 71 39
fax	(0)4 94 47 71 39
e-mail	p.robardet@wanadoo.fr

PROVENCE · ALPS · RIVIERA

If you crave a moment of utter tranquillity on your journey down the river of life, then Les Suants is a perfect green mooring to tie up to for a few days: the views of sliding hills, woods and pastures from the patio and bedroom are wonderfully restful. Fiona, a charming, integrated Englishwoman, speaks fluent French and has decorated her house and garden with great care. The bedroom has an antique chest of drawers, pastel walls, good linen and tall windows that open onto a pretty old tiled terrace. You have the run of the house, so why not pick a book and snuggle into a green sofa after a day discovering the local delights?

rooms	1 double with bath & wc.
price	€50 for two.
dinner	Good restaurant 2km.
closed	December-February & August.
directions	Exit A8 at Fréjus; D4 north to St Paul en Forêt; D55 left for Claviers & Draguignan, 2km; over bridge, 50m; right at Hurrell postbox.

Fiona Hurrell
Les Suanes,
83440 St Paul en Forêt, Var

tel	(0)4 94 76 32 39
fax	(0)4 94 76 32 39

Ève, a fascinating medieval history specialist, has decorated her large and spotlessly clean, cool villa in her own personal 'retro' style. She and Henri, a doctor, provide a generous breakfast that is usually served in the lovely garden under the spreading palm tree (self-service before 8am); one of the ground-floor rooms actually opens onto the garden and the top bedrooms have a big private balcony. The house is only 15 minutes' walk from old Cannes and its famous star-crossed Croisette (they close during The Festival to avoid the curling faxes strewn on the floor at 4am) and your hosts are really worth getting to know.

rooms	4: 1 double, 2 twins, 1 triple, all with bath & wc.
price	€75-€100 for two.
dinner	Restaurants 15 minutes' walk.
closed	Rarely.
directions	From A8 exit 'Cannes Centre' Bd Carnot. At 69 Bd Carnot (Le Kid café) right Rue René Vigieno; up hill 150m; house on right on small r'bout; entrance at back.

Ève & Henri Daran
L'Églantier,
14 rue Campestra,
06400 Cannes, Alpes-Maritimes
tel (0)4 93 68 22 43
fax (0)4 93 38 28 53
web www.bnbnet.com/bfr/fr00042.html

PROVENCE · ALPS · RIVIERA

The paradise of a garden, blending into the pine-clothed hillside, is a lesson in Mediterranean flora, æons away from the potteries and madding fleshpots of nearby Vallauris, and Madame makes marmalade with the oranges. The Roncés restored this old building on a terraced vineyard after leaving hectic Paris: they understand the value of peace. Pamper yourself by the pool, relax to the sound of chirruping cicadas. The bedrooms – one large, with kitchenette, one small, with garden view – have in common their comfort and cheery fabrics. Your hosts may seem rather distant – is it shyness or a desire not to intrude? *Italian spoken.*

rooms	2: 1 double with bath & wc; 1 twin with shower & wc.
price	€70-€80 for two.
dinner	Good bistro walking distance; choice in town.
closed	Rarely.
directions	From A8 Antibes exit to Vallauris; D135 Rte de Grasse; over 2 r'bouts, slow after hairpin bend; left down track signposted Mas du Mûrier. Telephone if lost.

M & Mme G. Roncé
Mas du Mûrier,
1407 route de Grasse,
06220 Vallauris, Alpes-Maritimes
tel (0)4 93 64 52 32
fax (0)4 93 64 52 32

Panko is a riot of colour: the sheltered (no-smoking) garden has clumps of orange, mauve and scarlet flowers; real and fake flowers invade the living room and fight with the cheerful pictures that cover the variegated walls; upstairs are rainbow sheets, patchwork bedcovers, painted furniture and *objets* galore, fine big towels and myriad toiletries; big outdoor breakfasts are served on colourful china. Madame's energy drives it all – she'll organise your stay to a tee, galleries and museums a speciality. It is quiet, exclusive, six minutes from several small beaches – superb! *Book early. Minimum 5 nights April-October.*

rooms	2 double/twin, both with bath & wc; 2 extra beds.
price	€100-€115 for two.
dinner	Good choice of restaurants 10 minutes' walk.
closed	Christmas, New Year, 2 weeks August.
directions	From Antibes for Cap d'Antibes; palm-tree r'bout for 'Cap d'Ant. Direct'; next junc. for Cap d'Ant.; 1st right Ch. du Crouton; 1st left cul-de-sac; at end, left on drive; at no. 17, 2nd house on right.

Clarisse & Bernard Bourgade
Villa Panko,
17 chemin du Parc Saramartel,
06160 Cap d'Antibes,
Alpes-Maritimes
tel (0)4 93 67 92 49
fax (0)4 93 61 29 32

PROVENCE · ALPS · RIVIERA

Blushes of pelargonium and cascades of bougainvillea tumble over this 1930s villa, and grapes dangle into your hand at breakfast. From the pretty garden you enter your delightful little sitting room with its country antiques, then through a basic shower room to a rather cramped and minimalist bedroom. But your hosts are so genuinely, generously welcoming – fresh flowers in the rooms, delicious breakfast – and take such great care of you that this is a minor thorn among the roses. It is remarkably quiet and, although this is a dull piece of suburbia, sweet old seaside Antibes is only a 20-minute walk away. *Min. 2 nights.*

rooms	1 double with small sitting room, shower & wc.
price	€68 for two.
dinner	Wide choice of restaurants in Antibes.
closed	Rarely.
directions	In Antibes centre from Place de Gaulle take Rue Aristide Briand; left at r'bout, follow railway 600m; right Impasse Lorini with barrier marked 'Privé'; house at end on right.

Martine & Pierre Martin
Villa Maghoss,
8 impasse Lorini,
06600 Antibes, Alpes-Maritimes
tel (0)4 93 67 02 97
fax (0)4 93 67 02 97

This very appealing Provençal-type villa is a happy marriage of modern technique and traditional design; the setting is entrancing, with umbrella pines, palms, the southern skies and Mediterranean heat. In the cool interior all is well-ordered and smart. Your charming, efficient and enthusiastic hosts have created old out of new, paved their generous terrace with lovely old squares, and furnished the rooms with an appropriate mix of the antique and the contemporary. There is an excellent dayroom/kitchen for guests and a beautifully tended green garden (and 10 golf courses within a five-kilometre radius).

rooms	3: 2 double/twins, 1 double, all with bath & wc.
price	€60–€76 for two.
dinner	Two excellent restaurants 300m.
closed	Rarely, please book ahead.
directions	From A8 exit for Antibes D103; over Bouillides r'bout for Valbonne village 3km; 100m after Bois Doré restaurant, before Petite Ferme bus stop, ring at iron gate No. 205; up lane, house on left at top.

Alain & Christine Ringenbach
Le Cheneau,
205 route d'Antibes,
06560 Valbonne, Alpes-Maritimes
tel (0)4 93 12 13 94
fax (0)4 93 12 91 85
e-mail ringbach@club-internet.fr

PROVENCE · ALPS · RIVIERA

Annick, a well-travelled, kind and restful person, is a former riding instructress, now more likely to be helping people into hammocks than onto horses. Her peaceful garden, with its awesomely ancient olive trees dotted about the terraces and among the lush grass, is ideal for a siesta. Over this looks the garden suite, a treat for those who want to self-cater: its delightful kitchen is light-filled and quarry-tiled. The smaller blue room is charming with its own entrance, a vast antique wardrobe, fine linen, an old wooden bed. If it's too hot for the terrace, breakfast is in the lovely saffron-yellow living room.

rooms	2: 1 double with shower & wc; 1 double with bath, wc & kitchenette.
price	€55–€70 for two.
dinner	Restaurants in village; self-catering available.
closed	November-mid-December.
directions	From Grasse D2085 to Le Rouret; through village, left D7 for La Colle sur Loup & Cagnes; on leaving village, hard right down steep track; house on right.

Annick Le Guay
Les Coquelicots,
30 route de Roquefort,
06650 Le Rouret, Alpes-Maritimes
tel (0)4 93 77 40 04
fax (0)4 93 77 40 04

Honey grows in Provence, of course, so breakfast here includes 12 kinds. The *objets* and goodies set out for guests' delight are to scale. And the house? Twenty years ago there was a little Provençal sheep-shed here on 5,000m² of wild land, then a vast open-plan villa and thoroughly manicured garden took the limelight and the sheep-shed became a fully-equipped suite with a bedroom up narrow steep stairs and its own patio. Marianne, bubbling serenely, welcomes and provides for all. Tennis and golf nearby, as well as the artistic treasures of the coast. Amazing house, hospitable people. *Sensible dogs welcome.*

rooms	2: 1 double, 1 suite for 2 with sitting room, shower & wc.
price	€70 for two.
dinner	Choice of restaurants within easy drive.
closed	October-March.
directions	From A8 exit 47 D2085 for Grasse 17km. 1km after Le Rouret hard left before Mercedes garage, imm'ly right Chemin Reinards 800m, right Chemin Clamarquier, right to 34 in cul-de-sac.

Marianne & Éric Prince
34 chemin de Clamarquier,
06650 Le Rouret, Alpes-Maritimes
tel (0)4 93 77 42 97
fax (0)4 93 77 42 97
e-mail meprince@wanadoo.fr

PROVENCE · ALPS · RIVIERA

Breakfast in heaven on Michelle's finely-laid spread before a vast and magic sea view, birdsong thrilling from the lush subtropical vegetation and Beethoven from the house. The terraced garden drops down to the sheltered pool, the house is done with antiques and taste. Your hosts, a devoted couple who adore children, make all who come near them feel happier: he, a partially blind former soldier, makes olive-wood carvings and fascinating conversation; Madame, a management consultant of charm and intelligence, is now Cultural Attachée to the Mairie. Wonderful hosts, super dog Oomba.

rooms	4: 1 double/twin, 2 doubles, all with bath, shower & wc; 1 family suite with bath & wc.
price	€70-€110 for two; under 10s free.
dinner	€15, wine €3; restaurants in village.
closed	Occasionally in winter.
directions	From A8 exit St Laurent du Var; over r'bout for Zone Ind.; over 2nd r'bout; 3rd r'bout left D118 to St Jeannet; through village to top, Rue St Claude. (Owners will send map.)

Guy & Michelle Benoît Sère
L'Olivier Peintre,
136 rue Saint Claude,
06640 St Jeannet, Alpes-Maritimes
tel (0)4 93 24 78 91
fax (0)4 93 24 78 77
e-mail Mbenoitsere@aol.com

Both Alain and Michelle, a delightfully happy and enthusiastic couple, are fiercely and rightly proud of this very pretty old house which they saved up for while working for France Télécom. In an ideal setting on the upper fringe of a very pretty village, the house and garden have been lovingly renovated to create a really super place to stay. The bedrooms, each with its own terrace onto the garden, are separate from yet cleverly integrated with the rest of the house. Dinners are amazing. Ask Alain about his vintage wines. *Minimum 2 nights.*

rooms	2: 1 double, 1 suite for 4, both with shower or bath & wc.
price	€46-€52 for two.
dinner	€16 with wine, by arrangement.
closed	October-February.
directions	From Cagnes sur Mer centre D18 to La Gaude; left 100m after Cupola; left into Place des Marronniers; walk up behind grocer's Rue des Marroniers to house. (Alain will fetch luggage.)

Alain & Michelle Martin
13 Montée de la Citadelle,
06610 La Gaude, Alpes-Maritimes
tel (0)4 93 24 71 01
fax (0)4 93 24 71 01

PROVENCE · ALPS · RIVIERA

Such engaging hosts a game of *pétanque*, a chat about horticulture, some help with planning your trip – nothing is too much trouble. And what a classic Côte d'Azur setting: look from your elegant bedroom over immaculate lawns – and palms imported from Egypt. Inside, there's heaps of southern style – family antiques, Persian carpets on marble floors, pristine modern bathrooms – yet the atmosphere is not the least intimidating. Breakfast can be either full English or continental. "Super inside, super outside and super people". *Min. 2 nights. Open by request during carnival.*

rooms	3: 2 doubles, 1 suite, all with bath & wc.
price	€100 for two; suite €167 for four.
dinner	Restaurants in Nice.
closed	Rarely.
directions	From Nice Route Grenoble for airport; on past Leroy Merlin shopping centre; right at Agencement Cuisine sign.

Jean-Claude & Brigitte Janer
La Tour Manda,
682 route de Grenoble,
06200 Nice, Alpes-Maritimes
tel (0)4 93 29 81 32
fax (0)4 93 29 81 32
e-mail latourmanda@wanadoo.fr

Madame, calm, kind, supremely elegant *and* a lively, talented painter, loves her house to bits and has much fun sharing it. It is like a doll's house; indeed, the small single room is full of antique dolls. The main bedroom, also quite small, looks onto the rambling, lushly Mediterranean, statue-decorated, terraced garden with many reading corners whence you can see the sea. It has delightful French antiques, a good kitchenette, a (very small) shower room, and a cosy open-fire sitting room perfect for winter guests. Amazing quiet so near Nice, with good walking and cycling paths nearby. *Min. 2 nights.*

rooms	1 suite (double & single) with shower & wc.
price	€64 for two.
dinner	Restaurants 3-7km.
closed	Rarely.
directions	From A8 exit 54 Nice Nord D14 for Gairaut & Aspremont for 4km; left at junc. for Aspremont; Av. Panéra 800m on left; house 50m on right.

Mme Pia Malet-Kanitz
Villa Pan'É Râ,
8 avenue Panéra –
Gairaut Supérieur,
06100 Nice, Alpes-Maritimes
tel (0)4 92 09 93 20
fax (0)4 92 09 93 20

PROVENCE · ALPS · RIVIERA

Way up above Nice and the lowly quarters (the drive up is part of the adventure), drowned in bougainvillea, the great Italianate villa stands in a veritable jungle of scented garden – the 'enchanted' tag is not usurped. Your hosts are new to B&B, enthusiastic, attentive and enjoying it lots. Rooms, all big, one very big with its own veranda, are almost lavish in their rich Provençal colours, excellent furnishings and superb bathrooms unmatched by any hotel we know. Served on the sunny terrace, a brilliant breakfast includes cheese, cereals and fresh fruit salad. And a super pool to finish the picture.

rooms	3: 2 doubles, 1 suite for 4, all with bath, shower & wc.
price	€100 for two.
dinner	Vast choice in town, 2km (walk down, taxi back?).
closed	Rarely.
directions	From Pl. St Philippe, under expressway, left Av. Estienne d'O. 600m, over level crossing, after sharp right-hand bend, hard back left private track climbing to house.

Mme Martine Ferrary
Le Castel Enchanté,
61 route de Saint Pierre de Féric,
06000 Nice, Alpes-Maritimes
tel (0)4 93 97 02 08
fax (0)4 93 97 13 70
e-mail contact@castel-enchante.com
web www.castel-enchante.com

You are bang in the heart of Nice, a quick trot from markets, restaurants and the Promenade des Anglais. Your roomy, ground-floor, 1920s apartment, where monks once lived (there's a church next door), has wood-finished floors and is freshly decorated in whites, corals, and azure blue. One room opens to a garden bursting with vines, roses and bougainvillea: no noise, blissfully – just the cooing of doves. It's a stylish place to stay, with the books and piano, and Martine and Bernard are wonderful, cosmopolitan people, happy to share their wide knowledge of the "hidden Riviera". *Min. 2 nights.*

rooms	2: 2 doubles, with shower or bath & wc.
price	€70-€90 for two.
dinner	Huge choice of restaurants in Nice.
closed	Rarely.
directions	From airport to Promenade des Anglais; Bd Gambetta left just before Negresco hotel; follow Gambetta under railway bridge; 3rd right Rue Vernier; 2nd left at Kodak on corner.

Bernard & Martine Deloupy
Un Jardin en Ville,
40 bis rue Vernier,
06000 Nice, Alpes-Maritimes

tel	(0)4 93 82 43 02
fax	(0)4 93 82 45 29
e-mail	martine@deloupy.com
web	www.unjardinenville.com

map: 18 entry: 789

Paul, who is French, and his English wife Dorothy have been here since the 60s and have made the most of every square inch of the steep site. He is very proud of his handiwork: his latest creation is a bridge over the water garden. The views – of wooded valley leading to distant sea – are stupendous and make it entirely worth braving the narrow approach roads through the outskirts of Old Menton. Bedrooms open off a south-facing terrace, have satin bedspreads, simple furniture and functional bathrooms. Breakfast may be on that pretty shaded terrace and it's deliciously breezy by the pool in summer. *Gîte space for 13 people.*

rooms	4 doubles, all with bath & wc.
price	€54 for two.
dinner	Wide choice of restaurants in Menton.
closed	December-January, except by arrangement.
directions	From Menton D24 for Castellar (not Ciappes de Castellar). Follow numbers (odds on left) & park above house.

M & Mme Paul Gazzano
151 route de Castellar,
06500 Menton, Alpes-Maritimes

tel	(0)4 93 57 39 73
e-mail	natie06@yahoo.fr

map: 18 entry: 790

Was that Sleeping Beauty yawning in the mysterious woods? Set in gentle isolation just a dramatic drive up from hot Riviera vulgarity, the slightly faded Italianate mansion is home to a trio of highly cultured, artistic, English-fluent people who have re-awakened its 19th-century magic. No clutter, either of mind or matter, here. Breakfast is in the atmospheric old kitchen. White bedrooms have pretty fabrics, simple antiques and views of trees where birds burst their lungs and Marcel Mayer's superb sculptures await you. Come for dreamy space, natural peace, intelligent conversation. Or ride a horse into the hills for a day.

rooms	4: 3 doubles, 1 triple, all with shower & wc.
price	€55-€75 for two.
dinner	Several restaurants in Sospel, 2km.
closed	Rarely.
directions	From Menton D2566 to Sospel; at entrance to village left for Col de Turini 1.9km; left for 'La Vasta' & 'Campings'. Paraïs 1.3km along, hard back on right after ranch & sharp bend.

Marie Mayer & Marcel Mayer
Domaine du Paraïs,
La Vasta,
06380 Sospel, Alpes-Maritimes
tel (0)4 93 04 15 78
fax (0)4 93 04 15 78

Looking east over the yacht-studded bay, south over the onion domes of a *fin de siècle* Persian palace, here is a warmly human refuge from the fascinating excesses that are Monaco. Michelle's sober, white-painted flat is decorated with wood, marble and lots of contemporary art, her own and her friends'. Living room: arched doors, little fireplace, little breakfast table, wide balcony; guest room: white candlewick bedcover, big gilt-framed mirror, sea view; bathroom: gloriously old-fashioned beige. Space everywhere, and Michelle is as good a hostess as she is an artist.

rooms	1 double/twin with bath & wc.
price	€90 for two.
dinner	Wide choice of restaurants in Monaco.
closed	August.
directions	From A8 exit 56 Monaco for centre (tunnel); past Jardin Exotique; on right-hand bend (pharmacie on corner) left; left at end Malbousquet; park opposite No. 26 to unload.

Michelle Rousseau
Villa Nyanga,
26 rue Malbousquet,
98000 Principauté de Monaco,
tel (00) 377 93 50 32 81
fax (00) 377 93 50 32 81
Please note this includes code for Monaco.
e-mail michelle.rousseau@mageos.com
web www.bbfrance.com/rousseau.html

WHAT'S IN THE BACK OF THE BOOK? ...

FRENCH WORDS AND EXPRESSIONS

French words and expressions used in this book

Table d'hôtes	Dinner with the owners of the house: fixed price set menu, that must be booked ahead.

Types of houses:

Gîte Panda	May be either a *chambre d'hôtes* or a self-catering house in a national or regional park; owners provide information about flora and fauna, walking itineraries, sometimes guided walks and will lend you binoculars, even rucksacks.
Château	A mansion or stately home built for aristocrats between the 16th and 19th centuries.
Bastide	Has several meanings: it can be a stronghold, a small fortified village or, in Provence, it can simply be another word for *mas*.
Bergerie	Sheep fold, sheep shed.
Longère	A long, low farmhouse made of Breton granite.
Maison bourgeoise Maison de maître	Big, comfortable houses in quite large grounds and built for members of the professions, captains of industry, trade, etc.
Maison vigneronne	Vine-worker's cottage.
Mas	A Provençal country house, usually long and low and beautifully typical in its old stone walls, pan-tiled roof and painted shutters.
Moulin	A mill – water or wind.

Other words and expressions:

Armoire	Wardrobe, often carved.
Brocante	Secondhand furniture, objects, fabric, hats, knick-knacks.
Confit	Parts of goose or duck preserved in their own fat then fried.
Châtelain/e	Lord/lady of the manor.
Clafoutis	Fruit flan.
Garrigue	Typical scrub vegetation on Mediterranean hillsides.
Boules, pétanque	Bowling game played with metal balls on a dirt surface.
Lavoir	Public washing place.
Lit clos	Old-fashioned panel-enclosed box bed.
Marais	Marsh or marshland.
Maquis	Wild scrubland.
Objets/objets trouvés	Objects, bric-a-brac, ornaments, finds (lost property).
Paysan	Not peasant in the English sense but smallholder, modest farmer.
Pelote	Basque ball game, with similarities to squash.
Potage/potager	Vegetable soup/vegetable garden.
Pressoir	Press for olives/grapes/apples.
Salle de chasse	Gun room.
Salon	Sitting or drawing room.

TIPS FOR TRAVELLERS IN FRANCE

Phonecard If you are not wedded to a mobile phone buy a phonecard (*télécarte*) on arrival; they are on sale at post offices and tobacconists' (*tabac*).

Public holidays Be aware of public holidays; many national museums and galleries close on Tuesdays, others close on Mondays (e.g. Monet's garden in Giverny) as do many country restaurants, and opening times may be different on the following days:

Movable feasts in 2003 & 2004

New Year's Day (1 January) May Day (1 May)
Liberation 1945 (8 May) Bastille Day (14 July)
Assumption (15 August) All Saints (1 November)
Armistice (11 November)
Easter Sunday 20 April 2003 (11 April 2004)
Ascension Thursday 29 May 2003 (20 May 2004)
Whit Sunday & Monday (Pentecost) 8 & 9 June 2003 (30 & 31 May 2004)

Beware also of the mass exodus over public holiday weekends, both the first day – outward journey – and the last – return journey.

Medical & emergency procedures If you are an EC citizen, have an E111 form with you for filling in after any medical treatment. Part of the sum will subsequently be refunded, so it is advisable to take out private insurance.

French emergency services are: the public service called SAMU or the Casualty Department – *Services des Urgences* – of a hospital; the private service is called SOS MÉDECINS.

Other Insurance It is probably wise to insure the contents of your car.

Roads & driving Current speed limits are: motorways 130 kph (80 mph), RN national trunk roads 110 kph (68 mph), other open roads 90 kph (56 mph), in towns 50 kph (30 mph). The road police are very active and can demand on-the-spot payment of fines.

One soon gets used to driving on the right but complacency leads to trouble; take special care coming out of car parks, private drives, one-lane roads and coming onto roundabouts.

Directions in towns The French drive towards a destination and use road numbers far less than we do. Thus, to find your way *à la française*, know the general direction you want to go, i.e. the towns your route goes through, and when you see *Autres Directions* or *Toutes Directions* in a town, forget road numbers, just continue towards the place name you're heading for or through.

AVOIDING CULTURAL CONFUSION

En suite

'En suite' is not used in France to describe bathrooms off the bedroom and to do so can lead to confusion. To be clear, simply ask for a room *'avec salle de bains et wc'*.

Greetings and forms of address

We Anglo-Saxons drop far more easily into first-name terms than the French. This reluctance on their part is not a sign of coldness, it's simply an Old National Habit, to be respected, we feel, like any other tribal ritual. So it's advisable to wait for the signal from them as to when you have achieved more intimate status.

The French do not say *"Bonjour Monsieur Dupont"* or *"Bonjour Madame Jones"* – this is considered rather familiar. They just say *"Bonjour Monsieur"* or *"Bonjour Madame"* – which makes it easy to be lazy about remembering people's names.

Breakfast

À table

In simple houses there may be only a bowl/large cup and a teaspoon per person on the table. If so, you are expected to butter your bread on your hand or on the tablecloth (often the kitchen oilcloth) using the knife in the butter dish, then spread the jam with the jam spoon.

A well-bred English lady would never dream of 'dunking' her croissant, toast or teacake in her cup – it is perfectly acceptable behaviour in French society.

Lunch/dinner

Cutlery is laid concave face upwards in 'Anglo-Saxon' countries; in France it is proper to lay forks and spoons convex face upwards (crests are engraved accordingly). Do try and hold back your instinctive need to turn them over!

To the right of your plate, at the tip of the knife, you may find a knife-rest. This serves two purposes: to lay your knife on when you are not using it, rather than leaving it in your plate; to lay your knife and fork on (points downwards) if you are asked to *garder vos couverts* (keep your knife and fork) while the plates are changed – e.g. between starter and main dish.

Cheese comes before pudding in France – that's the way they do it. Cut a round cheese as you would cut a round cake – in triangular segments. When a ready-cut segment such as a piece of Brie is presented, the rule is to 'preserve the point', i.e. do not cut it straight across but take an angle which removes the existing point but makes another one.

ALASTAIR SAWDAY'S

French Bed & Breakfast
Edition 8
£15.99

British Bed & Breakfast
Edition 7
£14.99

British Hotels, Inns & Other Places
Edition 4
£12.99

French Hotels, Inns & Other Places
Edition 2
£11.99

French Holiday Homes
Edition 1
£11.99

Paris Hotels
Edition 3
£8.95

SPECIAL PLACES TO STAY SERIES

Garden Bed & Breakfast
Edition 1
£10.95

London
Edition 1
£9.99

Ireland
Edition 3
£10.95

Spain
Edition 4
£11.95

Italy
Edition 2
£11.95

Portugal
Edition 1
£8.95

WHAT IS ALASTAIR SAWDAY PUBLISHING?

These books owe their style and mood to Alastair's miscellaneous career and his interest in the community and the environment

A dozen or more of us work in two converted barns on a farm near Bristol, close enough to the city for a bicycle ride and far enough for a silence broken only by horses and the occasional passage of a tractor. Some editors work in the countries they write about, e.g. France; others work from the UK but are based outside the office. We enjoy each other's company, celebrate every event possible and work in an easy-going but committed environment.

These books owe their style and mood to Alastair's miscellaneous career and his interest in the community and the environment. He has taught overseas, worked with refugees, run development projects abroad, founded a travel company and several environmental organisations. There has been a slightly mad streak evident throughout, not least in his driving of a waste-paper-collection lorry for a year, the manning of stalls at jumble sales and the pursuit of causes long before they were considered sane.

Back to the travel company: trying to take his clients to eat and sleep in places that were not owned by corporations and assorted bandits he found dozens of very special places in France – farms, châteaux, etc – a list that grew into the first book, French Bed and Breakfast. It was a celebration of 'real' places to stay and the remarkable people who run them.

The publishing company grew from that first and rather whimsical French book. It started as a mild crusade, and there it stays – full of 'attitude', and the more appealing for it. For we still celebrate the unusual, the beautiful, the individual. We are passionate about rejecting the banal, the ugly, the pompous and the indifferent and we are passionate too about 'real' food. Alastair is a trustee of the Soil Association and keen to promote organic growing and consuming by owners and visitors.

It is a source of deep pleasure to us to know that there are many thousands of people who share our views. We are by no means alone in trumpeting the virtues of resisting the destruction and uniformity of so much of our culture – and the cultures of other nations, too.

We run a company in which people and values matter. We love to hear of new friendships between those in the book and those using it, and to know that there are many people – among them farmers – who have been enabled to pursue their decent lives thanks to the extra income the book brings them.

WWW.SPECIALPLACESTOSTAY.COM

Britain
France
Ireland
Italy
Portugal
Spain...

all in one place!

On the unfathomable and often unnavigable sea of internet accommodation pages, those who have discovered www.specialplacestostay.com have found it to be an island of reliability. Not only will you find a database full of honest, trustworthy, up-to-date information about Special Places to Stay across Europe, but also:

- Links to the web sites of well over a thousand places from the series
- Colourful, clickable, interactive maps to help you find the right place
- The facility to make most bookings by e-mail – even if you don't have e-mail yourself
- Online purchasing of our books, securely and cheaply
- Regular, exclusive special offers on titles from the series
- The latest news about future editions, new titles and new places
- The chance to participate in the evolution of the site and the books

The site is constantly evolving and is frequently updated. We've revised our maps, adding more useful and interesting links, providing news, updates and special features that won't appear anywhere else but in our window on the worldwide web.

Just as with our printed guides, your feedback counts, so when you've surfed all this and you still want more, let us know – this site has been planted with room to grow.

Russell Wilkinson, Web Producer
website@specialplacestostay.com

If you'd like to receive news and updates about our books by e-mail, send a message to newsletter@specialplacestostay.com

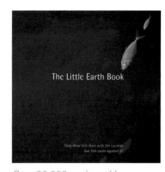

ORDER FORM UK

All these Special Places to Stay books and The Little Earth Book are available in major bookshops or you may order them direct. Post and packaging are FREE.

		Price	No. copies
French Bed & Breakfast	Edition 8	£15.99	
French Hotels, Inns and other places	Edition 2	£11.99	
French Holiday Homes	Edition 1	£11.99	
Paris Hotels	Edition 3	£8.95	
British Bed & Breakfast	Edition 7	£14.99	
British Hotels, Inns and other places	Edition 4	£12.99	
Garden Bed & Breakfast	Edition 1	£10.95	
London	Edition 1	£9.99	
Ireland	Edition 3	£10.95	
Spain	Edition 4	£11.95	
Portugal	Edition 3	£8.95	
Italy	Edition 2	£11.95	
The Little Earth Book	Edition 2	£5.99	
Please make cheques payable to Alastair Sawday Publishing	**Total £**		

Please send cheques to: Alastair Sawday Publishing, The Home Farm Stables, Barrow Gurney, Bristol BS48 3RW. For credit card orders call 01275 464891 or order directly from our website www.specialplacestostay.com

Title First name

Surname

Address

Postcode

Tel

If you do not wish to receive mail from other like-minded companies, please tick here ☐

If you would prefer not to receive information about special offers on our books, please tick here ☐

FBB8

ORDER FORM USA

All these books are available at your local bookstore, or you may order direct. Allow two to three weeks for delivery.

		Price	No. copies
Portugal	Edition 1	$14.95	
Spain	Edition 4	$19.95	
Ireland	Edition 3	$17.95	
Paris Hotels	Edition 3	$14.95	
Garden Bed & Breakfast	Edition 1	$17.95	
British Hotels, Inns and other places	Edition 4	$17.95	
French Hotels, Inns and other places	Edition 2	$19.95	
British Bed & Breakfast	Edition 7	$19.95	
London	Edition 1	$12.95	
Italy	Edition 2	$17.95	
French Holiday Homes	Edition 1	$17.95	
	Total $		

Shipping in the continental USA: $3.95 for one book, $4.95 for two books, $5.95 for three or more books.
Outside continental USA, call (800) 243-0495 for prices.
For delivery to AK, CA, CO, CT, FL, GA, IL, IN, KS, MI, MN, MO, NE, NM, NC, OK, SC, TN, TX, VA, and WA, please add appropriate sales tax.

Please make checks payable to: The Globe Pequot Press Total $

To order by phone with MasterCard or Visa: (800) 243-0495, 9am to 5pm EST; by fax: (800) 820-2329, 24 hours; through our web site: www.globe-pequot.com; or by mail: The Globe Pequot Press, P.O. Box 480, Guilford, CT 06437

Date

Name

Address

Town

State

Zip code

Tel

Fax

FBB8

REPORT FORM

Comments on existing entries and new discoveries

If you have any comments on entries in this guide, please let us have them. If you have a favourite house, hotel, inn or other new discovery, not just in France, please let us know about it.

Book title: ______________________

Entry no: ______________ Edition no: ______________

New recommendation: ______________________

Country: ______________________

Name of property: ______________________

Address: ______________________

____

____

Postcode: ______________________

Tel: ______________________

Date of stay: ______________________

Comments: ______________________

____

____

From: ______________________

Address: ______________________

____

____

Postcode: ______________________

Tel: ______________________

Please send the completed form to:

Alastair Sawday Publishing,
The Home Farm Stables, Barrow Gurney, Bristol BS48 3RW
or go to www.specialplacestostay.com and click on 'contact'.

Thank you.

FBB8

BOOKING FORM

À l'attention de:
To:

Date:

Madame, Monsieur
Veuillez faire la réservation suivante au nom de:
Please make the following booking for (name):

Pour *nuit(s)* *Arrivée le jour:* *mois* *année*

For night(s) Arriving: day month year
Départ le jour: *mois* *année*
Leaving: day month year

Si possible, nous aimerions *chambres, disposées comme suit:*
We would like rooms, arranged as follows

À grand lit *À lits jumeaux*
Double bed Twin beds

Pour trois *À un lit simple*
Triple Single

Suite *Appartement* *ou autre*
Suite Apartment or other

Nous sommes accompagnés de *enfant(s) âgé(s) de* *ans.*
Avez-vous un/des lit(s) supplémentaire(s), un lit bébé; si oui, à quel prix?
We are travelling with childern, aged years. Please let us know if you have an extra bed/extra beds/a cot and if so, at what price.

Notre chien/chat sera-t-il le bienvenu dans votre maison?
Si oui, y a-t-il un supplément à payer?
We are travelling with our dog/cat. Will it be welcome in your house? If so, is there a supplement to pay?

Nous aimerions également réserver le dîner pour *personnes.*
We would also like to book dinner for people.

Veuillez nous envoyer la confirmation à l'adresse ci-dessous:
Please send confirmation to the following address:

Nom: Name:

Adresse: Address:

Tel No: E-mail:

Fax No:

QUICK REFERENCE INDICES

Wheelchair friendly

If you need rooms which are wheelchair-friendly, contact these places.

Alsace • 94 • Burgundy • 132 • 134 • Normandy • 183 • 195 • Brittany • 268 • Western Loire • 303 • 308 • 336 • 361 • 363 • Loire Valley • 422 • 431 • Poitou · Charentes • 444 • 465 • 466 Aquitaine • 500 • 531 • Limousin • 554 • Languedoc · Roussillon • 679 • 687 • Rhône Valley · Alps • 697 • 721

Limited mobility

These houses have bedrooms and bathrooms that are accessible for people of limited mobility. Please check for details.

The North • 9 • 10 • 14 • 15 • 16 •36 • 44 • Picardy • 49 • 51• 55 • 57 • 58 • 59 • 62• 71 • Champagne · Ardenne • 122 • Paris · Île de France • 142 • 145 • Normandy • 171• 175 • 180 • 186 • 194 • 201• 218 • 220 • 222 • 226 • 231• 238 • 242 • 246 • 252• 254 • Brittany • 269 • 291• 295 • Western Loire • 301• 312• 314• 318 • 319 • 320 • 325 • 328 • 330 • 332 • 333 • 334 • 335 • 337• 344• 345 • 346 • 352 • 356 • 358 • 364 • 366 • 367 • Loire Valley • 376 • 377 • 381• 383 • 384 • 391• 394 • 397• 400 • 401• 402 • 404 • 406 • 410 • 413 • 414 • 416 • 417• 424 • 429 • 430 • 433 • 435 • 436 • 438 • 439 • Poitou · Charentes • 443 • 446 • 447• 450 • 451• 453 • 454 • 456 • 469 • 470 • 474 • 484 • Aquitaine • 488 • 501• 515• 516 • 517• 518 • 520 • 537 • Limousin • 544• 546 • 553 • 558 • Auvergne • 560 • 561• 564• 572 • Midi · Pyrénées • 582• 584• 592• 601• 603 • 611• 622 • 636 • Languedoc · Roussillon • 643 • 644 • 662• 665• 666• 672• 682• 686 • Rhône Valley · Alps • 714 • 716 • 718 • 724 • 728 • 735 • Provence · Alps · Riviera • 740 • 743 • 746 • 749 • 750 • 755 • 760 • 762 • 763 • 764• 771• 772 • 774 • 784

No Car?

Owners of these B&Bs have told us that they can be reached by public transport and/or that they are happy to collect you from the nearest bus or train station – please check when booking. There may be a small charge. (Other owners not on this list may be just as helpful, so do ask.)

The North •1 • 3 • 6 •10 • 12 • 15 • 18 • 21 • 28 • 31 • 34 • 35 • 37 • 39 • 41 • 42 • 43 • Picardy • 45 • 47 • 59 • 62 • 65 • 68 • Champagne · Ardenne • 82 • 86 • Lorraine • 87 • 89 • Alsace • 93 • Franche Comté • 97 • 101 • Burgundy • 103 • 109 • 112 • 113 • 114 • 116 • 118 • 120 • 121 • 122 • 123 • 124 • 132 • 133 • Paris · Île de France • 139 • 142 • 149 • 151 • 152 • 153 • 154 • 155 • 156 • 157 • 158 •159 • 160 • 161 • 166 • Normandy • 169 • 170 • 171 • 172 • 174 • 176 • 177 • 178 • 179 • 180 •

181 • 182• 184 • 185 • 187 • 190 • 191 • 192 • 194 • 199 • 202 • 207 • 209 • 211 • 219 • 220 • 222 • 224 • 229 • Brittany • 260 • 262 • 263 • 264 • 270 • 275 • 280 • 282 • 285 • 288 • 289 • 293 • 296 • 298 • 299 • Western Loire • 304 • 306 • 307 • 309 • 313• 317 • 319 • 321 • 326 • 327 • 329 • 336 • 338 • 341 • 343 • 346 • 347 • 353 • 355 • 356 • 362 • 366 • Loire Valley • 368 • 370 • 371 • 372 • 373 • 376 • 377 • 378 • 379 • 380 • 382 • 384 • 386 • 395 • 400 • 403 • 404 • 405 • 409 • 411 • 412 • 414 • 421 • 425 • 427 • 429 • 432 • 433 • 435 • 436 • 439 • 440 • Poitou · Charentes • 443 • 444 • 446 • 449 • 453 • 454 • 458 • 460 • 461 • 464 • 465 • 466 • 468 • 473 • 476 • Aquitaine • 487 • 488 • 490 • 499 • 500 • 501 • 504 • 505 • 509 • 512 • 520 • 522 • 527 • 533 • Limousin • 545 • 555 • Auvergne • 559 • 563 • 564 • 573 • 574 • Midi · Pyrénées 576 • 580 • 581 • 583 • 584 • 587 • 589 • 592 • 596 • 607 • 611 • 613 • 616 • 617 • 620 • 623 • 626 • 628 • 631 • 635 • 637 • 638 • Languedoc · Roussillon • 642 • 648 • 654 • 655 • 660 • 661 • 666 • 667 • 669 • 675 • 676 • 679 • 683 • Rhône Valley · Alps • 692 • 694 • 695 • 698 • 703 • 710 • 714 • 715 • 716 • 718 • 722 • 723 • 724 • 725 • 725a • Provence · Alps · Riviera • 730 • 734 • 736 • 737 • 740 • 743 • 751 • 752 • 753 • 755 • 756 • 763 • 766 • 767 • 777 • 784 • Monaco • 792

Organic

Owners of these B&Bs use organic produce wherever possible.

The North • 34 • Picardy • 59 • Champagne · Ardenne • 80 • Franche Comté • 101 • Burgundy • 112 • 115 • Western Loire • 338 • Loire Valley • 400 • Poitou · Charentes • 458 • 465 • 469 • Aquitaine • 521 • 525 • Limousin • 545 • Midi · Pyrénées • 588 • 595 • 603 • 605 • 616 • 630 • 638 • 639 • Languedoc · Roussillon • 641 • Rhône Valley · Alps • 688 • 697 • 716 •718 • 721 • Provence · Alps · Riviera • 763

Courses, workshops, lessons

Aromatherapy - Yoga - Relaxation

Picardy • 68 • Franche Comté • 101 • Paris • 166 • Normandy • 172 • 240 • Western Loire • 338 • Aquitaine • 488 • 493 • 501 • 503 • Midi · Pyrénées • 591 • 603 • Languedoc · Roussillon • 643 • 667 • Rhône Valley · Alps • 693 • Provence · Alps · Riviera • 738 • 752 •

Cookery

The North • 31 • Picardy • 47 • 59 • Champagne · Ardenne • 82 • Burgundy • 121 • 124 • 127 • 134 • Normandy •192 • Brittany • 263 • 277 • 289 • Western Loire • 313 • 362 •

Local flora & fauna

These places are surrounded by interesting flora and fauna and have owners who are knowledgeable about them. Some are Gîtes Panda.

INDEX – SURNAMES

INDEX – SURNAMES

INDEX – SURNAMES

INDEX – SURNAMES

INDEX – SURNAMES

INDEX – SURNAMES

INDEX – SURNAMES

INDEX – PLACES

INDEX – PLACES

INDEX – PLACES

INDEX – PLACES

INDEX – PLACES

INDEX – PLACES

THE ENVIRONMENT

We try to reduce our impact on the environment by:

- planting trees. We are officially Carbon Neutral®. The emissions directly related to our office,and the paper production, printing and distribution of this book have been 'neutralised' through the planting of indigenous woodlands with Future Forests.
- re-using paper, recycling stationery, tins, bottles, etc.
- encouraging staff use of bicycles (they are loaned free) and car sharing.
- celebrating the use of organic, home-grown and locally-produced food.
- publishing books that support, in however small a way, the rural economy and small-scale businesses.
- running an Environmental Benefit Trust to stimulate business interest in the environment.
- working to establish an organic standard for B&B's.
- publishing The Little Earth Book (www.littleearth.co.uk), a collection of essays on environmental issues. We also have a new title in production called The Little Food Book, another hard-hitting analysis – this time of the food industry.

CONVERSION TABLE

Euro €	US $	£ Sterling
1	0.98	0.63
5	4.91	3.17
7	6.87	4.44
10	9.82	6.34
15	14.73	9.52
20	19.64	12.69
30	29.46	19.03
40	39.28	25.38
50	49.10	31.72

September 2002

EXPLANATION OF SYMBOLS

Treat each one as a guide rather than a statement of fact and check important points when booking.

Children are positively welcomed, with no age restrictions, but cots, high chairs etc are not necessarily available.

Full and approved wheelchair facilities for at least one bedroom and bathroom and access to all ground-floor common areas.

Ground-floor bedrooms for people of limited mobility.

Your hosts speak English, whether perfect or not.

No smoking anywhere in the house.

Smoking restrictions exist usually, but not always, in the dining room and some bedrooms. For full restrictions, check when booking.

Pets are welcome but may have to sleep in an outbuilding or your car. Check when booking.

This house has pets of its own that live in the house: dog, cat, duck, parrot …

Credit cards accepted; most commonly Visa and MasterCard.

Vegetarians catered for with advance warning. All hosts can cater for vegetarians at breakfast.

Most, but not necessarily all, ingredients are organically grown, home-grown or locally grown.

Working farm.

You can borrow or hire bikes.

Good hiking nearby.

Swimming pool on the premises.

Cover photo credits. Thank you to:
1. Image Bank
2. Corbis
3. La Maison Neuve (appearing in French Holiday Homes, entry no. 146, www.specialplacestostay.com)
4. Corbis
5. Red Cover
Photo of Alastair Sawday Fiona Duby